AUTOCOURSE ™

The World's Leading Grand Prix Annual

100% PRESTIGE
100% PERFORMANCE

TAG Heuer
WHAT ARE YOU MADE OF ?

DAVID COULTHARD AND HIS TAG HEUER KIRIUM FORMULA ONE

SWISS AVANT-GARDE SINCE 1860

CONTENTS

AUTOCOURSE
2003–2004
is published by:
Hazleton Publishing Ltd,
5th Floor, Mermaid House,
2 Puddle Dock, London,
EC4V 3DS.

Colour reproduction by
Radstock Repro,
Midsomer Norton, Somerset

Printed in England by
Butler and Tanner Ltd,
Frome, Somerset

Hazleton Publishing Ltd is a member
of Profile Media Group Plc.

ISBN: 1 903135 20 6

DISTRIBUTORS

UNITED KINGDOM
Haynes Publishing plc
Sparkford
Near Yeovil
Somerset BA22 7JJ
Telephone: 01963 442030
Fax: 01963 440001

NORTH AMERICA
Motorbooks International
PO Box 1
729 Prospect Avenue
Osceola
Wisconsin 54020, USA
Telephone: (1) 715 294 3345
Fax: (1) 715 294 4448

REST OF THE WORLD
Menoshire Ltd
Unit 13
21 Wadsworth Road
Perivale
Middlesex UB6 7LQ
Telephone: 020 8566 7344
Fax: 020 8991 2439

Dust-jacket photograph: Six-time World Champion Michael Schumacher driving his Scuderia Ferrari Marlboro F2003-GA.

Title page photograph: Runner up in the World Drivers' Championship, Finland's Kimi Räikkönen in the West McLaren Mercedes MP4/17D.
Photographs: Darren Heath

editor
ALAN HENRY

director
ROBERT YARHAM

managing editor
IAN PENBERTHY

art editor
STEVE SMALL

business development manager
PETER MERCER

sales promotion
LAURA FELL

results and statistics
DAVID HAYHOE
EMMA HENRY

f1 illustrations
IAN HUTCHINSON
NICOLA CURTIS

f1 illustrations reference
MICHAEL FISHER

chief photographer
DARREN HEATH

chief contributing photographers
BRYN WILLIAMS/crash.net
PATRICK GOSLING
LAT PHOTOGRAPHIC

Acknowledgements

The Editor of AUTOCOURSE wishes to thank the following for their assistance while compiling the 2003–2004 edition.
Eire: Jordan Grand Prix (Eddie Jordan, Ian Phillips, Gary Anderson, Helen Temple and Henri Durand); **France:** ACO, Federation Française du Sport Automobile, FIA (Max Mosley, Bernie Ecclestone, Alan Donnelly, Richard Woods, Agnes Kaiser, Charlie Whiting, Herbie Blash, Pat Behar and Amy Saward), Formula One Management (Pasquale Latteneddiu), Michelin (Pierre Dupasquier and Severine Ray), Renault F1 (Flavio Briatore, Mike Gascoyne, Pat Symonds, Patrizia Spinelli, Serena Santolamazza and Bradley Lord); **Germany:** Formula 3 Vereinigung; BMW Motorsport (Gerhard Berger, Mario Theissen and Jorg Kottmeier), Mercedes-Benz (Norbert Haug, Wolfgang Schattling, Frank Reichert and Tanya Severin), Sabine Kehm, Katja Heim; **Great Britain:** Autocar, British American Racing (David Richards, Craig Pollock, Geoffrey Willis, Hugh Chambers, Nick Fry, Alastair Watkins, Iain Brown, Tracy Novak and Jane Chapman), Matt Bishop, Martin Brundle, Timothy Collings, Bob Constanduros, Paul Edwards, Peter Foubister, Maurice Hamilton, Emma Henry, Nick Henry, Ian Hutchinson, Cosworth Engineering (Bernard Ferguson), Ford (Jost Capito, Sophia Claughton-Wallin and Becky Lowth), Jaguar Racing (Tony Purnell, David Pitchforth, Mark Gillan, Stuart Dyble, Nav Sidhu and Jane Stewart), McLaren International (Ron Dennis, Martin Whitmarsh, Adrian Newey, Justine Blake, Beverley Keynes, Ellen Kolby, Clare Robertson, Lyndy Redding, Simon Points, Neil Oatley, Steve Hallam and Peter Stayner), Stan Piecha, Nigel Roebuck, Eric Silbermann, Sir Jackie Stewart, Jules Kulpinski, Professor Sid Watkins, WilliamsF1 (Sir Frank Williams, Patrick Head, Dickie Stanford, Sam Michael, Frank Dernie, Jonathan Williams, Silvia Hoffer and Liam Clogger); **Italy:** Commisione Sportiva Automobilistica Italiana, Scuderia Ferrari (Jean Todt, Ross Brawn, Antonio Ghini, Luca Colajanni, Stefania Bocci, Jane Parisi and Regine Rettner), 'George' Piola; **Japan:** Bridgestone (Hirode Hamashima, Hisao Suganuma and Rachel Ingham), Honda Racing (Robert Watherston and Charlie Reid), Toyota (Ove Andersson, John Howett, Andrea Ficarelli, Chris Hughes, Silke Albus and Virginie Papin); **Switzerland:** Sauber (Peter Sauber, Hans-Peter Brack and Josef Leberer); **USA:** CART, Daytona International Speedway, Indianapolis Motor Speedway, NASCAR, Roger Penske, SportsCar.

Photographs published in AUTOCOURSE 2003–2004 have been contributed by:

Chief Photographer: Darren Heath; *Chief Contributing Photographers:* Bryn Williams/crash.net; Patrick Gosling; LAT Photographic: Steven Tee, Charles Coates, Lorenzo Bellanca, Peter Spinney, Michael Cooper, Mike Weston, Jack Atley, Malcolm Griffiths, Gary Hawkins, John Tingle, Jeff Bloxham, Glenn Dunbar, Phil Abbott, Greg Bauders, Will Kuhn, Gavin Lawrence, Richard Dole, Robert Le Sieur; GP Photo/Peter Nygaard; John Marsh/redzoneimages.com.

www.autocourse.com

FOREWORD

by MICHAEL SCHUMACHER

I still remember the party we had in Suzuka after the last race of the 2003 season; it was wonderful. We were singing and dancing and drinking together – you have to understand we had gone through a very tough season with a lot of bad moments. That's why our victories in Suzuka were so sweet.

A lot of people were telling me about my record breaking sixth title, but, honestly, the fifth constructors' title for Ferrari in a row means much more to me. That's something no other team has ever achieved. That's our era Ferrari. I am extremely proud of having participated in that record, as I am proud to be part of that team.

I have said this very often, and I have the feeling it becomes stronger and stronger, and more and more true: 'La Ferrari' is my second family. I am passionate for this Scuderia, which is so passionate itself. Even in difficult moments, this team never gives up and always stays united. That's the unique thing about what we have created in the past years. That's what makes working with all those guys so sweet.

I am deeply grateful to all of them. They deserve to be celebrated. It's they who are the legend now, not me. Because it's they who revive the myth.

Photograph: Darren Heath

D.G.M 2.079.2/03

Mercedes-AMG supports the Eric Clapton Crossroads Foundation

The sportier the car

The CL

► Of course you can get from A to B faster in a Mercedes-Benz AMG. But if you're sitting in the CLK 55 AMG, you may well find yourself wanting to take a few detours to C and D, to prolong the sheer pleasure of driving. Especially if you have a look at all the things we've given the CLK 55 AMG to help it on its way. Such as the AMG 5.5-litre V8 engine, which delivers 270 kW (367 hp) and a torque of no less than 510 Nm. Then there are the high-performance AMG braking system, the AMG suspension and, not least, the AMG SPEEDSHIFT automatic transmission with steering-wheel shift. Every detail – including

the longer the journey

55 AMG

the exclusive interior – is designed to make driving this car an exceptional experience for you. When you look at it like that, it's not surprising that, with the CLK 55 AMG, you tend to look forward to the driving rather than reaching your destination. The quickest way to get to know the CLK 55 AMG is to visit your Mercedes-Benz dealer, or alternatively just have a look at our website on www.mercedes-benz.com/amg.

CHALLENGING TIMES

By ALAN HENRY

IT was a simply towering achievement. By the time the chequered flag fell to mark the end of the 2003 Japanese Grand Prix at Suzuka, Michael Schumacher had finally clinched that all-time record sixth world championship. He had 70 wins to his credit, and Ferrari, the blue riband powerhouse of F1 domination these past four seasons, had secured its fifth straight constructors' title.

Obviously, it is too soon to place Schumacher's F1 achievements in a fair and accurate historical perspective. It would be pleasant to be able to record that his on-track activities eclipsed the sport's political dimension. Yet, in reality, Michael's latest success was forged and shaped to a very large degree in the white hot flames of the Ferrari political crucible, which has played a major role in dictating the shape of the sport for the past half-century.

Michael is a genius and he drives for a team that is brilliantly adept at harnessing any sort of advantage, whether sporting or political, on track or off. The template crafted by the team's sporting director, Jean Todt, calls for winning at all costs. And if that means fanning the flames of controversy over the width of rival Michelin front-tyre contact patches at a moment when the championship battle is becoming precariously tight, so be it. Winning is Todt's only priority, and if the manner in which he achieves that aim sometimes has the fans up in arms, then that's a price they have to pay.

However, you would be hard pressed to argue anything other than that the best man won the championship, even though the wafer-thin advantage of two points that Michael eventually enjoyed over emergent rival Kimi Räikkönen came at the end of a race in which the multiple title winner looked less convincing than he had done for many a day.

Michael is worshipped by the *tifosi* and deeply respected by his contemporaries and rivals. Yet it is hard to discern the warmth and affection that accrued to Juan Manuel Fangio from his competitors. When Fangio's Maserati took the Ferraris of Mike Hawthorn and Peter Collins to the cleaners in the 1957 German Grand Prix at the Nürburgring, the two British drivers were suffused with admiration for his efforts.

Contrast this with the lack of any comment whatsoever from Räikkönen and David Coulthard after the McLaren drivers finished second and third at Suzuka, and were asked where they thought Michael stood in the pantheon of all-time great racing drivers. We are told that times have changed and that the professionalism required in this business now eclipses the gung-ho attitude that prevailed in the 1950s. Perhaps so, but the affection and regard of one's peers is a quantifiable factor that transcends such generational boundaries.

The season began on an uncertain note. FIA President Max Mosley had initiated a raft of rule changes that included one-lap Indy-style qualifying – but with a key difference. From now on, the second qualifying session on Saturday afternoon would be regarded, in effect, as the first few laps of the race. Cars would be confined to a *parc fermé* area after that session and no fuel could be added before they took their places on the starting grid the following afternoon.

The one-shot qualifying format was adjudged a success by many, even though the difficulties in assessing what sort of fuel load – and therefore how much additional weight – was being carried by each competing car, made life difficult for those television commentators who were trying to offer an informative analysis of events on the circuit. The changes did not please everybody, however. As this was being written, McLaren and Williams still had arbitration pending over the manner in which the FIA had implemented its revised regulations for 2003, which the two teams believed was, in itself, a clear breach of the governing body's own rules. The matter is likely to drag on into 2004. It remains to be seen whether the whole issue runs out of steam on its own or becomes a major issue again next season.

Nevertheless, Mosley claimed that the changes – which included awarding championship points down to eighth place – would still result in the best driver winning the title, but his task would take a little longer. In that respect, the FIA president probably judged things correctly, and television ratings, F1's commercial lifeblood, began to stabilise, then show signs of rising slowly during the course of the season.

Even so, Ferrari had an overwhelmingly impressive run. Michael never suffered a mechanical failure and retired only once during the course of the season, when he spun off in heavy rain in Brazil. Yet six times out of the season's 16 races, Rubens Barrichello outqualified the world champion, and there were occasions when the Brazilian certainly looked the more convincing runner, most notably at Silverstone and Suzuka, where he scored superb wins. In

Left: **The season saw a fifth consecutive constructors' title for Ferrari.**

Inset, below far left: **It's a record! Michael Schumacher is embraced by Jean Todt after the race at Suzuka.**

Inset, below left: **The tifosi were happy with Ferrari's domination; the uncommitted, less so.**
Photographs: Darren Heath

Top: **Michael Schumacher was made to work harder than ever for his sixth title success.**

Above: **The Prancing Horse. The most powerful symbol in F1.**
Photographs: Darren Heath

addition, he clearly had the upper hand during qualifying at Hockenheim, Hungaroring and Indianapolis, and could well have added Austria to his tally of victories, had it not been for a delay during a refuelling stop.

Barrichello's formidable form made up just one element of the wide ranging challenge facing Schumacher in 2003. Kimi Räikkönen and Fernando Alonso posted maiden grand prix victories during the course of the season, both underscoring their eligibility as future title challengers. Juan Pablo Montoya won two races, as did Ralf Schumacher, but neither BMW Williams nor McLaren Mercedes had their admittedly competitive machinery consistently honed to the levels required to get on terms with Ferrari. Despite this, there was sufficient evidence to indicate that life will become more difficult for Michael Schumacher in terms of hard competition over the next few years.

Away from the tracks, concerns about the sport's finances continued to dominate the F1 arena, in particular the car makers' challenge to the status quo with their proposed GPWC series, due to start after the expiry of the current Concorde agreement at the end of 2007. Put simply, GPWC is a device designed primarily to ensure what the teams regard as a more equitable distribution of the sport's commercial-rights revenue.

Of course, this debate is as old as the hills and centres on whether one believes that F1 is best served by Bernie Ecclestone's autocratic management style or would benefit from a broader-based consensus, which would give more scope for the motor industry's voice to be heard. It is certainly a ticklish issue and one that, despite hints to the contrary, looked no closer to being solved at the end of the year than it had at the beginning.

Ferrari, of course, occupied a central role in these negotiations, as it has done on many other occasions in motor racing history. F1 is nothing without the famous Italian team, as its chairman, Luca di Montezemolo, warned in May, making the point that the three banks that had financed the now bankrupt Kirch media empire's $2.2 billion bid for 75 per cent of Bernie Ecclestone's SLEC empire, would have to agree to sharing more of the sport's profits. Initially, he set a deadline of 31 December 2003 for the finalisation of a deal – or GPWC would go it alone.

The bottom line is that Ecclestone and the GPWC brethren have both made bids to secure Ferrari's allegiance to their respective series, offering financial sweeteners that effectively recognise the Italian team's unique place in the sport's history. That in itself indicates just how fragmented and indecisive the car manufacturers

really are. At one end of the spectrum, one has DaimlerChrysler as the most committed advocate of the GPWC line; at the other are Ford and Honda (not a GPWC member), who are understandably more concerned about securing the success of their own F1 operations than plunging ever farther into a complex battle that may become prohibitively costly for all concerned.

Keeping costs under control is another area that has preoccupied the smaller teams. Hints from DaimlerChrysler, Renault and Toyota that they might be prepared to sign up to a customer F1 engine budget of around $10 million under the new regime, which requires one engine per car to last a full grand prix weekend from the start of 2004, were inevitably greeted with sighs of relief all round among the less-wealthy operations.

Eventually, however, only Cosworth looked like coming up with the goods – at least for 2004 – and as we went to press, it was clear that the manufacturer would be hard pressed to keep the price down to the level encouraged by the FIA. Jordan and Minardi were the two tail-enders upon whom this state of affairs impinged, but with no alternative engine supply available – and Cosworth's need to generate income for the Ford empire – there is no choice but for them to reach an eventual accommodation.

Elsewhere, the F1 calendar seemed poised for further expansion outside Europe, with both Bahrain and Shanghai scheduled to hold debut races in 2004. Inevitably, this put pressure on European events and, with Austria being dropped from the calendar at the end of the 2003 season, the British Grand Prix at Silverstone was also subject to more than its fair share of critical scrutiny by Max Mosley and Bernie Ecclestone. The rights and wrongs of whether this event should benefit from direct government funding, at a time when just about every other fixture on the FIA F1 World Championship calendar enjoys such support, remains a matter for ongoing detailed debate.

Outside the hermetically sealed F1 environment, there was much other racing to be seen. In the sports car world, Bentley succeeded in realising its ambition to return to the winner's circle at Le Mans, while in the USA, CART and the IRL continued the process of trying to evolve their respective series in distinctly different directions to maximise their future potential for growth.

Penske ace Gil de Ferran beat team-mate Helio Castroneves to win the Indianapolis 500 before announcing his retirement at the end of the season. Twice CART champion de Ferran also rounded off his career by winning the final IRL round at Texas in October, a race that saw Kiwi Scott Dixon crowned as the series' champion. A few weeks later, former Penske driver Paul Tracy clinched the CART crown after a dominant season.

Yet these remain very much supporting members of the international motor racing cast. The equilibrium of international racing has become distorted and unbalanced over the past two decades as grand prix racing has sucked the sport dry of every penny. For the race fan, at least, there is thin fare indeed away from the high price tag of the F1 spectator enclosure.

That puts even more responsibility on the shoulders of the FIA, the teams and the car manufacturers to ensure that F1 not only is conducted equitably, but also demonstrably continues to offer value for money. The changes to the format for 2003 were like the proverbial curate's egg. Good in parts.

Maintaining the momentum of such changes, to make F1 more user friendly for paying spectator and TV viewer alike, remains one of the key challenges facing the sport over the next few years. F1 is striving for market share at a time when there has never been more competition for the public's leisure-time attention. It must be nurtured carefully if it is to be sure of winning the battle.

Alan Henry,
Tillingham,
Essex
November 2003

THE WINNING STREAK CONTINUES

2001 MALAYSIAN GRAND PRIX
FRENCH GRAND PRIX
1999 EUROPEAN G
1999 MALAYSIAN GRAND P
'02 SPANISH GRAND PRIX
1999 JAPANESE GR
RITISH GRAND PRIX
'002 MONACO GRAND P
2000 AUSTRALIAN GRA
2000 BRITISH GR
2000 BRAZILIAN G
2003 AUSTRALIAN GRAND
2003 ITALIAN GRAND PR
2000 HUNGARIAN GRAND P
2003 JAPANESE GRAND PRIX

UNDISPUTED CLUTCH AND BRAKE
CHAMPIONS - YEAR AFTER YEAR

With an unbroken run of 69 Grand Prix wins (since Luxembourg 1999) and a tally of 545 since the current Formula 1 began in 1950, AP Racing also look the favourites for 2004!

In anyone's book, this is a fantastic achievement - a tribute to our designers, engineers and technicians who make it their business to keep AP Racing ahead of the game - and your team ahead of the pack.

The spin-off from our success in the highest form of motorsport benefits all our race and road customers - join them.

Getting away fast or stopping quicker - AP Racing have the science covered.

AP RACING
WHELER ROAD
COVENTRY
CV3 4LB
ENGLAND
TEL **+44 (0)24 7663 9595**
FAX +44 (0)24 7663 9559
EMAIL: sales@apracing.co.uk

THE SCIENCE OF FRICTION

www.apracing.com

AP-WS1

FIA FORMULA 1
WORLD CHAMPIONSHIP 2003

TOP TEN DRIVERS

Chosen by the Editor, taking
into account their racing
performances and the
equipment at their disposal

photography by
DARREN HEATH

MICHAEL SCHUMACHER

1

Date of birth: *3 January 1969*

Team: *Scuderia Ferrari Marlboro*

Grand Prix starts in 2003: *16*

World Championship placing: *1st*

Wins: *6*

Poles: *5*

Points: *93*

MICHAEL Schumacher's analytical brilliance continued to underpin the Ferrari team's efforts throughout the eighth year of their partnership, although briefly that all-time record sixth World Championship looked as though it might slip from his grasp during an unexpected mid-summer performance drop-off. Much was made of the fact that Michael looked more under pressure than in any recent season, although trying to pin this on any slackening of his motivation would be unfair.

Ferrari started the 2003 campaign with the previous season's F2002, and it certainly looked as though the team was pushing the old car's performance boundaries to the limit in the early races. Michael didn't post his first win until Imola, the last race for the F2002, and a fortnight later he celebrated the debut of the F2003-GA with a measured victory over Fernando Alonso's Renault at Barcelona. Michael alone knew just how overdue the replacement car had been, admitting that it wouldn't have been possible to beat Alonso had he been forced to drive its predecessor. The new car was certainly better in every respect, but Michelin was relentlessly closing the gap, regularly bringing Williams, McLaren and Renault within range of the Ferrari squad. Nevertheless, Michael won brilliantly in Austria and, most notably, Canada, where he managed to vault ahead of the Williams-BMWs and keep the pace of the race down to a level at which he could conserve his brakes to the chequered flag, while still remaining at the front.

Thereafter, Michael's form suffered a brief wobble. A punctured tyre delayed him at Hockenheim, where he drove out of his skin to hold second place in the closing stages, never in the same league as Montoya's victorious Williams-BMW. Then, in Hungary, he had to endure a lamentable run to eighth, during which he was lapped by Alonso's winning Renault. But two impressive wins at Monza and Indianapolis brought his career tally to a remarkable 70 victories.

If Michael Schumacher made mistakes in 2003, it was because circumstances demanded that he pushed harder than at any other time during his Formula 1 career. That he was able to muster the determination and focus to do that, in his 12th full season under the spotlight, speaks volumes of his genius.

WHEN he won the Hungarian Grand Prix, Fernando Alonso became the youngest winner in the history of the official World Championship. In doing so, he beat a record established by Bruce McLaren that had endured since the 1959 US Grand Prix at Sebring. Over four decades ago, McLaren had arrived on the scene as a bright young talent, yet the signs are that Alonso is more than simply promising. He is a dynamic driver with the potential to win world championships.

That's certainly the view of Flavio Briatore, the Renault F1 team principal. Briatore might be accused of bias, since he steers the young Spaniard's career as well as running the French team on a day-to-day basis. But you can't fault his ability when it comes to selecting new talent. He placed Alonso at Minardi in 2001, then paced the development of his career by bringing him in as Renault test driver for the 2002 season. For 2003, his promotion to the big time was a seamless, trouble-free transition.

Alonso qualified brilliantly on pole position in Malaysia and led the opening stages of the race, finishing an excellent third to sample the view from the podium for the first time in his F1 career. He really got into his stride at Barcelona, where he almost split the Ferraris on the run down to the first corner and then jumped Barrichello at the first round of refuelling stops, thereafter maintaining relentless pressure on Michael Schumacher for the remainder of the race to finish second. This was a brilliant performance, which inevitably raised the level of F1 interest in Spain and helped consolidate not only Alonso's burgeoning reputation, but also the television viewing figures in that country. A week later, when he demonstrated the Renault in the streets of Madrid, more than 100,000 enthusiasts turned out to cheer him on.

Renault team insiders believe passionately that this unassuming young man has boundless potential as F1's most promising new star, and they have no doubts that he will win many more races in the future as well as world championships. Like all great drivers, Alonso's speed and competitiveness flow easily from his finger tips. Even at this early stage of his career, he is one of the most complete performers on the grid.

Date of birth: 29 July 1981

Team: Mild Seven Renault F1 Team

Grand Prix starts in 2003: 16

World Championship placing: 6th

Wins: 1

Poles: 2

Points: 55

2

FERNANDO ALONSO

KIMI RÄIKKÖNEN

3

THIS was the man who carried the championship battle all the way to the very last race of the season, the young Finn with the unassuming, unruffled confidence that definitely marks him out as a potential world champion. In a future post-Michael Schumacher era, whenever that might arrive, the prospect of repeated three-way title battles between Kimi Räikkönen, Fernando Alonso and Juan Pablo Montoya is enough to make the average race fan salivate with optimism. And Räikkönen is seriously fast enough to take on all comers.

Like so many of those rivals pitched into battle with Schumacher's Ferrari, it is all too easy just to recall the downside of their efforts. In Kimi's case, this included losing victory in Australia due to a speed-limiter glitch on his McLaren-Mercedes and the engine failure that cost him a potentially sublime triumph in the European GP at the Nürburgring. There were also the driving errors that gradually eroded his points tally, most notably the major qualifying mistakes that consigned him to the back of the grid at Barcelona and Montreal. All conspired to nibble away at his championship chances and meant that he went to Suzuka with a mountain to climb if he was going to get the job done.

On the credit side, Kimi drove a storming race to post his first grand prix victory in Malaysia, and thoroughly deserved to win at Nürburgring and Indianapolis, only losing the latter event to Michael Schumacher thanks to the performance edge exerted by the Ferrari's Bridgestone rain tyres over the McLaren's Michelins.

Räikkönen was put on earth to be a McLaren driver, sharing the team's ingrained introspection and caution when it comes to dealing with the media. Coaxing him out of his shell to shape an image of Kimi Räikkönen, the international sporting hero, will not be the work of a moment. Yet his team-mates respect and admire their latest Finn for his instinctive driving genius, his unruffled temperament and his refusal to be intimidated by his key rivals. All those who witnessed him eyeballing it wheel-to-wheel with Michael Schumacher's Ferrari at Melbourne, in a manoeuvre that saw the World Champion pushed wide over a kerb, will have realised beyond doubt the strength of Räikkönen's claim to a future title crown.

Date of birth: 17 October 1979

Team: West McLaren Mercedes

Grand Prix starts in 2003: 16

World Championship placing: 2nd

Wins: 1

Poles: 2

Points: 91

HE is one of the most exciting drivers of the current era, of that there can be no shred of doubt. Hugely talented and motivated, Juan Pablo Montoya combines his on-track skill with an off-circuit charisma and charm that is enormously attractive. On the face of it, his tough, no-nonsense approach appears to make him ideal as a Williams driver, so it is sad that fissures developed during 2003 between the Colombian and his team, which seem likely to herald a switch to the McLaren squad at the end of 2004.

Initially, Montoya and team-mate Ralf Schumacher had struggled with the development of the all-new Williams-BMW FW25, so it was disappointing that a late-race driving slip cost him victory in the season opener at Melbourne. Later, he drove a brilliant race at Monaco to score his first win of the season, but short-term tensions boiled over after the French GP at Magny-Cours, where Juan Pablo lost his cool after Ralf Schumacher stayed ahead by a few yards after the third round of refuelling stops.

The affair was eventually calmed down after the race, and Montoya appeared to understand. But it led to a heightening of tension with Frank Williams and Patrick Head, and the chemistry of Montoya's relationship with the team seemed never quite the same again.

Subsequently strengthening his title challenge with a fine victory in the German GP at Hockenheim, Juan Pablo missed out on a crucial pole position at Monza, which effectively cost him a realistic chance of beating Michael Schumacher's Ferrari in what turned out to be the race of the year in terms of flat-out motoring and unrelenting competition between these two top drivers.

Montoya's title challenge came to an end at Indianapolis after a poor overall showing by the Williams team, which included refuelling problems and a drive-through penalty incurred after he pitched Barrichello's Ferrari into a gravel trap. Yet despite this and two other potentially crucial spins at Montreal and Hungaroring, Montoya emerged from the season with his reputation and credibility suitably enhanced.

Date of birth: 20 September 1975

Team: BMW WilliamsF1 Team

Grand Prix starts in 2003: 16

World Championship placing: 3rd

Wins: 2

Poles: 1

Points: 82

JUAN PABLO MONTOYA

4

No matter how you slice it, the role of Michael Schumacher's team-mate gets no easier as the seasons roll by. Yet the hugely popular Rubens Barrichello continues to master the tricky balancing act between husbanding his own personal career prospects and not offending the Maranello system, which revolves exclusively around Michael, seen as the brightest star in its firmament.

Barrichello won just a two races in 2003, both of which were superb. The first was a win from pole position at Silverstone, where his impeccable showing in qualifying tipped Schumacher into a rare driving error as he battled to top the Brazilian's best lap. The second, no less impressive, came when he dominated Suzuka, again from pole position. During the course of the season, Barrichello out-qualified Schuey on no fewer than six occasions, but his biggest disappointment came in the Brazilian Grand Prix at Interlagos, where he started from pole position in front of his home crowd, only to run out of fuel while leading due to a telemetry problem.

A mid-season lull in Barrichello's campaign saw him produce disappointing performances in the Monaco, Canadian and French GPs, and inevitably this raised speculation that he might be replaced when his current contract expires at the end of 2004. Interestingly, his former team boss, Jackie Stewart, believes that if Barrichello were as pampered at Ferrari as Michael Schumacher clearly is, then he would be even closer to the multiple World Champion's performance level. Ultimately, he has the talent to lead the team should 'The Master' opt for retirement in the forseeable future.

It is a measure of Rubens' mature and balanced temperament that he instantly assumed a degree of the blame for the collision at Indianapolis that put him out of the race and resulted in his good friend, Juan Pablo Montoya, receiving a drive-through penalty. The problem for Barrichello is that it appears that Ferrari takes him a little too much for granted, although, to be fair, Ross Brawn did offer a ringing endorsement of his talent and status after his victory at Silverstone. He may be a veteran of a decade in the F1 business, but if Ferrari doesn't want him for 2005, there will almost certainly be several rival teams that do.

Date of birth: 23 May 1972

Team: Scuderia Ferrari Marlboro

Grand Prix starts in 2003: 16

World Championship placing: 4th

Wins: 2

Poles: 3

Points: 65

RUBENS BARRICHELLO

5

RALF SCHUMACHER

6

Date of birth: *30 June 1975*

Team: *BMW WilliamsF1 Team*

Grand Prix starts in 2003: *15*

World Championship placing: *5th*

Wins: *2*

Poles: *3*

Points: *58*

THE psychological pressure of having to race an elder brother who holds such an overwhelmingly pre-eminent position in the sport remained the biggest single challenge facing Ralf Schumacher in 2003, yet by and large the younger sibling did an excellent job after a shaky start. At one point, it even looked as though the two brothers might end up battling down to the wire for the title crown, but the consequences of a first-corner collision that eliminated Ralf from the German GP effectively dealt a setback to his prospects from which he never recovered.

Initially, Ralf struggled with the lack of front-end grip from the Williams FW25 but, in fairness, always remained upbeat about the team's prospects, reporting early in the season that he had never known the team to have worked so consistently hard since he had signed up at the start of 1999. His first setback came when he lost the Monaco GP after qualifying commandingly on pole position, and he attracted a degree of criticism from those who felt he might have made a more robust effort to pass his brother's Ferrari during a chase that lasted much of the Canadian GP and ended with Ralf taking the chequered flag just a couple of lengths behind.

However, he drove brilliantly to score consecutive wins in the European and French GPs, prompting Niki Lauda to admit that he really did have a very credible chance of winning the World Championship. It seemed as though he had developed the knack of getting the best out of the FW25, but then came disappointment at Silverstone, where technical problems prevented him from scoring points for the first time in the season. After this, there was the controversy of Hockenheim, where the prospect of a ten-place penalty in the Hungarian GP hung over his head until it was replaced by a fine.

Ultimately, Ralf's title hopes were dashed when he was involved in a massive crash during testing at Monza, Marc Gené subbing for him in the Italian GP, and he had disappointing races at Indianapolis and Suzuka. Taken as a whole, however, Schumacher junior had a good year. He has a laid-back style and easy fluency that makes him an attractive personality. Also he has proved, at last, that, from time to time, he has some of his brother's steel as well.

MARK WEBBER

7

Date of birth: *27 August 1976*

Team: *Jaguar Racing*

Grand Prix starts in 2003: *16*

World Championship placing: *9th=*

Wins: *0*

Poles: *0*

Points: *17*

MARK Webber followed hard on the heels of Fernando Alonso as the Minardi team's most celebrated F1 graduate, although the fact that the Spaniard spent the 2002 season on the subs' bench as Renault's test driver meant that the pair of them entered their second full season of racing at the start of 2003.

A former F3000 front runner, Webber had also made a name for himself as test driver with the Renault team during its previous incarnation under the Benetton flag. His recruitment to the Jaguar F1 effort was former principal Niki Lauda's most enduring legacy to the team and, from the very start, the unassuming, notably well-balanced Australian proved himself not only to be a very fine racing driver, but also a huge motivational spur to the team's workforce.

When Mark qualified third on the grid at the Brazilian GP at Interlagos, pit-lane cynics dismissed his achievement as a fluke produced by running with a light fuel load. In fact, his fuel loads had been comparable with his rivals, thus marking him out as a man who could make a difference, boosting the prospects of a middle-ranking car to the point where eyebrows were raised in admiration. Admittedly, he failed to finish, having inadvertently triggered the huge accident that led to the race being red-flagged, but in Spain, Austria and Canada he was seventh, and he followed that up with sixth places at Nürburgring and Magny-Cours.

Yet the key to 26-year-old Webber's appeal is his sheer normality. His gregarious Australian spirit is tempered by a natural friendliness as he hangs around the Jaguar motorhome, chatting with all and sundry with a refreshing lack of ego or pretence.

Webber says that his ambition is to remain with Jaguar Racing and grow with the team to race-winning maturity. Having put in all the groundwork, he says that he would hate to see somebody else reap the pay-off. Truth be told, Webber's star is rising faster than Jaguar's and a top team may come a-calling with a large cheque before too long. It will be nothing more than he deserves.

THIS was the season in which the popular Scot was expected to deliver his most convincing challenge for the World Championship. As things turned out, it developed into the most disappointing campaign of Coulthard's nine-year F1 career. He opened the year with a lucky win in Australia, yet it was not long before his title prospects had sunk without a trace, thanks to his inability to come to terms with the newly introduced one-lap qualifying format.

In Malaysia, it looked as though he was in with a good chance of winning, until he was sidelined by a frustrating technical failure. Then, at Interlagos, he led the lion's share of the laps, only to be in the pits refuelling when the race was stopped prematurely. Psychologically, this seemed to be something of a turning point. From then on, David simply failed to get the job done in qualifying and, although his race pace was often comparable with Räikkönen's, he was never sufficiently close to the front of the grid to make a worthwhile impact on the outcome of any of the events. After his win in Melbourne, he did not appear on the podium again until the German GP at Hockenheim, where he finished second, almost a minute behind Montoya. Thereafter, his only other podium finish came at Suzuka, where he finished third behind Barrichello and Räikkönen.

Coulthard's mental equilibrium cannot have been helped by paddock rumours circulating from mid-season onward to the effect that McLaren had lost faith in his performance potential and was attempting to negotiate Montoya's release from Williams as a replacement for 2004.

Despite this, McLaren confirmed that Coulthard would be on the team's driving strength for 2004 and that it retained an option on his services for the following year. That said, it's difficult to imagine that McLaren will continue to employ him after the end of 2004, as the team is determined to have two drivers of Räikkönen's stature and potential. Just how much this will impact on Coulthard's performance next season is difficult to say, but it certainly won't help matters.

Date of birth: *27 March 1971*

Team: *West McLaren Mercedes*

Grand Prix starts in 2003: *16*

World Championship placing: *7th*

Wins: *1*

Poles: *0*

Points: *51*

8

DAVID COULTHARD

JENSON BUTTON

9

ourth places in the Austrian and Japanese Grands Prix represented the high-water marks of Button's 2003 season. Frankly, it was a minimal reward for the British driver's efforts throughout a difficult year, during which his biggest single challenge was trying to blend together the best elements of the BAR chassis, Honda V10 engine and Bridgestone tyre performance. Bringing these to the boil at the same moment was never an easy task, but there was the odd impressive moment, most notably at Indianapolis, where an astute late change to just the right choice of Bridgestone rain tyres in a chaotic event saw Button pop up in the lead for several laps before he was overwhelmed by winner Michael Schumacher's Ferrari.

This was the race that should have seen Jenson take the first podium finish of his four-year F1 career. He was well ahead of Heinz-Harald Frentzen's Sauber, which eventually claimed third behind Schumacher and Kimi Räikkönen's McLaren, but then the Honda engine unstitched itself in a spectacular cloud of smoke right in front of the pits and his day was done.

Another major task for Button at the start of 2003 was to get the upper hand over Jacques Villeneuve, who had been a fixture at BAR since the team had been established and shaped around him at the beginning of 1999. Initially, the Canadian had been sniffy about Jenson's credentials, hinting that he had no real pedigree and that it was up to him to make his name in the team. Button did just that, more often than not shading Villeneuve in the process, but earning his respect at the same time.

Button's paucity of hard results inevitably is leading him into that curious limbo land that bridges the gulf between a driver perceived as a bright young star and one seen as an established old hand. He has a good relationship with BAR team principal David Richards, who continues to insist that he has World Championship potential. The ease and assurance that Jenson radiated as he led those laps at Indianapolis, and sped to a solid fourth in Japan, served as a compelling reminder of what he might achieve if BAR can give him consistently competitive equipment in the future.

Date of birth: *19 January 1980*

Team: *Lucky Strike BAR Honda*

Grand Prix starts in 2003: *15*

World Championship placing: *9th=*

Wins: *0*

Poles: *0*

Points: *17*

Date of birth: *19 September 1973*

Team: *Panasonic Toyota Racing*

Grand Prix starts in 2003: *16*

World Championship placing: *13th*

Wins: *0*

Poles: *0*

Points: *10*

THIS affable Brazilian earned his Toyota F1 seat as a reward for winning the CART title in 2002, and initially there was a feeling that the company had been rather unreasonable in ditching both Mika Salo and Allan McNish at the end of that season. Nobody was really quite certain about da Matta's true credentials, but he quickly proved himself to be a feisty and resilient little performer with a cheerful nature and a tough streak just below his chirpy exterior.

Switching from a Champ car to an F1 machine running on grooved rubber was always going to be a challenge for da Matta, but he quickly got the knack of the technique required to turn in on the brakes and certainly was in no way intimidated by the exalted company in which he found himself. In the Spanish GP, he first displayed his potential by hassling Ralf Schumacher's Williams-BMW all the way to the chequered flag. Then, when the intervention of the safety car unexpectedly shuffled the pack early in the British GP, he suddenly found himself leading the race. Under pressure from Kimi Räikkönen's McLaren, da Matta handled Silverstone's high-speed swerves with an unruffled precision that served as a reminder of just how seasoned a racer this pint-sized Brazilian really is.

The Toyota team also believes that da Matta is extremely tough mentally, perhaps even tougher than his equally quick team-mate, Olivier Panis. The Japanese car maker is fully confident that this driving partnership can earn it some really worthwhile results in 2004 after a somewhat disappointing time over the past 16 races. Da Matta certainly has the potential to deliver on his early promise, and his progress will be watched with fascination by those who understand that Toyota is playing the long game and will not be happy until it is a consistent winning force in this business.

CRISTIANO DA MATTA

10

JUAN PABLO MONTOYA

SHOOTING STAR

By ALAN HENRY

BUT for a handful of minor driving errors and a dash of mechanical unreliability from his Williams-BMW FW25, Juan Pablo Montoya could have become an even bigger hero in his native Colombia during the 2003 season. As it was, he finished a strong third in the drivers' title chase, 11 points behind six-times champion Michael Schumacher. More crucially, he consolidated his reputation as a natural and instinctive racer, and took another key step toward establishing his credentials as a front-line F1 competitor.

Having completed his third season of F1 with the BMW Williams squad, Montoya is one of a small handful of competitors who isn't the slightest bit intimidated by Michael Schumacher's overwhelming status. And he has largely sustained the form that he demonstrated initially when he forced his way ahead of Schumacher's Ferrari to take the lead of the 2001 Brazilian GP, only his third F1 race.

Aggressive and sometimes slightly impetuous, Montoya is also a driver who likes to make the best of the opening lap while his rivals are still jostling for position. Sometimes, this gets him into a few scrapes. Witness the '02 Brazilian GP, where he was insufficiently circumspect when dealing with Schumacher and consequently lost his car's nose section against the Ferrari's rear wheel. But he relishes close wheel-to-wheel jousting and makes it his business to ensure that he is not edged out in tight situations.

Montoya is volatile and effervescent, but also there is a slight emotional streak to his character, which is a potential weakness. Yet his freewheeling style made him very popular at Williams from the moment he arrived. That said, his brief outburst over the radio to the engineers during the 2003 French GP, when he suspected they had adopted a refuelling strategy that favoured his teammate, Ralf Schumacher, caused tempers to be strained briefly.

Initially, it was felt by some team insiders that Montoya wasn't quite as fit as he needed to be for top F1 competition, but he had improved physically for 2003. On the downside, he demonstrated that he could be prone to unforced errors, which cost him dear in the title battle. He spun in the Australian, Canadian and Hungarian GPs, and was lucky to be able to resume in all three cases. The lapse in Melbourne, of course, robbed him of victory in the first race of the season, handing it instead to David Coulthard.

'I think the first time I ever heard of Juan Pablo's name was when Betise, my wife, was down doing a little bit of freelance promotional work for a Brazilian driver called Max Wilson,' recalled Patrick Head. 'She was down at the Formula 3000 race at Pau, in south-west France, during 1997 to do a bit of press work for him. I rang her up on the Friday and asked her how things were going. She said, "Fine." Then I asked her how Max was going. She said, "Fine, but there's a guy here you want to take some notice of. A chap called Montoya, who's a second-and-a-half faster than anybody else, and he looks pretty good to me."'

Patrick grinned as he continued, 'So the first person who noticed it was Mrs H – even though she hadn't become Mrs H at that particular time – and so I obviously began to take an interest in him then as he continued through Formula 3000. He finished runner-up to Ricardo Zonta in 1997.

'Then we brought him to meet Frank [Williams] and we kept an eye on him. He was clearly very good, so we decided to give him a contract as a Formula 1 test driver, and he took to it like a duck to water, so to speak. So you could tell straight away that the step up from Formula 3000 to F1 wasn't going to cause him any problems.'

Having the right driver pairing at the right moment always

Above: Montoya in the Williams at Hungary, where he finished third after a late-race spurt.

Right: An off-course excursion in the US GP, the race that wrecked his title ambitions.

Facing page: Blue in Green. Behind his trademark shades in Malaysia.
Photographs: Darren Heath

Right: Riding the kerbs in Japan.

Below: Colombia's finest waves to the crowd after his dominant win in Germany.
Both photographs: Darren Heath

Above: With his wife Connie as she reads about the season ahead at the Australian GP.
Photograph: Patrick Gosling

Far right: Montoya took a superb win at Monaco.
Photograph: Darren Heath

poses something of a challenge in the F1 business. It's often the case that a particular driver is contractually available when there is no vacant place with a team that might be interested in securing his services. Meshing these different requirements and schedules is not always the easiest task, as Williams found at the start of the '99 season.

At the end of the previous season, both Williams drivers – Jacques Villeneuve and Heinz-Harald Frentzen – had left the team. Villeneuve embarked on what would turn out to be a fruitless five-year odyssey with BAR, while Frentzen – who'd managed only a single race win during his time with Williams – joined Eddie Jordan's squad.

Head recounted, 'Then we took on Alex Zanardi for 1999 and there was the possibility that we might run Juan in the second car. But Frank and I discussed it and decided that having one chap coming in from another formula [Zanardi was reigning CART champion] and a rookie in the other car wasn't going to make an ideal mix. As a result, we took on Ralf Schumacher instead of Juan, but as Zanardi had come out of Chip Ganassi's CART team in the USA, it seemed logical for Frank to talk to Chip about Juan going over there for a couple of years.

'He did just that, and I think it turned out to be very good experience for Juan, and as a direct result of that move, he now has a CART championship title and a victory in the Indy 500 on his record, which doesn't do any harm on his CV.

'We duly brought him back to Formula 1 at the start of the 2001 season, when he replaced Jenson Button, and he immediately impressed us with his sheer speed and the fact that he so obviously enjoyed it... It didn't seem to take anything out of him; the speed came easily. He's not a driver who has to struggle. It's not a stressful activity for him; he really enjoys what he is doing.'

Inevitably, many compare Juan Pablo to Michael Schumacher,

in terms of his competitiveness and potential future achievements. Montoya is sanguine about this, and in no way intimidated.

'You can learn a lot from watching guys like Michael,' he admitted. 'But I don't measure myself against anybody. I just go out and try to do my best to beat everybody. You just go out and give it your best shot. Sometimes, that means pole position, sometimes tenth place on the grid.

'I'll admit that it's obviously interesting to race against Michael. He's a tough guy, he's been in F1 for a long time and you can learn a lot from him. But you can also learn a lot from many other people in F1.'

Patrick Head believes that Montoya matured into a rounded performer during the 2003 season. 'He is really fast and a very tough character as well,' he said. 'Sometimes, he can get a little bit excitable when he's setting up the car, but he's become much better in this respect, I would say, over the past season or so.

'All in all, and to sum him up, I would have to say that Juan Pablo is very fast, has excellent judgement and has learned enough about Formula 1 to know when he needs to be quick. And when he doesn't.'

BMW Motorsport's outgoing competitions director, Gerhard Berger, also recognises Montoya's sheer quality from an astute driver's perspective. He has no doubts as to his potential.

'I think it's very clear what Juan Pablo is able to do,' he said. 'He's a bloody quick guy, very Latin, emotional. This is an advantage, disadvantage, whatever. The good side is that the way he goes about his overtaking, when he makes it so simple, you think, "Anybody can overtake, so why don't they ever do it."

'The other side is that you have to set these cars up in a cool and analytical way, and if he gets in a mood, then it can be difficult. But he's definitely a winner. He's won championships before. And he has the ability to do the same in the future.'

The clouds still hover over Silverstone's long-term future as a grand prix venue.
Photograph: Darren Heath

MAKING
TRACKS

By ERIC SILBERMANN

THE British Grand Prix should be a showcase for Formula 1. The majority of teams are UK based, and a host of small British engineering firms literally keep the wheels of the sport turning. However, once again this year, the Silverstone weekend was held under a cloud, of the financial rather than meteorological sort.

Dragging the grey skies along behind them were Bernie Ecclestone and Max Mosley, claiming that circuit owner the BRDC (British Racing Drivers Club) had to get its act together and improve circuit facilities or face losing the race. The BRDC is widely perceived as a bunch of charming, yet bumbling, aristocrats with a penchant for blue blazers, cloth caps and equally cloth ears. But it did listen and was even forced into an arranged marriage with Brands Hatch owner Octagon Motorsport (now Brands Hatch Leisure).

Main photograph: Rubens Barrichello and his Ferrari are dwarfed by the vast expanse of Silverstone. The style of the grandstands harks back to another era.

Below: Barcelona's state-of-the-art main grandstand.

Photographs: Darren Heath

Circuit de Catalunya

Great things were promised for Silverstone at the Wedding Breakfast, but sadly the blushing bride's dowry proved smaller than expected: just enough this year for some nice tarmac car parks and a few more toilets. Even more embarrassing for a venue best described as shabby, the one oasis of modernity at Silverstone was the very expensive BRDC clubhouse. While Sir Jackie Stewart stalked the paddock, rallying the media to the Silverstone cause, it did not help that those very same journalists had spent a frustrating time finding their car park, because the signs used by every other grand prix on the calendar were mysteriously not in evidence and we were sent on a tour of the English countryside. Making matters worse, once we had found 'Ye Olde Car Parke', we had to work in 'Ye Olde Media Centre', a stifling, airless building where the only improvement for this year was – yes, you've guessed it – more toilets!

But come the afternoon of Sunday 20 July, dear old Silverstone, bless her, despite having had more facelifts than an ageing Hollywood starlet, hitched up her skirts and showed us some real racing with real overtaking. Okay, it might have involved some intervention from the Almighty, in the form of one of his more eccentric followers taking a walk down the track, just inches from the speeding cars, but despite its faults, a real race track delivered the goods.

Happily, Silverstone does feature on the 2004 calendar, although race day clashes with the finals of the European Football Championship and some tennis tournament played out on the lawns of south London, which might lessen its appeal for the casual viewer.

Looking at the rest of the 17-race calendar, we will be experiencing Bahrain and China for the first time. These two circuits were designed by Hermann Tilke, the man who created the Sepang track in Malaysia, rejigged Hockenheim and the Nürburgring, and

apparently drew up plans for the new state-of-the-art grandstand in Barcelona.

Looking out of the press-office window at Silverstone this year, I did wonder how the fans felt about shelling out enough money to have taken their families for a week's holiday on the Costa Brava to sit on hard plastic seats with no roof over their heads, but I can't help feeling the new generation of race track, with its emphasis on luxury facilities, is missing the point.

Joni Mitchell's seminal sixties proto-eco protest song, 'Big Yellow Taxi', contains the lyrics, 'Don't it always seem to go, that you don't know what you've got 'til it's gone?' That's an apt phrase to describe what is happening to our race circuits, both old and new, as the emphasis seems to have shifted away from the track itself to the surrounding amenities.

Leaf through the literature for any of these new circuits and entire pages are devoted to Mr Tilke's plans to reflect the culture of the host country in the design of the buildings. We are informed that ample parking is available for the Paddock Club guests, who can watch the race in air-conditioned splendour. The pit complex is big enough to host a motor show, while debriefing rooms are built above the garages so that the Formula 1 drivers don't run the risk of bumping into a member of the public while walking across the paddock.

Apparently, the roof of the Sepang grandstand was designed in the shape of a chrysanthemum, and the layout of the Shanghai track follows the outline of the city's emblem. Yet I cannot remember discussing gardening with Michael Schumacher, nor do I recall hearing Juan Pablo Montoya delivering a dissertation on Chinese hieroglyphics.

Look for information about the actual track at these new state-of-the-art venues and comments seem to be limited to how wide is the road, how grippy the tarmac, how big the run-off areas and

how safe it is. Big deal! These comments could apply to any half-decent motorway.

It is no coincidence that along with Silverstone, most drivers love racing at Interlagos, Spa and Suzuka, where working conditions and facilities are not first rate, but the tracks are. All these circuits have their faults, but that only serves to give them character and make the drivers think about what they are doing. It is time for these newly wealthy countries, who wish to flaunt their cash, to realise that they should put more effort into designing proper tracks, rather than displaying their architectural prowess.

While there is no such thing as a perfect race track, there are a few key elements that could be incorporated to guarantee excitement. The number-one priority is that a circuit should be high-speed, a statement on which all racing drivers seem to agree.

Formula 1 cars are supposed to be frighteningly quick and we do not want to see them skittering around first-gear corners like Touring Cars. Throw in a couple of tight turns at the end of quick straights to provide passing opportunities, some rapid changes of direction – but please, no chicanes – along with steep climbs, blind crests and frightening descents, as well as some very long, quick corners. The surface does not need to be as smooth as a billiard table, while the odd section of negative camber would not go amiss. Actually, it has all been done before, and I think it was called Brands Hatch!

Already I hear the Thought Police, the Nanny States and the

Do-Gooders cry out in alarm that all this sounds rather dangerous. And your point would be? Motor racing is supposed to be dangerous. No one wants to see a return to the days when grand prix racing regularly lost a handful of drivers every season, but what guarantees that a grand prix report moves from the sports pages to the front page of a national newspaper?

A crash of course. Given that we the spectators cannot begin to understand the skills involved in piloting a Formula 1 car, we need to know that the men driving them are heroes, risking their lives for our entertainment. The modern antiseptic race tracks are in danger of reducing the sport to a 3D computer race game.

Give the crowd a good show and they won't give a fig for chrysanthemums, if I can mix my botanical metaphors. A good show on a real race track will also serve to raise the sport's profile and that, in turn, will attract more sponsors. So yes, we do need lavish and luxurious hospitality areas, good access and plentiful parking to keep the people who pay for our sport happy, but these should be the icing on the cake, not its base.

The FIA and teams are currently discussing slashing engine capacity from its present three litres to two, in a bid to control the speed of the modern F1 car. Maybe they should also turn their attention to creating new circuits that present a worthwhile challenge and preserving those that already do so, warts and all. To quote our song writing friend, Joni, again: 'Give me spots on apples and leave me the birds and the bees.'

Top: Despite improvised working conditions for Formula 1 personnel, Monaco remains at the core of the grand prix calendar.
Photograph: Darren Heath

Above left: Barcelona, the archetypal modern circuit. To the left, The Paddock Club atop the press room offers its patrons a tremendous view over the pit lane, while opposite a magnificent grandstand houses the paying spectators.

Above and far left: The Indianapolis Motor Speedway and the Sepang circuit in Malaysia have set new standards for spectator facilities.
Photographs: Patrick Gosling

JACQUES VILLENEUVE INTERVIEW

FREE SPIRIT

By NIGEL ROEBUCK

GOODBYE, Jacques, or is it *au revoir*? As of late October, the only certainties were that, after five years, Villeneuve had been unceremoniously dropped by BAR, and that no obvious vacancy existed elsewhere. Inconceivable as once it might have seemed, the 1997 World Champion was on the street, his last grand prix perhaps run.

'It's a shame,' said Flavio Briatore, always a Villeneuve fan. 'A few years ago, I tried very hard to sign Jacques, and I think he's still good now. Plus, I like him personally, because he's a character, and F1 needs characters, needs *stars*.'

A character Villeneuve undoubtedly is – not an easy one, in the way that his father was, but similar in the sense that he says what he thinks and looks you in the eye. Jacques, though, is a harder, darker, man than was Gilles, and a more solitary one, too.

From the beginning, he developed an intense dislike of the constant references to his father. 'I'm very proud of everything he achieved,' he said, 'but I don't want always to be thought of as Gilles Villeneuve's son – I'm Jacques Villeneuve, a person in my own right…'

Look at his helmet: in design, it is similar to his father's, but the colours are different.

At the time of Gilles's death, in 1982, Jacques was a month past his 11th birthday. Soon he was sent off to boarding school in Switzerland, where he excelled as a skier, his instructor one Craig Pollock, who would become his mentor and, later, his manager.

Villeneuve's career began with karts, then progressed to F3 in Italy, where, not surprisingly, the constant references to, and comparisons with, his father drove him to distraction. On the advice of his godfather, Patrick Tambay, he opted for a season in Japan.

He flourished there, too. Previously, his talent had seemed unremarkable, but in Japanese F3 he began to win. Unlike other foreign drivers in the series, he did not dash home at every opportunity, but stayed put for a year. It was an alien environment for a young Westerner, and perhaps his inherent feistiness, the sense that he is essentially a loner, was fostered there.

After many later successes in America – including becoming CART champion and winning the Indianapolis 500 – Villeneuve came to F1 in 1996, having been signed by Williams-Renault. At Melbourne, he became only the third driver to start his first grand prix from pole position, and only an engine problem kept him from winning the race.

At the end of that year, Patrick Head considered the team's latest star: 'As a driver, he reminds me a little bit of Piquet, in that he's very, very in control in the cockpit, as Nelson was. You'd be thinking, "Why isn't he going faster?" In fact, he was just doing his homework, working away – but then, when it was time to go faster, he could just dive into it. I don't think Jacques gets flustered very easily.

'As a bloke, I think he's a bit of a one-off, really. Very self-contained. Maybe he needs Jock Clear, his race engineer, in his camp, but the impression he gives is that he doesn't really need the rest of us. It's almost as if he doesn't want to make any form of bond with the team – or with people generally, although he's got certain "insiders". You'd have to say he's very self-confident.'

Second to team-mate Damon Hill in the '96 World Championship, Villeneuve went one better the following year, and in circumstances to make you believe that maybe there is a God after all. In the title-decider at Jerez, Michael Schumacher was leading, but Jacques reeled him in; when he went for the lead, Schumacher tried to take him out. For once, happily, the biter got bit.

Oddly, though, Villeneuve's has been an F1 career in reverse, in the sense that all his successes came early. There were 11 victories in his first 31 races; there has been none in the 100 since. In the course of three years with Williams, he scored 180 points; in five with BAR, the total was 39.

You could say, with some justification, therefore, that Jacques scuppered his career by deciding, in July 1998, to leave Williams for BAR, the new team put together by Pollock, his manager. Certainly, the money was enticing – only Michael Schumacher has earned more than Villeneuve in the last five years – but the future, on the face of it, was uncertain,

Jacques insists that dollars were not the reason that made him move: 'In '98, Williams went downhill, because we didn't have a factory engine deal, and in that situation you just create negative energy, and you need something fresh. At the time, it was the right thing to move. It wasn't really true that I did it for the money, although I know people assume I did.

'OK, the first BAR contract I signed was risky, but it made some

Above: Halcyon days. Celebrating victory in the Austrian GP in 1997. Poised on the edge of the World Championship, who could have imagined then that this would be Villeneuve's last GP win to date?

Below: Champion driver in 1997, piloting the Williams FW19-Renault.

Left: Villeneuve off track, not a social beast.
Photographs: Darren Heath

Above: 1998 was a year of toil and struggle. In the Canadian GP, Jacques locks a front left wheel on his Williams FW20 in an attempt to keep Fisichella's Benetton at bay.
Photograph: Darren Heath

Below: Sixth place at Monza proved to be the last points Villeneuve would score for BAR Honda.
Photograph: Bryn Williams/crash.net

Right: New kid on the block. Villeneuve in his 1996 debut season with Williams.
Photograph: Darren Heath

sense to me. What's more difficult to understand is the second time I signed! Again, it wasn't just money – in fact, I had an almost identical contract ready for signing somewhere else, so money wasn't a factor.'

That other contract had been with Renault, of course, and there must have been countless occasions when Villeneuve regretted turning down Briatore's offer. 'I stayed with BAR because Honda told me they wanted me to stay, that it was important for them,' he said. 'I had confidence in them, but…'

As he pointed out, though, there are different factions within Honda, which came sharply to light in 2003, as JV's future came under scrutiny. BAR, conscious that he remained 'a name', wished him to continue with the team, as did the engineering staff at Honda. The marketing people, though, had a preference for one of their own, Takuma Sato, and their will appears to have prevailed.

It must said, however, that in many ways Villeneuve did not make it easy for himself. On the one hand, there was the mammoth retainer; on the other, a distinct lack of results. You can argue that a BAR-Honda, on Bridgestones, was not the most competitive package around (albeit rather more so than in previous years), and also that the reliability of Jacques's car was lamentable, with eight retirements in 15 races.

Inescapably, though, his quirky personality worked against him, in the sense that not too many in the team were sorry to see him go. Back in the Williams days, they used to say that, Jock Clear apart, he knew by name few of the folk who worked on his car; the paradox is that fundamentally he is not an unfriendly man.

Many in the F1 paddock have a distaste for the intrusion of PR

in motor racing these days, and plenty found attractive Jacques's obvious lack of enthusiasm for it. He would argue that his task was to make the car faster, to drive it to his maximum, and at one time that would have been enough – particularly if he had been winning races.

Being nice, or otherwise, to the sponsors is one thing, though; being on friendly terms with everyone in your team quite another. One of the reasons everyone at Ferrari loved Gilles was that he lived in a motorhome and spent endless evening hours in the garage with the mechanics. Quite often, little Jacques would be there, too, but he seems not to have absorbed the importance of good relationships within a team. As Patrick Head had said, seven years earlier, 'It's almost as if he doesn't want to make any form of bond with the team…'

Villeneuve himself puts it this way, 'I'm not a social beast, no. My work ethics are to work with the engineers, and that's it. I won't fake all this stuff of going to the factory and waving to everybody! What's important to me is the work. I've got a reputation, too, for not doing PR work, and, all right, I've never said I *loved* it, and it's not something I have fun doing, but I'm a professional, and I do it.'

Among his friends, like David Coulthard, though, he is reckoned to be very much 'a social beast', very good company, very gregarious.

'Sure,' Jacques said, 'with a certain group. But it takes me a while to build up a relationship with people – and it's the same with a work relationship, too.'

After five years with BAR, that sounds a little hollow, and perhaps it played a significant part in the decision not to extend Villeneuve's contract. If true, it's a shame, but perhaps not too difficult to understand.

In terms of results, Jacques may not have achieved much since winning his championship all those years ago, but it will be a tragedy if F1 has seen the last of him, for free spirits are very thin on the ground in today's world, and so are racing purists.

JV is both.

'You can't police traction control, so we might as well have it, I guess, but I hate it, because it takes away part of your trade. Anything that's taken away from you, from your control, makes what *you* do less important,' he said. 'With traction control, you don't pay for mistakes as much as you used to – as much as you should. I'd ban it, and get rid of all telemetry, as well. Just talk with the engineers, get in and drive.

'Taking risks for yourself is one thing; putting other people at risk is something else, and it goes beyond what I consider acceptable – but if you can sleep at night with that, then you're okay, I guess. The line to follow is don't do something that you wouldn't want someone else to do to you, but if you're Michael Schumacher, and believe you're a higher being than everybody else, I guess you're allowed to do anything you want…

'I need to get a buzz from everything in life, and if I don't get it in a car, I'll get it somewhere else. When I'm older, I don't see myself living differently until…until the day I'm not here any more, I guess. I'll still ski like a maniac! I think the day I don't enjoy that rush any more, I'll just give up on life.'

A character, as Briatore said.

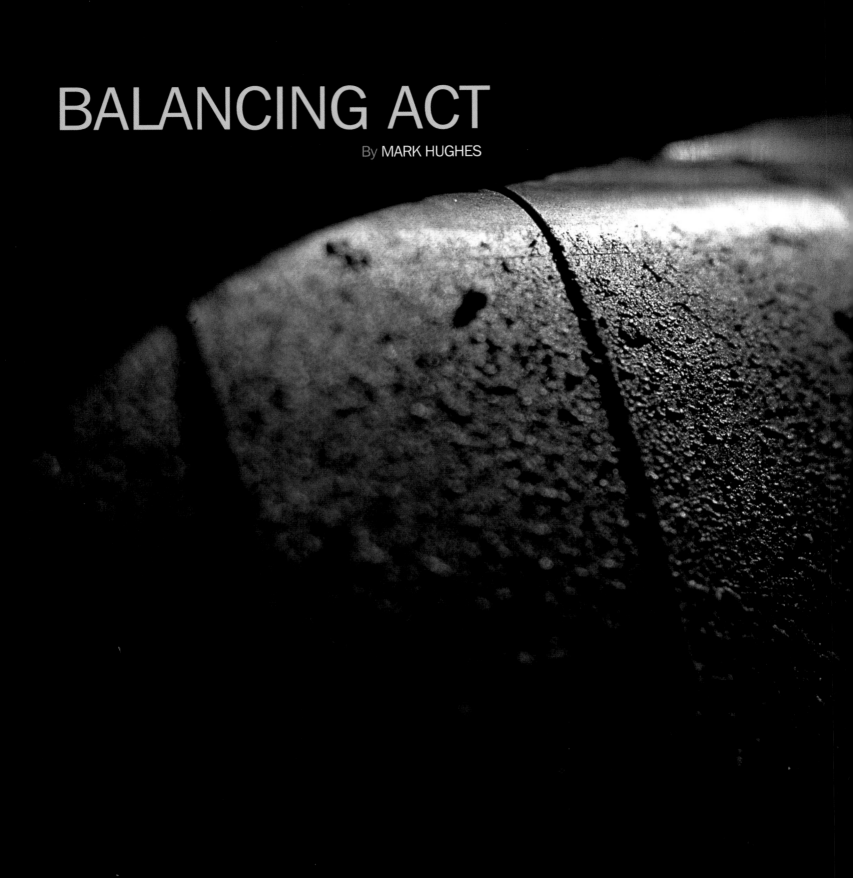

BALANCING ACT

By MARK HUGHES

THE obvious conundrum of the new one-lap qualifying format – of where to make the compromise between the one-lap speed and effective race strategy – was only the beginning. The subtleties went way beyond what even the teams were probably expecting.

Tyre behaviour and tyre management largely determined the whole question of strategy. Previously, the primary considerations had been the lap time penalty for extra weight at the circuit in question and fuel consumption. (In other words, by how much did weight hurt lap time – something that varies from track to track – and how quickly did that weight come off?) This still applied, but was often overshadowed by tyre considerations.

A good case study was McLaren. Into its second year with Michelin, the team had a much better understanding of the tyre, and the MP4/17D's rear suspension – arguably the key point of distinction between the car and the previous MP4/17 – worked the rubber much more effectively. Going into the new season, the car was suddenly a contender, aided by Williams's initial struggle to understand its new FW25. However, as the season wore on and the potential of the Williams was tapped, so it became clear that while the MP4/17D was a major improvement, its tyre usage remained its limiting factor.

Although the McLaren was quite kind to its tyres during a race, the reasons for this contributed directly to its inability to generate enough heat in them for a single lap of qualifying – explaining the propensity for Kimi Räikkönen to shunt on Saturday and David Coulthard to be slow. One way of getting more heat into the rubber is to load more fuel into the car. That would usually bring with it a theoretically better race strategy (in terms of the old-fashioned weight penalty on lap time versus time taken for pit stops and traffic delays). It seemed the obvious way to go for a car that was making inefficient use of a light fuel load over one lap. But the problem with this was the impact the heavy-fuel grid position had on that theoretically ideal race strategy; vital chunks of time were lost on the opening laps to the concertina effect as cars were forced to make room for each other. The farther back on the grid a driver was, the more he suffered the effects of the phenomenon. McLaren was caught between a strategic rock and a hard place – all because of how the car used its tyres. This clearly illustrated

that what is still called Saturday qualifying should really be considered the first lap of the race.

To gain a better understanding of the infinitely complex range of factors governing tyre performance, it's worth considering the specific, but inter-related, limitations: degradation, wear, blistering and 'graining'.

Degradation refers to performance drop-off from one lap to the next. It can occur because the tyre has surpassed its optimum temperature, because it is too worn, because it has blistered or because it has 'grained'. Degradation can vary massively according to the track and track temperature.

Sometimes, there was more degradation on the Michelin than the Bridgestone, but only because the former was starting from a point of higher performance – that is, it was a faster qualifying tyre. If some of that performance wore off after a few laps so that it brought the tyre down to about the same level of performance as the Bridgestone, its user was still ahead. Sometimes, the Michelin would show higher degradation on Friday, but the rate at which it degraded would reduce as the weekend went on, the layer of track rubber coming to its aid. Usually, the Michelin would produce better performance from higher track temperatures, once beyond a critical point (around 30 degrees C), and so start from a higher level, yet still suffer less degradation than the Bridgestone.

At Magny-Cours – and sometimes Barcelona – degradation is so severe that the tyres lose more performance on each lap than the car gains through its lower fuel load. Therefore, in terms of track positioning, it's an advantage if a driver's stint is of shorter duration than his rival's. This is the reverse of the usual situation.

Wear concerns the amount of rubber left on the tyre. It's not often an issue *per se*, but when it reaches a certain point, even though there's still rubber on the tyre, performance drops off – that is, the rate of degradation rises. In this situation, the rubber is no longer flexible enough to grip the tarmac and support the load, behaving almost like a harder-compound tyre. This 'springiness' and its effect on grip is known as hysteresis.

Tyres blister when they reach around 200 degrees C. At some tracks – notably Montreal and Hockenheim – drivers can live with blistering because the penalty is less than the gain provided by the softer-compound tyre that has induced

it. But they're walking a tightrope because it's a process that can snowball dramatically if allowed to go too far. A lot depends on the discipline of the driver in keeping the car to a set pace. Surrendering to the temptation of pushing harder will ensure that the blistering is terminal – witness Jarno Trulli's final Hockenheim stint.

'Graining' is the process whereby the shoulder of the tread block tears. When this occurs, the load borne by the tyre moves across to the next block. With the four-groove tyre, there are five blocks. Normally, only when 'graining' has affected the entire width of the tyre will it stop, as the reduced height of the blocks means that no longer is there enough leverage to cause the tears. This phenomenon tended to be more pronounced on the Michelin than the Bridgestone. The 'graining' was more common, lasted longer and the lap-time drop-off was greater when it did occur. But unlike last year, it wasn't so critical for Michelin because of the tyre's usual performance advantage in qualifying.

Bear in mind that none of the performance curves – degradation, wear, blistering, 'graining' – is linear. They tend to reach certain points, then sweep dramatically one way or the other. These curves are even less predictable as weight – that is, fuel – is loaded into the car and as the track temperature changes. Thus, for the teams, it is a very delicate

game of maintaining inter-related factors at optimum levels, and doing it without full data and with some other elements – primarily track temperature – beyond their control. Do you go for the better hysteresis of a softer compound and live with the 'graining' or blistering? Can you get away with not suffering that penalty? If you go for the harder compound, does one-lap tyre grip suffer so much that you may as well put in more fuel?

Under the new format, there is much less track time on which to base decisions before you have to commit to a strategy. Therefore, it's become more black art and fine feel, less hard data. The value of intuitive and experienced hands like Renault's Pat Symonds has gone exponential.

Generally, the Michelin offered a higher level of performance for its users to work with, helping them in their battle against Ferrari. But in their fight against each other, Williams, McLaren and Renault had to develop individual methods of tweaking the tyres' characteristics. Partly, these were inherent in the car and, in this respect, the Renault, with its width, low centre of gravity and high-stiffness vee-angle, had a built-in advantage (although this was offset by a sheer lack of grunt).

It's a difficult situation to balance. It's necessary to work the tyres hard in one lap qualifying to bring them up to the

Above: Ralf Schumacher found that his Williams-BMW was able to negotiate the balance of qualifying and race permutations better than its similarly-shod Michelin rivals.

Left: Tyres waiting for Mark Webber's Jaguar.

Below: Tucked into their warmers and ready for action at Monaco.

Bottom: Tread carefully. A used Michelin showing the wear.

Photographs: Darren Heath

optimum temperature, but on the other hand, they should not be pushed past the optimum for the race. The Jaguar's weight distribution and rear suspension geometry made for a car that heated its tyres spectacularly well over one lap, but abused them in the race. The McLaren was the opposite, but closer to the overall ideal. Although better on its tyres in both situations than the McLaren, the Renault still could have done with putting more heat into them over one lap. The Williams had the balance spot-on from Saturday at Monaco and for the rest of the season. It generated plenty of heat in them during qualifying (not as close to the qualifying optimum as the Jag, but closer than anyone else) and didn't mistreat them in the race. Weight distribution was the key. In fact, in some races, the Williams was easier on the rubber than the McLaren and as good as the Renault, but without the horsepower penalty.

The Williams's balance of grip, rubber durability, aero and engine performance meant that the team could often ignore the random variable of the penalty of grid position. The team would start from the front and simply divide its race into the theoretical optimum stint lengths unencumbered – a luxury denied the rest. Ultimately, however, that wasn't enough to overcome the early-season struggle to unlock the potential of the FW25.

HEALTHY OUTLOOK

By TONY DODGINS

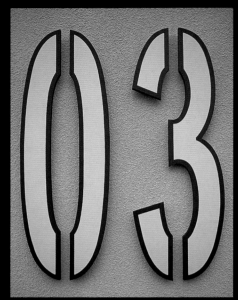

LIKE a child kicking against a parent's exhausted patience, grand prix racing was dragged screaming into an era of new rules for the 2003 season. When the F1 team principals met in the winter of '02, the agenda was cost reduction and a better Show. But they agreed little, and when one of them doubted they'd saved enough to cover the cost of the sandwiches they'd just eaten, Max Mosley decided he'd had enough.

For the FIA president, procrastination was not an option. Amid an economic down-turn, he recognised unease among sponsors, TV networks and race promoters. He acted. We would have one-lap qualifying, bespoke tyres, a revised scoring system, *parc fermé* betwixt qualifying and race, and, crucially, no refuelling after qualifying. The ramifications of this last 'detail' were enormous.

McLaren's Ron Dennis had apoplexy. Word was, he'd spent a fortune on his 'qualifying' car, which, at a stroke, had been rendered obsolete.

The sporting regulations, say the rules, may be changed prior to 31 October of the previous year, subject to unanimous agreement.

'We know the Concorde Agreement [the document by which F1 is run] has flaws,' said Dennis, 'but none that allow someone to take a dictatorial position. Or so we thought.'

Amazingly, the news that they could no longer refuel after qualifying – laughably on the grounds of safety – was broken to F1's technical directors in a fax from Charlie Whiting (the FIA's race director and technical delegate) on 12 February! In other words, a few days before the freight left for Melbourne.

Perhaps unsurprisingly, Dennis and Williams announced their decision to go to arbitration with the International Chamber of Commerce. Mosley, they said, had driven a bus through Concorde, wholly exceeding his authority.

It was hard to argue, at least about process, even if you were intrigued by the prospects, a most welcome bonus after a soporific 2002 season. According to Mosley, it was 'strict reinterpretation of existing rules.' Insert John McEnroe catch-phrase here. You couldn't help thinking that, for the FIA president, this had better work.

Nine months on, 'the boy Mosley got a result', in football parlance. For much of it, Max deserves great credit. Some, though, was more luck than judgement.

Heading for the finale at Suzuka, we could reflect on a superb season, the best for years: eight different winners, a championship that went down to the wire and vastly renewed interest. ITV's viewing figures were up for 65 per cent of the races.

The most significant change was the need to qualify in race trim. In one fell swoop, this did away with qualifying cars and shook up the grid. For decades, we'd spent a couple of days making sure that the fastest car started at the front, and then wondered why we didn't get a motor race on Sunday

The mechanics of race tactics would make a feature in itself, but Renault's director of engineering,

Above: Plenty of gripping moments for the tifosi.

Left: Max Mosley's rule changes gave Formula 1 a much needed shot in the arm in 2003.

Right: Michael Schumacher was made to work harder than ever to take his record sixth title.

Photographs: Darren Heath

Pat Symonds, one of the best strategists in the business, says that the new format made it much more complex and involved.

Take Monte Carlo, for example. Many figured that given the impossibility of overtaking, the way forward was a short first stint so as not to compromise grid position. But Symonds and Ferrari's Ross Brawn, for whom the fuel-heavy Jarno Trulli and Michael Schumacher qualified fourth and fifth respectively, thought otherwise and probably were right.

'Chances were, you'd get stuck in traffic running a short first stint because of the crocodile that develops at Monte Carlo,' Symonds said. 'But what I did not anticipate was da Matta's Toyota running so slowly with people stuck behind. It left a window to drop into, which, in fact, meant that an earlier stop would have been advantageous.'

On fuel-adjusted times, pole man Montoya would have qualified eighth. But the Colombian did manage to stop relatively early and still give the resurgent Williams team its first win in the principality for 20 years. Trulli could not stay with the leading trio on his heavier fuel load and also held up Schumacher's Ferrari. In the end, Montoya, Räikkönen and Schumacher crossed the line separated by 1.72s – the fifth-closest podium of all time. Previously, Schumacher would simply have taken the pole and cleared off.

Artificial, yell the purists. Maybe so. Or just different?

Canada, a fortnight later, was even closer, with just 1.35s covering the podium finishers. And Silverstone was superb, one of the best races anyone could remember for years.

Why was it so good? Again, it was a function of the need to qualify in race trim, giving a mixed grid, allied to the nuances of varying tyre performance on a circuit where overtaking is feasible. Not forgetting the religious nutter who chose Hangar Straight for his Sunday-afternoon jog.

On single-lap qualifying, there was more dissent. 'Call me an enthusiast or an anorak,' David Coulthard said, 'but I know that Ayrton Senna took 65 poles, and that means something.

Top: Mr E and (above) Williams's Frank Dernie, neither of whom are great fans of the current qualifying rules.

Below: Montoya, who was on top form at Monaco, is not happy about the rules either.
Photographs: Darren Heath

The fans want to know who is the fastest. That's part of the sport's history and it's lost to us.'

Coulthard could not get on with one-lap qualifying, and Juan Pablo Montoya hated it as well.

'I don't think it shows true driver performance,' the Colombian said. 'It sucks! You are basically driving a bag of s**t.'

I'm not sure Patrick Head and co. would appreciate such a glowing description of the FW25, but you get the drift. Montoya, the man who started from the pole seven times last year, could not 'dance on the edge' like he could with a lightweight car in pure qualifying trim. In fact, on qualifying performance over the season, he was trounced by Ralf Schumacher, which was a surprise.

Bernie Ecclestone was not a fan.

'It's horrible,' said Mr E in Malaysia. 'First, the drivers are not on the limit, and then they complete only one lap, come back to the pits and can only watch. They don't have the chance to beat a rival who has bettered their time. There's no fighting. The excitement has gone.'

What did the TV men think?

ITV's James Allen: 'I don't like Friday because the quick men go first and then it seems to peter out. But Saturday is fine, the mixed grids are exciting and it's good that we don't know how much fuel people are carrying. It makes it more interesting. There was talk of published car weights, but I'm pleased that didn't happen.'

Whatever you may think of the various qualifying scenarios, the point to remember is that, in Britain at any rate, two-and-a-half-times as many people watched the race in 2003. Vastly improved races are a good trade-off against a little lost excitement provided by multi-car qualifying, especially when there is no guarantee that the television director will catch it anyway.

I mentioned that Mosley had enjoyed some luck. It involved the reduced competitiveness of Ferrari's F2003-GA.

An illuminating piece of journalism from Mark Hughes of *Autosport*, who writes elsewhere in *AUTOCOURSE*, revealed that Ferrari had designed its new car around a longer wheelbase, partly to provide it with more options in terms of qualifying set-up.

Ross Brawn explained that the concessions made when designing a qualifying car and a race car are all to do with weight distribution. There were times in '02 when a Ferrari was overheating its front tyres toward the end of a qualifying lap. Because F1's rear tyres are too narrow relative to the fronts, the idea is to load up the front to do more work – more difficult with a short-wheelbase car.

Ferrari, therefore, had given itself more set-up options for qualifying – which suddenly it didn't need and couldn't use – and fewer options for race set-up. This goes some way to explaining why, at circuits where qualifying was especially important, like Hungary, the F2003-GA struggled in the race. It was interesting that Williams had gone the other way, toward a short-wheelbase car, had changed the weight distribution and made such strong progress. Mosley, then, benefited

from a coincidental mismatch between that 11th-hour rule change and a development direction to which Ferrari was committed.

At least you've got to hope it was coincidental. Hell, where would F1 be without Machiavellian theory? It will be interesting to see what happens next year.

With a goodly proportion of the philosophy behind Brawn's '03 car redundant, you had to giggle when, during a prickly Monza press conference in the aftermath of the Michelin tyre controversy, someone asked whether it had ever been known for the FIA to interpret or clarify a rule other than in Ferrari's favour.

'There's this perception that the FIA favours Ferrari, but nothing done over the winter favoured us one jot,' Ross Brawn pointed out. 'We were dominating F1, we had everything together, a good way of working, and it all got turned upside-down.'

It's a reasonable point. The *parc fermé* law condensed the timetable and, safety issues apart, you might have expected it to impact on reliability, a Ferrari strong suit. In fact, it didn't. Ferrari and Williams headed to the last race with just one mechanical failure apiece – a credit to both. In 2002, Schumacher had the title under lock and key by July, which meant eight months before the F1 World Championship was seriously in anyone's consciousness again. The FIA wanted to put that right, and it did so by revising the points system.

The four-point win-to-second-place margin was halved and points were awarded down to eighth. No doubt this helped team principals not belonging to the manufacturer elite who preferred to speak to their paymasters with some points to show for all the effort and expenditure.

Undoubtedly, it worked, although not everyone was keen. Williams's Frank Dernie had been in and out of F1 paddocks for nigh on 30 years and he was no fan.

'It's ironic that Michael Schumacher and Luca di Montezemolo were complaining at the start of the season that the new points system was really bad because it was going to be so hard to catch Räikkönen. But then suddenly, with Juan Montoya bearing down on Michael later on, it was their biggest ally!

'But I do think the new system is rubbish – a massive step backwards. You've now got a situation where you could quite easily win the championship without any race wins at all.'

By way of illustration, Kimi Räikkönen went to Suzuka with an outside chance of claiming the title with two wins to Schumacher's six. Can that be right? A few years back, everyone was screaming that champions should be winners and first place was suddenly worth ten points instead of nine, partly to reflect that.

Inevitably, given the scale of change, there were anachronisms and anomalies along the way. Michael Schumacher, for example, was having a pre-race snooze at Interlagos,

blissfully unaware that, because of the heavy rain, Charlie Whiting had allowed everyone to change their wing settings. Unarguably valid on safety grounds, but the champion had factored expected rain into his qualifying set-up, compromising his performance, then had lost his advantage. He was not best pleased.

And a single-wet-tyre rule, intended to save money, meant that everyone tried to make do with a shallow-groove wet, which was more adaptable across a range of conditions, but pretty useless in proper rain. That gave us the farce we saw later that same afternoon in Brazil. Again, though, this was promptly addressed.

Undoubtedly, allowing tyre manufacturers to provide their customers with different rubber helped the Michelin teams because there was more than one front-running outfit on the French tyres. But that's as it should be. It negated another Ferrari advantage, given that Bridgestone always developed rubber almost exclusively around the Italian team. The idea that a car should be compromised by having to run a tyre suitable for a rival, given the amount of money spent in F1, was always nonsense.

As a championship and as entertainment, Formula 1 was terrific in 2003. Whether or not you agree that Dr Mosley's patient was terminally sick in the first place, you'd be hard pushed to argue that the magic potions pulled from his black bag have done other than help to return it to rude health.

Above: Canada provided an entertaining race for the home crowd and the worldwide TV audience.
Photograph: Darren Heath

THE CLASS OF '03

By MIKE DOODSON

EIGHT different winners in 16 races was the satisfying reward for FIA President Max Mosley's decision to impose a note of unpredictability on to the 2003 season's qualifying procedure. Yes, the new 'full fuel and race tyres' format may have been artificial and contrived, and it did not meet with the approval of all the team owners, but generally the drivers welcomed it.

Of the eight winners, three were newcomers to the podium. Giancarlo Fisichella at last managed to claim a victory in his eighth season of F1, thanks to a Brazilian downpour, but Kimi Räikkönen (in Malaysia) and Fernando Alonso (in Hungary) were comparative tyros, being in their third and second full seasons respectively. It is impossible, of course, to say whether the three new winners would have had the same opportunities under the pre-2003 regulations. Surely nobody would deny, though, that at least two potential stars of the future twinkled brightly in 2003, and that they would surely have done so regardless of Mosley's cunning intervention.

Top: **Fernando Alonso became the youngest ever grand prix winner.**
Photograph: Darren Heath

Above: **Kimi Räikkönen admires the winner's trophy on the podium in Malaysia.**
Photograph: Patrick Gosling

Left: **Kimi in action in Malaysia.**

Facing page: **Alonso qualifies the Renault fastest in Malaysia, making him the youngest pole-position starter as well.**
Photographs: Darren Heath

After his quietly impressive debut season (9 points, tenth place in the championship) with Sauber in 2001, Räikkönen was a logical choice for McLaren in 2002. It was an expensive acquisition for Ron Dennis, with figures for Sauber's compensation of up to $10 million being bandied about. Nevertheless, it promises to pay off handsomely. Not only did the new Finn take over seamlessly where his retired predecessor Mika Häkkinen had left off, but also he almost tasted victory in his first year with the Silver Arrows. It failed to happen only because a French marshal at Magny-Cours didn't deploy his flags promptly enough to signal the oil from an exploding Toyota that cost Räikkönen an off-track excursion when he was within six laps of defeating Michael Schumacher.

When the first win finally came, in Malaysia 2003, it was at the expense of Alonso, who had qualified on pole with a smaller load of fuel. Despite the Spaniard suffering from a serious dose of flu, it was a tough chase, and Rubens Barrichello – who had separated the two by finishing second – made the unusually generous observation afterward that both men were future world champions.

Because he prefers driving to talking, Kimi has gained a reputation as the most taciturn driver ever to land a seat in an F1 car. It is true that his answers to journalists' questions, delivered in a monotone croak that suggests his voice has only just broken, are brief to the point of brusqueness. But he has an immensely quick mind and a discernible sense of humour, leavened by a frustratingly well developed sense of discretion. He fits in perfectly at McLaren and almost imperceptibly has assumed the position of *de facto* team leader.

Kimi is the younger of two brothers with motor sporting ambitions. Their parents poured their life savings into the boys' careers,

and one account suggests that it wasn't until the younger sibling landed his contract with Sauber that the family home gained an inside toilet. Although the Räikkönens were offered the opportunity of retiring by their son, only his father was happy to be padding around at home instead of driving the road roller that was once his speciality. 'My dad is not working any more, but although my mum was off work last year, she decided that she still wants to carry on,' said Kimi. His brother's rallying career, meanwhile, seems to have lost some of its impetus.

It was Kimi's extraordinary consistency that allowed him to get to the end of the season still with a chance of wresting the title from Michael Schumacher. One important reason for this was his willingness to test whenever the call came, which kept the McLaren MP4/17D competitive, and he continues to dazzle his engineers with good feedback and inspired ideas to improve the car. Although he botched a couple of qualifying sessions, he extracted some exceptional speed from the McLaren on Saturday afternoons, despite the fact that it's extremely nervous to drive on the limit. He out-qualified team-mate David Coulthard by 10–6 and took 91 championship points to the Scot's 51.

Despite the Finn's loyalty to McLaren, it was inevitable that there was some frustration over the lack of progress with the much vaunted, but unreliable, MP4/18, which ended up with tens of thousands of test miles behind it, but not not one in a race. 'The 17D is almost exactly the same as it was for the first race [in Australia],' he confided in September. 'We haven't really had any new parts for it the whole season, and it was only really for Monza when we got some development parts which really made a difference you could notice.'

Above: Alonso – flat out all the way.

Below: Fernando's big day, winning in Hungary.
Both photographs: Patrick Gosling

As for Alonso, he bested his team-mate, Jarno Trulli, 9–6 in qualifying and claimed 55 points to the Italian's 33. His greatest advantage, like Räikkönen's, was his consistency in a car whose performance varied alarmingly from track to track. Also like Räikkönen, he is close to his engineers and maintains an almost non-stop radio conversation with them throughout the races. When it came to grasping opportunities in 2003, the Spaniard rarely missed, in contrast with Trulli, who tended to panic when under pressure.

Alonso was spotted by Flavio Briatore after a masterly F3000 win at Spa-Francorchamps in 2000. He was signed to a long-term management contract and loaned out for 2001 to Minardi, where he utterly outclassed the Brazilian Tarso Marques. In 2002, he was retained as a test driver with the Briatore-managed Renault team, honing his talent for analytical feedback and putting a hefty mileage behind him before returning to full-time competition in 2003 as Briatore's choice over Jenson Button.

Another similarity with Räikkönen is that Alonso comes from a humble background. He was born in the north-western Spanish city of Oviedo, facing the Atlantic, where his father, José Luis, was the manager of an explosives factory. Family encouragement started early: the boy was given his first kart at the age of three. There are some remarkable parallels with the career of Michael Schumacher here, for José Luis had the knack of putting together raceworthy karts from bits that had been thrown away by others. The family photo album has pictures of Fernando with trophies that were sometimes almost as big as he was. José Luis now works for the booming sports promotion agency started by ex-F1 driver Adrian Campos.

By the time he was 17, Fernando had won a clutch of national titles and a world karting championship. He immediately went into the Euro-Open Movistar Nissan single-seater series, where nine pole positions and six wins took him to the title and earned him an F3000 ride for 2001 with Astromega. The win at Spa helped him to an eventual fourth place in the championship.

There is something Schumacher-like, too, in the sheer tenacity displayed by Alonso. It got the better of him in the Renault at a rainy Interlagos, where he failed to slow down, despite a flurry of yellow flags warning of Mark Webber's smash at the corner before the pits. The Renault hit one of the Jaguar's flying wheels and the ensuing impact with the wall, at virtually flat-out speed, looked grave indeed. But the youngster gave a cheery thumbs-up as he was stretchered away. It was surely fortunate for him that he was unavailable for interview when the stewards reviewed the incident.

Alonso had already become the youngest man ever to take a pole position in a championship GP when he set the fastest time in qualifying in Malaysia. His big day was to come in Hungary, where literally he ran away from the field on a circuit that particularly suited the Renault. By the end of the race, he had lapped both his team-mate and Michael Schumacher's Ferrari. Later, he celebrated having broken Bruce McLaren's 34-year-old youth crown as he became the sport's youngest ever winner at the age of 22 years and 26 days.

'The thing about Fernando is he only knows one way to drive,' Renault technical boss Mike Gascoyne told *The Guardian* at Monaco. 'He enjoys it; he gets in and goes flat out. With Fernando, it's flat out all the way. That's as quick as it goes – flat out. Gets out, shrugs his shoulders and says, "That's it," sort of thing.

'A lot of people commented on the choice when we took him instead of Jenson, but really we said it at the time: the guy has the spark of a world champion about him, and I don't think there is anyone who doubts it.'

No sooner had Alonso won in Hungary than the rumour mill began to suggest that he was the likely candidate to take over from Michael Schumacher, some sources indicating that the move was imminent. Briatore, understandably, quickly disabused the pundits of any such imaginings, but it is difficult not to speculate on just how suitable the Spaniard would be for the role.

With Michael apparently minded to honour his contract with Ferrari, albeit not necessarily all the way to the end of 2006, finding a replacement will be on the minds of Montezemolo and Todt. Räikkönen and Alonso probably did better than either of them expected in 2003, and they are committed to their existing teams for long periods. But inevitably their names must be high on the Ferrari shopping list – and if the call should eventually come, resisting it will be difficult.

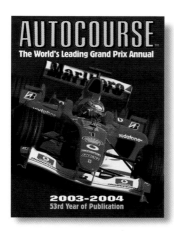
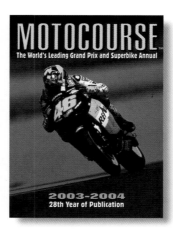

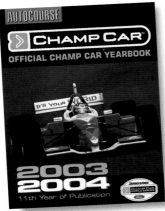

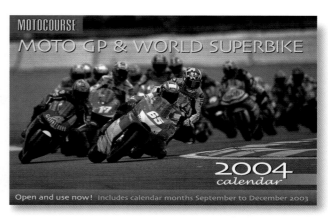
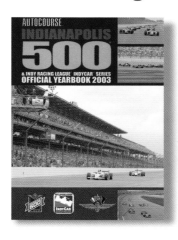
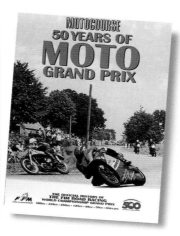
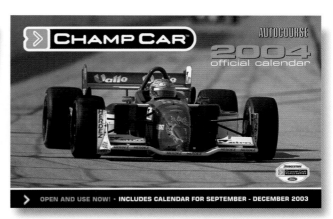

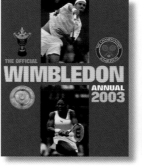

MANFRED von Brauchitsch, the sole surviving member of the epic Mercedes-Benz 'Silver Arrows' Grand Prix team of the 1930s, died on 5 February, 2003, at the age of 97. He was one of the unluckiest drivers of the period, winning just three major international races for Mercedes between 1934 and '39.

Born in Hamburg into a Prussian dynasty of army officers, von Brauchitsch enlisted in the forces immediately after finishing secondary school. He had risen to the rank of sergeant by 1923, when he was invalided out of the army, but his uncle, Walther von Brauchitsch, went on to become a general in 1938 and later was promoted to commander-in-chief of Hitler's armies.

Manfred's first triumph came at the 1934 Eifel GP at the Nürburgring, the weekend when the *Silberpfeile* earned their informal nickname after the Mercedes W25s had to be stripped of their white paint and raced with bare aluminium bodywork to bring them below the 750-kg maximum weight limit.

Von Brauchitsch memorably lost the 1935 German Grand Prix to Tazio Nuvolari's underpowered Alfa Romeo after his Mercedes suffered a tyre failure on the final lap. Three years later, he received another disappointment in this race when his car caught fire during a refuelling stop. When he resumed the race, he discovered that the removable steering wheel had not been refitted properly, with the result that it came off its spindle and he spun gently into a ditch.

MANFRED von BRAUCHITSCH

In 1937, he won the Monaco Grand Prix ahead of team-mate Rudolf Caracciola, a success achieved against team orders, which put him in bad odour with the charismatic Mercedes team manager, Alfred Neubauer. Despite these tensions, he regarded Caracciola as his closest friend in the team and the finest driver he had raced against.

Von Brauchitsch also won the 1938 French Grand Prix at Reims. He spent the war working as private secretary to a general in Berlin before moving briefly to Argentina after hostilities ceased. He returned to Germany in 1948.

He never raced after the war, but despite having decamped to East Germany following lurid problems in his personal life, Manfred von Brauchitsch visited the West on several occasions, notably for the historic event at Dijon-Prenois, which supported the 1974 French Grand Prix, and the opening of the new Nürburgring ten years later.

After the reunification of Germany in 1989, the patrician von Brauchitsch became a regular visitor to many Mercedes-Benz functions and was cast almost in the role of royalty. He was fit and alert until a few months before his death. He had outlived Hermann Lang, the other surviving member of the Silver Arrows squad, by more than a decade.

KARL Kling, who partnered Juan Manuel Fangio in the Mercedes W196 squad during 1954, died at Hemmenhofen, on Lake Constance, on 18 March, 2003, at the age of 92. By no means the greatest of F1 exponents, Kling was nevertheless a versatile and loyal member of the Mercedes team, whose greatest success was his victory in the 1952 Carrera Panamericana road race through Mexico, which he won sharing a Mercedes 300SL coupé with compatriot Hans Klenk.

Kling started out as a reception clerk in the PR department of Daimler-Benz in 1936, and he competed with Mercedes production cars in rallies and reliability trials up to the outbreak of the Second World War. He serviced aircraft for the Luftwaffe during the war, then began racing again in 1946 with a BMW 328 before graduating to a Veritas. He was invited into the Mercedes sports car and Formula 1 teams in the early 1950s.

He was runner-up to Fangio in the 1954 French Grand Prix, but his career was not without controversy. In that year's German Grand Prix, he raced through to wrest the lead from Fangio, openly defying standing team orders and urgent signals from Neubauer and fellow drivers Hermann Lang and Hans Herrmann in the pits.

KARL KLING

Eventually, he had to make a pit stop to repair damaged suspension, receiving a roasting from Mercedes director Dr Fritz Nallinger, who initially wanted him to be fired. 'A man who's incapable of team discipline and who drives his car to death is no use to us,' he fumed. Later, it became clear that Kling was running with a lighter fuel load than Fangio and would have had to make another refuelling stop. When that was explained, Nallinger relented.

Eventually, Kling was permitted his moment of glory in the non-championship *Avusrennen* at the famous circuit in Berlin, leading home Fangio and Hans Herrmann in a Mercedes 1-2-3. He retired from racing in 1955 and succeeded Neubauer as head of the Daimler-Benz sports department. In 1959, he won the 14,000-km Algiers-to-Cape Town rally in a Mercedes 180D, and two years later repeated the feat in the 11,500-km Algiers-Lagos-Algiers rally in a Mercedes 200SE. In 1990, Hermann and von Brauchitsch were among many Mercedes luminaries who turned out to celebrate Kling's 80th birthday at the company's Stuttgart museum.

TEDDY YIP

TEDDY Yip was a larger-than-life character whose Theodore Racing F1 team scored a memorable victory in the rain-soaked 1978 Silverstone International Trophy race, with future world champion Keke Rosberg at the wheel.

Teddy was the ultimate international wheeler-dealer. Born in Indonesia and educated in Holland, he was one of the commercial driving forces behind the Macau Grand Prix, and had raced there himself in 1956 at the wheel of a Jaguar XK120. Yip may have been a hard-nosed and successful businessman, but also he was an absolutely passionate motor racing fan, and his death in July, at the age of 96, certainly deprived the sport of one of its more colourful personalities.

He first became involved in international racing as a backer of Brian Redman in Formula 5000 in 1974, a relationship that brought him into contact with team boss Sid Taylor. There followed further involvement in America with Vern Schuppan and, consequently, Dan Gurney's Eagle team.

Yip supported Schuppan's drives in Formula 1 with the Ensign team in 1974 and continued to back the Australian in America. Then, he sponsored Alan Jones, who won two F5000 events for the team in 1976.

Later, Yip would provide support for the Ensign team before commissioning Ron Tauranac to design and build the Theodore TR1, which Rosberg used to such great effect at Silverstone. His F1 involvement ended with backing for the Ensign team again in 1983.

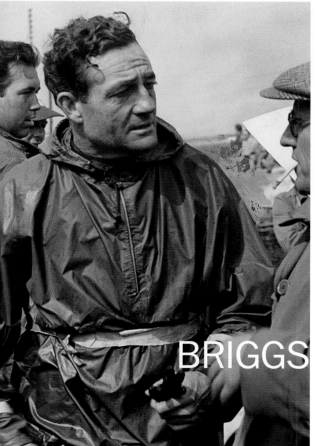

BRIGGS Cunningham, the Yale-educated multi-millionaire American sportsman, who financed his own team of Cunningham sports cars at Le Mans in the early 1950s, died on 2 July, 2003, aged 96.

The son of a wealthy financier from Cincinnati, who had made a fortune from the meat packing business and had been one of the first backers of Proctor & Gamble, Cunningham was born with a silver spoon in his mouth and fielded a wide variety of cars – usually Jaguars – for many years after his own machines ceased to compete.

When he retired from driving, he turned to his second love, ocean yacht racing, and captained the US entry *Columbia* when it won the 1958 America's Cup. He also founded the Cunningham auto museum at Costa Mesa, California, which thrived for over 30 years until its eventual closure in 1985 due to its owner's old age.

BRIGGS CUNNINGHAM

Formula 1 review

Contributors
BOB CONSTANDUROS
MAURICE HAMILTON
ALAN HENRY

F1 illustrations
IAN HUTCHINSON
NICOLA CURTIS

F1 illustrations reference
MICHAEL FISHER

Photograph: Darren Heath

MICHAEL SCHUMACHER

RUBENS BARRICHELLO

Photographs: Darren Heath

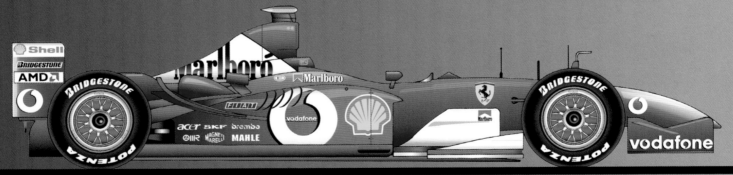

N. Curtis 2003

FERRARI F2003-GA

SPONSORS	Marlboro, Shell, Vodafone, Fiat, Bridgestone, AMD, Olympus, Acer, Brembo, Magneti Marelli
ENGINE	Type: Ferrari 052 No. of cylinders (vee angle): V10 (90°) Sparking Plugs: NGK Electronics: Magneti Marelli Fuel: Shell Oil: Shell
TRANSMISSION	Gearbox: Ferrari seven-speed longitudinal automatic Clutch: Hand-operated
CHASSIS	Front suspension: independent, pushrod-activated torsion spring Rear suspension: independent, pushrod-activated torsion spring
	Wheel diameter: front: 13 in. rear: 13 in. Wheels: BBS Tyres: Bridgestone Brake pads: Brembo Brake discs: Brembo Brake calipers: Brembo
	Steering: Ferrari power-assisted Battery: Magneti Marelli Instruments: Magneti Marelli
DIMENSIONS	Formula weight: 1322.8 lb/600 kg including driver

**Above left: Michael and the Ferrari F2003-GA
winning in Canada.**

**Above, from top: Jean Todt, Ross Brawn and
Rory Byrne.**
Photographs: Darren Heath

F Ferrari's success in 2002 came relatively easily, that certainly was not the case in 2003. The Italian team's bid for the championship went all the way to the wire. Michael Schumacher gained his record sixth world title by just two points with his eighth place at Suzuka, his equal worst position of the year, while the Scuderia clinched its 13th constructors' title by 14 points after rival Williams failed to score for the first and only time during 2003.

Ferrari itself only failed to score once, early in the season in Brazil, when Michael Schumacher crashed and Rubens Barrichello ran out of fuel. But a mid-summer dip – when Michael finished seventh and eighth in the German and Hungarian Grands Prix respectively – provided a wake-up call for the team, which went on to win the last three races.

It was a crucial, character-building period, as technical director Ross Brawn emphasised: 'When you have some races like we had in Hockenheim and Hungary, you try and understand what actually happened. You go through everything, to try to piece together why you are not competitive, and then you also look at things that you can physically and feasibly do.

'We could see we were struggling a little bit in a couple of areas. We took another view on the tyres with Bridgestone, as to what approach we should take. We stepped back a bit and had another look to see whether we were going in the right direction on tyres, and we came to the conclusion we weren't. Not Bridgestone's fault, Ferrari's fault.'

He added, 'We'd gone in a certain direction on tyres which, in retrospect, probably wasn't the right direction, so we went back a few steps and reassessed where we were and took a slightly different direction. Along with some improvements to the car, that was enough to turn it around.'

As in 2002, Ferrari began the season with its previous year's challenger, used mainly for tyre testing during the off-season, with engine updates that were possible to initiate retrospectively, as the old and new power units were very similar.

'We didn't do an awful lot to the 2002 car for the beginning of the season,' explained Brawn. 'It was very much the same car and, looking back, it was the right decision to concentrate on the 2003 car because I think the 2002 car, at that stage of the season, was perfectly competitive. We didn't make the best of it for other reasons. We had other things that stopped us, but the car was more than capable of winning races or scoring good points at the beginning of the season, so it very much served its purpose.'

True, Michael put the F2002 on pole for Australia, with Rubens alongside, but a tardy first pit stop, being put on the grass by Räikkönen and losing a bargeboard relegated him to fourth at the chequered flag. A collision with Trulli on lap one in Malaysia resulted in a stop for a new front wing and a drive-through penalty, which dropped Michael to 14th, but eventually he finished sixth, while Barrichello came home a fine second to Räikkönen.

In the Brazilian rain, pole-man Barrichello was leading when he ran out of fuel. Team-mate Schumacher had already crashed his car, ending a run of continuous points finishes dating back to the 2001 Hungarian Grand Prix. It was the first time since the 1999 European Grand Prix that the Scuderia had failed to score any points in a race, while the previous occasion upon which neither of its cars had seen the chequered flag was the Belgian GP of 1998.

At this stage, Ferrari was third in the championship, 23 points behind the leader, McLaren, and nine adrift of second-place Renault. Räikkönen led the drivers' series with 24 points; Ferrari's men had eight each. It was from this point onward that Ferrari hit form. Still using the 2002 car, and in spite of being in mourning for his mother, Elisabeth, who had died the previous evening, Michael demonstrated the strength of his character by winning commandingly at Imola, giving the F2002 a fine send-off. Michael was now third in the championship, the team second.

From this point on, the team would only use the F2003-GA, the suffix honouring Giovanni Agnelli, who had passed away earlier in the year. Brawn described the car as the best Ferrari ever. 'It was a good step aerodynamically, and with the rules having been stable for so long, it was quite difficult to make progress aerodynamically,' he said.

Even though the new car did not make its debut until early May,

it was not possible to accommodate any ideas that the team might have had in respect of the new regulations, introduced in January. But it would change during the rest of the season.

'We've not changed the suspension very much at all,' explained Brawn. 'We've run through a range of adjustments within the scope of the system, damper work, all the traditional stuff.

'Aerodynamically, there's just been a constant update. Every race or every few races, there have been changes on the car. We've had two or three versions of the turning vanes behind the front wheels, several front wings, several rear wings, several floors – they're just coming along all the time. These days, quite frankly, you're prepared to make pieces for relatively small improvements because the improvements are so difficult to find.

'But we've had quite a catalogue of aerodynamic changes during the season. Obviously, some of them are very specific, like a Monaco package or a Monza package, which are two extremes of downforce levels.'

There had been developments on Paolo Martinelli's engines as well. 'There have been some useful steps,' explained Brawn. 'If I look at what we had at the beginning of the season, and what we've got at the end – we had another nice step at Indianapolis – it is quite a reasonable improvement. But it's come in a few horsepower here, a few horsepower there – nice incremental improvements all year long. We are a good step in power over and above what we had in the first races this season.'

Your Vision, Our Future

A PERFECT CAMERA
FOR A GREAT MOMENT

The Olympus μ[mju:] 400 DIGITAL:

Voted the best Digital Consumer Camera
in the TIPA European Photo & Imaging Awards 2003/2004.

4 million pixels in a weatherproof* metal body.

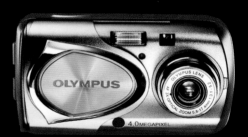

www.olympus.co.uk
0800 072 0070

Above: Michael Schumacher and Ferrari bounced back at Monza from their mid-season dip in form.
Photograph: Bryn Williams/crash.net

With the new car, Michael and Rubens repeated their first and third in Spain, and a similar result in Austria saw Ferrari take the lead of the constructors' championship, only to lose it again at Monaco, where Michael finished third and Rubens eighth. Then, first and fifth in Canada saw Michael and Ferrari emerge as leaders of both championships. Michael suffered a spin in the next race, at the Nürburgring, when battling with Montoya, which dropped him to fifth, although he came back to third in France a week later.

This was the start of the team's dip in the series, which would culminate in the major rethink post-Hungary. It did a phenomenal amount of testing with Bridgestone – some 120 days and around 200 different compound/construction combinations. After all, Ferrari was the only major team running those tyres, following McLaren's defection to Michelin.

Felipe Massa had replaced Luciano Burti alongside Luca Badoer as test driver in a somewhat bizarre, yet amicable, turn-around, and it was at this juncture that the effects of Ferrari's 'wrong turn' began to be felt. The team tended to be quite conservative with its tyre choice, particularly as it was fairly confident. It usually chose a tyre that had been used before, plus a tyre that it was fairly sure would work. The team even tended to run quite a lot of fuel.

One bright spot during the summer was Rubens Barrichello's thrilling British Grand Prix win, whereas Michael finished fourth. Two weeks later, however, in Germany, Rubens was involved in the start-line accident and, after suffering a puncture, Michael finished seventh.

It was even worse in Hungary, where Rubens crashed, and Michael salvaged one point and was lapped. 'Hungary was a low point,' admitted Brawn, 'but that was a combination of things: the car didn't work very well, Michael didn't have a great race. You have a couple of things you're not quite on top of and you get lapped.

'When you find yourself being beaten, you have to dig a bit deeper, and I think the major consideration was to make sure that we had absolutely the best tyres that Bridgestone could offer. I think we found a good combination. So we had a very good test where we were able to pick the optimum tyre for Monza.

'It was also a very good test in terms of the set-up of the car. We arrived with a car which was working very well to begin with, so I think everyone just realised that we couldn't make any mistakes. We had to be more than 100 per cent throughout the test and throughout the race weekend, and that's what happened.'

The team won at Monza and then, in difficult conditions, Michael took the chequered flag again in the United States GP at Indianapolis while all about him fell by the wayside, once more proving his talent and strength. The finale was a thriller, with Michael starting 14th, yet climbing up to claim the vital eighth point as Rubens obeyed team orders. 'We told him to win,' joked Jean Todt. Barrichello duly deprived Räikkönen of the ten points he needed.

The team's reliability had been phenomenal and there had been few changes. Chris Dyer had taken over from Luca Baldisseri as Michael's race engineer, having been promoted from support engineer.

Brawn is very much building a team for the future. 'I've been there seven years now and I'm seeing guys who joined us back then who are now becoming very important people in our organisation,' he explained.

The factory is growing too: 'We're building some new facilities for engines, for gearboxes. We're expanding the aero group. We're growing in capacity. I'm thinking about the future while I'm at Ferrari, and perhaps even the future when I'm not at Ferrari.'

The opposition had been warned.

Bob Constanduros

MAHLE makes Winners

Nowhere else are engines put to a tougher test than in big international races. High engine speeds above 18,000 rpm and piston head temperatures of more than 300°C call for supreme skill in development and the highest standard of perfection in technology. MAHLE has been a leading system supplier for decades to the World Champions in Formula One, to the winners of the 24 Hours of Le Mans, and to the winners of all categories in touring car, sports and racing car events.

And when the favourites set out on the next races, MAHLE pistons and engine components will once again be there on the road to victory.

So that millions of motorists the world over benefit every day from MAHLE top technology proven time and again in motor racing.

More Information: MAHLE GmbH, Pragstr. 26–46, D-70376 Stuttgart
www.mahle.com

PISTONS AND ENGINE COMPONENTS
FILTER SYSTEMS VALVE TRAIN SYSTEMS

3

Photograph: Darren Heath

JUAN PABLO MONTOYA

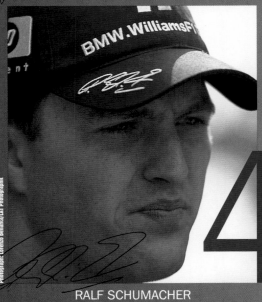

Photograph: Lorenzo Bellanca/LAT Photographic

RALF SCHUMACHER

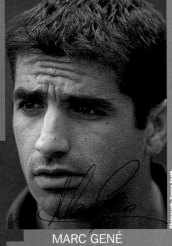

4

Photograph: Darren Heath

MARC GENÉ

N. Chris Volpe   2003

WILLIAMS FW25-BMW

SPONSORS	BMW, Hewlett Packard, Castrol, Petrobras, Accenture, Allianz, Budweiser, FedEx, NiquitinCQ, PPG, Reuters, Western Union, 7UP, Michelin, MAN, Nike, Oris, OZ Racing, Willy Bogner, Xilinx, CIBER Solutions Partners
ENGINE	Type: BMW P83 No. of cylinders (vee angle): V10 (90°) Sparking plugs: Champion Electronics: BMW Fuel: Petrobras Oil: Castrol
TRANSMISSION	Gearbox: WilliamsF1 six-speed longitudinal semi-automatic Driveshafts: WilliamsF1/Pankl Clutch: AP Racing hand-operated
CHASSIS	Front suspension: Torsion bars Rear suspension: Torsion bars, coil springs Dampers: WilliamsF1
	Wheel diameter: front: 13 in. rear: 13 in. Wheels: OZ Racing Tyres: Michelin Brake discs: Carbone Industrie
	Brake pads: Carbone Industrie Calipers: AP Racing Steering: Power-assisted Fuel tank: ATL Instruments: WilliamsF1 digital display
DIMENSIONS	Formula weight: 1322.8 lb/600 kg including driver

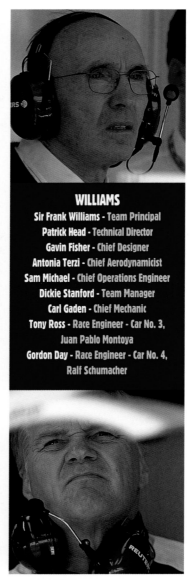

THE scene at Suzuka summed up the season for BMW Williams as Patrick Head emerged from the engineers' office to face the media.

First question: 'You must be disappointed, Patrick.'

Answer: 'Of course I'm disappointed! What sort of question is THAT?'

A silly one in view of what had happened in the final race. Juan Pablo Montoya had been leading when his car stuttered to a halt as the hydraulics went awry. Meanwhile, Ralf Schumacher, potentially a pole-position contender, but consigned to the back of the grid when rain fell during qualifying, was spinning his way to 12th place. It meant zero points for the first time in the season. Worse than that, it meant that BMW WilliamsF1 had lost the battle with Ferrari for the constructors' championship. And this 14 days after Montoya had been eliminated from the contest for the drivers' title. It was a massive disappointment.

In a perfect world, Williams should have cleaned up. With Ferrari and Bridgestone struggling, and McLaren-Mercedes shooting itself in the foot with the unraced MP4/18, the Williams FW25 should have been the car to do the job. Ultimately, it was, as four poles and four wins confirm. But it took too long to get there.

'After what had been a disappointing season in 2002, we had looked very critically at ourselves and decided on the areas where we needed to make big changes,' said Head. 'There was a lot of hard work by Gavin Fisher and Sam Michael – and, to some extent, myself – but not all of that came together at the beginning of the year. When the FW25 first ran, it certainly had a disappointing performance, but I think we were fairly clear that the fundamental building blocks that we wanted to put in place were encapsulated in that car.'

As the season got going and Montoya spun away the lead in Melbourne, the aerodynamics department in particular became extremely productive as the drivers and engineers learned about setting up and running the car. They were helped in part by the return of former aerodynamicist Frank Dernie, who employed his wide operational experience to good effect in utilising the aforementioned building blocks.

After a mildly chaotic Imola, thanks to a combination of errors by drivers and team in the pit stops, the popular perception that Monaco, a few months later, marked a turning point was encouraged by a pole for Schumacher and a faultless win for Montoya. In fact, Montoya ought to have won the previous race in Austria.

'Juan Pablo was steadily pulling away from Kimi Räikkönen when we had an engine failure which resulted from a leak in the water circuit,' said Head. 'So it's not true to say that everything was a disaster up to Monaco. But the results certainly started coming very strongly from Monaco onwards.'

It was a sign of the team's intention that Frank Williams and Head were disappointed with second and third places at the next race in Canada. Sure enough, that level of expectation was satisfied with two wins in succession for Ralf, followed by a victory, two races later, for Montoya at Hockenheim. Now the Williams momentum was on a roll and the championship battle was intensifying. But, within the team, the impetus was suddenly switching from one driver to the other.

'Up until Silverstone, Ralf had a slight edge on Juan Pablo,' said Head. 'Then Ralf put a wheel over the edge and broke one of the guide vanes on the car, and that sent the water temperature off the clock. The pit stop to have it removed destroyed his race. And then, of course, he had the accident at the start at Hockenheim. Those two things suddenly meant that, because Juan finished second at Silverstone and won at Hockenheim, he went forward relative to Ralf by 18 points.'

Montoya's impetus would continue as he closed the gap on Michael Schumacher to just one point. Then came Indianapolis, where a collision with the Ferrari of Rubens Barrichello brought a drive-through penalty, which was handed out at the moment when JPM needed to switch to wet-weather tyres. The time lost on both counts effectively ended his championship hunt.

'It was a fairly aggressive move,' said Head, referring to Montoya's challenge. 'But, without that penalty, Juan probably would have come to the final race still in a position to compete in the championship, so it was a championship-excluding decision. Of course, I'm in the position of believing it to be an unnecessarily harsh penalty, but I'm still flabbergasted when recalling what happened between Michael [Schumacher] and [Fernando] Alonso at Silverstone, where he [Schumacher] literally crossed from one side of the track to the other and pushed Alonso completely off on

Above left: Montoya winning at Monaco.
Photograph: Bryn Williams/crash.net

Top: Sir Frank Williams was happy to see his cars challenging again for the championship.
Photograph: Charles Coates/LAT Photographic

Above centre: Patrick Head continued to set high standards for the Williams engineering team.

Above: BMW's Mario Theissen.
Photographs: Darren Heath

Above: Ralf Schumacher took a dominant victory in the French Grand Prix.
Photograph: Darren Heath

Top left: Test driver Marc Gené stood in for the indisposed Schumacher at Monza and drove beautifully into fifth place.
Photograph: Bryn Williams/crash.net

Top right: Ralf Schumacher's first of two wins of the year came in Europe.
Photograph: Darren Heath

to the grass at 200 mph – and that was considered perfectly okay.'

Meanwhile, in the background, word was that Montoya was looking to leave and join McLaren. It was a strange decision, sparked a few months previously by more than the thought that Schumacher was on a considerably larger retainer. Montoya's relationship with the team had taken a serious dive at Magny-Cours when he simply could not beat Ralf and took it out on the team with a volley of abuse over the radio.

'Juan [lying second to Ralf] had decided he wanted to come in a lap early,' said Head. 'He knew what lap Ralf was coming in, so he thought he would be able to jump him. So he came in and returned with a very fast lap. But Ralf on that lap asked if he could come in early, and Sam could hardly say no when we were in a position to do so. When Juan came round and found Ralf coming out of the pits, still in the lead, he became very upset because he thought that, in response to him coming in early, we'd said to Ralf, "Oh, you'd better come in a lap early, otherwise Juan's going to get you." But that wasn't the case; it was Ralf who had initiated it.'

Montoya was called to the Williams headquarters, where he received a forthright speech. He may not have liked it, but that did not affect his efforts in the car for the rest of the season as he exploited the excellent mix of Williams, BMW and the continuing rise of Michelin.

'Towards the latter part of 2002, the Michelin tyres took a big step forward in terms of their durability and stability,' said Head.

'We started to be in a position where we were less influenced by the heavy "graining" that had made it very difficult to develop the car. That was a big advantage to us. Michelin certainly did a great job in 2003, even if work needs to be done on the wet-weather tyres.'

BMW also stepped up to the plate with the P83, a new V10 that, according to the Munich firm's post-season summary, did not suffer a single race failure; a stuffy remark in the light of the Austrian blow-up that reflected the occasional tension evident between the two firms.

'Certainly, BMW has done an excellent job,' said Head. 'Generally, the reliability of the engine at the races and tests has been simply better than it has been before.'

The Williams engineering department is not resting in its quest to match the progress of its engine partner. A new wind-tunnel will improve the testing methodology and offer the capability of making many more runs than the present facility. In the short term, however, it is clear that the lesson from 2003 has hit home.

'You can always improve,' said Head. 'The target is to do something that we haven't achieved for the last five years. And that's to come out at the beginning of the following season with a car that can run at the front right from the very first race. That's the challenge.'

Maurice Hamilton

BMW.WilliamsF1 Team
Technical Sponsor

This season, it wasn't just Montoya's piston heads that kept moving.

A perfectly balanced car. The closest, most fiercely fought championship for over a decade. And ultimately, Castrol's lubricant technology delivering the power, performance and reliability to keep the WilliamsF1 BMW FW25's piston heads moving – and that has meant a few other heads have turned, too.

A Successful Formula

Photograph: Steven Tee/LAT Photographic

DAVID COULTHARD

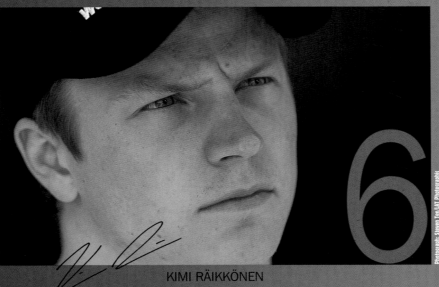

Photograph: Steven Tee/LAT Photographic

KIMI RÄIKKÖNEN

N. Curtis 2003

McLAREN MP4/17D-MERCEDES-BENZ

SPONSORS	West, Mobil 1, Siemens Mobile, Michelin, BAE Systems, Computer Associates, Sun Microsystems, Loctite, SAP, Warsteiner, Hugo Boss, Schueco, Advanced Composite Group, Canon, Charmiles, GS Battery, Yamazaki Mazak, TAG Heuer, Targetti, Enkei, Sonax, Sports Marketing Surveys, Kenwood, T-Mobile
ENGINE	Type: Mercedes-Benz FO110M No. of cylinders (vee angle): V10 (90°) Electronics: TAG Electronic Systems Fuel: Mobil Oil: Mobil 1
TRANSMISSION	Gearbox: McLaren seven-speed longitudinal semi-automatic Driveshafts and CV assemblies: McLaren Clutch: Hand-operated
CHASSIS	Front suspension: double wishbone, inboard torsion-bar/damper system, pushrod and bell crank-activated Rear suspension: double wishbone, inboard torsion-bar/damper system, pushrod and bell crank-activated Dampers: Penske/McLaren Wheels: Enkei Tyres: Michelin Brake discs: Hitco Brake calipers: AP Racing Steering: McLaren power-assisted Fuel tank: ATL Battery: GS Instruments: TAG Electronic Systems
DIMENSIONS	Formula weight: 1322.8 lb/600 kg including driver

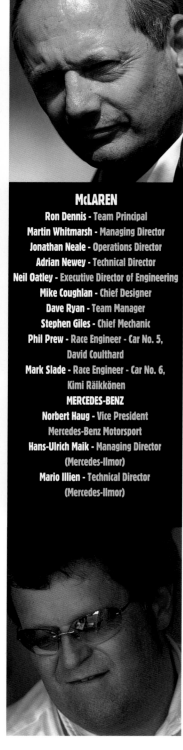

Top and above: Team Principal Ron Dennis and Mercedes-Benz's Norbert Haug — expecting better results in 2004.

Above left: Kimi Räikkönen at Imola.
Photographs: Darren Heath

THERE was a time in F1 when one could set one's watch by the arrival of a new car from each team at the start of every season. Cars that had completed a season's racing simply became redundant at the end of the year and were sold, or stored away, while the team cleared the decks for an all-new challenger with which to tackle the following season. Not any more.

McLaren's year encapsulated that reality. The MP4/17, dating from the 2002 season, was subjected to a major revamp while the team wrestled to make sense of its much-touted replacement, the MP4/18, an all-new machine that was intended to raise the team's game and carry the front-running F1 fight to Ferrari. Yet this ambitious development turned out to be a significant failure for McLaren, despite the efforts of the team's senior management to put a philosophical and upbeat gloss on the project. It is extremely rare for a leading F1 team to invest in a radical new machine and then never get around to using it in the heat of battle, but that was the story of MP4/18.

The new car was born out of work on a whole variety of concepts that were being evaluated by both McLaren and Mercedes Ilmor, a process that reached a defining moment in August 2002 while the team was in the middle of a season's racing with the existing McLaren-Mercedes MP4/17.

'Looking at our competitiveness vis-à-vis our principal rival, namely Ferrari, we decided we were going to have to take a more aggressive approach to the technical programme in order to take a bigger jump forward,' explained McLaren's managing director, Martin Whitmarsh, the man who bore the brunt of criticism for the new car's failure from within the organisation.

'We looked at what we had in mind at the time and decided that we felt we could do a better job with MP4/17. There was potential in the car to improve its performance, so we saw an opportunity there to improve that car while at the same time give ourselves more time, both on the engine and chassis front, to maybe take a bigger step forward.

'At that point, we knew that, in order to do that, we would be missing the first races of the season with the new car, so we embarked on a programme to develop MP4/17. Some of the first fruits of that were seen at the end of the last [2002] season.' These included a revised front suspension package, which enabled the

team to reassert its position ahead of the rival BMW Williams squad in the last few races of the year.

Already in August 2003, it had been decided to bypass the Mercedes F0110N engine programme in favour of a more ambitious approach – the F0110P – in a bid to complement McLaren's intention to make the MP4/18 chassis a very special production.

Yet even though the new car was to prove potentially very quick, its testing programme was strewn with problems, never mind the fact that it failed the FIA side-impact tests twice. It was also beset by excessive vibration from the all-new, lighter and lower Mercedes F0110P V10 engine, which caused knock-on effects in terms of secondary component failures. Worse, there were two very big accidents – one involving Alex Wurz at Jerez, the other Räikkönen in Barcelona – which left two chassis very badly damaged.

The result was that an improved MP4/17D was fielded from the start of the season. Uprated with further revised aerodynamics, some gearbox changes and subtle internal chassis modifications, the 'interim' car began the year brilliantly with victories for David Coulthard in Melbourne and Kimi Räikkönen in Malaysia. The team nearly made it a hat trick of wins in Brazil, where both MP4/17Ds took turns at leading, success only being snatched away when the race was abruptly red-flagged following the accidents involving Mark Webber and Fernando Alonso.

Räikkönen had taken the championship lead from Coulthard in Malaysia, and he held it successfully through to the Canadian GP at Montreal, almost three months later. Looked at objectively, the McLaren driver could have won the world championship easily, having done everything that was asked of him in terms of capitalising on Michael Schumacher's weak start to the season. While Coulthard was written out of the title battle early on, through his inability to come to terms with the new one-lap qualifying format, Räikkönen could reflect on two major errors in qualifying at Barcelona and Montreal, which forced him to the back of the grid with disastrous consequences.

A high-profile Mercedes engine failure also cost Räikkönen what looked like a runaway victory at the Nürburgring, so when those problems are factored into the equation, the Finn did well to wind up just two points behind the world champion by the end of

Above: Martin Whitmarsh had an upbeat view of his team's decision not to race the much-touted MP4/18 during the season.
Photograph: Darren Heath

the season. The failure at the German race was particularly galling, as this was the only time in the season's 32 race starts that the very reliable Mercedes V10 suffered an internal breakage.

Initially, the MP4/18's race debut had been optimistically pencilled in for the 'fifth or sixth' race, but Barcelona and the A1-Ring came and went without any sign of it. Then the British Grand Prix was mentioned, but by the time it became clear that the new car would not appear for Silverstone, Whitmarsh was coming close to acknowledging that it would probably only compete as a test vehicle right at the end of the season.

'I guess it becomes unfeasible [to run it] when we ship the cars to Japan,' he said, referring to the final race of the season at Suzuka on 12 October. 'But I think we will race the MP4/18. What we are saying is that, with the self-imposed test ban, it is not appropriate to introduce it before Italy.

'We have got a test after the end of that ban, at Monza, [and] we will be taking it there. We are doing a fair amount of work on the car in that intervening period and that has got to be our goal, to be racing in Italy. But we will decide after that test if we are comfortable with the reliability and performance of the car.' But the MP4/18 never appeared.

Meanwhile, McLaren was faced with a delicate balancing act in terms of determining just how much effort should be split between the MP4/18 and the work necessary to maintain the MP4/17D's competitiveness.

'Make no mistake about it, this was a well-developed car,' reflected Whitmarsh. 'Of course, the reality was that during the first one-third of the season, we were distracted by concentrating on the new car and, by Canada, it was clear that we needed to apply more energy into the MP4/17D project to maintain its championship assault.'

For Montreal, the race car's front suspension and brake cooling systems were uprated, but by the time it ran at Hockenheim and Hungary, this particular McLaren was becoming a touch breathless compared to its front-running opposition. Consequently, a new engine upgrade and aerodynamic package were brought on stream at Monza as a matter of some urgency.

'If we hadn't had that new package at Monza, we would have looked a bit sad,' said Whitmarsh. 'It wasn't designed to help us close on the leaders; it was intended to help us keep up and not drop back farther down the grid.'

In reality, less obvious features from the MP4/18 also had been incorporated in the 17D during the course of the year. 'The Monza update included elements from the 18, including developing the brakes, launch system and engine systems, although there were elements from the new car which obviously couldn't be used, such as the brake cooling package and so on,' continued Whitmarsh.

In fact, although the season yielded only two race wins, the McLaren Mercedes squad could be moderately satisfied with its achievements under somewhat trying circumstances. The strategy for 2004 is intended to be very different, the new MP4/19 being scheduled to test well before the end of November '03 in a bid to hit the ground running in Melbourne with a reliable and competitive car capable of taking the fight squarely to Ferrari.

'We laser-etch the chassis type on to most of the components of our cars,' said one McLaren insider wryly. 'The real test for outsiders will be to get close enough to the MP4/19 to see how many of its parts will have "MP4/18" etched on them.'

Alan Henry

MILD SEVEN RENAULT F1 TEAM

7

Photograph: Peter Spinney/LAT Photographic

JARNO TRULLI

8

Photograph: Michael Cooper/LAT Photographic

Alonso FERNANDO ALONSO

RENAULT R23

SPONSORS	Mild Seven, Renault, Elf, Michelin, Hanjin, 3D Systems, Magneti Marelli, Charmilles, Novell
ENGINE	Type: Renault F1 RS23 No. of cylinders: V10 Sparking plugs: Champion Electronics: Magneti Marelli Fuel: Elf Oil: Elf
TRANSMISSION	Gearbox: Renault F1 six-speed longitudinal semi-automatic Driveshafts: Renault F1 integrated tri-lobe Clutch: AP Racing hand-operated
CHASSIS	Front suspension: Double wishbones, pushrod-activated torsion bars Rear suspension: Double wishbones, pushrod-activated torsion bars
	Suspension dampers: Penske Wheel diameter: front: 13 in. rear: 13 in. Wheels: OZ Tyres: Michelin Brake pads: Hitco Brake discs: Hitco Brake calipers: AP Racing
	Steering: Renault F1 power-assisted Radiators: Marston Fuel tank: ATL Instruments: Renault F1
DIMENSIONS	Track: front: 1450 mm rear: 1420 mm Gearbox weight: 45 kg Chassis weight (tub): 65 kg Formula weight: 1322.8 lb/600 kg including driver

RENAULT was probably unique in realising more than it set out to achieve in 2003. The expectation had been to consolidate fourth place in the championship and possibly challenge for third with a number of podium finishes. In the event, Fernando Alonso and Jarno Trulli made it to the rostrum a total of five times (the lion's share going to the Spaniard). Renault even held second place very briefly before dropping to third and then accepting a comfortable fourth in the constructors' championship, way ahead of the rest.

Not on the agenda – although, of course, always the ultimate aim of any team – was a stunning victory, in Hungary, and there were a couple of near-misses, too. For a team with a modest budget compared to Ferrari, Williams and McLaren, Renault enjoyed a very respectable year. In fact, the season was amazing when you consider that this Anglo-French alliance turned up at the first race wondering why it had bothered.

'I remember being in the scrutineering bay in Melbourne, absolutely convinced that we could not finish a race,' said Pat Symonds, executive director of engineering. 'It was that very day when, for the first time, we had achieved a race distance with the engine on the dyno. Otherwise, there was not a scrap of evidence to say that we would finish.'

The engine in question was the latest version of Renault's 111-degree V10. Despite everyone's fears, it not only finished in Australia, but also helped both drivers score points. That may have been a reassuring start, but what happened next would blow away everyone's doubts.

The blue and yellow cars filled the front row at the Malaysian Grand Prix and went on to finish third (Alonso) and fifth. It was an impressive performance, if only because it highlighted the team's ability to deal with the latest qualifying rules better than anyone else at this early stage. Mike Gascoyne – who left to join Toyota during the season – may have been Renault's capable and energetic technical director, but it was the diligence and experience of Symonds that paid tactical dividends. While everyone else played the conservative game during final qualifying, Renault made some bold decisions.

'We were faced with a whole new approach,' explained Symonds. 'We did a fantastic amount of work and half figured out how we were going to deal with the single-lap qualifying/*parc fermé* situation. In Australia, we took our first step and qualified reasonably well, but I wouldn't say we got things quite right. I looked at what other people were doing and I thought, "Oh sh**, I've got this wrong! Everyone else is just being totally conventional."

'But I stuck with it and suddenly we were on the front row in Malaysia. Obviously, I knew how much fuel we had on board, and the more I listened to people claiming we must be stopping very early to refuel, the more I realised we were looking good. That [a reasonably short first stint] later became the norm, and I've had a huge amount of pleasure from being the first to devise the strategy.'

Shrewd thinking also accounted for Renault bucking the top-team trend by signing up for the Friday-morning test session at the expense of limited testing between races. It would be a successful three-car operation that was absolutely right for this team.

'That helped us very specifically and had a direct bearing on our performance,' said Symonds. 'When the option became available, we took it seriously, whereas some of the other teams didn't even consider it. We spent days and days looking at the pros and cons, how we would structure it, the budget projections and so on.

'It's a big, big effort to run three cars and very hard to keep on top of. I think a measure of our seriousness was employing Allan [McNish] who was an absolutely paramount and fundamental part of doing it. I wanted him and basically no one else because of his ability and his knowledge. He made a very real contribution to the development of the car.

'In effect, the whole thing gave us what I call "Near Real-Time Testing". Okay, the circuit was a little bit green, but we had the correct surface with more or less the correct temperature and more or less the correct spec of car. With the limited resources we had, it was without a doubt the best thing for our team.'

If the R23 had a weak point, it was the engine torque in the medium and high ranges. Otherwise, Michelin made a major contribution, and the chassis and aerodynamics packages were second to none. That really came into play on the Hungaroring, where Alonso led every lap from pole and became the youngest driver

Top: Patrick Fauré ensured that support was unflagging from the Renault corporate hierarchy.
Photograph: Charles Coates/LAT Photographic

Above: Flavio Briatore's enigmatic management style gave the team its distinctive identity.
Photograph: Darren Heath

Above left: Alonso was possibly the most outstanding driver of the year.
Photograph: Bryn Williams/crash.net

Right: Allan McNish made a great contribution to developing the Renault R23.
Photograph: Patrick Gosling

Above: Jarno Trulli had an extremely promising season, despite several disappointments.
Photograph: Bryn Williams/crash.net

ever to win a grand prix. Just as satisfying was his chase of Michael Schumacher's winning Ferrari in Barcelona.

'If Hungary hadn't been such a dominant win,' said Symonds, 'I think I would have put second at Barcelona as more of an achievement. Malaysia was about being one step ahead of the others, but Barcelona was about performance and being there all the way on as level a playing field as you can have.'

Barcelona summed up the varying fortunes of the Renault drivers. Alonso stole the glory, while Trulli, after qualifying an excellent fourth, became involved in a collision with David Coulthard at the first corner.

'I hate talking about luck,' said Symonds, 'but, dear me, there was nothing Jarno was doing wrong, but yet, if something was going to go wrong, it would happen to Jarno. At the same time, Fernando joined the race team and settled in immediately because he had been testing with us for a year. As the season went on, things evened out a lot more and, coming up to Hungary, Jarno was the dominant driver.

'We wanted two drivers who are as equal as they can be and, essentially, that's what we've had, even if it isn't obvious when you look at the hard results. Sure, people make a lot of fuss about

Fernando – and quite rightly so – but Jarno is still a very quick driver. If Jarno has a fault, it's his race craft under pressure. He is a very good qualifier, but, in the race, his ability is sometimes clouded by this one deficiency.

'They get on extremely well, perhaps better than any driver pairing I have ever known, and it's perfect for our team as we continue to grow and develop. We've had this steady build-up ever since Renault became the owners of the team [in 2000] and started to put money in. We're no longer having to directly pay for engines, and that has released money into other areas. In terms of overall competitiveness, the money spent on people, engineering and specifically in the wind-tunnel has had a very positive effect on our performance.

'We have again shown some solid progress and provided a realistic and a believable stepping-stone to finishing higher in the championship. When I say believable, I don't mean believable by people in the team; I mean believable by those outside Renault. Now we are able to say that we are a team to be reckoned with.'

Maurice Hamilton

CRÉATEUR D'AUTOMOBILES

Clio **RENAULT** *sport*

Va Va Voom Voom Voom Voom Voom Voom Voom Voom Voom Voom Voom Voom Voom Voom Voom Voom Voom Voom Voom Voom Voom Voom Voom Voom Voom Voom Voom Voom Voom Voom Voom Voom Voom Voom Voom Voom Voom Voom Voom Voom Voom Voom Voom Voom Voom Voom Voom Voom Voom Voom Voom Voom Voom Voom Voom Voom Voom Voom Voom Voom Voom Voom Voom Voom Voom Voom Voom Voom Voom Voom Voom Voom Voom Voom Voom Voom Voom Voom Voom Voom Voom Voom Voom Voom Voom Voom Voom Voom Voom Voom Voom Voom Voom Voom Voom.

For more details call 0800 52 51 50 or visit www.renault.co.uk

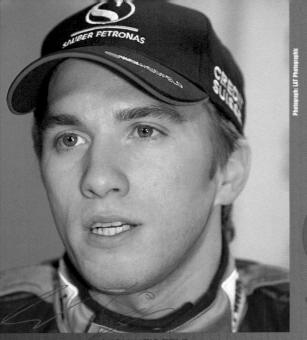

NICK HEIDFELD

HEINZ-HARALD FRENTZEN

SAUBER'S principal aim in 2003 was to hang on to its fifth place from the 2002 championship. With two rounds to go, it didn't look good, as the team was down in a distant ninth spot. A fortuitous result in the penultimate race, at Indianapolis, propelled the Swiss outfit to fifth, but an equally good performance by BAR in Japan pushed it back to sixth at the end, although it was top privateer. This was an achievement with which it could be pleased. After all, the team had worked to a similar budget as in the previous year, but felt its challengers, such as BAR, Jaguar and Toyota, had considerably greater resources and were likely to have sorted out their problems of 2002. So Sauber knew that it was going to be a tough year and not easy to hang on to that fifth place. But no one expected the season to be as tough as it turned out.

Not much changes at Sauber unless that is what the team wants. People don't leave – there's nowhere to go. So the team remains healthy and stable, and insiders say that there's no lack of motivation. Technical Director Willy Rampf and Seamus Mullarkey, leading a 32-strong aerodynamics department, were at the forefront of the engineering effort, although there was still no chief designer. And the budget came with the usual support of Petronas, Credit Suisse and Red Bull. Certainly, Sauber continues to attract finance.

Although the C21 had been a development of the C20, the 2003 car, the C22, had been a clean-sheet project, built largely of all-new components. There were several priorities, one of which was to make better use of the tyres, and to this end the aerodynamic package was improved. However, initial testing revealed a lack of downforce, so further aerodynamic work was targeted immediately.

As usual, the Sauber ran Ferrari's rebadged engine from the previous season, driving through the team's own gearbox. The engine was upgraded twice during the year: once for Montreal qualifying, after which it was raced at the Nürburgring, and again for Monza. 'In each case, the benefit was something the drivers felt straight away,' said Rampf.

However, after a reasonable start with eight points from the first three races, when the team's established engine's reliability stood it in good stead as others faced new-car and engine problems, it was Sauber's turn to suffer from engine unreliability, which took some two months to cure.

'We couldn't find the origin of this problem,' said Rampf. Eventually, it was traced to the starting procedure, which had caused several embarrassing failures in the valve-train. Indeed, in the four races from Spain to Canada, team returnee Heinz-Harald Frentzen completed fewer than 50 laps – although this was not due to engine problems – while team-mate Nick Heidfeld had two engine failures. It was a particularly lean period.

At the same time, Sauber was developing the car and, in particular, its aerodynamics. The team wanted to improve aerodynamic efficiency and stability. Since its own advanced wind-tunnel was still being constructed, it continued to use the government facility at Emmen - an old-fashioned 50-per-cent design with a narrow section that produces turbulence – where it had bought 2,200 hours. This was less than a third of Renault's wind-tunnel time, however.

SAUBER C22-PETRONAS

SPONSORS	Petronas, Credit Suisse, Red Bull, Mobile Telesystems (MTS), Bridgestone, Active O2, Plenexis, Giugiaro, Puma, Microsoft, Magneti Marelli, Paninfo, Walter Meier AG, Käser Kompressoren, Toshiba, MSC Software, Catia, Ericsson, Emil Frey AG, Temenos, Mercedes-Benz Truck Division
ENGINE	Type: Petronas 03A/B/C No. of cylinders: V10 Electronics: Magneti Marelli Fuel: Petronas Oil: Petronas
TRANSMISSION	Gearbox: Sauber seven-speed longitudinal semi-automatic Clutch: Sachs hand-operated
CHASSIS	Front suspension: double wishbones, pushrod-activated, inboard spring/damper units Rear suspension: double wishbones, pushrod-activated, inboard spring/damper units Wheel diameter: front: 13 in. rear: 13 in. Wheels: OZ Tyres: Bridgestone Brake pads: Brembo Brake discs: Brembo Brake calipers: Brembo Radiators: Calsonic Fuel tank: ATL Battery: Sauber
DIMENSIONS	Wheelbase: 3100 mm Track: front: 1470 mm rear: 1410 mm Formula weight: 1322.8 lb/600 kg including driver

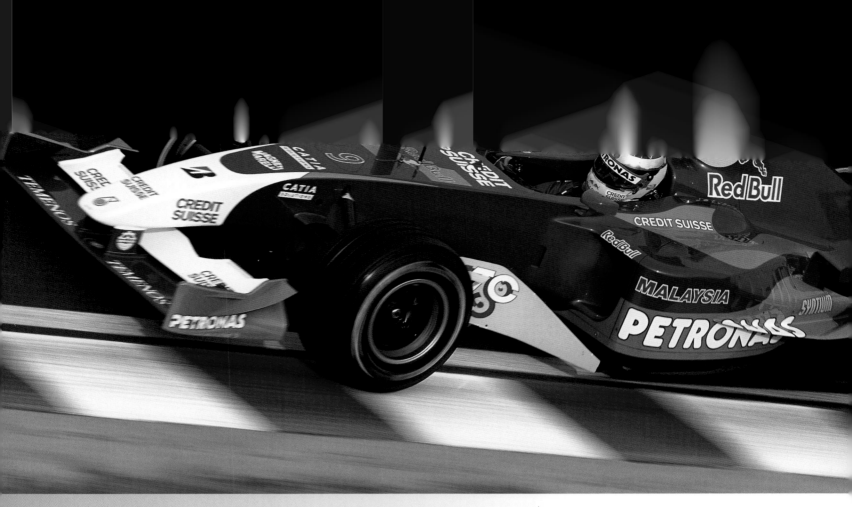

'We have a lot of ideas, but we have to concentrate on a certain number of ideas to be able to work things out in the wind-tunnel,' explained Rampf. 'At the beginning of the season, we worked a lot on the front wing. We had a variety of front wings plus flaps and made only small steps. Then we concentrated on one front wing, but we almost had a different flap and end-plate arrangement for each track.

'But after the first few races, we saw that by concentrating on the front wing, we could not achieve what we wanted to achieve. The steps were too small to see any improvements, to really catch up with the competition. That's the reason why we changed our philosophy.

'So we then concentrated on the rear end of the car, that means the rear wing and also the engine cover. We had different modifications up to the new-shaped engine cover at Indianapolis. From Silverstone onwards, we had aerodynamic modifications to the rear wing and the floor, which really paid off. We could see there was an upward trend.'

However, it wasn't quite that simple. Firstly, Sauber had to travel to Lola's wind-tunnel to compare its findings, and when, after the summer break, the team tested the new rear end, it found that this produced so much downforce that it couldn't balance the front end, which gave substantial understeer in the Lesmos and Parabolica during Monza testing in August.

Little winglets that were part of the modification were too weak and fell off, so they needed repairing. Then Heidfeld crashed, and it was only after the Italian Grand Prix that the new arrangement was sorted out for the final two races of the year.

The new rear end, plus the Sauber's apparent natural ease in wet weather, helped Frentzen and Heidfeld to third and fifth places respectively at the United States Grand Prix at Indianapolis, almost the first points since Brazil. It was a huge relief to the team. And a Sauber had led a grand prix for the first time in the team's 11-year history.

There had been other changes, as well. The team had tried different front suspension geometry and worked hard on the car's damping system. Another aim was to keep the tyres more consistent so that the drop-off in race performance wasn't so great, but that was only apparent at the end of the season. However, the team did feel that it had suffered due to Bridgestone's lack of performance in the summer. It also found that the new tyres that appeared subsequently were only marginally better than their predecessors. Bridgestone had reacted to its rival's resurgence, but only just in time.

Peter Sauber was honest enough not to blame his drivers for the year's performance, even if subsequently he said that they would not be staying for 2004. It was felt that the team needed a new start. The availability of Giancarlo Fisichella – whom Sauber had been eyeing for several years – and the end of Felipe Massa's instructive year at Ferrari meant that they would be taking over from the German duo, who now were redundant.

With Sauber's 60-per-cent wind-tunnel likely to take several months to commission, it will be mid-July 2004 before any benefit can be derived from the facility. Consequently, the team is expecting another tough year to come.

Bob Constanduros

Above: Nick Heidfeld signs off his Sauber career at Suzuka in Japan.
Photograph: Darren Heath

Below left: The services of Heinz-Harald Frentzen were also dispensed with just one season after the German returned.
Photograph: Bryn Williams/crash.net

Below: Team principal Peter Sauber: conservative, cool and composed.
Photograph: Peter Spinney/LAT Photographic

SAUBER

Peter Sauber - Team Principal
Willy Rampf - Technical Director
Osamu Goto - Engine Director
Seamus Mullarkey - Senior Aerodynamicist
Dirk de Beer - Senior Aerodynamicist
Beat Zehnder - Team Manager
Urs Kuratle - Chief Mechanic
Rémy Decorzent - Race Engineer - Car No. 9,
Nick Heidfeld
Jacky Eeckelaert - Race Engineer - Car No. 10,
Heinz-Harald Frentzen

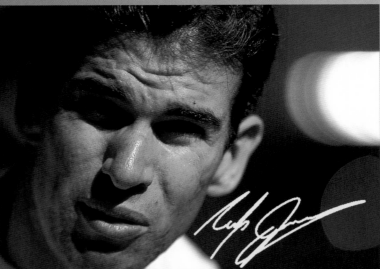

JORDAN FORD

11

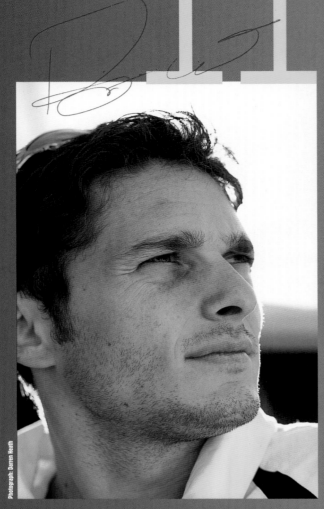

GIANCARLO FISICHELLA

12

ZSOLT BAUMGARTNER

JORDAN EJ-13-FORD COSWORTH

SPONSORS	Ford, B&H, Damovo, Bridgestone, Brother, Liqui-Moly, Remax, Imation, Cosworth, Puma, Vielife, Powermarque, Sparco, Grundig, Laurent-Perrier, Schroth, Touchpaper, Extreme, Piaggio
ENGINE	Type: Ford Cosworth RS1 No. of cylinders (vee angle): V10 (72°) Sparking Plugs: Champion Electronics: PI/Cosworth Fuel: Elf Oil: Elf
TRANSMISSION	Gearbox: Jordan seven-speed longitudinal automatic Clutch: AP Racing hand-operated
CHASSIS	Front suspension: Double wishbones, pushrod-activated torsion bars Rear suspension: Double wishbones, pushrod-activated torsion bars Dampers: Jordan/Penske
	Wheel diameter: front: 13 in. rear: 13 in. Wheels: BBS Tyres: Bridgestone Brake pads: Brembo/Carbone Industrie Brake discs: Brembo/Carbone Industrie
	Brake calipers: AP Racing Steering: Jordan power-assisted Radiators: Marston/Secan Fuel tank: ATL Battery: Panasonic Instruments: Jordan/TAG/PI
DIMENSIONS	Wheelbase: 3180 mm Track: front: 1800 mm rear: 1800 mm Formula weight: 1322.8 lb/600 kg including driver

IT'S not often that a team wins a grand prix, yet finishes the season propping up the constructors' championship. Then again, Jordan never was a run-of-the-mill outfit. In the roller-coaster ride initiated by Eddie Jordan more than a decade ago, 2003 was described by 'EJ' as one of his darkest years.

Even allowing for Irish hyperbole, it was an adequate description of a season in which the team went from winning in Brazil, to famously losing an expensive and questionable court case in London, and on to being saved by investors from Ireland. There were times when Jordan Grand Prix was on the point of closing its doors, yet the team finished the season talking optimistically about the future. The reality probably lies somewhere in between.

If Eddie Jordan was looking for money, then Technical Director Gary Anderson's search for downforce proved to be just as difficult. The EJ-13, an entirely new car, was produced on schedule, but that was when progress ground to a halt. No money meant no development. And no development meant no improvement.

'We started off the year with a few reliability issues with the car,' said Anderson. 'But our main problem as the season went on was a lack of development. I'm talking about component changes as well as testing. The car was reasonable when it first ran. But it wasn't as big a step as that made by some of our rivals. Once you recognise that, you've just got to move forward, and we didn't.

'Aerodynamics are the ultimate performance of any given car, and you have to get new bits and find more performance. We had a planned update for Silverstone and that never materialised. The season went by without anything happening. The car we had at Suzuka was the more or less the same car we had for the first race in Melbourne. You just can't go racing like that.

'The problem wasn't just financial. Okay, if the money had been available from the beginning, it would have meant we had to develop the car and there would have been a different attitude. But we needed to find the development before we had the money, and that was just as difficult to cope with. There appeared to be a lack of belief inside the company concerning the direction we had to go. We changed small stuff but, do that, and you only get a small return.'

Anderson's dissatisfaction was evident throughout the season as Giancarlo Fisichella and Ralph Firman complained endlessly about a lack of downforce and grip. As head of race engineering, he bore the brunt of their frustration, since he was in the front line at the track. Henri Durand, as director of design and development, remained back at base. In simple terms, Anderson looked after the build and running of the cars, and Durand was responsible for the speed. The partnership became strained as Anderson pushed for development and very little came because of financial restraints.

Matters became even worse psychologically when Eddie Jordan was humiliated by defeat in a court case pursuing allegedly promised funds from Vodafone. But as his reputation took a battering, 'EJ' bounced back by arranging for the 49.9-per-cent stake held in Jordan by the private equity firm Warburg Pincus, to be bought by a consortium of Irish businessmen.

Anderson, meanwhile, had been striving for results on the race track, the situation at the start of the season not being helped by a switch from a works Honda deal to customer engines from Ford and Cosworth.

'That does set you back a bit,' said Anderson. 'But Cosworth are very good people and we worked well with them. It was a bit disappointing, though, because the development steps were late and, when they did come, they tended to be a bit unreliable. So, all told, the car never moved forward and the drivers began to lose motivation.'

Fisichella had returned to Jordan at the beginning of 2002 and had struggled with a car that did not match his undoubted talent. It was even worse in 2003, and he became a familiar sight on the back half of the grid. In Brazil, he was 11th fastest. It may have been his second-best qualifying performance of the season, but not even the most optimistic Jordan fan could have expected the win that came at the end of a race disrupted by rain.

'We took a big risk in Brazil and did something a bit different,' said Anderson. 'We had a gut feeling and then the race fell into our hands. Jordan has always been a team that will try things like that and, given our competitiveness in 2003, it was our only way of hoping to get a result. Give us an opportunity like Brazil and we'll have a go. Others have to be more defensive and cautious; we don't. We weren't competitive in our own right, but we bought a lottery ticket and it came up. If you don't buy the ticket, you can't possibly win.'

Some thought Jordan was gambling by signing Firman on the basis of his Formula Nippon championship. The insistence that the Englishman with the Irish licence was not bringing money was not widely believed, particularly when he produced only the occasional glimmer of promise (Spain, Monaco and Suzuka). To be fair to Firman, it was a tough baptism in a difficult car, which failed badly enough in Hungary to put him out of two races, Zsolt Baumgartner acting as a solid, but uninspiring, stand-in.

'It was tough on Ralph, no question,' said Anderson. 'And he was up against a team-mate with lots of natural talent. The problem with Giancarlo, however, is that you don't get total commitment if the car isn't competitive. And the problem for Jordan in 2003 was that we were far from that. This team has a great bunch of guys who deserve far better. The highs were very high, but the lows were desperate; even lower than we expected.'

Maurice Hamilton

JORDAN

Eddie Jordan - Team Principal/Chief Executive
Gary Anderson - Director of Race and Test Engineering
Henri Durand - Technical Director
John McQuilliam - Chief Designer
Nicolo Petrucci - Senior Aerodynamicist
Tim Edwards - Team Manager
Andy Stevens - Chief Mechanic
Rob Smedley - Race Engineer - Car No. 11, Giancarlo Fisichella
Dominic Harlow - Race Engineer - Car No. 12, Ralph Firman

Above: Eddie Jordan, ever resilient.

Below: Giancarlo Fisichella, struggling for a second season.
Photographs: Darren Heath

Photograph: Darren Heath

MARK WEBBER

Photograph: Darren Heath

ANTONIO PIZZONIA

Photograph: Peter Spinney/LAT Photographic

JUSTIN WILSON

AFTER riding a management roller-coaster for the two previous years, which had claimed the scalps of high-profile team principals Bobby Rahal and Niki Lauda, the Jaguar F1 team sailed into more tranquil waters in 2003 under the stewardship of Tony Purnell and his MD, David Pitchforth. Jaguar had been a highly charged political battleground for too long, and the management realised that they might be drinking at the 'Last Chance Saloon' if they didn't do something about achieving hard results. And do it quickly.

The first challenge was to put the baggage of 2002 behind them. The Jaguar R3 had been a big disappointment, and while Eddie Irvine had offered some glimmers of hope toward the end of the year with a sixth place at Spa, followed by third at Monza, the car simply wasn't good enough.

Nevertheless, at the end of the season, Irvine's contract was not renewed and he retired from F1, while Pedro de la Rosa was negotiated out of his deal and eventually turned up at McLaren as a test driver. They were replaced by Mark Webber and former Williams test driver Antonio Pizzonia, who appeared, at first glance, to be a well-balanced pairing.

The team also needed reorganising. 'It was not just the management at the top level, but at every level of the organisation,' explained Pitchforth. 'One of the first things I did was to write down what everybody did and who they worked for. Now you might have laughed at this and assumed that this happens in every company where everybody knows who they work for. But in this company, they didn't.

'There were people who, when you wrote it all down in an organisation chart, were doubling up and doing the same job, while in other areas things were just dropping into a big hole. Yet there were a lot of good people still there who had worked for Stewart Grand Prix. It was easier to organise when it was slightly smaller at that time, then it got bigger and more disorganised, and now we've made it slightly smaller again and I think we're now better organisationally at every level than it has been before.'

The overwhelming priority, of course, was for Jaguar Racing to produce a better car. The aerodynamic team, under former Renault engineer Ben Agathangelou, previously had done a promising job sorting out the aerodynamics of the R3. But when it came to the R4, a much stiffer chassis structure was required to develop the aerodynamic programme.

'The big thing was that we wrote down what we were going to do in a specification,' explained Pitchforth. 'We then tested it before it ever hit the track and made sure that everything, hopefully, was structurally sound. There is a bit of a belief in some quarters of motor sport that the only way to test is with a racing driver on a track. We feel it is not. The best thing to do it is on

N. Curtis Jaffe 2003

JAGUAR R4-COSWORTH

SPONSORS	AT&T, Becks, Castrol, DuPont, EDS, HP, HSBC, Japhiro, Lear, Michelin, MSC Software, Mumm, Pioneer, Puma, Rolex, Volvo, 3D Systems
ENGINE	Type: Cosworth CR5 No. of cylinders (vee angle): V10 (90°) Sparking plugs: Champion Electronics: Pi VCS integrated engine/chassis electronic control system
	Fuel: Castrol Oil: Castrol
TRANSMISSION	Gearbox: Jaguar seven-speed longitudinal automatic sequential Driveshafts: Jaguar Clutch: AP Racing hand-operated
CHASSIS	Front suspension: Double wishbones, pushrods, torsion bars Rear suspension: Double wishbones, pushrods, torsion bars Dampers: Jaguar/Penske
	Wheels: OZ Racing Tyres: Michelin Brake pads: Carbone Industrie or Brembo Brake discs: Carbone Industrie or Brembo Brake calipers: AP Racing
	Steering: Jaguar power-assisted
DIMENSIONS	Formula weight: 1322.8 lb/600 kg including driver

the test rigs, in the laboratory, if you like, then take it to the track when it is sound.

'So the big gains we made were making sure that everything was working properly before we went to the circuit. There was also some good basic design philosophy which said let's not do anything which is too rash. What we needed was a good, sound, all-round racing car. That's what we specified and that's what we built.

'The other big gain has been in the area of aerodynamics. We started on the new aero package in March 2002, developed them on R3 and then applied what we learned to the new R4. It was an evolutionary design.'

Webber ran well from the beginning of the season, although irritating minor unreliability problems bugged the R4 during its early races. Pitchforth commented, 'At the beginning of the season, we experienced some annoying reliability issues which were really the result of R4 being so late. Because we started the programme by improving R3 and then moving on to R4, the actual amount of miles which R4 got under its belt before Melbourne was too small. We never properly did enough race distances in testing.

'So when we went out to do a race distance, it was warmer than it had been before, and part of a driveshaft bearing overheated and burnt out, which eventually seized and caused the driveshaft to punch the suspension out. It looked like a suspension failure, but it was actually a small bearing in the driveshaft which failed. That was because we hadn't done enough testing.'

Jaguar's engine partner, Cosworth, made a good effort with the promising 90-degree CR5 V10, which was produced exclusively for its number-one collaborator. Therefore, it was a disappointment that the team did not achieve sufficient mileage with the new unit prior to the start of the season.

'Cosworth did a great job, but the idea was to have the new engine running at the end of '02 in a hybrid R3 test car,' said Pitchforth. 'But that didn't quite work as it should have, so they were then farther behind than they should have been in the number of miles they should have put on the engine.

'They also had some problems on parts carried over from previous engines, but because they'd changed the design, you started moving stresses around. But again, they adjusted very quickly as well, and although sometimes it looked as though we were having the same sort of failures twice…in reality we weren't.'

The R4 was certainly a tough piece of kit, as Webber proved when he crashed heavily in the closing stages of the Brazilian GP at Interlagos. He'd qualified third on the grid at the Sao Paulo circuit, and although he failed to make the finish, it heralded a generally promising season that saw the pleasant Australian finishing seventh in Spain, Austria and Canada, then

sixth in the European, French and Hungarian races. His quiet mood of commitment and determination struck a popular chord within the Jaguar squad.

'He has been very good technical input and he's been heavily involved in the specification of R5 [for 2004] as well,' said Pitchforth. 'He's done a sanity check on what we're changing, just to make sure we're not going off on a wild-goose chase. And once he's happy we're doing that, he leaves us alone. He understands the data, works well with the engineers and is a good motivational influence on the whole workforce.'

Pizzonia's disappointing initial form, by contrast, seemed baffling. Jaguar scored a PR own-goal when it became clear that the team was trying to ditch him in favour of McLaren tester Alex Wurz immediately after the Spanish GP. But the deal came to nothing and Jaguar had to back-track embarrassingly, giving public commitments that the young Brazilian would remain with the team for the full season.

Those assurances flew out of the window after the British GP – ironically, Pizzonia's most convincing drive so far – and he was replaced by Justin Wilson, like Webber, a graduate of Paul Stoddart's F1 academy at Minardi. 'That was unfortunate with Antonio, but it just became obvious that he wasn't improving,' said Pitchforth. 'Justin fitted in well, good motivational force.'

Be that as it may, at the end of the season, Pizzonia returned to test for Williams, where he was just as quick and consistent as he'd been before his detour to Jaguar. The whole episode remained a mystery.

Jaguar established itself as a credible F1 force in 2003, even though it was short of sponsorship cash and needs more finance to make a decisive step forward for 2004.

'When it comes to R5, we intend to do more testing with R4 at the end of the season and then try to do better quality, better organised testing with R5 prior to next year's season,' summed up Pitchforth.

He continued, 'We also had some other niggling problems which were a by-product of trying to do too much too quickly. So on one side, we did a good job getting the car out, it showed good pace, but on the other, we paid the price with some niggling problems.

'As long as you learn from a bad result, and don't repeat it, then that's okay. And I'm very pleased that we haven't had recurrent problems.'

Jaguar might have done better in 2003, but on the other hand, it probably achieved more – and looked more promising – than many had expected.

Alan Henry

JAGUAR

Tony Purnell - *CEO Premier Performance Division*

Dave Pitchforth - *Managing Director*

Sir John Allison - *Operations Director*

Ian Pocock - *Director of Engineering*

Ben Agathangelou - *Head Aerodynamicist*

David Stubbs - *Team Manager*

Mark Gillan - *Head of Vehicle Performance*

Malcolm Oastler - *Chief Engineer*

Robert Taylor - *Head of Vehicle Design*

Darren Nicholls - *Chief Mechanic*

Peter Harrison - *Race Engineer - Car No. 14, Mark Webber*

Stefano Sordo - *Race Engineer - Car No. 15, Justin Wilson*

Above: Tony Purnell helped steer the team into calmer waters after Niki Lauda's departure.
Photograph: Darren Heath

Below: Mark Webber assumed the team leadership with great confidence.
Photograph: Bryn Williams/crash.net

LUCKY STRIKE BAR HONDA

JACQUES VILLENEUVE

Photograph: Steven Tee/LAT Photographic

TAKUMA SATO

Photograph: Lorenzo Bellanca/LAT Photographic

Photograph: Darren Heath

JENSON BUTTON

IT may have taken a long time and cost a lot of money, but BAR finally made a move forward in 2003. Having dropped down the World Championship order during the previous two years, the team not only met its budget in 2003, but also reversed the trend and claimed fifth place in the championship – and it led two grands prix!

This was also the first full season for both team principal David Richards (who arrived in late 2001) and technical director Geoff Willis (arrived spring, 2002), so it was very much a building year. With a new driver in Jenson Button joining the increasingly disillusioned Jacques Villeneuve, and Honda concentrating on BAR exclusively, it was a year when expectations were ultimately met, but only just.

The team certainly couldn't be faulted for trying hard. It tested a lot, developments came thick and fast, and Richards ran a tight ship. 'This year's budget was marginally reduced,' he explained. 'It didn't affect anything. We've just become far more efficient in the way we operate. We were operating on a head count of 20 per cent less than we originally started with.' That works out at around 350 people.

The exclusive relationship with Honda was strengthened, too. There was a massive engine development programme throughout 2003, but Richards was eager to establish a far more co-operative

N. Chris Jolliffe 2003

BRITISH AMERICAN RACING BAR 005-HONDA

SPONSORS	Lucky Strike, Honda, Bridgestone, Intercond, Brunotti, Sina, Alpinestars
ENGINE	Type: Honda RA003E No. of cylinders: V10 Sparking plugs: NRG Electronics: Di/Athena Fuel: Elf Oil: Nisseki
TRANSMISSION	Gearbox: BAR/Xtrac seven-speed longitudinal semi-automatic Driveshafts: Pankl Clutch: AP triple-plate hand-operated
CHASSIS	Front suspension: double wishbones, pushrod-activated torsion bars Rear suspension: double wishbones, pushrod-activated torsion bars Suspension dampers: Koni
	Wheel diameter: front: 14 in. rear: 14 in. Wheels: BBS Tyres: Bridgestone Brake pads: Brembo Brake discs: Brembo Brake calipers: AP Racing
	Steering: BAR power-assisted rack and pinion Radiators: IMI Marston/Showa Fuel tank: ATL Battery: Yuasa Instruments: BAR
DIMENSIONS	Wheelbase: 3140 mm Track: front: 1460 mm rear: 1420 mm Formula weight: 1322.8 lb/600 kg including driver

Left: Villeneuve parted company from BAR before the last race of the season.
Photograph: Bryn Williams/crash.net

Below: David Richards helped turn around the team's fortunes.
Photograph: Steven Tee/LAT Photographic

approach. So gone were the parallel programmes, to be replaced by one technical structure, a step away from his ultimate collaboration with the team's Japanese partner.

The year started with an all-new chassis from a design team that was 'skeletal' when the project was started in August 2002, but subsequently was strengthened by a further 15 engineers. 'We knew we had to be reasonably conservative in a number of areas because we simply couldn't afford to have any of the problems of the previous car,' said Willis. 'The biggest problem with that car was its lack of turn-in stability. So we kept the wheelbase on the long side and worked very hard on lowering the centre of gravity, building in aerodynamic characteristics which were going to help with its stability.'

The team's strong composite department made a very light chassis, which passed all its crash tests immediately. 'We believe [it is] one of the lightest in the pit lane,' said Willis.

He continued, 'We picked up a few more mechanical engineers and then focused on all the other issues, including engine installation, mechanical power steering, hydraulics. We basically re-engineered the whole car, always with the focus of "right first time" design, simple, sensible use of materials, and design and manufacturing resource.

'So as it rolled out, all the big bits of the car were as we wanted them to be – right first time. We made a mistake on engine installation. We had some big reliability problems in our second and third tests, where we had to revert to an earlier concept, which I had wanted to start with, but allowed myself to get talked into being more adventurous.' That, and a shortage of parts, resulted in just 8,000 km of pre-season testing. Willis would have preferred double that figure.

There was also an all-new Honda engine, which first ran on the dyno in August 2002 and was in a car right from the first Barcelona winter test. The policy was to improve it throughout the off-season, with a further five upgrades in power (giving between 0.3 and 1.5–2.0 per cent) and weight reduction (a total of between five and ten per cent) during the year. In fact, the team had to go back a step in Melbourne after a batch problem with camshafts caused problems, but that had been corrected by Malaysia.

The first power upgrade from the Japanese-based development team was introduced at Imola, with the second in Canada, taking the output to over 900 bhp. The third was incorporated for Silverstone, the fourth for Monza and the fifth for Suzuka, where development on 'a major component which we have been working on all year' resulted in Button leading for three laps. There was a significant increase in power, as well as revs, which it was hoped would have a bearing on the 2004 engine.

The first weight reduction – in the valve-train – was made for Monaco, the second for Silverstone, followed by a block reduction in Hungary. Further slimming took place for the outings at Indianapolis and Suzuka, where Button enjoyed stints at the head of the pack.

Willis's commitment to getting things right first time worked well: 'We've had no real redesigns of anything on the car, so we've been able to focus most things on aerodynamic developments. We've had four or five big steps and they've all worked very well.' Those steps included increased downforce for Monaco and reduced downforce for Monza, plus a major change at Silverstone: a lighter roll hoop, plus new bodywork, diffuser and side-pods. There were four front-wing upgrades, and two lower and five upper rear wings. Also, there was a lighter-weight front anti-roll bar layout, lighter gearbox internals and experimental geometry changes.

However, in spite of a massive testing schedule, assisted by test drivers Takuma Sato and Anthony Davidson, the relentless pace took its toll. 'Reliability has been very poor,' said Richards,

'and those are issues that can be levelled at both ourselves and Honda. But collectively, it's just an approach and a catch-up process that has meant that everyone's been moving rather too fast, instead of making a far more strategic approach to things.'

Although both drivers finished the first race – out of the points – it wasn't until Round Six that they both finished again. There was a problem with hydraulic pumps, while Villeneuve was stopped by electrical problems twice in the first six races, and once because of the gearbox. Button crashed in the wet in Brazil, and again – more heavily – in Monaco, but he had finished in the points three times up to that point, including a fine fourth in Austria. As a result, the team was usually in fifth or sixth position in the constructors' series.

Yet the mid-season was poor, with more retirements for Villeneuve and only minimal points for Button at Nürburgring and Silverstone. 'We really struggled in Canada, Magny-Cours and Nürburgring on low-grip conditions,' admitted Willis. 'We've not been able to use new tyres as well as we've been able to use old tyres. Typically, on race fuel, we've been pretty competitive.'

In fact, BAR's Bridgestone tyre choice varied considerably, sometimes with two vastly differing compounds or constructions, which made things difficult. 'A couple of times, we've tried very new compounds that have been successful on some occasions and have bitten us badly on others. We have tried to go our own way when we think Ferrari are wrong,' said Willis. By the end of the season, BAR was seeking a move to Michelin.

After Villeneuve's sixth place at Monza came a breakthrough at Indianapolis. 'We were struggling on the Friday,' explained Willis, 'and then we made a big car change on Saturday, and we learned quite a lot from that. Maybe we should have done that a bit earlier.' Qualifying eleventh, Button led from lap 23 to 38, but blew up four laps later. Villeneuve also stopped with engine failure, blamed on ancillary parts that let go. Honda said they were only the team's second and third race engine failures of the year.

It was too much for Villeneuve. It had already been announced that he would be replaced by Sato for the coming year. 'There's a well-known saying that continuing to do the same thing time after time, and expecting a different result, is the definition of insanity,' explained Richards of his decision.

On the Thursday of Suzuka, the last race, Villeneuve quit. It was ironic that Jacques should not have been part of the team's finest hour. Button finished fourth, and his new team-mate, Takuma Sato, sixth, regaining BAR's fifth place in the championship. On that basis, the team and its engine partner headed into what they hoped would be a new era.

Bob Constanduros

Left: Geoffrey Willis led the technical group that made worthwhile progress on the chassis development programme.
Photograph: Darren Heath

JUSTIN WILSON

NICOLAS KIESA

JOS VERSTAPPEN

YEAR three in Paul Stoddart's five-year plan for Minardi was meant to have been rewarded by regular points, but none came the way of the Anglo-Italian team. It shouldn't have been like that claimed Stoddart: 'We came in with a fantastic engine and probably the best driver line-up Minardi's ever had, and it all turned to sh** because we didn't have the money to develop the car.'

The highlight was Jos Verstappen's fastest time on Friday at Magny-Cours. But only because it rained.

Money was what the season was all about. Running on a budget of less than $25 million meant that Stoddart's team managed only 12 days in the Fondmetal wind-tunnel all year. It hadn't been planned that way, but Stoddart rued '30 per cent of your planned budget knocked out almost on day one.' That was the so-called fighting fund, a lifeline of $8 million promised on 15 January, which, according to some, was conditional. In the end, only a small part of it was paid, nothing like the amount expected.

Then there was Gazprom, which represented 40 per cent of the budget, and it wasn't until May that Minardi realised that nothing was going to come of that. Matteo Bobbi was given some Friday-morning test drives on the promise of 600,000 euros, which never turned up, and finally Italian toolmaker Stayer didn't pay either, causing the loss of a further 400,000 euros. 'It was our worst year for cash,' said Stoddart.

It all came to a head after Monaco, and in Canada, the much publicised meetings and press conference eventually resulted in a commitment to the team from Bernie Ecclestone. 'In the end, he didn't actually have to invest any money, but the association with Bernie certainly helped the position, and I suppose it eased the pressure a bit,' explained Stoddart. 'A lot of people thought Minardi wouldn't make it, and that has actually held back sponsors and investors because they figured that we were going to do an Arrows or a Prost and go down. Announcing to the world that Bernie was prepared to back us enabled us to get through without any help.'

Other sponsors turned up, such as Trust, a household name in Holland, but Stoddart admits that the sponsorship was probably sold for a ridiculously small sum. The presence of Jos Verstappen certainly helped the team's balance sheet.

The Dutchman teamed up with former F3000 champion Justin Wilson at the beginning of the year, making Stoddart's dream team. But up to the moment that Wilson left to go to Jaguar, Verstappen had only outqualified him 6–4, even though he had competed in 91 more grands prix. Wilson's place was taken by Denmark's Nicolas Kiesa, who finished every one of his five

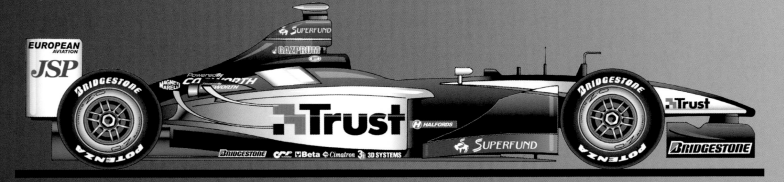

EUROPEAN MINARDI PS03-COSWORTH

SPONSORS	Cosworth Racing, European Aviation, Trust International, Superfund, Halfords, Muermans Group, Wilux, Brevi, Allegrini, Carrera Jeans, Bridgestone,
	Magneti Marelli, 3D Systems, Cimatron, Puma, Beta, Leaseplan, Poderi Morini
ENGINE	Type: Cosworth CR3 No. of cylinders (vee angle): V10 (72°) Sparking Plugs: Champion Electronics: Magneti Marelli Fuel: Elf Oil: Elf
TRANSMISSION	Gearbox: Minardi six-speed longitudinal semi-automatic sequential Driveshafts: Minardi Clutch: AP Racing hand-operated
CHASSIS	Front suspension: double wishbone pushrod-activated torsion bars Rear suspension: double wishbone pushrod-activated torsion bars Suspension dampers: Sachs
	Wheel diameter: front: 13 in. rear: 13 in. Wheels: OZ Racing Tyres: Bridgestone Brake pads: Hitco Brembo Brake discs: Hitco Brembo Brake calipers: Brembo
	Steering: Minardi power-assisted rack and pinion Radiators: Minardi/Secan Fuel tank: ATL Battery: Fiamm Instruments: Magneti Marelli
DIMENSIONS	Wheelbase: 3095 mm Track: front: 1480 mm rear: 1410 mm Formula weight: 1322.8 lb/600 kg including driver and camera

Left: Justin Wilson holds off Jacques Villeneuve during the European GP.
Photograph: Darren Heath

Below: Paul Stoddart may have been short of cash, but he wasn't short of nerve.
Photograph: Jack Atley/LAT Photographic

Bottom: Jos Verstappen in the British GP.
Photograph: Darren Heath

grands prix, if not very quickly. Stoddart was proud that 40 per cent of the field in Germany were, or had been, Minardi drivers.

The drivers were just part of the usual annual turnover for Minardi. Gone too were Asiatech's engines, KL sponsorship and Michelin. After an initial hiccough when the team had to test on Avons, Bridgestone eventually agreed to supply tyres. Cosworth came up with its largely undeveloped CK 72-degree V10 (slightly longer than Jordan's LK), but there was no title sponsor.

Minardi's staff remained fairly static, however: Gabriele Tredozzi headed the 17-strong drawing office, aided by Fabio Sansavini, chief aerodynamicist Loïc Bigois and structural head Paolo Marabini. 'We work well together,' said Tredozzi.

Tredozzi sees the irony in working for the Faenza team. 'Normally, we only change the engine,' he said of the differences in the 2003 car, 'but the engine involved many things in the car, like the gearbox bellhousing, oil system, water system, engine mounting in the chassis, and then electronic system, looms, all the software, everything. And after that, the main problem was to fit Justin Wilson in the car.

'We maintained the same wheelbase as last year, but the distance from the rear edge of the cockpit to the rear axle was a bit shorter, and we moved the front wheels forward. We moved the front wing forward as well, and introduced a new one in the middle of the season and new bodywork. The rear suspension was the same as before, but we had new front suspension with new wishbones because we had moved the wheels forward.'

There were small developments during the year, but without the finance to develop the car, and with no wind-tunnel time, Friday-morning testing remained the only way of checking them –

which sometimes cost the team race preparation time. Otherwise, Minardi did some testing at Monza prior to the grand prix, but that was all.

Reliability, on the face of it, was average, Wilson finishing only two of his first eight races, but the first three retirements were because of a holed radiator, physical problems and a fuelling glitch, something similar to which was repeated two races later. Verstappen suffered from trouble with the electrics at Imola, launch control in Austria, the gearbox in Canada and hydraulics in Germany. Not once was either driver let down by the Cosworth engine during a race.

'One of the things that needs to be stressed is that it isn't that Minardi have done any better or worse than in the last couple of years,' said Stoddart, 'but that last year we could count on a not-so-hot Jaguar, a not-so-great BAR, a very conservative Toyota, and on a bad day, maybe we could capture a Sauber or a Jordan.

'This year, all those cars, perhaps with the exception of Jordan, who's obviously had the same kind of problems we've had, have actually gone light years ahead. They've sorted out their problems. All of the teams this year picked up their act big time, and that made us actually look a bit worse in terms of what we've done.

'I think we've done a great job, but the history books won't show that, apart from perhaps some people might forget that it rained in Magny-Cours on the Friday, which gave us our best day of the year. But that really was the highlight of the year, and that's so sad. This year the rest of the competition moved away from us.'

Bob Constanduros

MINARDI

Paul Stoddart - Team Principal
Gabriele Tredozi - Technical Director
Andy Tilley - Chief Engineer
Mark Parish - Engine Liaison Manager
Loïc Bigois - Senior Aerodynamicist
John Walton - Sporting Director
Paulo Piancastelli - Chief Mechanic
Alex Varnava - Race Engineer - Car No. 18, Justin Wilson/Nicolas Kiesa
Greg Wheeler - Race Engineer - Car No. 19, Jos Verstappen

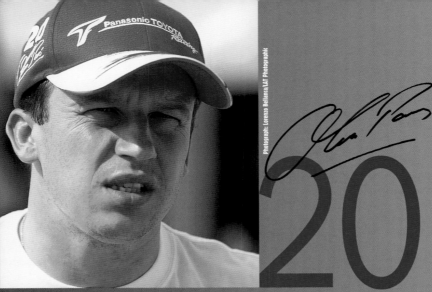

OLIVIER PANIS

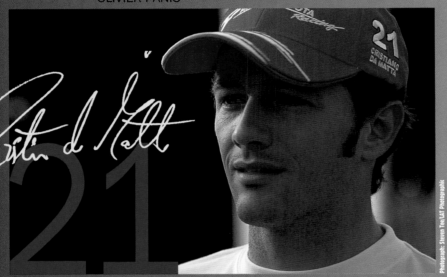

CRISTIANO DA MATTA

PANASONIC TOYOTA RACING

TOYOTA may have won the race to be the first F1 team to test its 2003 challenger, but the Japanese company's second season of racing in motor sport's premier category delivered perhaps rather less than was anticipated. That was disappointing, particularly bearing in mind that the team's 2002 driver line-up of Mika Salo and Allan McNish had been swept aside in favour of the experienced Olivier Panis and F1 novice Cristiano da Matta, the CART champion and winner of the previous year's Indianapolis 500.

Track temperatures were barely above freezing when Panis edged the first TF103 out on to the circuit at Paul Ricard last winter, to the accompaniment of optimistic predictions about its future form. Nevertheless, Panis did manage to strike a slightly cautionary note while giving a generally upbeat signal.

'When I first drove the [interim] test car, I was very impressed with its new V10 engine, but a little concerned about the lack of aerodynamic downforce,' he said. 'But the new car has reaped the benefit of the team's new wind-tunnel, which is working 15 hours every day.

'The new car is a big step forward. The drivability and the torque of the new engine are very impressive.' Then he added ironically, 'For me, it is much better than what I had to drive last year.' Considering the pleasant Frenchman had been driving an unreliable BAR-Honda in 2002, this was not a complete surprise.

The TF103 seemed to some people to have taken some visual clues from the dominant Ferrari F2002, particularly in the shape of the side-pods, engine cover, 'periscope' exhausts and the positioning of the radiators. The TF103 was around 20 kg lighter than its predecessor, thereby facilitating more strategic positioning of ballast, and the new, slightly shorter, RVX-03 engine developed by Luca Marmorini's team was expected to develop around 850 bhp at just under 19,000 rpm.

At the car's launch, team principal Ove Andersson said, 'Realistically, we should be aiming for top-ten qualifying positions in every race and to challenge for points on a regular basis.'

Ten months later, Toyota had achieved only part of that ambition. The team had qualified in the top ten just 14 times out of 32 race starts. It had not achieved a single podium finish. And it wound up a disappointing eighth in the constructors' championship, trailing the big fight for fifth place – 'best of the rest' – behind BAR Honda, Sauber and Jaguar. Only Jordan and Minardi were lower in the final reckoning.

At Suzuka, Norbert Kreyer, general manager of race and test engineering, reflected ruefully on the season's 16 races. 'We made clear targets that if everything goes well, we can achieve 15 points and perhaps, if it goes very well, get a podium,' he said.

TOYOTA TF103

SPONSORS	Panasonic, AOL Time Warner, Avex, BBS, Catia and Enovia Solutions, DEA, Ebbon-Dacs, EMC, EOS, Exxon Mobil, Future Sports, Kärcher, KDDI, KTC, Magneti Marelli,
	MAN, MBA Production, Météo France, Michelin, Nolan, Puma, Sika, Sparco, St Georges, Technogym, Travelex, Vuarnet, Wella, Yamaha, ZF Sachs
ENGINE	Type: Toyota RVX-03 No. of cylinders (vee angle): V10 (90°) Sparking plugs: Denso Electronics: Toyota/Magneti Marelli Fuel: Esso Oil: Esso
TRANSMISSION	Gearbox: Toyota seven-speed longitudinal semi-automatic Driveshafts: Toyota Clutch: Sachs/AP Racing hand-operated
CHASSIS	Front suspension: Pushrod with torsion bar front and rear Rear suspension: Pushrod with torsion bar front and rear Suspension dampers: Sachs
	Wheel diameter: front: 13 in. rear: 13 in. Wheels: BBS Tyres: Michelin Brake pads: Brembo Brake discs: Brembo Brake calipers: Brembo
	Steering: Toyota power-assisted Radiators: Nippon-Denso Fuel tank: ATL Battery: Panasonic
DIMENSIONS	Wheelbase: 3090 mm Track: front: 1425 mm rear: 1411 mm Formula weight: 1322.8 lb/600 kg including driver and camera

'At the moment [prior to the Japanese GP], we have 14 points and no podium. This wasn't a "must", but it was a worthwhile target.

'We began the season with a fuel system problem in Australia. Olivier started from fifth position on the grid, and then we get a problem. A problem which was a mixture of pick up and boiling the fuel – the temperature was too hot; throughout the winter, we'd been testing in cool conditions and simulations, then we went to Australia to encounter this fuel overheating.

'The next problem was a refuelling-rig problem in Malaysia, which we eventually solved for Brazil. But by the time we'd got this under control, we'd obviously lost the potential for some points.'

He continued, 'By the end of the season, more aero improvements. Hard learning curve; we learn from our mistakes: for example, the tyre choice at Indianapolis. Our realistic starting position was seventh and tenth, I think, so anything better than that a bonus.

'We made roughly four steps – 5–6 bhp a time – during the course of the year from the engine side, then also major aero update in Silverstone. We were still learning how to harness the best aero package and how to get the best out of the tyre performance.'

The Toyota TF103s actually ran in 1-2 formation during the British Grand Prix at Silverstone, having made luckily timed first refuelling stops during the first safety-car phase of the unpredictable race. However, while it was undeniably satisfying to watch da Matta confidently fending off Kimi Räikkönen through the fast swerves of the British circuit, it was qualifying at Indianapolis, where Panis lined up third on the grid, that gave the team probably the most satisfaction.

'We had a good position at Indy, but we lost that,' said Kreyer. 'For Toyota, the drivers are fine and okay. We are a young team, we have to improve. They have done a good job. Olivier brings huge experience, and I must say that Cristiano has done a very good job, particularly as he had to learn the tracks. I was particu- larly impressed by the way in which he learned Suzuka so quickly. I think he can do well next season.

'I think it is possible that we may be ready to challenge for wins in 2005 and 2006. We have to be realistic. Meanwhile, we will be testing an interim car, with an engine capable, we hope, of running 750 km, from mid-November.'

For their part, the two drivers had delivered pretty well what the team had expected from them. Panis's huge experience and testing know-how enabled the team to make the most of its developing technical resources, while da Matta looked like a real discovery. If anything, he was mentally slightly tougher than his team-mate, focused and very determined in his own quiet way.

Perhaps the most wry assessment of Toyota's progress in 2003 came from Allan McNish. Displaced from the squad after a single season, he kept his name well in play within the F1 ranks by switching to Renault as a test driver.

But was he bitter or resentful about the treatment meted out to him by Toyota? 'I would say disappointed, rather than bitter,' he said. 'I think I was disappointed because I couldn't have done anything to change the circumstances. But I think 2003 has proved two things. Firstly, it has proved that I have the capability to be in F1 which, to put it bluntly, there was a question mark over last season. The second thing is that changing Mika [Salo] and myself was not the key to [improving] anything at my previous team.'

That was an understandably harsh assessment. Toyota has the ingredients to become successful in the long term, as well as the necessary resources and single-mindedness. From the touchlines, however, you could see perhaps why McNish had reached his conclusion.

Alan Henry

TOYOTA

Tsutomu Tomita - Team Chairman
Ove Andersson - Team Principal
John Howett - Team President
Toshiro Kurusu - Team Vice President
Keizo Takahashi - General Manager Car Design & Development
Luca Marmorini - General Manager Engine Department
Gustav Brunner - Chief Designer
Rene Hilhorst - Senior Manager Aerodynamics
Norbert Kreyer - General Manager Race & Test Engineering
Ange Pasquali - Team Manager
Dieter Gass - Chief Race Engineer
Humphrey Corbett - Race Engineer - Car No. 20, Olivier Panis
Ossi Oikarinen - Race Engineer - Car No. 21, Cristiano da Matta

Photograph: Darren Heath

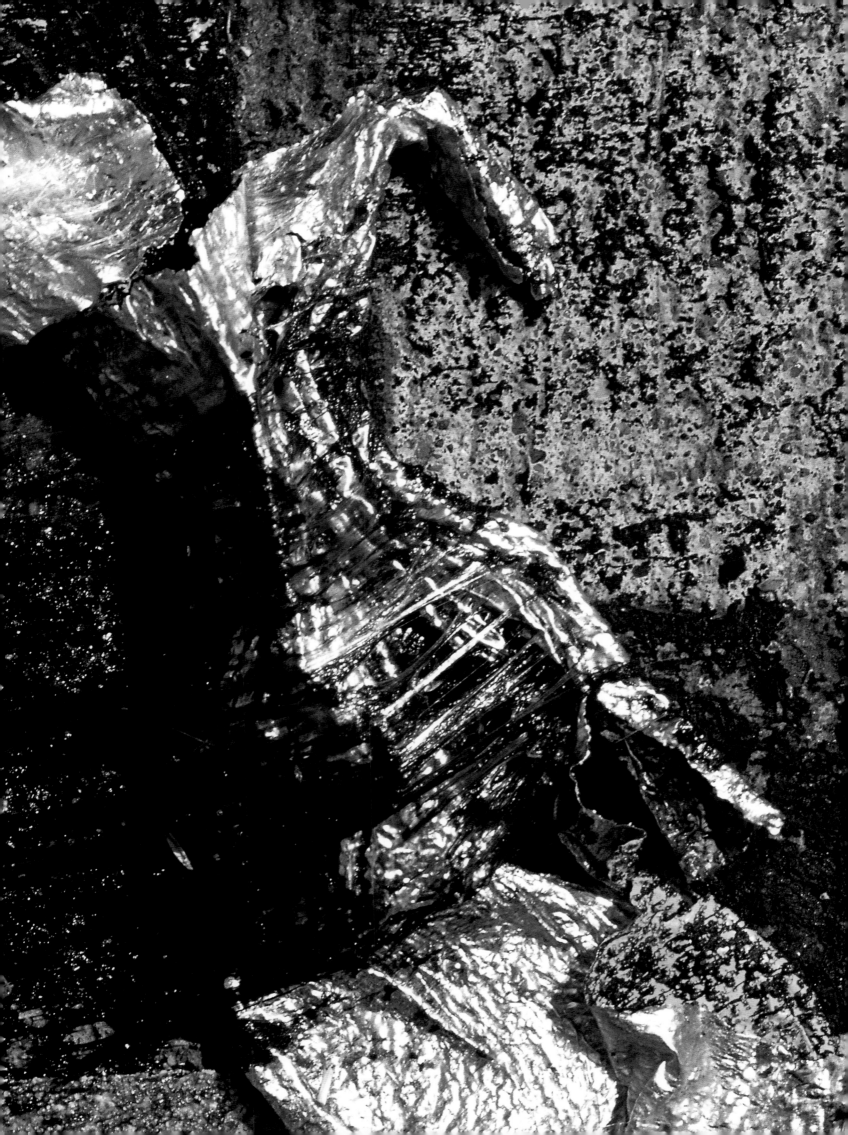

AUSTRALIANGP
MELBOURNE

Main photograph: Clever strategy by McLaren put David Coulthard into a winning position, and the Scot took his chance with aplomb.

Inset far left: Coulthard takes station behind the safety car.

Inset left: The remains of Rubens Barrichello's Ferrari.

Photographs: Darren Heath

Four teams would eventually opt to take part in the new Friday-morning test session: Renault, Jaguar, Jordan and Minardi. The two-hour slot saw Jarno Trulli set fastest time at 1m 28.125s in his Renault R23, ahead of Mark Webber's Jaguar R4 (1m 28.213s), Giancarlo Fisichella's Jordan EJ-13 (1m 28.225s) and Fernando Alonso's Renault (1m 28.339s).

While Jaguar, Minardi and Jordan were intent on employing the Friday sessions as a means of less-expensive testing while, at the same time, giving their novice drivers more track experience in unfamiliar settings, from the outset Renault was determined to use the extra laps as a valuable springboard to raise its technical game. To that end, a dedicated third car was on hand for the team's newly recruited test driver, the highly experienced Allan McNish.

'I think it has been a big benefit for us,' said Renault technical director Mike Gascoyne. 'We were quick in every session, the drivers were very happy with the car, and by the time we got to the pre-qualifying warm-up, they said that the set-up was perfect.'

Friday's hour-long qualifying session saw Rubens Barrichello's Ferrari fastest, ahead of Kimi Räikkönen's McLaren, Jacques Villeneuve's BAR-Honda and Michael Schumacher's Ferrari. Yet despite the fact that Schumacher made his one-lap run for grid position fourth from the end of the queue, his magical touch ensured that he achieved the 51st pole position of his career with a 1m 27.173s best. And Rubens joined him on the front row less than 0.3s slower.

However, Michael made a mistake during Saturday's free practice, damaging the front of his Ferrari and having to work with Barrichello's chassis settings for the rest of the day. 'He did a much better job with the set-up,' admitted the world champion.

'Today we got a better insight into the effects of the new sporting regulations,' said Jean Todt. 'The changing of components after free practice, a very hectic 15-minute warm-up and then everything played out over just one lap. That aside, the F2002 again gave satisfaction with another all-red front row.'

In the McLaren camp, Räikkönen had impressed with an excellent second-fastest time on Friday, but crashed heavily on Saturday morning and then ran wide in the T-car during qualifying, dropping to 15th (1m 29.470s) and scattering debris all over the circuit, which slightly wrong-footed Barrichello, the final driver out.

'Today's qualifying was the first time this weekend I have had a problem,' said the Brazilian. 'I was on a good lap when I saw the oil/debris flags after turn six. With the new rules, you are supposed to be alone on the track, so I was not sure what to do and lost concentration. Kimi's car was on the correct side of the track, but there were bits of car on the road. I'm not complaining, but I could have done a better time.'

Juan Pablo Montoya qualified his Williams-BMW FW25 third at 1m 28.101s, admitting that it was a real challenge to qualify an F1 car over a single lap with a heavier quantity of fuel than before. 'I tell you, it takes a lot more out of you than a car on a light fuel load that you've just spent three runs getting the set-up right for,' he grinned.

Heinz-Harald Frentzen ran a relatively light fuel load to place his Sauber C22 fourth at 1m 28.274s, ahead of Olivier Panis's Toyota TF103 (1m 28.288s), while the BAR-Hondas of Jacques Villeneuve (1m 28.420s) and Jenson Button (1m 28.682s) sandwiched Nick Heidfeld's Sauber (1m 28.464s) in sixth and eighth places.

The BAR team's weekend had started on a troubled note on Friday after a faulty batch of incorrectly machined camshafts caused the failure of two Honda RA003E V10 engines. That promised a busy few hours for the mechanics, but the cars appeared to be in good shape on Saturday.

Ralf Schumacher and David Coulthard made mistakes on their runs and started from ninth and 11th as a consequence, while both the Renault drivers also produced less-than-perfect qualifying laps. Jaguar opted for the harder of the two Michelin tyre compounds, and Mark Webber confessed that his resultant 14th place on the grid represented a somewhat conservative effort.

Ralph Firman, Cristiano da Matta, Antonio Pizzonia and Justin Wilson were all learning the ropes, and the Minardi team took advantage of the rule permitting anybody who abandoned their qualifying lap to start at the back of the grid with no parc fermé restrictions. That was what they chose to do and perhaps what McLaren might usefully have done with Räikkönen as well.

D AVID Coulthard began his eighth season as a McLaren Mercedes F1 driver with a brilliantly mature run to victory at Melbourne's Albert Park circuit. But his success owed as much to the team's astute last-moment change of strategy as to the Scot's admirable capacity to avoid the silly mistakes that hobbled many of the front-runners.

Qualifying had proved to be a nightmare for McLaren. Coulthard made a mistake on the first corner of his sole flying lap, squandering a competitive grid position, and had to be content with a distant 11th. His team-mate, Kimi Räikkönen, was 15th after almost throwing his MP4/17D off the track.

Then, in the cool and rainy conditions that prevailed on race morning, McLaren altered its tactics. Both cars had left the pit lane on rain tyres and were set for a two-stop strategy. However, mid-way around their out lap, both drivers realised that the circuit was drying out very quickly.

As a result, Räikkönen went straight into the pits at the end of that lap, fuelling up for a one-stop run and switching to dry-weather rubber before lining up to take his start from the end of the pit lane. Jos Verstappen also started from there in the spare Minardi PS03 after his race machine developed an oil leak.

Meanwhile, Barrichello's Ferrari was beginning to creep ominously from its position on the outside of the front row, even though the Brazilian had his foot firmly on the brake pedal. Then the fifth red light went out and Michael Schumacher accelerated smoothly into the first corner, ahead of his team-mate with Juan Pablo Montoya's Williams FW25, Olivier Panis's Toyota TF103 and the Sauber C22s of Heinz-Harald Frentzen and Nick Heidfeld leading the pursuit.

As Michael and Barrichello pulled clear, Coulthard aimed for the pit entry lane at the end of lap two, following Räikkönen's example. He rejoined 20th and last, but now was in a strong tactical position on the right rubber and facing the prospect of one more refuelling stop.

Ironically, the jumbled grid resulting from the varying fuel loads carried during the one-shot qualifying session almost ensured that the Ferraris would run away in the early stages rather than have their performance capped in any way. At the end of the opening lap, Schumacher and Barrichello were a staggering 5.6s ahead of Heidfeld in third, the speed of his Sauber having been artificially distorted by a low-fuel qualifying run.

It was the slippery early laps, dirty track surface and variety of tyre choices among the 20-car field that really turned the race on its ear. On lap two, Juan Pablo Montoya forced his Williams-BMW FW25 up into third place, then inherited second when Barrichello crashed heavily mid-way around the sixth lap.

Next time around, F1 debutant Ralph Firman lost his Jordan-Ford at the same right-hander, then Schumacher took his Ferrari into the pits for an early stop at the end of lap eight, switching to dry rubber, but suffering from a lengthy 14.2s service caused by a sticking wheel nut.

Barrichello blamed his accident on the new HANS head-and-neck support system, which had become mandatory in F1 from the start of the new season. Ferrari had customised the upper torso support in an attempt to make it more comfortable for the driver, a process that involved positioning inflatable insulating pads between the carbon fibre of the support arms and the driver's race suit. Unfortunately, in Barrichello's case, one of the support pads lost its air pressure and the carbon fibre began to chafe directly on his collar-bone.

'The mistake was mine,' shrugged Rubens. 'I got on to the dirty part of the track and slid wide. But at the end of the day, you need to concentrate and it was hurting so much. To be perfectly honest, my concentration wasn't fixed on the track because of the HANS device and it was hurting like hell, so much so that I doubt I would have been able to finish the race.'

For his part, Firman, who had climbed to eighth place thanks to the team's correct call on the tyre front, was slightly bewildered about the cause of his own accident. 'I was well within myself, but then suddenly had major oversteer, lost the car and hit the barrier,' he mused. 'Rubens went off there, and I understand there was a possibility of some oil on the track, but honestly I don't know.'

That left Montoya slip-sliding his way around in the lead, ahead of the Renault R23s of Fernando Alonso and Jarno Trulli, but then the safety car was deployed to clear up the mess created by Barrichello and Firman as well as allowing the retrieval of Cristiano da Matta's Toyota, which had spun into a gravel trap on lap eight.

Panis, Giancarlo Fisichella's Jordan, Antonio Pizzonia's Jaguar and the Minardi of Justin Wilson all headed for the pits when the safety car came out, leaving the order at the head of the field as Montoya, Alonso, Trulli, Ralf Schumacher (Williams), Webber, Räikkönen, Michael Schumacher and Coulthard. On lap ten,

Above: But for a pit-lane speeding infringement, Kimi Räikkönen could have been the winner in Australia.

Opposite: Ralph Firman's hands betray the anxious wait for one-shot qualifying.
Photographs: Darren Heath

RUNNERS AND RIDERS FOR 2003

SCUDERIA FERRARI MARLBORO
Michael Schumacher and Rubens Barrichello starting their fourth straight season as team-mates, the Scuderia relying on an uprated version of the dominant F2002 with which to start the season. All-new F2003-GA – so titled in memory of the late Fiat patriarch Gianni Agnelli – unveiled only a month before the start of the season with its race debut scheduled for Imola at the earliest. New car described by technical director Ross Brawn as being possibly the biggest year-on-year improvement the team had managed in recent seasons. Felipe Massa, fresh from debut F1 season with Sauber, joined Luca Badoer on the test driving squad.

BMW WILLIAMSF1 TEAM
A huge sense of expectation surrounded the shorter-wheelbase, smaller-tank Williams FW25 powered by the latest, prodigiously powerful 90-degree BMW P83 V10, although the car made its debut at Melbourne without its definitive new rear-end set-up, which includes a smaller gearbox and torsion-bar suspension. Ralf Schumacher and Juan Pablo Montoya hoping that a combination of much improved Michelin rubber and a better aerodynamic package will help their challenge at the front of the pack.

WEST MCLAREN MERCEDES
David Coulthard and Kimi Räikkönen eager to get their challenge under way with an uprated MP4/17D featuring a smaller gearbox and more tightly packaged rear suspension layout. Backed up by test driver Alex Wurz – and with Pedro de la Rosa soon to be signed in a similar role – the team looked set to benefit further with the initiation of a separate, dedicated Michelin test programme apart from its regular chassis effort. Work behind the scenes progressing flat-out on the striking new MP4/18A, which was not expected to race much before the season's half-way point.

MILD SEVEN RENAULT F1 TEAM
All-new Renault R23 still powered by wide-angle, 110-degree Renault V6, but tipped as much improved, fully integrated design for the first time since the French car maker purchased the former Benetton team. Fernando Alonso replaces Jenson Button alongside the experienced Jarno Trulli, and much is expected from this new driver combination.

SAUBER PETRONAS
Conservative driver line-up of Heinz-Harald Frentzen and Nick Heidfeld paired with latest customer Ferrari V10 engine makes for few material changes in the Sauber squad, although $45 million investment in full-sized wind-tunnel tipped to strengthen longer-term technical strength. An experienced and seasoned line-up that can be expected to spring the occasional surprise near the front of the field.

JORDAN FORD
The cash-strapped British team negotiated a worthwhile severance payment, allowing Honda to terminate its engine supply contract with a year still to run and freeing Jordan to enter a lease deal for Cosworth CR4 V10 engines at a cost of around $18 million. Lack of sponsorship has also obliged Jordan to recruit Formula Nippon champion Ralph Firman, who indirectly brings some funds to the party, while Giancarlo Fisichella remains on strength as team leader. Eddie Jordan predicts that 2003 will be a 'back to basics year' for his Silverstone-based operation.

JAGUAR RACING
Facing the new year after more off-season blood letting – Niki Lauda deposed as team principal. New, stiffer, more promising R4 chassis with highly rated drivers Mark Webber and Antonio Pizzonia, powered by latest Cosworth CR5, high-revving lightweight V10.

LUCKY STRIKE BAR HONDA
All-new BAR-Honda 005 representing the first complete design from the technical team directed by former Williams aerodynamicist Geoffrey Willis. Powered by the latest evolutionary version of Honda's V10 package, first tested at the end of last season, the Japanese manufacturer having spent much effort in improving reliability and power output. Jenson Button replaces Olivier Panis in the driver line-up alongside Jacques Villeneuve, promising a somewhat sparky personal partnership.

EUROPEAN MINARDI COSWORTH
Asiatech V10s have given way to Cosworth CR3 engines in the financially hard-pressed Minardi squad, which sports a new line-up of Jos Verstappen and Justin Wilson in place of Mark Webber and Alex Yoong. Wilson purchased the drive with the help of a public flotation of his racing career, which yielded around $1 million in individual $700 stakes. A specially lengthened chassis is required to accommodate the British driver's 6-ft 3-in frame. Team switched from Michelin to Bridgestone tyres for this season.

PANASONIC TOYOTA RACING
Latest TF103 design reflects many more hours of wind-tunnel development – directed by Gustav Brunner – than the car's immediate predecessor. Uprated V10 engine and seven-speed gearbox exhaustively tested over the winter, with Olivier Panis and CART champion Cristiano da Matta taking over from Mika Salo and Allan McNish.

Main photograph: Mark Webber settled easily into the Jaguar camp.
Photograph: Darren Heath

Above: Jenson Button rebuilding his career with the BAR team.

Above right: Justin Wilson realised his F1 dream at last with Minardi.

Right: CART champion Cristiano da Matta was typically committed on his Toyota debut.
Photographs: Bryn Williams/crash.net

Above: Michael Schumacher lost his chance of victory, paying the price for running high on the kerb and damaging a bargeboard.
Photograph: Patrick Gosling

Right: Montoya was left to reflect on a late-race spin, which dropped him behind Coulthard.
Photograph: Darren Heath

Alonso pitted, dropping his Renault to the tail of the field and allowing Trulli to move into second.

Hardly had the race resumed its rhythm than Mark Webber's Jaguar R4 wobbled to a standstill with broken suspension after a plucky run in the thick of the action. Once again, the safety car was sent out.

'It was disappointing, but I remain positive because of the clear potential we showed today,' said Webber. 'Once the race began, the performance of the car was good and I thoroughly enjoyed myself out there. I was on a two-stop strategy and even though I knew that Michael Schumacher was probably running a little heavier than me on fuel, it was a very nice feeling indeed to be fighting him on the race track.'

The second safety-car period prompted Montoya, Trulli and Ralf Schumacher to make their first stops, Ralf's visit taking an overlong 18.2s after problems with a sticking right rear wheel nut. Leaving the pits in frustration, the younger Schumacher went wheel-to-wheel with Alonso into the first corner, forcing the Renault driver out over the gravel and pitching himself into a spin.

Meanwhile, Justin Wilson's F1 debut had come to an end with a holed water radiator after only 16 laps. 'It was fantastic to have the opportunity of getting towards the mid-field and being able to race some of the other guys and drive past them,' he grinned broadly.

On lap 21, the race restarted with Räikkönen leading, ahead of Michael Schumacher, Coulthard and the BAR-Hondas of Jacques Villeneuve and Jenson Button. At the end of lap 25, both BARs headed for the pit lane, a furious Button being subjected to a time-consuming delay as he waited behind his team-mate for service.

'I had radio problems, so it was very difficult to communicate with the pit wall and both cars ended up pitting at the same time,' said Villeneuve. 'It took a long time to get the tyres working and I didn't get enough time on any set.'

Button, who clearly believed that Villeneuve had deliberately pitted in a bid to spoil his efforts, was not amused. 'Jacques did not come in when he was supposed to,' he said. 'I was a little bit shocked when he came in because I knew I was on the right lap.

'He did apologise, which was needed, I think. But I am not very impressed. It is very annoying. It was a bit of a nightmare for everyone.'

Meanwhile, Schumacher was piling on the pressure behind Räikkönen's McLaren, but the Finn wasn't to be ruffled. The pair edged away from Coulthard, and on lap 29 Michael made a deliberately short pit stop, determined to vault ahead of the McLaren and leave sufficient time for a late-race 'splash and dash' to retain the advantage.

Räikkönen stopped four laps later, but a slight glitch with the

ECCLESTONE SLAMS FERRARI

On the eve of the Australian Grand Prix, F1 commercial rights holder Bernie Ecclestone fired a warning shot across Ferrari's bows by describing the team as 'arrogant' in its approach to the sport.

In a BBC Radio 5 Live interview, he added, 'McLaren won 15 races [in 1988] with Prost and Senna, but they were racing each other and nobody cared. It was two guys having a race – one won one and the next weekend the other won.

'At the moment, two guys are racing, and only one is allowed to win. And that's what the public don't want to see and I don't want to see. I want to see McLaren and Williams chasing Michael.'

He continued, 'The thing that upsets people and upsets me as well is that Schumacher gets protection from a second driver who does what he is told.'

Bernie extended his criticism by adding that he thought that the way in which Bridgestone made tyres exclusively for Michael Schumacher was also wrong: 'The whole Ferrari set-up is for Michael, so Michelin, who make tyres for Williams, Renault and McLaren, find it hard to compete. If Michelin was in a position to make tyres for David Coulthard or Montoya and no one else, they would be three seconds a lap quicker.'

That said, Ecclestone admitted that he was not concerned about the prospect of Schumacher winning a sixth world championship. 'It is good to have a superstar,' he said. 'I don't think that is a problem; it's the way they [Ferrari] win. We don't want him to win the title too early in the season.'

engine electronics meant that he exceeded the pit-lane speed limit by a mere 1 kph, sufficient nevertheless for him to be hauled back for the inevitable drive-through penalty.

While Räikkönen was under investigation, and before he had taken the penalty, Schumacher had attempted to muscle ahead of the McLaren driver at the first corner. The result was that Michael veered wide on to the grass as Kimi kept to his line. Two laps later, Räikkönen entered the pits for his penalty, but the crucial time lost by Schumacher had surely wiped out his prospect of a win, given the need for that final extra stop.

Montoya made his final fuel stop on lap 42, and now it seemed as though all Schumacher would have to do was nurse his 11s lead. In reality, he had to press on to build a sufficient cushion for that extra stop. During that sprint, he bottomed his Ferrari heavily, riding high up the kerb on the exit of turn five, after which the bargeboards started to disintegrate.

Race officials gave him the black and orange flag, signifying a mechanical defect, and he came in for what would otherwise have been his final stop, refuelling quickly and resuming in fourth, behind Räikkönen.

Now Montoya looked as though he had it in the bag, just 2.5s ahead of Coulthard, who had run unspectacularly, but efficiently, on his heavy fuel load for much of the race.

Then, just 12 laps from the finish, the hapless Montoya spun, handing the race to Coulthard .

'What was so frustrating was that I kept it off all the walls when it was slippery in the early stages,' said Montoya, 'then spun when I was under no pressure. It was my fault, but I felt the traction control may have kicked in a little late.'

Räikkönen, who'd survived two spells of tyre 'graining' during the race, fended off Schumacher to the end. Behind the Ferrari, the Renaults of Jarno Trulli and Fernando Alonso sandwiched Heinz-Harald Frentzen's sixth-place Sauber at the chequered flag. Ralf Schumacher claimed the final point for eighth place, while the BAR-Hondas and Jos Verstappen's Minardi were the only other runners to make it to the chequered flag.

Heidfeld had retired with a suspension failure, possibly the legacy of a collision in traffic, while Panis's Toyota hopes had been thwarted when he was forced to call it a day with a fuel pick-up problem.

A lucky win for Coulthard? The Scot was under no illusions. 'I have very high standards,' he admitted. 'From a pure satisfaction viewpoint, the best way to win a race is start from pole, set fastest lap and lead all the way. I don't feel as good about that result as some I've achieved, but it is a win nonetheless and I am happy to take it.'

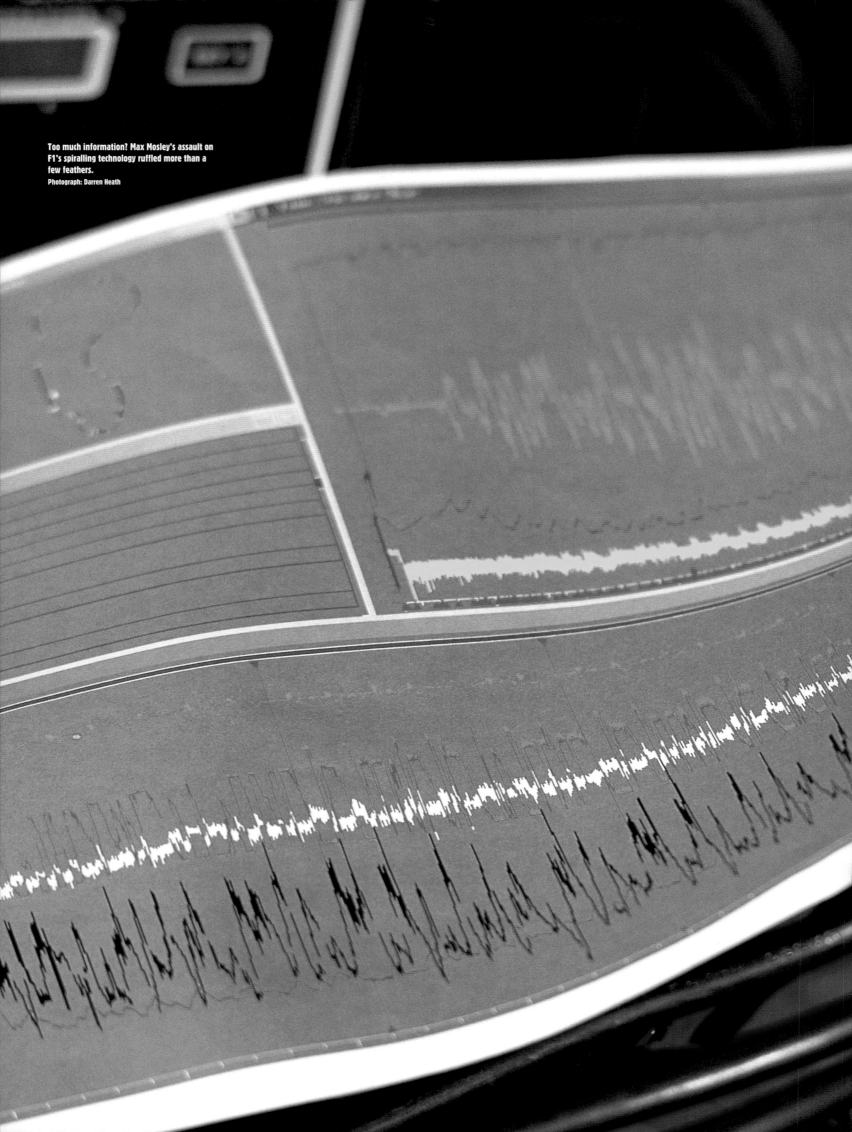

Too much information? Max Mosley's assault on F1's spiralling technology ruffled more than a few feathers.
Photograph: Darren Heath

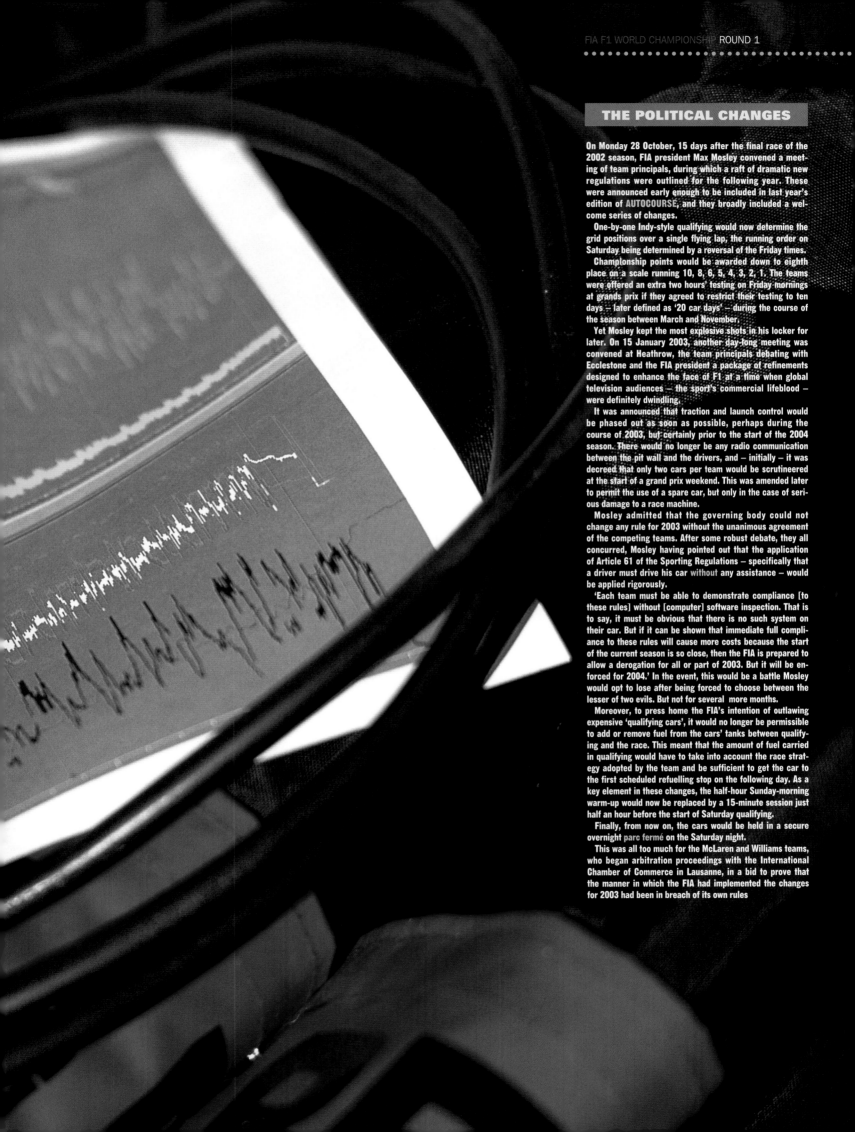

THE POLITICAL CHANGES

On Monday 28 October, 15 days after the final race of the 2002 season, FIA president Max Mosley convened a meeting of team principals, during which a raft of dramatic new regulations were outlined for the following year. These were announced early enough to be included in last year's edition of AUTOCOURSE, and they broadly included a welcome series of changes.

One-by-one Indy-style qualifying would now determine the grid positions over a single flying lap, the running order on Saturday being determined by a reversal of the Friday times.

Championship points would be awarded down to eighth place on a scale running 10, 8, 6, 5, 4, 3, 2, 1. The teams were offered an extra two hours' testing on Friday mornings at grands prix if they agreed to restrict their testing to ten days – later defined as '20 car days' – during the course of the season between March and November.

Yet Mosley kept the most explosive shots in his locker for later. On 15 January 2003, another day-long meeting was convened at Heathrow, the team principals debating with Ecclestone and the FIA president a package of refinements designed to enhance the face of F1 at a time when global television audiences – the sport's commercial lifeblood – were definitely dwindling.

It was announced that traction and launch control would be phased out as soon as possible, perhaps during the course of 2003, but certainly prior to the start of the 2004 season. There would no longer be any radio communication between the pit wall and the drivers, and – initially – it was decreed that only two cars per team would be scrutineered at the start of a grand prix weekend. This was amended later to permit the use of a spare car, but only in the case of serious damage to a race machine.

Mosley admitted that the governing body could not change any rule for 2003 without the unanimous agreement of the competing teams. After some robust debate, they all concurred, Mosley having pointed out that the application of Article 61 of the Sporting Regulations – specifically that a driver must drive his car without any assistance – would be applied rigorously.

'Each team must be able to demonstrate compliance [to these rules] without [computer] software inspection. That is to say, it must be obvious that there is no such system on their car. But if it can be shown that immediate full compliance to these rules will cause more costs because the start of the current season is so close, then the FIA is prepared to allow a derogation for all or part of 2003. But it will be enforced for 2004.' In the event, this would be a battle Mosley would opt to lose after being forced to choose between the lesser of two evils. But not for several more months.

Moreover, to press home the FIA's intention of outlawing expensive 'qualifying cars', it would no longer be permissible to add or remove fuel from the cars' tanks between qualifying and the race. This meant that the amount of fuel carried in qualifying would have to take into account the race strategy adopted by the team and be sufficient to get the car to the first scheduled refuelling stop on the following day. As a key element in these changes, the half-hour Sunday-morning warm-up would now be replaced by a 15-minute session just half an hour before the start of Saturday qualifying.

Finally, from now on, the cars would be held in a secure overnight parc fermé on the Saturday night.

This was all too much for the McLaren and Williams teams, who began arbitration proceedings with the International Chamber of Commerce in Lausanne, in a bid to prove that the manner in which the FIA had implemented the changes for 2003 had been in breach of its own rules

FIA F1 WORLD CHAMPIONSHIP • ROUND 1

FOSTER'S
AUSTRALIAN GRAND PRIX

MELBOURNE
7–9 MARCH 2003

Photograph: Darren Heath

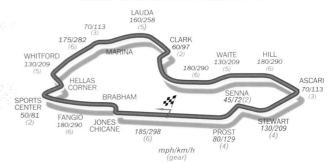

MELBOURNE – ALBERT PARK
CIRCUIT LENGTH: 3.295 miles/5.303 km

LAUDA 160/258 (5)
70/113 (3)
175/282 (6)
CLARK 60/97 (2)
MARINA
WHITFORD 130/209 (5)
WAITE 130/209 (5)
HILL 180/290 (6)
180/290 (6)
HELLAS CORNER
ASCARI 70/113 (3)
SPORTS CENTER 50/81 (2)
BRABHAM
SENNA 45/72 (2)
FANGIO 180/290 (6)
JONES CHICANE
185/298 (6)
PROST 80/129 (4)
STEWART 130/209 (4)
mph/km/h (gear)

RACE DISTANCE: 58 laps, 191.117 miles/307.574 km
RACE WEATHER: Initially wet, then sunny and dry (track 20/25°C, air 18/20°C)

Pos.	Driver	Nat.	No.	Entrant	Car/Engine	Tyres	Laps	Time/Retirement	Speed (mph/km/h)	Gap to leader	Fastest race lap
1	David Coulthard	GB	5	West McLaren Mercedes	McLaren MP4/17D-Mercedes F0110M V10	M	58	1h 34m 42.124s	121.085/194.868		1m 28.272s lap 28
2	Juan Pablo Montoya	COL	3	BMW WilliamsF1 Team	Williams FW25-BMW P83 V10	M	58	1h 34m 50.799s	120.901/194.571	+8.675s	1m 27.942s lap 39
3	Kimi Räikkönen	FIN	6	West McLaren Mercedes	McLaren MP4/17D-Mercedes F0110M V10	M	58	1h 34m 51.316s	120.889/194.553	+9.192s	1m 27.724s lap 32
4	Michael Schumacher	D	1	Scuderia Ferrari Marlboro	Ferrari F2002-051 V10	B	58	1h 34m 51.606s	120.883/194.543	+9.482s	1m 27.759s lap 27
5	Jarno Trulli	I	7	Mild Seven Renault F1 Team	Renault R3-RS23 V10	M	58	1h 35m 20.925s	120.264/193.546	+38.801s	1m 28.638s lap 44
6	Heinz-Harald Frentzen	D	10	Sauber Petronas	Sauber C22-Petronas 03A V10	B	58	1h 35m 26.052s	120.156/193.373	+43.928s	1m 29.096s lap 35
7	Fernando Alonso	E	8	Mild Seven Renault F1 Team	Renault R3-RS23 V10	B	58	1h 35m 27.198s	120.132/193.334	+45.074s	1m 28.170s lap 35
8	Ralf Schumacher	D	4	BMW WilliamsF1 Team	Williams FW25-BMW P83 V10	M	58	1h 35m 27.869s	120.118/193.312	+45.745s	1m 28.617s lap 37
9	Jacques Villeneuve	CDN	16	Lucky Strike BAR Honda	BAR 005-Honda RA003E V10	B	58	1h 35m 47.660s	119.704/192.646	+65.536s	1m 28.770s lap 57
10	Jenson Button	GB	17	Lucky Strike BAR Honda	BAR 005-Honda RA003E V10	B	58	1h 35m 48.098s	119.695/192.631	+65.974s	1m 28.600s lap 57
11	Jos Verstappen	NL	19	European Minardi Cosworth	Minardi PS03-Cosworth CR3 V10	B	57			+1 lap	1m 31.785s lap 29
12	Giancarlo Fisichella	I	11	Jordan Ford	Jordan EJ-13-Ford Cosworth RS1 V10	B	52	Gearbox			1m 29.274s lap 49
13	Antonio Pizzonia	BR	15	Jaguar Racing	Jaguar R4-Cosworth CR5 V10	M	52	Suspension			1m 29.217s lap 37
	Olivier Panis	F	20	Panasonic Toyota Racing	Toyota TF103-RVX-03 V10	M	31	Fuel system			1m 29.694s lap 23
	Nick Heidfeld	D	9	Sauber Petronas	Sauber C22-Petronas 03A V10	B	20	Broken suspension			1m 33.519s lap 14
	Justin Wilson	GB	18	European Minardi Cosworth	Minardi PS03-Cosworth CR3 V10	B	16	Radiator			1m 33.139s lap 13
	Mark Webber	AUS	14	Jaguar Racing	Jaguar R4-Cosworth CR5 V10	M	15	Suspension			1m 29.697s lap 14
	Cristiano da Matta	BR	21	Panasonic Toyota Racing	Toyota TF103-RVX-03 V10	M	7	Spun			1m 33.753s lap 7
	Ralph Firman	IRL	12	Jordan Ford	Jordan EJ-13-Ford Cosworth RS1 V10	B	6	Crash			1m 36.644s lap 6
	Rubens Barrichello	BR	2	Scuderia Ferrari Marlboro	Ferrari F2002-051 V10	B	5	Crash			1m 37.086s lap 5

Fastest lap: Kimi Räikkönen, on lap 32, 1m 27.724s, 135.224 mph/217.623 km/h (record for modified track layout).
Previous lap record: Michael Schumacher (Ferrari F2001-050 V10), 1m 28.214s, 134.473 mph/216.414 km/h (2001).

19th: JOS VERSTAPPEN Minardi-Cosworth
started from pit lane

17th: RALPH FIRMAN Jordan-Ford Cosworth

15th: KIMI RÄIKKÖNEN McLaren-Mercedes
started from pit lane

13th: GIANCARLO FISICHELLA Jordan-Ford Cosworth

11th: DAVID COULTHARD McLaren-Mercedes

20th: JUSTIN WILSON Minardi-Cosworth

18th: ANTONIO PIZZONIA Jaguar-Cosworth

16th: CRISTIANO DA MATTA Toyota

14th: MARK WEBBER Jaguar-Cosworth

12th: JARNO TRULLI Renault

Grid order	1	2	3	4	5	6	7	8	9	10	11	12	13	14	15	16	17	18	19	20	21	22	23	24	25	26	27	28	29	30	31	32	33	34	35	36	37	38	39	40	41	42	43	44
1 M. SCHUMACHER	1	1	1	1	1	1	3	3	3	3	3	3	3	3	3	3	6	6	6	6	6	6	6	6	6	6	6	6	6	6	6	3	3	3	3	3	3	3	3	3	1	1	1
2 BARRICHELLO	2	2	2	2	2	3	8	8	7	7	7	7	7	7	1	1	1	1	1	1	1	1	1	1	1	5	5	3	6	6	6	6	6	1	1	1		3	3	3
3 MONTOYA	9	3	3	3	8	7	7	7	4	4	4	4	4	4	5	5	5	5	5	5	5	5	5	5	3	3	3	10	10	10	10	1	1	5	5	5	5	5	5
10 FRENTZEN	3	9	10	10	8	7	4	4	4	14	14	6	6	6	6	16	16	16	16	16	16	16	3	3	3	3	10	10	10	11	1	1	1	5	5	5	6	8	8	7	7	7
20 PANIS	10	10	9	8	10	4	14	14	14	6	6	1	1	1	1	17	17	17	17	17	17	17	20	20	20	20	11	11	11	5	5	5	5	7	7	7	7	7	6	6	6
16 VILLENEUVE	17	17	8	9	7	14	20	6	6	1	1	14	14	14	14	5	20	20	20	20	3	3	3	3	10	10	10	10	1	1	1	7	7	7	8	8	8	4	6	8	10	10
9 HEIDFELD	16	16	17	17	4	20	6	1	1	5	5	5	5	5	5	5	3	3	3	20	20	20	20	11	11	11	11	7	7	7	7	8	8	4	4	4	6	10	10	8	8
17 BUTTON	8	8	16	17	9	12	1	5	5	16	16	16	16	16	17	10	10	10	10	10	10	7	7	7	20	19	8	8	4	4	4	10	10	10	16	16	4	4	4
4 R. SCHUMACHER	7	7	7	20	14	6	11	20	16	20	20	17	17	17	20	11	11	11	11	11	11	11	11	11	19	19	19	19	9	15	4	16	16	16	16	16	10	10	16	11	11	11
8 ALONSO	5	18	20	4	20	9	15	16	20	17	20	20	20	20	10	7	7	7	7	7	7	7	15	15	15	8	16	16	11	15	15	15	15	15	11	11	16	16	16
5 COULTHARD	20	20	18	14	12	11	21	21	10	10	10	10	10	10	19	19	19	19	19	19	19	8	8	8	8	4	20	15	15	17	17	17	17	17	17	17	17	17	17	17	17
7 TRULLI	18	4	4	18	5	1	10	10	17	19	19	19	19	19	9	9	9	9	9	9	8	4	4	4	20	17	17	11	11	11	11	11	11	15	15	15	15	15
11 FISICHELLA	4	14	14	12	18	21	18	19	19	19	19	19	19	19	4	9	9	9	8	8	8	16	16	16	16	16	17	17	19	19	19	19	19	19	19	19	19
14 WEBBER	14	12	12	6	11	18	16	19	19	15	15	15	15	18	15	9	8	8	8	4	4	4	17	17	17	17	17	19
21 DA MATTA	12	6	6	15	15	5	17	15	9	9	9	18	18	15	9	8	4	4	4
12 FIRMAN	15	15	15	11	10	10	18	9	18	18	9	9	9	9	8
15 PIZZONIA	6	11	11	21	5	16	9	18	8	8	8	8	8
18 WILSON	11	21	21	5	17	17	9
6 RÄIKKÖNEN	21	19	19	19	19	19
19 VERSTAPPEN	19	5	5	16	16

Pit stop
One lap behind leader

TIME SHEETS

SATURDAY QUALIFYING determines race grid order
Sunny and dry (track 22/23°C, air 18/19°C)

Pos.	Driver	Lap time	Sector 1	Sector 2	Sector 3
1	Michael Schumacher	1m 27.173s	29.152s	23.168s	34.853s
2	Rubens Barrichello	1m 27.418s	29.215s	23.313s	34.890s
3	Juan Pablo Montoya	1m 28.101s	29.278s	23.323s	35.500s
4	Heinz-Harald Frentzen	1m 28.274s	29.511s	23.244s	35.519s
5	Olivier Panis	1m 28.288s	29.468s	23.313s	35.507s
6	Jacques Villeneuve	1m 28.420s	29.490s	23.402s	35.528s
7	Nick Heidfeld	1m 28.464s	29.342s	23.448s	35.652s
8	Jenson Button	1m 28.682s	29.590s	23.512s	35.580s
9	Ralf Schumacher	1m 28.830s	29.783s	23.316s	35.731s
10	Fernando Alonso	1m 28.928s	29.308s	23.397s	36.223s
11	David Coulthard	1m 29.105s	29.867s	23.520s	35.718s
12	Jarno Trulli	1m 29.136s	29.702s	23.580s	35.854s
13	Giancarlo Fisichella	1m 29.344s	29.996s	23.722s	35.626s
14	Mark Webber	1m 29.367s	30.307s	23.538s	35.522s
15	Kimi Räikkönen	1m 29.470s	29.465s	23.224s	36.781s
16	Cristiano da Matta	1m 29.538s	29.640s	23.809s	36.089s
17	Ralph Firman	1m 31.242s	30.392s	23.840s	37.010s
18	Antonio Pizzonia	1m 31.723s	30.790s	24.117s	36.816s
19	Jos Verstappen	No time	31.284s	24.656s	38.836s
20	Justin Wilson	No time	31.363s	24.363s	37.155s

FRIDAY QUALIFYING determines Sat running order
Sunny and dry (track 32/35°C, air 24/26°C)

Pos.	Driver	Lap time
1	Rubens Barrichello	1m 26.372s
2	Kimi Räikkönen	1m 26.551s
3	Jacques Villeneuve	1m 26.832s
4	Michael Schumacher	1m 27.103s
5	Jenson Button	1m 27.159s
6	David Coulthard	1m 27.242s
7	Fernando Alonso	1m 27.255s
8	Olivier Panis	1m 27.352s
9	Jarno Trulli	1m 27.411s
10	Juan Pablo Montoya	1m 27.450s
11	Cristiano da Matta	1m 27.478s
12	Nick Heidfeld	1m 27.510s
13	Heinz-Harald Frentzen	1m 27.563s
14	Giancarlo Fisichella	1m 27.633s
15	Mark Webber	1m 27.675s
16	Ralf Schumacher	1m 28.266s
17	Ralph Firman	1m 29.977s
18	Jos Verstappen	1m 30.053s
19	Antonio Pizzonia	1m 30.092s
20	Justin Wilson	1m 30.479s

PRIVATE TESTING
Sunny and dry (track: 26/28°C, air 19/22°C)

Pos.	Driver	Laps	Time
1	Jarno Trulli	35	1m 28.125s
2	Mark Webber	40	1m 28.213s
3	Giancarlo Fisichella	28	1m 28.225s
4	Fernando Alonso	38	1m 28.339s
5	Allan McNish	46	1m 29.557s
6	Ralph Firman	29	1m 30.325s
7	Jos Verstappen	25	1m 30.458s
8	Antonio Pizzonia	16	1m 30.502s
9	Justin Wilson	30	1m 31.187s

FRIDAY FREE PRACTICE
Sunny and dry (track 30/32°C, air 22/24°C)

Pos.	Driver	Laps	Time
1	Kimi Räikkönen	18	1m 26.509s
2	David Coulthard	23	1m 26.988s
3	Jarno Trulli	7	1m 27.286s
4	Rubens Barrichello	21	1m 27.459s
5	Mark Webber	13	1m 27.654s
6	Michael Schumacher	25	1m 27.666s
7	Fernando Alonso	8	1m 27.671s
8	Nick Heidfeld	17	1m 27.918s
9	Juan Pablo Montoya	12	1m 27.929s
10	Ralf Schumacher	24	1m 27.982s
11	Antonio Pizzonia	13	1m 28.092s
12	Heinz-Harald Frentzen	19	1m 28.207s
13	Olivier Panis	12	1m 28.362s
14	Jenson Button	10	1m 28.493s
15	Cristiano da Matta	24	1m 28.698s
16	Giancarlo Fisichella	6	1m 29.327s
17	Ralph Firman	15	1m 29.531s
18	Jos Verstappen	14	1m 30.198s
19	Justin Wilson	17	1m 30.606s
20	Jacques Villeneuve	5	1m 31.529s

SATURDAY FREE PRACTICE
Sunny and dry (track 18/20°C, air 18/19°C)

Pos.	Driver	Laps	Time
1	Jarno Trulli	23	1m 26.928s
2	Jenson Button	30	1m 27.415s
3	Fernando Alonso	29	1m 27.424s
4	Michael Schumacher	23	1m 27.517s
5	Rubens Barrichello	27	1m 27.558s
6	Juan Pablo Montoya	32	1m 27.700s
7	Ralf Schumacher	29	1m 27.814s
8	Nick Heidfeld	18	1m 28.049s
9	David Coulthard	18	1m 28.090s
10	Cristiano da Matta	23	1m 28.177s
11	Olivier Panis	29	1m 28.360s
12	Mark Webber	26	1m 28.421s
13	Jacques Villeneuve	16	1m 28.509s
14	Kimi Räikkönen	10	1m 28.564s
15	Heinz-Harald Frentzen	27	1m 28.590s
16	Giancarlo Fisichella	28	1m 28.619s
17	Ralph Firman	26	1m 29.814s
18	Antonio Pizzonia	10	1m 30.551s
19	Justin Wilson	20	1m 30.857s
20	Jos Verstappen	19	1m 31.066s

WARM-UP
Sunny and dry (track 21°C, air 17°C)

Pos.	Driver	Laps	Time
1	Rubens Barrichello	7	1m 27.738s
2	Michael Schumacher	7	1m 27.844s
3	Fernando Alonso	4	1m 28.142s
4	Jarno Trulli	4	1m 28.654s
5	David Coulthard	5	1m 28.692s
6	Jacques Villeneuve	6	1m 28.694s
7	Ralf Schumacher	6	1m 28.895s
8	Kimi Räikkönen	4	1m 28.903s
9	Jenson Button	7	1m 29.205s
10	Olivier Panis	5	1m 29.346s
11	Heinz-Harald Frentzen	4	1m 29.485s
12	Nick Heidfeld	6	1m 29.653s
13	Giancarlo Fisichella	6	1m 29.888s
14	Mark Webber	4	1m 29.991s
15	Jos Verstappen	3	1m 30.288s
16	Juan Pablo Montoya	4	1m 30.325s
17	Justin Wilson	4	1m 31.063s
18	Ralph Firman	5	1m 32.229s
19	Antonio Pizzonia	4	1m 32.414s
20	Cristiano da Matta	1	No time

POINTS TABLES: CONSTRUCTORS
1	McLaren	16
2	Williams	9
3	Renault	6
4	Ferrari	5
5	Sauber	3

FOR THE RECORD

First grand prix start
Cristiano da Matta

Ralph Firman

Antonio Pizzonia

Justin Wilson

First grand prix point
Fernando Alonso

9th: RALF SCHUMACHER Williams-BMW

7th: NICK HEIDFELD Sauber-Petronas

5th: OLIVIER PANIS Toyota

3rd: JUAN PABLO MONTOYA Williams-BMW

Pole: MICHAEL SCHUMACHER Ferrari

10th: FERNANDO ALONSO Renault

8th: JENSON BUTTON BAR-Honda

6th: JACQUES VILLENEUVE BAR-Honda

4th: HEINZ-HARALD FRENTZEN Sauber-Petronas

2nd: RUBENS BARRICHELLO Ferrari

Lap chart (laps 46–58)

46	47	48	49	50	51	52	53	54	55	56	57	58	
3	3	5	5	5	5	5	5	5	5	5	5	5	1
5	5	3	3	3	3	3	3	3	3	3	3	3	2
1	6	6	6	6	6	6	6	6	6	6	6	6	3
6	1	1	1	1	1	1	1	1	1	1	1	1	4
7	7	7	7	7	7	7	7	7	7	7	7	7	5
10	10	10	10	10	10	10	10	10	10	10	10	10	6
8	8	8	8	8	8	8	8	8	8	8	8	8	7
4	4	4	4	4	4	4	4	4	4	4	4	4	8
11	11	11	11	11	11	11	16	16	16	16	16	16	
16	16	16	16	16	16	16	17	17	17	17	17	17	
17	17	17	17	17	17	17	19	19	19	19	19		
15	15	15	15	15	15	15							
19	19	19	19	19	19	19							

CHASSIS LOG BOOK

1	Michael Schumacher	F2002/225
2	Rubens Barrichello	F2002/222
	Spare	F2002/219
3	Juan Pablo Montoya	FW25/04
4	Ralf Schumacher	FW25/03
	Spare	FW25/02
5	David Coulthard	MP4/17D-06
6	Kimi Räikkönen	MP4/17D-08
	Spare	MP4/17D-09
7	Jarno Trulli	R23/03
8	Fernando Alonso	R23/02
	Allan McNish	R23/01
	Spare	R23/01
9	Nick Heidfeld	C22/01
10	Heinz-Harald Frentzen	C22/03
	Spare	C22/02
11	Giancarlo Fisichella	EJ-13/04
12	Ralph Firman	EJ-13/02
	Spare	EJ-13/01
14	Mark Webber	R4/01
15	Antonio Pizzonia	R4/03
	Spare	R4/02
16	Jacques Villeneuve	BAR005/3
17	Jenson Button	BAR005/4
	Spare	BAR005/2
18	Justin Wilson	PS03/04
19	Jos Verstappen	PS03/01
	Spare	PS03/02
20	Olivier Panis	TF103/03
21	Cristiano da Matta	TF103/02
	Spare	TF103/04

POINTS TABLES: DRIVERS
1	David Coulthard	10
2	Juan Pablo Montoya	8
3	Kimi Räikkönen	6
4	Michael Schumacher	5
5	Jarno Trulli	4
6	Heinz-Harald Frentzen	3
7	Fernando Alonso	2
8	Ralf Schumacher	1

Kimi Räikkönen became the second-youngest
grand prix winner with his victory in Malaysia.
Photograph: Darren Heath

MALAYSIANGP
SEPANG

SEPANG QUALIFYING

Qualifying certainly produced a few surprises. Before the start of the season, McLaren chairman Ron Dennis had jocularly referred to the Renault squad as 'one of the Friday-morning track sweepers' after its decision to opt for the extra test session. 'And now I refer to McLaren as our test team,' grinned Renault technical director Mike Gascoyne after Alonso and Trulli had buttoned up the front row of the grid.

Gascoyne's riposte reflected the fact that McLaren had undertaken an exhaustive test of Michelin's latest soft-compound tyre at Jerez prior to the Malaysian race. Alonso (1m 37.044s) and Trulli (1m 37.217s) had used it to excellent effect, qualifying ahead of Michael Schumacher and Coulthard.

'The extra Friday test session benefited us [here] more than I expected in terms of pure driving,' said Gascoyne. 'The tyre choice was very clear after we completed 120 laps on it during the morning, but ultimately we were on pole because Fernando didn't make even the slightest mistake. All credit to Jarno, too, who watched Fernando do the perfect lap, then [virtually] matched it.'

On the inside of the second row, Michael Schumacher ended up with a 1m 37.393s best. 'Tomorrow we will find out how much fuel the front-runners really have on board,' said Maranello technical chief Ross Brawn thoughtfully.

Schumacher seemed certain to be carrying more fuel than the Renaults, yet opting for the harder Bridgestone choice with durability in mind meant that he was forced to settle for the second row. Both Williams and McLaren drivers were left battling to dial out understeer during pre-qualifying practice.

David Coulthard wound up fourth at 1m 37.454s followed by Rubens Barrichello's Ferrari (1m 37.579s), Nick Heidfeld's Sauber (1m 37.766s) and Räikkönen (1m 37.858s), the Finn having run wide at the final corner as he fought for crucial tenths of a second.

In the Williams camp, both Juan Pablo Montoya and Ralf Schumacher were struggling for balance with their FW25s. Montoya posted an eighth-fastest 1m 37.974s, admitting that he was particularly worried after watching Ralf's earlier run, which only netted the German driver a distant 17th at 1m 38.789s.

However, the younger Schumacher was clearly preoccupied because of German tabloid press stories about his personal life, and he admitted that he had lost crucial time through driving errors on a couple of corners. 'Despite this, I think we have a good strategy compared to the other teams and our performance will improve for Sunday,' he predicted correctly.

Jenson Button wound up ninth at 1m 38.073s, heading his team-mate, Jacques Villeneuve (1m 38.289s), by three places in the final line-up. 'It's nice to be inside the top ten, but I didn't think the lap was going to be as quick as it was,' said Button. 'The first sector seemed good to me, and then I made a mistake in each of the last two sectors.' Villeneuve admitted that the team had improved the balance of his car over the weekend, but he made an error at the hairpin and lost time.

Over at Toyota, Olivier Panis was guardedly optimistic about the progress made by the TF103 after posting a tenth-fastest 1m 38.094s. 'We struggled with the set-up in free practice yesterday,' said the Frenchman, 'so we worked a lot overnight and made some real improvements.' A clutch problem forced Cristiano da Matta to take the spare car, but he managed a respectable 11th-fastest time, just 0.003s behind his team-mate.

Heinz-Harald Frentzen's Sauber, carrying significantly more fuel than Heidfeld's, lined up 13th at 1m 38.291s, while Giancarlo Fisichella managed a respectable 1m 38.416s, despite opting for the harder Bridgestone tyre choice. Firman battled with excessive oversteer during the last sector of the lap and wound up a slightly disappointing 20th on 1m 40.910s.

The Jaguar R4s of Antonio Pizzonia (1m 38.516s) and Mark Webber (1m 38.624s) qualified 15th and 16th after struggling with fuel pick-up problems on the first day. Pizzonia kept things nice and smooth without any dramatics, despite having suffered plenty of technical problems in Melbourne, while Webber admitted that he had lost around 0.3s on the final corner after a good effort up to that point.

With Firman last in the line-up, the Minardi PS03s of Jos Verstappen (1m 40.417s) and Justin Wilson (1m 40.599s) were 18th and 19th. 'We improved the car as the day progressed,' said Wilson, 'and although the time this afternoon isn't quite what we'd hoped for, I'm not too disappointed, all things considered.'

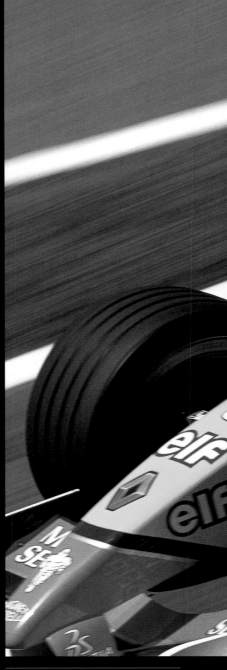

ECCLESTONE CRITICISES QUALIFYING FORMAT

F1 commercial rights holder Bernie Ecclestone offered his verdict on the new qualifying format after the Malaysian Grand Prix – and it was less than positive.

Speaking to the Brazilian news agency Agencia Estado immediately after Kimi Räikkönen's victory at Sepang, he said, 'Did you like it? Did you have fun with what you saw? It's horrible.

'First, the drivers are not driving on the limit in qualifying, and then they complete only one fast lap and they return to the pits and do nothing. There's no fighting – the excitement of qualifying has gone.'

Although the FIA president Max Mosley said he believed that the new qualifying format should be given time to 'bed in', Ecclestone was adamant that it should be changed as quickly as possible.

'When you go to see the doctor and he gives you a pill and that doesn't heal you, he changes your medication,' said Ecclestone. 'The new system is not working. We are going to wait a bit longer and then we are going to change it, yes. They want to transform our sport into a show. But did you see a show today?'

THE names of Kimi Räikkönen and Fernando Alonso were writ large in the F1 record books after a storming Malaysian Grand Prix at Sepang. The brilliant Finn became the second-youngest winner in the sport's history at the end of a tactically perfect race, while Alonso became the youngest ever pole winner in the Renault RS3.

Fittingly, the 23-year-old Finn's achievement was bettered only by Bruce McLaren, founder of the team for which he was driving, who had won the 1959 United States Grand Prix at Sebring when he was 22. McLaren, who died in a testing accident at Goodwood a decade before Räikkönen was born, certainly would have approved of the man who gave the team its latest success.

Rubens Barrichello finished an excellent second for Ferrari on a day when Michael Schumacher made one of his occasional mistakes, barging into Jarno Trulli's Renault on the second corner of the race in his haste to stay ahead of Melbourne winner David Coulthard's McLaren-Mercedes.

Alonso and Trulli had buttoned up the front row of the grid after a very convincing qualifying performance, but as the two Renaults scrambled into the first long right-hander in first and second places, Schumacher tried to take a tight line into the following left-hander in a bid to stop Coulthard's McLaren, by then level with the Ferrari on Michael's right, from actually making up the place.

It only took a split second for Michael to glance right, assess Coulthard's position and then look ahead again, to see that Trulli was braking hard for the second left-hander. Michael manhandled his Ferrari on to the kerb in a bid to avoid Jarno, but the F2002's right front wheel smacked firmly into the Renault's left rear and spun it around.

'Honestly, I think we missed a good opportunity today,' said Trulli after fighting back to fifth. 'Everything was going smoothly, but then Michael pushed me out. He apologised, but my race had been spoiled.' Farther back, Antonio Pizzonia's Jaguar R4 was shunted into Juan Pablo Montoya's Williams FW25 by Jos

Verstappen's Minardi PS03 as the traffic banked up in the wake of the front-runners' tangle.

Schuey's error earned him a drive-through penalty, but he stormed back to finish sixth, passing Jenson Button's BAR-Honda on the final lap. As it transpired, Michael could have usefully saved himself this impetuosity, as Coulthard went out early on with an electrical fault.

At the end of the opening lap, Alonso led by 2.4s from Coulthard, Nick Heidfeld's Sauber C22, Kimi Räikkönen's McLaren MP4/17D and the rest of the pack.

Others already in trouble included Cristiano da Matta, who had started from the pit lane after an electrical problem and was running with a full fuel tank in a bid to head-off any repeat of the pick-up troubles experienced by the team in Melbourne, while Jacques Villeneuve didn't even manage to start the race at all. Just before his car left the garage prior to the final parade lap, it developed an electrical fault, which was fixed but returned at the start of the parade lap, damaging the gearbox. It seems that the main vehicle computer reset itself due a sudden voltage spike in the system. That effectively scrambled the car's gear-selection capability, causing the transmission to attempt to engage two gears at once and damaging the selectors.

Second time around and Räikkönen nipped past on the outside of Heidfeld to take second place, just as Coulthard rolled to a halt at the side of the track after a broken electrical connection had shut down his Mercedes V10. Understandably, he was absolutely furious about this rare lapse in McLaren preparation and was not reticent in saying so.

'It was frustrating, disappointing and all the things which go with giving away opportunities like that,' said Coulthard. 'I said to the team on the radio when I ground to a halt, "Look guys, we all know this was a lost opportunity."'

At this point, Alonso was leading Räikkönen by 5.9s and Michael Schumacher pitted to replace his Ferrari's front wing,

DIARY

Ferrari president Luca di Montezemolo and sporting director Jean Todt are given bonuses of $19.2 million and $3.2 million respectively for their contributions to the prestige value of the Italian car maker.

Niki Lauda rules out any interest in running for the FIA presidency at any stage in the future.

Frank Williams writes to Bernie Ecclestone urging him to take steps to protect the future of the British Grand Prix.

Gil de Ferran is badly concussed in high-speed collision with Michael Andretti during IRL race at Phoenix.

German former GP driver Karl Kling dies at the age of 92.

which had been damaged slightly in the first-corner fracas, the world champion rejoining the chase in 14th position. On lap five, Rubens Barrichello's Ferrari F2002 and Olivier Panis's Toyota TF103 overtook Jenson Button's BAR-Honda to take fourth and fifth places, while the recovering Trulli nipped ahead of Justin Wilson's fast-starting Minardi to take ninth.

By this stage of the race, it was clear that the HANS restraint system would surface again as a potentially controversial issue. Barrichello, who had been complaining about a slight hernia, had been checked out by FIA medical delegate Syd Watkins prior to the event, and the doctor had agreed that the Brazilian should not use the device in Malaysia.

Subsequently, that decision would incense FIA president Max Mosley, who formally announced that no such exceptions would be granted in the future. 'If any driver is unable to wear the device for medical or any other reasons, the team concerned will have to replace him, just as they would if he could not wear a crash helmet or seat belts,' he said.

Wilson was actually forced to withdraw from the race due to the acute pain caused by an ill-fitting HANS device. The pain was so bad that eventually it paralysed his arms, and the team took several minutes to lift him from the cockpit of the Minardi, which did not have the benefit of power steering. He was flown by helicopter to hospital where he was given pain killers and the feeling eventually returned to his arms before he flew home.

'The [retaining] belts slipped off the HANS device after a few laps and I was flopping around in the car,' said Wilson. 'After a while, the pain got too much, but I feel better now and should be fine for Brazil.'

On lap nine, Michael Schumacher entered the pit lane to take

his drive-through penalty for 'causing an avoidable accident', and by lap 13 the race had lost the hapless Olivier Panis, whose Toyota had ground to a halt out on the circuit, half a lap after rejoining from its first refuelling stop on lap 12.

On closer examination, it appeared that the Toyota had developed a pressure build-up in its fuel tank, something that effectively fooled the refuelling rig into believing it had delivered its full load when, in fact, no fuel had gone into the car. It was another bitter disappointment for Panis on a day when he'd looked in good shape, running right up there with Rubens and the Ferrari.

Alonso, who had started with a modest 39 litres of fuel in his Renault, led until he made the first of two scheduled stops after 14 of the race's 56 laps. He was stationary for 9.2s and resumed in fourth place. In the meantime, Räikkönen had assumed the lead and held on to it until his own first stop on lap 19, allowing Barrichello to take over at the front of the pack until he also stopped on lap 22. Thereafter, Räikkönen was never headed, retaining his lead through his second pit stop on lap 40 to win by a commanding 39.2s.

'I wasn't expecting a win today from seventh on the grid, but nonetheless it's nice to get one,' said Kimi. 'On the warm-up lap, the car felt good and I knew we had a chance. In the last 20 laps, I was just driving pretty easily, bringing the car home. The car set-up was fantastic and the car perfect.'

Barrichello took second, explaining that the slight delay caused by avoiding the Schumacher/Trulli incident at the first corner had compromised his race and he had not been able to claw back the deficit.

'When I was running with nothing ahead of me, I could tell that Kimi was pulling away a bit,' said Rubens. 'Then, after the second

stop, I had a slight misfire, but I kept pushing until, with 15 laps to go, the team told me to hold position.'

Alonso, exhausted by the effects of a flu-like virus and consequently suffering with a high temperature in the sweltering conditions, had to switch to the manual gearchange mechanism for the last ten laps, as well as deal with the loss of fifth gear, on his way to third place. His impressive performance made him the first Spaniard to mount the F1 podium since the Marquis de Portago had shared the second-place Ferrari in the 1956 British Grand Prix at Silverstone.

'Today is the best day of my life,' said Alonso with such a genuine blend of spontaneity and youthful enthusiasm that it came straight from the heart. 'It's a great feeling to finish on the podium, especially as I was forced to shift manually for the second half of the race. Frankly, I thought I wasn't going to finish and instead got this great result!'

In the Williams camp, pre-race form seemed to have been turned on its head. Ralf Schumacher had vaulted through from a disappointing 17th on the grid to finish fourth, while the hapless Montoya had lost three laps having a new rear wing fitted, after being savaged by Pizzonia on the opening lap, and wound up 12th. 'Also my drinks bottle stopped working after a dozen laps, which made the rest of my race today very, very hard,' he reported.

At BAR Honda, there was some late-race disappointment for Jenson Button when he dropped from fifth to seventh on the final lap behind Michael Schumacher's Ferrari and Trulli's Renault. 'It was a very tiring race and the car was so difficult to drive,' said Button. 'I had very low grip and the oversteer got progressively worse towards the end. It destroyed the rear tyres. I held off Jarno for as long as I could, then on the last corner I braked where I normally would and the rear just locked up. I went straight on and Michael was able to get through.'

In eighth and ninth places came the Sauber C22s of Nick Heidfeld and Heinz-Harald Frentzen. Heidfeld had lost time with gearchange problems at his refuelling stops, and Frentzen's engine had stalled when he was in the pits, but Heinz-Harald still managed to force his way ahead of Ralph Firman's well-driven Jordan on the final lap when the EJ-13 spluttered low on fuel. Neither Jaguar R4 made it to the chequered flag, Mark Webber being withdrawn with an oil-consumption problem after 35 laps, while Antonio Pizzonia spun off with a suspected brake problem.

Räikkönen and McLaren Mercedes now led their respective championship points tables after two of the 16 races, leaving Michael Schumacher apparently on the back foot after mistakes had cost him dearly at Melbourne and Sepang. Yet nobody in their right mind was about to write off the reigning world champion.

Main photograph: The unfortunate Jarno Trulli is tipped into a spin by Michael Schumacher's Ferrari. Juan Pablo Montoya and Rubens Barrichello take avoiding action.
Photograph: Darren Heath

Inset: Räikkönen takes the chequered flag to the delight of his West McLaren Mercedes team.
Photograph: John Marsh/redzoneimages.com

Jenson Button flashes past in his BAR-Honda. A straight-on moment on the final lap lost him a place to Michael Schumacher.
Photograph: Darren Heath

FIA F1 WORLD CHAMPIONSHIP • ROUND 2

PETRONAS MALAYSIAN GRAND PRIX

SEPANG 21–23 MARCH 2003

Photograph: Darren Heath

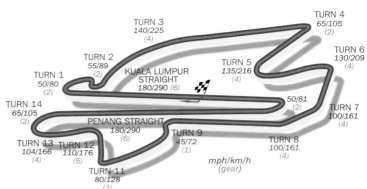

SEPANG
CIRCUIT LENGTH: 3.444 miles/5.543 km

TURN 1 50/80 (2)
TURN 2 55/89 (2)
TURN 3 140/225 (4)
TURN 4 65/105 (2)
TURN 5 135/216 (4)
TURN 6 130/209 (4)
TURN 7 100/161 (4)
TURN 8 100/161 (4)
TURN 9 45/72 (1)
TURN 11 80/128 (3)
TURN 12 110/176 (5)
TURN 13 104/166 (4)
TURN 14 65/105 (2)
KUALA LUMPUR STRAIGHT 180/290 (6)
PENANG STRAIGHT 180/290 (6)
50/81 (2)
mph/km/h (gear)

RACE DISTANCE: 56 laps, 192.878 miles/310.408 km RACE WEATHER: Hot and dry (track 41°C, air 25°C)

Pos.	Driver	Nat.	No.	Entrant	Car/Engine	Tyres	Laps	Time/Retirement	Speed (mph/km/h)	Gap to leader	Fastest race lap	
1	Kimi Räikkönen	FIN	6	West McLaren Mercedes	McLaren MP4/17D-Mercedes F0110M V10	M	56	1h 32m 22.195s	125.286/201.629		1m 36.764s	10
2	Rubens Barrichello	BR	2	Scuderia Ferrari Marlboro	Ferrari F2002-051 V10	B	56	1h 33m 01.481s	124.405/200.210	+39.286s	1m 36.542s	24
3	Fernando Alonso	E	8	Mild Seven Renault F1 Team	Renault R3-RS23 V10	B	56	1h 33m 26.202s	123.856/199.327	+64.007s	1m 37.078s	12
4	Ralf Schumacher	D	4	BMW WilliamsF1 Team	Williams FW25-BMW P83 V10	M	56	1h 33m 50.221s	123.327/198.476	+88.026s	1m 38.071s	24
5	Jarno Trulli	I	7	Mild Seven Renault F1 Team	Renault R3-RS23 V10	M	55			+ 1 lap	1m 37.484s	53
6	Michael Schumacher	D	1	Scuderia Ferrari Marlboro	Ferrari F2002-051 V10	B	55			+1 lap	1m 36.412s	45
7	Jenson Button	GB	17	Lucky Strike BAR Honda	BAR 005-Honda RA003E V10	B	55			+1 lap	1m 38.413s	10
8	Nick Heidfeld	D	9	Sauber Petronas	Sauber C22-Petronas 03A V10	B	55			+1 lap	1m 38.528s	9
9	Heinz-Harald Frentzen	D	10	Sauber Petronas	Sauber C22-Petronas 03A V10	B	55			+1 lap	1m 39.287s	19
10	Ralph Firman	IRL	12	Jordan Ford	Jordan EJ-13-Ford Cosworth RS1 V10	B	55			+1 lap	1m 39.665s	14
11	Cristiano da Matta	BR	21	Panasonic Toyota Racing	Toyota TF103-RVX-03 V10	M	55			+1 lap	1m 38.156s	35
12	Juan Pablo Montoya	COL	3	BMW WilliamsF1 Team	Williams FW25-BMW P83 V10	M	53			+3 laps	1m 37.787s	26
13	Jos Verstappen	NL	19	European Minardi Cosworth	Minardi PS03-Cosworth CR3 V10	B	52			+4 laps	1m 39.667s	3
	Antonio Pizzonia	BR	15	Jaguar Racing	Jaguar R4-Cosworth CR5 V10	M	42	Spun off			1m 38.572s	3
	Justin Wilson	GB	18	European Minardi Cosworth	Minardi PS03-Cosworth CR3 V10	B	41	Withdrew			1m 39.752s	12
	Mark Webber	AUS	14	Jaguar Racing	Jaguar R4-Cosworth CR5 V10	M	35	Oil system			1m 38.464s	6
	Olivier Panis	F	20	Panasonic Toyota Racing	Toyota TF103-RVX-03 V10	M	12	Fuel pick-up			1m 38.176s	7
	David Coulthard	GB	5	West McLaren Mercedes	McLaren MP4/17D-Mercedes F0110M V10	M	2	Spark box			1m 38.021s	2
	Giancarlo Fisichella	I	11	Jordan Ford	Jordan EJ-13-Ford Cosworth RS1 V10	B	0	Left on grid				
	Jacques Villeneuve	CDN	16	Lucky Strike BAR Honda	BAR 005-Honda RA003E V10	B	0	Electronics/gearbox				

Fastest lap: Michael Schumacher, on lap 45, 1m 36.412s, 128.607 mph/206.974 km/h (record).

Previous lap record: Juan Pablo Montoya (Williams FW24-BMW P82 V10), 1m 38.049s, 126.460 mph/203.518 km/h (2002).

19th: JUSTIN WILSON Minardi-Cosworth

17th: RALF SCHUMACHER Williams-BMW

15th: ANTONIO PIZZONIA Jaguar-Cosworth

13th: HEINZ-HARALD FRENTZEN Sauber-Petronas

11th: CRISTIANO DA MATTA Toyota started from pit lane

20th: RALPH FIRMAN Jordan-Ford Cosworth

18th: JOS VERSTAPPEN Minardi-Cosworth

16th: MARK WEBBER Jaguar-Cosworth

14th: GIANCARLO FISICHELLA Jordan-Ford Cosworth

12th: JACQUES VILLENEUVE BAR-Honda did not start

Grid order	1	2	3	4	5	6	7	8	9	10	11	12	13	14	15	16	17	18	19	20	21	22	23	24	25	26	27	28	29	30	31	32	33	34	35	36	37	38	39	40	41	42	43
8 ALONSO	8	8	8	8	8	8	8	8	8	8	8	8	8	6	6	6	6	6	6	2	2	2	6	6	6	6	6	6	6	6	6	6	6	6	6	6	6	6	6	6	6	6	6
7 TRULLI	5	5	6	6	6	6	6	6	6	6	6	6	6	8	2	2	2	2	2	6	6	6	8	8	8	8	8	8	8	8	8	8	8	8	8	2	2	2	2	8	8	8	8
1 M. SCHUMACHER	9	9	9	9	9	9	9	9	2	2	2	2	2	17	17	8	8	8	8	8	2	2	2	2	2	2	2	2	2	2	2	2	2	2	2	8	8	8	8	8	8	8	8
5 COULTHARD	6	6	17	17	2	2	2	2	9	9	9	9	17	17		8	4	4	4	4	4	4	4	4	4	4	4	4	4	4	4	4	4	4	4	4	4	4	4	4	4	4	4
2 BARRICHELLO	17	17	2	2	20	20	20	20	20	20	20	17	9	4	4	4	17	17	17	17	17	17	17	17	17	17	17	17	17	17	17	17	17	17	17	7	7	7	17	17	17	1	1
9 HEIDFELD	2	2	20	20	17	17	17	17	17	17	17	20	4	7	7	7	7	12	12	12	12	12	7	7	7	7	7	7	7	7	7	7	17	17	17	7	7	7	7	17	17	17	17
6 RÄIKKÖNEN	20	20	18	4	4	4	4	4	4	4	4	4	7	14	14	14	12	7	7	7	7	7	12																				
3 MONTOYA	18	18	4	14	14	14	14	14	7	7	7	7	14	12	12	21	21	9	9	9	9	9	1	1	1	21	21	21	21	21	21	14	14	14	9	9	9	9	9	9	9	9	9
17 BUTTON	4	4	14	18	7	7	7	7	14	14	14	14	18	21	21	10	10	1	1	1	1	1	21	21	21	14	14	14	14	14	14	1	1	1	21	21	21	21	21	21	21	21	21
20 PANIS	14	14	7	7	18	18	18	18	18	18	18	18	12	10	10	9	9	21	21	21	21	21	14	14	14	1	1	1	1	21	10	10	12	12	12	12	12	12	12	12	12	12	12
10 FRENTZEN	12	1	12	12	12	12	12	12	12	12	12	21	9	9	1	1	14	14	14	14	14	14	10	10	10	10	10	10	10	10	1	21	10	10	10	10	10	10	10	10	10	10	10
11 FISICHELLA	1	12	1	21	21	21	21	21	21	21	21	10	1	1	18	12	12	10	10	10	10	10	15	12	12	12	12	12	12	12	12	12	15	15	15	15	15	15	15	5	5	5	3
15 PIZZONIA	7	7	21	10	10	10	10	10	10	10	10	10	10	18	18	18	18	18	18	18	18	18	18	15	15	15	15	15	15	15	15	15	18	18	18	18	18	18	18	18	18	3	19
14 WEBBER	21	21	10	1	1	1	1	1	1	1	1	1	15	15	15	15	15	15	15	15	15	15	15	15	15	15	15	15	15	15	15	15	3	3	3	3	3	3	3	3	3	19	
4 R. SCHUMACHER	10	10	15	15	15	15	15	15	15	15	15	15	19	19	19	3	3	3	3	3	3	3	3	3	3	3	3	3	3	3	3	3	19	19	19	19	19	19	19	19	19		
19 VERSTAPPEN	3	15	19	19	19	19	19	19	19	19	19	19	3	3	3	19	19	19	19	19	19	19	19	19	19	19	19	19	19	19	19	19											
18 WILSON	15	19	3	3	3	3	3	3	3	3	3	3																															
12 FIRMAN	19	3																																									
21 DA MATTA																																											
16 VILLENEUVE																																											

Pit stop
One lap behind leader

TIME SHEETS

SATURDAY QUALIFYING determines race grid order
Very hot and dry (track 51/52°C, air 35/37°C)

Pos.	Driver	Lap time	Sector 1	Sector 2	Sector 3
1	Fernando Alonso	1m 37.044s	24.892s	32.533s	39.619s
2	Jarno Trulli	1m 37.217s	24.934s	32.756s	39.527s
3	Michael Schumacher	1m 37.393s	24.932s	32.507s	39.954s
4	David Coulthard	1m 37.454s	24.869s	32.725s	39.860s
5	Rubens Barrichello	1m 37.579s	24.944s	32.628s	40.007s
6	Nick Heidfeld	1m 37.766s	24.919s	32.755s	40.092s
7	Kimi Räikkönen	1m 37.858s	24.991s	32.814s	40.053s
8	Juan Pablo Montoya	1m 37.974s	25.037s	32.628s	40.309s
9	Jenson Button	1m 38.073s	25.083s	32.770s	40.220s
10	Olivier Panis	1m 38.094s	24.970s	33.184s	39.940s
11	Cristiano da Matta	1m 38.097s	25.104s	33.023s	39.970s
12	Jacques Villeneuve	1m 38.289s	24.965s	33.066s	40.258s
13	Heinz-Harald Frentzen	1m 38.291s	24.990s	32.949s	40.352s
14	Giancarlo Fisichella	1m 38.416s	25.205s	32.735s	40.476s
15	Antonio Pizzonia	1m 38.516s	25.196s	32.884s	40.436s
16	Mark Webber	1m 38.624s	25.445s	32.692s	40.487s
17	Ralf Schumacher	1m 38.789s	25.098s	33.398s	40.293s
18	Jos Verstappen	1m 40.417s	25.273s	34.199s	40.945s
19	Justin Wilson	1m 40.599s	25.507s	34.052s	41.040s
20	Ralph Firman	1m 40.910s	25.429s	33.915s	41.566s

FRIDAY QUALIFYING determines Sat running order
Hot and dry (track 47°C, air 35°C)

Pos.	Driver	Lap time
1	Michael Schumacher	1m 34.980s
2	Rubens Barrichello	1m 35.681s
3	Juan Pablo Montoya	1m 35.939s
4	Kimi Räikkönen	1m 36.038s
5	David Coulthard	1m 36.297s
6	Jarno Trulli	1m 36.301s
7	Nick Heidfeld	1m 36.407s
8	Heinz-Harald Frentzen	1m 36.615s
9	Jenson Button	1m 36.632s
10	Fernando Alonso	1m 36.693s
11	Cristiano da Matta	1m 36.706s
12	Giancarlo Fisichella	1m 36.759s
13	Ralf Schumacher	1m 36.805s
14	Olivier Panis	1m 36.995s
15	Jacques Villeneuve	1m 37.585s
16	Mark Webber	1m 37.669s
17	Ralph Firman	1m 38.240s
18	Jos Verstappen	1m 38.904s
19	Justin Wilson	1m 39.354s
20	Antonio Pizzonia	No time

POINTS TABLES: CONSTRUCTORS

1	McLaren	26
2 =	Ferrari	16
2 =	Renault	16
4	Williams	14
5	Sauber	4
6	BAR	2

FOR THE RECORD

First pole position
Fernando Alonso
First grand prix win
Kimi Räikkönen

Photograph: Darren Heath

PRIVATE TESTING
Hot and dry (track 30/35°C, air 29/32°C)

Pos.	Driver	Laps	Time
1	Fernando Alonso	40	1m 37.693s
2	Giancarlo Fisichella	29	1m 37.815s
3	Jarno Trulli	41	1m 37.851s
4	Allan McNish	36	1m 38.851s
5	Ralph Firman	20	1m 40.296s
6	Antonio Pizzonia	33	1m 40.784s
7	Jos Verstappen	19	1m 40.923s
8	Justin Wilson	23	1m 41.929s
9	Mark Webber	8	1m 49.907s

FRIDAY FREE PRACTICE
Hot and dry (track 40°C, air 33°C)

Pos.	Driver	Laps	Time
1	David Coulthard	20	1m 36.102s
2	Fernando Alonso	15	1m 36.231s
3	Jarno Trulli	13	1m 36.372s
4	Juan Pablo Montoya	18	1m 36.998s
5	Ralf Schumacher	21	1m 37.045s
6	Jenson Button	23	1m 37.060s
7	Michael Schumacher	20	1m 37.313s
8	Jacques Villeneuve	22	1m 37.357s
9	Rubens Barrichello	20	1m 37.497s
10	Olivier Panis	18	1m 37.748s
11	Giancarlo Fisichella	20	1m 37.847s
12	Nick Heidfeld	17	1m 37.906s
13	Heinz-Harald Frentzen	11	1m 37.951s
14	Cristiano da Matta	24	1m 37.992s
15	Kimi Räikkönen	15	1m 38.515s
16	Ralph Firman	13	1m 38.516s
17	Antonio Pizzonia	13	1m 38.839s
18	Mark Webber	3	1m 38.870s
19	Jos Verstappen	13	1m 39.183s
20	Justin Wilson	14	1m 39.695s

SATURDAY FREE PRACTICE
Very hot and dry (track 48/50°C, air 35°C)

Pos.	Driver	Laps	Time
1	Kimi Räikkönen	24	1m 36.557s
2	David Coulthard	23	1m 36.777s
3	Fernando Alonso	29	1m 36.849s
4	Michael Schumacher	18	1m 36.990s
5	Cristiano da Matta	34	1m 37.093s
6	Jarno Trulli	26	1m 37.198s
7	Juan Pablo Montoya	36	1m 37.218s
8	Jenson Button	31	1m 37.418s
9	Rubens Barrichello	31	1m 37.422s
10	Ralf Schumacher	31	1m 37.436s
11	Giancarlo Fisichella	30	1m 37.443s
12	Olivier Panis	23	1m 37.623s
13	Heinz-Harald Frentzen	37	1m 37.751s
14	Antonio Pizzonia	34	1m 37.947s
15	Mark Webber	27	1m 37.980s
16	Nick Heidfeld	30	1m 38.090s
17	Ralph Firman	32	1m 38.282s
18	Jacques Villeneuve	29	1m 38.329s
19	Jos Verstappen	19	1m 40.382s
20	Justin Wilson	14	1m 40.638s

WARM-UP
Very hot and dry (track 50/51°C, air 36°C)

Pos.	Driver	Laps	Time
1	Kimi Räikkönen	4	1m 37.506s
2	David Coulthard	4	1m 37.848s
3	Rubens Barrichello	5	1m 38.060s
4	Fernando Alonso	4	1m 38.122s
5	Olivier Panis	5	1m 38.187s
6	Jarno Trulli	4	1m 38.443s
7	Jenson Button	7	1m 38.468s
8	Juan Pablo Montoya	4	1m 38.615s
9	Jacques Villeneuve	4	1m 38.621s
10	Ralf Schumacher	4	1m 38.640s
11	Mark Webber	4	1m 38.680s
12	Nick Heidfeld	6	1m 38.700s
13	Cristiano da Matta	4	1m 38.876s
14	Antonio Pizzonia	4	1m 38.907s
15	Heinz-Harald Frentzen	4	1m 38.933s
16	Michael Schumacher	3	1m 39.483s
17	Justin Wilson	6	1m 40.588s
18	Giancarlo Fisichella	5	1m 41.202s
19	Jos Verstappen	3	1m 41.458s
20	Ralph Firman	4	1m 42.884s

9th: JENSON BUTTON BAR-Honda

7th: KIMI RÄIKKÖNEN McLaren-Mercedes

5th: RUBENS BARRICHELLO Ferrari

3rd: MICHAEL SCHUMACHER Ferrari

Pole: FERNANDO ALONSO Renault

10th: OLIVIER PANIS Toyota

8th: JUAN PABLO MONTOYA Williams-BMW

6th: NICK HEIDFELD Sauber-Petronas

4th: DAVID COULTHARD McLaren-Mercedes

2nd: JARNO TRULLI Renault

	44	45	46	47	48	49	50	51	52	53	54	55	56	
	6	6	6	6	6	6	6	6	6	6	6	6	6	1
	2	2	2	2	2	2	2	2	2	2	2	2	2	2
	8	8	8	8	8	8	8	8	8	8	8	8	8	3
	4	4	4	4	4	4	4	4	4	4	4	4	4	4
	17	17	17	17	17	17	17	17	17	17	17	7		5
	7	7	7	7	7	7	7	7	7	7	7	1		6
	1	1	1	1	1	1	1	1	1	1	1	17		7
	9	9	9	9	9	9	9	9	9	9	9	9		8
	21	21	21	21	21	12	12	12	12	12	12	10		
	12	12	12	12	12	10	10	10	10	10	10	12		
	10	10	10	10	10	21	21	21	21	21	21			
	3	3	3	3	3	3	3	3	3	3				
	19	19	19	19	19	19	19	19	19					

CHASSIS LOG BOOK

1	Michael Schumacher	F2002/225
2	Rubens Barrichello	F2002/222
	Spare	F2002/219
3	Juan Pablo Montoya	FW25/04
4	Ralf Schumacher	FW25/03
	Spare	FW25/02
5	David Coulthard	MP4/17D-08
6	Kimi Räikkönen	MP4/17D-09
	Spare	MP4/17D-06
7	Jarno Trulli	R23/03
8	Fernando Alonso	R23/02
	Allan McNish	R23/01
	Spare	R23/01
9	Nick Heidfeld	C22/01
10	Heinz-Harald Frentzen	C22/03
	Spare	C22/02

11	Giancarlo Fisichella	EJ-13/04
12	Ralph Firman	EJ-13/02
	Spare	EJ-13/01
14	Mark Webber	R4/01
15	Antonio Pizzonia	R4/03
	Spare	R4/02
16	Jacques Villeneuve	BAR005/3
17	Jenson Button	BAR005/4
	Spare	BAR005/2
18	Justin Wilson	PS03/04
19	Jos Verstappen	PS03/01
	Spare	PS03/02
20	Olivier Panis	TF103/05
21	Cristiano da Matta	TF103/02
	Spare	TF103/04

POINTS TABLES: DRIVERS

1	Kimi Räikkönen	16
2	David Coulthard	10
3 =	Juan Pablo Montoya	8
3 =	Rubens Barrichello	8
3 =	Fernando Alonso	8
3 =	Michael Schumacher	8
3 =	Jarno Trulli	8
8	Ralf Schumacher	6
9	Heinz-Harald Frentzen	3
10	Jenson Button	2
11	Nick Heidfeld	1

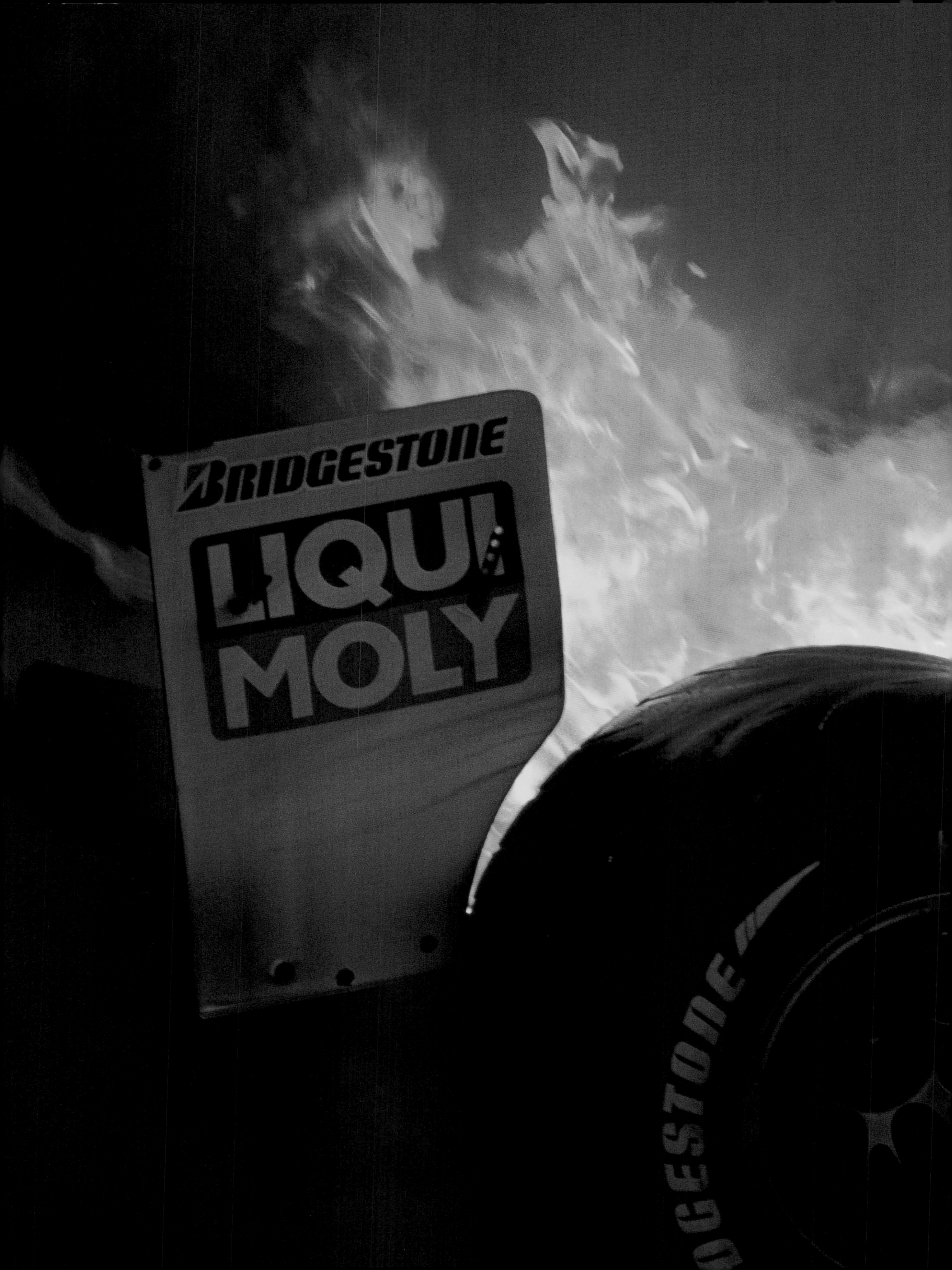
BRIDGESTONE
LIQUI
MOLY
BRIDGESTONE

FIA F1 WORLD CHAMPIONSHIP • ROUND 3

BRAZILIANGP
INTERLAGOS

Inset top: Fisichella took full advantage of the race chaos to snatch his maiden grand prix victory.
Photograph: Patrick Gosling

Main photograph: Fisichella's Jordan goes up in flames after the Italian had pulled into the pit lane at the end of the race.

Inset left: A wistful Giancarlo sprays the champagne as he accepts his initial second-place finish behind Kimi Räikkönen.
Photographs: Darren Heath

INTERLAGOS QUALIFYING

A perfect job by Rubens Barrichello earned him the adulation of his delighted home crowd after he planted his Ferrari F2002 on pole position with a well-controlled lap in 1m 13.807s. On this occasion, it was Michael Schumacher who made a slight slip at the first corner, costing the world champion crucial tenths, which dropped him back to seventh on 1m 14.130s.

'I feel fantastic,' admitted Barrichello. 'Ever since I was a kid, all I wanted to do was to be here in a competitive car, waving at the crowd from pole position. On my lap, I concentrated on not over-driving and not making any mistakes. Usually, I have the split-times on my [cockpit] display, but today I wanted to be on my own out on the track and asked the team to switch it off.'

Rubens was joined on the front row by his old friend and long-time rival David Coulthard, who took the McLaren MP4/17D around in 1m 13.818s, what the Scot described as a reasonably tidy qualifying lap: 'I wasn't happy with the balance of the car during the 15-minute warm-up, so we changed it back to how we ran it during this morning's practice and everything felt fine.'

Kimi Räikkönen wound up fourth on 1m 13.866s, but the most impressive display of the afternoon came from Mark Webber in the Jaguar R4, who charged around to split the McLarens on 1m 13.851s. 'The car felt great out there, and this was as close to a near-perfect lap as I could have done,' said the popular Australian.

In the Renault camp, Jarno Trulli was happy with his fifth-fastest 1m 13.953s, while Fernando Alonso was a little disappointed with 1m 14.384s, which put him on the outside of the fifth row, tenth quickest. 'I am quite happy with my lap time because I didn't make any mistakes and the car felt good,' said the Spanish driver brightly.

Ralf Schumacher admitted that he had made a couple of slight mistakes that cost him time, so his sixth-fastest 1m 14.124s with the Williams-BMW FW25 was not too disappointing. The car featured front wing changes for his race as well as employing its definitive gearbox and torsion-bar rear-end package for the first time. Juan Pablo Montoya settled for ninth on 1m 14.223s, admitting that a touch too much understeer had lost him crucial time at the final corner.

Giancarlo Fisichella was confident about the feel of his Jordan-Ford EJ-13, setting an eighth-fastest 1m 14.191s, but his team-mate, Ralph Firman, not only made a set-up change between the two Saturday sessions, but also a mistake on his qualifying lap, a 16th-fastest 1m 15.240s. 'Despite this, it was still my best lap time of the weekend, so overall I'm happy because the car is good for the race,' said Ralph.

Jenson Button (1m 14.504s) and Jacques Villeneuve (1m 14.668s) made disappointing runs to 11th and 13th positions on the grid for the BAR Honda team. Button felt that his lap was not too bad, but that he had been down a couple of tenths in the final sector of the lap. Villeneuve, however, reported that his Honda V10 had seemed to lose power, which knocked the edge off his lap times.

The Sauber C22s of Nick Heidfeld (1m 14.631s) and Heinz-Harald Frentzen (1m 14.839s) were also closely matched in 12th and 14th positions. 'I think I lost out a bit because I had to run so early in the session,' said Heidfeld, 'but compared to the rest of the weekend, I was quite happy with the way the C22 performed today.'

By contrast, Toyota's, Olivier Panis was left mentally kicking himself after making a crucial error on his best lap, ending up 15th at 1m 14.839s. 'When I started my qualifying lap, everything was fine with the car,' said the Frenchman. 'I tried to push hard, but I made a big mistake in the second sector. I really want to say sorry to the team because the car is really good in terms of performance.'

Cristiano da Matta qualified the other TF103 in 18th spot on 1m 15.641s, separated from Panis by only Firman's Jordan and Antonio Pizzonia's Jaguar R4. The back row of the grid was shared by the two Minardis of Jos Verstappen (1m 16.542s) and Justin Wilson (1m 16.586s). 'There were no problems,' explained Wilson. 'I drove a pretty clean lap and the time is certainly acceptable for the fuel load we were carrying.'

G IANCARLO Fisichella finally scored his maiden F1 victory in Brazil, yet it was in circumstances so convoluted and bizarre that the Italian driver had to wait five days for his success to be confirmed – and ten days before he got his hands on the winner's trophy. Only when the stewards reconvened for a meeting in Paris, on the Friday following the race at Interlagos, was the first victory for an Italian driver since Riccardo Patrese's 1992 triumph at Suzuka added to the record books.

It was the Jordan team's fourth ever grand prix win, and an achievement that ensured its V10 Ford Cosworth-engined machine reached the winner's podium before arch-rival Jaguar.

Fisichella was propelled into the limelight when Mark Webber, struggling for grip on worn Michelins, crashed spectacularly in the fast left-hand kink before the pits. Webber's car ended up alongside the barrier on the left of the track, its driver shaken but unhurt, although parts of the Jaguar were strewn across the circuit.

As the dust settled, Fisichella jinked through the debris, but then Fernando Alonso arrived over the crest at speed and slammed straight into one of the Jaguar's wheels, which was lying in the middle of the track. That, in turn, hurled the young Spanish driver sharp right into the retaining wall. Both impacts were in excess of 30 G, and it says much for the standards of contemporary F1 car construction that Alonso escaped with nothing more serious than bruised legs, although he was taken to hospital for a precautionary check-up.

By any standards, it took an embarrassingly long time to make sense of the official timekeeping at Interlagos. This most remarkable race of changing fortunes initially ended with Kimi Räikkönen being awarded victory, even though his McLaren-Mercedes MP4/17D was actually entering the pit lane at the time. The result

was originally determined under the provisions of a rule that counts back two laps from that on which the leader is running when the event is red-flagged prematurely to a halt.

For some reason, the official timing display momentarily indicated 55 laps completed for Fisichella, then flicked back to 54. That would have meant that he was on his 55th lap at the moment the red flag was shown, so the count-back went to lap 53, when Räikkönen was ahead.

In fact, Eddie Jordan was absolutely certain that his team's own timing system indicated that his man was over 10s into his 56th lap when the race ended. These findings were duly presented to the FIA; they agreed that the evidence was valid and amended the result, and Fisichella was rightfully credited with that extra lap.

Yet if there was an award for the driver who most deserved to win at Interlagos, it would have been shared by David Coulthard and pole winner Rubens Barrichello. On a day when the outcome of the race was shaped largely by the respective performances of the Bridgestone and Michelin wet-weather rubber, the McLaren and Ferrari rivals were the most canny and consistent performers.

The onset of heavy rain on race morning posed a serious potential problem for the Michelin runners, including McLaren, Williams and Jaguar. Their choice of designated race tyre was closer to a deep-grooved full wet tyre than the relatively shallow-grooved intermediate, which was available to the Bridgestone users.

The FIA officials announced at 12.30 pm, with almost painful formality, that a 'change in climatic conditions had occurred.' In other words, it was tipping it down in the manner only known to Brazil, and therefore it was permissible to change various chassis settings and switch to rain tyres.

Unfortunately for the Michelin-shod cars, when the track was at its wettest – and therefore when they could have derived the most benefit from the tyres – the safety car was deployed, negating their advantage. Therefore, it was no surprise that the rule permitting just a single wet-specification tyre per weekend attracted much consideration and debate during the Brazilian GP weekend. Some drivers considered it a potentially dangerous state of affairs, but others, notably Jacques Villeneuve, took the view that the best drivers in the world should be able to handle the challenge, atrocious though the conditions were.

Yet for a short period, it really looked as though the Brazilian GP might not take place at all. Even with the cars lined up on the starting grid, the conditions seemed too bad to take the gamble. Eventually, it was decided that the race would start 15 minutes late, and it would be run behind the safety car for the first few laps.

Both Heinz-Harald Frentzen and Jos Verstappen, in the Sauber C22 and Minardi PS03 spare cars respectively, elected to start from the pit lane, as did Ralph Firman and Antonio Pizzonia – to give themselves the ability to top up their cars and switch from a two- to one-stop strategy.

For eight laps, the pack circulated steadily behind the safety car, then Bernd Mayländer aimed the silver Mercedes CLK coupé toward the sanctuary of the pit lane and the pack was unleashed. David Coulthard surged through immediately to take the lead from Barrichello going into the first corner after the pits.

Mid-way around lap ten, Kimi Räikkönen squeezed through into second place and the two McLarens finished the lap just 0.1s apart. On lap 11, Räikkönen grabbed the lead from Coulthard, while Juan Pablo Montoya's Williams-BMW FW25 also slipped through into second. Webber was fourth and, farther back, Ralf Schumacher's Williams overtook Jarno Trulli's Renault for sixth

DIARY

ITV viewing figures for the Brazilian GP peak at 13 million just before the end of the race. The coverage averages 6.9 million viewers for the duration of the event.

Peter Sauber writes to FIA president Max Mosley, expressing his disapproval of the manner in which the sport's governing body has implemented the F1 rule changes for the 2003 season.

Jaguar F1 team puts Antonio Pizzonia's progress under close scrutiny after the young Brazilian driver produces another disappointing performance at Interlagos.

place, but shortly after the German driver spun and Trulli lost crucial time avoiding him.

By lap 13, Räikkönen was 3.6s in front of Montoya, with Coulthard third followed by Webber and Michael Schumacher, who had moved his Ferrari ahead of team-mate Barrichello to take fifth. On lap 14, Coulthard was back into second place and making up ground on Räikkönen, closing to 1.4s on lap 17.

Going into lap 18, Ralph Firman's Jordan suffered a failure of the right front suspension as it approached the braking area for the left-hander after the pits at around 175 mph. The wheel folded up on to the nose of the yellow car and Firman became a passenger as it slid into the back of Olivier Panis's Toyota TF103, eliminating both cars from the race. With debris all over the track, the safety car was deployed for the second time of the afternoon.

Panis shrugged off his disappointment with characteristic stoicism. 'With the race starting under the safety car due to the wet conditions, we took advantage of this to refuel the car and we had a good strategy,' he explained. 'Unfortunately it was a bit difficult to drive the car with a full tank. I felt a big impact from the rear of my car and didn't really understand what had happened until Ralph Firman spoke with me and explained he had hit me.'

Räikkönen stayed out behind the safety car, but the next ten cars dived into the pits to top up their fuel tanks while the pack was still running at reduced speed. At the start of lap 23, the field was unleashed again, Räikkönen completing that lap 1.7s ahead of Coulthard, followed by Michael Schumacher who was third.

Behind him came Barrichello and Cristiano da Matta's Toyota (which had yet to stop).

Even though the track was beginning to dry by this stage, rivulets of water were coursing across the circuit at turn three. On lap 25, Montoya became the first casualty of this slippery section, sliding off the road and crashing into the barrier. He was soon followed by Antonio Pizzonia. Then, on lap 27, Michael Schumacher spun off, triggering the third safety-car period of the race.

'The weather conditions were difficult, but acceptable today,' reflected the world champion. 'As for my accident, I was aquaplaning and in that situation you are just a passenger in the car.'

The order behind the safety car was Coulthard, Barrichello, Ralf Schumacher, Webber, Button (BAR Honda), da Matta, Alonso and the remarkable Verstappen (Minardi), who was one place ahead of eventual winner Fisichella. Räikkönen had pitted to refuel.

On lap 30, the race restarted and Räikkönen surged immediately past Fisichella and Verstappen to take seventh place. Next time around, Verstappen spun off at turn three, much to the frustration of team chief Paul Stoddart, who hurled his radio headphones across the Minardi garage in despair.

Yet Verstappen was in good company. On lap 33, Button slammed off the road at turn three in a startlingly heavy impact. 'I just caught the standing water a little too much,' said Jenson. 'I tried to save it, but that just sent me into the tyre wall. I went in quite heavily and my back is aching a little, but it could have been much worse. It's disappointing, but that's the way it goes.'

Alonso third ahead of the hapless Coulthard and Heinz-Harald Frentzen's Sauber. Jacques Villeneuve survived to take sixth place, his comments again obliquely admonishing some of his rivals. 'It was a very difficult race,' he admitted. 'The track was tough to drive, but if you took care of yourself then it wasn't too bad. There wasn't that much water really. It's down to the drivers to be less crazy in those conditions, and there was some crazy driving out there.

'Some drivers were overtaking under yellow flags. Half-way through the race, I saw Alonso overtake under the flags. I think it's that kind of driving that leads to big accidents. We saw the same thing in the pit stops, with the drivers chopping across the field on the exit, then having to lift half-way down the straight to stop them going off on to the grass. It's the sort of thing that creates the danger, not just the conditions themselves.'

Webber dropped to ninth, behind Ralf Schumacher and Trulli in the revised running order, a result that was not an accurate reflection of the excellence of the Australian driver's performance prior to his accident.

Crucially, in the days that followed, there was no firm explanation from either the FIA or the race organisers as to precisely how the initial results glitch had been caused. TAG Heuer, the official timekeeper to the F1 world championship, insisted that it had not been at fault. It had accurately collated and communicated the information to the race officials. How they chose to interpret and/or amend the data was not, in TAG Heuer's view, its business to say. Or, more specifically, its fault.

Fisichella eventually received the winner's trophy from Kimi Räikkönen, its initial recipient, at a pleasant presentation on the start/finish line before practice for the San Marino Grand Prix at Imola ten days after his win.

'I'm glad to have won at last, but I still feel annoyed that I was prevented from celebrating on the podium immediately after my success,' said Giancarlo.

Ron Dennis summed it up well: 'While it would have been nice for us to start the season with a hat trick of victories, once it was established that the situation had been resolved, we were happy to applaud our friends at Jordan at the end of what had been a remarkable and unpredictable race of changing fortunes.'

F1 TEAMS GIVE SUPPORT TO GPWC

The major car manufacturers took a step closer to a major confrontation with F1 commercial rights holder Bernie Ecclestone on the Friday after the Brazilian Grand Prix, when all ten F1 team principals signed a 'memorandum of understanding' to support the proposed GPWC series from 2008.

The meeting took place in Munich where GPWC offered a new deal that promised the teams a 75-per-cent cut in the net television broadcasting rights income, plus 50 per cent of the sport's pre-tax profits. In addition, GPWC pledged to channel all the monies from trackside advertising, on-track advertising and other commercial income – currently also controlled by Ecclestone's companies – for distribution among the teams.

A statement from GPWC said, 'The meeting was part of an ongoing development process and represents a key step for GPWC and the F1 teams towards realising their common goals; achieving long-term stability for the sport, significantly increasing team payments and creating a more transparent commercial environment.

'Following today's meeting, GPWC intends to meet with Max Mosley and Bernie Ecclestone to update them on the details.'

It is also understood that the GPWC pledged to help smaller teams to survive by agreeing to make available engine packages at a competitive price, a move that ostensibly would improve the sport's long-term stability.

Far left: The suspension of Ralph Firman's Jordan collapses while running behind team-mate Giancarlo Fisichella and Toyota's Olivier Panis.

Left: What happened? A bemused Panis after his car was taken out by Firman.
Photographs: Darren Heath

Below: Kimi Räikkönen was judged the winner before Jordan's successful appeal.
Photograph: Patrick Gosling

Button's departure from the fray brought out the safety car for the fourth time. Four laps later, on lap 37, the race started yet again and, next time around, Räikkönen vaulted past Alonso and Ralf Schumacher to take third. By now, Coulthard was just 0.6s ahead of Barrichello, whose intermediate Bridgestones were allowing him to lap significantly faster than the McLaren driver.

By the end of lap 41, Barrichello was only 0.2s adrift, and when Coulthard ran slightly wide through the first corner going into lap 45, he seized the opportunity to pass. Meanwhile, Alonso had been signalled into the pits for a drive-through penalty after overtaking under yellow flags.

Barrichello's lead had grown to 4.2s by lap 46, and Coulthard looked as though he was beaten. Yet on lap 47, the Brazilian's moment of glory ended as his car spluttered to a halt, apparently out of fuel, thanks to a strategic miscalculation. Coulthard moved back into the lead and made his second refuelling stop at the end of lap 52, now apparently on course for victory.

At that point, all hell broke loose on the startline straight as Webber crashed heavily. With wreckage all over the track, the safety car was deployed for the fifth time, but then Alonso smashed into the debris and it was promptly decided to red-flag the race to a halt, Fisichella just having scrambled ahead of Räikkönen to take the lead.

When the dust settled and the FIA finally accepted that Fisichella had been ahead, counting back two laps meant that the Jordan driver had won by a mere 0.945s from Räikkönen, with

1ST GEAR

Photograph: Darren Heath

GRANDE PRÊMIO DO BRASIL

INTERLAGOS 4–6 APRIL 2003

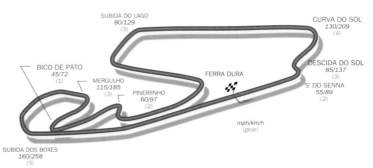

INTERLAGOS, SÃO PAULO
AUTODROMO CARLOS PACE

CIRCUIT LENGTH: 2.677 miles/4.309 km

SUBIDA DO LAGO 80/129 (3)
CURVA DO SOL 130/209 (4)
BICO DE PATO 45/72 (1)
MERGULHO 115/185 (3)
PINEIRINHO 60/97 (2)
FERRA DURA
DESCIDA DO SOL 85/137 (3)
S' DO SENNA 55/89 (2)
mph/km/h (gear)
SUBIDA DOS BOXES 160/258 (5)

RACE DISTANCE: 54 laps, 144.584 miles/232.686 km **RACE WEATHER:** Heavy rain, later drying slowly (track 19/21°C, air 18/20°C)

Pos.	Driver	Nat.	No.	Entrant	Car/Engine	Tyres	Laps	Time/Retirement	Speed (mph/km/h)	Gap to leader	Fastest race lap	
1	Giancarlo Fisichella	I	11	Jordan Ford	Jordan EJ-13-Ford Cosworth RS1 V10	B	54	1h 31m 17.748s	95.009/152.902		1m 23.454s	51
2	Kimi Räikkönen	FIN	6	West McLaren Mercedes	McLaren MP4/17D-Mercedes F0110M V10	M	54	1h 31m 18.693s	94.993/152.876	+0.945	1m 24.104s	39
3	Fernando Alonso	E	8	Mild Seven Renault F1 Team	Renault R3-RS23 V10	B	54	1h 31m 24.096s	94.899/152.725	+6.348s	1m 23.770s	41
4	David Coulthard	GB	5	West McLaren Mercedes	McLaren MP4/17D-Mercedes F0110M V10	M	54	1h 31m 25.844s	94.868/152.676	+8.096s	1m 23.132s	40
5	Heinz-Harald Frentzen	D	10	Sauber Petronas	Sauber C22-Petronas 03A V10	B	54	1h 31m 26.390s	94.859/152.661	+8.642s	1m 23.089s	53
6	Jacques Villeneuve	CDN	16	Lucky Strike BAR Honda	BAR 005-Honda RA003E v10	B	54	1h 31m 33. 802s	94.731/152.455	+16.054s	1m 22.713s	54
7	Ralf Schumacher	D	4	BMW WilliamsF1 Team	Williams FW25-BMW P83 V10	M	54	1h 31m 56.274s	94.345/151.834	+38.526s	1m 24.778s	46
8	Jarno Trulli	I	7	Mild Seven Renault F1 Team	Renault R3-RS23 V10	M	54	1h 32m 03.675s	94.219/151.631	+45.927s	1m 25.036s	43
9	Mark Webber	AUS	14	Jaguar Racing	Jaguar R4-Cosworth CR5 V10	M	53	Accident/DNF			1m 24.956s	50
10	Cristiano da Matta	BR	21	Panasonic Toyota Racing	Toyota TF103-RVX-03 V10	M	53			+1 lap	1m 27.080s	47
	Rubens Barrichello	BR	2	Scuderia Ferrari Marlboro	Ferrari F2002-051 V10	B	46	Fuel system			1m 22.032s	46
	Jenson Button	GB	17	Lucky Strike BAR Honda	BAR 005-Honda RA003E V10	B	32	Accident			1m 26.042s	17
	Jos Verstappen	NL	19	European Minardi Cosworth	Minardi PS03-Cosworth CR3 V10	B	30	Spun off			1m 28.010s	25
	Michael Schumacher	D	1	Scuderia Ferrari Marlboro	Ferrari F2002-051 V10	B	26	Accident			1m 24.040s	18
	Juan Pablo Montoya	COL	3	BMW WilliamsF1 Team	Williams FW25-BMW P83 V10	M	24	Accident			1m 25.814s	24
	Antonio Pizzonia	BR	15	Jaguar Racing	Jaguar R4-Cosworth CR5 V10	M	24	Accident			1m 27.990s	24
	Olivier Panis	F	20	Panasonic Toyota Racing	Toyota TF103-RVX-03 V10	M	17	Accident			1m 30.494s	17
	Ralph Firman	IRL	12	Jordan Ford	Jordan EJ-13-Ford Cosworth RS1 V10	B	17	Front suspension			1m 29.159s	13
	Justin Wilson	GB	18	European Minardi Cosworth	Minardi PS03-Cosworth CR3 V10	B	15	Spun off			1m 28.023s	15
	Nick Heidfeld	D	9	Sauber Petronas	Sauber C22-Petronas 03A V10	B	8	Engine cut			2m 11.396s	4

Fastest lap: Rubens Barrichello, on lap 46, 1m 22.032s, 117.502 mph/189.101 km/h.

Lap record: Michael Schumacher (F1 Ferrari F-2000-V10), 1m 14.755s, 128.940 mph/207.509 km/h (2000).

20th: JUSTIN WILSON Minardi-Cosworth

18th: CRISTIANO DA MATTA Toyota

16th: RALPH FIRMAN Jordan-Ford Cosworth
started from pit lane

14th: HEINZ-HARALD FRENTZEN Sauber-Petronas
started from pit lane

12th: NICK HEIDFELD Sauber-Petronas

19th: JOS VERSTAPPEN Minardi-Cosworth
started from pit lane

17th: ANTONIO PIZZONIA Jaguar-Cosworth
started from pit lane

15th: OLIVIER PANIS Toyota

13th: JACQUES VILLENEUVE BAR-Honda

11th: JENSON BUTTON BAR-Honda

Grid order	1	2	3	4	5	6	7	8	9	10	11	12	13	14	15	16	17	18	19	20	21	22	23	24	25	26	27	28	29	30	31	32	33	34	35	36	37	38	39	40
2 BARRICHELLO	2	2	2	2	2	2	2	2	5	5	6	6	6	6	6	6	6	6	6	6	6	6	6	6	6	6	5	5	5	5	5	5	5	5	5	5	5	5	5	5
5 COULTHARD	5	5	5	5	5	5	5	5	2	6	3	3	3	5	5	5	5	5	5	5	5	5	5	5	5	5	6	2	2	2	2	2	2	2	2	2	2	2	2	2
14 WEBBER	14	14	14	14	14	14	14	14	6	3	5	5	5	3	3	1	1	1	1	1	1	1	1	1	1	1	2	4	4	4	4	4	4	4	4	6	6	6		
6 RÄIKKÖNEN	6	6	6	6	6	6	6	6	14	2	14	14	14	14	1	3	3	3	3	21	21	21	2	2	2	4	14	14	14	14	8	8	8	8	8	4	4	8		
7 TRULLI	7	7	7	7	7	7	7	7	3	14	1	1	1	14	14	14	2	2	2	2	23	3	21	21	14	17	17	17	17	17	6	6	6	6	8	8	4			
4 R. SCHUMACHER	4	4	4	4	4	4	4	4	7	4	2	2	2	2	2	2	14	8	3	3	3	21	14	14	17	8	8	8	8	14	11	11	11	11	11	11	11			
1 M. SCHUMACHER	1	1	1	1	1	1	1	1	4	7	8	8	8	8	8	8	8	8	14	15	15	15	15	15	4	4	21	19	19	6	6	6	11	7	7	7	7	7		
11 FISICHELLA	11	11	11	11	11	11	3	3	1	1	17	17	17	17	17	17	17	17	17	10	10	10	14	14	17	8	11	11	11	11	7	10	10	10	10	14	14	14		
3 MONTOYA	3	3	3	3	3	8	8	8	8	7	7	7	7	7	7	7	14	14	14	17	4	19	19	6	6	16	16	16	16	16	14	16	10	10	10					
8 ALONSO	8	8	8	8	8	8	11	17	17	17	16	4	4	4	4	4	4	17	17	4	17	11	8	11	16	16	6	7	7	16	21	14	14	21	16	16	16			
17 BUTTON	17	17	17	17	17	17	17	9	16	16	4	16	16	16	16	16	16	19	19	8	11	16	7	7	10	10	21	14	21	16	16	21	21							
9 HEIDFELD	9	9	9	9	9	9	9	16	18	18	18	18	18	21	21	21	4	4	19	11	19	8	11	16	7	10	10	21	21	21										
16 VILLENEUVE	16	16	16	16	16	16	16	21	21	21	21	21	21	15	15	15	15	8	11	11	16	16	7	7	10	21	21	10												
20 PANIS	21	21	21	21	21	21	21	18	10	10	15	15	15	10	10	10	10	11	16	16	16	8	8	10	10															
21 DA MATTA	18	18	18	18	18	18	18	19	19	15	10	10	10	19	19	19	19	3	19	16	8	7	7	7																
18 WILSON	18	19	19	19	19	19	19	8	19	19	19	19	19	19	20	21	3	18	7	8	8	10	10																	
10 FRENTZEN	20	10	10	10	10	10	10	15	20	20	20	20	20	20	11	11																								
12 FIRMAN	10	15	15	15	15	15	15	20	11	11	11	11	11	12	12																									
15 PIZZONIA	15	20	20	20	20	20	20	11	12	12	12	12	12	12																										
19 VERSTAPPEN	12	12	12	12	12	12	12	12																																

Pit stop

One lap behind leader

TIME SHEETS

SATURDAY QUALIFYING determines race grid order
Dry and hot (track 33/38°C, air 25/26°C)

Pos.	Driver	Lap time	Sector 1	Sector 2	Sector 3
1	Rubens Barrichello	1m 13.807s	18.911s	37.670s	17.226s
2	David Coulthard	1m 13.818s	18.818s	37.769s	17.231s
3	Mark Webber	1m 13.851s	18.874s	37.444s	17.533s
4	Kimi Räikkönen	1m 13.866s	18.848s	37.857s	17.161s
5	Jarno Trulli	1m 13.953s	18.994s	37.359s	17.600s
6	Ralf Schumacher	1m 14.124s	18.859s	38.017s	17.248s
7	Michael Schumacher	1m 14.130s	19.061s	37.661s	17.408s
8	Giancarlo Fisichella	1m 14.191s	18.891s	37.957s	17.343s
9	Juan Pablo Montoya	1m 14.223s	18.984s	37.872s	17.179s
10	Fernando Alonso	1m 14.384s	19.132s	37.556s	17.696s
11	Jenson Button	1m 14.504s	18.906s	38.173s	17.425s
12	Nick Heidfeld	1m 14.631s	18.969s	38.329s	17.333s
13	Jacques Villeneuve	1m 14.668s	18.940s	38.380s	17.348s
14	Heinz-Harald Frentzen	1m 14.839s	18.930s	38.417s	17.492s
15	Olivier Panis	1m 14.839s	19.056s	38.323s	17.310s
16	Ralph Firman	1m 15.240s	19.152s	38.661s	17.427s
17	Antonio Pizzonia	1m 15.317s	19.060s	38.454s	17.803s
18	Cristiano da Matta	1m 15.641s	19.292s	38.764s	17.529s
19	Jos Verstappen	1m 16.542s	19.411s	39.403s	17.728s
20	Justin Wilson	1m 16.586s	19.715s	39.057s	17.814s

FRIDAY QUALIFYING determines Sat running order
Track wet, drying later (track 24/25°C, air 22/23°C)

Pos.	Driver	Lap time
1	Mark Webber	1m 23.111s
2	Rubens Barrichello	1m 23.249s
3	Kimi Räikkönen	1m 24.607s
4	David Coulthard	1m 24.655s
5	Michael Schumacher	1m 25.585s
6	Olivier Panis	1m 25.614s
7	Jacques Villeneuve	1m 25.672s
8	Antonio Pizzonia	1m 25.764s
9	Fernando Alonso	1m 26.203s
10	Heinz-Harald Frentzen	1m 26.375s
11	Cristiano da Matta	1m 26.554s
12	Jarno Trulli	1m 26.557s
13	Ralf Schumacher	1m 26.709s
14	Giancarlo Fisichella	1m 26.726s
15	Jos Verstappen	1m 26.886s
16	Nick Heidfeld	1m 27.111s
17	Juan Pablo Montoya	1m 27.961s
18	Ralph Firman	1m 28.083s
19	Justin Wilson	1m 28.317s
20	Jenson Button	No time

POINTS TABLES: CONSTRUCTORS

1	McLaren	41
2	Renault	23
3	Ferrari	16
4	Williams	14
5 =	Jordan	8
5 =	Sauber	8
7	BAR	5
8	Jaguar	2

FOR THE RECORD

50 grand prix points
Kimi Räikkönen

100 grand prix starts
Jarno Trulli

200 grand prix starts
Jordan

First grand prix win
Giancarlo Fisichella

PRIVATE TESTING
Cloudy, then rainy (track 20/22°C, air 20/21°C)

Pos.	Driver	Laps	Time
1	Jarno Trulli	41	1m 14.262s
2	Antonio Pizzonia	34	1m 14.464s
3	Mark Webber	35	1m 14.492s
4	Fernando Alonso	39	1m 14.680s
5	Giancarlo Fisichella	23	1m 15.092s
6	Allan McNish	16	1m 16.087s
7	Jos Verstappen	18	1m 16.322s
8	Ralph Firman	27	1m 16.559s
9	Justin Wilson	24	1m 16.615s

FRIDAY FREE PRACTICE
Wet and changeable (track 23/24°C, air 20/21°C)

Pos.	Driver	Laps	Time
1	Michael Schumacher	9	1m 28.060s
2	David Coulthard	10	1m 28.188s
3	Jenson Button	10	1m 28.903s
4	Jarno Trulli	4	1m 29.607s
5	Juan Pablo Montoya	10	1m 30.885s
6	Rubens Barrichello	6	1m 31.462s
7	Olivier Panis	5	1m 31.518s
8	Cristiano da Matta	6	1m 31.548s
9	Giancarlo Fisichella	7	1m 32.603s
10	Heinz-Harald Frentzen	9	1m 33.131s
11	Mark Webber	3	1m 33.714s
12	Ralf Schumacher	9	1m 35.013s
13	Jos Verstappen	3	1m 37.226s
14	Nick Heidfeld	7	1m 38.728s
15	Jacques Villeneuve	8	1m 48.359s
16	Ralph Firman	3	1m 57.783s
17	Kimi Räikkönen	2	No time
18	Antonio Pizzonia	2	No time
19	Justin Wilson	2	No time
20	Fernando Alonso	3	No time

SATURDAY FREE PRACTICE
Dry and hot (track 31/33°C, air 23/24°C)

Pos.	Driver	Laps	Time
1	Olivier Panis	36	1m 13.457s
2	Michael Schumacher	32	1m 13.546s
3	Jarno Trulli	30	1m 13.621s
4	David Coulthard	33	1m 13.893s
5	Juan Pablo Montoya	34	1m 13.929s
6	Kimi Räikkönen	31	1m 13.946s
7	Rubens Barrichello	34	1m 13.993s
8	Mark Webber	42	1m 14.102s
9	Ralf Schumacher	35	1m 14.192s
10	Fernando Alonso	41	1m 14.209s
11	Giancarlo Fisichella	33	1m 14.224s
12	Jenson Button	44	1m 14.464s
13	Antonio Pizzonia	42	1m 14.511s
14	Jacques Villeneuve	43	1m 14.523s
15	Nick Heidfeld	35	1m 14.744s
16	Cristiano da Matta	37	1m 14.819s
17	Heinz-Harald Frentzen	36	1m 14.921s
18	Ralph Firman	31	1m 15.475s
19	Jos Verstappen	33	1m 15.610s
20	Justin Wilson	25	1m 16.067s

WARM-UP
Dry and hot (track 33/38°C, air 25/26°C)

Pos.	Driver	Laps	Time
1	Kimi Räikkönen	4	1m 13.886s
2	Rubens Barrichello	7	1m 14.002s
3	Michael Schumacher	6	1m 14.166s
4	David Coulthard	5	1m 14.253s
5	Juan Pablo Montoya	5	1m 14.321s
6	Mark Webber	4	1m 14.584s
7	Jenson Button	7	1m 14.690s
8	Ralf Schumacher	3	1m 14.719s
9	Jacques Villeneuve	5	1m 14.768s
10	Nick Heidfeld	6	1m 14.773s
11	Jarno Trulli	6	1m 14.863s
12	Giancarlo Fisichella	4	1m 14.913s
13	Fernando Alonso	4	1m 14.934s
14	Antonio Pizzonia	4	1m 15.245s
15	Heinz-Harald Frentzen	4	1m 15.291s
16	Cristiano da Matta	6	1m 15.352s
17	Olivier Panis	5	1m 15.401s
18	Ralph Firman	4	1m 16.115s
19	Jos Verstappen	3	1m 16.744s
20	Justin Wilson	4	1m 16.935s

10th: FERNANDO ALONSO Renault

8th: GIANCARLO FISICHELLA Jordan-Ford Cosworth

6th: RALF SCHUMACHER Williams-BMW

4th: KIMI RÄIKKÖNEN McLaren-Mercedes

2nd: DAVID COULTHARD McLaren-Mercedes

9th: JUAN PABLO MONTOYA Williams-BMW

7th: MICHAEL SCHUMACHER Ferrari

5th: JARNO TRULLI Renault

3rd: MARK WEBBER Jaguar-Cosworth

Pole: RUBENS BARRICHELLO Ferrari

Lap Chart

43	44	45	46	47	48	49	50	51	52	53	54	•	
5	5	2	2	5	5	5	5	5	5	5	6	11	1
2	2	5	5	6	6	6	6	6	11	11		6	2
6	6	6	6	4	11	11	11	11	11	8	8	8	3
4	4	4	4	11	4	8	8	8	8	5	5	4	4
11	11	11	11	7	7	7	10	10	10	10	10	5	5
7	7	7	7	10	8	10	7	7	16	16	6	6	6
14	10	10	10	8	10	16	16	16	16	4	4	7	7
10	8	8	8	16	16	14	14	14	14	7	7	8	8
8	16	16	16	14	14	4	4	4	4	14			
16	14	14	14	21	21	21	21	21	21				
21	21	21	21										

CHASSIS LOG BOOK

No.	Driver	Chassis
1	Michael Schumacher	F2002/225
2	Rubens Barrichello	F2002/222
	Spare	F2002/219
3	Juan Pablo Montoya	FW25/04
4	Ralf Schumacher	FW25/03
	Spare	FW25/02
5	David Coulthard	MP4/17D-08
6	Kimi Räikkönen	MP4/17D-09
	Spare	MP4/17D-06
7	Jarno Trulli	R23/03
8	Fernando Alonso	R23/02
	Allan McNish	R23/01
	Spare	R23/01
9	Nick Heidfeld	C22/01
10	Heinz-Harald Frentzen	C22/03
	Spare	C22/02
11	Giancarlo Fisichella	EJ-13/04
12	Ralph Firman	EJ-13/02
	Spare	EJ-13/01
14	Mark Webber	R4/01
15	Antonio Pizzonia	R4/03
	Spare	R4/02
16	Jacques Villeneuve	BAR005/2
17	Jenson Button	BAR005/4
	Spare	BAR005/3
18	Justin Wilson	PS03/04
19	Jos Verstappen	PS03/01
	Spare	PS03/02
20	Olivier Panis	TF103/05
21	Cristiano da Matta	TF103/02
	Spare	TF103/01

POINTS TABLES: DRIVERS

1	Kimi Räikkönen	26
2	David Coulthard	15
3	Fernando Alonso	14
4	Jarno Trulli	9
5 =	Juan Pablo Montoya	8
5 =	Giancarlo Fisichella	8
5 =	Rubens Barrichello	8
5 =	Michael Schumacher	8
9	Heinz-Harald Frentzen	7
10	Ralf Schumacher	6
11	Jacques Villeneuve	3
12 =	Jenson Button	2
12 =	Mark Webber	2
14	Nick Heidfeld	1

SAN MARINOGP
IMOLA

See the light. Michael Schumacher scored his first grand prix win of the season in personally sad circumstances.
Photograph: Darren Heath

IMOLA QUALIFYING

DIARY

Antonio Pizzonia rumoured to be on the verge of losing his Jaguar F1 drive.

Frank Williams denies reports that Ralf Schumacher could be dropped before the start of the 2004 season.

DaimlerChrysler confirms there is a possibility that it could increase its 40-percent stake in the McLaren organisation at some point in the future.

Max Mosley again hints that he is considering standing again for the FIA presidency when his current term of office ends in 2005.

For Michael and Ralf Schumacher, qualifying at Imola was dominated by thoughts of their gravely ill mother, Elisabeth, who had lapsed into a coma in a Cologne hospital. Immediately after the two men had qualified first and second on the grid, they flew back to Germany to spend some time at her bedside. She died later that evening.

Yet Michael was still capable of rationalising and explaining what went into his 52nd career pole position. 'Today, what we refer to as the "old" car proved what it could do and what we knew it was capable of,' he said after posting a 1m 22.327s, 'yet, at the same time, I knew before the season started that we weren't going to have a year like last year when everything was perfect.' His team-mate, Rubens Barrichello, pulled back from a spin into gravel at Rivazza during the 15-minute pre-qualifying warm-up to line up third with a 1m 22.557s.

With the rival McLaren-Mercedes MP4/17Ds qualifying with heavier fuel loads in anticipation of two-stop refuelling strategies, the shoot-out for pole was between the Ferraris and Williams-BMWs, all of which were committed to a three-stop tactic.

Ralf suffered a setback on Saturday morning when he spun off at the Variante Alta, damaging his race car badly enough to need the spare FW25 for the one-shot qualifying session. 'After the first sector, where I was not very fast, I thought my qualifying lap had been compromised, then surprisingly I made it,' said Ralf. 'I must say thanks to the T-car team, as they did a very good job getting my car ready, which I had to use after the mistake I made this morning.'

Montoya wound up fourth on 1m 22.789s, but it was Mark Webber who was outstanding again in the Jaguar R4, posting a 1m 23.015s to take fifth place on the inside of the third row. 'I was aiming for a top-six position and it's great to have managed P5 on the grid for tomorrow,' he said. 'In some ways, the lap was quite conservative. I didn't want to make any silly mistakes or over-push the car. Knowing how to control your aggression isn't easy over this one-lap qualifying challenge, and there's a very fine line between going too slowly and too fast.'

Kimi Räikkönen lined up the best placed McLaren alongside the Jaguar in sixth with a 1m 23.148s, but Coulthard made a mistake, locking a wheel at Rivazza, and paid a high price with a 1m 23.818s best. That left him down on the sixth row in 12th place.

With Jarno Trulli having been forced to take the spare Renault R23 at short notice, Fernando Alonso's performance in setting an eighth-fastest 1m 23.169s was a more representative reflection of the car's true potential. The young Spaniard found himself sandwiched on the grid by the BAR-Honda 005s of Jacques Villeneuve (1m 23.160s) and Jenson Button (1m 23.381s).

'I'm very happy with my lap because it's quicker than we had been expecting,' explained Villeneuve. 'We've been working all weekend towards race set-up, so to get a good lap in qualifying is great. There was still a tenth to be had in the last corner, but I think the signs are good for the race tomorrow.'

Button commented, "The first two sectors of my qualifying lap were okay, but then I went a bit wide in the high-speed chicane up the hill and lost a bit of time. I also had a bit too much understeer in the high-speed corners.'

Olivier Panis did a good job to qualify tenth on 1m 23.460s, happy that things seemed to be coming together well after a troubled Friday session, during which he had lost time with a brake problem. Cristiano da Matta recorded a 1m 23.838s, which earned him 13th place on the grid for his Monza debut. 'The track conditions were a little slippery, but my lap was quite good,' he said.

In the Sauber camp, Nick Heidfeld admitted that he'd been struggling all weekend to find a good balance from his race car, so switched to the spare C22 just before the warm-up. It was a move that left him pretty satisfied and he managed a 1m 23.700s for 11th fastest, placing him three spots ahead of team-mate Heinz-Harald Frentzen (1m 23.932s), whose car needed a hurried engine change prior to the warm-up after a failure during the morning.

Antonio Pizzonia was learning his way in the Jaguar and had to be satisfied with 15th fastest at 1m 24.147s, which put him ahead of the hapless Trulli, while both Jordans were mixed in with the Minardis on the last two rows. Giancarlo Fisichella was running a lot of fuel and Ralph Firman had flat-spotted a tyre under braking for the first corner. Justin Wilson avoided the back row of the grid with an 18th-fastest time, but Jos Verstappen crashed at the Variante Alta on his qualifying run and failed to finish his flying lap.

IN many ways, the San Marino GP was the most difficult race of Michael Schumacher's career. Mourning the death of his mother, who had passed away only a few hours before the start, Michael scored a psychologically crucial victory in Ferrari's heartland, locking in to Maranello's familiar winning streak while, at the same time, emerging triumphant on the final outing for that remarkable, prolific winner, the Ferrari F2002. The early laps were enlivened by a poignant battle between Michael and his brother Ralf in the Williams-BMW FW25, which had started from second place on the front row and out-accelerated the Ferrari into the first corner.

Both brothers were on three-stop strategies, but while Michael's race ran seamlessly to schedule, Ralf's was beset by pit-lane glitches that left him trailing in fourth place at the chequered flag, behind Kimi Räikkönen's McLaren-Mercedes MP4/17D and the other Ferrari F2002 of Rubens Barrichello.

Jos Verstappen started the race from the pit lane after crashing his Minardi PS03 in Saturday qualifying, while Justin Wilson came in at the end of the parade lap to refuel, as did Ralph Firman in his Jordan. Meanwhile, Ralf Schumacher accelerated cleanly into the lead, edging out brother Michael's Ferrari as the pack jostled into the Tamburello chicane.

Farther back, both Jaguars were suffering launch-control problems. Mark Webber had to switch hurriedly to manual gear selection when his R4 was reluctant to move as he removed his finger from the start button. Antonio Pizzonia was also left on the line, subsequently being pushed to the pits from where he started his race one lap down on the remainder of the field.

By the end of lap one, Ralf Schumacher led from Michael by 0.5s, with Rubens Barrichello's Ferrari next up from Juan Pablo Montoya's Williams and Kimi Räikkönen's McLaren. Olivier Panis's Toyota was seventh, the hapless Webber down to 11th.

Second time around and Ralf was hanging on to the lead by the skin of his teeth, his brother darting about under his rear wing. Barrichello was edging close, and by the end of lap four the first three were absolutely nose to tail, while Montoya was only a few lengths behind in fourth.

With all the competitors on the softest rubber available, lack of grip caused by the initial spell of 'graining' affected the Michelin and Bridgestone runners to different degrees. The Michelin performance drop-off in the early laps was more marked and longer-lived than the slight deterioration in grip suffered by the Michelins. The result was that Ralf Schumacher appeared to be under increasing pressure as the laps rolled by.

Eventually, at the end of lap 16, Ralf made the first of the Williams team's three planned refuelling stops, receiving service in 6.4s. The FW25 lurched forward and almost stalled as he selected the wrong gear when he set off down the pit lane. That put Michael's Ferrari safely into the lead, and the world champion pitted for his first stop in 8.2s at the end of lap 18, resuming third, behind Räikkönen and David Coulthard.

Coulthard made a 9.8s first stop at the end of lap 21, dropping back to sixth, while Räikkönen came in from the lead on lap 22, an 8.6s effort putting him back into the race in fourth, behind Michael Schumacher, Ralf Schumacher and Barrichello, and ahead of Juan Pablo Montoya, Coulthard, Fernando Alonso (Renault R23) and Olivier Panis. Montoya had made his first foray into the pits at the end of lap 17, slightly overshooting his allotted stopping point with the result that he dragged the refuelling rig out of position.

Farther back, Webber's tribulations with the Jaguar had continued. On lap 15, the Australian had entered the pits for the first of his three refuelling stops, but inadvertently exceeded the pit-lane speed limit, which meant that he was back for a drive-through penalty five laps later, and that dropped him to 12th.

On lap 21, Justin Wilson had also refuelled, but the rig had malfunctioned, forcing him to return next time around, only for the problem to recur. While he'd been stationary for a second time, the Minardi had dumped most of its coolant over the pit lane, putting him out.

'After the first four or five laps of the race, the car started to slide around quite a bit,' said Wilson, 'so I decided to maintain the best pace I could and just hang on to the pit stop. I didn't realise there was a problem until they called me back to the pits on the

Left: Juan Pablo Montoya kicks up the dirt.
Photograph: Darren Heath

Bottom left: Following Jordan's successful appeal, Giancarlo Fisichella was presented with the winner's trophy from the Brazilian Grand Prix on the Imola start line.
Photograph: John Marsh/redzoneimages.com

Below: Ralf Schumacher leads the two Ferraris during the early stages of the race.
Photograph: Patrick Gosling

Above: Rubens Barrichello ensured that both Ferrari F2002 drivers were on the podium at the end of this classic car's final race.
Photograph: Darren Heath

Above right: Another win for Ferrari kept the Tifosi happy.
Photograph: Patrick Gosling

Above far right: Michael and Rubens embrace.

Centre right: McLaren mechanics keep a watchful eye on their man's progress.

Right: Ron Dennis was typically forthright on the subject of traction control.
Photographs: Darren Heath

next lap and told me the fuel hadn't been delivered. Up to that point, the car had been running fine. It's fair to say that it's been a disappointing day.'

On lap 30, Juan Pablo Montoya came in for his second refuelling stop, but the Williams rig malfunctioned and the FW25 was short-changed. As a result, the Colombian needed a top-up on lap 32, after which he resumed in a frustrating eighth place.

This all left the Williams team a little flustered and, to compound its difficulties, when Ralf made his second refuelling stop (7.8s) from second place at the end of lap 31, he received Montoya's allocated fuel load, which was good for a couple of laps less than had been planned. Ultimately, this caused Ralf to lose places to Räikkönen and Barrichello, as he had to make his final stop a little early, on lap 48, and rejoined just 0.5s behind Räikkönen. Had he taken on his originally planned fuel load, he would have squeezed in a couple of extra laps and, at the speed he was lapping at that point in the race, probably would have retained his second place.

Michael Schumacher came in for his second pit stop (7.0s) on lap 49, briefly allowing Barrichello ahead until the Brazilian made his second scheduled stop next time around, this being a slow 13.3s affair thanks to a sticking left front wheel nut.

At the end of lap 52, Barrichello out-accelerated Ralf Schumacher's Williams to take third place coming out of the final corner. Meanwhile, at the head of the field, Michael Schumacher was able to ease back in the closing stages, any potential challenge from Räikkönen being blunted by the fact that the Finn had been forced to drive in what one McLaren insider described as 'engine conservation mode' to coax his car to the chequered flag.

Late in the race, both Jordan-Fords succumbed to engine problems. Giancarlo Fisichella had lost time during his first refuelling stop due to a misunderstanding that led him to believe he had

been given the signal to move away while the car was still being refuelled. Later, he suffered a hydraulics problem, although this had stabilised shortly before the engine failed on lap 58.

Ralph Firman had been held up by the Minardis at the start of the race, but once he had worked his way clear of them, he was able to push quite hard, although he reported that the car was suffering from slight oversteer turning into the corners. Then the clutch developed a problem and finally he stopped with engine failure on lap 52.

For all the understandable personal grief assailing the Schumacher boys, Michael's victory had been a truly remarkable swan-song for the Ferrari F2002, which had won 15 of its 19 races since making its victorious debut at Interlagos the previous year.

'It was very difficult for Michael today and he did the job because he felt he wanted to do the job, and he did fantastic work for the team,' said Jean Todt. 'On top of that, he's a driver. I think it is important that he shows what he is as a man and that's maybe the most important thing today. Obviously, we have deserved better than what we've had so far with the potential of the team, the drivers, the car, but that's racing. It was very important to win here at Imola and it was important to give a good end to this unbelievable car.'

Barrichello was guardedly upbeat after steering his way to a podium finish. 'It was a good fight, a clear one,' he said. 'Obviously, my race was kind of done by the strategy of Williams because I couldn't overtake Ralf the way Michael did at the first stop, and then on the second stop it was so close, again I lost a lot of time, otherwise it could have been a little bit different. But it was a fun race and I was quite enthusiastic about the overtaking.'

Ralf Schumacher wound up a good fourth after a demanding race and, like Michael, he absented himself from the media conference. 'In general, our chassis improvements became visible at

Imola,' said Sam Michael, Williams's chief operations engineer. 'However, our race was hampered by a few things. We went for a three-stop strategy which promised to be the quicker one, which is proven by the fact that the race winner stopped three times too. But this strategy does not leave any margin if anything goes wrong, and we had several problems at the pit stops, the worst one being a malfunctioning fuel rig.'

Behind Coulthard, Fernando Alonso was delighted with his sixth place in the underpowered Renault R23. 'A perfect finish to a good weekend for me,' he said. 'Today I couldn't hope for a better result. The car felt very good, I was competitive from the start, and it was great to be able to race and fight with the top teams.'

By contrast, Jarno Trulli had been forced to switch to the spare R23, set up for Alonso, after he had suffered a late engine failure prior to qualifying. That was responsible for his poor grid position and he struggled with the car all afternoon, finishing a disappointing 13th.

Montoya was seventh, followed by Jenson Button, who was extremely vexed that a two-stop strategy had yielded him only eighth place, even allowing for the fact that he had been boxed in behind Webber during the early stages. Jacques Villeneuve made a poor start and dropped to 13th; he was the race's first retirement, with a wiring-loom fire, after just 19 laps.

Olivier Panis finished a lapped ninth for Toyota, ahead of the two Saubers of Heidfeld and Frentzen, da Matta, the off-form Trulli and Pizzonia's Jaguar.

In the final reckoning, Räikkönen retained a comfortable lead in the drivers' championship stakes, but now Coulthard was under serious threat from the emergent Michael Schumacher. One left Imola with the impression that this race had been the most important pointer to future form we'd seen all season. And the new Ferrari was yet to come.

NEW ROW OVER TRACTION CONTROL

The FIA and F1 teams were facing another confrontation during the San Marino GP weekend, the reason being the vexed issue of whether or not traction-control systems should be re-admitted for 2004. In addition, the engine manufacturers were hinting that their plans to deliver subsidised engine packages to independent teams could be compromised by the costs involved in developing a new breed of F1 engine without the use of electronic aids.

'The teams, or most of them, are quite keen to hang on to traction control and launch control, [while] we are equally keen not to do that,' said FIA president Max Mosley. 'The main issue is one of cheating and enforcement and certainty, and we've agreed we're going to have a major meeting about that in the very near future to try and reach agreement, but the FIA position is very clear: that we would not be happy with the idea that drivers should continue to use traction control, launch control, fully automatic gearboxes and so forth after the beginning of 2004.'

McLaren chairman Ron Dennis commented, 'There is an understandable desire by the purists, of which I am one, to see the maximum opportunity for the drivers to demonstrate their skill. But there is a misconception because of a lack of knowledge of what electronics do. Brazil is a classic example of their lack of contribution, because with these systems, drivers were still making mistakes.'

Making tracks. Fernando Alonso at full speed down the home straight on his way to a heartening sixth place in the San Marino GP.
Photograph: Darren Heath

Photograph: Darren Heath

FIA F1 WORLD CHAMPIONSHIP • ROUND 4

GRAN PREMIO FOSTER'S DI SAN MARINO

IMOLA 18–20 APRIL 2003

IMOLA – AUTODROMO DINO E ENZO FERRARI

CIRCUIT LENGTH: 3.065 miles/4.933 km

TRAGUARDO 55/89 (2) — ACQUE MINERALI 70/113 (3) — PIRATELLA 105/169 (4) — TOSA 55/89 (2) — VILLENEUVE 85/137 (3) — 175/281 (6) — VARIANTE ALTA 75/121 (3) — RIVAZZA 65/105 (2) — TAMBURELLO 100/161 (3) — VARIANTE BASSA 180/290 (6) — mph/km/h (gear)

RACE DISTANCE: 62 laps, 189.896 miles/305.609 km **RACE WEATHER:** Overcast and warm (track 24/27°C, air 19/20°C)

Pos.	Driver	Nat.	No.	Entrant	Car/Engine	Tyres	Laps	Time/Retirement	Speed (mph/km/h)	Gap to leader	Fastest race lap	
1	Michael Schumacher	D	1	Scuderia Ferrari Marlboro	Ferrari F2002-051 V10	B	62	1h 28m 12.058s	129.179/207.894		1m 22.491s	17
2	Kimi Räikkönen	FIN	6	West McLaren Mercedes	McLaren MP4/17D-Mercedes FO110M V10	M	62	1h 28m 13.940s	129.134/207.821	+1.882s	1m 22.810s	21
3	Rubens Barrichello	BR	2	Scuderia Ferrari Marlboro	Ferrari F2002-051 V10	B	62	1h 28m 14.349s	129.124/207.805	+2.291s	1m 22.775s	49
4	Ralf Schumacher	D	4	BMW WilliamsF1 Team	Williams FW25-BMW P83 V10	M	62	1h 28m 20.861s	128.965/207.549	+8.803s	1m 23.265s	29
5	David Coulthard	GB	5	West McLaren Mercedes	McLaren MP4/17D-Mercedes FO110M V10	M	62	1h 28m 21.469s	128.950/207.525	+9.411s	1m 23.200s	20
6	Fernando Alonso	E	8	Mild Seven Renault F1 Team	Renault R3-RS23 V10	B	62	1h 28m 55.747s	128.122/206.192	+43.689s	1m 23.844s	60
7	Juan Pablo Montoya	COL	3	BMW WilliamsF1 Team	Williams FW25-BMW P83 V10	M	62	1h 28m 57.329s	128.084/206.131	+45.271s	1m 22.946s	32
8	Jenson Button	GB	17	Lucky Strike BAR Honda	BAR 005-Honda RA003E V10	B	61			+1 lap	1m 23.972s	15
9	Olivier Panis	F	20	Panasonic Toyota Racing	Toyota TF103-RVX-03 V10	M	61			+1 lap	1m 25.123s	36
10	Nick Heidfeld	D	9	Sauber Petronas	Sauber C22-Petronas 03A V10	B	61			+1 lap	1m 25.329s	38
11	Heinz-Harald Frentzen	D	10	Sauber Petronas	Sauber C22-Petronas 03A V10	B	61			+1 lap	1m 24.874s	34
12	Cristiano da Matta	BR	21	Panasonic Toyota Racing	Toyota TF103-RVX-03 V10	M	61			+1 lap	1m 24.705s	15
13	Jarno Trulli	I	7	Mild Seven Renault F1 Team	Renault R3-RS23 V10	M	61			+1 lap	1m 25.444s	13
14	Antonio Pizzonia	BR	15	Jaguar Racing	Jaguar R4-Cosworth CR5 V10	M	60			+2 laps	1m 24.733s	36
15	Giancarlo Fisichella	I	11	Jordan Ford	Jordan EJ-13-Ford Cosworth RS1 V10	B	57	Engine			1m 24.730s	27
	Mark Webber	AUS	14	Jaguar Racing	Jaguar R4-Cosworth CR5 V10	M	54	Driveshaft			1m 24.258s	30
	Ralph Firman	IRL	12	Jordan Ford	Jordan EJ-13-Ford Cosworth RS1 V10	B	51	Engine			1m 25.539s	45
	Jos Verstappen	NL	19	European Minardi Cosworth	Minardi PS03-Cosworth CR3 V10	B	38	Electrical			1m 26.835s	35
	Justin Wilson	GB	18	European Minardi Cosworth	Minardi PS03-Cosworth CR3 V10	B	23	Refuelling problem			1m 26.354s	23
	Jacques Villeneuve	CDN	16	Lucky Strike BAR Honda	BAR 005-Honda RA003E V10	B	19	Oil fire			1m 24.108s	16

Fastest lap: Michael Schumacher, on lap 17, 1m 22.491s, 133.769 mph/215.281 km/h (record).

Previous lap record: Rubens Barrichello (Ferrari F2002-051 V10), 1m 24.170s, 131.101 mph/210.987 km/h (2002).

19th: RALPH FIRMAN Jordan-Ford Cosworth
started from pit lane

17th: GIANCARLO FISICHELLA Jordan-Ford Cosworth
started from pit lane

15th: ANTONIO PIZZONIA Jaguar-Cosworth

13th: CRISTIANO DA MATTA Toyota

11th: NICK HEIDFELD Sauber-Petronas

20th: JOS VERSTAPPEN Minardi-Cosworth
started from pit lane

18th: JUSTIN WILSON Minardi-Cosworth
started from pit lane

16th: JARNO TRULLI Renault

14th: HEINZ-HARALD FRENTZEN Sauber-Petronas

12th: DAVID COULTHARD McLaren-Mercedes

Grid order	1	2	3	4	5	6	7	8	9	10	11	12	13	14	15	16	17	18	19	20	21	22	23	24	25	26	27	28	29	30	31	32	33	34	35	36	37	38	39	40	41	42	43	44	45	46	47
1 M. SCHUMACHER	4	4	4	4	4	4	4	4	4	4	4	4	4	4	4	1	1	1	6	6	6	6	6	1	1	1	1	1	1	1	1	1	1	1	1	1	1	1	1	1	1	1	1	1	1	1	1
4 R. SCHUMACHER	1	1	1	1	1	1	1	1	1	1	1	1	1	1	1	4	2	6	5	5	5	1	4	4	4	4	4	4	4	2	2	6	6	6	6	6	6	6	6	6	4	4	4	4	4	4	4
2 BARRICHELLO	2	2	2	2	2	2	2	2	2	2	2	2	2	2	2	2	3	5	1	1	1	4	2	2	2	2	2	2	2	6	4	4	4	4	4	4	4	4	4	4	2	2	2
3 MONTOYA	3	3	3	3	3	3	3	3	3	3	3	3	3	3	3	6	4	4	4	2	6	6	6	6	6	6	6	4	2	2	2	2	2	2	2	2	2	2	5	6	6
14 WEBBER	6	6	6	6	6	6	6	6	6	6	6	6	6	6	6	5	2	2	2	3	3	3	3	3	3	3	3	5	5	5	5	5	5	5	5	5	5	5	5	6	5	5
6 RÄIKKÖNEN	8	8	8	8	8	8	8	8	8	8	8	8	8	8	8	3	5	5	5	3	3	5	5	5	5	5	3	8	8	8	8	8	8	3	3	3	3	3	3	3
16 VILLENEUVE	20	20	20	20	20	20	20	20	20	20	20	20	5	5	5	17	17	16	16	8	8	8	8	8	8	8	8	8	8	8	8	8	8	17	17	17	17	17	3	8
8 ALONSO	5	5	5	5	5	5	5	5	5	5	9	9	17	14	16	8	8	20	20	20	20	20	20	20	20	17	17	17	17	3	3	3	3	3	10	10	10	17	17	17	17	17	17
17 BUTTON	9	9	9	9	9	9	9	9	9	9	17	17	14	16	8	11	11	17	17	17	17	17	17	17	9	9	9	14	10	10	10	10	10	17	17	20	20	20	9	9	14	14
20 PANIS	17	17	17	17	17	17	17	17	17	17	14	14	16	8	11	9	9	9	9	9	9	9	9	21	14	14	20	20	20	20	20	20	20	9	9	9	14	14	20	20
9 HEIDFELD	14	14	14	14	14	14	14	14	14	14	21	7	11	10	20	20	20	21	21	21	21	21	14	10	10	20	9	9	9	9	9	14	14	14	20	20	9	9
5 COULTHARD	21	21	21	21	21	21	21	21	16	16	7	10	7	7	17	17	21	21	21	21	14	14	14	14	14	7	7	7	7	7	7	7	7	21	21	10	10	10
21 DA MATTA	16	16	16	16	16	16	16	16	7	7	10	20	20	20	7	7	7	7	7	7	7	7	7	7	10	10	10	10	10	11
10 FRENTZEN	7	7	7	7	7	7	7	7	11	11	20	11	11	21	21	21	21	11	11	11	11	11	21	21	11	11	11	21	21	21	21	21	11	11	11	11	21	21
15 PIZZONIA	11	11	11	11	11	11	11	11	10	10	9	9	21	21	21	11	11	12	12	12	12	11	11	11	11	11	11	11	11	12	12	12	12	12	12	12	12
7 TRULLI	10	10	10	10	10	10	10	10	20	20	12	12	12	12	12	12	7	7	12	12	12	12	12	7	7	7	7	7
11 FISICHELLA	19	19	19	19	19	19	19	19	12	12	19	18	18	18	18	15	15	15	15	15	15	15	15	15
18 WILSON	12	12	12	12	12	12	12	12	18	18	18	19	19	19	18
12 FIRMAN	18	18	18	18	18	18	18	18	19	19	15	15	15	15	15	15
19 VERSTAPPEN	15	15	15	15	15	15	15	15	15	15	15	15	15	15

Pit stop

One lap behind leader

SATURDAY QUALIFYING determines race grid order
Cloudy, becoming sunny (track 23/26°C, air 19/22°C)

Pos.	Driver	Lap time	Sector 1	Sector 2	Sector 3
1	Michael Schumacher	1m 22.327s	23.464s	27.467s	31.396s
2	Ralf Schumacher	1m 22.341s	23.715s	27.525s	31.101s
3	Rubens Barrichello	1m 22.557s	23.726s	27.465s	31.366s
4	Juan Pablo Montoya	1m 22.789s	23.595s	27.925s	31.269s
5	Mark Webber	1m 23.015s	23.962s	27.756s	31.297s
6	Kimi Räikkönen	1m 23.148s	23.890s	27.813s	31.445s
7	Jacques Villeneuve	1m 23.160s	23.639s	27.853s	31.668s
8	Fernando Alonso	1m 23.169s	23.898s	27.869s	31.402s
9	Jenson Button	1m 23.381s	23.762s	27.922s	31.697s
10	Olivier Panis	1m 23.460s	24.065s	27.711s	31.684s
11	Nick Heidfeld	1m 23.700s	23.978s	28.016s	31.706s
12	David Coulthard	1m 23.818s	23.956s	27.823s	32.039s
13	Cristiano da Matta	1m 23.838s	24.190s	27.706s	31.942s
14	Heinz-Harald Frentzen	1m 23.932s	24.079s	28.034s	31.819s
15	Antonio Pizzonia	1m 24.147s	24.167s	28.325s	31.655s
16	Jarno Trulli	1m 24.190s	24.311s	28.064s	31.815s
17	Giancarlo Fisichella	1m 24.317s	24.311s	27.982s	32.024s
18	Justin Wilson	1m 25.826s	24.859s	28.696s	32.271s
19	Ralph Firman	1m 26.357s	24.931s	28.613s	32.813s
20	Jos Verstappen	No time	–	–	–

FRIDAY QUALIFYING determines Sat running order
Sunny and dry (track 29/36°C, air 21/24°C)

Pos.	Driver	Lap time
1	Michael Schumacher	1m 20.628s
2	Rubens Barrichello	1m 21.082s
3	Ralf Schumacher	1m 21.193s
4	Juan Pablo Montoya	1m 21.490s
5	Mark Webber	1m 21.669s
6	Jenson Button	1m 21.891s
7	Jacques Villeneuve	1m 21.926s
8	Kimi Räikkönen	1m 22.147s
9	David Coulthard	1m 22.326s
10	Heinz-Harald Frentzen	1m 22.531s
11	Giancarlo Fisichella	1m 22.724s
12	Olivier Panis	1m 22.765s
13	Fernando Alonso	1m 22.809s
14	Nick Heidfeld	1m 22.911s
15	Antonio Pizzonia	1m 22.919s
16	Jarno Trulli	1m 23.100s
17	Ralph Firman	1m 24.360s
18	Cristiano da Matta	1m 24.854s
19	Jos Verstappen	1m 24.990s
20	Justin Wilson	1m 25.195s

PRIVATE TESTING
Sunny and dry (track 18/22°C, air 17/20°C)

Pos.	Driver	Laps	Time
1	Antonio Pizzonia	33	1m 23.099s
2	Giancarlo Fisichella	31	1m 23.239s
3	Mark Webber	37	1m 23.457s
4	Ralph Firman	30	1m 23.885s
5	Jarno Trulli	25	1m 24.003s
6	Fernando Alonso	45	1m 24.298s
7	Alan McNish	20	1m 25.264s
8	Jos Verstappen	24	1m 25.905s
9	Justin Wilson	30	1m 26.374s
10	Matteo Bobbi	17	1m 29.433s

FRIDAY FREE PRACTICE
Sunny and dry (track 27/29°C, air 20/21°C)

Pos.	Driver	Laps	Time
1	Ralf Schumacher	20	1m 21.335s
2	Juan Pablo Montoya	18	1m 21.409s
3	Mark Webber	21	1m 22.056s
4	David Coulthard	22	1m 22.121s
5	Fernando Alonso	17	1m 22.561s
6	Jenson Button	20	1m 22.669s
7	Heinz-Harald Frentzen	18	1m 22.714s
8	Jarno Trulli	19	1m 23.051s
9	Rubens Barrichello	26	1m 23.057s
10	Michael Schumacher	9	1m 23.057s
11	Giancarlo Fisichella	9	1m 23.267s
12	Antonio Pizzonia	8	1m 23.426s
13	Kimi Räikkönen	24	1m 23.557s
14	Nick Heidfeld	17	1m 23.834s
15	Ralph Firman	11	1m 24.007s
16	Cristiano da Matta	23	1m 24.117s
17	Olivier Panis	14	1m 24.565s
18	Jacques Villeneuve	13	1m 25.153s
19	Jos Verstappen	17	1m 25.180s
20	Justin Wilson	4	1m 25.706s

SATURDAY FREE PRACTICE
Cloudy and dry (track 17/25°C, air 15/19°C)

Pos.	Driver	Laps	Time
1	Rubens Barrichello	31	1m 22.819s
2	Ralf Schumacher	23	1m 22.897s
3	Mark Webber	19	1m 22.958s
4	Kimi Räikkönen	35	1m 22.962s
5	Michael Schumacher	35	1m 22.974s
6	Fernando Alonso	41	1m 23.042s
7	David Coulthard	34	1m 23.198s
8	Juan Pablo Montoya	33	1m 23.769s
9	Jacques Villeneuve	33	1m 24.098s
10	Olivier Panis	31	1m 24.099s
11	Giancarlo Fisichella	24	1m 24.132s
12	Jenson Button	40	1m 24.178s
13	Jarno Trulli	38	1m 24.322s
14	Cristiano da Matta	40	1m 24.683s
15	Nick Heidfeld	32	1m 24.747s
16	Ralph Firman	27	1m 24.763s
17	Heinz-Harald Frentzen	7	1m 25.332s
18	Jos Verstappen	25	1m 25.745s
19	Justin Wilson	22	1m 25.945s
20	Antonio Pizzonia	17	1m 26.195s

WARM-UP
Cloudy and dry (track 23°C, air 20°C)

Pos.	Driver	Laps	Time
1	David Coulthard	4	1m 23.349s
2	Michael Schumacher	5	1m 23.452s
3	Juan Pablo Montoya	5	1m 23.509s
4	Ralf Schumacher	4	1m 23.514s
5	Jenson Button	8	1m 23.750s
6	Olivier Panis	4	1m 23.893s
7	Fernando Alonso	4	1m 24.002s
8	Kimi Räikkönen	4	1m 24.019s
9	Jacques Villeneuve	5	1m 24.028s
10	Mark Webber	5	1m 24.231s
11	Cristiano da Matta	7	1m 24.332s
12	Nick Heidfeld	4	1m 24.377s
13	Heinz-Harald Frentzen	7	1m 24.527s
14	Antonio Pizzonia	5	1m 25.029s
15	Giancarlo Fisichella	4	1m 25.191s
16	Jarno Trulli	3	1m 25.554s
17	Justin Wilson	4	1m 26.169s
18	Ralph Firman	4	1m 26.191s
19	Rubens Barrichello	3	1m 26.198s
20	Jos Verstappen	7	1m 26.746s

9th: JENSON BUTTON BAR-Honda

7th: JACQUES VILLENEUVE BAR-Honda

5th: MARK WEBBER Jaguar-Cosworth

3rd: RUBENS BARRICHELLO Ferrari

Pole: MICHAEL SCHUMACHER Ferrari

10th: OLIVIER PANIS Toyota

8th: FERNANDO ALONSO Renault

6th: KIMI RÄIKKÖNEN McLaren-Mercedes

4th: JUAN PABLO MONTOYA Williams-BMW

2nd: RALF SCHUMACHER Williams-BMW

49	50	51	52	53	54	55	56	57	58	59	60	61	62	●
1	2	1	1	1	1	1	1	1	1	1	1	1	1	1
2	1	6	6	6	6	6	6	6	6	6	6	6	6	2
6	6	4	2	2	2	2	2	2	2	2	2	2	2	3
4	4	2	4	4	4	4	4	4	4	4	4	4	4	4
5	5	5	5	5	5	5	5	5	5	5	5	5	5	5
3	8	8	8	8	8	8	8	8	8	8	8	8	8	6
8	3	3	3	3	3	3	3	3	3	3	3	3	3	7
17	17	17	17	17	17	17	17	17	17	17	17	17		8
14	14	14	14	14	20	20	20	20	20	20	20	20		
20	20	20	20	20	9	9	9	9	9	9	9	9		
9	9	9	9	9	10	10	10	10	10	10	10	10		
10	10	10	10	10	11	11	11	11	21	21	21	21		
11	11	11	11	11	21	21	21	21	7	7	7	7		
21	21	21	21	21	7	7	7	7	15	15	15			
7	7	7	7	7	14	15	15	15						
12	12	12	12	15	15	15								
15	15	15												

CHASSIS LOG BOOK

1	Michael Schumacher	F2002/225
2	Rubens Barrichello	F2002/222
	Spare	F2002/219
3	Juan Pablo Montoya	FW25/04
4	Ralf Schumacher	FW25/03
	Spare	FW25/02
5	David Coulthard	MP4/17D-08
6	Kimi Räikkönen	MP4/17D-06
	Spare	MP4/17D-07
7	Jarno Trulli	R23/03
8	Fernando Alonso	R23/05
	Allan McNish	R23/01
	Spare	R23/01
9	Nick Heidfeld	C22/03
10	Heinz-Harald Frentzen	C22/04
	Spare	C22/06

11	Giancarlo Fisichella	EJ-13/04
12	Ralph Firman	EJ-13/03
	Spare	EJ-13/01
14	Mark Webber	R4/01
15	Antonio Pizzonia	R4/02
	Spare	R4/03
16	Jacques Villeneuve	BAR005/2
17	Jenson Button	BAR005/4
	Spare	BAR005/3
18	Justin Wilson	PS03/04
19	Jos Verstappen	PS03/01
	Matteo Bobbi	PS03/02
	Spare	PS03/02
20	Olivier Panis	TF103/05
21	Cristiano da Matta	TF103/02
	Spare	TF103/01

Main photograph: **Michael Schumacher and the new Ferrari F2003-GA, which he gave a debut victory on the Circuit de Catalunya.**

Inset below: **New boy Fernando Alonso joins the Ferrari party hosted by Michael Schumacher and Rubens Barrichello.**
Photographs: Darren Heath

FIA F1 WORLD CHAMPIONSHIP • ROUND 5

SPANISHGP
BARCELONA

MICHAEL Schumacher certainly gave the new Ferrari F2003-GA a commanding debut win in the Spanish Grand Prix at the Circuit de Catalunya, but local hero Fernando Alonso also did enough to signal that the superb Michelin-shod Renault R23 would continue to keep the established front-runners on their toes for the rest of the season.

'We always expected a tough fight with the Renault performing so well,' said Schumacher, acknowledging just how hard he had been forced to work for the victory. 'We're lucky to be here with the new car because I don't think the old one would have made it.'

The 22-year-old Spaniard drove a flawless race in front of 96,000 of his compatriots to finish just 5.7s behind Michael's scarlet machine, having vaulted ahead of Rubens Barrichello's Ferrari at the first of his three scheduled refuelling stops. The three-stop strategy was calculated to be around 8s quicker over the 65-lap race distance than a two-stop schedule, both Ferrari and Renault proving that this was the fastest route to the finish.

The consistent performance of the hard-compound Michelins at least gave heart to the McLaren Mercedes squad on a day when it should have been up there challenging the new Ferrari. Points leader Kimi Räikkönen qualified last after an off-track moment in practice, then smashed into the back of Antonio Pizzonia's stalled Jaguar R4 on the starting grid, resulting in the safety car being deployed to slow the field for the first five laps while the wreckage was cleared from the circuit.

It almost seemed as though nothing could get worse for the young Brazilian. On Friday morning, he'd entered the pit lane a touch too quickly during the two-hour test session and hit Jaguar team mechanic Andy Saunders, throwing him several feet into the air. Saunders was taken to the medical centre suffering from cuts, bruises and slight concussion after what many regarded as an extremely lucky escape.

Now, thanks to another apparent glitch with his car's launch-control system, Pizzonia was left stranded as the race started. Although Justin Wilson managed successfully to weave his Minardi around the stationary Jaguar, Räikkönen had been unable to miss it and had paid a high price for his error in qualifying.

At the end of the day, the convoluted sequence of events surrounding Pizzonia's impending dismissal from the Jaguar team would be resolved when it declined an invitation from McLaren to pay around $1.7 million to secure the services of Alexander Wurz for the balance of the season. Jaguar would stick with the young Brazilian for the rest of the year, or so it seemed.

At the start, Schumacher's Ferrari accelerated cleanly away from pole position, but Alonso nipped ahead of Barrichello to squeeze momentarily between the two Italian cars. Under braking for the first corner, however, Rubens went around the back of the Spaniard and braked late on the outside, effectively edging him out again.

For his part, Michael braked deep into the corner and the two Ferraris brushed wheels as Barrichello rode over the outside kerbing, losing momentum. He held second place, ahead of Alonso, but Trulli and Coulthard tangled in their wake, Jarno's Renault spinning firmly into the barrier.

'I had a good start and was making my way smoothly, keeping on my line, when, at the second corner, I saw Coulthard's car cutting through from the outside,' said Trulli. 'He hit me and I was out. A real shame, because I know this could have been an excellent race for me.'

After the Räikkönen/Pizzonia collision, the safety car remained out until the end of lap five. Next time around, Michael Schumacher was already 0.9s ahead of Barrichello, with Alonso third, followed by Ralf Schumacher and Montoya in their Williams FW25s, the Colombian having slipped ahead of Jenson Button's BAR-Honda in a very bold move under braking as they started their first serious racing lap.

With ten laps completed, the two Ferraris were separated by 2.4s at the head of the field, and this gap had opened to 3.2s by the end of lap 12, when Jacques Villeneuve's race came to a premature end with another electrical fire.

'It's a shame that we spend the weekend working on race strategy and set-up, and we compromise our qualifying position to give us the best shot at the race,' he said. 'Then we can't even make use of that work because we don't finish on Sunday.'

On the face of it, the new Ferrari F2003-GA certainly rewrote the 2003 F1 performance parameters, most noticeably with its outstanding straight-line speed, which came in part from a major improvement in Maranello's aerodynamic package and extra power produced by the latest version of the V10 engine.

Michael Schumacher winged his way to an unchallenged pole position with a best of 1m 17.762s, 0.25s faster than team-mate Rubens Barrichello, who joined him on the front row. As would be emphasised in Sunday's race, the 'Schumacher factor' proved a premium benefit for the Italian squad, for Barrichello only just kept Fernando Alonso's Renault R23 off the front row by a scant 0.21s.

'This weekend is the first time I have driven the new car at this track and so it was not easy to find the right direction in terms of set-up, but today's result shows we seem to have got it right,' said Schumacher. 'My lap was not perfect, as I had a bad line through turn nine and turn eleven and, as Rubens had been very quick, I thought I might be behind him, but in the end I was quicker.'

Barrichello was satisfied, although he admitted, 'It was not a great lap for me.'

In the Renault camp, of course, there was much elation, as Alonso had done a brilliant job, the team feeling more than ever that its commitment to the extra two-hour Friday test session was continuing to reap valuable performance dividends.

Although 11 mph slower than Schumacher's Ferrari at the end of the startline straight, it said much for the entire Renault driver/chassis/aerodynamic package that the young Spaniard only just missed out on a front-row start.

'This is a special day for me, since, as I had hoped, I was able to place my car on the second row in front of my home crowd,' grinned Alonso. 'I felt the car much more competitive today than yesterday. In qualifying, it was perfectly balanced and I did an excellent lap.'

Jarno Trulli was well satisfied with fourth place on the grid, a 1m 18.615s ensuring that he just pipped an on-form Jenson Button's BAR-Honda for a place on the outside of the second row.

Button managed 1m 18.704s and admitted he was delighted. 'I am really pleased with fifth today,' he said. 'It felt like a quick lap, but I did make a couple of mistakes. I pushed a bit too hard in some of the corners and got a bit of oversteer, but it's nothing that can't be sorted out for tomorrow.'

Button's team-mate, Jacques Villeneuve, had experienced a rather more bumpy ride. He had opted to use the spare BAR 005 after struggling with his race chassis' set-up during the Friday sessions, but on the Saturday morning had an off-track excursion that damaged the rear end of the spare. A fresh engine, gearbox and rear suspension were fitted in time for qualifying and he lined up 11th at 1m 19.563s.

'We were a little bit lost yesterday, and the car was undrivable,' said Jacques, 'but we've been able to work on that for today. It was a good clean lap, nothing special, but I'm quite happy.'

Toyota's Olivier Panis was delighted to have qualified his TF103 sixth fastest on 1m 18.811s, and with his inexperienced team-mate, Cristiano da Matta, managing a 1m 19.623s for 13th on the grid, this was a good day for the Cologne-based outfit.

Less promising was the form displayed by the Williams-BMW FW25s of Ralf Schumacher (1m 19.006s) and Juan Pablo Montoya (1m 19.377s), who battled rear-end instability on their way to seventh and ninth in the final line-up, more than a second shy of the new Ferrari. Both men had grappled with an abrupt transition from understeer to oversteer, it proving impossible to achieve a decent and consistent handling balance.

For the McLaren team, problems seemed to come thick and fast. David Coulthard's MP4/17D developed an engine problem, and a fresh Mercedes V10 was installed just before he made his qualifying run, although the Scot decided to stick to the spare car, which had been set up originally for Kimi Räikkönen.

Under the circumstances, Coulthard did well to split the Williams duo with an eighth-fastest 1m 19.128s. For his part, Räikkönen had taken a trip across the gravel at turn seven, which had forced him to abort his run and start from the back of the grid.

Heinz-Harald Frentzen qualified his Sauber C23 tenth on 1m 19.427s, while Mark Webber managed 1m 19.615s to take a promising 12th for Jaguar, four places ahead of his beleaguered team-mate, Antonio Pizzonia, who found himself the subject of unsettling speculation over his future with the British F1 team.

Nick Heidfeld was 14th fastest in the other Sauber, while for Jordan-Ford Ralph Firman managed a respectable 15th-fastest 1m 20.215s, two places ahead of a troubled Giancarlo Fisichella on 1m 20.976s, the Italian having missed the pre-qualifying warm-up while an engine change was completed.

'There was still a problem, so I switched to the T-car, which was set up for Ralph, and I had not driven it all weekend,' shrugged Fisichella. 'It's been quite a frustrating weekend and it will be difficult tomorrow.'

Bringing up the rear were the two Minardis, although on this occasion Justin Wilson found himself elevated off the back row into 18th place, thanks to Räikkönen's crucial driving error.

BERGER SLAMS WILLIAMS F1

Gerhard Berger, the BMW motorsports director, propelled himself into the centre of controversy by predicting that the German car maker would never win a world championship as long as it was in partnership with the Williams F1 team.

'The high expectations could not be fulfilled,' said Berger. 'BMW has been building the best engines for several seasons now, but is always slowed down by Williams cars. This means we may win one or two races, where our super engine will help, but the world championship will remain a dream.'

Berger's criticism came in the wake of another disappointing outing for the Williams-BMWs in the Spanish Grand Prix. It was made during an Austrian television interview as negotiations continued between the two parties over prospects for continuing their alliance beyond the end of 2004.

Frank Williams would not comment on the issue, while BMW attempted to play down the significance of the remarks, suggesting that perhaps they had been taken out of context as 'somewhat stronger' than Berger's intended tone.

Despite these observations from Munich, most F1 insiders believed that Berger had touched a sensitive nerve and that his comments were intended to galvanise Williams into modifying its position in negotiations with BMW.

Although there was inevitable speculation that BMW might switch allegiance to another F1 team, it was difficult to see how they would find a partner with a proven track record to equal that of Williams. The only other feasible route seemed to be for BMW to commit to build its own car, an option that it had repeatedly ruled out in the past.

Above: **Cristiano da Matta scored points for Toyota.**

Left: **Under pressure. Antonio Pizzonia's race seat at Jaguar appeared to be under threat.**

Right: **Ralph Firman was delighted to score his first World Championship point, bringing his Jordan-Ford home in eighth place.**
Photographs: Darren Heath

DIARY

Safety standards at Silverstone put under the spotlight after Juan Pablo Montoya crashes heavily during testing prior to the Spanish Grand Prix, his Williams FW25 becoming lodged under the tyre barrier at Becketts corner.

Sébastien Bourdais wins CART Champ Car race on Brands Hatch Indy circuit.

Bentley sets blistering pace at Le Mans test day.

Peter 'Possum' Bourne, the multiple Asia-Pacific, Australian and New Zealand Rally champion, dies in hospital after an accident in New Zealand.

By lap 16, Michael had opened his lead to 3.6s. During lap 18, Alonso made his first refuelling stop in 7.2s. Michael brought the Ferrari in for its first scheduled visit to the pits on lap 19, followed by Barrichello a lap later, but Alonso just managed to squeeze through into second place before Rubens rejoined. At this point, the young Spaniard looked set to give 100 per cent as he made his bid to hunt down the world champion.

Farther back, McLaren fortunes suffered another blow with Coulthard's retirement on lap 18. Going into the first right-hander after the pits, Jenson Button had attempted to out-brake the McLaren, the two cars collided and David's race ended in the gravel trap. Button was forced to head for the pits to replace a damaged nose section and a punctured front tyre, and was delayed sufficiently to be two laps down at the finish.

Predictably, Michael Schumacher seemed up to Alonso's challenge, although this would certainly be no push-over. By lap 22, his advantage was 2.6s, which he extended to 5.3s. Then Alonso trimmed it back to 4.8s, but as they lapped a torrid battle between the two Minardis and Jordans, Fernando dropped back to 7.9s behind the Ferrari.

Yet by the time Michael made his second refuelling stop, in 6.9s on lap 35, the Renault driver was just 6.4s adrift, and he managed to stay ahead of Barrichello after making his own stop at the end of lap 36. Now, however, he found himself behind the rather obstructive Ralf Schumacher for a couple of laps until the German driver slid off into the gravel at turn three, ripping the guide vanes off his FW25's diffuser and badly damaging the floor.

On lap 41, Ralf made an 8.8s stop from third place, allowing Barrichello back into third, ahead of Montoya, who came in for service (8.6s) on lap 42. On the same lap, Olivier Panis's hopes of a decent result were dashed when his Toyota TF103 rolled to a standstill with suspected gearbox failure. 'Obviously, I'm very annoyed,' said the Frenchman, who was clearly vexed about this latest failure. 'We have been so strong here all weekend, and in the race we were looking good on a two-stop strategy and up into the points again. I'm so disappointed. We really need to stop losing points like this.'

Four laps later, the Jordan team suffered a major blow when Giancarlo Fisichella's EJ-13 limped into the pits with an engine failure, having progressively lost power over the previous few laps. 'I had a lot of problems,' said Fisichella. 'First of all in the pit stop, we had a rig failure and had to use the other rig, then put too much fuel into the car. Then, after a few laps, the bargeboard broke and I lost a lot of grip, making it very difficult to drive. And finally there was an engine problem.'

At the front of the field, Michael Schumacher was still exerting his authority over the ambitious new star in the Renault. By lap 46, the Ferrari was 5.3s ahead, then 4.9s on lap 48, a lap before Michael made his third refuelling stop in 6.9s.

Alonso, now revelling in leading a grand prix, came in next time around for a 6.6s effort – an achievement duplicated exactly by Barrichello at the same time. From then on, the Spaniard could only chase as hard as he knew how, Michael opening the lead to almost 10s before easing off to win by 5.716s. He'd made his point, asserted his authority. But his young rival had also made an indelible mark. Unquestionably, it had been a great performance from Alonso, but with commendable self-analysis, the youngster didn't believe he had a real chance of winning in Barcelona – not even if he'd run ahead of Barrichello from the very start.

'In reality, I think Michael controlled the gap quite easily with me and it was not possible to beat him,' he said. 'We had a perfect car for 64 laps, no mistakes from my side, perfect pit stops, so there was nothing more to take from that race, I think.'

Barrichello was clearly rather disappointed to end up third. 'My tyres were good for the first five to ten laps of each stint, but after that I could not maintain my pace,' he explained. 'That was why Fernando managed to pull away, because when I should have been pushing to pass the five cars which were racing one another, I was struggling a bit.

'I made some changes to the settings from the cockpit, and during the last pit stop the team changed the front wing settings. The car was much better after that, which is proved by the fact I set the fastest lap, but by then it was too late to catch up.'

Behind Barrichello, the Williams-BMWs of Juan Pablo Montoya and Ralf Schumacher finished fourth and fifth, the German driver grappling with a major handling imbalance after damaging his car's undertray in that off-track moment. The remaining points were scored by the forceful Cristiano da Matta (Toyota), Mark Webber (Jaguar) and a satisfied Ralph Firman in the sole surviving Jordan-Ford, the British driver scoring his first championship point.

Although Räikkönen finished the day still leading the championship, David Coulthard plummeted from second to fifth in the table. Even so, team chief Ron Dennis remained upbeat about his team's prospects for the balance of the season, quietly confident that the forthcoming MP4/18A challenger would be a match for the new Ferrari.

At this stage, the new McLaren had yet to be tested for the first time, but all the available data suggested that it would be a quantum leap forward from the MP4/17D. There was speculation that the new car might debut in Canada, but in the meantime, Michael Schumacher looked set to keep racking up the points.

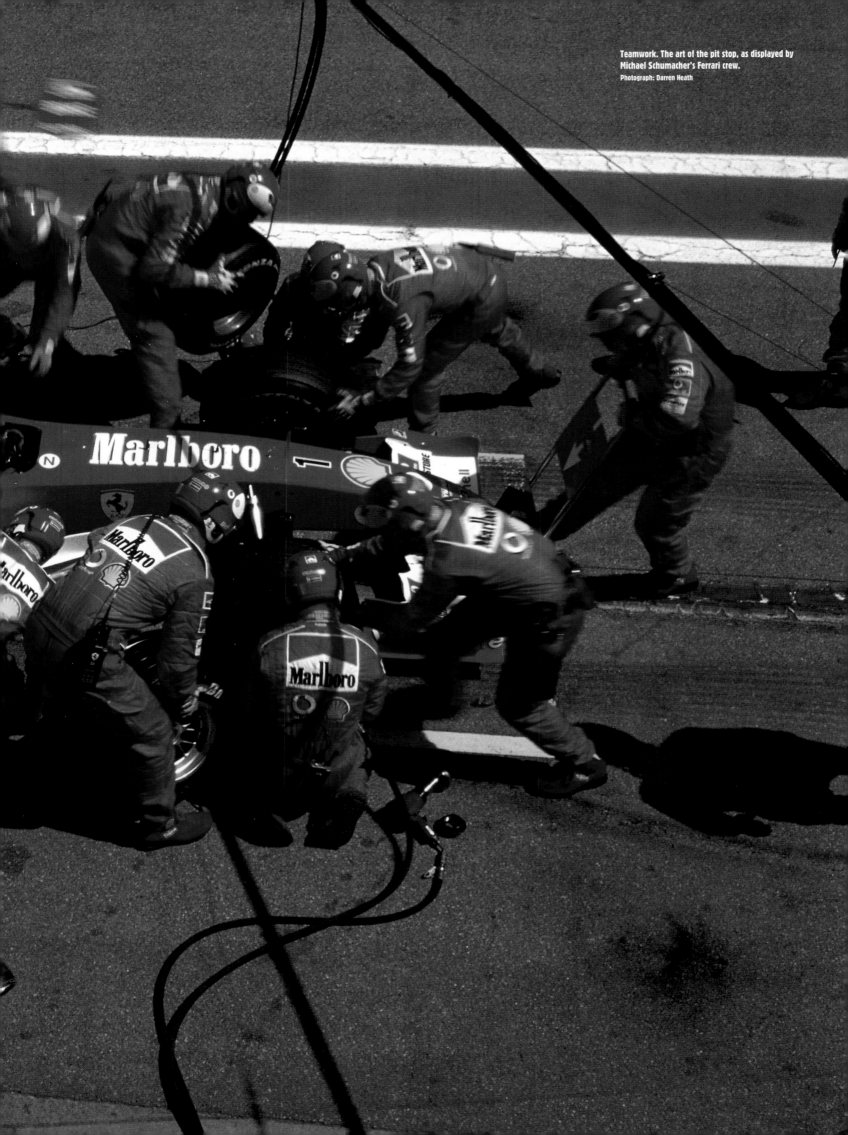

Teamwork. The art of the pit stop, as displayed by
Michael Schumacher's Ferrari crew.
Photograph: Darren Heath

FIA F1 WORLD CHAMPIONSHIP · ROUND 5

GRAN PREMIO MARLBORO de ESPAÑA

CATALUNYA 2–4 MAY 2003

Photograph: Darren Heath

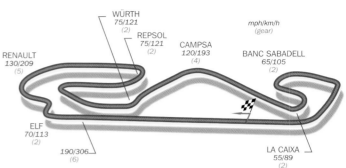

CATALUNYA CIRCUIT – BARCELONA

CIRCUIT LENGTH: 2.939 miles/4.730 km

RENAULT 130/209 (5)

WÜRTH 75/121 (2)

REPSOL 75/121 (2)

CAMPSA 120/193 (4)

BANC SABADELL 65/105 (2)

mph/km/h (gear)

ELF 70/113 (2)

190/306 (6)

LA CAIXA 55/89 (2)

RACE DISTANCE: 65 laps, 190.962 miles/307.324 km   **RACE WEATHER:** Dry, hot and sunny (track 38/40°C, air 27/28°C)

Pos.	Driver	Nat.	No.	Entrant	Car/Engine	Tyres	Laps	Time/Retirement	Speed (mph/km/h)	Gap to leader	Fastest race lap	
1	Michael Schumacher	D	1	Scuderia Ferrari Marlboro	Ferrari F2003-GA-051 V10	B	65	1h 33m 46.933s	122.173/196.619		1m 20.307s	51
2	Fernando Alonso	E	8	Mild Seven Renault F1 Team	Renault R3-RS23 V10	M	65	1h 33m 52.649s	122.050/196.420	+5.716s	1m 20.476s	42
3	Rubens Barrichello	BR	2	Scuderia Ferrari Marlboro	Ferrari F2003-GA-051 V10	B	65	1h 34m 04.934s	121.784/195.992	+18.001s	1m 20.143s	52
4	Juan Pablo Montoya	COL	3	BMW WilliamsF1 Team	Williams FW25-BMW P83 V10	M	65	1h 34m 48.955s	120.842/194.476	+62.022s	1m 21.448s	21
5	Ralf Schumacher	D	4	BMW WilliamsF1 Team	Williams FW25-BMW P83 V10	M	64			+1 lap	1m 20.798s	8
6	Cristiano da Matta	BR	21	Panasonic Toyota Racing	Toyota TF103-RVX-03 V10	M	64			+1 lap	1m 20.935s	22
7	Mark Webber	AUS	14	Jaguar Racing	Jaguar R4-Cosworth CR5 V10	M	64			+1 lap	1m 21.967s	20
8	Ralph Firman	IRL	12	Jordan Ford	Jordan EJ-13-Ford Cosworth RS1 V10	B	63			+2 laps	1m 22.719s	29
9	Jenson Button	GB	17	Lucky Strike BAR Honda	BAR 005-Honda RA003E V10	B	63			+2 laps	1m 21.300s	7
10	Nick Heidfeld	D	9	Sauber Petronas	Sauber C22-Petronas 03A V10	B	63			+2 laps	1m 22.568s	34
11	Justin Wilson	GB	18	European Minardi Cosworth	Minardi PS03-Cosworth CR3 V10	B	63			+2 laps	1m 23.222s	7
12	Jos Verstappen	NL	19	European Minardi Cosworth	Minardi PS03-Cosworth CR3 V10	B	62			+3 laps	1m 22.942s	16
	Giancarlo Fisichella	I	11	Jordan Ford	Jordan EJ-13-Ford Cosworth RS1 V10	B	43	Engine			1m 22.900s	17
	Olivier Panis	F	20	Panasonic Toyota Racing	Toyota TF103-RVX-03 V10	M	41	Gearbox			1m 20.803s	14
	Heinz-Harald Frentzen	D	10	Sauber Petronas	Sauber C22-Petronas 03A V10	B	38	Suspension			1m 21.791s	32
	David Coulthard	GB	5	West McLaren Mercedes	McLaren MP4/17D-Mercedes F0110M V10	M	17	Collision with Button			1m 22.577s	10
	Jacques Villeneuve	CDN	16	Lucky Strike BAR Honda	BAR 003-Honda RA003E V10	B	12	Engine			1m 22.175s	9
	Jarno Trulli	I	7	Mild Seven Renault F1 Team	Renault R3-RS23 V10	M	0	Collision with Coulthard				
	Antonio Pizzonia	BR	15	Jaguar Racing	Jaguar R4-Cosworth CR5 V10	M	0	Stalled/accident				
	Kimi Räikkönen	FIN	6	West McLaren Mercedes	McLaren MP4/17D-Mercedes F0110M V10	M	0	Collision with Pizzonia				

Fastest lap: Rubens Barrichello, on lap 52, 1m 20.143s, 132.023 mph/212.470 km/h (record).

Previous lap record: Michael Schumacher (F1 Ferrari F2002 V10), 1m 20.355s, 131.672 mph/211.909 km/h (2002).

19th: JOS VERSTAPPEN Minardi-Cosworth

17th: GIANCARLO FISICHELLA Jordan-Ford Cosworth

15th: RALPH FIRMAN Jordan-Ford Cosworth

13th: CRISTIANO DA MATTA Toyota

11th: JACQUES VILLENEUVE BAR-Honda

20th: KIMI RÄIKKÖNEN McLaren-Mercedes

18th: JUSTIN WILSON Minardi-Cosworth

16th: ANTONIO PIZZONIA Jaguar-Cosworth

14th: NICK HEIDFELD Sauber-Petronas

12th: MARK WEBBER Jaguar-Cosworth

Grid order	1	2	3	4	5	6	7	8	9	10	11	12	13	14	15	16	17	18	19	20	21	22	23	24	25	26	27	28	29	30	31	32	33	34	35	36	37	38	39	40	41	42	43	44	45	46	47	48	49	50	5
1 M. SCHUMACHER	1	1	1	1	1	1	1	1	1	1	1	1	1	1	1	1	1	2	1	1	1	1	1	1	1	1	1	1	1	1	1	1	1	1	1	1	8	8	1	1	1	1	1	1	1	1	1	1	1	1	
2 BARRICHELLO	2	2	2	2	2	2	2	2	2	2	2	2	2	2	2	2	2	1	2	2	2	2	2	2	2	2	2	2	2	2	2	2	2	2	2	8	1	4	4	8	8	8	8	8	8	8	8	8	8	2	
8 ALONSO	8	8	8	8	8	8	8	8	8	8	8	8	8	8	8	4	4	3	8	2	2	2	2	2	2	2	2	2	2	2	2	2	2	2	2	4	4	8	8	2	2	2	2	2	2	2	2	2	2		1
7 TRULLI	4	4	4	4	4	4	4	4	4	4	4	4	4	4	4	8	3	8	4	4	4	4	4	4	4	4	4	4	4	4	4	4	4	4	1	3	3	2	2	4	3	21	21	21	21	21	21		3		
17 BUTTON	17	17	17	17	17	3	3	3	3	3	3	3	3	3	3	8	4	3	3	3	3	3	3	3	3	3	3	3	3	3	3	3	3	3	2	2	3	3	21	4	4	4	3	3	4	4					
20 PANIS	3	3	3	3	17	17	17	17	17	17	17	21	21	11	11	11	11	21	21	21	21	21	21	21	20	20	20	20	20	20	20	20	20	21	4	5	4	21	21	2											
4 R. SCHUMACHER	16	16	16	16	16	16	16	16	16	16	21	21	17	20	11	21	21	11	12	20	20	20	20	21	21	21	21	21	21	21	21	21	21	14	14	14	14	14	14	14	14	14	14	14	14	14	14	14	14	14	1
5 COULTHARD	21	21	21	9	21	21	21	21	21	21	18	20	20	21	21	14	14	12	12	12	20	12	10	10	10	10	10	14	14	14	14	14	14	14	14	14	14	12	17	12	12	12	12	12	12						
3 MONTOYA	18	18	18	21	18	18	18	18	18	18	11	18	18	11	14	5	17	10	10	10	20	10	10	12	9	9	9	14	14	9	9	10	10	10	10	12	12	12	17	9	9	9	9	9	9						
10 FRENTZEN	9	9	9	18	11	11	11	11	11	11	20	11	11	14	5	17	12	20	20	20	10	9	9	14	14	14	9	9	10	10	12	12	12	12	12	17	17	17	9	12	17	17	17	17	1						
16 VILLENEUVE	11	11	11	11	9	20	20	20	20	14	14	14	5	17	10	9	9	9	14	14	14	18	18	12	12	12	12	17	17	17	17	9	9	5	11	11	19	18	18	18	18	1									
14 WEBBER	12	19	19	19	20	20	20	14	14	14	5	17	18	10	9	14	14	14	18	18	18	17	17	17	9	9	9	10	11	19	19	19	19	1																	
21 DA MATTA	19	20	20	20	14	14	14	5	5	5	19	19	12	12	12	11	18	18	18	18	11	11	11	18	18	18	18	11	19	19	19	18	1																		
9 HEIDFELD	20	14	14	14	12	5	5	5	19	19	12	10	10	10	20	18	19	11	11	11	12	11	17	11	11	11	11	11	18	18	18																				
12 FIRMAN	10	12	12	12	10	12	12	12	12	12	10	10	9	9	18	19	17	17	17	17	17	17	19	19	19	19	19	19	19	19																					
15 PIZZONIA	5	10	10	10	5	10	10	10	10	9	9	19	19	19	19																																			
11 FISICHELLA	14	5	5	5	9	9	9	9	9	9	16																																								
18 WILSON																																																			
19 VERSTAPPEN																																																			
6 RÄIKKÖNEN																																																			

Pit stop
One lap behind leader

TIME SHEETS

SATURDAY QUALIFYING determines race grid order
Dry, hot and sunny (track 37/39°C, air 26/27°C)

Pos.	Driver	Lap time	Sector 1	Sector 2	Sector 3
1	Michael Schumacher	1m 17.762s	22.486s	30.983s	24.293s
2	Rubens Barrichello	1m 18.020s	22.455s	31.149s	24.416s
3	Fernando Alonso	1m 18.233s	22.788s	31.067s	24.378s
4	Jarno Trulli	1m 18.615s	22.956s	31.308s	24.351s
5	Jenson Button	1m 18.704s	22.818s	31.266s	24.620s
6	Olivier Panis	1m 18.811s	22.888s	31.108s	24.815s
7	Ralf Schumacher	1m 19.006s	23.097s	31.331s	24.578s
8	David Coulthard	1m 19.128s	23.154s	31.329s	24.645s
9	Juan Pablo Montoya	1m 19.377s	23.157s	31.523s	24.697s
10	Heinz-Harald Frentzen	1m 19.427s	23.107s	31.603s	24.717s
11	Jacques Villeneuve	1m 19.563s	23.299s	31.523s	24.741s
12	Mark Webber	1m 19.615s	23.324s	31.536s	24.755s
13	Cristiano da Matta	1m 19.623s	22.981s	31.561s	25.081s
14	Nick Heidfeld	1m 19.646s	23.127s	31.800s	24.719s
15	Ralph Firman	1m 20.215s	23.395s	31.724s	25.096s
16	Antonio Pizzonia	1m 20.308s	23.414s	31.903s	24.991s
17	Giancarlo Fisichella	1m 20.976s	23.708s	32.130s	25.138s
18	Justin Wilson	1m 22.104s	23.878s	32.681s	25.545s
19	Jos Verstappen	1m 22.237s	23.968s	32.759s	25.510s
20	Kimi Räikkönen	No time	–	–	–

FRIDAY QUALIFYING determines Sat running order
Dry, hot and sunny (track 34/36°C, air 26/27°C)

Pos.	Driver	Lap time
1	Michael Schumacher	1m 17.130s
2	Jarno Trulli	1m 17.149s
3	Rubens Barrichello	1m 17.218s
4	Cristiano da Matta	1m 17.443s
5	Jenson Button	1m 17.613s
6	Olivier Panis	1m 17.746s
7	Mark Webber	1m 17.793s
8	Kimi Räikkönen	1m 17.862s
9	David Coulthard	1m 18.060s
10	Fernando Alonso	1m 18.100s
11	Ralf Schumacher	1m 18.409s
12	Jacques Villeneuve	1m 18.461s
13	Antonio Pizzonia	1m 18.528s
14	Juan Pablo Montoya	1m 18.607s
15	Giancarlo Fisichella	1m 18.879s
16	Heinz-Harald Frentzen	1m 18.909s
17	Nick Heidfeld	1m 19.050s
18	Ralph Firman	1m 19.195s
19	Jos Verstappen	1m 20.822s
20	Justin Wilson	1m 21.100s

POINTS TABLES: CONSTRUCTORS

1	McLaren	51
2	Ferrari	48
3	Renault	34
4	Williams	32
5	Jordan	11
6	Sauber	8
7	BAR	6
8	Toyota	3
9	Jaguar	2

FOR THE RECORD

First grand prix point

Ralph Firman

Cristiano da Matta

PRIVATE TESTING
Dry and sunny (track 25/28°C, air 21/23°C)

Pos.	Driver	Laps	Time
1	Jarno Trulli	43	1m 17.706s
2	Giancarlo Fisichella	39	1m 17.991s
3	Fernando Alonso	37	1m 18.048s
4	Alan McNish	52	1m 18.625s
5	Antonio Pizzonia	44	1m 18.699s
6	Mark Webber	53	1m 18.731s
7	Ralph Firman	43	1m 18.761s
8	Justin Wilson	31	1m 21.036s
9	Jos Verstappen	29	1m 21.294s

FRIDAY FREE PRACTICE
Dry, hot and sunny (track 28/32°C, air 23/25°C)

Pos.	Driver	Laps	Time
1	Ralf Schumacher	17	1m 17.015s
2	Jarno Trulli	7	1m 17.138s
3	Fernando Alonso	11	1m 17.184s
4	David Coulthard	20	1m 17.209s
5	Olivier Panis	13	1m 17.220s
6	Juan Pablo Montoya	18	1m 17.897s
7	Mark Webber	17	1m 17.933s
8	Jenson Button	29	1m 17.966s
9	Cristiano da Matta	26	1m 18.101s
10	Rubens Barrichello	25	1m 18.303s
11	Antonio Pizzonia	18	1m 18.350s
12	Ralph Firman	18	1m 18.639s
13	Heinz-Harald Frentzen	16	1m 18.691s
14	Jacques Villeneuve	23	1m 18.731s
15	Michael Schumacher	24	1m 18.738s
16	Giancarlo Fisichella	18	1m 18.954s
17	Nick Heidfeld	19	1m 19.219s
18	Kimi Räikkönen	17	1m 19.337s
19	Justin Wilson	21	1m 20.264s
20	Jos Verstappen	12	1m 20.559s

SATURDAY FREE PRACTICE
Dry, hot and sunny (track 20/29°C, air 16/23°C)

Pos.	Driver	Laps	Time
1	Fernando Alonso	24	1m 17.670s
2	Rubens Barrichello	31	1m 18.214s
3	Jarno Trulli	29	1m 18.263s
4	Michael Schumacher	27	1m 18.623s
5	Olivier Panis	34	1m 18.985s
6	Kimi Räikkönen	26	1m 19.012s
7	David Coulthard	30	1m 19.150s
8	Jenson Button	31	1m 19.159s
9	Mark Webber	37	1m 19.172s
10	Antonio Pizzonia	38	1m 19.262s
11	Cristiano da Matta	44	1m 19.342s
12	Jacques Villeneuve	30	1m 19.525s
13	Heinz-Harald Frentzen	26	1m 19.729s
14	Giancarlo Fisichella	25	1m 19.773s
15	Juan Pablo Montoya	27	1m 19.819s
16	Ralf Schumacher	36	1m 19.846s
17	Ralph Firman	30	1m 20.298s
18	Nick Heidfeld	25	1m 20.349s
19	Jos Verstappen	20	1m 21.945s
20	Justin Wilson	27	1m 21.960s

WARM-UP
Dry, hot and sunny (track 34°C, air 25°C)

Pos.	Driver	Laps	Time
1	Rubens Barrichello	7	1m 18.872s
2	Fernando Alonso	4	1m 18.928s
3	Jenson Button	4	1m 19.245s
4	Michael Schumacher	4	1m 19.260s
5	Kimi Räikkönen	4	1m 19.419s
6	Ralf Schumacher	6	1m 19.439s
7	Olivier Panis	5	1m 19.792s
8	Juan Pablo Montoya	6	1m 19.958s
9	Jacques Villeneuve	6	1m 19.998s
10	Cristiano da Matta	5	1m 20.039s
11	Nick Heidfeld	6	1m 20.116s
12	David Coulthard	4	1m 20.127s
13	Mark Webber	4	1m 20.405s
14	Ralph Firman	6	1m 20.478s
15	Antonio Pizzonia	4	1m 20.836s
16	Jos Verstappen	3	1m 21.997s
17	Justin Wilson	6	1m 22.002s
18	Jarno Trulli		No time
19	Heinz-Harald Frentzen		No time
20	Giancarlo Fisichella		No time

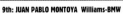
9th: JUAN PABLO MONTOYA Williams-BMW

7th: RALF SCHUMACHER Williams-BMW

5th: JENSON BUTTON BAR-Honda

3rd: FERNANDO ALONSO Renault

Pole: MICHAEL SCHUMACHER Ferrari

10th: HEINZ-HARALD FRENTZEN Sauber-Petronas

8th: DAVID COULTHARD McLaren-Mercedes

6th: OLIVIER PANIS Toyota

4th: JARNO TRULLI Renault

2nd: RUBENS BARRICHELLO Ferrari

52	53	54	55	56	57	58	59	60	61	62	63	64	65	•	
1	1	1	1	1	1	1	1	1	1	1	1	1	1		1
8	8	8	8	8	8	8	8	8	8	8	8	8	8		2
2	2	2	2	2	2	2	2	2	2	2	2	2	2		3
3	3	3	3	3	3	3	3	3	3	3	3	3	3		4
4	4	4	4	4	4	4	4	4	4	4	4	4	4		5
21	21	21	21	21	21	21	21	21	21	21	21	21	21		6
14	14	14	14	14	14	14	14	14	14	14	14	14	14		7
12	12	12	12	12	12	12	12	12	12	12	12				8
9	17	17	17	17	17	17	17	17	17	17	17				
17	9	9	9	9	9	9	9	9	9	9	9				
18	18	18	18	18	18	18	18	18	18	18	18				
19	19	19	19	19	19	19	19	19	19	19					

CHASSIS LOG BOOK

1	Michael Schumacher	F2003-GA/229
2	Rubens Barrichello	F2003-GA/227
	Spare	F2003-GA/228
3	Juan Pablo Montoya	FW25/06
4	Ralf Schumacher	FW25/05
	Spare	FW25/04
5	David Coulthard	MP4/17D-09
6	Kimi Räikkönen	MP4/17D-06
	Spare	MP4/17D-07
7	Jarno Trulli	R23/03
8	Fernando Alonso	R23/04
	Allan McNish	R23/01
	Spare	R23/01
9	Nick Heidfeld	C22/03
10	Heinz-Harald Frentzen	C22/04
	Spare	C22/02
11	Giancarlo Fisichella	EJ-13/04
12	Ralph Firman	EJ-13/03
	Spare	EJ-13/02
14	Mark Webber	R4/04
15	Antonio Pizzonia	R4/03
	Spare	R4/02
16	Jacques Villeneuve	BAR005/2
17	Jenson Button	BAR005/4
	Spare	BAR005/3
18	Justin Wilson	PS03/03
19	Jos Verstappen	PS03/04
	Spare	PS03/02
20	Olivier Panis	TF103/05
21	Cristiano da Matta	TF103/02
	Spare	TF103/01

POINTS TABLES: DRIVERS

1	Kimi Räikkönen	32
2	Michael Schumacher	28
3	Fernando Alonso	25
4	Rubens Barrichello	20
5	David Coulthard	19
6	Ralf Schumacher	17
7	Juan Pablo Montoya	15
8	Giancarlo Fisichella	10
9	Jarno Trulli	9
10	Heinz-Harald Frentzen	7
11 =	Jacques Villeneuve	3
11 =	Cristiano da Matta	3
11 =	Jenson Button	3
14	Mark Webber	2
15 =	Nick Heidfeld	1
15 =	Ralph Firman	1

FIA F1 WORLD CHAMPIONSHIP • ROUND 6

AUSTRIANGP
A1-RING

...chael Schumacher locked the rear wheels of his Ferrari and was 0.2s down on Räikkönen at the first timing ...lit during his Saturday qualifying run, and it seemed ...te pole position, on this occasion at least, was lost to ...e world champion.

...et in what must have been one of the greatest laps in ...e Ferrari ace's distinguished career, Michael clawed ...ck the time to post his 54th career pole position at ...at might have been the last ever GP to be staged at ...e spectacular circuit in the Styrian mountains.

The world champion's 1m 09.150s best just edged ...ikkönen out by 0.039s at the end of the day. 'At the ...cond corner, I had a little wobble, but I did not lose ...o much time because I was able to catch it before the ...ex,' said Schumacher. 'After that, I had a good run. ...e did a great job finding the right handling balance ...om the start of the weekend.'

...By contrast, Michael's team-mate, Rubens Barrichello, ...uld only manage 1m 9.784s for fifth fastest, which left ...n a little frustrated. 'I must admit that I did not expect ... be as far back as fifth on the grid,' he said. 'On my lap, ...e track was not perfectly clean, but I went down a dif-...rent route to my team-mate in terms of the car [set-up] ...d I hope it will pay off in the race.'

...Räikkönen was well satisfied with his place on the ...ont row, but David Coulthard made an error again on ...s single qualifying lap, running wide over the kerb on ...e final corner. Admittedly, he was carrying more fuel ...an Kimi, but ending up 14th on 1m 10.893s was a ...ge disappointment, not to mention handicap, for his ...ce prospects.

'I have been struggling with the balance throughout ...e weekend and didn't have the confidence to attack,' ...id the Scot. 'I ran wide in the last corner, which cost ...e some time, but to be honest, I don't think the lap ...uld have been that good anyway.'

...n the Williams camp, the whole weekend's pro-...amme was being played out against the backdrop of ...e constantly tense negotiations with BMW over the ...estion of extending the technical partnership with the ...itish team. Juan Pablo Montoya did a good job qualify-...g third on 1m 9.391s, but Ralf Schumacher spun into ...e gravel on his Friday qualifying run and wound up ...nth on Saturday with a 1m 10.279s.

'After I had spun off during first qualifying, I had to ...pe with the disadvantage of being first on the track and, of course, there is less grip at the start of the session,' he said. 'When it came to it, I also lost some tenths in the first corner, so it wasn't a good lap and, as a consequence, maybe I should not be too disappointed with my grid position.'

Sauber's Nick Heidfeld was extremely satisfied with his fourth-fastest 1m 9.725s best on a light fuel load, a time achieved after switching to the spare C22 following the pre-qualifying warm-up. His team-mate, Heinz-Harald Frentzen, adopted a more conservative approach — that's to say running with more fuel — and he wound up 15th (1m 11.307s) as a result.

Jarno Trulli was comfortably the quickest Renault R23 driver on 1m 9.890s in sixth place after Fernando Alonso had pushed too hard and spun off on his qualifying run, ending up 19th on 1m 20.113s. He was just ahead of Jos Verstappen in the Minardi, who had spun off, but had not managed to recover and complete the lap as the young Spanish driver had done.

Of the BAR-Honda duo, Jenson Button wound up seventh on 1m 9.935s, five places ahead of Jacques Villeneuve (1m 10.618s). Both men ran pretty comparable fuel loads, but while Button had experienced a touch too much oversteer, Villeneuve admitted that he had pushed too hard.

'The car felt amazing on old tyres this morning, but we couldn't get the best out of new tyres this afternoon,' explained the Canadian. 'I tried to compensate, but I drove too aggressively and made a big mistake in turn one, which basically cost me the lap. A lot of people were driving too hard today and I was one of them.'

Antonio Pizzonia had a good run with the Jaguar R4 (1m 10.045s), his eighth place on the grid putting him at the head of the Cosworth brigade, fractionally in front of Giancarlo Fisichella's Jordan (1m 10.105s). Unfortunately, Mark Webber had followed Villeneuve out on his run and lost grip on those corners where Jacques had left dust and debris in his wake.

Both Toyota TF103s were struggling for balance at this circuit, so under the circumstances Olivier Panis judged his 1m 10.402s effort for 11th spot on the grid not too bad. He was just two places ahead of team-mate Cristiano da Matta.

For his part, Ralph Firman suffered from slightly too much understeer with his Jordan and could only manage 1m 11.505s for 16th fastest, two places ahead of Justin Wilson in the Minardi PS03.

DIARY

...ercedes denies speculation that Ilmor co-founder ...ario Illien is preparing to leave the team to join ...enault.

...rnie Ecclestone says that F1 teams may be ...rced to accept more than 17 races on the ...alendar if they are to avoid losing some of the ...assic European events. He made those comments ...s it seemed very likely that the A1-Ring fixture ...ould be dropped in 2004.

...auber test driver Neel Jari has his first outing in a ...am car at the Spanish Valencia circuit.

...ary Paffett poised to sign deal to drive in the DTM ...r Mercedes.

...oyota tables bid to lure Mike Gascoyne from his ...osition as Renault F1 technical director.

Right: Nick Heidfeld raised Sauber's profile with a

SIX races, three wins. That was ... record after taking the che... end of an impressive perform... GA. It was the second straight win f... dominated its debut outing at the S...

Michael achieved his 67th career ... Kimi Räikkönen's McLaren-Merced... managing to fend off Rubens Barr... quered flag to take second place and ... by two points.

Michael won with a two-stop strat... catching fire during its first visit to t... quick squirt with the fire extinguish... which was emanating from a sea... Michael accelerated straight back in...

'Seeing fire is not nice, but the g... their fire extinguishers and I manage... wasn't tempted to jump out of the ... what might have been damaged, but ...

Barrichello, who qualified fifth or ... stone tyre compounds, had been ex... race, but lost over 10s during his fi... ning third on lap 21. Without that ... gested that his pre-race content... strategy seemed to have been just... was the one whose remarkable goo... straight day.

Even before the start, the event ... chaos. Cristiano da Matta stalled hi... was aborted and the Brazilian drive... grid for the restart, at which point h...

'For the [second] restart and the pit stops, we decided not to risk it and did manual starts.'

Fernando Alonso had opted to start from the pit lane in his spare Renault R23 after his qualifying woes, while Mark Webber fell foul of an unfortunate interpretation of the regulations when he was handed a 10s stop-go penalty for refuelling in the pit lane before the start. 'We fuelled the car for a long first stint, but because the race didn't officially start until the third attempt, our fuel top-up was declared illegal and consequently we were given the penalty,' said Mark Gillan, the team's head of vehicle performance.

Unruffled by the repeated delays, Michael Schumacher accelerated neatly into the lead, with Juan Pablo Montoya slotting in ahead of Kimi Räikkönen. Farther back, Jos Verstappen's Minardi PS03 rolled to a standstill on the approach to the first corner with an apparent launch-control failure, resulting in the safety car being deployed immediately so that the abandoned car could be removed from its dangerous position.

Olivier Panis took advantage of the safety car to refuel at the end of the second lap, and Justin Wilson followed his example next time around. Both competitors rejoined at the tail of the field in time for the race proper to start when the safety car was withdrawn at the end of lap four.

One lap later, Schumacher's Ferrari was already 1.4s ahead of Montoya, whose Williams had been showing signs of overheating from the start due to a malfunction of a pressure valve in the FW25's cooling system. By lap seven, Michael was 2.8s ahead of the Colombian, with Räikkönen another 1.5s back in third place,

With 12 laps completed, Schumacher's Ferrari was 6.7s ahead of Montoya, while Räikkönen was coming under increasing pressure from Barrichello. Nick Heidfeld was leading the rest of the pack from Antonio Pizzonia's Jaguar, Jarno Trulli's Renault and Jenson Button's BAR-Honda.

Pizzonia made his first refuelling stop in 12.1s on lap 14, followed by Ralph Firman in 10.6s. A couple of laps later, Michael

Schumacher ran wide at the first corner when a light rain shower began to douse sections of the circuit. Suddenly Michael's lead slipped from 7.1s to 3s. He eased it back to 3.4s over Montoya on lap 19 and the pressure was relaxed slightly when the Williams driver headed for the pits to refuel on lap 20, dropping from second to sixth place.

On lap 21, Barrichello came in, several laps earlier than planned, in a bid to leap-frog ahead of Räikkönen's McLaren, but as he entered the pit lane, problems were already brewing. His fuel rig could not be made to function, so the team switched to Michael's rig – primed with sufficient fuel for a long second stint – which meant that Rubens went back into the race with a heavier car than was ideal after being stationary for 19.8s.

Then, on lap 23, Michael Schumacher came in, and the team was forced to use the faulty refuelling rig, which caused the flash fire. As a consequence, he would have to press hard through a shorter-than-expected middle stint to make up the time lost in the incident. In fact, it was remarkable that the Ferrari was only stationary for 20.4s and he went back into the race in third place, close behind Räikkönen who, in turn, was just over 3s adrift of Montoya's leading Williams.

In the Ferrari garage, the mechanics were faced with the urgent task of disassembling the refuelling nozzle on the troublesome rig, examining it in detail and then reassembling it carefully, all against the deadline of Michael's impending second refuelling stop. As it transpired, they completed the job perfectly and in plenty of time.

By lap 30, Montoya had eased open his lead to 4.1s, but on lap 32 his BMW engine expired coming out of the uphill right-hand Remuskurve. In reality, it was almost certain that the V10 had been doomed from the start due to a problem with the water-pressure control valve.

'This was not working correctly,' said BMW Motorsport director Mario Theissen. 'We knew it was not going to last, as we saw a big

Above: Rubens Barrichello added to Ferrari's joy with a podium finish.
Photograph: Darren Heath

FERRARI SANGUINE OVER REFUELLING DRAMA

The Ferrari team was surprisingly relaxed about the drama that resulted in Michael Schumacher's car being enveloped in flame during its first refuelling stop. Technical director Ross Brawn insisted that this minor glitch certainly did not form the basis for any proposed prohibition of the technique that has been legal since the start of 1994.

'I don't think it's a clear-cut argument [one way or the other] and I don't think what we saw today is necessarily a crucial event in the decision as to whether we carry on with refuelling or not,' said Brawn. 'Almost more disappointing for us was the fact that the fuel rig didn't work at all for Rubens and almost certainly lost him second place. We had a lot of trouble today and we need to sit down with Intertechnique [the French supplier of the rigs] and the FIA, and go through everything to find how we can solve these problems.'

Brawn added that he had not been concerned that the extinguishant could have damaged the car. 'The foam and the compounds used now are not as aggressive as before,' he said. 'One of the extinguishers went virtually straight on the engine and that almost caused it to stop, just because there was no oxygen getting to it. Michael thought we were suffering an engine failure, because as he drove down the pit lane there was no power after the extinguisher had gone into the engine.'

However, McLaren chairman Ron Dennis suggested that the rig malfunction experienced by Ferrari reflected the lack of zeal displayed by Intertechnique when it came to resolving problems with their products.

'They are, to be honest, appalling,' he said. 'Most of the efforts to optimise the equipment have been made by the teams and the FIA.'

increase in [water] pressure, but as Juan was leading, we didn't want to retire him.'

For Michael Schumacher, Montoya's retirement provided a double bonus. Not only was he able to make up a point at the Colombian's expense, but also he vaulted ahead of Räikkönen to take the lead after Kimi was momentarily wrong-footed by the slowing Williams. Michael just drove around the outside of the McLaren, then pulled steadily away into the distance.

'That was a tricky little moment,' explained Schumacher. 'Not extremely tricky because there was a sort of gap and I was already by [alongside] Kimi at this stage, but the point was I didn't know what Juan Pablo was going to do, whether he would stay off line or he was going to suddenly pull over and think he was still racing, so it was a little bit concerning.

'But in the end, he stayed off line and he did a proper job.' Then he added an ironic barb: 'He could probably have stopped a little bit earlier instead of continuing around for the rest of the lap with an oily engine, but I guess he was lazy and didn't want to walk back to the pits.'

On lap 35, Barrichello overtook Button for third place, and two laps later Alonso, who had climbed to fifth place thanks to a near-full tank at the start, finally came in for fuel and dropped back to eighth. Unfortunately, the Spaniard would not have much longer in the chase, eventually retiring after 44 laps with a rare Renault engine failure.

'I started the race from the pits with the T-car and made good progress,' said Alonso. 'The one-stop strategy was correct, but it

was disappointing that I failed to make it to the finish, as this is the first time I haven't finished a race all season. Hopefully, it will also be the last!'

Michael Schumacher took the Ferrari in for a second 12.6s stop on lap 42, dropping to third place, behind Räikkönen and Barrichello, who were separated by 13.9s. Alonso's engine failure had made the first uphill right-hander after the pits particularly slippery, and several cars ran wide over the next few laps.

On lap 49, Räikkönen made his second pit stop, followed by Barrichello a lap later, thereby restoring the status quo at the head of the pack, with Michael leading by 8.3s. Now only mechanical failure could deprive him of his 67th grand prix victory and he duly reeled off the laps to complete the job in characteristically confident style, allowing his advantage to dwindle to 3.362s at the chequered flag. With Barrichello only 0.58s behind Räikkönen in third place, the final sprint to the line looked much closer from the touchlines than it was in reality.

Räikkönen was moderately satisfied. 'The car was quite good,'he said, 'and it was good to finish second, but I'm still a little disappointed not to have won the race. When it started to rain, I think the Michelins worked a little bit better than the Bridgestones under those conditions and we were able to go a little bit quicker, but it was not enough.'

Barrichello, who had struggled with a cold and fever for much of the weekend, clearly regarded the outcome of his personal race as something of a missed opportunity. 'I didn't actually feel good for the whole weekend because I have a little bit of a cold,' he said. 'It was hard to push because I was sweating quite a lot in the car, but, having said that, it was a great race. It was a pity about the pit stop because it's frustrating when you feel that you could have won the race or you could have done better and you lose time, but things like that happen and I still finished on the podium. The car felt good the whole time. I had probably the most consistent of the quick times, so I was quite pleased.'

Jenson Button enjoyed a strong run to fourth place in the BAR-Honda, which made up for some of the disappointments in earlier races of the season.

'I had a great race today, I really enjoyed it,' said Button. 'I matched my best ever race finish today, so it's great to be back up there getting the point today. This is just what the team needed and deserved, but it wasn't a fluke. We really earned our result today.'

David Coulthard, who had made a couple of mistakes in qualifying, buckled down to a good solid run from 14th place on the starting grid to fifth at the finish.

'Sixth place was the best I was expecting on the basis of our pre-race simulation,' he said, 'so it was a bit of a bonus to gain another place, but not enough points to go with it. I didn't change my front tyres at the second pit stop because the car felt better on worn rubber and I didn't want to lose time during that period of "graining" [low grip] which we often experience on new tyres.'

Webber came home seventh, ahead of Trulli, while Pizzonia just missed out on his first championship point, finishing ninth and less than a second behind the sole surviving Renault. Da Matta survived to tenth, ahead of Firman and a highly frustrated Jacques Villeneuve, who was bedevilled by an almost complete failure of the car's electronic control systems.

'I had no limiter button, no idea of which gear I was in, no neutral, nothing,' he shrugged. 'My race engineer was even counting my speed down for me coming into the pits. We had decided not to change the steering wheel at the first stop because it can mess up the electronics, but after the car stalled, we changed it and had to wait for the system to reset. It was a fairly disastrous stop and I lost a lot of time.'

Six years had passed since Villeneuve had won the Austrian Grand Prix on the way to gaining his world championship title for the Williams team. He'd switched to BAR two years later, suffused with optimism and high hopes. As he was lapped by Michael Schumacher, on this occasion Jacques could have been forgiven for wondering where it had all gone wrong.

Above: Jenson Button's fourth place for BAR Honda equalled his career-best results.

Above left: Cristiano da Matta on the grid before the start. The Brazilian was to endure electronic glitches, which would cause two restarts.

Left: Kimi Räikkönen kept his championship hopes on track by splitting the Ferraris.
Photographs: Darren Heath

Far left: Refuelling-rig problems beset Ferrari, but the team handled these setbacks with characteristic composure.
Photograph: Patrick Gosling

FIA F1 WORLD CHAMPIONSHIP • ROUND 6

A1 GRAND PRIX VON ÖSTERREICH

A1-RING 16–18 MAY 2003

Photograph: Darren Heath

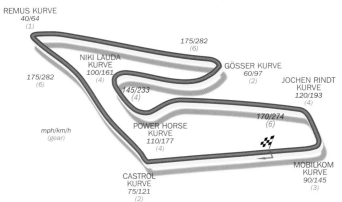

ZELTWEG – A1-RING
CIRCUIT LENGTH: 2.688 miles/4.326 km

REMUS KURVE 40/64 (1)

NIKI LAUDA KURVE 100/161 (4)

175/282 (6)

GÖSSER KURVE 60/97 (2)

JOCHEN RINDT KURVE 120/193 (4)

175/282 (6)

145/233 (4)

170/274 (6)

mph/km/h (gear)

POWER HORSE KURVE 110/177 (4)

CASTROL KURVE 75/121 (2)

MOBILKOM KURVE 90/145 (3)

RACE DISTANCE: 69 laps, 185.475 miles/298.494 km RACE WEATHER: Dry, occasional light showers (track 20/36°C, air 19/22°C)

Pos.	Driver	Nat.	No.	Entrant	Car/Engine	Tyres	Laps	Time/Retirement	Speed (mph/km/h)	Gap to leader	Fastest race lap	
1	Michael Schumacher	D	1	Scuderia Ferrari Marlboro	Ferrari F2003-GA-051 V10	B	69	1h 24m 04.888s	132.354/213.003		1m 08.337s	41
2	Kimi Räikkönen	FIN	6	West McLaren Mercedes	McLaren MP4/17D-Mercedes F0110M V10	M	69	1h 24m 08.250s	132.265/212.861	+3.362s	1m 08.423s	45
3	Rubens Barrichello	BR	2	Scuderia Ferrari Marlboro	Ferrari F2003-GA-051 V10	B	69	1h 24m 08.839s	132.250/212.836	+3.951s	1m 08.913s	44
4	Jenson Button	GB	17	Lucky Strike BAR Honda	BAR 005-Honda RA003E V10	B	69	1h 24m 47.131s	131.255/211.234	+42.243s	1m 09.828s	22
5	David Coulthard	GB	5	West McLaren Mercedes	McLaren MP4/17D-Mercedes F0110M V10	M	69	1h 25m 04.628s	130.805/210.510	+59.740s	1m 09.626s	64
6	Ralf Schumacher	D	4	BMW WilliamsF1 Team	Williams FW25-BMW P83 V10	M	68			+1 lap	1m 10.246s	40
7	Mark Webber	AUS	14	Jaguar Racing	Jaguar R4-Cosworth CR5 V10	M	68			+1 lap	1m 08.966s	68
8	Jarno Trulli	I	7	Mild Seven Renault F1 Team	Renault R3-RS23 V10	M	68			+1 lap	1m 10.358s	68
9	Antonio Pizzonia	BR	15	Jaguar Racing	Jaguar R4-Cosworth CR5 V10	M	68			+1 lap	1m 09.978s	67
10	Cristiano da Matta	BR	21	Panasonic Toyota Racing	Toyota TF103-RVX-03 V10	M	68			+1 lap	1m 10.466s	67
11	Ralph Firman	IRL	12	Jordan Ford	Jordan EJ-13-Ford Cosworth RS1 V10	B	68			+1 lap	1m 10.659s	68
12	Jacques Villeneuve	CDN	16	Lucky Strike BAR Honda	BAR 005-Honda RA003E V10	B	68			+1 lap	1m 09.764s	64
13	Justin Wilson	GB	18	European Minardi Cosworth	Minardi PS03-Cosworth CR3 V10	B	67			+2 laps	1m 11.267s	67
	Giancarlo Fisichella	I	11	Jordan Ford	Jordan EJ-13-Ford Cosworth RS1 V10	B	60	Fuel system			1m 11.019s	60
	Nick Heidfeld	D	9	Sauber Petronas	Sauber C22-Petronas 03A V10	B	46	Engine			1m 10.516s	12
	Fernando Alonso	E	8	Mild Seven Renault F1 Team	Renault R3-RS23 V10	M	44	Engine			1m 10.526s	34
	Juan Pablo Montoya	COL	3	BMW WilliamsF1 Team	Williams FW25-BMW P83 V10	M	32	Engine/water pressure			1m 10.112s	28
	Olivier Panis	F	20	Panasonic Toyota Racing	Toyota TF103-RVX-03 V10	M	6	Hit debris/suspension			1m 13.097s	6
	Jos Verstappen	NL	19	European Minardi Cosworth	Minardi PS03-Cosworth CR3 V10	B	0	Launch control				
DNS	Heinz-Harald Frentzen	D	10	Sauber Petronas	Sauber C22-Petronas 03A V10	B	0	Clutch				

Fastest lap: Michael Schumacher, on lap 41, 1m 08.337s, 141.607 mph/227.894 km/h (record).

Previous lap record: Michael Schumacher (F1 Ferrari F2002 V10), 1m 09.298s, 139.642 mph/224.733 km/h (2002).

19th: FERNANDO ALONSO Renault
started from pit lane

17th: MARK WEBBER Jaguar-Cosworth
started from pit lane

15th: HEINZ-HARALD FRENTZEN Sauber-Petronas
did not start

13th: CRISTIANO DA MATTA Toyota
started from back of grid

11th: OLIVIER PANIS Toyota

20th: JOS VERSTAPPEN Minardi-Cosworth

18th: JUSTIN WILSON Minardi-Cosworth

16th: RALPH FIRMAN Jordan-Ford Cosworth

14th: DAVID COULTHARD McLaren-Mercedes

12th: JACQUES VILLENEUVE BAR-Honda

Grid order	1	2	3	4	5	6	7	8	9	10	11	12	13	14	15	16	17	18	19	20	21	22	23	24	25	26	27	28	29	30	31	32	33	34	35	36	37	38	39	40	41	42	43	44	45	46	47	48	49	50	51	52	53	5
1 M. SCHUMACHER	1	1	1	1	1	1	1	1	1	1	1	1	1	1	1	1	1	1	1	1	1	1	1	3	3	3	3	3	3	3	3	1	1	1	1	1	1	1	1	1	1	1	6	6	6	6	6	6	6	2	1	1	1	
6 RÄIKKÖNEN	3	3	3	3	3	3	3	3	3	3	3	3	3	3	3	3	3	3	3	6	6	6	6	6	6	6	6	6	6	6	6	6	6	6	6	6	6	6	6	6	2	2	2	2	2	2	2	2	1	6	6	6		
3 MONTOYA	6	6	6	6	6	6	6	6	6	6	6	6	6	6	6	6	6	6	6	2	17	17	1	1	1	1	1	1	17	17	17	2	2	2	2	2	2	2	2	1	1	1	1	1	6									
9 HEIDFELD	2	2	2	2	2	2	2	2	2	2	2	2	2	2	2	2	2	2	2	17	3	3	17	17	17	17	17	17	2	2	17	17	17	17	17	17	17	17	17	17	17	16	5	5	17	17	17							
2 BARRICHELLO	9	9	9	9	9	9	9	9	9	9	9	9	9	7	7	17	17	17	17	16	16	2	2	2	2	2	2	2	8	8	8	8	4	4	4	4	16	16	16	16	5	16	4	4	4									
7 TRULLI	15	15	15	15	15	15	15	15	15	15	15	15	17	17	16	16	16	16	3	2	8	8	8	8	8	4	4	4	8	16	16	16	16	5	5	5	17	17	4	5	5	5												
17 BUTTON	7	7	7	7	7	7	7	7	7	7	7	7	4	4	5	5	5	5	5	4	4	4	4	4	4	3	16	16	16	16	5	5	5	5	4	4	4	4	14	14	14	14												
15 PIZZONIA	17	17	17	17	17	17	17	17	17	17	17	15	16	5	21	21	8	8	4	9	9	9	9	9	9	5	5	5	8	8	15	15	15	14	14	7	7																	
11 FISICHELLA	4	4	4	4	4	4	4	4	4	4	4	11	11	21	7	8	4	4	9	18	11	11	11	11	11	11	16	11	11	11	11	11	11	15	14	14	7	7	15	15	15	15												
4 R. SCHUMACHER	11	11	11	11	11	11	11	11	11	11	11	16	5	8	8	4	9	18	18	11	16	16	16	16	16	5	11	11	11	9	12	12	15	15	7	7	15	15	11	11	11													
20 PANIS	16	16	16	16	16	16	16	16	16	16	5	21	4	4	4	9	18	11	16	5	5	5	5	5	11	12	12	12	12	12	14	14	7	11	11	11	21	21	21	21														
16 VILLENEUVE	5	5	18	5	12	12	12	12	12	12	12	8	9	9	18	18	11	16	5	14	14	14	14	14	12	12	7	7	7	15	15	14	14	7	21	21	12	12	12	12														
5 COULTHARD	20	20	5	12	5	5	5	5	5	5	21	14	18	11	11	12	7	7	7	7	7	12	7	21	21	14	9	7	21	21	12	12	12	16	16	16																		
10 FRENTZEN	12	12	12	21	18	21	21	21	21	21	18	4	7	18	18	11	14	14	12	7	7	7	7	7	15	21	21	12	14	14	7	21	12	12	18	9	18	18	18	18														
12 FIRMAN	18	18	21	8	8	8	8	8	8	8	8	18	14	14	14	14	7	7	7	7	7	15	15	15	15	15	21	14	14	14	21	21	18	18	9	18																		
18 WILSON	21	21	8	14	14	14	14	14	14	14	14	9	8	15	15	15	15	15	21	21	21	21	21	14	14	18	18	18	18	18	18	18	9	9	9																			
19 VERSTAPPEN	8	8	14	20	20	20	18	18	18	18	18	12	14	12	15	21	21	21	21	21	18	18	18	18	18	18																												
21 DA MATTA	14	14	20	18	18	18																																																	
14 WEBBER																																																						
8 ALONSO																																																						

Pit stop
One lap behind leader

TIME SHEETS

SATURDAY QUALIFYING determines race grid order
Dry, warm and sunny (track 30/33°C, air 19/20°C)

Pos.	Driver	Lap time	Sector 1	Sector 2	Sector 3
1	Michael Schumacher	1m 09.150s	17.238s	29.518s	22.394s
2	Kimi Räikkönen	1m 09.189s	17.079s	29.629s	22.481s
3	Juan Pablo Montoya	1m 09.391s	17.221s	29.676s	22.494s
4	Nick Heidfeld	1m 09.725s	17.307s	29.604s	22.814s
5	Rubens Barrichello	1m 09.784s	17.352s	29.585s	22.847s
6	Jarno Trulli	1m 09.890s	17.491s	29.657s	22.742s
7	Jenson Button	1m 09.935s	17.208s	29.664s	23.063s
8	Antonio Pizzonia	1m 10.045s	17.451s	29.856s	22.738s
9	Giancarlo Fisichella	1m 10.105s	17.303s	29.704s	23.098s
10	Ralf Schumacher	1m 10.279s	17.597s	30.038s	22.644s
11	Olivier Panis	1m 10.402s	17.352s	30.207s	22.843s
12	Jacques Villeneuve	1m 10.618s	17.788s	29.807s	23.023s
13	Cristiano da Matta	1m 10.834s	17.515s	30.381s	22.938s
14	David Coulthard	1m 10.893s	17.284s	30.036s	23.573s
15	Heinz-Harald Frentzen	1m 11.307s	17.517s	30.464s	23.326s
16	Ralph Firman	1m 11.505s	17.348s	30.367s	23.646s
17	Mark Webber	1m 11.662s	18.411s	30.365s	22.886s
18	Justin Wilson	1m 14.508s	17.799s	31.076s	24.662s
19	Fernando Alonso	1m 20.113s	–	–	–
20	Jos Verstappen	No time	–	–	–

FRIDAY QUALIFYING determines Sat running order
Dry, cool and cloudy (track 28/31°C, air 17/18°C)

Pos.	Driver	Lap time
1	Michael Schumacher	1m 07.908s
2	Rubens Barrichello	1m 08.187s
3	Mark Webber	1m 08.512s
4	Jacques Villeneuve	1m 08.680s
5	Jenson Button	1m 08.831s
6	Juan Pablo Montoya	1m 08.839s
7	David Coulthard	1m 08.947s
8	Kimi Räikkönen	1m 08.978s
9	Antonio Pizzonia	1m 09.024s
10	Giancarlo Fisichella	1m 09.281s
11	Jarno Trulli	1m 09.450s
12	Nick Heidfeld	1m 09.479s
13	Fernando Alonso	1m 09.680s
14	Olivier Panis	1m 09.764s
15	Heinz-Harald Frentzen	1m 10.055s
16	Cristiano da Matta	1m 10.370s
17	Jos Verstappen	1m 10.894s
18	Justin Wilson	1m 11.056s
19	Ralph Firman	1m 11.171s
20	Ralf Schumacher	No time

FOR THE RECORD
100 laps led
Kimi Räikkönen

POINTS TABLES: CONSTRUCTORS
1	Ferrari	64
2	McLaren	63
3 =	Renault	35
3 =	Williams	35
5 =	Jordan	11
5 =	BAR	11
7	Sauber	8
8	Jaguar	4
9	Toyota	3

PRIVATE TESTING
Warm and dry (track 25/31°C, air: 15/20°C)

Pos.	Driver	Laps	Time
1	Giancarlo Fisichella	37	1m 09.781s
2	Antonio Pizzonia	50	1m 09.907s
3	Mark Webber	39	1m 10.036s
4	Jarno Trulli	49	1m 10.338s
5	Fernando Alonso	64	1m 10.380s
6	Alan McNish	59	1m 10.395s
7	Ralph Firman	35	1m 10.763s
8	Justin Wilson	31	1m 11.280s
9	Jos Verstappen	36	1m 11.717s

FRIDAY FREE PRACTICE
Cool and sunny (track 25/31°C, air 15/20°C)

Pos.	Driver	Laps	Time
1	David Coulthard	22	1m 08.836s
2	Jarno Trulli	28	1m 08.944s
3	Antonio Pizzonia	17	1m 08.961s
4	Michael Schumacher	33	1m 08.968s
5	Mark Webber	26	1m 09.023s
6	Fernando Alonso	25	1m 09.071s
7	Jenson Button	28	1m 09.374s
8	Nick Heidfeld	26	1m 09.374s
9	Jacques Villeneuve	23	1m 09.429s
10	Juan Pablo Montoya	28	1m 09.530s
11	Heinz-Harald Frentzen	26	1m 09.800s
12	Rubens Barrichello	31	1m 09.826s
13	Ralf Schumacher	24	1m 09.961s
14	Kimi Räikkönen	28	1m 10.019s
15	Giancarlo Fisichella	20	1m 10.089s
16	Ralph Firman	24	1m 10.296s
17	Cristiano da Matta	28	1m 10.494s
18	Olivier Panis	21	1m 10.504s
19	Jos Verstappen	14	1m 10.903s
20	Justin Wilson	16	1m 11.060s

SATURDAY FREE PRACTICE
Dry, warm and sunny (track 26/29°C, air 17°C)

Pos.	Driver	Laps	Time
1	Rubens Barrichello	45	1m 09.241s
2	Juan Pablo Montoya	37	1m 09.301s
3	Michael Schumacher	36	1m 09.331s
4	Ralf Schumacher	41	1m 09.418s
5	Jarno Trulli	52	1m 09.704s
6	Jacques Villeneuve	47	1m 09.708s
7	Kimi Räikkönen	34	1m 09.870s
8	Mark Webber	43	1m 09.891s
9	Fernando Alonso	46	1m 09.923s
10	Giancarlo Fisichella	28	1m 10.018s
11	Nick Heidfeld	40	1m 10.044s
12	Antonio Pizzonia	38	1m 10.057s
13	Olivier Panis	39	1m 10.076s
14	Jenson Button	34	1m 10.212s
15	David Coulthard	38	1m 10.222s
16	Cristiano da Matta	39	1m 10.370s
17	Heinz-Harald Frentzen	40	1m 10.456s
18	Ralph Firman	36	1m 11.413s
19	Jos Verstappen	22	1m 11.546s
20	Justin Wilson	31	1m 11.936s

WARM-UP
Dry, warm and sunny (track 27/30°C, air 18°C)

Pos.	Driver	Laps	Time
1	Juan Pablo Montoya	5	1m 09.323s
2	Kimi Räikkönen	4	1m 09.628s
3	Michael Schumacher	8	1m 09.639s
4	Jarno Trulli	5	1m 09.973s
5	Fernando Alonso	5	1m 10.108s
6	Mark Webber	5	1m 10.153s
7	David Coulthard	5	1m 10.184s
8	Antonio Pizzonia	5	1m 10.202s
9	Jenson Button	7	1m 10.243s
10	Nick Heidfeld	8	1m 10.413s
11	Giancarlo Fisichella	5	1m 10.552s
12	Jacques Villeneuve	7	1m 10.702s
13	Rubens Barrichello	6	1m 10.852s
14	Heinz-Harald Frentzen	5	1m 10.961s
15	Cristiano da Matta	8	1m 10.988s
16	Olivier Panis	8	1m 11.243s
17	Ralph Firman	4	1m 12.045s
18	Jos Verstappen	8	1m 12.230s
19	Ralf Schumacher	3	1m 12.560s
20	Justin Wilson	4	1m 12.817s

9th: GIANCARLO FISICHELLA Jordan-Ford Cosworth

7th: JENSON BUTTON BAR-Honda

5th: RUBENS BARRICHELLO Ferrari

3rd: JUAN PABLO MONTOYA Williams-BMW

Pole: MICHAEL SCHUMACHER Ferrari

10th: RALF SCHUMACHER Williams-BMW

8th: ANTONIO PIZZONIA Jaguar-Cosworth

6th: JARNO TRULLI Renault

4th: NICK HEIDFELD Sauber-Petronas

2nd: KIMI RÄIKKÖNEN McLaren-Mercedes

Lap chart (laps 55–69)

55	56	57	58	59	60	61	62	63	64	65	66	67	68	69	
1	1	1	1	1	1	1	1	1	1	1	1	1	1	1	1
6	6	6	6	6	6	6	6	6	6	6	6	6	6	6	2
2	2	2	2	2	2	2	2	2	2	2	2	2	2	2	3
17	17	17	17	17	17	17	17	17	17	17	17	17	17	17	4
4	4	5	5	5	5	5	5	5	5	5	5	5	5	5	5
5	5	4	4	4	4	4	4	4	4	4	4	4	4	4	6
14	14	14	14	14	14	14	14	14	14	14	14	14	14	14	7
7	7	7	7	7	7	7	7	7	7	7	7	7	7	7	8
15	15	15	15	15	15	15	15	15	15	15	15	15			
11	11	11	11	11	11	11	21	21	21	21	21	21	21		
21	21	21	21	21	21	21	12	12	12	12	12	12	12		
12	12	12	12	12	12	16	16	16	16	16	16	16			
16	16	16	16	16	16	18	18	18	18	18	18				
18	18	18	18	18	18										

CHASSIS LOG BOOK

1	Michael Schumacher	F2003-GA/229		11	Giancarlo Fisichella	EJ-13/04
2	Rubens Barrichello	F2003-GA/228		12	Ralph Firman	EJ-13/03
	Spare	F2003-GA/230			Spare	EJ-13/02
3	Juan Pablo Montoya	FW25/06		14	Mark Webber	R4/04
4	Ralf Schumacher	FW25/05		15	Antonio Pizzonia	R4/03
	Spare	FW25/04			Spare	R4/02
5	David Coulthard	MP4/17D-08		16	Jacques Villeneuve	BAR005/3
6	Kimi Räikkönen	MP4/17D-09		17	Jenson Button	BAR005/4
	Spare	MP4/17D-07			Spare	BAR005/2
7	Jarno Trulli	R23/03		18	Justin Wilson	PS03/04
8	Fernando Alonso	R23/04		19	Jos Verstappen	PS03/03
	Alan McNish	R23/01			Spare	PS03/02
	Spare	R23/01				
9	Nick Heidfeld	C22/02		20	Olivier Panis	TF103/05
10	Heinz-Harald Frentzen	C22/04		21	Cristiano da Matta	TF103/07
	Spare	C22/03			Spare	TF103/04

POINTS TABLES: DRIVERS
1	Kimi Räikkönen	40
2	Michael Schumacher	38
3	Rubens Barrichello	26
4	Fernando Alonso	25
5	David Coulthard	23
6	Ralf Schumacher	20
7	Juan Pablo Montoya	15
8 =	Giancarlo Fisichella	10
8 =	Jarno Trulli	10
10	Jenson Button	8
11	Heinz-Harald Frentzen	7
12	Mark Webber	4
13 =	Jacques Villeneuve	3
13 =	Cristiano da Matta	3
15 =	Nick Heidfeld	1
15 =	Ralph Firman	1

FIA F1 WORLD CHAMPIONSHIP • ROUND 7

MONACO GP
MONTE CARLO

Juan Pablo Montoya leads Kimi Räikkönen and
Michael Schumacher on his way to a memorable
second career F1 victory.
Photograph: Darren Heath

Saturday's free practice was punctuated by a near disaster when Jenson Button crashed his BAR-Honda coming out of the tunnel, the car slamming sideways into a protective barrier on the edge of the chicane escape road. It was an absolute carbon copy of Karl Wendlinger's terrifying crash in practice for the 1994 race, which resulted in the German driver being hospitalised in a near-fatal coma for over a fortnight.

Thankfully, the huge improvements in lateral cockpit protection meant that Jenson escaped with little more than concussion and a severe shaking. He was taken to hospital, where he remained overnight as a precaution, although it was suggested that he might take part in the race, starting from the pit lane. In the event, wisely, he gave it a miss. 'I've never really had a big accident in F1, but it doesn't scare me at all, which is great,' he said. 'You never know if it will, but it didn't scare me at all in this one.'

'I'm looking forward to getting back in the car, but I also don't want to be silly about it,' he continued. 'I want to go through all the training regime first and make sure everything's good. I don't want to get back into the car and hurt myself. We have to make sure everything's okay before I do that.'

Button admitted that he had been pushing too hard. 'And what makes it so frustrating is that it was a bloody good lap,' he told his father, John, who visited his bedside later in the day. It certainly was a great shame, as Jenson had been third fastest, behind the two Ferraris, during Thursday's first qualifying session and looked a strong contender on his fourth outing at Monaco.

Ferrari remained confident that it could make its F2003-GA work perfectly on the softer-compound Bridgestones, but unexpected 'graining' on the third sector of the lap meant that Michael Schumacher (1m 15.644s) and Rubens Barrichello (1m 15.820s) were left grappling with oversteer, and they wound up a disappointed fifth and seventh in the final grid order. Interestingly, unlike McLaren and Williams, the Ferrari team did not install fresh V10s immediately before qualifying, apparently wishing to conceal details of its engine installation and the intricacies of its rear suspension as much as possible in the cramped and confined Monaco pit lane.

'Obviously, I am not happy with this qualifying result,' said Schumacher, 'but I am not particularly concerned about it. I drove a lap which was error-free, but right from this morning we could see we were not as competitive in the second and third sectors.'

The track temperature had risen from 26 to 35 degrees C between the two sessions on Saturday, and this was responsible in part for the soft Bridgestones' tendency toward 'graining' in the later part of the lap.

In the Williams camp, Ralf Schumacher had dug deep into his personal store of determination to post a pole winning 1m 15.259s in the Williams-BMW FW25. 'Looking at this morning's times, I really did not expect to be on pole position and I'm clearly very pleased about the second pole of my career,' he said, 'and thanks to the Michelin tyres, which seem to be very consistent here.'

Ralf's team-mate, Juan Pablo Montoya, wound up on the second row of the grid, third fastest at 1m 15.415s. 'The car had a good balance, even though on my qualifying lap the car was bottoming slightly and I lost some time because of it,' he said.

Kimi Räikkönen did a superb job to post a 1m 15.295s in the McLaren-Mercedes MP4/17D, but David Coulthard – comfortably fastest in the morning's free practice session – made a last-minute set-up adjustment that dulled the fine edge of his car's handling and he had to settle for sixth on 1m 15.700s.

'We had a very good set-up in the morning, but we then made some adjustments after the warm-up, which was intended to further improve the car for the race,' said Coulthard. 'Unfortunately, this caused some understeer and I also got it wrong at the swimming-pool chicane, which ultimately ruined my lap.'

Jarno Trulli continued his tradition of producing strong performances at Monaco with a 1m 15.500s best, earning fourth fastest on the grid, while Fernando Alonso did well to take eighth (1m 15.884s) after sliding into a barrier during the morning's free practice session and losing crucial track time as a result.

Mark Webber did a good job in the Jaguar R4, a 1m 16.237s earning him ninth on the grid, while Antonio Pizzonia showed signs of raising his game with a 1m 17.103s, which earned him 13th-fastest qualifying time on his first visit to Monaco at the wheel of an F1 car.

Jacques Villeneuve was left to fly the BAR-Honda flag alone after Button's accident, the Canadian qualifying 11th on 1m 16.755s, immediately behind Cristiano da Matta's Toyota TF103 (1m 16.744s) and ahead of Giancarlo Fisichella's Jordan (1m 16.967s).

The Italian driver had expected better. 'On Thursday our performance level wasn't too bad,' said Fisichella, 'but we lost a lot of grip just in the qualifying session and the car was very nervous. Because of that, I made quite a few mistakes.' Team-mate Ralph Firman grappled with a touch of understeer and wound up 16th on 1m 17.452s.

Nick Heidfeld and Heinz-Harald Frentzen were 14th and 15th, presumably taking a tactical view of the race with a fair amount of fuel aboard for a long opening stint, while Olivier Panis had a miserable qualifying session, struggling with lack of grip. 'It's all a bit depressing,' said Ove Andersson, 'a case of back to the drawing-board, if you like.'

Monaco-based marketing company PPG1 attempts to have BAR-Honda cars impounded prior to Monaco GP in wrangle over payment of sponsorship commission.

Toyota rejects an invitation to join GPWC, preferring to commit itself to the existing F1 structure.

McLaren denies the accusation that it has poached a major Russian sponsor, Gazprom from Minardi.

Michael Jourdain Jnr wins first CART Champ Car victory at Milwaukee.

Dodge threatens legal action in response to top Winston Cup team Bill Davis Racing's links with Toyota and its plans to enter NASCAR in 2004.

Opposite: Ralf Schumacher took pole with a breathtaking lap.
Photograph: Darren Heath

Above, left to right: Despite being stretchered off to hospital, Jenson Button was fortunate to escape uninjured from his high-speed crash in practice. The Briton was unable to take part in the race.
Photographs: Bryn Williams/crash.net

Left: Kimi Räikkönen tests the Michelin rubber to the extreme in his quest for pole.
Photograph: Peter Nygaard/GP Photo

SEVEN laps from the end of the Monaco Grand Prix, the Williams crew radioed Juan Pablo Montoya and told him to cut the revs of his BMW engine. If he wanted to reach the chequered flag, he would have to take things easy.

Briefly, he complied. But soon he was back on the radio. 'If I do that for much longer, Räikkönen is going to tow past me in the tunnel,' he said. The BMW engine was on the verge of overheating, just as it had done in Austria a fortnight earlier, but Montoya pressed on, kept his fingers crossed and finished the job.

Juan Pablo had driven superbly to clinch his second GP victory by a scant 0.6s from the determined McLaren-Mercedes driver. It had been a great chase all afternoon and one of the closest races ever seen in the Principality, with Michael Schumacher's Ferrari storming up to within 1.1s of the second-place McLaren at the chequered flag.

Not that Kimi had been without his problems. The Mercedes engineers had been obliged to make a precautionary valve change on his V10 engine prior to the start, but it didn't miss a beat during the event itself.

Amazingly, this was the first Williams victory at Monaco for 20 years. Keke Rosberg, the man who had scored that previous success, was present to witness it, watching from his yacht moored in the harbour.

'It was all different then,' he said, recalling his memorable win in the agile little Cosworth V8-engined Williams FW08C. 'I finished the race with the palm of my gearchange hand absolutely mashed to jelly. Today, I suppose my medical guru would have escorted me away from the car. All I did was clear off to Ibiza, stuck my hand in the salt water and said, "Pour me a beer."'

From the end of lap two to the end of lap four, the safety car was deployed following an accident involving Heinz-Harald Frentzen, who had crashed his Sauber Petronas at the swimming-pool chicane, the car being removed by the emergency services. This represented a major handicap for Ralf Schumacher, who had made a last-minute adjustment by increasing his tyre pressures in a bid to obtain an early advantage in the opening stint of the race.

When the safety car was withdrawn, Ralf and Montoya sprinted away from the pack, and 2.3s separated the two Williams-BMWs by the end of lap six. Michael Schumacher, outgunned by Trulli's Renault in the rush to Ste Devote on the opening lap, was already 7.4s behind the leader, and Coulthard, running seventh in the other McLaren, was 9.2s behind Ralf's Williams. It was a graphic illustration of how time lost at Monaco in the early stages of any race is time lost more or less for ever.

Montoya soon began to chisel into Ralf's advantage, cutting it to less than 2s by lap 14, just as Mark Webber made an early stop from ninth place to investigate a problem with his Jaguar R4's pneumatic valve gear. He resumed at the tail of the field for another two laps before calling it a day.

By lap 18, Räikkönen had edged forward to make it a three-way party at the head of the field; the trio was covered by 2.9s at the

end of that lap. At this point, Ralf was struggling with loss of grip from his left front tyre and consequently was called in for his first pit stop at the end of lap 21, a lap earlier than scheduled. He was away again in 7.8s, but after Montoya made an 8.2s stop at the end of lap 23, the Colombian went back into the race ahead of his team-mate.

This put Räikkönen briefly in the lead, and he was stretching the MP4/17D to its limit in a bid to create a cushion prior to his own first visit to the pits when he was balked momentarily on lap 24 as he lapped Jacques Villeneuve's BAR-Honda. He duly pitted at the end of lap 25 for an 8.2s turn-around, but he couldn't quite keep his track place and resumed in seventh between the two Williams-BMWs. Now Trulli led by 0.9s from Michael Schumacher until the Italian took the Renault in for a 7.6s stop at the end of lap 27, allowing Schumacher's Ferrari to lead by 2.1s from Fernando Alonso's Renault and the second Ferrari of Rubens Barrichello. Meanwhile, Montoya moved up to fourth.

Alonso made an 8.3s stop at the end of lap 29, followed next time around by second-place Barrichello (9.2s). Michael finally made his first visit to the pits at the end of lap 31 and rejoined the race in third, behind Montoya and Räikkönen. Trulli dropped to fifth after this shake-out.

'You know, the hardest pressure was when they told me I had to get a gap to Kimi before my stop because he was going longer than me,' said Montoya later. 'It was quite hard. I managed to pull away from two seconds to four before I stopped, but then when I managed to get a couple of laps into the race until his stop, I still managed to get ahead of him and then just backed off a little bit and paced myself.'

Meanwhile, Coulthard pitted for the first time from fourth position on lap 27 (7.6s) and resumed in eighth. After the first round of refuelling stops had been completed, Kimi was running second, behind Montoya, while David was up to sixth.

After Montoya's second stop (6.7s), on lap 49, Kimi took the lead again. On this lap, he posted a new lap record of 1m 14.545s. The Finn made his second pit stop on lap 53 (8.9s), after which he resumed in third position.

Three laps later, Coulthard pitted for the second time (7.6s). As in his first stop, he came in right behind Jarno Trulli (Renault), who had been running just in front of him for most of the race. He narrowly failed to overtake Trulli as the two cars rejoined the race and slid into eighth position.

After Rubens Barrichello's Ferrari headed for the pits for the second time, on lap 60, David moved into seventh and took the chequered flag 18 laps later in the same position. Kimi closed up behind Montoya, reducing the Colombian's lead from 3s to less than 1s and pressed him all the way to the chequered flag, but on the narrow streets of Monaco, he could not find a way past.

Understandably, Montoya felt elated at the end of the afternoon. 'Really, you've got to say that I had quite a few races where I had a chance to win,' he grinned. 'The last one was Melbourne. I threw that away, so there was a bit of pressure not to make basically any mistakes. It was definitely worth waiting for. I won Monza [in 2001] and now this. It's fantastic. I'm so happy. It's just unreal.'

For his part, Räikkönen was philosophical about his inability to capitalise on running later in the opening stint. 'Yeah, I'm not very lucky with second place on the starting grid,' he said. 'I always seem to get bad starts. Okay, the race was just a little bit following

Montoya to try and get past, but here you don't have any chances to get past if they don't make any mistakes.

'I knew I would run a little bit longer, but on both pit stops I always had traffic when he went into the pits and that completely destroyed the chance to get past him.'

In the later stages of the race, Michael Schumacher had closed in relentlessly on the leading pair, but that early stint boxed in behind Trulli had made the situation irretrievable. 'The fact is that if I wouldn't have been stuck behind Trulli, I guess I could have kept the situation closer to Kimi,' he speculated. 'We tried everything, but we have to say clearly that this weekend we probably weren't strong enough.'

Ralf Schumacher finished a disappointed fourth, hobbled by a moment when he had skidded straight on at Rascasse, losing 12s while he reversed out to regain the track. However, he wound up well clear of Fernando Alonso who, thanks to staying out five laps longer than his key rivals before making his second stop, managed to vault both Trulli and Coulthard to take a good fifth.

Behind the eighth-place Barrichello, who had experienced a disappointing race with consistently bad breaks in heavy traffic, Cristiano da Matta (Toyota) just fended off Giancarlo Fisichella (Jordan), while Nick Heidfeld (Sauber), Ralph Firman (Jordan) and the hapless Olivier Panis – worn out by a one-stop race in the gripless Toyota – completed the list of finishers.

It had been a great day for Montoya, yet it was also the first decisive indication that supremacy in the tyre war was beginning to swing in the direction of Michelin. For sure, Michael Schumacher remained Bridgestone's secret weapon, but Monaco '03 reminded everybody that even he could be put under pressure.

Above: The Renaults of Jarno Trulli and Fernando Alonso sandwich Michael Schumacher's Ferrari, compromising the German's race strategy.
Photograph: Darren Heath

CAR MAKERS RAPPED OVER CHEAP ENGINES

FIA president Max Mosley held everybody's attention at the Monaco GP by warning the major car manufacturers that he expected them to fulfil their promises to supply realistically priced engine packages to the independent F1 teams in 2004. If they did not toe the line, the governing body was poised to tear up its proposed amnesty on electronic driver aids and insist on a ban on anti-wheelspin traction-control systems from the start of next season.

'I would be very surprised if the manufacturers did not stick to their initial undertakings on this,' said Mosley, 'but I don't want to comment further until I have had the opportunity of talking to them in detail. If they are not prepared to supply these engines, then obviously the FIA will have to consider its position.'

Another FIA insider added, 'It is perfectly clear that the interests of the sport as a whole would be well served by getting rid of traction control. It's only a matter of compromise to keep it as long as the engine suppliers help ensure the survival of the independent Formula One teams.'

Early in 2003, Mercedes-Benz indicated that it would be prepared to supply customer engines to independent teams for around $10 million from the start of the 2004 season. Renault and Toyota also suggested that they were prepared to consider similar schemes.

However, Patrick Fauré, chairman and CEO of the Renault F1 team, made it clear that his company could not commit to supplying an additional team with engines until 2005 at the earliest, and said that the price tag would have to be raised.

'I think they would be more expensive than $10 million, nearer $15 million perhaps,' he commented. 'I don't think that anybody can impose an obligation on us to supply engines. But we will not sell them for $10 million.'

Fauré also said that he believed a final decision as to whether or not the new GPWC series would go ahead would be reached within three months.

The car manufacturers were continuing to negotiate with Bernie Ecclestone and the three bankers controlling the interests of the bankrupt Kirch media group over purchasing a stake in SLEC, the company founded by Ecclestone to manage the F1 commercial rights.

'I think probably now we are in the final phase of our talks and negotiations,' Fauré speculated. 'We will soon know whether we will have an agreement or the negotiations have reached their end.'

However, the FIA retains the right of approval of any transfer of shares that results in a change of control over those commercial rights, and could exercise its veto unless the car manufacturers commit to looking after the interests of the independent teams.

Top: A typically relaxed Juan Pablo Montoya in pit-lane discussion.
Photograph: Darren Heath

Above: It's a beautiful day. Bono was one of the many celebrities to take in the action.
Photograph: Bryn Williams/crash.net

Left: Kimi Räikkönen at speed on his way to a very close second place.
Photograph: Patrick Gosling

Left: Max Mosley took a robust view toward what he felt were the car manufacturers' obligations.

Right: Jos Verstappen working hard with his tail-end Minardi PS03.

Far right: Another fast Marlboro man, MotoGP racer Loris Capirossi.
Photographs: Darren Heath

Michael Schumacher attacks the kerb as he
hustles his Ferrari F2003-GA through the harbour-
front chicane.
Photograph: Darren Heath

FIA F1 WORLD CHAMPIONSHIP • ROUND 7

GRAND PRIX DE MONACO

MONTE CARLO 29 MAY–1 JUNE 2003

Photograph: Darren Heath

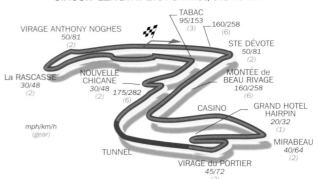

MONACO – MONTE CARLO GRAND PRIX CIRCUIT

CIRCUIT LENGTH: 2.075 miles/3.340 km

TABAC 95/153 (3)
160/258 (6)
VIRAGE ANTHONY NOGHES 50/81 (2)
STE DÉVOTE 50/81 (2)
La RASCASSE 30/48 (2)
NOUVELLE CHICANE 30/48 (2)
175/282 (6)
MONTÉE de BEAU RIVAGE 160/258 (6)
CASINO
GRAND HOTEL HAIRPIN 20/32 (1)
mph/km/h (gear)
MIRABEAU 40/64 (2)
TUNNEL
VIRAGE du PORTIER 45/72 (2)

RACE DISTANCE: 78 laps, 161.879 miles/260.520 km **RACE WEATHER:** Dry, warm and sunny (track 26/30°C, air 23/26°C)

Pos.	Driver	Nat.	No.	Entrant	Car/Engine	Tyres	Laps	Time/Retirement	Speed (mph/km/h)	Gap to leader	Fastest race lap	
1	Juan Pablo Montoya	COL	3	BMW WilliamsF1 Team	Williams FW25-BMW P83 V10	M	78	1h 42m 19.010s	94.928/152.772		1m 14.902s	47
2	Kimi Räikkönen	FIN	6	West McLaren Mercedes	McLaren MP4/17D-Mercedes F0110M V10	M	78	1h 42m 19.612s	94.919/152.757	+0.602s	1m 14.545s	49
3	Michael Schumacher	D	1	Scuderia Ferrari Marlboro	Ferrari F2003-GA-051 V10	B	78	1h 42m 20.730s	94.901/152.729	+1.720s	1m 14.707s	30
4	Ralf Schumacher	D	4	BMW WilliamsF1 Team	Williams FW25-BMW P83 V10	M	78	1h 42m 47.528s	94.489/152.066	+28.518s	1m 14.768s	77
5	Fernando Alonso	E	8	Mild Seven Renault F1 Team	Renault R3-RS23 V10	M	78	1h 42m 55.261s	94.371/151.875	+36.251s	1m 15.397s	58
6	Jarno Trulli	I	7	Mild Seven Renault F1 Team	Renault R3-RS23 V10	M	78	1h 42m 59.982s	94.299/151.759	+40.972s	1m 15.679s	51
7	David Coulthard	GB	5	West McLaren Mercedes	McLaren MP4/17D-Mercedes F0110M V10	M	78	1h 43m 00.237s	94.295/151.753	+41.227s	1m 15.439s	51
8	Rubens Barrichello	BR	2	Scuderia Ferrari Marlboro	Ferrari F2003-GA-051 V10	B	78	1h 43m 12.276s	94.112/151.458	+53.266s	1m 15.307s	59
9	Cristiano da Matta	BR	21	Panasonic Toyota Racing	Toyota TF103-RVX-03 V10	M	77			+1 lap	1m 16.282s	51
10	Giancarlo Fisichella	I	11	Jordan Ford	Jordan EJ-13-Ford Cosworth RS1 V10	B	77			+1 lap	1m 16.647s	72
11	Nick Heidfeld	D	9	Sauber Petronas	Sauber C22-Petronas 03A V10	B	76			+2 laps	1m 16.835s	75
12	Ralph Firman	IRL	12	Jordan Ford	Jordan EJ-13-Ford Cosworth RS1 V10	B	76			+2 laps	1m 17.208s	51
13	Olivier Panis	F	20	Panasonic Toyota Racing	Toyota TF103-RVX-03 V10	M	74			+4 laps	1m 17.777s	70
	Jacques Villeneuve	CDN	16	Lucky Strike BAR Honda	BAR 005-Honda RA003E V10	B	63	Engine			1m 16.292s	50
	Justin Wilson	GB	18	European Minardi Cosworth	Minardi PS03-Cosworth CR3 V10	B	29	Fuel pick-up			1m 19.169s	19
	Jos Verstappen	NL	19	European Minardi Cosworth	Minardi PS03-Cosworth CR3 V10	B	28	Fuel pick-up			1m 19.146s	25
	Mark Webber	AUS	14	Jaguar Racing	Jaguar R4-Cosworth CR5 V10	M	16	Engine pneumatics			1m 18.004s	13
	Antonio Pizzonia	BR	15	Jaguar Racing	Jaguar R4-Cosworth CR5 V10	M	10	Electrics			1m 19.437s	8
	Heinz-Harald Frentzen	D	10	Sauber Petronas	Sauber C22-Petronas 03A V10	B	0	Accident				
DNS	Jenson Button	GB	17	Lucky Strike BAR Honda	BAR 005-Honda RA003E V10	B		Practice accident				

Fastest lap: Kimi Räikkönen, on lap 49, 1m 14.545s, 100.226 mph/161.298 km/h (record for new track layout).

Previous lap record: Rubens Barrichello (F1 Ferrari F2002 V10), 1m 18.023s, 96.618 mph/155.492 km/h (2002).

18th: JOS VERSTAPPEN Minardi-Cosworth

16th: RALPH FIRMAN Jordan-Ford Cosworth

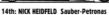

14th: NICK HEIDFELD Sauber-Petronas

12th: GIANCARLO FISICHELLA Jordan-Ford Cosworth

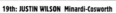

19th: JUSTIN WILSON Minardi-Cosworth

17th: OLIVIER PANIS Toyota

15th: HEINZ-HARALD FRENTZEN Sauber-Petronas

13th: ANTONIO PIZZONIA Jaguar-Cosworth

11th: JACQUES VILLENEUVE BAR-Honda

Grid order	1 2 3 4 5 6 7 8 9 10 11 12 13 14 15 16 17 18 19 20 21 22 23 24 25 26 27 28 29 30 31 32 33 34 35 36 37 38 39 40 41 42 43 44 45 46 47 48 49 50 51 52 53 54 55 56 57 58 59 60
4 R. SCHUMACHER	4 4 4 4 4 4 4 4 4 4 4 4 4 4 4 4 4 4 4 4 3 6 6 7 7 1 1 3 3 3 3 3 3 3 3 3 3 3 3 3 3 3 6 6 6 1 1 1 1 1 1 3 3
6 RÄIKKÖNEN	3 3 3 3 3 3 3 3 3 3 3 3 3 3 3 3 3 3 3 3 6 6 7 7 1 1 8 8 2 3 6 6 6 6 6 6 6 6 6 6 6 6 1 1 1 3 3 3 3 3 3 6 6
3 MONTOYA	6 6 6 6 6 6 6 6 6 6 6 6 6 6 6 6 7 7 1 1 8 8 2 2 3 6 1 1 1 1 1 1 1 1 1 1 1 1 1 1 3 3 3 3 6 6 6 6 6 6 1 8
7 TRULLI	7 7 7 7 7 7 7 7 7 7 7 7 7 7 7 7 7 1 1 8 8 5 5 3 3 6 4 4 4 4 4 4 4 4 4 4 4 4 4 7 7 7 7 7 7 7 8 8 8 1
1 M. SCHUMACHER	1 1 1 1 1 1 1 1 1 1 1 1 1 1 1 1 1 1 8 8 5 5 2 2 6 6 4 7 7 7 7 7 7 7 7 7 7 7 7 7 7 5 5 5 5 5 5 2 2 2 4
5 COULTHARD	8 8 8 8 8 8 8 8 8 8 8 8 8 8 8 8 8 8 4 4 5 5 5 5 5 5 5 5 5 5 5 5 5 8 8 8 8 8 8 8 7 4 4 2
2 BARRICHELLO	5 5 5 5 5 5 5 5 5 5 5 5 5 5 5 5 2 2 3 3 6 6 7 7 7 8 8 8 8 8 8 8 8 8 8 8 2 2 2 2 2 2 5 5 7 7 7
8 ALONSO	2 2 2 2 2 2 2 2 2 2 2 2 2 2 2 2 2 4 4 4 4 5 5 5 8 2 2 2 2 2 2 2 2 2 2 2 4 4 4 4 4 4 5 5 5 5
14 WEBBER	14 14 14 14 14 14 14 14 14 14 14 21 21 21 21 21 21 21 11 11 16 16 16 16 16 16 16 16 16 16 16 16 16 16 16 16 16 16 16 16 16 16 16 16 16 16 16 16 16 11 11 16 16 16
21 DA MATTA	21 21 21 21 21 21 21 21 21 21 21 11 11 11 11 11 11 11 16 16 16 21 21 21 21 21 21 21 21 21 21 21 21 21 21 21 21 11 11 11 11 11 11 16 16 21 21 21
16 VILLENEUVE	11 11 11 11 11 11 11 11 11 11 11 16 16 16 16 16 16 16 12 12 12 11 11 11 11 11 11 11 11 11 11 11 11 11 11 21 21 21 21 21 21 21 11 11 11
11 FISICHELLA	9 9 9 9 9 9 9 9 9 9 9 9 9 9 9 9 16 16 12 21 21 9 9 9 9 9 9 12 12 12 12 12 12 12 12 12 12 12 12 12 12 12 12 12
15 PIZZONIA	16 16 16 16 16 16 16 16 16 16 12 12 12 12 9 9 9 20 9 9 12 12 12 12 12 12 12 12 9 9 9 9 9 9 9 9 12 12 12 12 12
9 HEIDFELD	15 15 15 15 15 15 15 12 12 12 14 19 19 19 19 19 9 9 9 20 20 20 20 20 20 20 20 20 20 20 20 20 20 20 20 20 20 20 20 20
10 FRENTZEN	12 12 12 12 12 12 12 15 15 15 19 19 14 14 18 18 18 18 18 18 18 20
12 FIRMAN	19 19 19 19 19 19 19 19 19 18 18 18 18 20 20 20 20 20 20 20 20 20
20 PANIS	18 18 18 18 18 18 18 18 20 20 20 20 20
19 VERSTAPPEN	20 20 20 20 20 20 20 20 20
18 WILSON	

Pit stop
One lap behind leader

TIME SHEETS

SATURDAY QUALIFYING determines race grid order
Dry, warm and sunny (track 32/36°C, air 24/27°C)

Pos.	Driver	Lap time	Sector 1	Sector 2	Sector 3
1	Ralf Schumacher	1m 15.259s	19.781s	37.237s	18.241s
2	Kimi Räikkönen	1m 15.295s	19.787s	37.251s	18.257s
3	Juan Pablo Montoya	1m 15.415s	19.811s	37.407s	18.197s
4	Jarno Trulli	1m 15.500s	19.716s	37.623s	18.161s
5	Michael Schumacher	1m 15.644s	19.678s	37.622s	18.344s
6	David Coulthard	1m 15.700s	19.799s	37.648s	18.253s
7	Rubens Barrichello	1m 15.820s	19.805s	37.496s	18.519s
8	Fernando Alonso	1m 15.884s	19.786s	37.651s	18.447s
9	Mark Webber	1m 16.237s	19.881s	37.989s	18.367s
10	Cristiano da Matta	1m 16.744s	20.128s	38.058s	18.558s
11	Jacques Villeneuve	1m 16.755s	20.141s	38.034s	18.580s
12	Giancarlo Fisichella	1m 16.967s	20.034s	38.364s	18.569s
13	Antonio Pizzonia	1m 17.103s	20.146s	38.394s	18.563s
14	Nick Heidfeld	1m 17.176s	20.048s	38.317s	18.811s
15	Heinz-Harald Frentzen	1m 17.402s	20.120s	38.347s	18.935s
16	Ralph Firman	1m 17.452s	19.889s	38.375s	19.188s
17	Olivier Panis	1m 17.464s	20.193s	38.536s	18.735s
18	Jos Verstappen	1m 18.706s	20.508s	39.199s	18.999s
19	Justin Wilson	1m 20.063s	21.081s	39.642s	19.340s
20	Jenson Button	No time	–	–	–

THURSDAY QUALIFYING determines Sat running order
Dry and sunny, then cloudy (track 38/44°C, air: 27/32°C)

Pos.	Driver	Lap time
1	Michael Schumacher	1m 16.305s
2	Rubens Barrichello	1m 16.636s
3	Jenson Button	1m 16.895s
4	Jarno Trulli	1m 16.905s
5	David Coulthard	1m 17.059s
6	Ralf Schumacher	1m 17.063s
7	Giancarlo Fisichella	1m 17.080s
8	Juan Pablo Montoya	1m 17.108s
9	Mark Webber	1m 17.637s
10	Nick Heidfeld	1m 17.912s
11	Kimi Räikkönen	1m 17.926s
12	Jacques Villeneuve	1m 18.109s
13	Ralph Firman	1m 18.286s
14	Fernando Alonso	1m 18.370s
15	Antonio Pizzonia	1m 18.967s
16	Jos Verstappen	1m 19.421s
17	Justin Wilson	1m 19.680s
18	Olivier Panis	1m 19.903s
19	Cristiano da Matta	1m 20.374s
20	Heinz-Harald Frentzen	No time

POINTS TABLES: CONSTRUCTORS

1	McLaren	73
2	Ferrari	71
3	Williams	50
4	Renault	42
5 =	Jordan	11
5 =	BAR	11
7	Sauber	8
8	Jaguar	4
9	Toyota	3

FOR THE RECORD

50 grand prix points

Jarno Trulli

100 grand prix points

Juan Pablo Montoya

200 grand prix points

Ralf Schumacher

PRIVATE TESTING
Warm and dry (track 28/30°C, air 25/28°C)

Pos.	Driver	Laps	Time
1	Jarno Trulli	35	1m 16.888s
2	Giancarlo Fisichella	44	1m 17.569s
3	Mark Webber	36	1m 18.420s
4	Alan McNish	51	1m 18.438s
5	Fernando Alonso	29	1m 18.600s
6	Ralph Firman	50	1m 18.714s
7	Antonio Pizzonia	43	1m 19.521s
8	Justin Wilson	40	1m 19.923s
9	Jos Verstappen	30	1m 19.978s

THURSDAY FREE PRACTICE
Hot, dry and sunny (track 34/38°C, air 29/32°C)

Pos.	Driver	Laps	Time
1	Mark Webber	21	1m 16.373s
2	Jenson Button	25	1m 16.476s
3	David Coulthard	25	1m 16.505s
4	Fernando Alonso	17	1m 16.578s
5	Jarno Trulli	14	1m 16.800s
6	Michael Schumacher	33	1m 16.915s
7	Giancarlo Fisichella	20	1m 16.930s
8	Juan Pablo Montoya	22	1m 17.173s
9	Kimi Räikkönen	22	1m 17.218s
10	Rubens Barrichello	31	1m 17.372s
11	Heinz-Harald Frentzen	27	1m 17.550s
12	Jacques Villeneuve	25	1m 17.710s
13	Olivier Panis	21	1m 17.811s
14	Antonio Pizzonia	15	1m 17.913s
15	Ralf Schumacher	26	1m 18.039s
16	Ralph Firman	21	1m 18.133s
17	Nick Heidfeld	24	1m 18.660s
18	Justin Wilson	19	1m 18.952s
19	Jos Verstappen	21	1m 19.026s
20	Cristiano da Matta	29	1m 19.956s

SATURDAY FREE PRACTICE
Dry, warm and sunny (track 32/36°C, air 24/27°C)

Pos.	Driver	Laps	Time
1	David Coulthard	24	1m 14.747s
2	Juan Pablo Montoya	29	1m 15.098s
3	Michael Schumacher	25	1m 15.255s
4	Ralf Schumacher	35	1m 15.303s
5	Jarno Trulli	31	1m 15.517s
6	Kimi Räikkönen	32	1m 15.604s
7	Rubens Barrichello	30	1m 15.861s
8	Mark Webber	39	1m 15.886s
9	Giancarlo Fisichella	27	1m 16.311s
10	Jacques Villeneuve	34	1m 16.810s
11	Jenson Button	27	1m 16.895s
12	Antonio Pizzonia	39	1m 17.113s
13	Heinz-Harald Frentzen	38	1m 17.232s
14	Fernando Alonso	21	1m 17.290s
15	Cristiano da Matta	38	1m 17.686s
16	Ralph Firman	28	1m 17.986s
17	Olivier Panis	25	1m 18.101s
18	Nick Heidfeld	29	1m 18.167s
19	Jos Verstappen	32	1m 18.425s
20	Justin Wilson	29	1m 18.606s

WARM-UP
Dry, warm and sunny (track 30/32°C, air 23/24°C)

Pos.	Driver	Laps	Time
1	David Coulthard	6	1m 15.596s
2	Kimi Räikkönen	6	1m 15.798s
3	Fernando Alonso	8	1m 15.931s
4	Jarno Trulli	4	1m 16.052s
5	Michael Schumacher	6	1m 16.127s
6	Rubens Barrichello	6	1m 16.313s
7	Mark Webber	5	1m 16.434s
8	Ralf Schumacher	7	1m 16.754s
9	Jacques Villeneuve	6	1m 16.986s
10	Juan Pablo Montoya	6	1m 17.002s
11	Heinz-Harald Frentzen	6	1m 17.316s
12	Nick Heidfeld	6	1m 17.463s
13	Antonio Pizzonia	7	1m 18.053s
14	Cristiano da Matta	9	1m 18.123s
15	Olivier Panis	8	1m 18.745s
16	Giancarlo Fisichella	5	1m 19.431s
17	Justin Wilson	6	1m 19.517s
18	Jos Verstappen	4	1m 19.705s
19	Ralph Firman	7	1m 20.670s

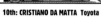
10th: CRISTIANO DA MATTA Toyota

8th: FERNANDO ALONSO Renault

6th: DAVID COULTHARD McLaren-Mercedes

4th: JARNO TRULLI Renault

2nd: KIMI RÄIKKÖNEN Mclaren-Mercedes

9th: MARK WEBBER Jaguar-Cosworth

7th: RUBENS BARRICHELLO Ferrari

5th: MICHAEL SCHUMACHER Ferrari

3rd: JUAN PABLO MONTOYA Williams-BMW

Pole: RALF SCHUMACHER Williams-BMW

62	63	64	65	66	67	68	69	70	71	72	73	74	75	76	77	78	
3	3	3	3	3	3	3	3	3	3	3	3	3	3	3	3	3	1
6	6	6	6	6	6	6	6	6	6	6	6	6	6	6	6	6	2
1	1	1	1	1	1	1	1	1	1	1	1	1	1	1	1	1	3
4	4	4	4	4	4	4	4	4	4	4	4	4	4	4	4	4	4
8	8	8	8	8	8	8	8	8	8	8	8	8	8	8	8	8	5
7	7	7	7	7	7	7	7	7	7	7	7	7	7	7	7	7	6
5	5	5	5	5	5	5	5	5	5	5	5	5	5	5	5	5	7
2	2	2	2	2	2	2	2	2	2	2	2	2	2	2	2	2	8
16	16	21	21	21	21	21	21	21	21	21	21	21	21	21			
21	21	11	11	11	11	11	11	11	11	11	11	11	11	11			
11	11	9	9	9	9	9	9	9	9	9	9	9	9	9			
9	9	12	12	12	12	12	12	12	12	12	12	12	12				
12	12	20	20	20	20	20	20	20	20	20	20	20					
20	20																

CHASSIS LOG BOOK

1	Michael Schumacher	F2003-GA/229
2	Rubens Barrichello	F2003-GA/228
	Spare	F2003-GA/219
3	Juan Pablo Montoya	FW25/06
4	Ralf Schumacher	FW25/05
	Spare	FW25/02/04
5	David Coulthard	MP4/17D-06
6	Kimi Räikkönen	MP4/17D-09
	Spare	MP4/17D-05/07
7	Jarno Trulli	R23/03
8	Fernando Alonso	R23/04
	Allan McNish	R23/00/01
	Spare	R23/00/01
9	Nick Heidfeld	C22/02
10	Heinz-Harald Frentzen	C22/04
	Spare	C22/03/05
11	Giancarlo Fisichella	EJ-13/04
12	Ralph Firman	EJ-13/03
	Spare	EJ-13/02
14	Mark Webber	R4/04
15	Antonio Pizzonia	R4/03
	Spare	R4/02
16	Jacques Villeneuve	BAR005/3
17	Jenson Button	BAR005/4
	Spare	BAR005/2
18	Justin Wilson	PS03/04
19	Jos Verstappen	PS03/03
	Spare	PS03/02
20	Olivier Panis	TF103/04
21	Cristiano da Matta	TF103/07
	Spare	TF103/05/06

POINTS TABLES: DRIVERS

1	Kimi Räikkönen	48
2	Michael Schumacher	44
3	Fernando Alonso	29
4	Rubens Barrichello	27
5 =	Juan Pablo Montoya	25
5 =	David Coulthard	25
5 =	Ralf Schumacher	25
8	Jarno Trulli	13
9	Giancarlo Fisichella	10
10	Jenson Button	8
11	Heinz-Harald Frentzen	7
12	Mark Webber	4
13 =	Cristiano da Matta	3
13 =	Jacques Villeneuve	3
15 =	Nick Heidfeld	1
15 =	Ralph Firman	1

CANADIANGP

MONTREAL

Arm aloft, Michael Schumacher celebrates one of his best ever victories. Behind, Ralf had no answers and had to play second fiddle to his older brother.

Photograph: Darren Heath

MONTREAL QUALIFYING

Heavy rain for most of Friday's practice and qualifying sessions had made it extremely difficult for the teams to select the most suitable dry-weather tyres for this circuit, where it is not possible to stage pre-event testing. In that respect, the Renault and Jaguar teams were at a theoretical advantage, having taken part in the extra two-hour test session on Friday morning, to which they had committed themselves at the start of the season in exchange for limiting their testing away from the races.

Consequently, Renault driver Fernando Alonso and Jaguar's Mark Webber and Antonio Pizzonia had convinced themselves that the grippier, soft-compound Michelin tyres would last the 70-lap race and enable them to get closer to the pace-setting Williams drivers. The latter had used the harder-compound Michelins to claim their places at the front of the grid.

When it came to Saturday's hour-long qualifying session, the Williams-BMW duo simply blew away the opposition, Ralf Schumacher (1m 15.529s) and Juan Pablo Montoya (1m 15.923s) buttoning up the front row in impressive style. That said, Ralf remained a little cautious. 'The car was very well balanced,' he remarked, 'but as Monaco showed, it is only the race that counts.' Montoya added, 'I changed my tyres just before the start of the session and so made a few mistakes.'

Michael Schumacher had to be content with third fastest on 1m 16.047s, two places ahead of Rubens Barrichello (1m 16.143s). However, since Kimi Räikkönen had spun his McLaren into the tyre barrier at the first corner as he started his qualifying lap, Michael's key title rival would be at the back of the grid on this occasion.

'The track was very green,' said Ferrari technical director Ross Brawn. 'This did not help us, but it looks as though it was an advantage for the Michelin runners. I hope when the rubber goes down, it will be easier for us.' Michael admitted that he had come close to duplicating Räikkönen's mistake, while Barrichello flat-spotted a tyre at the same point. 'After that, the vibration was so bad I could hardly see the track,' he said.

With Räikkönen effectively out of the equation, McLaren hopes seemed to rest on David Coulthard, who produced a disappointing 1m 17.024s for 11th-fastest time. 'The car stepped sideways over the kerb at the final corner,' shrugged the Scot. 'I guess I could have been sixth or seventh.

We will have to see what happens in the race, but it is pretty difficult from back there.'

Alonso's fourth place in 1m 16.048s delighted the Renault team, while Jarno Trulli also did a good job to take eighth on 1m 16.718s, after being forced to switch to the spare R23 – set up for his team-mate – following a crash during the warm-up. 'Taking that into account, I think I can be pleased that I am starting eighth,' he said.

Mark Webber was well satisfied with sixth fastest (1m 16.182s) in the Jaguar R4. 'To be honest, we surprised ourselves,' he admitted. 'We did not expect to be that quick. It would have been nice to have beaten one of the Ferraris, but it is not bad to be disappointed when you get beaten by a Ferrari.' Antonio Pizzonia wound up 13th on 1m 17.337s, admitting that he had run wide at the first corner, which may have cost him around 0.2s.

For Toyota, there was a modest degree of satisfaction after Olivier Panis managed a seventh-fastest 1m 16.598s, while Cristiano da Matta was ninth on 1m 16.826s. 'I'm happy with this result,' said Panis, 'because I spun during the morning session, which caused a bit of damage to the car.' Da Matta also spun on Saturday morning, but his car was repaired.

Sauber's Heinz-Harald Frentzen (1m 16.939s) and Nick Heidfeld (1m 17.086s) did good jobs to sandwich Coulthard's McLaren, but the BAR-Honda squad had a miserable afternoon, with Jacques Villeneuve 14th on 1m 17.347s and Jenson Button – fully recovered from his Monaco accident – 17th on 1m 18.205s. Villeneuve had spun during Friday qualifying with the result that he had to run first on Saturday.

'Naturally, we are very disappointed,' said technical director Geoff Willis. 'For some reason, we did not get the best out of the car when it mattered. Jacques made a small mistake on the third sector, while Jenson made an even bigger mistake at the last corner and that gave him a very slow time.'

The Jordan-Fords of Giancarlo Fisichella (1m 18.036s) and Ralph Firman (1m 18.692s) could only manage 16th and 19th, both drivers flat-spotting their tyres during their runs. Jos Verstappen did a good job to take 15th for Minardi on 1m 18.014s, and Justin Wilson returned an 18th-fastest 1m 18.560s.

MICHAEL Schumacher drove a superbly controlled race to post his 68th F1 victory in the Canadian Grand Prix, running just fast enough to keep his Ferrari ahead of brother Ralf's Williams-BMW FW25 in a tactical battle that lasted the entire 70-lap distance.

The closing stages of the race saw mounting excitement as what had been a two-car joust between the Schumachers for most of the afternoon expanded into a four-car contest when Juan Pablo Montoya (Williams-BMW) and Fernando Alonso (Renault R23) began to close in on their tails. The four were covered by just 4.4s as they flashed past the flag in one of the closest finishes in recent history.

On the face of it, the win looked like a routine success for Michael. In reality, it was one of his very best victories, as later it emerged that his Ferrari's braking performance had given cause for concern. The Ferrari telemetry had revealed that the F2003-GA's brake wear had been so acute during the early stages of the race that Ross Brawn judged that the brakes had around 20 laps left in them when Michael made his first pit stop at the end of lap 21. Thus, Schumacher was forced into conservation mode and, having pushed his way through into the lead, ran the race at his own pace to preserve the brakes over the remaining 49 laps to the chequered flag.

When called upon to deliver, Schumacher's Ferrari could demonstrate a small, but decisive, edge, running around 4 mph faster than the Williams-BMWs on the start/finish straight. He kept as much braking performance as possible in hand on the punishing circuit by allowing his brother to close right up on his tail for periods of time, but then used the power of the latest Ferrari V10 engine to create vital breathing space when needed.

'It doesn't get much better than that, really. It was obviously the ideal result,' said Michael. 'It was a tight race, a tough race. We had to be very careful on our brake side, so I wasn't able to push all the way through and just drove the pace I needed to, and during the pit-stop area, that's the area I started to sort of open the gap a little bit.'

It was a success that propelled Schumacher and Ferrari into the lead of the drivers' and constructors' world championships as the season reached its half-way point and a reversal of the memorable 1-2 success achieved by the German brothers at this circuit two years before, when Ralf had emerged the winner after a similarly close contest.

The younger Schumacher, who later was criticised for not pressing his brother more aggressively, remained philosophical at what was clearly a disappointing outcome to the afternoon. 'Obviously, it was a bit disappointing because we had a better race pace,' he concluded. 'I can't see where he took the advantage, but anyway, I know he was in a different race, but I was always able to follow him and with a clear road, I could have gone quicker. I think we had a better tyre today, as we had last year. But in 2001, I won like this, now it's his turn, so why not?'

Fifth place was taken by the other Ferrari driven by Rubens Barrichello, which had been delayed early in the race after a minor collision and subsequently suffered a handling imbalance when one of his car's aerodynamic side deflectors fell off during the course of the event.

Kimi Räikkönen, who had begun the race leading the world championship, paid a heavy price for a qualifying accident that had forced him to start last from the pit lane. He finished sixth, with Mark Webber (Jaguar) and Olivier Panis (Toyota) completing the points scorers in seventh and eighth places.

Qualifying had seen the Williams-BMWs of Ralf Schumacher and Montoya monopolise the front row of the grid, Michael Schumacher's Ferrari F2003-GA being off the front row for the second successive race, this time in third place, ahead of the impressive Fernando Alonso's Renault R23.

At the start, Ralf Schumacher accelerated into an immediate lead, while Montoya locked a wheel as the pack braked hard for the first tight left-hander. Ralf led Montoya by 0.7s at the end of the opening lap, with Michael's Ferrari and Fernando Alonso's Renault next up. Already a gap was opening to Rubens Barrichello, who'd touched the Spaniard's car at the start and who could feel that something wasn't quite right at the front of his Ferrari.

At the tail of the field, Antonio Pizzonia's Jaguar R4 ran into the back of Jarno Trulli's Renault at the second hairpin on the opening lap, although responsibility for the accident was certainly not clear-cut according to David Coulthard, who was making up ground from his lowly grid position and felt that the Italian had braked too early.

Trulli disagreed. 'At the start, I seemed to find a lot of traffic on the run to the first corner,' he said. 'Then Pizzonia hit the rear of my car, which punctured a tyre.'

The Brazilian countered, 'I ran into the back of Jarno, who was being passed around the outside by David, and he braked very suddenly. In the process, I lost the nose-cone of my car.'

Second time around and Montoya spun on the fast ess-bend before the pits, dropping from second to fifth, but he was soon back into the swing of things and only took one more lap to repass

Above: Montoya recovered to take third place in his Williams-BMW.

Far left: The long walk home for Kimi Räikkönen. Having spun out of his qualifying lap, the Finn had to start the race from the back of the grid.

Bottom left: Practice was affected by wet weather. But it provided some spectacular action as Michael Schumacher blasted his Ferrari past the BAR-Honda of Jacques Villeneuve.

Photographs: Darren Heath

DIARY

NASCAR star Jeff Gordon tries 2002 Williams FW24 during demonstration test at Indianapolis.

BAR test driver Anthony Davidson hospitalised, but unhurt, after 175-mph Le Mans accident in his Prodrive Ferrari 550.

BMW hints that it may quit the proposed GPWC after having second thoughts about taking part in the new series.

Felipe Massa poised to return to Sauber in 2004 after a year as Ferrari test driver.

CART series boss Chris Pook confirms that the US-based single-seater series could be up for sale later in the year.

Mark Webber's Jaguar R4. Yet it effectively wrote the Colombian out of the race winning equation.

Although it took only until lap ten for Montoya to climb back to third place, ahead of Alonso, by that stage he was 11.2s behind Michael's second-place Ferrari. In the meantime, Jacques Villeneuve's hopes of a half-decent home race had begun to fade as his BAR 005's brake pedal was starting to go soft following an early spurt up to ninth place.

'From lap two or three, the brakes started going off and the pedal was going down, so I radioed in saying, "Well, there's a leak or something,"' he said. 'Well, it felt like a leak. So every time I was hitting the brakes, I was looking where I would go if the pedal went down, just to make sure I had a little somewhere to escape. I tightened the belts as well, just in case.' He called it a day after just 14 laps.

Ralf Schumacher succeeded in holding the early lead through the period of initial grip loss suffered by his Michelin rubber and, having experienced such 'graining', elected not change his front tyres at either of his pit stops.

Ralf was leading by 0.9s when he made an 8.8s first refuelling stop after 20 laps. Michael stayed out a lap longer before coming in for a 10.6s turn-around, and thanks to a fractionally faster 'in' lap, he managed to squeeze out ahead of his brother's Williams. Had Montoya been where he should have been – namely in that second-place 'buffer zone' between Ralf and Michael – the race might have yielded Ralf's fifth grand prix victory rather than Michael's 68th.

Alonso ran strongly from the start, holding third place behind the Schumacher brothers in the opening stages, then surging into the lead on lap 21 when they made their first refuelling stops. The young Spaniard enjoyed his stint at the head of the field until the end of lap 26, when he pitted to take on fuel, allowing Michael Schumacher to slip into the lead for the first time.

The detailed mathematics of the situation were frustrating for Williams. Because Ralf had come in early, Ferrari could see how much fuel he'd taken on and then topped up the F2003-GA accordingly to run at extra couple of laps before Michael's second stop. Ralf came in for the second time on lap 46 for an 8.2s stop – a lap after Montoya – but Michael stayed out until lap 48, easily keeping his lead.

Both Ralf and Montoya, in second and third, were troubled by flapping rear-view mirrors, which were most distracting to the Williams drivers. Moreover, Juan Pablo's problems were compounded by his having to use the manual downshift system almost from the start of the race. It appears that the electronic timing trigger on the Colombian's FW25 was faulty and was adversely affecting not only the automatic change system, but also its traction control and the operation of its differential.

'I had instability into the corners,' said Montoya, 'especially the chicane. I missed it twice, and when they told me I couldn't miss it again, I had to brake early. Then sometimes it would downshift, sometimes not, so I couldn't slow the car quickly enough. It was a bit of a nightmare.'

Alonso did a fine job to finish fourth. 'For the first time this year, we were really fighting for the win and it was a good feeling,' said Fernando. 'I lost some time during my first stint, but managed to catch it up again at the end, even though I could not get past the car in front.'

Alonso finished 59.7s ahead of Barrichello's Ferrari, while Kimi Räikkönen at least salvaged a half-decent result from what initially had looked like developing into a particularly bad day. Having crashed in qualifying, he started from the pit lane and had climbed to fifth place with a heavy fuel load when his right rear Michelin tyre flew apart as he approached the pit-lane entrance on lap 33. He managed to steer his stricken McLaren in for a fresh set of tyres and a top-up of fuel, but the delay dropped him to a distant tenth place.

Räikkönen had climbed back to sixth at the finish, ahead of Mark Webber's Jaguar R4; the Australian had suffered from slight brake problems and oversteer during the course of the race. His team-mate, Pizzonia, trailed home tenth, although he had to call it a day on the penultimate lap due to severe brake wear. The two Jaguars were split by Olivier Panis's Toyota TF103 and Jos Verstappen's Minardi at the chequered flag.

Villeneuve's early departure from the fray heralded an unpromising afternoon for the BAR Honda squad. Jenson Button had battled worsening understeer in the early stages, then he lost fourth gear and, despite his efforts to short-shift to conserve the transmission, subsequently fifth, sixth and seventh before retiring after 51 laps.

David Coulthard's McLaren retired with a transmission failure, while Giancarlo Fisichella's Jordan-Ford expired with a similar problem. Ralph Firman suffered an oil leak that triggered an engine failure, so it could hardly have been worse for the Silverstone-based squad.

At the end of the day, the Canadian Grand Prix had been another celebrated event where Michael Schumacher had displayed his extra helping of driving genius precisely when it was needed. Yet the Williams-BMWs had certainly given Maranello something to think about. And plenty more of that would be coming soon.

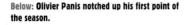

Below: Olivier Panis notched up his first point of the season.

Bottom: Alonso leads Montoya. They finished third and fourth in reverse order.
Photographs: Darren Heath

ECCLESTONE THROWS LIFELINE TO MINARDI

Bernie Ecclestone certainly sprung a surprise among the F1 brethren when he threw a lifeline to the cash-strapped Minardi team, which was at the centre of a major row immediately prior to the Canadian GP.

After Paul Stoddart, the Minardi team principal, had angered McLaren and Williams by claiming that they had gone back on a deal to provide additional finance for the smaller teams in the F1 pit lane, Ecclestone offered to take a majority shareholding in Minardi, which would guarantee that the team could continue racing until at least the end of the season.

It was believed that Ecclestone had helped to the tune of $4 million, thereby plugging the hole in Minardi's operating budget. Stoddart believed that this should have been filled from the £8 million 'fighting fund', which originally was to have been split between his team and Jordan in a share-out of television monies originally accruing to the Arrows team, subsequently bankrupted at the start of the season.

'Having Bernie as a shareholder in the team came completely out of the blue,' said Stoddart, 'and I hope that now I can get on with making the team what I always wanted it to be, but did not have the money to make happen.

'At the end of the day, I am here to race cars and not to be a politician. Having Bernie as a shareholder puts me in a very powerful position. I think what he has done is to ensure that there are ten healthy teams in Formula One, and I am now looking forward to trying to build the team up.'

Ecclestone added, 'It is time to get on with the sport and go racing.'

Yet Ecclestone's position seemed slightly ambiguous, as he had made the offer to invest in Minardi only hours after saying that such small teams had no place in the sport, and claiming that originally he had told Stoddart that the Australian should have got out of F1 at the end of last season.

'If he hasn't got the money, he shouldn't be competing,' Ecclestone had said on Saturday morning. 'It's like if you started a business and then things go bad and you are asking your competitors, "Please can you give me some money to help me compete against you?"'

There was speculation that Ecclestone could have been poised to broker the sale of Minardi to a consortium of Italian businessmen, and that Stoddart, who had gained the reputation of being an uncomfortably outspoken loose cannon within the secretive world of F1 business affairs, might quietly drop out of the sport.

For the moment, however, Stoddart remained upbeat and confident. 'When it comes to Bernie, when the chips were down, he was there for me,' he said. 'The big teams and the automobile manufacturers were not. It is a good day for Minardi, but the people I am happiest for are the guys in the team. It has not been easy for them and this effectively guarantees their future.'

Above: Mark Webber produced another strong performance for Jaguar.

Below: This is how much I own! Bernie makes his point to Paul Stoddart.
Photographs: Darren Heath

FIA F1 WORLD CHAMPIONSHIP • ROUND 8
GRAND PRIX AIR CANADA
MONTREAL 13–15 JUNE 2003

Photograph: Darren Heath

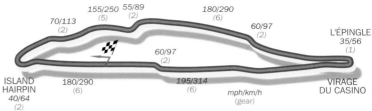

MONTREAL – CIRCUIT GILLES VILLENEUVE

CIRCUIT LENGTH: 2.710 miles/4.361 km

155/250 (5)   55/89 (2)   180/290 (6)

70/113 (2)   60/97 (2)   L'ÉPINGLE 35/56 (1)

60/97 (2)

ISLAND HAIRPIN 40/64 (2)   180/290 (6)   195/314 (6)   mph/km/h (gear)   VIRAGE DU CASINO

RACE DISTANCE: 70 laps, 189.686 miles/305.270 km   **RACE WEATHER:** Dry, cloudy and windy (track 28/32°C, air 20/24°C)

Pos.	Driver	Nat.	No.	Entrant	Car/Engine	Tyres	Laps	Time/Retirement	Speed (mph/km/h)	Gap to leader	Fastest race lap	
1	Michael Schumacher	D	1	Scuderia Ferrari Marlboro	Ferrari F2003-GA-051 V10	B	70	1h 31m 13.591s	124.757/200.777		1m 16.378s	46
2	Ralf Schumacher	D	4	BMW WilliamsF1 Team	Williams FW25-BMW P83 V10	M	70	1h 31m 14.375s	124.739/200.748	+0.784s	1m 16.599s	48
3	Juan Pablo Montoya	COL	3	BMW WilliamsF1 Team	Williams FW25-BMW P83 V10	M	70	1h 31m 14.946s	124.726/200.727	+1.355s	1m 16.349s	39
4	Fernando Alonso	E	8	Mild Seven Renault F1 Team	Renault R3-RS23 V10	M	70	1h 31m 18.072s	124.654/200.612	+4.481s	1m 16.040s	53
5	Rubens Barrichello	BR	2	Scuderia Ferrari Marlboro	Ferrari F2003-GA-051 V10	B	70	1h 32m 17.852s	123.309/198.447	+64.261s	1m 16.368s	35
6	Kimi Räikkönen	FIN	6	West McLaren Mercedes	McLaren MP4/17D-Mercedes F0110M V10	M	70	1h 32m 24.093s	123.170/198.223	+70.502s	1m 16.699s	67
7	Mark Webber	AUS	14	Jaguar Racing	Jaguar R4-Cosworth CR5 V10	M	69			+1 lap	1m 17.592s	45
8	Olivier Panis	F	20	Panasonic Toyota Racing	Toyota TF103-RVX-03 V10	M	69			+1 lap	1m 17.904s	40
9	Jos Verstappen	NL	19	European Minardi Cosworth	Minardi PS03-Cosworth CR3 V10	B	68			+2 laps	1m 18.521s	38
10	Antonio Pizzonia	BR	15	Jaguar Racing	Jaguar R4-Cosworth CR5 V10	M	66	Brakes			1m 17.324s	54
11	Cristiano da Matta	BR	21	Panasonic Toyota Racing	Toyota TF103-RVX-03 V10	M	64	Suspension			1m 17.787s	38
	Justin Wilson	GB	18	European Minardi Cosworth	Minardi PS03-Cosworth CR3 V10	B	60	Transmission			1m 18.039s	42
	Jenson Button	GB	17	Lucky Strike BAR Honda	BAR 005-Honda RA003E V10	B	51	Gearbox			1m 17.562s	22
	David Coulthard	GB	5	West McLaren Mercedes	McLaren MP4/17D-Mercedes F0110M V10	M	47	Gearbox			1m 17.088s	23
	Nick Heidfeld	D	9	Sauber Petronas	Sauber C22-Petronas 03A V10	B	47	Engine			1m 17.769s	44
	Jarno Trulli	I	7	Mild Seven Renault F1 Team	Renault R3-RS23 V10	M	22	Collision damage			1m 18.696s	16
	Giancarlo Fisichella	I	11	Jordan Ford	Jordan EJ-13-Ford Cosworth RS1 V10	B	20	Gearbox			1m 17.186s	20
	Ralph Firman	IRL	12	Jordan Ford	Jordan EJ-13-Ford Cosworth RS1 V10	B	20	Oil leak			1m 19.453s	18
	Jacques Villeneuve	CDN	16	Lucky Strike BAR Honda	BAR 005-Honda RA003E V10	B	14	Brakes			1m 19.780s	6
	Heinz-Harald Frentzen	D	10	Sauber Petronas	Sauber C22-Petronas 03A V10	B	6	Electronics			1m 20.043s	3

Fastest lap: Fernando Alonso, on lap 53, 1m 16.040s, 128.291 mph/206.465 km/h.

Lap record: Juan Pablo Montoya (F1 Williams FW24-BMW V10), 1m 15.960s, 128.426 mph/206.682 km/h (2002).

19th: RALPH FIRMAN Jordan-Ford Cosworth
started from pit lane

17th: JENSON BUTTON BAR-Honda

15th: JOS VERSTAPPEN Minardi-Cosworth

13th: ANTONIO PIZZONIA Jaguar-Cosworth

11th: DAVID COULTHARD McLaren-Mercedes

20th: KIMI RÄIKKÖNEN McLaren-Mercedes
started from pit lane

18th: JUSTIN WILSON Minardi-Cosworth

16th: GIANCARLO FISICHELLA Jordan-Ford Cosworth

14th: JACQUES VILLENEUVE BAR-Honda

12th: NICK HEIDFELD Sauber-Petronas

Grid order	1	2	3	4	5	6	7	8	9	10	11	12	13	14	15	16	17	18	19	20	21	22	23	24	25	26	27	28	29	30	31	32	33	34	35	36	37	38	39	40	41	42	43	44	45	46	47	48	49	50	51	52	53
4 R. SCHUMACHER	4	4	4	4	4	4	4	4	4	4	4	4	4	4	4	4	4	4	1	8	8	8	8	8	1	1	1	1	1	1	1	1	1	1	1	1	1	1	1	1	1	1	1	1	1	1	1	1	8	8	8	8	8
3 MONTOYA	3	1	1	1	1	1	1	1	1	1	1	1	1	1	1	1	1	1	8	1	1	1	1	1	4	4	4	4	4	4	4	4	4	4	4	4	4	4	4	4	4	4	4	4	4	8	8	8	1	1	1	1	1
1 M. SCHUMACHER	1	8	8	8	8	8	8	8	3	3	3	3	3	3	3	3	3	8	4	4	4	4	4	3	3	3	3	3	3	3	3	3	3	3	3	3	3	3	3	8	4	4	4	4	4	4	4	4	4	4	4	4	4
8 ALONSO	8	14	14	3	3	3	3	3	8	8	8	8	8	8	8	8	8	3	5	5	5	5	3	8	8	8	8	8	8	8	8	8	8	8	8	8	8	8	8	3	3	3	3	3	3	3	3	3	3	3	3	3	3
2 BARRICHELLO	2	3	3	14	14	14	14	14	14	14	14	14	14	14	14	14	14	5	3	3	3	6	6	6	6	6	6	6	6	6	2	2	2	2	5	5	5	14	14	2	2	2	2	2	2	2	2	2	2	2	2	2	2
14 WEBBER	14	20	20	20	20	20	20	20	20	20	20	20	5	5	5	11	11	17	6	2	2	2	2	2	2	5	14	14	14	5	5	5	14	14	14	14	5	2	5	5	6	6	6	6	6	6	6	6	6	6	6	6	6
20 PANIS	20	21	21	21	21	21	21	21	21	21	5	5	21	9	11	17	6	6	2	5	5	5	5	5	5	14	14	14	14	2	2	2	2	2	2	5	6	14	14	14	14	14
7 TRULLI	21	5	5	5	5	5	5	5	5	5	21	21	21	9	11	11	6	2	14	14	14	14	14	14	14	20	20	20	20	20	20	20	21	6	6	17	14	21	21	21	21	21
21 DA MATTA	5	16	16	16	16	16	16	16	16	16	16	9	11	17	6	2	14	14	20	20	20	20	20	20	20	21	21	21	21	21	6	17	17	14	21	20	20	20	20	20	20
10 FRENTZEN	7	10	10	10	10	18	18	18	18	18	9	11	17	6	6	2	14	14	20	20	21	21	21	21	21	21	21	6	6	6	6	6	17	9	21	21	20	17	17	17	18	18
5 COULTHARD	16	18	18	18	9	9	9	9	9	6	2	20	20	21	17	17	17	17	17	17	17	17	17	17	17	17	7	9	21	20	20	17	18	18	18	19	19
9 HEIDFELD	10	9	9	9	11	11	11	11	11	6	21	20	21	21	9	9	9	9	9	9	9	9	9	9	9	9	20	20	17	19	19	19	15	15
15 PIZZONIA	18	19	19	19	11	11	11	11	17	6	2	20	20	21	21	18	18	18	18	18	18	18	18	18	18	18	18	15	15	15
16 VILLENEUVE	19	17	11	11	11	11	17	17	17	6	6	2	12	12	12	12	9	9	18	18	18	18	18	18	18	19	19	19	19	19	19
19 VERSTAPPEN	9	11	17	17	6	6	6	6	6	2	12	12	19	19	19	15	15	15	15	15	15	15	15	15	15	15	15	15	15	15	15
11 FISICHELLA	17	6	6	6	2	2	12	12	18	18	18	18	18	18	7	7
17 BUTTON	11	12	12	12	12	12	2	2	12	19	19	16	15	15	15
18 WILSON	6	2	2	2	2	15	15	15	15	15	15	7	7	7	7	7
12 FIRMAN	12	7	7	15	15	15	7	7	7	7	7	7	7
6 RÄIKKÖNEN	15	15	15	7	7	7

Pit stop
One lap behind leader

SATURDAY QUALIFYING determines race grid order

Dry, cloudy and light wind (track 18/21°C, air 16/17°C)

Pos.	Driver	Lap time	Sector 1	Sector 2	Sector 3
1	Ralf Schumacher	1m 15.529s	21.458s	24.244s	29.827s
2	Juan Pablo Montoya	1m 15.923s	21.687s	24.297s	29.939s
3	Michael Schumacher	1m 16.047s	21.610s	24.406s	30.031s
4	Fernando Alonso	1m 16.048s	21.301s	24.466s	30.281s
5	Rubens Barrichello	1m 16.143s	21.797s	24.275s	30.071s
6	Mark Webber	1m 16.182s	21.375s	24.384s	30.423s
7	Olivier Panis	1m 16.598s	21.626s	24.612s	30.360s
8	Jarno Trulli	1m 16.718s	21.625s	24.765s	30.328s
9	Cristiano da Matta	1m 16.826s	21.669s	24.612s	30.545s
10	Heinz-Harald Frentzen	1m 16.939s	21.581s	24.676s	30.682s
11	David Coulthard	1m 17.024s	21.713s	24.595s	30.716s
12	Nick Heidfeld	1m 17.086s	21.618s	24.820s	30.648s
13	Antonio Pizzonia	1m 17.337s	22.080s	24.605s	30.652s
14	Jacques Villeneuve	1m 17.347s	21.692s	24.777s	30.878s
15	Jos Verstappen	1m 18.014s	22.210s	25.091s	30.713s
16	Giancarlo Fisichella	1m 18.036s	22.008s	25.499s	30.529s
17	Jenson Button	1m 18.205s	21.783s	25.012s	31.410s
18	Justin Wilson	1m 18.560s	22.189s	25.368s	31.003s
19	Ralph Firman	1m 18.692s	22.424s	25.153s	31.115s
20	Kimi Räikkönen	No time	–	–	–

FRIDAY QUALIFYING determines Sat running order

Rain increasing, drying later (track 15°C, air 16°C)

Pos.	Driver	Lap time
1	Rubens Barrichello	1m 30.925s
2	Michael Schumacher	1m 31.969s
3	Nick Heidfeld	1m 32.778s
4	Ralph Firman	1m 34.759s
5	Fernando Alonso	1m 35.173s
6	Kimi Räikkönen	1m 35.373s
7	Heinz-Harald Frentzen	1m 35.776s
8	David Coulthard	1m 36.463s
9	Mark Webber	1m 36.699s
10	Olivier Panis	1m 37.313s
11	Jos Verstappen	1m 37.426s
12	Juan Pablo Montoya	1m 37.479s
13	Justin Wilson	1m 38.088s
14	Jenson Button	1m 38.109s
15	Ralf Schumacher	1m 38.210s
16	Cristiano da Matta	1m 38.244s
17	Antonio Pizzonia	1m 38.255s
18	Giancarlo Fisichella	1m 38.617s
19	Jarno Trulli	1m 41.413s
20	Jacques Villeneuve	1m 44.702s

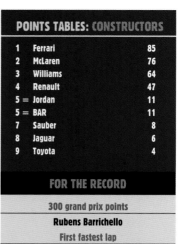
PRIVATE TESTING

Cloudy and breezy (track 22°C, air 20°C)

Pos.	Driver	Laps	Time
1	Fernando Alonso	52	1m 15.483s
2	Antonio Pizzonia	48	1m 16.253s
3	Mark Webber	42	1m 16.469s
4	Jarno Trulli	49	1m 16.629s
5	Allan McNish	46	1m 16.726s
6	Giancarlo Fisichella	38	1m 17.156s
7	Ralph Firman	41	1m 17.426s
8	Jos Verstappen	28	1m 17.852s
9	Justin Wilson	31	1m 18.495s

FRIDAY FREE PRACTICE

Dry, then rain (track 20°C, air: 20°C)

Pos.	Driver	Laps	Time
1	Antonio Pizzonia	11	1m 16.621s
2	Juan Pablo Montoya	16	1m 17.216s
3	Michael Schumacher	17	1m 17.228s
4	Mark Webber	13	1m 17.344s
5	Olivier Panis	16	1m 17.464s
6	Ralf Schumacher	21	1m 17.894s
7	Ralph Firman	12	1m 17.973s
8	Kimi Räikkönen	16	1m 18.155s
9	David Coulthard	16	1m 18.165s
10	Rubens Barrichello	24	1m 18.240s
11	Cristiano da Matta	23	1m 18.559s
12	Justin Wilson	16	1m 18.586s
13	Jacques Villeneuve	19	1m 18.716s
14	Heinz-Harald Frentzen	21	1m 19.765s
15	Nick Heidfeld	17	1m 23.061s
16	Jos Verstappen	15	1m 24.571s
17	Giancarlo Fisichella	11	1m 28.141s
18	Jenson Button	14	1m 28.872s
19	Fernando Alonso	8	1m 31.658s
20	Jarno Trulli	8	1m 32.552s

SATURDAY FREE PRACTICE

Cloudy, rain and light wind (track 17°C, air 15/16°C)

Pos.	Driver	Laps	Time
1	Michael Schumacher	42	1m 23.385s
2	Rubens Barrichello	40	1m 23.677s
3	Giancarlo Fisichella	30	1m 25.240s
4	Fernando Alonso	41	1m 25.382s
5	Ralf Schumacher	32	1m 25.668s
6	Jacques Villeneuve	37	1m 25.704s
7	David Coulthard	37	1m 25.839s
8	Jenson Button	39	1m 25.902s
9	Jarno Trulli	42	1m 25.961s
10	Mark Webber	39	1m 26.440s
11	Nick Heidfeld	30	1m 26.537s
12	Ralph Firman	38	1m 26.690s
13	Kimi Räikkönen	41	1m 26.771s
14	Justin Wilson	27	1m 27.018s
15	Antonio Pizzonia	40	1m 27.145s
16	Juan Pablo Montoya	32	1m 28.225s
17	Jos Verstappen	28	1m 28.246s
18	Heinz-Harald Frentzen	19	1m 29.190s
19	Cristiano da Matta	22	1m 29.215s
20	Olivier Panis	16	1m 30.410s

WARM-UP

Drying track, sunny (track 30/32°C, air 23/24°C)

Pos.	Driver	Laps	Time
1	Ralf Schumacher	6	1m 16.236s
2	Kimi Räikkönen	7	1m 16.697s
3	David Coulthard	8	1m 17.313s
4	Jarno Trulli	7	1m 17.560s
5	Fernando Alonso	7	1m 17.651s
6	Olivier Panis	8	1m 17.676s
7	Jacques Villeneuve	9	1m 17.689s
8	Juan Pablo Montoya	7	1m 17.799s
9	Mark Webber	6	1m 17.807s
10	Antonio Pizzonia	7	1m 17.930s
11	Nick Heidfeld	7	1m 17.979s
12	Cristiano da Matta	8	1m 17.983s
13	Giancarlo Fisichella	8	1m 18.328s
14	Heinz-Harald Frentzen	6	1m 18.339s
15	Jenson Button	7	1m 18.439s
16	Rubens Barrichello	7	1m 18.579s
17	Michael Schumacher	8	1m 18.845s
18	Justin Wilson	6	1m 18.893s
19	Jos Verstappen	7	1m 19.588s
20	Ralph Firman	6	1m 20.594s

9th: CRISTIANO DA MATTA Toyota

7th: OLIVIER PANIS Toyota

5th: RUBENS BARRICHELLO Ferrari

3rd: MICHAEL SCHUMACHER Ferrari

Pole: RALF SCHUMACHER Williams-BMW

10th: HEINZ-HARALD FRENTZEN Sauber-Petronas

8th: JARNO TRULLI Renault

6th: MARK WEBBER Jaguar-Cosworth

4th: FERNANDO ALONSO Renault

2nd: JUAN PABLO MONTOYA Williams-BMW

55	56	57	58	59	60	61	62	63	64	65	66	67	68	69	70	•
1	1	1	1	1	1	1	1	1	1	1	1	1	1	1	1	1
4	4	4	4	4	4	4	4	4	4	4	4	4	4	4	4	2
3	3	3	3	3	3	3	3	3	3	3	3	3	3	3	3	3
8	8	8	8	8	8	8	8	8	8	8	8	8	8	8	8	4
2	2	2	2	2	2	2	2	2	2	2	2	2	2	2	2	5
6	6	6	6	6	6	6	6	6	6	6	6	6	6	6	6	6
14	14	14	14	14	14	14	14	14	14	14	14	14	14	14		7
21	21	21	21	21	21	21	21	21	21	20	20	20	20	20		8
20	20	20	20	20	20	20	20	20	20	19	19	19	19			
18	18	18	18	18	18	19	19	19	15	15						
19	19	19	19	19	19	15	15	15	15							
15	15	15	15	15	15											

Back on top. Ralf Schumacher's title challenge gained real momentum with his win at the Nürburgring.
Photograph: Darren Heath

WILLIAMS AND BMW EXTEND PARTNERSHIP

Williams and BMW used the race at the Nürburgring as the opportunity to announce a five-year extension of their Formula 1 partnership, the Munich-based car maker agreeing to supply engines to the British team until the end of 2009.

This was a major coup for Williams, which had been struggling to regain its World Championship momentum in recent seasons, despite having won six grands prix with BMW power prior to Ralf's Nürburgring success, which came barely a month after Montoya's Monaco triumph.

'BMW has been an extremely impressive and highly motivated engine partner,' said Frank Williams. 'I have every confidence that with the structure of this new agreement, we will be able to draw from a deeper pool of BMW resource.'

This strongly suggested that the new contract, hammered out in a series of tense meetings over the course of three months, would see BMW having a greater say in the way that the technical programme was operated. For its part, Williams used the stability promised by the agreement to embark on an unprecedented level of technical investment, including the installation of a second £15-million wind-tunnel at its Oxfordshire headquarters.

Frank Williams acknowledged that it had been difficult for some members of the Grove-based team to accept the need for technical input on chassis development from its engine partner.

'Essentially, it was felt that if Williams have ten brains on a problem, then with another ten brains it should, in theory, provide a better solution,' he said. 'Even if it is only one per cent better because of the laws of diminishing returns, it is still worth a go.'

Williams added, 'For us, it was important to get long-term stability into the team, and if you considered too much what is happening after 2007 [regarding the threatened GPWC breakaway series], you would just wait and wait, then get to '07 and not be prepared.

'We believe F1 is going to stay as strong as it is for the long term, and we think this is the right decision.'

Kimi Räikkönen's first pole position was achieved superbly in the Michelin-shod McLaren-Mercedes MP4/17D, despite the fact that the cool Finn had not set a single fastest sector time in his polished efforts to edge out Michael Schumacher's Ferrari F2003-GA. It was clear that Michelin's rubber enjoyed a crucial performance edge at the Nürburgring and obviously kept the Bridgestone opposition on its toes.

'We are very keen to improve our tyre performance when running in the higher end of the temperature scale with softer compounds,' said Bridgestone's technical manager Hisao Suganuma. 'I feel we need more consistency in our tyre performance in that area and we will be doing some development work on that type of compound.'

In contrast to Räikkönen's front-running form, Coulthard's ongoing struggle to achieve a decent qualifying pace continued to baffle the Scot. 'I'm trying to understand it,' he said, after gaining ninth spot on the grid with a 1m 32.742s. 'I've got the support of the team in trying to replicate the pace I've had in the other sessions in qualifying.

'I was six-tenths slower in qualifying than I was in the warm-up. Obviously, will be making some changes for the next grand prix.'

McLaren managing director Martin Whitmarsh commented, 'David is a very analytical driver, and sometimes that is a useful quality. But it may not be useful when you have got to put it on the line over one lap.'

Of course, Michael Schumacher's unique talent helped propel his Ferrari into second place on the grid, Barrichello's sister car being the only other Bridgestone runner in a sea of Michelin-shod cars. Jenson Button's BAR-Honda was the next car on the grid wearing the Japanese tyres, and he was in 12th place.

'We have shown we are competitive here,' said Michael Schumacher, after posting a 1m 31.555s personal best. 'Yesterday, the Michelin runners benefited from a softer compound that they could not use today, and so today gave the true picture.' Barrichello was slightly disappointed with his fifth-fastest 1m 31.780s.

Ralf Schumacher's best of 1m 31.619s saw the Williams-BMW losing time in the third sector of the lap, although he said that the first couple of sectors had been okay. Montoya was less than delighted with his 1m 31.765s for fourth fastest. 'I am a bit disappointed,' he shrugged. 'I expected more, but with the fuel load we have, we should be looking good tomorrow. The balance of the car was not as good as in the morning, but I am confident for the race. The positive trend is continuing.'

Jarno Trulli managed an excellent 1m 31.976s for sixth on the grid, reporting that the Renault team had worked hard to improve the R23's handling balance and grip levels over the course of the first two days. Fernando Alonso had to be content with eighth fastest on 1m 32.424s.

'It was a good run for me,' he said. 'There were no mistakes, although the car balance still wasn't perfect. I haven't had any problems all day, and we worked hard to find the right compromise on set-up. I'm certainly happy to be starting from the top ten.'

In the Toyota camp, there was much satisfaction with Olivier Panis's performance, the Frenchman winding up a strong seventh on 1m 32.350s. 'We have been competitive all weekend,' said Panis. 'We had a good car from the first session yesterday and we are improving all the time.' Cristiano da Matta was also happy with a tenth-fastest 1m 32.949s

Mark Webber squeezed an 11th-fastest 1m 33.066s out of his Jaguar R4, but Antonio Pizzonia, who had gambled (wrongly) on car set-up changes just before the warm-up, was slightly dejected with his 16th-place 1m 34.159s. 'It was a lot worse than expected,' said the Brazilian. 'The car was worse and we could not go back and change everything in the time available.'

BAR Honda's Jenson Button did as good a job as his Bridgestones would permit to line up 12th on 1m 33.395s. 'I was pushing hard throughout the lap, but we were still struggling for grip, so the car was very twitchy,' he said. 'It's been a tough weekend so far and we've had to try a lot of things with the set-up to improve for today. The balance isn't too bad now; we're just not quick enough.'

Villeneuve was five places farther back with a 1m 34.596s best. His weekend had got off to a bad start when he spun off during first qualifying after a heavy rainstorm doused the circuit. That meant that he ran first on Saturday, which served to compound his woes.

'Today was a bad day,' he admitted. 'It's never a good thing to go out first for qualifying, but on top of that I had a bad lap. The car was sliding and I braked too late into turn one, locked the front wheels and lost a good half-second as a result. But we ran a good strategy fuel-wise, so there were a number of reasons for us being slower, but even without the mistake we would probably only have been 15th today.'

The Jordan place ahead of team-mate Ralph Firman (1m 33.827s). The two Minardis of Jos Verstappen and Justin Wilson were 18th and 19th, the Englishman having shone in the pouring rain on Friday afternoon. Despite slipping and sliding in the underpowered PS03, the lanky driver from Sheffield recorded a time over a second faster than Verstappen, an ac-

DIARY

Mobile phone giant Vodafone, a leading backer of the Marlboro-liveried Ferraris, had insisted that it would not sponsor any team that already carried tobacco advertising when it made its original decision to enter the F1 business. This fact emerges in the London High Court, where the Jordan team is pursuing a claim against Vodafone for failing to honour an agreement to become the Silverstone-based team's title sponsor from the start of the 2002 season.

Former F1 driver Alex Yoong claims he is owed $200,000 by Minardi in payment for his time with the team in 2002.

Honda Racing Development vice president Otmar Szafnauer confirms that Honda will increase its involvement with BAR chassis development from the start of the 2004 season.

McLaren managing director Martin Whitmarsh fuels speculation that the team's new MP4/18A challenger may never race. 'Anything is possible,' he replied enigmatically to inquiries on the matter. 'The reality is that if our assessment is that we can win the championship more reliably with the current car, then we would do that.'

This page: Kimi Räikkönen took his first pole position at the Nürburgring.

Above left: Frank Williams cemented his partnership with BMW with a new agreement.

Bottom left: Olivier Panis was very satisfied with seventh on the grid for Toyota.
Photographs: Darren Heath

IT was always odds-on that a Schumacher would win the European Grand Prix, but on this occasion it was Ralf, the younger sibling, who drove a perfect race in his Williams-BMW FW25. The memorable home victory brought the delighted local fans to their feet and was a timely success to cement the five-year extension of the partnership between the German car maker and the famous British team, which had been announced earlier in the weekend.

Schumacher finished 16.8s ahead of his team-mate, Juan Pablo Montoya, while Rubens Barrichello saved the day for Ferrari with a strong run to third place, avoiding the pitfalls that beset many of his more celebrated rivals.

Yet while the BMW top brass popped the champagne corks, their counterparts at Mercedes were left to lick their wounds after an engine failure cruelly robbed Kimi Räikkönen of a brilliant victory. His McLaren-Mercedes MP4/17D was running away with the race from the first pole position of the brilliant Finn's career when it was abruptly sidelined in an expensive plume of smoke, apparently because a piston failed.

'I made a textbook start from pole position and was able to control the race, pulling away until I had to retire with an engine failure,' explained Räikkönen. 'I had no indication it was going to happen and the car was feeling great. The gap to Michael can easily be closed with a good result and that is what we want to achieve next weekend.'

Before the start, Michael Schumacher had admitted privately that he wished he'd qualified third rather than second, because being off-line on the front row of the grid meant that he was on the dusty side of the circuit. So it proved. When the starting lights went out, Räikkönen accelerated cleanly into the lead, with Ralf Schumacher coming smartly through from third to ease his brother back another place as the cars jostled into the first tight right-hander.

As the pack disappeared through the corner, Nick Heidfeld accelerated after the pack from the pit lane, having decided to start

from there after suffering engine problems on Saturday and a gearbox downchange glitch, which had caused him to spin off at turn one during qualifying.

At the end of the opening lap, Räikkönen led by 1.8s from Ralf Schumacher, who was followed by the Ferrari F2003-GAs of Michael Schumacher and Rubens Barrichello, Juan Pablo Montoya in the other Williams-BMW and Jarno Trulli's Renault R23. Räikkönen, benefiting from a slightly lighter fuel load, was able to sprint away during the early stages of the race, building up a lead of 5.3s by the end of the sixth lap, by which time his hapless team-mate, David Coulthard, was already 14.2s down in the mid-field ruck.

This was a Michelin race, first and foremost. As if to emphasise the point, Jenson Button and Jacques Villeneuve's Bridgestone-shod BARs were reduced to battling at the tail of the field with the Michelin-tyred Minardis. Button would eventually salvage seventh place and a couple of championship points from the débâcle, but Villeneuve would continue to struggle near the back all afternoon.

On lap 14, Jacques compounded his problems by knocking his nose wing askew on one of the rubber bollards delineating the chicane just before the pits. Later, he would also spin at the chicane, and eventually he retired after 51 laps with a broken second gear.

Räikkönen made his first refuelling stop (8.8s) at the end of lap 16, as did Michael Schumacher from third place. That put Ralf ahead. Barrichello pitted on lap 17, Montoya on lap 18 and Ralf finally on lap 21, when his Williams-BMW also received a slight adjustment to its front wing. By staying out for the extra five laps, Ralf gained 4.3s on Räikkönen, effectively halving the McLaren-Mercedes driver's lead.

However, the advantage became academic mid-way around lap 25 when Kimi's machine began to emit an ominous trail of blue smoke. It was all over for the young Finn and, as he parked the car on the edge of the circuit, Ralf Schumacher surged through into a lead he was never to lose. History had repeated itself. In 1997, Mika Häkkinen had launched his McLaren-Mercedes from the first pole position here at the Nürburgring and had led the race only for

the engine to fail. Now the same fate had befallen his successor in the McLaren line-up.

While Ralf Schumacher took over from Räikkönen at the head of the field, his team-mate, Montoya, had a rather more fraught afternoon. The Colombian had struggled for grip on his first two sets of Michelin tyres, but then started to fly with a much better third set. Initially, he admitted that he had experienced difficulty in staying in touch with Barrichello.

'I had really bad "graining" and then the rears started to go off really badly,' he said of his first stint during the race. 'I kind of struggled a little bit and because I had so much oversteer, I decided to put on the new rears, and it went from massive oversteer to massive understeer. Probably going [for] new tyres all round [at the first stop] would have been better, but at the time I thought it was better to just stay with the old fronts, and I think I lost most of the time to Ralf there. Then for the last stop, we went for new tyres.'

Relishing the grip afforded by his new rubber, Montoya was in a different league. On lap 43, he ran down the outside of Michael Schumacher's Ferrari for third place going into the lower hairpin. In passing around the outside of the world champion, he pinched him slightly and the Ferrari spun. Michael did not stall the engine and, therefore, was able to restart, having been pushed from a place of danger.

'As for the collision with Juan Pablo, in my opinion it was a straightforward racing accident,' said Schumacher. 'He was faster than me, tried to pass and gave me just enough room to survive. Maybe I could have wished for a little more space, but I have no problem with Juan Pablo over this.'

Montoya was similarly philosophical. 'I braked late and gave him enough room to go round the corner on the inside,' he said. 'We touched and he spun. It was a racing incident, even if I must say that overtaking Michael at his home grand prix was much fun.'

Unaccountably, Ferrari technical director Ross Brawn lashed out at Montoya. 'I think it was a very crude manoeuvre from Montoya,' he said. 'He just gets alongside people and turns in. We all want to see overtaking, we all want to see exciting races, but he could have put both drivers out of the race. In past years, Mika [Häkkinen] and Michael had lots of great races, but they never did things like that. It just shows a complete lack of class from Juan Pablo Montoya.'

By any standards, this was an extraordinary verdict, which perhaps said more about the acute pressure placed on Ferrari to achieve success than Montoya's driving style, about which Michael himself was admirably sanguine.

The race now settled down, with Ralf Schumacher some 16.7s ahead of his team-mate, followed by Barrichello in third place and Coulthard chasing Alonso hard for fourth. This tussle for the place behind the Brazilian ended in tears on lap 57, when Coulthard speared into the gravel at high speed under braking for the final chicane, after apparently being brake tested by his Spanish rival. The Scot, obviously disappointed, graciously declined to contradict Alonso's claims that he had been struggling with heavy rear-tyre wear under hard braking. The stewards concluded eventually that Alonso had not transgressed any rule.

'I'm definitely not taking a biased view on this,' said the Scot. 'He may genuinely have had a problem, but he was inconsistent in the way he was dealing with it. But he certainly braked 10 metres earlier than he had done on the previous lap. I have my own views on the incident and I will discuss them privately with Alonso.

'Ultimately, though, I have not seen any evidence this season to make me think that Fernando is anything less than a very talented driver.'

Alonso seemed annoyed at having to defend himself for what he clearly regarded as Coulthard's mistake. 'I've just finished fourth ahead of a Ferrari and scored points for myself and the team,' he said. 'To spend half an hour speaking about the way Coulthard went off the road seems silly to me.'

Alonso just managed to keep ahead of Michael Schumacher's Ferrari to take fourth place, despite a friendly tap from the world champion at the final corner, while Mark Webber achieved his best result all season with sixth place in the Jaguar R4.

'Considering that my lead in the world championship has now increased to seven points, I really cannot complain about the result of the race,' said Michael, 'especially as with the new points system it takes longer to catch up, except in the case of a non-finish.'

Webber was slightly unhappy with the performance of the Jaguar R4. 'I'm a little disappointed not to have achieved a better balance on the car and, at times, the rear tyres were simply too good,' he said. 'I suffered understeer during the first two stints, but after my second stop the car came good and competitive.'

Jenson Button paid the price for being on Bridgestone tyres when the Michelins had the edge, but drove well to seventh place. 'I'm very happy to finish where we did, because we weren't really on the pace today at all,' he said. 'The start was poor and there must have been a 30-metre gap between me and the guys in front, but I caught up at the first corner and managed to get past Webber in the process. I was really struggling with oversteer and it was a tough old weekend, so I'm pleased we managed to get a couple of points.'

Button may have cast a sideways glance up at the Williams lads celebrating on the podium and reflected on the fact that Williams was where he had begun his F1 career three years before. If he did, he certainly didn't admit to it.

Kimi Räikkönen was the man of the weekend, taking pole position and leading the race until his McLaren-Mercedes failed him.
Photograph: Darren Heath

FIA F1 WORLD CHAMPIONSHIP • ROUND 9

ALLIANZ GRAND PRIX OF EUROPE

NÜRBURGRING 27–29 JUNE 2003

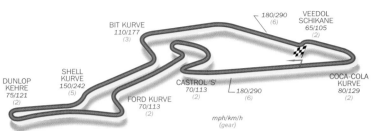

NÜRBURGRING – GRAND PRIX CIRCUIT

CIRCUIT LENGTH: 3.217 miles/5.148 km

BIT KURVE 110/177 (3)

VEEDOL SCHIKANE 65/105 (2)

180/290 (6)

SHELL KURVE 150/242 (5)

DUNLOP KEHRE 75/121 (2)

CASTROL 'S' 70/113 (2)

180/290 (6)

COCA-COLA KURVE 80/129 (2)

FORD KURVE 70/113 (2)

mph/km/h (gear)

RACE DISTANCE: 60 laps, 191.398 miles/308.863 km **RACE WEATHER:** Dry and warm (track 29°C, air 26°C)

Pos.	Driver	Nat.	No.	Entrant	Car/Engine	Tyres	Laps	Time/Retirement	Speed (mph/km/h)	Gap to leader	Fastest race lap	
1	Ralf Schumacher	D	4	BMW WilliamsF1 Team	Williams FW25-BMW P83 V10	M	60	1h 34m 43.622s	121.561/195.633s		1m 32.826s	34
2	Juan Pablo Montoya	COL	3	BMW WilliamsF1 Team	Williams FW25-BMW P83 V10	M	60	1h 35m 00.443s	121.202/195.056	+16.821s	1m 33.094s	59
3	Rubens Barrichello	BR	2	Scuderia Ferrari Marlboro	Ferrari F2003-GA-051 V10	B	60	1h 35m 23.295s	120.718/194.277	+39.673s	1m 33.200s	15
4	Fernando Alonso	E	8	Mild Seven Renault F1 Team	Renault R3-RS23 V10	M	60	1h 35m 49.353s	120.170/193.396	+65.731s	1m 33.307s	17
5	Michael Schumacher	D	1	Scuderia Ferrari Marlboro	Ferrari F2003-GA-051 V10	B	60	1h 35m 49.784s	120.162/193.382	+66.162s	1m 32.904s	34
6	Mark Webber	AUS	14	Jaguar Racing	Jaguar R4-Cosworth CR5 V10	M	59			+1 lap	1m 34.191s	37
7	Jenson Button	GB	17	Lucky Strike BAR Honda	BAR 005-Honda RA003E V10	B	59			+1 lap	1m 34.208s	14
8	Nick Heidfeld	D	9	Sauber Petronas	Sauber C22-Petronas 03B V10	B	59			+1 lap	1m 34.541s	23
9	Heinz-Harald Frentzen	D	10	Sauber Petronas	Sauber C22-Petronas 03B V10	B	59			+1 lap	1m 33.994s	33
10	Antonio Pizzonia	BR	15	Jaguar Racing	Jaguar R4-Cosworth CR5 V10	M	59			+1 lap	1m 34.915s	47
11	Ralph Firman	IRL	12	Jordan Ford	Jordan EJ-13-Ford Cosworth RS1 V10	B	58			+2 laps	1m 35.328s	29
12	Giancarlo Fisichella	I	11	Jordan Ford	Jordan EJ-13-Ford Cosworth RS1 V10	B	58			+2 laps	1m 34.656s	29
13	Justin Wilson	GB	18	European Minardi Cosworth	Minardi PS03-Cosworth CR3 V10	B	58			+2 laps	1m 36.709s	19
14	Jos Verstappen	NL	19	European Minardi Cosworth	Minardi PS03-Cosworth CR3 V10	B	57			+3 laps	1m 37.365s	3
15	David Coulthard	GB	5	West McLaren Mercedes	McLaren MP4/17D-Mercedes F0110M V10	M	56	Spun off			1m 33.236s	12
	Cristiano da Matta	BR	21	Panasonic Toyota Racing	Toyota TF103-RVX-03 V10	M	53	Engine			1m 33.398s	15
	Jacques Villeneuve	CDN	16	Lucky Strike BAR Honda	BAR 005-Honda RA003E V10	B	51	Transmission			1m 35.100s	45
	Jarno Trulli	I	7	Mild Seven Renault F1 Team	Renault R3-RS23 V10	M	37	Fuel pump			1m 33.348s	13
	Olivier Panis	F	20	Panasonic Toyota Racing	Toyota TF103-RVX-03 V10	M	37	Spun off/brakes			1m 33.583s	8
	Kimi Räikkönen	FIN	6	West McLaren Mercedes	McLaren MP4/17D-Mercedes F0110M V10	M	25	Engine			1m 32.621s	14

Fastest lap: Kimi Räikkönen, on lap 14, 1m 32.621s, 124.331 mph/200.092 km/h (record for modified track layout).

Previous lap record: Michael Schumacher (F1 Ferrari F2002-051 V10), 1m 32.226s, 124.816 mph/200.872 km/h (2002).

19th: JUSTIN WILSON Minardi-Cosworth

17th: JACQUES VILLENEUVE BAR-Honda

15th: HEINZ-HARALD FRENTZEN Sauber-Petronas

13th: GIANCARLO FISICHELLA Jordan-Ford Cosworth

11th: MARK WEBBER Jaguar-Cosworth

20th: NICK HEIDFELD Sauber-Petronas started from pit lane

18th: JOS VERSTAPPEN Minardi-Cosworth

16th: ANTONIO PIZZONIA Jaguar-Cosworth

14th: RALPH FIRMAN Jordan-Ford Cosworth

12th: JENSON BUTTON BAR-Honda

Grid order	1	2	3	4	5	6	7	8	9	10	11	12	13	14	15	16	17	18	19	20	21	22	23	24	25	26	27	28	29	30	31	32	33	34	35	36	37	38	39	40	41	42	43	44	45	46
6 RÄIKKÖNEN	6	6	6	6	6	6	6	6	6	6	6	6	6	6	6	6	4	4	4	4	4	6	6	6	6	4	4	4	4	4	4	4	4	4	4	4	4	4	4	4	4	4	4	4	4	4
1 M. SCHUMACHER	4	4	4	4	4	4	4	4	4	4	4	4	4	4	4	3	3		6	6	6	4	4	4	4	1	1	1	1	1	1	1	1	1	1	1	3	3	3		5	5	3	3	3	3
4 R. SCHUMACHER	1	1	1	1	1	1	1	1	1	1	1	1	1	1	2	2	8	1	1	1	1	2	2	2	2	2	2	2	2	2	2	2	2	2	2	2		5	5	5	1	1	2	2	2	3
3 MONTOYA	2	2	2	2	2	2	2	2	2	2	2	2	2	2	1	8	5	2	2	2	2	2	3	3	3	3	3	3	3	3	3	3	3	3	8		1	1	3	3	8	8	8
2 BARRICHELLO	3	3	3	3	3	3	3	3	3	3	3	3	3	3	3	5	6	3	3	3	3	8	8	8	8	8	8	8	8	8	8	8	7	1	2	2	2	2	5	5	5	5
7 TRULLI	7	7	7	7	7	7	7	7	7	7	7	7	7	7	8	6	1	8	7	7	7	7	7	7	7	7	7	7	7	7	7	5	2	8	8	8	8	1	1	1	1
20 PANIS	8	8	8	8	8	8	8	8	8	8	8	8	8	8	7	5	1	2	7	7	7	7	7	5	5	5	5	5	5	5	5	5	1	14	15	21	21	14	14	14	14
8 ALONSO	20	20	20	20	20	20	20	20	20	20	5	5	5	5	5	21	7	7	5	5	5	5	5	17	17	17	17	17	17	17	17	17	14	15	21	15	14	14	17	17	17
5 COULTHARD	5	5	5	5	5	5	5	5	5	21	21	21	21	7	21	21	21	21	21	21	21	21	17	20	20	20	20	20	20	20	20	14	17	21	14	14	17	17	10	10	9	9
21 DA MATTA	21	21	21	21	21	21	21	21	17	17	17	17	17	15	9	9	9	9	17	17	17	14	14	14	14	14	14	14	14	14	20	15	17	17	17	10	10	9	9	10	10
14 WEBBER	17	17	17	17	17	17	17	17	14	14	14	20	20	9	17	20	20	20	20	10	10	10	10	10	15	15	15	15	21	10	10	10	9	21	15	15	15
17 BUTTON	14	14	14	14	14	14	14	14	10	10	20	10	10	14	14	14	14	10	10	10	10	15	15	9	9	9	9	21	9	15	15	15	11	21	21
11 FISICHELLA	12	12	12	12	12	12	12	12	10	10	9	14	14	14	10	10	10	10	15	9	9	9	9	9	21	21	21	20	11	11	11	11	11
12 FIRMAN	10	10	10	10	10	10	10	10	15	15	15	10	14	20	10	10	15	15	15	9	21	21	21	9	10	10	10	12	12	12	12	12	12
10 FRENTZEN	15	15	15	15	15	15	15	15	11	9	9	9	10	10	15	15	9	9	9	9	21	11	11	11	11	16	16	16	16	16
15 PIZZONIA	11	11	11	11	11	11	11	11	12	9	18	18	18	18	18	12	12	12	12	12	12	18	18	18	18	18	18	18
16 VILLENEUVE	19	19	19	19	19	19	9	9	19	19	16	16	11	11	11	11	11	11	11	16	16	16	16
19 VERSTAPPEN	18	18	18	18	18	16	19	19	16	16	16	16	16	16	16	16	18	18
18 WILSON	16	16	16	16	16	9	9	18	18	16	16	19	19	19	19	19	19	19	19	19	19
9 HEIDFELD	9	9	9	9	9	9	18	18	16	16	12	11	11	16	16	16	16	16	16	16

TIME SHEETS

SATURDAY QUALIFYING determines race grid order
Sunny and warm (track 32°C, air 20°C)

Pos.	Driver	Lap time	Sector 1	Sector 2	Sector 3
1	Kimi Räikkönen	1m 31.523s	29.762s	38.240s	23.521s
2	Michael Schumacher	1m 31.555s	29.893s	38.070s	23.592s
3	Ralf Schumacher	1m 31.619s	29.741s	38.303s	23.575s
4	Juan Pablo Montoya	1m 31.765s	29.741s	38.326s	23.698s
5	Rubens Barrichello	1m 31.780s	29.890s	38.384s	23.506s
6	Jarno Trulli	1m 31.976s	29.869s	38.266s	23.841s
7	Olivier Panis	1m 32.350s	30.026s	38.458s	23.866s
8	Fernando Alonso	1m 32.424s	30.087s	38.554s	23.783s
9	David Coulthard	1m 32.742s	30.185s	38.882s	23.675s
10	Cristiano da Matta	1m 32.949s	30.410s	38.786s	23.753s
11	Mark Webber	1m 33.066s	30.456s	38.700s	23.910s
12	Jenson Button	1m 33.395s	30.734s	38.760s	23.901s
13	Giancarlo Fisichella	1m 33.553s	30.510s	39.148s	23.895s
14	Ralph Firman	1m 33.827s	30.679s	39.051s	24.097
15	Heinz-Harald Frentzen	1m 34.000s	30.556s	39.441s	24.003s
16	Antonio Pizzonia	1m 34.159s	30.725s	39.275s	24.159s
17	Jacques Villeneuve	1m 34.596s	31.128s	39.185s	24.283s
18	Jos Verstappen	1m 36.318s	31.280s	40.541s	24.497s
19	Justin Wilson	1m 36.485s	31.462s	40.499s	24.524s
20	Nick Heidfeld	No time	–	–	–

FRIDAY QUALIFYING determines Sat running order
Overcast, then rain (track 28°C, air 26°C)

Pos.	Driver	Lap time
1	Kimi Räikkönen	1m 29.989s
2	Michael Schumacher	1m 30.353s
3	Juan Pablo Montoya	1m 30.378s
4	Ralf Schumacher	1m 30.522s
5	Rubens Barrichello	1m 30.842s
6	David Coulthard	1m 30.903s
7	Jarno Trulli	1m 31.143s
8	Fernando Alonso	1m 31.533s
9	Giancarlo Fisichella	1m 32.196s
10	Heinz-Harald Frentzen	1m 32.201s
11	Jenson Button	1m 32.479s
12	Mark Webber	1m 35.972s
13	Nick Heidfeld	1m 52.300s
14	Ralph Firman	1m 53.893s
15	Justin Wilson	1m 54.546s
16	Jos Verstappen	1m 55.921s
17	Olivier Panis	1m 57.327s
18	Antonio Pizzonia	1m 57.435s
19	Cristiano da Matta	No time
20	Jacques Villeneuve	No time

PRIVATE TESTING
Sunny (track 24°C, air 22°C)

Pos.	Driver	Laps	Time
1	Jarno Trulli	48	1m 32.085s
2	Fernando Alonso	45	1m 32.311s
3	Antonio Pizzonia	41	1m 32.965s
4	Ralph Firman	45	1m 33.019s
5	Mark Webber	38	1m 33.174s
6	Allan McNish	30	1m 33.935s
7	Giancarlo Fisichella	35	1m 34.579s
8	Jos Verstappen	31	1m 34.857s
9	Justin Wilson	30	1m 35.455s

FRIDAY FREE PRACTICE
Dry and sunny (track 27°C, air 24°C)

Pos.	Driver	Laps	Time
1	Olivier Panis	22	1m 31.197s
2	Mark Webber	19	1m 31.224s
3	Kimi Räikkönen	19	1m 31.260s
4	Jarno Trulli	22	1m 31.513s
5	Fernando Alonso	18	1m 31.750s
6	Antonio Pizzonia	18	1m 31.794s
7	David Coulthard	22	1m 31.918s
8	Ralf Schumacher	22	1m 32.170s
9	Cristiano da Matta	26	1m 32.492s
10	Michael Schumacher	24	1m 32.560s
11	Juan Pablo Montoya	22	1m 32.590s
12	Rubens Barrichello	17	1m 32.607s
13	Giancarlo Fisichella	16	1m 32.692s
14	Heinz-Harald Frentzen	20	1m 32.792s
15	Jenson Button	23	1m 32.841s
16	Nick Heidfeld	18	1m 32.901s
17	Jacques Villeneuve	21	1m 33.602s
18	Ralph Firman	17	1m 33.643s
19	Jos Verstappen	9	1m 34.947s
20	Justin Wilson	14	1m 35.525s

SATURDAY FIRST FREE PRACTICE
Sunny and warm (track 29°C, air 19°C)

Pos.	Driver	Laps	Time
1	Olivier Panis	19	1m 31.181s
2	Rubens Barrichello	15	1m 32.039s
3	David Coulthard	14	1m 32.471s
4	Juan Pablo Montoya	17	1m 32.471s
5	Kimi Räikkönen	17	1m 32.803s
6	Michael Schumacher	17	1m 32.852s
7	Ralf Schumacher	18	1m 32.891s
8	Antonio Pizzonia	15	1m 33.127s
9	Cristiano da Matta	19	1m 33.140s
10	Jarno Trulli	15	1m 33.707s
11	Jacques Villeneuve	18	1m 34.127s
12	Fernando Alonso	17	1m 34.179s
13	Mark Webber	15	1m 34.564s
14	Jenson Button	13	1m 34.582s
15	Heinz-Harald Frentzen	13	1m 34.775s
16	Nick Heidfeld	14	1m 34.784s
17	Ralph Firman	14	1m 34.967s
18	Giancarlo Fisichella	13	1m 35.332s
19	Jos Verstappen	9	1m 36.845s
20	Justin Wilson	13	1m 37.001s

SATURDAY SECOND FREE PRACTICE
Sunny and warm (track 29°C, air 19°C)

Pos.	Driver	Laps	Time
1	Ralf Schumacher	11	1m 31.305s
2	Juan Pablo Montoya	15	1m 31.366s
3	Olivier Panis	18	1m 31.490s
4	David Coulthard	16	1m 31.608s
5	Kimi Räikkönen	13	1m 32.021s
6	Cristiano da Matta	22	1m 32.057s
7	Jarno Trulli	20	1m 32.356s
8	Fernando Alonso	18	1m 32.391s
9	Michael Schumacher	21	1m 32.652s
10	Rubens Barrichello	16	1m 33.010s
11	Antonio Pizzonia	18	1m 33.076s
12	Giancarlo Fisichella	20	1m 33.214s
13	Jenson Button	12	1m 33.474s
14	Mark Webber	18	1m 33.635s
15	Nick Heidfeld	22	1m 33.698s
16	Jacques Villeneuve	13	1m 34.085s
17	Ralph Firman	4	1m 34.827s
18	Heinz-Harald Frentzen	20	1m 34.940s
19	Justin Wilson	10	1m 36.026s
20	Jos Verstappen	9	1m 36.381s

WARM-UP
Sunny and warm (track 32°C, air 20°C)

Pos.	Driver	Laps	Time
1	Michael Schumacher	6	1m 31.981s
2	Rubens Barrichello	6	1m 32.097s
3	David Coulthard	4	1m 32.114s
4	Juan Pablo Montoya	6	1m 32.252s
5	Kimi Räikkönen	5	1m 32.385s
6	Olivier Panis	6	1m 32.545s
7	Ralf Schumacher	6	1m 32.547s
8	Jarno Trulli	4	1m 33.029s
9	Fernando Alonso	6	1m 33.068s
10	Cristiano da Matta	6	1m 33.306s
11	Jenson Button	7	1m 33.780s
12	Jacques Villeneuve	6	1m 34.114s
13	Mark Webber	4	1m 34.164s
14	Giancarlo Fisichella	4	1m 34.229s
15	Ralph Firman	7	1m 34.373s
16	Antonio Pizzonia	5	1m 34.746s
17	Justin Wilson	6	1m 36.559s
18	Jos Verstappen	5	1m 37.181s
19	Heinz-Harald Frentzen	5	No time
20	Nick Heidfeld	4	No time

9th: DAVID COULTHARD McLaren-Mercedes

7th: OLIVIER PANIS Toyota

5th: RUBENS BARRICHELLO Ferrari

3rd: RALF SCHUMACHER Williams-BMW

Pole: KIMI RÄIKKÖNEN McLaren-Mercedes

10th: CRISTIANO DA MATTA Toyota

8th: FERNANDO ALONSO Renault

6th: JARNO TRULLI Renault

4th: JUAN PABLO MONTOYA Williams-BMW

2nd: MICHAEL SCHUMACHER Ferrari

48	49	50	51	52	53	54	55	56	57	58	59	60	●
4	4	4	4	4	4	4	4	4	4	4	4	4	1
3	3	3	3	3	3	3	3	3	3	3	3	3	2
2	2	2	2	2	2	2	2	2	2	2	2	2	3
8	8	8	8	8	8	8	8	8	8	8	8	8	4
5	5	5	5	5	5	5	5	5	1	1	1	1	5
1	1	1	1	1	1	1	1	14	14	14			6
14	14	14	14	14	14	14	14	14	17	17	17		7
17	17	17	17	17	17	17	17	17	9	9	9		8
9	9	9	9	9	9	9	9	9	10	10	10		
10	10	10	10	10	10	10	10	10	15	15	15		
15	15	15	15	15	15	15	15	15	12	12			
21	21	21	21	21	21	21	12	12					
11	11	11	11	11	11	11	11	11	18	18			
12	12	12	12	12	18	18	18	19					
16	16	16	16	16	18	18	19	19					
18	18	18	18	18	19	19							
19	19	19	19										

Pit stop
One lap behind leader

CHASSIS LOG BOOK

1	Michael Schumacher	F2003-GA/229
2	Rubens Barrichello	F2003-GA/230
	Spare	F2003-GA/231
3	Juan Pablo Montoya	FW25/06
4	Ralf Schumacher	FW25/07
	Spare	FW25/04
5	David Coulthard	MP4/17D-07
6	Kimi Räikkönen	MP4/17D-09
	Spare	MP4/17D-06
7	Jarno Trulli	R23/05
8	Fernando Alonso	R23/04
	Allan McNish	R23/03
	Spare	R23/03
9	Nick Heidfeld	C22/01
10	Heinz-Harald Frentzen	C22/03
	Spare	C22/02

11	Giancarlo Fisichella	EJ-13/04
12	Ralph Firman	EJ-13/03
	Spare	EJ-13/02
14	Mark Webber	R4/04
15	Antonio Pizzonia	R4/05
	Spare	R4/03
16	Jacques Villeneuve	BAR005/3
17	Jenson Button	BAR005/5
	Spare	BAR005/4
18	Justin Wilson	PS03/04
19	Jos Verstappen	PS03/03
	Spare	PS03/02
20	Olivier Panis	TF103/05
21	Cristiano da Matta	TF103/07
	Spare	TF103/04

FRENCHGP
MAGNY-COURS

Making it two in a row. The French GP was Ralf Schumacher's second successive victory of 2003.
Photograph: Darren Heath

MAGNY-COURS QUALIFYING

Paul Stoddart's Minardi team certainly monopolised attention, both on and off the track, at Magny-Cours on the Friday of the French GP weekend. With Stoddart threatening to disrupt the political scene further at Silverstone a fortnight later, Minardi sprang a surprise when Jos Verstappen and Justin Wilson set fastest and second-fastest times during the saturated first qualifying session.

As F1's fastest runners slid and struggled for grip on a rain-soaked circuit, the Minardi duo made their one-lap qualifying runs at the end of the hour-long session, by which time the track surface had virtually dried out.

This left Verstappen just 0.1s in front of Wilson, with Ralph Firman's Jordan-Ford adding to the unreality in third place, ahead of Nick Heidfeld's Sauber, Olivier Panis's Toyota and the Jaguar of Antonio Pizzonia. Unfortunately, Wilson was stripped of his time when his car was found to be 2 kg below the minimum weight limit, the difference between a set of dry- and wet-weather tyres.

Meanwhile, Stoddart warned his rivals that a threat to the legality of their cars was in the pipeline. He wrote to them advising them that, as from Silverstone, Minardi would be removing all electronic driver aids from its cars. Then he hinted that his team would protest the other cars in the race under the provision in the rules that states that a driver must drive the car 'alone and unaided', there being no agreement on the validity of traction control and associated systems.

Stoddart was using this strategy as a means of forcing the top teams such as McLaren, Williams and Ferrari to allow the payment of $4 million each to Minardi and Jordan from a so-called 'fighting fund' to help the two cash-strapped small teams. This had been agreed originally in January, but the teams concerned had since declined to authorise payment. Thankfully, the whole affair blew over like the proverbial storm in a teacup.

In hot and humid conditions, Ralf Schumacher stormed to his third pole position of the season, posting a 1m 5.019s to ease out team-mate Juan Pablo Montoya by 0.11s and lead an all-Williams front row. 'I'm delighted with this pole, especially when I think that I went out fourth when the track had not reached its optimum condition,' said Ralf. 'My lap was reasonably clean, but it wasn't the best lap I've done due to some understeer in the third sector.'

Montoya reported that his car wasn't handling particularly well on his best effort, but obviously he was satisfied to be 0.34s ahead of Michael Schumacher's third-place Ferrari F2003-GA, clearly the fastest of the Bridgestone runners. Barrichello was unable to better eighth place with a disappointing 1m 16.166s. 'All of a sudden, the car was a lot worse than it was this morning,' said Rubens. 'I had terrible understeer and couldn't do anything about it. We lost most of our time in the second sector, which is due to traction and problems in the medium-fast corners.'

Kimi Räikkönen (1m 15.533s) and David Coulthard (1m 15.628s) wound up fourth and fifth fastest, the Scot at least feeling moderately content with this performance, even though he felt he could have driven harder.

'I was driving defensively,' admitted Coulthard, 'just keeping the lap tidy. Now I'm already looking back and I know I could have gone a couple of tenths quicker if I had pushed more.'

Jarno Trulli (1m 15.967s) and Fernando Alonso (1m 16.087s) in the Renault R23s proved closely matched in sixth and seventh positions on the grid, although Trulli admitted that he had experienced a little trouble in finding the right set-up on Saturday morning. Alonso was broadly satisfied with his performance.

The Jaguar squad was pleased with Mark Webber's ninth on 1m 16.308s, ahead of Antonio Pizzonia in 11th on 1m 16.965s. However, the weekend had got off to an unexpected start for Webber during Friday morning's practice, when Michael Schumacher's Ferrari was waved out of its pit straight into his left front wheel. Ferrari picked up a $10,000 fine for its inattentiveness.

For the BAR Honda team, missing Friday morning's free practice session while the legal squabbles were sorted out hardly helped Jenson Button or Jacques Villeneuve. Then the Englishman lost more track time on Saturday morning, thanks to an engine failure. Villeneuve would end up 12th on 1m 16.990s, while Jenson was two places farther back on 1m 17.077s.

Olivier Panis wound up tenth in the Toyota TF103 with a 1m 16.345s, and Cristiano da Matta was 13th on 1m 17.068s. The two Sauber C22s of Nick Heidfeld (1m 17.445s) and Heinz-Harald Frentzen (1m 17.562s) were next up, with the two Jordan-Fords and both Minardi-Cosworths side-by-side on rows nine and ten respectively.

DIARY

Hirotoshi Honda, the 61-year-old son of the late Soichiro Honda, is arrested in Japan on suspicion of a massive tax fraud relating to his Mugen company, which supplied F1 engines to the British Jordan team between 1998 and 2000.

World Champion Michael Schumacher describes Ferrari sporting director Jean Todt as 'a friend for life' in a touching tribute published in an Italian newspaper on the tenth anniversary of the Frenchman's arrival at Maranello.

American sports car racer Briggs Cunningham dies at the age of 96.

Anthony Davidson is lined up as reserve driver for the Jaguar F1 team. He is on loan from BAR Honda, where he is a test driver.

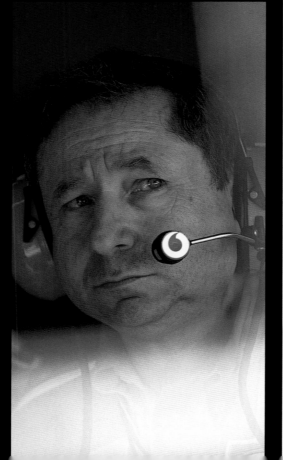

Left: Mark Webber continued to impress and score points for Jaguar.

Right: Ferrari sporting director Jean Todt received a warm tribute from Michael Schumacher.

Photographs: Darren Heath

WHAT a difference two months can make. At the A1-Ring, as Ralf Schumacher sat with his Williams-BMW's wheels spinning in a gravel trap during a qualifying session, you could almost touch the simmering sense of exasperation in the Williams team's pit-lane garage. Everything was going wrong. Williams was locked in a protracted debate with BMW over a new deal to extend their partnership beyond the end of 2004, but the cars were unreliable and the drivers inconsistent. Schumacher, in particular, had been driving erratically and with a lack of consistency that left his mechanics and engineers shaking their heads in despair.

There were even rumours that BMW might ditch Williams and join forces with another team. Yet at Magny-Cours, Ralf Schumacher continued the dramatic process of reinventing his front-line reputation with a matchless victory in the French Grand Prix, heading a Williams 1-2 in front of Juan Pablo Montoya for the second straight Sunday. He had started from pole position, driven with majestic poise and never looked in the slightest bit ruffled.

With the track temperature nudging steadily into the mid-30s as the cars accelerated away on their parade lap, there was much speculation as to whether or not the revamped layout at the Circuit de Nevers would produce a hotly contested race. As it transpired, the French GP would be yet another in the sequence of processional events that we've become used to over the years.

Ralf Schumacher surged straight into the lead from Montoya, while Kimi Räikkönen's McLaren slotted in ahead of Michael Schumacher's Ferrari, which had a wheel-to-wheel moment with David Coulthard's McLaren going into the first left-hand flick.

'At the start, Kimi got ahead because he made the better start,' said Michael immediately after the race. 'We will have to see if it was my reaction time or something on the car. David nearly came past as well and we ran side by side for a couple of corners, which was exciting.'

At the end of the opening lap, Ralf led from Juan Pablo, with Räikkönen still third, ahead of Michael's Ferrari, the quartet being covered by just 3.0s. Farther back, Rubens Barrichello spun on the revised left-hand kink before the pits, dropping from eighth to the tail of the field.

'I got my line wrong at the new chicane at the end of the first lap, as I was unsighted because I was following Alonso's Renault in front of me very closely,' explained Rubens later. 'When I turned in, I went up on the kerb, the car didn't want to respond and all I can say is that it was my mistake. My chances of a good result ended at that moment.'

The race quickly settled down into a procession, the leading foursome pulling steadily away, leaving Coulthard fifth, ahead of the two Renault R23s of Jarno Trulli and Fernando Alonso. These, in turn, were being tailed by Mark Webber's Jaguar in the opening phase of the chase.

A three-stop strategy had been calculated as the fastest way of completing the race distance, and Coulthard was the first of the serious runners to head for the pits on lap 15. He took on fuel in 7.0s. At this point, Ralf Schumacher was leading Montoya by 4.5s.

Räikkönen (6.8s), Trulli and Webber all made their first stops next time around, with Montoya (10.1s) and Alonso (7.3s) refuelling on lap 17, followed by Ralf on lap 18 (6.4s). The younger Schumacher rejoined the fray just over 6s ahead of Montoya. A sticking wheel nut had cost Juan Pablo about 3s, but the FW25 felt fine and the Colombian began to press on, chipping away at his team-mate's advantage. Meanwhile, Barrichello had recovered to eighth by the time he made his first 9.0s stop at the end of lap 20.

On the first anniversary of the announcement that he would be joining the BAR Honda team, Jenson Button was left pondering the latest in a succession of disappointing results in what he had hoped would be a positive and successful year. His race came to an abrupt end after 21 laps following a fuel-rig problem, which forced him to park his BAR 005 out on the circuit with a dry tank.

'It's obviously very disappointing to retire from a race with a problem like this,' he said. 'It's been a tough weekend, but the team put the problems behind it and made the best of things. The race was going well. The car's handling balance was good, even though we were slow.

'I was made aware by the team that there had been a fuel delivery problem, but then the car stopped out on the track before I had time to make another stop.'

One of the problems Button had referred to was the impounding of the BAR 005s on Thursday evening due to a legal wrangle over sponsorship commission allegedly owed to an agency. The local court reversed the initial decision to lock up the cars, but they missed the first practice session.

The second round of pit stops began on lap 31, with Räikkönen (7.9s) dropping from third to seventh. Coulthard, who had inherited

OBJETS
SAISIS
PAR LA S.C.P.
ETIENNE LAMOTTE
BRUNO GYS
ANDRE WAGNER
HUISSIERS DE JUSTICE
ASSOCIES
2 AVENUE SAINT JUST
58000 NEVERS

IMPORTANT :

BAR-HONDAS IMPOUNDED IN FRANCE

The BAR-Honda 005s were impounded and loaded into their transporters under the supervision of police and court officials on Thursday afternoon at Magny-Cours, as part of an ongoing legal action allegedly relating to unpaid commission on a sponsorship deal.

Around £2 million was being claimed by France Corbeil of the agency PPGI. He argued that he was owed the money under the terms of an agreement made with Craig Pollock, the founder of the BAR team, who had stood down as team principal at the end of 2001 to be replaced by David Richards.

BAR's lawyers were in court on Friday morning in a bid to have the cars released, but the issue was not resolved in time for them to be running at the start of the first free practice session at 11 am that day. However, they were freed by the court shortly after, the judge having ruled that the initial decision to impound the cars was invalid.

BAR had pointed out that the matter was being handled through the courts in Monaco and was due to be heard on 15 October. 'It was therefore surprising that PPGI should seek a seizure order on assets of the team when the due process and time-scale had already been established by the Monaco courts,' said a spokesperson.

The problem returned to haunt BAR on the Sunday evening after the race, when the team was made aware of further impending legal action by PPGI. The team issued a statement explaining that it was completely within its rights to remove its cars and equipment from the circuit and to return to the UK. It warned that it would be starting a counter-suit for damages caused by PPGI's 'unfounded statements'.

Above: David Richards had to sort out some irksome problems.

Top: The BAR Honda truck with the temporary injunction notice from the local court taped prominently to its door.

Above right: BAR on track. Jacques Villeneuve leads team-mate Button, Heidfeld, Frentzen and Verstappen.

Photographs: Darren Heath

third, refuelled on lap 32 in 6.6s. Montoya pitted (7.7s) from second on lap 34, while both Schumacher brothers came in for service next time around, Ralf taking 7.3s and Michael 7.0s. The status quo remained.

On lap 50, Montoya made his third pit visit in 8.1s, mistakenly figuring that Ralf would stay out for two more laps before refuelling. In fact, Schumacher took his FW25 in for a quick 7.6s stop and just squeezed out a fraction ahead of Montoya. Juan Pablo vented his frustration over the radio at the team whom, in the heat of the moment, he wrongly believed had connived against him.

Montoya said harsh things over the radio and later would receive a formal ticking off from the Williams management. Thereafter, he sulked and dropped back to finish a distant second, relinquishing a chance of having a tilt at the lead when Ralf made a slight mistake during the final stint and ran wide on one corner.

Renault, meanwhile, made a poor showing in its home race. Trulli's car began to lose performance on lap 42, retiring four laps later when a fuel leak into the engine airbox triggered a minor fire. Alonso went out on lap 44 with an engine failure, surprising his engineers, who had received no warning from the car's telemetry.

Similarly, David Coulthard was on the receiving end of more bad luck. During the last of his three refuelling stops, just as he

had been poised to vault ahead of his team-mate, Räikkönen, who had run third from the start, the refuelling rig malfunctioned. The team switched to the second rig, then David was waved back into the race before the mechanic refuelling the car had stepped clear of the left rear wheel.

The mechanic was knocked down as David accelerated away, but survived unscathed. In the chaos, a side deflector was knocked off the McLaren, although no other damage was sustained. However, by the time he had accelerated back into the race, David had lost the finely balanced fight to get on terms with Michael Schumacher's Ferrari, which eventually finished third.

'I made a good start and was fighting with Michael throughout turns one and two, but couldn't really get past,' said Coulthard. 'When the race settled down, Kimi and I were able to run at the same pace, but were not fast enough to challenge for the lead.

'Unfortunately, there were a couple of problems during my third pit stop. Initially, the fuel nozzle didn't attach correctly, we had to use the second one and then struggled when we had to remove it. Fortunately, nobody was injured, but I lost that possible third place.'

Yet while Coulthard might have regarded third place as something of a bonus, Michael Schumacher clearly regarded the whole

race as little more than an unmitigated disaster. His longer third stint had enabled him to vault ahead of Kimi in the closing stages, and the Finn was slowed further during the last few laps by brake problems, which culminated in a rear disc failure. After the race, Michael may have been the soul of tact and discretion when questioned about his Ferrari's performance, but when quizzed on the lacklustre performance of its Bridgestone tyres, his body language betrayed his annoyance and frustration.

'The car was as good as it could have been today, honestly,' said Schumacher, specifically avoiding any reference to the tyres. 'For us, it was sort of maximum. We had a bit of a struggle on the second set [of tyres]. The second stint was probably the slowest overall because afterwards it was pretty good for us.'

He added, 'Obviously, we need to be concerned about it. We see what they do, and we obviously work very hard at home to get our acts together to improve the situation.'

Behind Coulthard's eventually fifth-placed McLaren, Mark Webber repeated the sixth spot he had achieved at the Nürburgring the previous weekend, giving Jaguar personnel reason to be quietly satisfied. 'We had a good car today and it performed very well indeed,' he said.

Barrichello climbed back to seventh, ahead of Olivier Panis's Toyota, Jacques Villeneuve's BAR-Honda, the Jaguar of Antonio Pizzonia and the second Toyota of Cristiano da Matta. Panis felt that scoring a single point was certainly a positive result for the Cologne-based team, but da Matta had struggled with balance during the race. He put this down to the fact that he'd opted for the primary Michelin tyre rather than the optional compound.

'Looking ahead, I am very optimistic for Silverstone,' said the Brazilian. 'We had a positive test there recently and it is a track I enjoy.' Propitious words indeed.

Heinz-Harald Frentzen and Nick Heidfeld brought their Sauber C22s home in 12th and 13th places, ahead of Justin Wilson's Minardi, Ralf Firman in the sole surviving Jordan (Giancarlo Fisichella had succumbed to engine failure) and Jos Verstappen in the other Minardi.

At the end of the French GP, the FIA F1 World Championship seemed poised on the verge of a four-way shoot-out. But as Ferrari prepared to knuckle down to an intensive five-day, four-driver, three-circuit Bridgestone tyre testing blitz in preparation for Silverstone, many people left Magny-Cours carefully pondering the remaining six races of the year.

Perhaps this had been as bad as it would get for Michael Schumacher. And as good as it was going to get for Ralf.

FIA F1 WORLD CHAMPIONSHIP • ROUND 10

MOBIL 1
GRAND PRIX DE FRANCE
MAGNY-COURS 4–6 JULY 2003

Photograph: Darren Heath

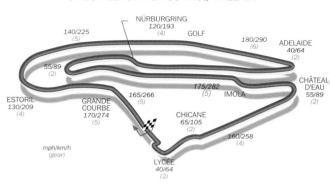

CIRCUIT DE NEVERS – MAGNY-COURS
CIRCUIT LENGTH: 2.756 miles/4.411 km

NÜRBURGRING 120/193 (4)
GOLF
140/225 (5)
180/290 (6)
ADELAIDE 40/64 (2)
55/89 (2)
CHÂTEAU D'EAU 55/89 (2)
175/282 (5)
IMOLA
165/266 (5)
ESTORIL 130/209 (4)
GRANDE COURBE 170/274 (5)
CHICANE 65/105 (2)
160/258 (4)
mph/km/h (gear)
LYCEE 40/64 (2)

RACE DISTANCE: 70 laps, 191.746 miles/308.586 km   RACE WEATHER: Hot and sunny (track 26/36°C, air 23/26°C)

Pos.	Driver	Nat.	No.	Entrant	Car/Engine	Tyres	Laps	Time/Retirement	Speed (mph/km/h)	Gap to leader	Fastest race lap	
1	Ralf Schumacher	D	4	BMW WilliamsF1 Team	Williams FW25-BMW P83 V10	M	70	1h 30m 49.213s	126.676/203.866		1m 15.698s	37
2	Juan Pablo Montoya	COL	3	BMW WilliamsF1 Team	Williams FW25-BMW P83 V10	M	70	1h 31m 03.026s	126.356/203.350	+13.813s	1m 15.512s	36
3	Michael Schumacher	D	1	Scuderia Ferrari Marlboro	Ferrari F2003-GA-051 V10	B	70	1h 31m 08.781s	126.223/203.136	+19.568s	1m 16.303s	19
4	Kimi Räikkönen	FIN	6	West McLaren Mercedes	McLaren MP4/17D-Mercedes F0110M V10	M	70	1h 31m 27.260s	125.798/202.452	+38.047s	1m 16.609s	19
5	David Coulthard	GB	5	West McLaren Mercedes	McLaren MP4/17D-Mercedes F0110M V10	M	70	1h 31m 29.502s	125.746/202.369	+40.289s	1m 15.981s	17
6	Mark Webber	AUS	14	Jaguar Racing	Jaguar R4-Cosworth CR5 V10	M	70	1h 31m 55.593s	125.151/201.412	+66.380s	1m 17.068s	47
7	Rubens Barrichello	BR	2	Scuderia Ferrari Marlboro	Ferrari F2003-GA-051 V10	B	69			+1 lap	1m 17.104s	47
8	Olivier Panis	F	20	Panasonic Toyota Racing	Toyota TF103-RVX-03 V10	M	69			+1 lap	1m 17.398s	36
9	Jacques Villeneuve	CDN	16	Lucky Strike BAR Honda	BAR 005-Honda RA003E V10	B	69			+1 lap	1m 17.786s	49
10	Antonio Pizzonia	BR	15	Jaguar Racing	Jaguar R4-Cosworth CR5 V10	M	69			+1 lap	1m 17.416s	67
11	Cristiano da Matta	BR	21	Panasonic Toyota Racing	Toyota TF103-RVX-03 V10	M	69			+1 lap	1m 17.870s	63
12	Heinz-Harald Frentzen	D	10	Sauber Petronas	Sauber C22-Petronas 03B V10	B	68			+2 laps	1m 18.099s	18
13	Nick Heidfeld	D	9	Sauber Petronas	Sauber C22-Petronas 03B V10	B	68			+2 laps	1m 18.994s	21
14	Justin Wilson	GB	18	European Minardi Cosworth	Minardi PS03-Cosworth CR3 V10	B	67			+3 laps	1m 19.588s	25
15	Ralph Firman	IRL	12	Jordan Ford	Jordan EJ-13-Ford Cosworth RS1 V10	B	67			+3 laps	1m 19.345s	13
16	Jos Verstappen	NL	19	European Minardi Cosworth	Minardi PS03-Cosworth CR3 V10	B	66			+4 laps	1m 18.754s	66
	Jarno Trulli	I	7	Mild Seven Renault F1 Team	Renault R3-RS23 V10	M	45	Engine			1m 17.025s	33
	Fernando Alonso	E	8	Mild Seven Renault F1 Team	Renault R3-RS23 V10	M	43	Engine			1m 17.029s	11
	Giancarlo Fisichella	I	11	Jordan Ford	Jordan EJ-13-Ford Cosworth RS1 V10	B	42	Engine			1m 19.093s	23
	Jenson Button	GB	17	Lucky Strike BAR Honda	BAR 005-Honda RA003E V10	B	21	Out of fuel			1m 17.149s	19

Fastest lap: Juan Pablo Montoya, on lap 36, 1m 15.512s, 130.669 mph/210.292 km/h (record for modified track layout).

Previous lap record: David Coulthard (F1 McLaren MP4/17-Mercedes V10), 1m 15.045s, 126.713 mph/203.925 km/h (2002).

20th: JUSTIN WILSON Minardi-Cosworth

18th: RALPH FIRMAN Jordan-Ford Cosworth

16th: HEINZ-HARALD FRENTZEN Sauber-Petronas

14th: JENSON BUTTON BAR-Honda

12th: JACQUES VILLENEUVE BAR-Honda

19th: JOS VERSTAPPEN Minardi-Cosworth

17th: GIANCARLO FISICHELLA Jordan-Ford Cosworth

15th: NICK HEIDFELD Sauber-Petronas

13th: CRISTIANO DA MATTA Toyota

11th: ANTONIO PIZZONIA Jaguar-Cosworth

Grid order	1	2	3	4	5	6	7	8	9	10	11	12	13	14	15	16	17	18	19	20	21	22	23	24	25	26	27	28	29	30	31	32	33	34	35	36	37	38	39	40	41	42	43	44	45	46	47	48	49	50	51	52	53
4 R. SCHUMACHER	4	4	4	4	4	4	4	4	4	4	4	4	4	4	4	4	4	4	4	4	4	4	4	4	4	4	4	4	4	4	4	4	4	4	4	4	4	4	4	4	4	4	4	4	4	4	4	4	4	4	4	4	4
3 MONTOYA	3	3	3	3	3	3	3	3	3	3	3	3	3	3	3	3	3	3	3	3	3	3	3	3	3	3	3	3	3	3	3	3	3	3	3	3	3	3	3	3	3	3	3	3	3	3	3	3	3	3	3	3	3
1 M. SCHUMACHER	6	6	6	6	6	6	6	6	6	6	6	6	6	6	6	1	6	6	6	6	6	6	6	6	6	6	6	6	6	6	6	5	1	1	1	8	6	6	6	6	6	6	6	6	6	6	5	1	1	1	1	1	
6 RÄIKKÖNEN	1	1	1	1	1	1	1	1	1	1	1	1	1	1	1	8	5	5	5	5	5	5	5	5	5	5	5	5	5	5	5	1	7	7	8	6	5	5	5	5	5	5	5	5	5	5	1	6	6	6	6	6	
5 COULTHARD	5	5	5	5	5	5	5	5	5	5	5	5	5	5	5	7	6	1	1	1	1	1	1	1	1	1	1	1	1	1	1	7	8	8	6	5	1	1	1	1	1	1	1	6	5	5	5	5	5	5	5	5	
7 TRULLI	7	7	7	7	7	7	7	7	7	7	7	7	7	7	7	8	7	7	7	7	7	7	7	7	7	7	7	7	7	8	6	5	6	1	7	7	7	7	7	8	14	14	14	14	14	14	14	14					
8 ALONSO	8	8	8	8	8	8	8	8	8	8	8	8	8	8	14		8	7	8	8	8	8	8	8	8	8	8	8	8	6	5	8	7	7	8	8	8	8	8	14	7	2	20	20	20	20	20	20	2				
2 BARRICHELLO	2	14	14	14	14	14	14	14	14	14	14	14	14	14	20	16	16	2	2	14	14	14	14	14	14	14	14	14	20	20	20	14	14	14	14	14	14	14	7	2	20	2	2	2	2	2	2	20					
14 WEBBER	14	15	15	15	15	15	15	15	15	15	15	15	15	20	5	17	21	21	14	15	15	15	15	15	15	15	20	14	14	16	16	2	2	2	2	2	2	20	7	16	16	16	16	16	16	16							
20 PANIS	15	20	20	20	20	20	20	20	20	20	20	20	20	16	16	2	14	15	20	20	20	20	20	20	20	16	16	16	2	2	16	20	20	20	20	20	21	21	15	15	15	15	15	15									
15 PIZZONIA	20	16	16	16	16	16	16	16	16	16	16	16	16	2	14	5	20	20	16	16	16	16	16	16	16	2	2	2	20	20	21	21	21	21	16	16	21	21	21	21	21	21	21	21									
16 VILLENEUVE	16	17	17	17	17	17	17	17	17	17	17	17	2	14	16	16	2	2	2	2	2	2	2	2	2	21	21	21	21	21	15	15	15	15	15	15	15	15	10	10	10	10	10	10									
21 DA MATTA	17	21	21	21	21	21	21	21	21	21	21	2	15	15	20	9	17	16	21	21	21	21	21	21	21	15	15	15	15	15	16	16	16	16	10	10	10	10	9	9	9	9	9	9									
17 BUTTON	21	9	9	9	9	9	2	2	2	2	2	15	20	9	16	21	21	10	10	10	10	10	10	10	9	9	9	9	9	10	10	10	10	9	9	18	18	18	18	18													
9 HEIDFELD	9	19	19	19	19	19	2	2	9	9	9	9	9	11	11	11	11	9	9	9	9	9	10	10	10	10	10	10	9	9	9	9	9	9	19	18	19	19	19	19													
10 FRENTZEN	19	10	10	10	2	19	19	19	10	10	10	10	10	10	18	11	11	11	11	11	11	11	11	11	11	11	11	11	11	11	11	11	11	18	18	12	12	12	12	12													
11 FISICHELLA	10	11	11	11	11	10	10	10	11	11	11	11	11	9	9	18	18	19	19	19	12	18	18	18	18	18	18	18	12	18	12	12	12	12	18																		
12 FIRMAN	11	12	12	12	11	11	11	11	12	12	12	12	12	18	18	18	10	18	18	18	18	9	19	19	19	19	19	19	18	12	18	18	18	18	12																		
19 VERSTAPPEN	12	18	2	18	18	18	18	12	18	18	18	18	19	19	19	19	9	12	12	12	19	19	12	12	12	12	12	12	19	19	19	19	19																				
18 WILSON	18	2	18	12	12	12	12	18	19	19	19	19	18	12	12	12	12	12	12	12	12	12	12	12	12																												

TIME SHEETS

SATURDAY QUALIFYING determines race grid order

Dry and hot (track 30°C, air 21°C)

Pos.	Driver	Lap time	Sector 1	Sector 2	Sector 3
1	Ralf Schumacher	1m 15.019s	24.238s	26.208s	24.573s
2	Juan Pablo Montoya	1m 15.136s	24.353s	26.146s	24.637s
3	Michael Schumacher	1m 15.480s	24.187s	26.547s	24.746s
4	Kimi Räikkönen	1m 15.533s	24.275s	26.337s	24.921s
5	David Coulthard	1m 15.628s	24.441s	26.387s	24.800s
6	Jarno Trulli	1m 15.967s	24.536s	26.562s	24.869s
7	Fernando Alonso	1m 16.087s	24.516s	26.584s	24.987s
8	Rubens Barrichello	1m 16.166s	24.426s	26.726s	25.014s
9	Mark Webber	1m 16.308s	24.853s	26.489s	24.966s
10	Olivier Panis	1m 16.345s	24.646s	26.580s	25.119s
11	Antonio Pizzonia	1m 16.965s	24.801s	27.022s	25.142s
12	Jacques Villeneuve	1m 16.990s	24.666s	26.943s	25.381s
13	Cristiano da Matta	1m 17.068s	24.812s	26.932s	25.324s
14	Jenson Button	1m 17.077s	24.545s	27.003s	25.529s
15	Nick Heidfeld	1m 17.445s	24.812s	27.147s	25.486s
16	Heinz-Harald Frentzen	1m 17.562s	24.967s	27.027s	25.568s
17	Giancarlo Fisichella	1m 18.431s	25.149s	27.222s	26.060s
18	Ralph Firman	1m 18.514s	25.269s	27.313s	25.932s
19	Jos Verstappen	1m 19.709s	25.363s	27.374s	25.972s
20	Justin Wilson	1m 19.619s	25.953s	27.625s	26.041s

FRIDAY QUALIFYING determines Sat running order

Damp track, becoming drier (track 24/28°C, air 21/22°C)

Pos.	Driver	Lap time
1	Jos Verstappen	1m 20.817s
2	Ralph Firman	1m 23.496s
3	Nick Heidfeld	1m 24.042s
4	Olivier Panis	1m 24.175s
5	Antonio Pizzonia	1m 24.642s
6	Jacques Villeneuve	1m 24.651s
7	Mark Webber	1m 25.178s
8	Heinz-Harald Frentzen	1m 26.151s
9	Cristiano da Matta	1m 26.975s
10	Rubens Barrichello	1m 27.095s
11	Michael Schumacher	1m 27.929s
12	Giancarlo Fisichella	1m 28.502s
13	David Coulthard	1m 28.937s
14	Juan Pablo Montoya	1m 28.988s
15	Jarno Trulli	1m 29.024s
16	Kimi Räikkönen	1m 29.120s
17	Ralf Schumacher	1m 29.327s
18	Fernando Alonso	1m 29.455s
19	Jenson Button	1m 30.731s
20	Justin Wilson*	–

* Time disallowed

POINTS TABLES: CONSTRUCTORS

1	Ferrari	103
2	Williams	100
3	McLaren	85
4	Renault	52
5	BAR	13
6	Jaguar	12
7	Jordan	11
8	Sauber	9
9	Toyota	5

FOR THE RECORD

150 grand prix starts

Renault

PRIVATE TESTING

Dry, rain later (track 18/20°C, air 17/19°C)

Pos.	Driver	Laps	Time
1	Fernando Alonso	38	1m 16.709s
2	Mark Webber	23	1m 17.017s
3	Jarno Trulli	50	1m 17.323s
4	Antonio Pizzonia	23	1m 17.946s
5	Giancarlo Fisichella	26	1m 18.771s
6	Franck Montagny	28	1m 18.823s
7	Jos Verstappen	24	1m 19.289s
8	Justin Wilson	16	1m 19.636s
9	Ralph Firman	35	1m 20.259s

FRIDAY FREE PRACTICE

Dry and warm (track 21/23°C, air 18/19°C)

Pos.	Driver	Laps	Time
1	Mark Webber	27	1m 26.915s
2	Ralf Schumacher	24	1m 28.082s
3	Fernando Alonso	20	1m 28.260s
4	Jarno Trulli	19	1m 28.296s
5	Antonio Pizzonia	30	1m 28.442s
6	Michael Schumacher	16	1m 28.681s
7	David Coulthard	21	1m 28.718s
8	Olivier Panis	20	1m 28.773s
9	Giancarlo Fisichella	16	1m 28.782s
10	Heinz-Harald Frentzen	21	1m 28.803s
11	Kimi Räikkönen	22	1m 28.846s
12	Nick Heidfeld	23	1m 29.317s
13	Juan Pablo Montoya	21	1m 29.608s
14	Ralph Firman	22	1m 29.640s
15	Rubens Barrichello	18	1m 29.813s
16	Cristiano da Matta	25	1m 30.791s
17	Jos Verstappen	19	1m 32.091s
18	Justin Wilson	17	1m 32.535s
19	Jenson Button		No time
20	Jacques Villeneuve		No time

SATURDAY FIRST FREE PRACTICE

Dry and cloudy (track 28°C, air 19°C)

Pos.	Driver	Laps	Time
1	Fernando Alonso	24	1m 16.076s
2	Rubens Barrichello	19	1m 16.190s
3	Ralf Schumacher	20	1m 16.291s
4	Michael Schumacher	15	1m 16.495s
5	Juan Pablo Montoya	21	1m 16.687s
6	David Coulthard	19	1m 16.840s
7	Kimi Räikkönen	13	1m 17.050s
8	Cristiano da Matta	25	1m 17.118s
9	Jarno Trulli	14	1m 17.123s
10	Olivier Panis	18	1m 17.186s
11	Mark Webber	21	1m 17.197s
12	Jenson Button	22	1m 17.341s
13	Jacques Villeneuve	20	1m 17.452s
14	Antonio Pizzonia	16	1m 17.959s
15	Heinz-Harald Frentzen	15	1m 18.295s
16	Nick Heidfeld	13	1m 18.455s
17	Giancarlo Fisichella	14	1m 18.749s
18	Ralph Firman	17	1m 18.876s
19	Jos Verstappen	21	1m 19.089s
20	Justin Wilson	17	1m 19.948s

SATURDAY SECOND FREE PRACTICE

Dry and cloudy (track 28°C, air 19°C)

Pos.	Driver	Laps	Time
1	Ralf Schumacher	17	1m 14.966s
2	Juan Pablo Montoya	17	1m 15.577s
3	David Coulthard	14	1m 15.600s
4	Michael Schumacher	19	1m 15.918s
5	Kimi Räikkönen	14	1m 16.012s
6	Fernando Alonso	20	1m 16.039s
7	Mark Webber	24	1m 16.112s
8	Olivier Panis	17	1m 16.133s
9	Rubens Barrichello	18	1m 16.345s
10	Jarno Trulli	22	1m 16.376s
11	Antonio Pizzonia	25	1m 17.036s
12	Jacques Villeneuve	21	1m 17.101s
13	Cristiano da Matta	22	1m 17.690s
14	Heinz-Harald Frentzen	23	1m 17.776s
15	Jenson Button	3	1m 17.808s
16	Giancarlo Fisichella	21	1m 17.908s
17	Nick Heidfeld	25	1m 18.057s
18	Ralph Firman	17	1m 18.670s
19	Jos Verstappen	8	1m 18.696s
20	Justin Wilson	18	1m 19.044s

WARM-UP

Dry and hot (track 30°C, air 21°C)

Pos.	Driver	Laps	Time
1	Ralf Schumacher	4	1m 15.092s
2	Juan Pablo Montoya	6	1m 15.697s
3	Kimi Räikkönen	5	1m 15.822s
4	David Coulthard	4	1m 15.823s
5	Michael Schumacher	6	1m 15.879s
6	Olivier Panis	4	1m 16.238s
7	Fernando Alonso	7	1m 16.262s
8	Rubens Barrichello	6	1m 16.332s
9	Mark Webber	4	1m 16.801s
10	Jenson Button	7	1m 17.091s
11	Antonio Pizzonia	5	1m 17.212s
12	Jacques Villeneuve	5	1m 17.304s
13	Heinz-Harald Frentzen	7	1m 17.378s
14	Cristiano da Matta	6	1m 17.382s
15	Nick Heidfeld	5	1m 17.945s
16	Ralph Firman	7	1m 18.300s
17	Giancarlo Fisichella	4	1m 18.427s
18	Jos Verstappen	5	1m 18.899s
19	Justin Wilson	5	1m 19.454s
20	Jarno Trulli	3	No time

10th: OLIVIER PANIS Toyota

8th: RUBENS BARRICHELLO Ferrari

6th: JARNO TRULLI Renault

4th: KIMI RÄIKKÖNEN McLaren-Mercedes

2nd: JUAN PABLO MONTOYA Williams-BMW

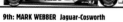

9th: MARK WEBBER Jaguar-Cosworth

7th: FERNANDO ALONSO Renault

5th: DAVID COULTHARD McLaren-Mercedes

3rd: MICHAEL SCHUMACHER Ferrari

Pole: RALF SCHUMACHER Williams-BMW

55	56	57	58	59	60	61	62	63	64	65	66	67	68	69	70	•
4	4	4	4	4	4	4	4	4	4	4	4	4	4	4	4	1
3	3	3	3	3	3	3	3	3	3	3	3	3	3	3	3	2
1	1	1	1	1	1	1	1	1	1	1	1	1	1	1	1	3
6	6	6	6	6	6	6	6	6	6	6	6	6	6	6	6	4
5	5	5	5	5	5	5	5	5	5	5	5	5	5	5	5	5
14	14	14	14	14	14	14	14	14	14	14	14	14	14	14	14	6
2	2	2	2	2	2	2	2	2	2	2	2	2	2	2		7
20	20	20	20	20	20	20	20	20	20	20	20	20	20	20		8
16	16	16	16	16	16	16	16	16	16	16	16	16	16	16		
15	15	15	15	15	15	15	15	15	15	15	15	15	15	15		
21	21	21	21	21	21	21	21	21	21	21	21	21	21	21		
10	10	10	10	10	10	10	10	10	10	10	10	10	10			
9	9	9	9	9	9	9	9	9	9	9	9	9	9			
18	18	18	18	18	18	18	18	18	18	18	18	18				
19	19	19	19	19	19	12	12	12	12	12	12	12				
12	12	12	12	12	12	19	19	19	19	19	19					

Pit stop

One lap behind leader

CHASSIS LOG BOOK

1	Michael Schumacher	F2003-GA/229
2	Rubens Barrichello	F2003-GA/230
	Spare	F2003-GA/231
3	Juan Pablo Montoya	FW25/06
4	Ralf Schumacher	FW25/07
	Spare	FW25/04
5	David Coulthard	MP4/17D-08
6	Kimi Räikkönen	MP4/17D-09
	Spare	MP4/17D-06
7	Jarno Trulli	R23/05
8	Fernando Alonso	R23/04
	Franck Montagny	R23/03
	Spare	R23/03
9	Nick Heidfeld	C22/01
10	Heinz-Harald Frentzen	C22/03
	Spare	C22/02
11	Giancarlo Fisichella	EJ-13/04
12	Ralph Firman	EJ-13/03
	Spare	EJ-13/02
14	Mark Webber	R4/04
15	Antonio Pizzonia	R4/05
	Spare	R4/03
16	Jacques Villeneuve	BAR005/3
17	Jenson Button	BAR005/4
	Spare	BAR005/5
18	Justin Wilson	PS03/04
19	Jos Verstappen	PS03/03
	Spare	PS03/02
20	Olivier Panis	TF103/05
21	Cristiano da Matta	TF103/07
	Spare	TF103/02

POINTS TABLES: DRIVERS

1	Michael Schumacher	64
2	Kimi Räikkönen	56
3	Ralf Schumacher	53
4	Juan Pablo Montoya	47
5 =	Rubens Barrichello	39
5 =	Fernando Alonso	39
7	David Coulthard	29
8	Jarno Trulli	13
9	Mark Webber	12
10 =	Giancarlo Fisichella	10
10 =	Jenson Button	10
12	Heinz-Harald Frentzen	7
13 =	Jacques Villeneuve	3
13 =	Cristiano da Matta	3
15 =	Olivier Panis	2
15 =	Nick Heidfeld	2
17	Ralph Firman	1

Feeling lucky? Rubens Barrichello celebrates his first win of the season, with friendly assistance from Montoya.
Photograph: Darren Heath

FIA F1 WORLD CHAMPIONSHIP • ROUND 11

BRITISH GP
SILVERSTONE

NiQuitinCQ

SILVERSTONE QUALIFYING

Rubens Barrichello is hugely popular with the British crowds, but his weekend got off to a shaky start in Friday qualifying when he speared into the gravel at the tight Luffield left-hander as a light drizzle brushed the circuit. That meant he was second in the queue to run in Saturday qualifying, behind Justin Wilson's Minardi, which had also failed to make a lap in the first session. This played into Rubens's hands, since the track surface was slightly cooler than when team-mate Michael Schumacher made his banzai run at the end of the practice period.

Michael was 0.006s faster than Barrichello at the first timing split, but slid wide over the kerb coming out of the Abbey chicane, which dropped him to fifth on the grid, behind his team-mate, Jarno Trulli's Renault R23B, Kimi Räikkönen's McLaren-Mercedes and Ralf Schumacher in the fastest of the Williams FW25s. Juan Pablo Montoya could only qualify seventh after being troubled by unpredictably gusting crosswinds on his quickest lap.

Thus, Barrichello's 1m 21.209s best came as a huge bonus after his disappointment of the previous day. 'Yesterday was just a little bit of a mishap in a way because the conditions were such where nobody had the track [conditions] exactly the same,' he said. 'I wanted to try things different and it worked out [for me] because I tried something completely new for that lap, which taught me that it didn't work, so I could start on a different [set-up] route this morning. But having said that, there is a little bit more pressure for you to be out as one of the first guys and you cannot make the same mistakes.'

Jarno Trulli was similarly delighted with his 1m 21.381s best, which earned him second place on the front row, relishing the performance of the revised aerodynamic package and engine spec upgrade sported by the Renault R23 for this race.

'I am extremely happy, but also surprised about my performance because I have been struggling all weekend with some trouble that stopped me improving my performance and car set-up,' he said. 'But then we got on top of it for qualifying.'

Trulli was the only driver who could make Michelin's softer tyre option work really well, his team-mate Fernando Alonso being forced to stay on the harder rubber after suffering blistering with the softer choice.

Alonso wound up eighth on 1m 22.404s. 'We had some problems with the set-up this morning,' he shrugged. 'I'm not sure if it was because of the change in track conditions, but the overall grip was not fantastic.'

Again it was Kimi Räikkönen who came out on top for the McLaren team,

posting a third-fastest 1m 21.695s in his MP4/17D. He was pleased with his lap, as he had been having difficulties with handling balance on Friday and had made some really worthwhile improvements to correct it. By contrast, David Coulthard had battled once more to get on the qualifying pace, ending up 12th on 1m 22.811s.

'I was really struggling with the balance of the car,' said Coulthard. 'As a result, I ran wide at Stowe, locked up the front under braking at Club and lost a lot of time. I was generally not hitting the apex of the corners, and we tried to make a few more changes after the warm-up, but they did not work out.'

Key rival BMW Williams also saw one of its drivers ending up in a good mood, the other less so. Ralf Schumacher posted a 1m 21.727s best to claim fourth place in his FW25, despite having to struggle with the balance of his car.

Juan Pablo Montoya was much less satisfied with a seventh-fastest 1m 22.214s. 'I am disappointed with this result because my car was very good and very stable this morning, and then it turned out to be not as positive in the warm-up and qualifying,' he explained. 'I didn't seem to have found the right balance as I was experiencing plenty of oversteer in some of the corners and generally poor traction. The car was very difficult to drive and very snappy.'

Cristiano da Matta produced a very assured performance to post sixth-fastest time on 1m 22.081s, winding up seven places ahead of his disappointed team-mate, Olivier Panis, who had suffered a major oversteering moment under braking during the last sector of the lap.

Another impressive performance came from Antonio Pizzonia, who managed a tenth-fastest 1m 22.634s, a tad faster than Jaguar R4 team-mate Mark Webber on this occasion; his 'reward' for this improved showing was to be dropped by the team in favour of Justin Wilson prior to the following race at Hockenheim.

In the BAR Honda camp, Jacques Villeneuve survived an engine failure and a spin on Saturday morning to post a ninth-fastest 1m 22.591s. That left Jenson Button to start his home grand prix 20th and last after he clipped a kerb at Becketts, breaking a front suspension pushrod, which caused him to abort his qualifying run.

Heinz-Harald Frentzen (1m 23.187s) and Nick Heidfeld (1m 23.844s) lined up their Sauber C22s 14th and 16th, sandwiching Giancarlo Fisichella's Jordan-Ford, while Ralph Firman and the two Minardis completed the grid line-up, ahead of the hapless Button.

DIARY

Justin Wilson signs for Jaguar as Antonio Pizzonia's replacement on the Monday after the British Grand Prix. Dane Nicolas Kiesa takes his place in the Minardi squad.

Giancarlo Fisichella visits the Sauber factory, fuelling speculation that he may join the Swiss team in 2004.

McLaren reaffirms its confidence that the new MP4/18A will race sometime during the 2003 season, despite failing its FIA side-impact test for the third time.

Alex Zanardi tries a specially adapted BMW racing saloon at Misano, the Italian toying with the idea of a return to racing.

IT may have been interrupted unexpectedly by a demonstrator on the track, but the British Grand Prix turned out to be easily the best F1 race so far of 2003. Rubens Barrichello drove immaculately to post his first win of the season, at a time when his future with Ferrari – beyond the expiry of his contract at the end of 2004 – had seemed in some doubt.

'This is a fantastic feeling,' enthused Barrichello. 'I came in for a lot of criticism after Canada and France, and I feel this performance answers my critics. I always leave my emotions behind when I get into the race car, but it is impossible for me not to want to cry when I hear the Brazilian anthem on the podium. It makes me think of my father, who sold his car so that I could start racing. Your last win is always your best, and this one certainly ranks highly.'

Yet if Barrichello was a worried man before the start, he certainly kept his concerns to himself. Outgunned in the early stages of the race by Jarno Trulli's Renault R23, which had started alongside his Ferrari F2003-GA on the front row of the grid, initially the Brazilian had been content to sit back in third place, behind Kimi Räikkönen's McLaren-Mercedes, and watch to see how the contest panned out.

It didn't take long for the race to develop into a tightly fought affair. After four laps, Trulli, Räikkönen, Barrichello, Ralf Schumacher (Williams-BMW) and Michael Schumacher (Ferrari) were covered by just 5.9s at the head of the pack. Earlier, Michael had attracted some adverse comment after ruthlessly chopping Fernando Alonso's Renault going into Stowe on the opening lap, forcing the Spanish driver to take to the grass.

The first unexpected development came on lap five, when David Coulthard's McLaren, in ninth place, shed its carbon-fibre cockpit surround, depositing debris on the circuit and triggering the first safety-car deployment. Ironically, the slow pace of the safety car reduced the negative effect on Coulthard's prospects by a 28.5s stop for repairs and enabled the Scot to stay in play for the rest of the afternoon.

He pitted at the same time as the Toyotas of Cristiano da Matta and Olivier Panis, and the race duly restarted when the safety car

was withdrawn at the end of lap eight. Trulli retained the lead from Räikkönen, Barrichello, Ralf and Michael Schumacher, Juan Pablo Montoya and Fernando Alonso.

Twelve laps into the 60-lap race, a lunatic protester wearing a kilt vaulted the spectator fence and began running up the Hangar Straight against the direction of the competing cars.

Although he didn't seem bent on suicide, it was a horrifying moment, which triggered the second safety-car period of the race. After cars swerved and wobbled dangerously at around 170 mph, the interloper was rugby tackled by an efficient marshal and dragged away by security staff to be arrested by the local police.

The protester – who turned out to be a religious activist and former priest called Neil Horan – had waved a sign with the message 'Read the Bible. The Bible is always right.' It was reported that previously he had carried out similar 'dances for peace' outside the Houses of Parliament and Newbury racecourse.

Later, it emerged that ITV commentator Jim Rosenthal had received a letter from the demonstrator prior to the race, warning that he was 'going to do something which will get you talking about me.'

Rosenthal had consigned the letter to the waste bin and was stunned to see 56-year-old Horan running on the circuit, just feet from cars travelling at high speed.

'Yes, I did receive a letter which turned out to be from this man,' said Rosenthal, 'but I would have to say in the commentating business you do tend to get some very strange mail from time to time.

'On this occasion, I must say that I read the first few lines and then threw it in the bin. His theme seemed to be, "Why do you spend all your time talking about racing cars when you should be reading the Bible." But I must stress he made no specific reference to the British Grand Prix.'

Rosenthal added, 'To be honest, it's terribly difficult to police many sports, not just racing. If somebody really wants to throw themselves in front of the 6.30 race at Windsor, then ultimately it's going to be pretty difficult to stop them.'

Nevertheless, Horan's presence on the circuit stunned the drivers. 'It absolutely blew me away,' said Mark Webber. 'It was all

Left: Rubens Barrichello took pole position with a stunning lap and made it count on race day.
Photograph: Bryn Williams/crash.net

Below left: Justin Wilson's F1 gamble appeared to have paid off with the announcement of a move to Jaguar.

Below: Jarno Trulli joined Barrichello on the front row, but encountered problems with grip and had to be satisfied with a sixth-place finish.
Photographs: Darren Heath

over in two-and-a-half seconds. Coming on to the straight, I was focusing on the car in front and saw a few different colours. Then I realised it was a person.

'The last thing you expect as you exit a high-speed corner is some idiot doing this. For a moment, I thought this was the end for me.'

This episode prompted the crucial tactical turning point of the race. No fewer than 14 cars took the opportunity to dive into the pits, scrambling frantically to refuel and change tyres while the safety car was circulating.

For a few chaotic minutes, the pit lane looked as crowded and as unpredictable as London's Strand during the rush hour, cars darting in and out among their impassive refuelling crews, often with only inches between them.

Everybody emerged intact, but this unscheduled round of stops played unexpectedly into the hands of the Toyota team. Having

opted for a three-stop refuelling strategy, but the 2002 CART champion had certainly laid down a crucial marker for the future.

'I thoroughly enjoyed that race and was quite happy with the way things went for us,' he said. 'I'm used to leading races, but this was the first time in Formula One, which was a very special feeling. I knew it wouldn't last long, so I enjoyed it while I could and pushed hard to build up as much time advantage as possible.'

Da Matta's golden moment in the limelight ended on lap 30, when he made his second refuelling stop, dropping to sixth and allowing Räikkönen through into the lead. The Finn held on until he refuelled for the second time on lap 35, after which Barrichello went ahead for three laps before pitting on lap 39.

Thereafter, the race settled down as a two-way battle between Räikkönen and Barrichello. Rubens slipped through into the lead after Räikkönen ran wide coming out of the tricky 130-mph Bridge right-hander on lap 42, and from then on he was never headed to the chequered flag.

'My engineers did a great job to give me such a good car so that I could attack and overtake,' Barrichello summed up. 'I lost two places at the start because I had to wait a long time for Trulli to come to the grid [so] my tyres lost temperature and I had no grip. But I knew I would be okay once the tyres came up to temperature.

'My passing move on Kimi was very close and I almost lost my nose. It was an aggressive, but fair fight.'

Räikkönen was in broad agreement: 'I was maybe a little quicker at the beginning of the race, but I was not able to get close enough to Jarno to be able to try and overtake. Then I started to lose the rear grip a little, and Rubens was so much stronger out of Club that I just wasn't able to hold him off.

'So I knew he had much better traction there and, while I tried to hold him off later, he got alongside me at Bridge and I just tried to go around the outside. But I got a little bit on the dirty track, ran slightly wide and he got past.'

Another small slip cost Räikkönen second place to Montoya, while Michael Schumacher wound up fourth after a day that had seen him running as low as 14th during the convoluted event.

Montoya was delighted with second. 'The only mistake I made was when I think a Jaguar blew up on the back straight and I was on the inside on every lap so I wouldn't go on the oil, and after the pit stop I thought it should be pretty good [cleared up] now and I braked on the oil and just went straight,' he explained. 'I think Kimi had the same problem when I passed him.'

Michael finished the day still leading the championship by seven points, ahead of Räikkönen, with Montoya emerging as the most likely Williams challenger for the title in third place, some 14 points behind the Ferrari driver.

'It was an interesting and very busy race,' said the world champion. 'To be honest, it was difficult to have an overview of what happened from the cockpit. Waiting in pit lane behind Rubens for the first stop meant we both lost a bit of time, and we lost some more as the mechanics had to wait for a gap in the traffic to let Rubens out. But it was definitely the right decision to come in and wait rather than do another lap. Rubens deserves his victory and I am happy for him.'

As for Coulthard, fifth place at Silverstone left him trailing in seventh on 33 points, his World Championship hopes all but written off for yet another season.

Trulli wound up a disappointing sixth after his car had lost grip following his first stop. 'Under the circumstances, I'm not sure whether to be satisfied or disappointed,' he mused after the race.

Da Matta came home seventh, ahead of the hard-charging Button, who'd driven well all afternoon from his starting position at the back of the grid. 'That was a lot of fun,' he grinned. 'It was always going to be hard from the back, but I don't think we could have done any better than that – it was one of the best performances of my career.

'I had a lot of fun carving my way through the field, and it was a great feeling for Jacques and I to be fighting with Michael.'

Ralf Schumacher took ninth, the first time he had been out of the points in the 2003 season, having been delayed when a guide vane came adrift and blocked the airflow to his FW25's water radiators. He crossed the line just over 5s ahead of Villeneuve, with Panis and Frentzen being the last unlapped runners in 11th and 12th places.

There were only three retirements. Fernando Alonso quit with electronic problems, his Renault R23 rolling to a standstill in front of the pits, while Pizzonia's Jaguar suffered an engine failure. Finally, Giancarlo Fisichella's miserable run of luck continued with a rear suspension failure at Becketts, of all places, after which he crawled back to the pits. Doubtless counting his lucky stars.

made their first refuelling stops during the previous safety-car period, Cristiano da Matta and Olivier Panis now went surging into first and second places, hotly pursued by Coulthard and Trulli.

Barrichello had lost a lot of time and dropped back to eighth, but the biggest losers turned out to be Montoya, Alonso and Michael Schumacher, all of whom had to wait for their teammates to be refuelled, rejoining respectively 12th, 13th and 14th. Jenson Button and Heinz-Harald Frentzen were similarly handicapped and were pushed back to 18th and 19th.

It took only another five laps for the on-form Räikkönen to muscle his way up to second place, behind da Matta, but if he thought the Brazilian was going to be a push-over, he was about to be disillusioned.

Da Matta, driving in only his 11th grand prix, spent the next 13 laps leading the field with a cool confidence that belied his inexperience. He would finish the afternoon in seventh place after Toyota

ECCLESTONE MAINTAINS PRESSURE ON SILVERSTONE

Silverstone had certainly spruced up its act for the 2003 British Grand Prix, with better facilities, more organised access roads and a general upbeat ambience, which reflected the amount of effort that had been expended on the track. Yet none of that prevented Bernie Ecclestone from continuing his relentless, sometimes slightly baffling, critique of the Northamptonshire circuit.

Ecclestone announced that he was giving Silverstone a one-month deadline to sort out its long-term programme of improvements or risk the prospect of being dropped from the World Championship calendar.

This was the uncompromising and continuing theme of his warnings, his thoughts largely being echoed by FIA president Max Mosley. Their firm message was that the British Racing Drivers' Club, which owns Silverstone, should borrow around £40 million to guarantee its continued programme of investment as well as secure some form of government backing to underwrite any future losses sustained by the race promoter, Brands Hatch Leisure (formerly Octagon Motorsport).

As Mosley schmoozed government ministers Peter Hain, Geoff Hoon and Patricia Hewitt in the FIA's hospitality area, Ecclestone renewed his attack on the BRDC, an organisation for which he is hard pressed to conceal his disdain.

'If by the middle of August, Silverstone can commit to building its originally planned pit complex [between Club corner and Abbey curve] and the government can come up with some guarantees to help the promoters, then we will give firm undertakings to the government that this race will be guaranteed at least until 2015,' said Ecclestone.

He warned, 'We keep raising the bar as far as circuit standards are concerned and the BRDC wants to keep it low. They have £13 million of the originally agreed £40 million fund for improvements remaining to finish off their five-year [development] plan.

'But all they managed to do was to spend £3 million on their clubhouse and built some car parks. They seem to think that it is quite unique to have roads and car parks. They have not husbanded their resources too well.'

Ecclestone, who had flown in by private jet from a holiday on his ocean-going yacht in the Mediterranean, continued to pour scorn on the claim by the BRDC president, Jackie Stewart, that the notion of the club borrowing £40 million to fund the improvements was 'unrealistic' and did not make economic sense.

'Basically, Octagon were too nice when they did the deal with the BRDC,' said Ecclestone. 'They rented a facility which wasn't suitable for the purpose. The BRDC says they can't afford it.'

Ecclestone firmly denied that he was trying to create some sort of financial crisis that would result in his purchasing Silverstone at a bargain-basement price. 'I wouldn't take it if they gave it to me,' he said.

He and Mosley also made it clear that they blamed Silverstone for torpedoing the original idea to revive a grand prix at Brands Hatch. 'The outrageous thing is that they stymied Brands Hatch and expect us to keep coming here and race in any conditions,' said Mosley.

Andrew Waller, the managing director of Brands Hatch Leisure admitted that improving Silverstone's status as a world-class F1 circuit was going to require sustained investment, but if it can be achieved, it will guarantee the circuit's long-term survival.

'I think at the end of the day we are all committed to ensuring Silverstone's future, but the precise specification of the [continued updating] scheme will be determined by the level of funding available,' he added.

Leading man. Cristiano da Matta gave Toyota a
brief taste of glory, comfortably holding Kimi
Räikkönen's McLaren at bay.
Photograph: Darren Heath

SILVERSTONE – GRAND PRIX CIRCUIT

CIRCUIT LENGTH: 3.194 miles/5.141 km

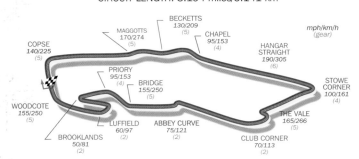

mph/km/h (gear)

- COPSE 140/225 (5)
- MAGGOTTS 170/274 (5)
- BECKETTS 130/209 (5)
- CHAPEL 95/153 (4)
- HANGAR STRAIGHT 190/305 (6)
- STOWE CORNER 100/161 (4)
- PRIORY 95/153 (4)
- BRIDGE 155/250 (5)
- WOODCOTE 155/250 (5)
- LUFFIELD 60/97 (2)
- ABBEY CURVE 75/121 (2)
- THE VALE 165/266 (5)
- BROOKLANDS 50/81 (2)
- CLUB CORNER 70/113 (2)

FIA F1 WORLD CHAMPIONSHIP • ROUND 11

FOSTER'S BRITISH GRAND PRIX

SILVERSTONE 18–20 JULY 2003

RACE DISTANCE: 60 laps, 191.603 miles/308.355 km   RACE WEATHER: Cloudy and bright (track 28/36°C, air 20/23°C)

Pos.	Driver	Nat.	No.	Entrant	Car/Engine	Tyres	Laps	Time/Retirement	Speed (mph/km/h)	Gap to leader	Fastest race lap	
1	Rubens Barrichello	BR	2	Scuderia Ferrari Marlboro	Ferrari F2003-GA-051 V10	B	60	1h 28m 37.554s	129.715/208.757		1m 22.236s	36
2	Juan Pablo Montoya	COL	3	BMW WilliamsF1 Team	Williams FW25-BMW P83 V10	M	60	1h 28m 43.016s	129.582/208.543	+5.462s	1m 22.938s	33
3	Kimi Räikkönen	FIN	6	West McLaren Mercedes	McLaren MP4/17D-Mercedes F0110M V10	M	60	1h 28m 48.210s	129.456/208.339	+10.656s	1m 22.911s	9
4	Michael Schumacher	D	1	Scuderia Ferrari Marlboro	Ferrari F2003-GA-051 V10	B	60	1h 29m 03.202s	129.093/207.755	+25.648s	1m 23.024s	10
5	David Coulthard	GB	5	West McLaren Mercedes	McLaren MP4/17D-Mercedes F0110M V10	M	60	1h 29m 14.381s	128.823/207.321	+36.827s	1m 22.692s	60
6	Jarno Trulli	I	7	Mild Seven Renault F1 Team	Renault R3-RS23 V10	M	60	1h 29m 20.621s	128.673/207.080	+43.067s	1m 22.797s	9
7	Cristiano da Matta	BR	21	Panasonic Toyota Racing	Toyota TF103-RVX-03 V10	M	60	1h 29m 22.639s	128.625/207.002	+45.085s	1m 23.528s	32
8	Jenson Button	GB	17	Lucky Strike BAR Honda	BAR 005-Honda RA003E V10	B	60	1h 29m 23.032s	128.615/206.986	+45.478s	1m 23.912s	53
9	Ralf Schumacher	D	4	BMW WilliamsF1 Team	Williams FW25-BMW P83 V10	M	60	1h 29m 35.586s	128.315/206.503	+58.032s	1m 22.943s	10
10	Jacques Villeneuve	CDN	16	Lucky Strike BAR Honda	BAR 005-Honda RA003E V10	B	60	1h 29m 41.123s	128.183/206.291	+63.569s	1m 23.705s	57
11	Olivier Panis	F	20	Panasonic Toyota Racing	Toyota TF103-RVX-03 V10	M	60	1h 29m 42.761s	128.144/206.228	+65.207s	1m 23.463s	47
12	Heinz-Harald Frentzen	D	10	Sauber Petronas	Sauber C22-Petronas 03B V10	B	60	1h 29m 43.118s	128.135/206.214	+65.564s	1m 23.933s	58
13	Ralph Firman	IRL	12	Jordan Ford	Jordan EJ-13-Ford Cosworth RS1 V10	B	59			+1 lap	1m 25.087s	33
14	Mark Webber	AUS	14	Jaguar Racing	Jaguar R4-Cosworth CR5 V10	M	59			+1 lap	1m 23.833s	28
15	Jos Verstappen	NL	19	European Minardi Cosworth	Minardi PS03-Cosworth CR3 V10	B	58			+2 laps	1m 27.021s	2
16	Justin Wilson	GB	18	European Minardi Cosworth	Minardi PS03-Cosworth CR3 V10	B	58			+2 laps	1m 25.859s	9
17	Nick Heidfeld	D	9	Sauber Petronas	Sauber C22-Petronas 03B V10	B	58			+2 laps	1m 24.537s	9
	Fernando Alonso	E	8	Mild Seven Renault F1 Team	Renault R3-RS23 V10	M	52	Electrics			1m 22.819s	37
	Giancarlo Fisichella	I	11	Jordan Ford	Jordan EJ-13-Ford Cosworth RS1 V10	B	44	Suspension			1m 23.823s	40
	Antonio Pizzonia	BR	15	Jaguar Racing	Jaguar R4-Cosworth CR5 V10	M	32	Engine			1m 23.158s	9

Fastest lap: Rubens Barrichello, on lap 38, 1m 22.236s, 139.842 mph/225.054 km/h (record).

Previous lap record: Rubens Barrichello (F1 Ferrari F2002-051 V10), 1m 23.083s, 138.416 mph/222.760 km/h (2002).

19th: JOS VERSTAPPEN Minardi-Cosworth

17th: RALPH FIRMAN Jordan-Ford Cosworth

15th: GIANCARLO FISICHELLA Jordan-Ford Cosworth

13th: OLIVIER PANIS Toyota

11th: MARK WEBBER Jaguar-Cosworth

20th: JENSON BUTTON BAR-Honda

18th: JUSTIN WILSON Minardi-Cosworth

16th: NICK HEIDFELD Sauber-Petronas

14th: HEINZ-HARALD FRENTZEN Sauber-Petronas

12th: DAVID COULTHARD McLaren-Mercedes

Grid order	1	2	3	4	5	6	7	8	9	10	11	12	13	14	15	16	17	18	19	20	21	22	23	24	25	26	27	28	29	30	31	32	33	34	35	36	37	38	39	40	41	42	43	44	45	46	47
2 BARRICHELLO	7	7	7	7	7	7	7	7	7	7	7	7	21	21	21	21	21	21	21	21	21	21	21	21	21	21	21	21	6	6	6	6	6	6	2	2	2	2	6	6	2	2	2	2	2	2	2
7 TRULLI	6	6	6	6	6	6	6	6	6	6	2	2	20	20	20	20	6	6	6	6	6	6	6	6	6	6	6	21	2	2	2	2	3	3	3	6	2	2	6	6	6	6	6	6	6	6	6
6 RÄIKKÖNEN	2	2	2	2	2	2	2	2	2	2	6	6	5	5	5	6	20	20	20	20	20	20	20	20	20	20	20	2	3	3	3	3	8	8	8	21	21	21	21	21	3	3	3	3			
4 R. SCHUMACHER	4	4	4	4	4	4	4	4	4	4	4	7	7	7	5	5	5	5	5	5	5	5	5	5	5	2	2	3	7	7	7	7	7	6	6	1	1	3	3	3	21	5	5	5			
1 M. SCHUMACHER	1	1	1	1	1	1	1	1	1	1	1	1	6	6	6	7	7	7	7	7	7	7	2	2	3	20	8	8	8	8	8	6	21	23	3	17	5	5	7	7	7						
21 DA MATTA	3	3	3	3	3	3	3	3	3	3	3	8	4	4	4	2	2	2	2	2	2	2	7	7	7	20	21	21	21	21	1	1	1	16	16	5	17	7	1	1	1						
3 MONTOYA	8	8	8	8	8	8	8	8	8	8	8	12	12	12	2	4	3	3	3	3	3	3	3	7	14	8	14	1	1	1	16	16	17	17	16	7	20	20	21	21	21						
8 ALONSO	21	21	21	21	21	15	16	16	16	16	16	16	2	2	12	3	4	12	12	12	12	12	14	14	8	14	12	12	12	16	4	4	5	5	7	20	1	1	20	14	8						
16 VILLENEUVE	5	5	5	5	5	21	14	14	14	14	14	14	14	3	12	14	14	14	14	15	14	8	8	12	12	1	16	16	16	4	17	17	4	7	20	1	14	14	14	8	17						
15 PIZZONIA	15	15	15	15	15	5	9	9	9	9	9	9	16	16	14	16	15	15	15	15	14	14	12	16	16	17	4	17	17	17	5	7	20	1	14	8	8	17	16								
14 WEBBER	16	16	16	16	16	17	17	17	17	11	11	19	19	19	16	16	16	16	16	1	1	17	17	17	17	1	4	4	17	11	11	5	10	20	14	14	8	17	17	16	14						
5 COULTHARD	14	14	14	14	14	14	11	11	11	11	3	3	3	8	8	8	8	16	1	1	17	11	5	5	10	7	10	10	8	16	16	16	4														
20 PANIS	20	20	20	20	20	9	10	10	10	10	17	3	8	8	8	1	1	1	17	17	17	11	11	4	7	5	10	7	20	14	4	4	16	16	4	4	20	20									
10 FRENTZEN	9	9	9	9	9	20	18	18	18	18	20	1	1	1	1	9	9	17	17	1	15	11	4	4	5	10	10	12	20	20	11	8	11	11	10	10	10	10									
11 FISICHELLA	17	17	17	17	17	17	19	21	21	21	10	11	11	11	11	11	11	11	11	11	10	10	10	10	5	20	20	20	20	14	14	14	10	10	10	12	12	12									
9 HEIDFELD	11	11	11	11	11	21	20	20	20	5	5	5	10	10	9	18	18	18	4	9	9	5	15	15	14	14	14	12	5	5	10	18	18	5	18	18	18	19	19	19	19						
12 FIRMAN	19	19	19	19	19	10	5	5	5	20	18	18	18	18	17	17	4	10	18	18	18	15	18	18	18	18	18	5	18	18	18	19	19	19	19	19	18	18									
18 WILSON	12	12	12	10	10	15	5	12	12	12	18	17	17	17	18	4	18	18	9	4	18	18	15	18	15	18	19	18	5	18	18	5	18	18	18	9	9	9									
19 VERSTAPPEN	18	18	18	18	18	5	12	19	19	19	19	10	9	9	4	9	9	9	18	19	19	19	9	9	18	18	9	18	9	9	9	9	9	9	9	9	9	11									
17 BUTTON	10	10	18	18	19	12	12	15	15	15	15	10	5	19	19	4	4	9	9	9	9	9	18	18	18																						

TIME SHEETS

SATURDAY QUALIFYING determines race grid order
Sunny, bright and windy (track 35/36°C, air 24/26°C)

Pos.	Driver	Lap time	Sector 1	Sector 2	Sector 3
1	Rubens Barrichello	1m 21.209s	26.313s	34.126s	20.770s
2	Jarno Trulli	1m 21.381s	26.577s	34.085s	20.719s
3	Kimi Räikkönen	1m 21.695s	26.479s	34.178s	20.949s
4	Ralf Schumacher	1m 21.727s	26.660s	34.110s	20.957s
5	Michael Schumacher	1m 21.867s	26.307s	34.593s	20.967s
6	Cristiano da Matta	1m 22.081s	26.844s	34.305s	20.932s
7	Juan Pablo Montoya	1m 22.214s	26.654s	34.443s	21.117s
8	Fernando Alonso	1m 22.404s	26.980s	34.347s	21.077s
9	Jacques Villeneuve	1m 22.591s	26.857s	34.784s	20.950s
10	Antonio Pizzonia	1m 22.634s	27.021s	34.468s	21.145s
11	Mark Webber	1m 22.647s	26.771s	34.831s	21.045s
12	David Coulthard	1m 22.811s	26.672s	34.948s	21.191s
13	Olivier Panis	1m 23.042s	26.801s	34.423s	21.818s
14	Heinz-Harald Frentzen	1m 23.187s	26.945s	35.130s	21.112s
15	Giancarlo Fisichella	1m 23.574s	27.533s	34.904s	21.117s
16	Nick Heidfeld	1m 23.844s	27.218s	35.309s	21.317s
17	Ralph Firman	1m 24.385s	27.660s	35.476s	21.249s
18	Justin Wilson	1m 25.468s	28.084s	35.818s	21.566s
19	Jos Verstappen	1m 25.759s	28.098s	35.819s	21.842s
20	Jenson Button	No time	–	–	–

FRIDAY QUALIFYING determines Sat running order
Sunny and dry (track 22/24°C, air 18/19°)

Pos.	Driver	Lap time
1	Michael Schumacher	1m 19.474s
2	Juan Pablo Montoya	1m 19.749s
3	Ralf Schumacher	1m 19.788s
4	Fernando Alonso	1m 19.907s
5	Olivier Panis	1m 19.959s
6	Jarno Trulli	1m 19.963s
7	David Coulthard	1m 19.968s
8	Mark Webber	1m 20.171s
9	Jenson Button	1m 20.569s
10	Cristiano da Matta	1m 20.765s
11	Antonio Pizzonia	1m 20.877s
12	Kimi Räikkönen	1m 21.065s
13	Jacques Villeneuve	1m 21.084s
14	Nick Heidfeld	1m 21.211s
15	Heinz-Harald Frentzen	1m 21.363s
16	Giancarlo Fisichella	1m 21.500s
17	Ralph Firman	1m 22.335s
18	Jos Verstappen	1m 23.418s
19	Rubens Barrichello	No time
20	Justin Wilson	No time

POINTS TABLES: CONSTRUCTORS

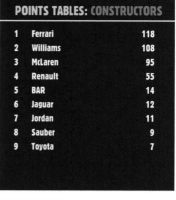

1	Ferrari	118
2	Williams	108
3	McLaren	95
4	Renault	55
5	BAR	14
6	Jaguar	12
7	Jordan	11
8	Sauber	9
9	Toyota	7

PRIVATE TESTING
Overcast, light rain (track 20/23°C, air 17/20°C)

Pos.	Driver	Laps	Time
1	Fernando Alonso	44	1m 21.547s
2	Jarno Trulli	35	1m 21.721s
3	Mark Webber	25	1m 22.060s
4	Allan McNish	34	1m 22.141s
5	Antonio Pizzonia	29	1m 22.834s
6	Giancarlo Fisichella	26	1m 22.864s
7	Ralph Firman	30	1m 24.006s
8	Jos Verstappen	23	1m 24.013s
9	Justin Wilson	29	1m 24.605s

FRIDAY FREE PRACTICE
Overcast with light rain (track 21/24°C, air 22/24°C)

Pos.	Driver	Laps	Time
1	David Coulthard	21	1m 20.039s
2	Mark Webber	17	1m 20.346s
3	Fernando Alonso	17	1m 20.485s
4	Rubens Barrichello	22	1m 20.604s
5	Olivier Panis	20	1m 20.693s
6	Jarno Trulli	19	1m 20.858s
7	Jenson Button	23	1m 20.933s
8	Antonio Pizzonia	14	1m 20.966s
9	Michael Schumacher	27	1m 20.992s
10	Cristiano da Matta	23	1m 21.027s
11	Ralf Schumacher	23	1m 21.029s
12	Juan Pablo Montoya	26	1m 21.182s
13	Jacques Villeneuve	24	1m 21.246s
14	Kimi Räikkönen	21	1m 21.407s
15	Heinz-Harald Frentzen	20	1m 21.969s
16	Giancarlo Fisichella	14	1m 22.028s
17	Ralph Firman	18	1m 22.135s
18	Jos Verstappen	15	1m 23.176s
19	Nick Heidfeld	25	1m 23.290s
20	Justin Wilson	9	1m 24.086s

SATURDAY FREE PRACTICE
Overcast and dry (track 30/33°C, air 24/26°C)

Pos.	Driver	Laps	Time
1	Kimi Räikkönen	11	1m 22.263s
2	Rubens Barrichello	14	1m 22.397s
3	Michael Schumacher	21	1m 22.659s
4	Juan Pablo Montoya	12	1m 23.141s
5	Fernando Alonso	11	1m 23.316s
6	Jacques Villeneuve	15	1m 23.591s
7	Ralf Schumacher	15	1m 23.596s
8	Jarno Trulli	17	1m 23.609s
9	David Coulthard	16	1m 23.888s
10	Mark Webber	19	1m 23.902s
11	Jenson Button	17	1m 23.925s
12	Nick Heidfeld	17	1m 23.939s
13	Olivier Panis	14	1m 24.484s
14	Cristiano da Matta	15	1m 24.532s
15	Heinz-Harald Frentzen	13	1m 24.573s
16	Antonio Pizzonia	15	1m 24.942s
17	Ralph Firman	15	1m 25.044s
18	Giancarlo Fisichella	15	1m 25.114s
19	Justin Wilson	17	1m 25.808s
20	Jos Verstappen	11	1m 26.262s

SATURDAY SECOND FREE PRACTICE
Overcast and dry (track 30/33°C, air 24/26°C)

Pos.	Driver	Laps	Time
1	Juan Pablo Montoya	12	1m 21.415s
2	Rubens Barrichello	18	1m 21.587s
3	Michael Schumacher	15	1m 21.608s
4	Ralf Schumacher	13	1m 21.711s
5	Olivier Panis	17	1m 22.257s
6	David Coulthard	15	1m 22.317s
7	Jarno Trulli	23	1m 22.332s
8	Kimi Räikkönen	15	1m 22.400s
9	Fernando Alonso	16	1m 22.462s
10	Cristiano da Matta	18	1m 22.614s
11	Mark Webber	20	1m 22.910s
12	Jacques Villeneuve	4	1m 23.326s
13	Jenson Button	21	1m 23.455s
14	Heinz-Harald Frentzen	19	1m 23.620s
15	Antonio Pizzonia	14	1m 23.703s
16	Giancarlo Fisichella	16	1m 23.944s
17	Nick Heidfeld	20	1m 23.945s
18	Ralph Firman	16	1m 23.981s
19	Jos Verstappen	13	1m 25.684s
20	Justin Wilson	14	1m 25.906s

WARM-UP
Sunny and bright. (track 34/35°C, air 25/26°C)

Pos.	Driver	Laps	Time
1	Rubens Barrichello	6	1m 21.094s
2	Kimi Räikkönen	4	1m 21.871s
3	Michael Schumacher	6	1m 22.074s
4	Mark Webber	6	1m 22.429s
5	Ralf Schumacher	6	1m 22.457s
6	Fernando Alonso	6	1m 22.498s
7	Antonio Pizzonia	6	1m 22.630s
8	David Coulthard	5	1m 22.722s
9	Jacques Villeneuve	7	1m 23.073s
10	Jenson Button	8	1m 23.235s
11	Heinz-Harald Frentzen	5	1m 23.376s
12	Olivier Panis	5	1m 23.462s
13	Giancarlo Fisichella	4	1m 23.792s
14	Nick Heidfeld	5	1m 24.295s
15	Ralph Firman	6	1m 24.692s
16	Jos Verstappen	4	1m 25.731s
17	Justin Wilson	4	1m 25.938s
18	Juan Pablo Montoya	5	1m 34.936s
19	Cristiano da Matta	2	No time
20	Jarno Trulli	3	No time

9th: JACQUES VILLENEUVE BAR-Honda

7th: JUAN PABLO MONTOYA Williams-BMW

5th: MICHAEL SCHUMACHER Ferrari

3rd: KIMI RÄIKKÖNEN McLaren-Mercedes

Pole: RUBENS BARRICHELLO Ferrari

10th: ANTONIO PIZZONIA Jaguar-Cosworth

8th: FERNANDO ALONSO Renault

6th: CRISTIANO DA MATTA Toyota

4th: RALF SCHUMACHER Williams-BMW

2nd: JARNO TRULLI Renault

48	49	50	51	52	53	54	55	56	57	58	59	60	
2	2	2	2	2	2	2	2	2	2	2	2	2	1
3	3	3	3	3	3	3	3	3	3	3	3	3	2
6	6	6	6	6	6	6	6	6	6	6	6	6	3
1	1	1	1	1	1	1	1	1	1	1	1	1	4
7	7	7	7	7	7	7	7	7	5	5	5	5	5
21	21	21	5	5	5	5	5	5	5	5	5	5	6
5	5	5	21	21	21	21	21	21	21	21	21	21	7
8	8	8	8	17	17	17	17	17	17	17	17	17	8
17	17	17	17	8	16	16	16	16	16	4	4		
16	16	16	16	16	4	4	4	4	4	16	16		
4	4	4	20	20	20	20	20	20	20				
20	20	20	20	10	10	10	10	10	10				
10	10	10	10	10	12	12	12	12	12	12			
12	12	12	12	12	14	14	14	14	14	14			
14	14	14	14	14	19	19	19	19	19				
19	19	19	19	19	18	18	18	18	18				
18	18	18	18	18	9	9	9	9	9				
9	9	9	9	9									

Pit stop
One lap behind leader

CHASSIS LOG BOOK

1	Michael Schumacher	F2003-GA/231
2	Rubens Barrichello	F2003-GA/230
	Spare	F2003-GA/228
3	Juan Pablo Montoya	FW25/06
4	Ralf Schumacher	FW25/07
	Spare	FW25/04
5	David Coulthard	MP4/17D-08
6	Kimi Räikkönen	MP4/17D-09
	Spare	MP4/17D-07
7	Jarno Trulli	R23/05
8	Fernando Alonso	R23/04
	Allan McNish	R23/03
	Spare	R23/03
9	Nick Heidfeld	C22/01
10	Heinz-Harald Frentzen	C22/03
	Spare	C22/02

11	Giancarlo Fisichella	EJ-13/04
12	Ralph Firman	EJ-13/03
	Spare	EJ-13/02
14	Mark Webber	R4/04
15	Antonio Pizzonia	R4/03
	Spare	R4/05
16	Jacques Villeneuve	BAR005/3
17	Jenson Button	BAR005/4
	Spare	BAR005/5
18	Justin Wilson	PS03/04
19	Jos Verstappen	PS03/03
	Spare	PS03/02
20	Olivier Panis	TF103/03
21	Cristiano da Matta	TF103/04
	Spare	TF103/07

POINTS TABLES: DRIVERS

1	Michael Schumacher	69
2	Kimi Räikkönen	62
3	Juan Pablo Montoya	55
4	Ralf Schumacher	53
5	Rubens Barrichello	49
6	Fernando Alonso	39
7	David Coulthard	33
8	Jarno Trulli	16
9	Mark Webber	11
10	Jenson Button	11
11	Giancarlo Fisichella	10
12	Heinz-Harald Frentzen	7
13	Cristiano da Matta	5
14	Jacques Villeneuve	3
15 =	Olivier Panis	2
15 =	Nick Heidfeld	2
17	Ralph Firman	1

FIA F1 WORLD CHAMPIONSHIP • ROUND 12

GERMAN GP
HOCKENHEIM

Facing page, main picture: **Juan Pabl**
made the most of other rivals' misfo
advance his championship chances w
dominant victory.
Photograph: Darren Heath

Facing page, inset: **Michael Schumach**
the pits with his left rear tyre deflate
Photograph: Bryn Williams/crash.net

Left: **A sequence of the opening seco**
race, when Ralf Schumacher's Willia
contact with the Ferrari of Rubens Ba
Kimi Räikkönen's McLaren. Montoya
the distance.
Photographs: Bryn Williams/crash.net

HOCKENHEIM QUALIFYING

It looked pretty flattering for Jaguar Racing new boy Justin Wilson on Friday, when he posted seventh-fastest time, a few tenths slower than his fourth-place team-mate, Mark Webber, and one place ahead of Michael Schumacher's Ferrari. In a sense, that told you all you needed to know about Hockenheim: it was a Michelin circuit from the viewpoint of sheer speed, although on the softer-compound choice, the Jaguar drivers were finding that the initial 'graining' period lasted as long as 12 laps in the torrid conditions.

Come the race, things didn't go so well. Webber spun off during a last-ditch attempt to wrest eighth place, and the final championship point, from Jenson Button's BAR-Honda, and Wilson's R4 succumbed to a gearbox problem.

By contrast, there were ominous initial problems with blistering on the Bridgestone rubber, although Michael Schumacher managed to rattle off four consecutive, very quick laps, which suggested that the Japanese tyres had consistency, if not the absolute pace. That proved a forlorn hope.

In the end, however, the excellent Williams-BMWs buttoned up the front row, with Montoya on 1m 15.167s, just 0.018s ahead of team-mate Ralf Schumacher. Barrichello made the softer Bridgestones work well for him, placing his Ferrari F2003-GA third in the line-up on 1m 15.488s, but then followed Michelin runners Jarno Trulli (1m 15.679s) and Kimi Räikkönen (1m 15.874s).

Michael Schumacher opted for the harder of the Bridgestone compounds. He ended up sixth on 1m 15.898s after an uncharacteristically frantic lap as he sought to put himself in the best possible position for what he believed would be a quick enough race pace, provided he was not too far back in the opening phase.

Schumacher conceded that he had pushed too hard in the middle sector of the lap. 'The car wasn't perfect,' he said, 'and I lost a bit of time there. It wasn't a great lap.'

The Toyota TF103s of Olivier Panis (1m 16.034s) and Cristiano da Matta (1m 16.550s) produced solid performances to qualify seventh and ninth, but like their Michelin-shod rivals, the Japanese team, using the softer rubber, was concerned about one-lap tyre temperatures with the track surface approaching 50 degrees C.

Fernando Alonso had a disappointing time, hobbled by binding brakes that knocked 4.4 mph off his top speed when compared with

Renault team-mate Trulli. The Spaniard had to be content with eighth on 1m 16.483s.

David Coulthard qualified tenth on 1m 16.666s, a starting position that reflected a generally troubled day, during which a problem with his car's electronic differential led to an argument with a tyre barrier.

'Until this morning's free practice, everything was going according to plan,' said the Scot. 'Unfortunately, I went off during the second session following a set-up change, the effects of which we underestimated, and I had to qualify the spare car. I was not as comfortable [with it] and seemed to be losing out on the low-speed sections of the track.'

Mark Webber was quite satisfied with what he described as 'a relatively clean lap', although he admitted to making a slight mistake in the final corner. He added, 'That's one-lap qualifying for you. There simply isn't any margin for mistake, and when it does happen, the price to be paid is high.'

Justin Wilson wound up 16th on his first Jaguar F1 outing at 1m 18.021s. 'Like Mark, I pushed too hard at the end of the lap to give my lap time a push,' he said. 'I lost a fair bit of time in the last sector, but that's where my inexperience with Jaguar and Michelin comes in.'

Just behind Webber came Giancarlo Fisichella's Jordan-Ford on 1m 16.831s, comfortably quicker than team-mate Ralph Firman, who could only manage a 1m 18.341s to line up in 18th place.

Jacques Villeneuve emerged the quickest contender for BAR Honda, a 1m 17.090s earning him 13th place. 'The car is lively and the balance not bad, so I could push hard today,' he said. 'The hardest thing was to get temperature into the tyres for one lap because they take around five or six laps to start working. I also lost some time in the last two corners where I picked up some understeer.'

The Canadian was at least happier than his team-mate, Jenson Button, who was left trailing in 17th on 1m 18.085s. 'It was a pretty terrible qualifying and very disappointing because the car is strong here,' said Button. 'Then in the second-to-last corner I made a big mistake when I got a lot of oversteer and ended up running off the circuit.'

Rounding off the grid were the two Minardis, Nicolas Kiesa doing a respectable job on his F1 debut to line up a tenth of a second shy of team-mate Jos Verstappen.

Above left: Justin Wilson created an immediate impression for Jaguar.

Above: Jacques Villeneuve pushing hard in his BAR-Honda.
Photographs: Darren Heath

Right: Ferrari and Bridgestone were on the back foot in the searing temperatures.

Far right: New boy Kiesa finds the limits of adhesion in his Minardi.
Photographs: Patrick Gosling

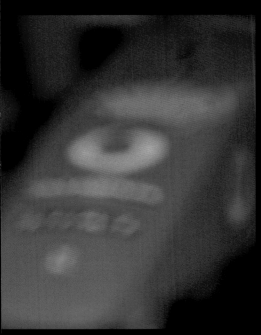

Above: For once, Michael Schumacher was unlucky, losing a hard-earned second place to a puncture.
Photograph: Patrick Gosling

Right: Jarno Trulli on the grid. The Italian driver had a good weekend, culminating in his first podium finish for Renault.
Photograph: Darren Heath

JUAN Pablo Montoya took another decisive step toward challenging for the 2003 World Championship at Hockenheim, but the Williams-BMW driver's flawless, dominant victory went down almost as a footnote to the main business of a torrid afternoon that saw track temperatures nudging 50 degrees C at one point during the 67-lap race. Montoya had qualified on pole position and was never challenged after his team-mate, Ralf Schumacher, alongside him on the front row, inadvertently forced Rubens Barrichello's Ferrari into Kimi Räikkönen's McLaren in the sprint to the first corner.

In the blink of an eye, and a shower of flying carbon fibre, the three title contenders were wiped out on the spot. All Juan Pablo was left to do was keep out of trouble, driving with metronomic precision to beat David Coulthard's McLaren MP4/17D to the chequered flag by just under a minute.

Given the fact that the McLaren-Mercedes wasn't as strong as the Williams-BMW in this sort of high-speed environment, Coulthard, using the spare car after having slid off on Saturday morning, drove a bold and audacious race. He started a distant tenth on the grid and profited from a long middle stint to haul himself into contention, despite grappling with understeer on his second and third sets of tyres, which made it difficult for him to run in close company. Eventually, the Scot stormed ahead of Michael Schumacher's Ferrari in the closing moments, when the world champion suffered a punctured left rear Bridgestone and had to limp to the pits.

Anybody on Michelin rubber was in the pound seats at Hockenheim; Jarno Trulli and Fernando Alonso ran consistently quickly on the softer of the two compounds to bring their Renault R23s home third and fourth, with Olivier Panis and Cristiano da Matta completing the top six for Toyota. Trulli complained of a loss of rear-end grip during the closing stages, allowing Alonso, who'd slid off the road earlier, to close to 0.2s at the line. As Montoya took the chequered flag to score the third GP win of his career, the race stewards were already meeting to consider his team-mate's culpability in that first-corner collision.

At the start, as the pack accelerated away to the first right-hander, the younger Schumacher moved to the left, toward Barrichello's Ferrari, which had nowhere to go, as the fast-starting Räikkönen's McLaren was pulling level on the other side. Schumacher's Williams squeezed the Ferrari into the McLaren, Räikkönen's car being pitched into a pirouette that spun it into the Williams before slamming wildly into the tyre barrier on the left side of the track.

As the race was slowed by the safety car to enable the debris to be cleared from the circuit, Schumacher drove his Williams-BMW FW25 around to the pits, where the car was retired with serious body damage.

The FIA stewards, Radovan Novak, Nazir Hoosein and Waltrand Wunsch, concluded that Ralf had been responsible for the incident and penalised him with a drop of ten grid positions from his qualifying place at the Hungarian GP on 24 August.

'Ralf Schumacher admitted to paying no attention to the position of the other cars during this manoeuvre,' read the official judgement. 'The stewards note that it is absolutely clear that Ralf Schumacher's car made contact with car number 2 [Barrichello], which in turn made contact with car number 6 [Räikkönen].

'Both drivers of cars number 2 and 6 were caught in a set of circumstances over which they had no control.'

Schumacher was defiantly unapologetic. 'You cannot think about what people around you are doing and sometimes these incidents do happen,' he said. 'I was just trying to defend my position and I didn't make any sudden move or anything, so there was all the time in the world for the other cars to move away from me.'

At first, Frank Williams indicated that the team would accept the penalty imposed on its driver and would not be appealing. Later, however, he had a change of heart and decided to support his driver, confirming that an appeal would be lodged.

For his part, Rubens Barrichello was critical of both Ralf Schumacher and Räikkönen. 'I think Ralf and Kimi took big risks, especially Kimi, who went very wide [to the left] to get past. Ralf moved to the left and gave me nowhere to go.'

Räikkönen added, 'I don't know who was to blame, and it doesn't really matter because there is nothing I can do about it, and at least I'm okay, apart from feeling a bit sore.'

After the safety car was withdrawn at the end of lap four, Montoya could look in his mirrors to see the two Renaults of Jarno Trulli and Fernando Alonso, safely behind him in second and third places, and conclude that they could be relied upon to provide a worthwhile cushion as he settled into an unchallenged rhythm at the front of the field.

With ten laps completed, Montoya led Trulli by 2.8s, while the first four back to Schumacher's Ferrari were covered by 6.8s. About five laps later, Juan Pablo realised that he couldn't quite obtain full power from the BMW V10. This was due to a slight throttle potentiometer glitch, but he quickly came to terms with the shortcoming, although initially it had given him a scare.

'I first noticed it in the stadium where I got on the throttle and it didn't accelerate properly,' he explained. 'I thought, "Oh no," because I thought I was about to retire. Then, as I was going down the back straight, I began hitting the rev-limiter. But even with it like this, it was easy. I couldn't believe that the others fell back the way they did.'

Most of the field had judged that a three-stop strategy was the fastest way through the race, but when Trulli took his Renault in for an 8.4s service on lap 14, it was clear that the French team was

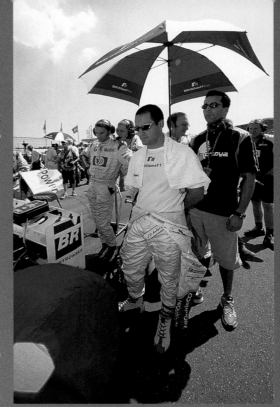

MONTOYA TO REPLACE COULTHARD?

David Coulthard's long-established role as a key member of the McLaren-Mercedes F1 team appeared to be under threat in the run-up to the German GP as speculation intensified that a deal had been made for him to be replaced by Juan Pablo Montoya in 2005.

Coulthard's singular failure to come to terms with the one-lap qualifying format introduced at the start of the 2003 season forced McLaren's senior management to the conclusion that a major reassessment of the team's driver line-up was called for. Yet Coulthard would be granted a lifeline of one further season with the team, even though McLaren had been desperately attempting to secure Montoya's services for 2004.

Montoya's manager, Julian Jakobi, acknowledged that the Colombian had a binding contract with Williams that ran until the end of 2004 and would not be seeking an early release from his obligations.

Frank Williams said, 'Both of our current drivers have firm contracts until the end of 2004 and that's all there is to it.'

McLaren simply employed its customary device to deflect further enquiries. 'We don't comment about media speculation,' said Martin Whitmarsh, the team's managing director. 'There is absolutely nothing to say on this issue.'

However, McLaren sources indicated that contact had certainly been made with Montoya. 'What you've got to ask yourself is which drivers Michael Schumacher really fears,' said one. 'The prospect of Kimi and Montoya taking on a Michael who might be just beginning to get past his peak in 2005 is certainly food for thought.'

It was also suspected that Ralf Schumacher's manager, Willi Weber, might have been trying to capitalise on the uncertainty surrounding Montoya's future in a bid to press Williams into extending his driver's contract beyond its expiry date at the end of the 2004 season. 'He's sniffed around McLaren and Toyota, and found there was nothing doing, and now Willi seems keen to raise a bit of speculation about how things might work out in the future,' said one paddock insider.

Whether this was an attempt to create a situation in which Frank Williams might come to the conclusion that he risked losing both men at the end of 2004, and that he would be advised to tie one of them down, was difficult to judge. The only certainty seemed to be McLaren's interest in Montoya.

aiming to make a two-stopper work. Montoya pitted for the first time (6.9s) on lap 17, briefly allowing Alonso into the lead; Michael Schumacher followed the Williams-BMW into the pit lane for an 8.0s turn-around.

Alonso made his first stop on lap 18, as did Coulthard in the McLaren. Montoya went straight back into the lead, but now he was over 12s ahead and he stretched that advantage to 16.4s over the next three laps, leaving Trulli, Alonso and the ever-determined Schumacher to squabble over third place.

On lap 31, Alonso finally buckled slightly under pressure from Schumacher, sliding off on to the grass coming into the stadium and allowing the Ferrari through into third place. Two laps later, Montoya pitted in 6.4s, storming back out with his lead intact. Then, on lap 38, Trulli (10.0s) led Schumacher (11.2s) in for the second spate of stops, Michael just failing to get the jump on the Renault as they accelerated back into the fray.

As Coulthard gradually worked his way up to the tail of this group, Schumacher redoubled his efforts to get past the second-place Renault, eventually managing to do so around the outside of the new hairpin on lap 59.

Trulli knew that by pushing hard in defence, his Michelin rear tyres would blister progressively. But Michael, whose Bridge-stones had been expected to suffer less heat degradation than the Michelins, had been stuck in traffic for so long that, even after he muscled his way ahead of Trulli, too much time had been lost to salvage the result he'd been looking for.

Although Michael now looked on course for second place, four laps from the finish he suffered a left rear puncture and had to crawl slowly around to the pits for attention. He wound up seventh, at least managing to add two more championship points to his tally.

'As I expected, Williams is now emerging as our main rival,' said Michael. 'I have to say that my car was working well through-out the race, even if I did not have the pace to catch Montoya, as he had built up a big lead by then.'

On lap 60, Coulthard had nipped ahead of Trulli and seemed to be headed for third place, but this became a well-won second after the Ferrari was delayed, the Scot having capitalised on a long mid-dle stint to vault ahead of Alonso's Renault.

'I was struggling a little bit at the start of that stint, because when I pitted [for the first time], the car was really well balanced and I thought I was in for a really strong afternoon,' said David. 'After the pit stop, I picked up quite a bit of understeer and it took a good ten laps or so for that to dial out, and that was the same on the third set, so that made it quite difficult to carry the pace behind the other cars that I could carry when I was alone.'

'Obviously, I was trying to size up Michael a lot to overtake when he had the manoeuvre on Jarno, and then I managed to pass him [Trulli] as well. I overcooked a little bit on the brakes, but then managed to get him at the next corner.'

With Trulli and Alonso coming home in the next two places, the Renault team was obviously well satisfied with its showing.

After reflecting on his first podium finish for Renault, Trulli said, 'I took advantage of the accident at the first corner and, during the first two stints, the car was very good.

'Montoya was faster than me, but I was controlling the people behind me. However, 15 laps from the end, I started suffering from blistering on the rear tyres. When the cars behind caught me, I lost two places, but Michael's problem was a stroke of luck which brought me a podium finish.'

Lapped by the winners in fifth and sixth places were the Toyota TF103s of Olivier Panis and Cristiano da Matta, each of whom had a trouble-free race on a three-stop strategy. 'The car was ab-solutely perfect,' said Panis. 'We have worked so hard this season and have demonstrated that we have a competitive package.'

Eighth and ninth were the two BAR-Hondas of Jenson Button and Jacques Villeneuve. The Canadian had been fuelled up for what was effectively a one-stop race after making a precautionary stop to check for signs of damage after being hit by Justin Wilson's Jaguar during the first-corner chaos.

Button finished ahead of him, the Englishman frustrated by locking rear wheels caused by a differential malfunction. 'It's a nightmare starting from the back of the grid,' he said, 'and I have to do better in Hungary because I'm just making life hard for my-self. We have to drive the car on the edge at the moment and sometimes it's very easy to slip over the limit.'

Villeneuve was similarly disappointed. 'Because of where we were on the track, we changed to a one-stop strategy,' he shrugged. 'This wasn't the best choice in the end, but we decided to take a gamble and it didn't work out.'

Nick Heidfeld finished tenth for Sauber, while Mark Webber made a rare mistake and spun off in the sole surviving Jaguar R4 three laps from the end, trying to wrest eighth place from Button. His team-mate, Wilson, making his Jaguar debut after a post-Silverstone switch from Minardi, retired with gearbox problems after being winged in the first-corner accident.

As Montoya celebrated, Ralf Schumacher looked on reflec-tively. What would happen at the FIA court of appeal hearing, he wondered? If he was to be demoted ten places on the grid in Hun-gary, his title hopes would be effectively sunk. To many F1 insid-ers, it seemed too harsh a penalty.

Facing page, main picture: David Coulthard shrugged aside rumours that his place at McLaren was under threat.

Facing page, inset: Juan Pablo Montoya seemed to be the man most likely to replace Coulthard should any change occur.

Below: Burnt offering. The exhaust outlet shroud on the Toyota of Olivier Panis was literally burnt to a crisp.
Photographs: Darren Heath

Photograph: Darren Heath

FIA F1 WORLD CHAMPIONSHIP • ROUND 12

GRÖSSER MOBIL 1 PREIS VON DEUTSCHLAND

HOCKENHEIM 1–3 AUGUST 2003

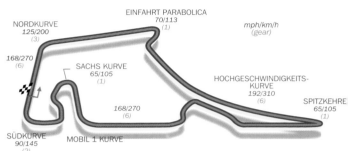

HOCKENHEIM
CIRCUIT LENGTH: 2.842 miles/4.574 km

EINFAHRT PARABOLICA 70/113 (1)

NORDKURVE 125/200 (3)

168/270 (6)

SACHS KURVE 65/105 (1)

mph/km/h (gear)

HOCHGESCHWINDIGKEITS-KURVE 192/310 (6)

SPITZKEHRE 65/105 (1)

168/270 (6)

SÜDKURVE 90/145 (2)

MOBIL 1 KURVE

RACE DISTANCE: 67 laps, 190.424 miles/306.458 km   RACE WEATHER: Hot and sunny (track 47/51°C, air 34/36°C)

Pos.	Driver	Nat.	No.	Entrant	Car/Engine	Tyres	Laps	Time/Retirement	Speed (mph/km/h)	Gap to leader	Fastest race lap	
1	Juan Pablo Montoya	COL	3	BMW WilliamsF1 Team	Williams FW25-BMW P83 V10	M	67	1h 28m 48.769s	128.646/207.036		1m 14.917s	14
2	David Coulthard	GB	5	West McLaren Mercedes	McLaren MP4/17D-Mercedes F0110M V10	M	67	1h 29m 54.228s	127.085/204.523	+65.459s	1m 16.003s	14
3	Jarno Trulli	I	7	Mild Seven Renault F1 Team	Renault R3-RS23 V10	M	67	1h 29m 57.829s	126.999/204.387	+69.060s	1m 15.740s	13
4	Fernando Alonso	E	8	Mild Seven Renault F1 Team	Renault R3-RS23 V10	M	67	1h 29m 58.113s	126.993/204.376	+69.344s	1m 16.060s	16
5	Olivier Panis	F	20	Panasonic Toyota Racing	Toyota TF103-RVX-03 V10	M	66			+1 lap	1m 15.883s	34
6	Cristiano da Matta	BR	21	Panasonic Toyota Racing	Toyota TF103-RVX-03 V10	M	66			+1 lap	1m 16.051s	35
7	Michael Schumacher	D	1	Scuderia Ferrari Marlboro	Ferrari F2003-GA-051 V10	B	66			+1 lap	1m 16.081s	36
8	Jenson Button	GB	17	Lucky Strike BAR Honda	BAR 005-Honda RA003E V10	B	66			+1 lap	1m 17.430s	41
9	Jacques Villeneuve	CDN	16	Lucky Strike BAR Honda	BAR 005-Honda RA003E V10	B	65			+2 laps	1m 18.235s	65
10	Nick Heidfeld	D	9	Sauber Petronas	Sauber C22-Petronas 03B V10	B	65			+2 laps	1m 18.036s	10
11	Mark Webber	AUS	14	Jaguar Racing	Jaguar R4-Cosworth CR5 V10	M	64			DNF	1m 17.754s	46
12	Nicolas Kiesa	DK	18	European Minardi Cosworth	Minardi PS03-Cosworth CR3 V10	B	62			+5 laps	1m 20.171s	26
13	Giancarlo Fisichella	I	11	Jordan Ford	Jordan EJ-13-Ford Cosworth RS1 V10	B	60			DNF	1m 18.145s	51
	Jos Verstappen	NL	19	European Minardi Cosworth	Minardi PS03-Cosworth CR3 V10	B	23	Hydraulics			1m 20.399s	6
	Justin Wilson	GB	15	Jaguar Racing	Jaguar R4-Cosworth CR5 V10	M	6	Stuck in gear			1m 19.441s	3
	Ralf Schumacher	D	4	BMW WilliamsF1 Team	Williams FW25-BMW P83 V10	M	1	Accident				
	Heinz-Harald Frentzen	D	10	Sauber Petronas	Sauber C22-Petronas 03B V10	B	1	Accident				
	Rubens Barrichello	BR	2	Scuderia Ferrari Marlboro	Ferrari F2003-GA-051 V10	B	0	Accident				
	Kimi Räikkönen	FIN	6	West McLaren Mercedes	McLaren MP4/17D-Mercedes F0110M V10	M	0	Accident				
	Ralph Firman	IRL	12	Jordan Ford	Jordan EJ-13-Ford Cosworth RS1 V10	B	0	Accident				

Fastest lap: Juan Pablo Montoya, on lap 14, 1m 14.917s, 136.574 mph/219.795 km/h (record).

Previous lap record: Michael Schumacher (F1 Ferrari F2002-051 V10), 1m 16.462s, 133.815 mph/215.354 km/h (2002).

19th: JOS VERSTAPPEN Minardi-Cosworth

17th: JENSON BUTTON BAR-Honda

15th: NICK HEIDFELD Sauber-Petronas

13th: JACQUES VILLENEUVE BAR-Honda

11th: MARK WEBBER Jaguar-Cosworth

20th: NICOLAS KIESA Minardi-Cosworth

18th: RALPH FIRMAN Jordan-Ford Cosworth

16th: JUSTIN WILSON Jaguar-Cosworth

14th: HEINZ-HARALD FRENTZEN Sauber-Petronas

12th: GIANCARLO FISICHELLA Jordan-Ford Cosworth

Grid order	1	2	3	4	5	6	7	8	9	10	11	12	13	14	15	16	17	18	19	20	21	22	23	24	25	26	27	28	29	30	31	32	33	34	35	36	37	38	39	40	41	42	43	44	45	46	47	48	49	50	51
3 MONTOYA	3	3	3	3	3	3	3	3	3	3	3	3	3	3	3	3	3	8	3	3	3	3	3	3	3	3	3	3	3	3	3	3	3	3	3	3	3	3	3	3	3	3	3	3	3	3	3	3	3	3	3
4 R. SCHUMACHER	7	7	7	7	7	7	7	7	7	7	7	7	7	7	8	8	8	3	7	7	7	7	7	7	7	7	7	7	7	7	7	7	7	7	7	7	7	8	5	5	5	7	7	7	7	7	7	7	7	7	7
2 BARRICHELLO	4	8	8	8	8	8	8	8	8	8	8	8	8	1	1	5	8	8	8	8	8	8	8	8	8	8	1	1	1	1	1	1	5	7	7	1	1	1	1	1	1	1	1	1	1	1	1	1	1	1	1
7 TRULLI	8	1	1	1	1	1	1	1	1	1	1	1	1	5	5	5	7	1	1	1	1	1	1	1	1	1	1	8	8	8	8	8	8	8	8	7	1	1	1	5	5	5	5	5	5	5	5	5	5	5	5
6 RÄIKKÖNEN	1	14	14	14	14	14	5	5	5	5	5	5	7	7	7	7	5	5																																	
1 M. SCHUMACHER	14	5	5	5	5	5	14	14	14	14	14	14	14	14	14	14	14	17	20	20	20	20	20	20	20	20	20	20	20	20	20	20	21	21	20	20	20	20	20	20	20	20	20	20	20	20	20	20	20	21	20
20 PANIS	5	20	20	20	20	20	20	20	20	20	20	20	20	20	20	21	21	17	17	14	20	21	21	21	21	21	21	21	21	21	20	20	21	21	21	21	21	21	21	21	21	21	21	21	21	21	21	21	21	20	21
8 ALONSO	20	21	21	21	21	21	21	21	21	21	21	21	21	17	17	21	20	20	20	21	16	16	16	16	16	16	16	16	16	16	16	16	16	16	17	17	17	17	17	17	14	17	17	17	17	17	17	17	17	17	17
21 DA MATTA	21	11	11	11	11	11	11	17	17	17	17	17	17	9	9	16	16	21	21	16	9	9	9	9	9	9	9	9	9	9	9	9	9	17	14	14	14	14	14	14	17	9	14	14	14	14	14	14	14	14	14
5 COULTHARD	11	9	9	9	9	9	9	9	9	9	9	9	9	9	9	9	20	16	20	21	16	9	9	17	17	17	17	17	17	17	17	17	17	14	9	9	9	9	9	9	9	14	9	9	9	9	9	9	9	9	9
14 WEBBER	9	17	17	17	17	17	17	11	16	16	16	16	16	16	16	20	9	9	9	9	14	14	14	14	14	14	14	14	14	9	16	16	16	16	16	16	16	16	16	16	16	16	16	16	16	16	16				
11 FISICHELLA	17	17	19	19	19	19	19	19	19	19	19	19	19	19	19	19	19	19	18	18	14	14	14	14	14	14	14	14	14	18	18	18	18	18	18	18	18	18	18	18	18	18	18	18	18	18	18	18	18		
16 VILLENEUVE	19	19	16	16	16	16	16	16	11	11	18	18	18	18	18	18	18	18	11	11	18	18	18	18	18	18	18	18	18	11	11	11	11	11	11	11	11	11	11	11	11	11	11	11	11	11	11	11	11	11	11
10 FRENTZEN	18	16	18	18	18	18	18	18	18	18	11	11	11	11	11	11	11	11	11	11	11																														
9 HEIDFELD	16	15	15	15	15	15																																													
15 WILSON	10																																																		
17 BUTTON	15																																																		
12 FIRMAN																																																			
19 VERSTAPPEN																																																			
18 KIESA																																																			

Pit stop
One lap behind leader

TIME SHEETS

SATURDAY QUALIFYING determines race grid order
Hot and sunny (track 45/48°C, air 33/34°C)

Pos.	Driver	Lap time	Sector 1	Sector 2	Sector 3
1	Juan Pablo Montoya	1m 15.167s	16.575s	35.237s	23.355s
2	Ralf Schumacher	1m 15.185s	16.522s	35.094s	23.569s
3	Rubens Barrichello	1m 15.488s	16.570s	35.385s	23.533s
4	Jarno Trulli	1m 15.679s	16.603s	35.514s	23.562s
5	Kimi Räikkönen	1m 15.874s	16.590s	35.405s	23.879s
6	Michael Schumacher	1m 15.898s	16.612s	35.736s	23.550s
7	Olivier Panis	1m 16.034s	16.733s	35.432s	23.869s
8	Fernando Alonso	1m 16.483s	16.808s	35.725s	23.950s
9	Cristiano da Matta	1m 16.550s	16.735s	35.617s	24.198s
10	David Coulthard	1m 16.666s	16.799s	35.649s	24.218s
11	Mark Webber	1m 16.775s	16.731s	35.515s	24.529s
12	Giancarlo Fisichella	1m 16.831s	16.670s	36.118s	24.043s
13	Jacques Villeneuve	1m 17.090s	16.877s	36.020s	24.193s
14	Heinz-Harald Frentzen	1m 17.169s	16.736s	36.268s	24.165s
15	Nick Heidfeld	1m 17.557s	17.164s	36.116s	24.277s
16	Justin Wilson	1m 18.021s	16.897s	36.145s	24.979s
17	Jenson Button	1m 18.085s	17.086s	36.060s	24.939s
18	Ralph Firman	1m 18.341s	16.960s	36.685s	24.696s
19	Jos Verstappen	1m 19.023s	17.279s	36.714s	25.030s
20	Nicolas Kiesa	1m 19.174s	17.623s	36.553s	24.998s

FRIDAY QUALIFYING determines Sat running order
Dry and sunny (track 35/44°C, air 28/30°C)

Pos.	Driver	Lap time
1	Ralf Schumacher	1m 14.427s
2	Juan Pablo Montoya	1m 14.673s
3	Jarno Trulli	1m 15.004s
4	Mark Webber	1m 15.030s
5	Fernando Alonso	1m 15.214s
6	Kimi Räikkönen	1m 15.276s
7	Justin Wilson	1m 15.373s
8	Rubens Barrichello	1m 15.399s
9	Michael Schumacher	1m 15.456s
10	Olivier Panis	1m 15.471s
11	David Coulthard	1m 15.557s
12	Jenson Button	1m 15.754s
13	Heinz-Harald Frentzen	1m 15.968s
14	Nick Heidfeld	1m 15.985s
15	Cristiano da Matta	1m 16.450s
16	Ralph Firman	1m 17.044s
17	Giancarlo Fisichella	1m 17.111s
18	Jos Verstappen	1m 17.702s
19	Jacques Villeneuve	No time

PRIVATE TESTING
Hot and sunny (track 33/38 °C, air 27/29°C)

Pos.	Driver	Laps	Time
1	Jarno Trulli	52	1m 16.074s
2	Fernando Alonso	47	1m 16.190s
3	Allan McNish	42	1m 16.304s
4	Mark Webber	48	1m 16.887s
5	Giancarlo Fisichella	37	1m 16.983s
6	Ralph Firman	42	1m 17.518s
7	Justin Wilson	49	1m 17.742s
8	Jos Verstappen	29	1m 18.518s
9	Zsolt Baumgartner	44	1m 18.912s
10	Nicolas Kiesa	39	1m 19.413s
11	Gianmaria Bruni	31	1m 19.865s

FRIDAY FREE PRACTICE
Hot and sunny (track 33/39°C, air 26/28°C)

Pos.	Driver	Laps	Time
1	David Coulthard	22	1m 15.523s
2	Jarno Trulli	11	1m 15.617s
3	Fernando Alonso	9	1m 15.797s
4	Mark Webber	25	1m 15.799s
5	Juan Pablo Montoya	23	1m 15.890s
6	Cristiano da Matta	28	1m 16.109s
7	Jenson Button	26	1m 16.187s
8	Ralf Schumacher	24	1m 16.401s
9	Justin Wilson	21	1m 16.568s
10	Olivier Panis	21	1m 16.602s
11	Michael Schumacher	30	1m 16.814s
12	Jacques Villeneuve	24	1m 16.945s
13	Giancarlo Fisichella	17	1m 17.050s
14	Heinz-Harald Frentzen	23	1m 17.137s
15	Kimi Räikkönen	23	1m 17.284s
16	Rubens Barrichello	25	1m 17.361s
17	Ralph Firman	19	1m 17.842s
18	Nick Heidfeld	26	1m 18.121s
19	Jos Verstappen	11	1m 18.791s
20	Nicolas Kiesa	15	1m 19.030s

SATURDAY FIRST FREE PRACTICE
Hot and sunny (track 41/45°C, air 31/32°C)

Pos.	Driver	Laps	Time
1	Juan Pablo Montoya	20	1m 15.668s
2	Rubens Barrichello	19	1m 15.853s
3	Ralf Schumacher	21	1m 15.890s
4	Michael Schumacher	21	1m 16.056s
5	Kimi Räikkönen	15	1m 16.193s
6	Jarno Trulli	18	1m 16.275s
7	Fernando Alonso	14	1m 16.371s
8	Olivier Panis	21	1m 16.560s
9	Mark Webber	17	1m 16.953s
10	Jenson Button	14	1m 16.957s
11	David Coulthard	18	1m 17.147s
12	Heinz-Harald Frentzen	19	1m 17.180s
13	Nick Heidfeld	15	1m 17.345s
14	Jacques Villeneuve	17	1m 17.353s
15	Giancarlo Fisichella	18	1m 17.419s
16	Cristiano da Matta	17	1m 17.662s
17	Justin Wilson	18	1m 18.083s
18	Ralph Firman	19	1m 18.293s
19	Jos Verstappen	15	1m 19.433s
20	Nicolas Kiesa	15	1m 19.766s

SATURDAY SECOND FREE PRACTICE
Hot and sunny (track 41/45°C, air 31/32°C)

Pos.	Driver	Laps	Time
1	Ralf Schumacher	13	1m 15.387s
2	Rubens Barrichello	16	1m 15.495s
3	Juan Pablo Montoya	7	1m 15.716s
4	Fernando Alonso	19	1m 16.277s
5	Jarno Trulli	13	1m 16.305s
6	Kimi Räikkönen	15	1m 16.320s
7	Mark Webber	17	1m 16.474s
8	Michael Schumacher	17	1m 16.493s
9	Jenson Button	24	1m 16.954s
10	Jacques Villeneuve	25	1m 16.957s
11	Olivier Panis	11	1m 17.169s
12	Heinz-Harald Frentzen	17	1m 17.334s
13	Cristiano da Matta	22	1m 17.426s
14	Giancarlo Fisichella	16	1m 17.583s
15	Nick Heidfeld	25	1m 17.647s
16	Justin Wilson	11	1m 17.766s
17	Ralph Firman	18	1m 18.403s
18	Jos Verstappen	20	1m 19.533s
19	Nicolas Kiesa	4	1m 20.408s
20	David Coulthard	2	No time

WARM-UP
Hot and sunny (track 45/49°C, air 32/33°C)

Pos.	Driver	Laps	Time
1	Juan Pablo Montoya	5	1m 15.385s
2	Fernando Alonso	6	1m 15.701s
3	Olivier Panis	5	1m 15.758s
4	Ralf Schumacher	6	1m 15.828s
5	Rubens Barrichello	6	1m 15.924s
6	Kimi Räikkönen	5	1m 15.964s
7	Cristiano da Matta	4	1m 16.341s
8	Jarno Trulli	4	1m 16.497s
9	Michael Schumacher	7	1m 16.532s
10	David Coulthard	6	1m 16.576s
11	Mark Webber	6	1m 16.908s
12	Jenson Button	7	1m 17.130s
13	Nick Heidfeld	4	1m 17.323s
14	Giancarlo Fisichella	6	1m 17.407s
15	Jacques Villeneuve	8	1m 17.421s
16	Heinz-Harald Frentzen	5	1m 17.796s
17	Ralph Firman	6	1m 17.840s
18	Justin Wilson	6	1m 17.903s
19	Jos Verstappen	6	1m 22.229s
20	Nicolas Kiesa	6	No time

9th: CRISTIANO DA MATTA Toyota

7th: OLIVIER PANIS Toyota

5th: KIMI RÄIKKÖNEN McLaren-Mercedes

3rd: RUBENS BARRICHELLO Ferrari

Pole: JUAN PABLO MONTOYA Williams-BMW

10th: DAVID COULTHARD McLaren-Mercedes

8th: FERNANDO ALONSO Renault

6th: MICHAEL SCHUMACHER Ferrari

4th: JARNO TRULLI Renault

2nd: RALF SCHUMACHER Williams-BMW

52	53	54	55	56	57	58	59	60	61	62	63	64	65	66	67	•	
3	3	3	3	3	3	3	3	3	3	3	3	3	3	3	3	1	
7	7	7	7	7	7	7	1	1	1	1	1	1	1	1	1	2	
1	1	1	1	1	1	1	7	5	5	5	7	7	7	7	7	3	
5	5	5	5	5	5	5	5	7	7	7	8	8	8	8	8	4	
8	8	8	8	8	8	8	8	8	8	8	20	20	20	20		5	
20	20	20	20	20	20	20	20	20	20	20	21	21	21	21		6	
21	21	21	21	21	21	21	21	21	21	21	1	1	1	1		7	
17	17	17	17	17	17	17	17	17	17	17	17	17	17	17		8	
14	14	14	14	14	14	14	14	14	14	14	14	14	16				
16	16	16	16	16	16	16	16	16	16	16	16	16	9				
9	9	9	9	9	9	9	9	9	9	9	9	9					
18	18	18	18	18	18	18	18	18	18	18							
11	11	11	11	11	11	11	11	11	11								

CHASSIS LOG BOOK

1	Michael Schumacher	F2003-GA/231	11	Giancarlo Fisichella	EJ-13/05
2	Rubens Barrichello	F2003-GA/230	12	Ralph Firman	EJ-13/03
	Spare	F2003-GA/229		Spare	EJ-13/04
3	Juan Pablo Montoya	FW25/06	14	Mark Webber	R4/04
4	Ralf Schumacher	FW25/07	15	Antonio Pizzonia	R4/05
	Spare	FW25/04		Spare	R4/03
5	David Coulthard	MP4/17D-07	16	Jacques Villeneuve	BAR005/3
6	Kimi Räikkönen	MP4/17D-09	17	Jenson Button	BAR005/4
	Spare	MP4/17D-06		Spare	BAR005/5
7	Jarno Trulli	R23/05	18	Nicolas Kiesa	PS03/01
8	Fernando Alonso	R23/04	19	Jos Verstappen	PS03/03
	Allan McNish	R23/03		Spare	PS03/02
	Spare	R23/03	20	Olivier Panis	TF103/08
9	Nick Heidfeld	C22/01	21	Cristiano da Matta	TF103/04
10	Heinz-Harald Frentzen	C22/03		Spare	TF103/02
	Spare	C22/02			

FIA F1 WORLD CHAMPIONSHIP • ROUND 13

HUNGARIANGP
HUNGARORING

Right: Ross Brawn and Michael Schumacher's race engineer, Chris Dyer, discuss tactics.
Photograph: Darren Heath

Below: Zsolt Baumgartner became Hungary's first ever grand prix driver, taking over Ralf Firman's Jordan-Ford.
Photograph: Patrick Gosling

HUNGARORING QUALIFYING

Prior to the race, Michelin competitions director Pierre Dupasquier reckoned that the French tyre maker was gaining a major benefit by pressing on with development programmes spread between four or five competitive teams. It certainly looked that way after second qualifying at the Hungaroring, where Fernando Alonso's Renault posted a m 21.688s best to out-qualify Ralf Schumacher's Williams (1m 21.944s), Mark Webber's Jaguar (1m 22.027s) and Juan Pablo Montoya's Williams (1m 22.180s), these four buttoning up the first two rows of the starting grid. Some insiders began to question whether Bridgestone had done the right thing by throwing all its development muscle behind the Ferrari squad.

Webber was measured in his assessment of the circuit changes, which theoretically held out the possibility of some overtaking moves into the first corner. 'Well, it's not going to be any worse than it was,' he said. 'Potentially, you can do something at the first corner, but it is unbelievably dirty off line, and the rubber on line even gets built up as the race goes on, so off line is even more hazardous, so we will see.'

Rubens Barrichello wound up fifth – matching Montoya's time exactly – while Michael Schumacher was only eighth 1m 22.755s). The Ferrari duo were the only Bridgestone runners to battle their way into the top ten.

'I did think we would have done better than that,' said Ferrari technical director Ross Brawn. 'Michael didn't feel he had the grip that was there in the warm-up, and Rubens had understeer towards the end of his run, so we didn't really optimise the car and tyres for qualifying. We'll see what we can do tomorrow.'

An assessment of the relative merits of the Bridgestone and Michelin tyres focused yet again on a key starting point: just how good was the Ferrari F2003-GA? Ross Brawn believed it represented a quantum leap forward over the F2002. So was Bridgestone losing ground? Or was Michelin closing the gap? In this specific instance, it seems that Michael's rear tyre pressures may have been set too low and they only came up to the optimum level in the third sector of the lap. Whatever the reason, he appeared to be struggling.

Splitting the two Ferraris were Jarno Trulli's Renault R23 (1m 22.610s) and Kimi Räikkönen's McLaren (1m 22.742s). 'It was not too bad,' shrugged Kimi. 'I made a little mistake in the last sector at corner 12, which cost me some time, and it feels good.'

Coulthard endured a slight drama with his McLaren's clutch just before his qualifying run, but the setback was quickly resolved and he qualified ninth on 1m 23.060s, fractionally ahead of Olivier Panis's Toyota TF103 (1m 23.369s). The Frenchman had been quickest in Friday morning's free practice session.

Justin Wilson lined up 12th on 1m 23.660s after a steady performance. 'My mileage with the Jaguar is still very low, and getting through a race distance will be valuable for me and the team,' he said. 'Anything above that will be a bonus.'

It was a busy weekend for Jordan. Ralph Firman wrote himself out of the race equation after surviving a 37-G, 175-mph shunt on Saturday morning, caused by his EJ-13 shedding its rear wing. Test driver Zsolt Baumgartner, the first Hungarian to race in F1 in the history of the official World Championship, was quickly issued a super licence by the FIA and drafted in as replacement. He qualified 19th on 1m 26.678s.

Meanwhile, Giancarlo Fisichella had decided on his escape route from the Jordan squad, having signed a deal with Sauber worth $7 million over the next two seasons. He lined up 13th on 1m 23.726s. 'We did a very good job, the lap was clean and the car balance good,' said the Italian. 'We did our best.'

The BAR-Hondas lined up 14th and 16th, Jenson Button posting a 1m 23.847s and Jacques Villeneuve a 1m 24.100s, the two being separated by Cristiano da Matta's Toyota (1m 23.982s). Button glanced a kerb quite hard during his run, and Villeneuve reported that his tyres went off slightly toward the end of his.

Sauber's Heinz-Harald Frentzen complained of poor balance problems on his way to a 1m 24.569s, 17th fastest, which was six places behind his team-mate, Nick Heidfeld. Right at the back, the Minardis of Jos Verstappen (1m 26.423s) and Nicolas Kiesa (1m 28.907s) sandwiched new boy Baumgartner in the Jordan.

FROM the moment he first strapped himself into the cockpit of a Renault R23, it was clear that Fernando Alonso was likely to become the youngest grand prix winner of all time. So it was hardly a surprise when, at the Hungaroring, with the track temperature sweltering in the upper 40-degree C bracket, the young Spaniard duly delivered a new record – at 22 years, 26 days old, Alonso was three months younger than the previous occupant of that privileged position, Bruce McLaren, when he had triumphed in the 1959 US Grand Prix at Sebring, behind the wheel of a spindly Cooper-Climax.

In securing this significant entry in the F1 record books, Alonso led all but one of the 70 laps of the Hungarian Grand Prix to win by 16.768s from Kimi Räikkönen in the McLaren-Mercedes MP4/17D. Immediately after stepping down from the rostrum, Flavio Briatore's latest protégé freely admitted that the whole experience had been slightly overwhelming.

'It's too early, it's like a dream at the moment,' said an ecstatic Alonso. 'With ten laps to go, I was hearing noises from the engine and the gearbox in my mind. It was fantastic. I need this victory to grow up this year and have more chance next season. I came here with a good feeling. I love the track here, and after qualifying I knew there was a good chance of finishing on the podium. Then, in the first stint, I started thinking that I could win, because after 12 laps or so I was 20 seconds ahead.

'We are not fighting for the championship, but my Renault was fantastic here this weekend. The chassis was excellent, and although the engine may not be the quickest, it is light, with a low centre of gravity which helped on these tight corners.'

The Hungaroring is all about lack of grip, unpredictable track conditions and a treacherous spin into the barriers that awaits

Above: **Jarno Trulli leads Montoya and both Schumachers early in the race.**
Photograph: Darren Heath

anybody who strays off line. And that's before taking into account the variations of grip that the F1 teams experienced on newly laid extensions to the tight little track near Budapest.

They'd lengthened the main straight in the hope that it might produce a touch more overtaking. It did, but not enough to prevent Mark Webber from keeping his Jaguar R4 in a seemingly impregnable second place – he was 20s ahead of the rest after only 11 laps. By the time the mid-field pack had muscled past the dogged Australian, the incredible Alonso had simply vanished into the distance. Webber eventually finished a strong and well-deserved sixth.

From the clean side of the circuit, Alonso was a good six lengths ahead by the time he arrived at the braking area for the first corner. With those on the right-hand side really struggling for grip, chaos reigned for the first couple of corners, Ralf Schumacher spinning out on turn two. He resumed with only Nicolas Kiesa's Minardi and Cristiano da Matta's Toyota behind him, the Brazilian having been pushed off the starting grid and having joined in late from the pit lane.

'I want to apologise to the team for that,' said da Matta. 'I got on the launch [control] button a bit too quickly, hit the brakes to avoid jump-starting, but there wasn't enough time for the anti-stall [mechanism] to kick in.'

Meanwhile, in the confusion at turn two, Montoya attempted to run around the outside of Michael Schumacher's Ferrari. 'On the first lap, I was going around the outside of him and he just threw his car at me completely,' shrugged Juan Pablo. 'I was a bit shocked by that, but if that's the way he's racing, then that's the way he's racing.'

At the end of the opening lap, Alonso came through 1.9s ahead

of Webber, with Rubens Barrichello's Ferrari F2003-GA holding third place. Then came Kimi Räikkönen's McLaren, Jarno Trulli's Renault, David Coulthard's McLaren, Michael Schumacher's Ferrari and a slow-starting Juan Pablo Montoya's Williams FW25.

Third time around and Barrichello attempted to pass Webber at the chicane, but bounced the Ferrari over its high kerbs and ended up losing out to both Räikkönen and Trulli. By lap six, Alonso led by 14s, and three laps later he was 17.5s ahead. Now there was no chance of anybody even remotely challenging the Renault ace, provided he kept his cool and refused to be ruffled. He managed both to perfection.

At the end of lap 13, both Alonso (6.4s) and Webber (7.2s) made their first refuelling stops. Fernando resumed just behind Räikkönen, the McLaren driver staying out for another two laps before topping up his car's tank in 7.6s; Trulli followed him in from third place. Barrichello came in for a 6.9s stop at the end of lap 16, and Michael pitted for fuel in the other Ferrari (9.3s) on lap 17. Montoya, who had stopped on the previous lap with Barrichello, vaulted ahead of the world champion thanks to a faster out lap.

Lap 15 was also marked by the race's first retirement, in the form of Jacques Villeneuve's BAR-Honda. The Canadian was hugely disappointed to have suffered yet another failure. 'We knew we would be much better in race set-up, and we were,' he said. 'It went really well at the start and I was able to make up six places in the first lap, despite having a lot of fuel on board, so things were looking good for a point or two. We knew for a couple of laps that things were starting to go wrong and I had reports that I was losing hydraulic pressure. In the end, I had no choice but to stop.'

At the end of lap 20, Rubens Barrichello's Ferrari suffered a

major failure of the left rear suspension, which tore virtually the whole corner off the car as he braked for the right-hander after the pits. The F2003-GA slammed into the tyre barrier, but Rubens hopped out without a scratch. Later, Ferrari would attribute the cause of the accident to Barrichello's earlier impact with the chicane kerb, although the team was quick to emphasise that it did not blame the Brazilian in any way.

Rubens commented, 'I was running a good race when, for reasons I don't know, I lost the left rear wheel and ended up in the crash barriers. Fortunately, I did not hurt myself at all and physically I am fine. However, I am not at all happy with the fact that I received no medical attention immediately after the accident and [or] shortly afterwards when I was back in the pits.'

The race now settled down with Alonso a commanding 24.1s ahead of Räikkönen by the end of lap 22. Webber was third, in front of Trulli, Montoya and Michael Schumacher. Trulli was struggling slightly with minor 'graining' problems on his second set of tyres and, as this group lapped Jordan stand-in Zsolt Baumgartner going into the first turn on lap 30, Montoya attempted to 'wipe out' Trulli against the backmarker.

However, the dogged Trulli was having none of it and chopped the Williams so fiercely that Montoya was forced to hoist his right front wheel on to the inside kerb in a bid to avoid contact. Right behind them, Ralf Schumacher continued his feisty recovery drive through the field by slicing ahead of brother Michael.

Alonso was ahead by 26.6s when he made his second 6.9s pit visit at the end of lap 30, easily retaining the lead, and the Renault driver was still over 25s in front of Räikkönen when the second round of refuelling stops had been completed.

On lap 34, Panis retired after suffering a gearbox breakage as he attempted to accelerate back into the race after taking on fuel. 'I heard a noise and knew instantly what had happened,' he said. 'I was making good progress through the field, and despite this result we are continuing to head in a good direction.'

Both Jordans succumbed to engine failure – making it five Cosworth breakages for the team over the weekend – and, on lap 39, Michael Schumacher suffered a heart-stopping moment when his Ferrari started to misfire out of fuel as he aimed for the pit lane. The car coasted into the pits, but with its engine having cut out, the hydraulics were not operating, delaying the opening of its refuelling flap. He resumed eighth, the slow turn-around having eliminated any chance of vaulting Trulli's seventh-place Renault.

Alonso made his third pit stop (7.7s) at the end of lap 49 and thereafter had a steady run through to the chequered flag. Räikkönen drove flat out all the way, and his fine performance saw him matching the winner's lap times for much of the afternoon.

'Of course, you want to win, but second place was the best we could do here today,' he said. 'The car in the race was good, I wasn't able to pass Webber's Jaguar in the opening stages; it was holding me up by about a second a lap. The car is basically the same as at the start of the season, but we will have a new aerodynamic package for the next race, so we're hoping that things will be even better.'

Williams-BMW drivers Montoya and Ralf Schumacher crossed the line separated by just over a second, in third and fourth places, good enough to propel the team into the lead of the constructors' championship with 129 points to Ferrari's 121. The younger Schumacher held fourth place in the championship on 58 points.

'I backed off a little bit when I was keeping an eye on Ralf,' said Montoya, who had survived a quick spin in the closing stages. 'I think if we'd had a good start, I think we had a big speed advantage in the street, so I think it was a matter of strategy. But by the second corner, I was eighth and Ralf was last.'

A switch to a two-stop plan earned Coulthard a good fifth, thanks in part to his excellent start and opening lap. 'The two-stop strategy was the right one, taking into consideration my ninth place on the starting grid,' he said. 'Apart from that, the 70 laps were rather uneventful and were all about keeping the guys with less fuel behind me.'

Trulli did a fine job to stay in front of Michael Schumacher all the way to the chequered flag, the world champion having been forced to work harder for his single championship point than possibly ever before. He was lapped by Alonso just after the beginning of lap 62.

'Obviously, it was not a great race for me,' said Michael with measured understatement. 'I spent a lot of time behind a slower car and so could not run at my maximum pace. Basically, a lot of things did not go the way we wanted. Now we have an important test session coming up at Monza, where I am confident we can improve our total package.'

There would be another three-week gap before the Italian GP at Monza beckoned. Yet in the scrutineering bay at the Hungaroring, the seeds of mistrust were emerging to signal the start of the most serious dispute of the season. And the most acrimonious.

DIARY

Former BRM chief engineer Tony Rudd dies at the age of 80.

Turkey confirms that it is on course to host its first grand prix in 2005.

Indy 500 winner Gil de Ferran announces that he will retire from racing at the end of the 2003 season. His place in the Penske IRL line-up will be taken by Sam Hornish.

Bernie Ecclestone repeats his belief that Sunday qualifying should be made a part of the grand prix weekend format in the near future.

Left: Fernando Alonso became grand prix racing's youngest ever winner.

Below: Kimi Räikkönen was the only driver who could match Alonso's speed.
Photographs: Darren Heath

RALF SCHUMACHER REPRIEVED BY FIA

Ralf Schumacher's somewhat forlorn championship bid was revitalised prior to the Hungarian GP when an FIA court of appeal dramatically quashed the draconian penalty that would have seen him demoted by ten places from his qualifying position in the Budapest race. In the event, of course, it made little difference, since he spun off on the second corner and spent the rest of the afternoon climbing back to finish fourth.

Schumacher had received the penalty after being held responsible for a multiple collision on the first corner of the German GP on 3 August. However, although the court confirmed the stewards' findings, it decided that the sanction imposed on the BMW Williams driver was excessive and instead substituted a $50,000 fine.

'I was delighted with the decision,' said Ralf Schumacher. 'After yesterday's hearing, I didn't expect too much, but I am very happy with the conclusion that was reached. I think the team presented a very thorough case and this helped a lot, I am sure.'

The court also heard evidence from the FIA technical and safety consultant Peter Wright, who had analysed the accident data recorders from Rubens Barrichello's Ferrari and Kimi Räikkönen's McLaren, the two cars with which Schumacher's Williams had collided as they accelerated away from the starting grid at Hockenheim.

Schumacher had squeezed Barrichello's Ferrari between his own car and Räikkönen's McLaren, which had been attempting to pass the slow-starting Brazilian on the left. However, it was believed that the data analysis revealed some evidence that Räikkönen actually had steered to the right and aggravated the already tight situation.

As a result, the court decided that the case should be referred back to the panel of stewards at the German Grand Prix, so that the conduct of Barrichello and Räikkönen could be reconsidered in the light of Wright's evidence.

This was duly carried out on the Friday at Budapest, but despite lengthy deliberations, it was decided that no sanction should be imposed on the other two drivers. The general view in the paddock was that this had been the correct outcome.

Above: Ralf Schumacher escaped demotion on the grid in Hungary.

Right: Mark Webber holds off Kimi Räikkönen, allowing Alonso to escape at the head of the field.
Photographs: Darren Heath

Photograph: Darren Heath

MARLBORO
MAGYAR NAGYDIJ

HUNGARORING 22–24 AUGUST 2003

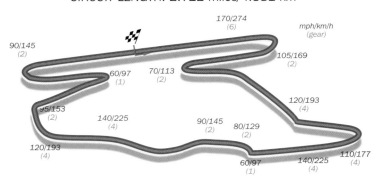

HUNGARORING
CIRCUIT LENGTH: 2.722 miles/4.381 km

170/274 (6)

mph/km/h (gear)

90/145 (2)

105/169 (2)

60/97 (1)   70/113 (2)

120/193 (4)

95/153 (2)   140/225 (4)   90/145 (2)   80/129 (2)

120/193 (4)

110/177 (4)

60/97 (1)   140/225 (4)

RACE DISTANCE: 70 laps, 190.551 miles/306.663 km **RACE WEATHER:** Hot and sunny (track 47/51°C, air 34/36°C)

Pos.	Driver	Nat.	No.	Entrant	Car/Engine	Tyres	Laps	Time/Retirement	Speed (mph/km/h)	Gap to leader	Fastest race lap	
1	Fernando Alonso	E	8	Mild Seven Renault F1 Team	Renault R3-RS23 V10	M	70	1h 39m 01.460s	115.457/185.810		1m 22.565s	47
2	Kimi Räikkönen	FIN	6	West McLaren Mercedes	McLaren MP4/17D-Mercedes F0110M V10	M	70	1h 39m 18.228s	115.132/185.287	+16.768s	1m 22.372s	66
3	Juan Pablo Montoya	COL	3	BMW WilliamsF1 Team	Williams FW25-BMW P83 V10	M	70	1h 39m 35.997s	114.789/184.736	+34.537s	1m 22.095s	37
4	Ralf Schumacher	D	4	BMW WilliamsF1 Team	Williams FW25-BMW P83 V10	M	70	1h 39m 37.080s	114.769/184.703	+35.620s	1m 22.319s	55
5	David Coulthard	GB	5	West McLaren Mercedes	McLaren MP4/17D-Mercedes F0110M V10	M	70	1h 39m 57.995	114.369/184.059	+56.535s	1m 23.193s	40
6	Mark Webber	AUS	14	Jaguar Racing	Jaguar R4-Cosworth CR5 V10	M	70	1h 40m 14.103s	114.062/183.566	+72.643s	1m 23.156s	49
7	Jarno Trulli	I	7	Mild Seven Renault F1 Team	Renault R3-RS23 V10	M	69			+1 lap	1m 24.100s	34
8	Michael Schumacher	D	1	Scuderia Ferrari Marlboro	Ferrari F2003-GA-051 V10	B	69			+1 lap	1m 23.207s	38
9	Nick Heidfeld	D	9	Sauber Petronas	Sauber C22-Petronas 03B V10	B	69			+1 lap	1m 24.267s	54
10	Jenson Button	GB	17	Lucky Strike BAR Honda	BAR 005-Honda RA003E V10	B	69			+1 lap	1m 23.376s	65
11	Cristiano da Matta	BR	21	Panasonic Toyota Racing	Toyota TF103-RVX-03 V10	M	68			+2 laps	1m 23.040s	36
12	Jos Verstappen	NL	19	European Minardi Cosworth	Minardi PS03-Cosworth CR3 V10	B	67			+3 laps	1m 26.559s	60
13	Nicolas Kiesa	DK	18	European Minardi Cosworth	Minardi PS03-Cosworth CR3 V10	B	66			+4 laps	1m 27.641s	47
	Heinz-Harald Frentzen	D	10	Sauber Petronas	Sauber C22-Petronas 03B V10	B	47	Out of fuel			1m 24.450s	45
	Justin Wilson	GB	15	Jaguar Racing	Jaguar R4-Cosworth CR5 V10	M	42	Engine			1m 24.936s	26
	Zsolt Baumgartner	H	12	Jordan Ford	Jordan EJ-13-Ford Cosworth RS1 V10	B	34	Engine			1m 26.464s	22
	Olivier Panis	F	20	Panasonic Toyota Racing	Toyota TF103-RVX-03 V10	M	33	Gearbox			1m 24.414s	17
	Giancarlo Fisichella	I	11	Jordan Ford	Jordan EJ-13-Ford Cosworth RS1 V10	B	28	Engine			1m 25.081s	13
	Rubens Barrichello	BR	2	Scuderia Ferrari Marlboro	Ferrari F2003-GA-051 V10	B	19	Accident			1m 24.583s	13
	Jacques Villeneuve	CDN	16	Lucky Strike BAR Honda	BAR 005-Honda RA003E V10	B	14	Hydraulic leak			1m 25.278s	13

Fastest lap: Juan Pablo Montoya, on lap 37, 1m 22.095s, 119.374 mph/192.114 km/h (record for new track configuration).

Previous lap record: Michael Schumacher (F1 Ferrari F2002-051 V10), 1m 16.207s, 116.680 mph/187.778 km/h (2002).

19th: ZSOLT BAUMGARTNER Jordan-Ford Cosworth

17th: HEINZ-HARALD FRENTZEN Sauber-Petronas

15th: CRISTIANO DA MATTA Toyota

13th: GIANCARLO FISICHELLA Jordan-Ford Cosworth

11th: NICK HEIDFELD Sauber-Petronas

20th: NICOLAS KIESA Minardi-Cosworth

18th: JOS VERSTAPPEN Minardi-Cosworth

16th: JACQUES VILLENEUVE BAR-Honda

14th: JENSON BUTTON BAR-Honda

12th: JUSTIN WILSON Jaguar-Cosworth

Grid order	1	2	3	4	5	6	7	8	9	10	11	12	13	14	15	16	17	18	19	20	21	22	23	24	25	26	27	28	29	30	31	32	33	34	35	36	37	38	39	40	41	42	43	44	45	46	47	48	49	50	51	52	53	54	55
8 ALONSO	8	8	8	8	8	8	8	8	8	8	8	8	8	6	8	8	8	8	8	8	8	8	8	8	8	8	8	8	8	8	8	8	8	8	8	8	8	8	8	8	8	8	8	8	8	8	8	8	8	8	8	8	8	8	8
4 R. SCHUMACHER	14	14	14	14	14	14	14	14	14	14	14	6	8	6	2	5	5	6	6	6	6	6	6	6	6	6	6	6	6	3	3	6	6	6	6	6	6	6	6	6	6	6	6	6	6	6	6	6	6	6	6	6	6	6	6
14 WEBBER	2	2	6	6	6	6	6	6	6	6	6	14	7	2	5	1	6	14	14	14	14	14	14	14	14	14	14	14	14	3	6	6	1	1	1	5	5	5	3	3	3	3	3	3	3	4	3	3
3 MONTOYA	6	6	7	7	7	7	7	7	7	7	7	7	7	2	7	1	4	14	7	7	7	7	7	7	7	7	7	7	7	4	1	1	5	5	5	3	3	3	5	14	14	4	4	4	4	4	3	3	4	4
2 BARRICHELLO	7	7	2	2	2	2	2	2	2	2	2	2	2	5	4	9	7	2	3	3	3	3	3	3	3	3	3	3	1	1	4	5	3	3	3	14	14	14	4	14	14	14	14	14	7	7	5	5
7 TRULLI	5	5	5	5	5	5	5	5	5	5	5	5	1	3	6	2	3	1	1	1	1	1	1	1	4	4	7	5	5	14	14	14	14	14	4	7	7	7	7	7	7	5	5	14	14	14
6 RÄIKKÖNEN	1	1	1	1	1	1	1	1	1	1	1	1	3	9	14	3	1	4	4	4	4	4	4	4	1	1	5	9	14	4	4	4	4	7	7	7	5	5	5	5	5	5	14	14	7	7	7
1 M. SCHUMACHER	3	3	3	3	3	3	3	3	3	3	3	3	9	4	6	7	1	5	5	5	5	5	5	5	5	5	1	5	5	9	14	9	7	7	7	7	1	1	1	1	1	1	1	1	9	1	1	1	1
5 COULTHARD	9	9	9	9	9	9	9	9	9	9	9	9	4	9	14	2	17	4	10	10	9	9	9	9	9	9	9	14	20	7	9	9	9	9	9	9	9	9	9	9	9	1	9	9	9
20 PANIS	16	16	16	16	16	16	16	16	4	4	4	20	20	7	17	4	9	9	20	20	20	20	20	20	20	20	20	7	17	17	17	17	17	17	17	10	10	10	10	17	17	17	17	17
9 HEIDFELD	11	11	11	11	15	15	15	4	16	16	16	14	17	3	9	10	20	20	15	15	15	15	15	15	15	15	15	10	9	9	9	9	9	21	21	21	21	21	21	21	21	21
15 WILSON	15	15	15	20	4	4	4	15	15	15	20	20	14	17	10	17	17	17	17	17	17	17	17	17	21	21	21	21	21	19	19	19	19	19	19
11 FISICHELLA	19	19	19	20	4	20	20	20	20	20	11	11	10	20	11	11	11	11	11	11	10	10	10	19	19	19	19	19	19	18	18	18	18	18
17 BUTTON	10	10	20	4	11	11	11	11	11	11	15	17	10	15	15	11	11	10	10	10	10	19	12	12	12	21	21	21	18	18	18
21 DA MATTA	20	20	10	10	10	10	10	19	19	19	19	17	17	10	11	11	11	12	19	19	19	21	19	19	21	18	18	18	18	18	18
16 VILLENEUVE	12	4	10	10	10	10	10	10	17	10	10	12	11	11	12	12	12	21	21	21	21	21	18
10 FRENTZEN	17	17	17	17	17	17	17	17	10	17	17	15	16	19	19	19	19	18	18	18	18	18
19 VERSTAPPEN	4	18	18	12	12	12	12	12	12	12	19	18	18	18	21	18	18	18
12 BAUMGARTNER	18	12	12	18	18	18	18	18	18	18	18	18	21	21	21	21
18 KIESA	21	21	21	21	21	21	21	21	21	21	21	21	21

Pit stop

One lap behind leader

TIME SHEETS

SATURDAY QUALIFYING determines race grid order
Sunny with light winds (track 44°C, air 32°C)

Pos.	Driver	Lap time	Sector 1	Sector 2	Sector 3
1	Fernando Alonso	1m 21.688s	29.180s	29.553s	22.955s
2	Ralf Schumacher	1m 21.944s	28.629s	30.034s	23.281s
3	Mark Webber	1m 22.027s	29.046s	29.662s	23.319s
4	Juan Pablo Montoya	1m 22.180s	28.954s	30.114s	23.112s
5	Rubens Barrichello	1m 22.180s	28.876s	29.846s	23.458s
6	Jarno Trulli	1m 22.610s	29.264s	29.896s	23.450s
7	Kimi Räikkönen	1m 22.742s	29.147s	29.978s	23.617s
8	Michael Schumacher	1m 22.755s	29.139s	30.353s	23.263s
9	David Coulthard	1m 23.060s	29.157s	30.531s	23.372s
10	Olivier Panis	1m 23.369s	29.119s	30.755s	23.495s
11	Nick Heidfeld	1m 23.621s	29.457s	30.504s	23.660s
12	Justin Wilson	1m 23.660s	29.677s	30.435s	23.548s
13	Giancarlo Fisichella	1m 23.726s	29.425s	30.572s	23.729s
14	Jenson Button	1m 23.847s	29.433s	30.599s	23.815s
15	Cristiano da Matta	1m 23.982s	29.414s	30.924s	23.644s
16	Jacques Villeneuve	1m 24.100s	29.414s	30.579s	24.107s
17	Heinz-Harald Frentzen	1m 24.569s	29.745s	31.086s	23.738s
18	Jos Verstappen	1m 26.423s	30.076s	31.982s	24.365s
19	Zsolt Baumgartner	1m 26.678s	30.345s	31.833s	24.460s
20	Nicolas Kiesa	1m 28.907s	30.487s	33.473s	24.947s

FRIDAY QUALIFYING determines Sat running order
Dry and warm (track 42°C, air 32°C)

Pos.	Driver	Lap time
1	Jarno Trulli	1m 22.358s
2	Ralf Schumacher	1m 22.413s
3	Mark Webber	1m 22.625s
4	David Coulthard	1m 22.786s
5	Rubens Barrichello	1m 22.892s
6	Fernando Alonso	1m 22.953s
7	Olivier Panis	1m 22.986s
8	Juan Pablo Montoya	1m 23.305s
9	Michael Schumacher	1m 23.430s
10	Nick Heidfeld	1m 23.482s
11	Heinz-Harald Frentzen	1m 23.660s
12	Kimi Räikkönen	1m 23.695s
13	Jenson Button	1m 24.313s
14	Jacques Villeneuve	1m 24.333s
15	Justin Wilson	1m 24.343s
16	Giancarlo Fisichella	1m 24.725s
17	Ralph Firman	1m 25.223s
18	Jos Verstappen	1m 26.052s
19	Nicolas Kiesa	1m 27.023s
20	Cristiano da Matta	1m 55.138s

POINTS TABLES: CONSTRUCTORS

1	Williams	129
2	Ferrari	121
3	McLaren	115
4	Renault	78
5 =	BAR	15
5 =	Jaguar	15
7	Toyota	14
8	Jordan	11
9	Sauber	9

PRIVATE TESTING
Dry and warm (track: 40/41°C, air 29/30°C)

Pos.	Driver	Laps	Time
1	Fernando Alonso	42	1m 22.230s
2	Allan McNish	42	1m 22.855s
3	Jarno Trulli	43	1m 23.092s
4	Mark Webber	27	1m 23.748s
5	Justin Wilson	40	1m 24.209s
6	Jos Verstappen	28	1m 25.321s
7	Zsolt Baumgartner	39	1m 26.006s
8	Nicolas Kiesa	34	1m 26.252s
9	Ralph Firman	38	1m 26.600s
10	Gianmaria Bruni	30	1m 27.036s
11	Giancarlo Fisichella	7	1m 27.399s

FRIDAY FREE PRACTICE
Dry and warm (track 41°C, air 31°C)

Pos.	Driver	Laps	Time
1	Olivier Panis	24	1m 21.770s
2	Jarno Trulli	13	1m 22.464s
3	Juan Pablo Montoya	25	1m 22.592s
4	Rubens Barrichello	21	1m 22.594s
5	Cristiano da Matta	25	1m 22.700s
6	Mark Webber	23	1m 22.741s
7	Ralf Schumacher	25	1m 22.757s
8	David Coulthard	24	1m 22.797s
9	Michael Schumacher	20	1m 22.842s
10	Fernando Alonso	4	1m 23.214s
11	Kimi Räikkönen	23	1m 23.532s
12	Heinz-Harald Frentzen	25	1m 23.586s
13	Jenson Button	26	1m 23.723s
14	Jacques Villeneuve	23	1m 23.817s
15	Giancarlo Fisichella	16	1m 24.474s
16	Ralph Firman	21	1m 24.502s
17	Nick Heidfeld	23	1m 24.535s
18	Justin Wilson	5	1m 24.669s
19	Jos Verstappen	18	1m 25.579s

SATURDAY FIRST FREE PRACTICE
Sunny with light winds (track 33/35°C, air 27/29°C)

Pos.	Driver	Laps	Time
1	Fernando Alonso	7	1m 22.950s
2	Michael Schumacher	12	1m 23.274s
3	Rubens Barrichello	12	1m 23.432s
4	Ralf Schumacher	15	1m 23.758s
5	Jarno Trulli	9	1m 23.796s
6	Juan Pablo Montoya	16	1m 24.142s
7	Olivier Panis	14	1m 24.251s
8	Mark Webber	10	1m 24.328s
9	Heinz-Harald Frentzen	9	1m 24.617s
10	Nick Heidfeld	10	1m 24.734s
11	Justin Wilson	12	1m 24.800s
12	Kimi Räikkönen	10	1m 24.837s
13	David Coulthard	11	1m 25.379s
14	Jenson Button	11	1m 25.397s
15	Cristiano da Matta	16	1m 25.545s
16	Giancarlo Fisichella	6	1m 25.566s
17	Jacques Villeneuve	19	1m 25.815s
18	Ralph Firman	6	1m 26.618s
19	Jos Verstappen	8	1m 26.976s
20	Nicolas Kiesa	11	1m 27.188s

SATURDAY SECOND FREE PRACTICE
Sunny with light winds (track 35/39°C, air 30/31°C)

Pos.	Driver	Laps	Time
1	Ralf Schumacher	18	1m 21.939s
2	Michael Schumacher	16	1m 22.313s
3	Rubens Barrichello	12	1m 22.467s
4	Juan Pablo Montoya	13	1m 22.494s
5	Mark Webber	23	1m 22.848s
6	Kimi Räikkönen	14	1m 22.876s
7	Fernando Alonso	18	1m 22.902s
8	Jarno Trulli	13	1m 23.074s
9	David Coulthard	13	1m 23.293s
10	Olivier Panis	17	1m 23.789s
11	Jenson Button	22	1m 23.805s
12	Nick Heidfeld	22	1m 23.838s
13	Justin Wilson	22	1m 23.853s
14	Heinz-Harald Frentzen	19	1m 24.006s
15	Jacques Villeneuve	25	1m 24.154s
16	Giancarlo Fisichella	14	1m 24.343s
17	Cristiano da Matta	13	1m 24.401s
18	Jos Verstappen	15	1m 26.498s
19	Nicolas Kiesa	13	1m 27.295s

WARM-UP
Sunny with light winds (track 45 °C, air 33°C)

Pos.	Driver	Laps	Time
1	Michael Schumacher	6	1m 22.210s
2	Fernando Alonso	6	1m 22.460s
3	Juan Pablo Montoya	5	1m 22.521s
4	Mark Webber	6	1m 22.654s
5	Ralf Schumacher	6	1m 22.766s
6	Jarno Trulli	4	1m 23.102s
7	Rubens Barrichello	6	1m 23.457s
8	Olivier Panis	6	1m 23.582s
9	David Coulthard	4	1m 23.822s
10	Nick Heidfeld	4	1m 24.046s
11	Giancarlo Fisichella	5	1m 24.250s
12	Jenson Button	7	1m 24.268s
13	Cristiano da Matta	5	1m 24.789s
14	Jacques Villeneuve	5	1m 25.066s
15	Justin Wilson	5	1m 25.106s
16	Zsolt Baumgartner	7	1m 26.346s
17	Jos Verstappen	4	1m 26.362s
18	Nicolas Kiesa	4	1m 31.376s
19	Kimi Räikkönen	5	1m 33.177s
20	Heinz-Harald Frentzen	4	1m 49.249s

9th: DAVID COULTHARD McLaren-Mercedes

7th: KIMI RÄIKKÖNEN McLaren-Mercedes

5th: RUBENS BARRICHELLO Ferrari

3rd: MARK WEBBER Jaguar-Cosworth

Pole: FERNANDO ALONSO Renault

10th: OLIVIER PANIS Toyota

8th: MICHAEL SCHUMACHER Ferrari

6th: JARNO TRULLI Renault

4th: JUAN PABLO MONTOYA Williams-BMW

2nd: RALF SCHUMACHER Williams-BMW

Lap chart (laps 56–70)

56	57	58	59	60	61	62	63	64	65	66	67	68	69	70	
8	8	8	8	8	8	8	8	8	8	8	8	8	8	8	1
6	6	6	6	6	6	6	6	6	6	6	6	6	6	6	2
3	3	3	3	3	3	3	3	3	3	3	3	3	3	3	3
4	4	4	4	4	4	4	4	4	4	4	4	4	4	4	4
5	5	5	5	5	5	5	5	5	5	5	5	5	5	5	5
14	14	14	14	14	14	14	14	14	14	14	14	14	14	14	6
7	7	7	7	7	7	7	7	7	7	7	7	7	7	7	7
1	1	1	1	1	1	1	1	1	1	1	1	1	1	1	8
9	9	9	9	9	9	9	9	9	9	9	9	9			
17	17	17	17	17	17	17	17	17	17	17	17	17			
21	21	21	21	21	21	21	21	21	21	21	21				
19	19	19	19	19	19	19	19	19	19	19					
18	18	18	18	18	18	18	18	18	18	18					

FOR THE RECORD
First grand prix win: **Fernando Alonso**

First grand prix start: **Zsolt Baumgartner**

CHASSIS LOG BOOK

1	Michael Schumacher	F2003-GA/231
2	Rubens Barrichello	F2003-GA/232
	Spare	F2003-GA/229
3	Juan Pablo Montoya	FW25/06
4	Ralf Schumacher	FW25/07
	Spare	FW25/04
5	David Coulthard	MP4/17D-08
6	Kimi Räikkönen	MP4/17D-09
	Spare	MP4/17D-07
7	Jarno Trulli	R23/05
8	Fernando Alonso	R23/04
	Allan McNish	R23/03
	Spare	R23/03
9	Nick Heidfeld	C22/01
10	Heinz-Harald Frentzen	C22/03
	Spare	C22/02
11	Giancarlo Fisichella/	EJ-13/03
	Zsolt Baumgartner	
12	Ralph Firman	EJ-13/03
	Spare	EJ-13/05
14	Mark Webber	R4/03
15	Justin Wilson	R4/05
	Spare	R4/04
16	Jacques Villeneuve	BAR005/6
17	Jenson Button	BAR005/4
	Spare	BAR005/5
18	Nicolas Kiesa	PS03/01
19	Jos Verstappen	PS03/02
	Spare	PS03/03
20	Olivier Panis	TF103/04
21	Cristiano da Matta	TF103/07
	Spare	TF103/08

POINTS TABLES: DRIVERS

1	Michael Schumacher	72
2	Juan Pablo Montoya	71
3	Kimi Räikkönen	70
4	Ralf Schumacher	58
5	Fernando Alonso	54
6	Rubens Barrichello	49
7	David Coulthard	45
8	Jarno Trulli	24
9	Mark Webber	15
10	Jenson Button	12
11	Giancarlo Fisichella	10
12	Cristiano da Matta	8
13	Heinz-Harald Frentzen	7
14	Oliver Panis	6
15	Jacques Villeneuve	3
16	Nick Heidfeld	2
17	Ralph Firman	1

Main picture: Juan Pablo Montoya and Michael Schumacher get the race under way without incident, but at the back of the grid, Fernando Alonso's Renault has made contact with Jos Verstappen's Minardi.

Inset: Michael Schumacher celebrates his 50th grand prix win for Ferrari with Ross Brawn.

Photographs: Darren Heath

FIA F1 WORLD CHAMPIONSHIP • ROUND 14

ITALIANGP
MONZA

MONZA QUALIFYING

Ferrari arrived in Monza with new front and rear wings for their F2003-GAs, plus uprated V10 engines topping the 900-bhp mark. Using scrubbed front Bridgestones to minimise the effects of slight 'graining' for their qualifying runs, Michael Schumacher (1m 20.963s) and Rubens Barrichello (1m 21.242s) qualified first and third after a heartening performance for the madly passionate tifosi.

'This is confirmation of all the hard work we have been doing,' said Schumacher. 'We are back on top in qualifying, and that has been our weakness in the last few races. A lot of detailed work went into achieving this with aerodynamic and engine improvements, and Bridgestone gave us good tyres. The lap time shows that we are a match for Montoya.'

Barrichello reckoned he could have gone slightly quicker had it not been for a problem under braking at the first chicane. 'The car was good in the warm-up,' he shrugged. 'I locked up the fronts at the first chicane and lost all my time there.'

Montoya was certainly a formidable challenger. The Colombian's Williams-BMW was 0.1s faster to the second timing split, but he clipped the inside kerb on the entry to Variante Ascari just a little too hard, which threw him a tad wide on the exit. It was enough to dissipate his advantage, and he wound up second, 0.051s behind Michael.

'I went wide in the first of the three corners,' said Juan Pablo, 'and I knew that it was over. We were 5 kph down on the Ferraris on top speed.'

In the other Williams FW25, test driver Marc Gené had been pressed into service on Saturday morning to stand in for Ralf Schumacher who, despite the all-clear from the circuit doctors, was still feeling the after-effects of a 170-mph accident that had occurred during testing at Monza a week before the race. 'Ralf seemed okay on Friday, but he was certainly a little quiet in the team debrief,' said Patrick Head, the Williams technical director. 'We asked him if he felt quite well and he said yes, but he wanted to go back to his hotel to relax and have an early night.

'The next morning, he came and talked to Frank [Williams] and I and told us that he'd had an awful headache for much of the previous night. It was clear he wasn't quite up to the mark, so we told him that we wouldn't be asking him to drive this weekend, which I think was what he wanted to hear, although I must stress he didn't ask to withdraw.'

At that point, Gené was trapped in a traffic jam on his way from the centre of Monza and the team had to send one of its staff to rescue him, the Spaniard abandoning his rental car by the side of the road. Having completed around 10,000 miles of testing in the FW25 so far this season, he slipped confidently behind the wheel and qualified it superbly in fifth place, just 0.4s away from team-mate Juan Pablo Montoya.

Kimi Räikkönen managed a 1m 21.466s to take fourth place, but David Coulthard lost track time with a steering problem on Saturday morning and had to be content with a 1m 22.471s best for eighth-fastest time.

Jarno Trulli's Renault R23 was fitted with revised cylinder heads for the race, producing a slight power boost, and he qualified well in sixth place on 1m 21.944s. Unfortunately, Fernando Alonso was the victim of a major electronic problem, which caused his traction control to disengage as he negotiated the first corner after the pits, spinning him out of contention and down to the back of the grid.

Among the BAR Honda team there was a mood of controlled optimism after Jenson Button (1m 22.301s) qualified seventh, three places ahead of team-mate Jacques Villeneuve (1m 22.717s). 'I am pretty pleased with that,' said the Englishman. 'I actually thought eighth would be about right, so seventh is a bonus.'

Toyota's Olivier Panis (1m 22.488s) was confident that he could score points from ninth on the grid, but Cristiano da Matta (1m 22.914s) was disappointed with his 12th spot in the line-up.

Mark Webber was satisfied with an 11th-fastest 1m 22.754s, while Justin Wilson was 15th on 1m 23.484s. 'I did not think we would do this well at Monza,' said Jaguar team boss Tony Purnell. 'And I am not sure that things will be too bad for the race. We're in there as a little bit of a predator for points.'

Giancarlo Fisichella (1m 22.992s) stretched the Jordan-Ford to post 13th-fastest time. Ralph Firman's place in the team was taken by Zsolt Baumgartner (1m 25.881s) for the second straight race while the Englishman continued to recuperate from the accident he had suffered during practice for the Hungarian GP.

Both Saubers were dogged by slight brake problems, leaving Heinz-Harald Frentzen (1m 23.216s) and Nick Heidfeld (1m 23.803s) 14th and 16th. The two Minardis of Jos Verstappen (1m 25.078s) and Nicolas Kiesa (1m 26.778s) were 17th and 19th.

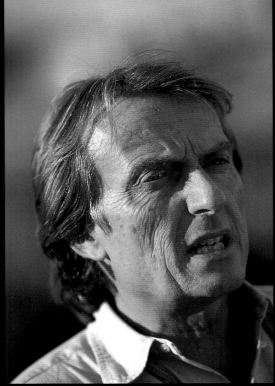

TYRE ROW THREATENS CHAMPIONSHIP BATTLE

Controversy over the legality of Michelin's F1 tyres erupted after Bridgestone tipped off Ferrari that – in its view – the French company's products could, in certain circumstances, infringe the rule specifying that the maximum front contact patch must not exceed 270 mm. Objections were raised immediately after the Hungarian Grand Prix, where Michael Schumacher had finished a lapped eighth, inevitably prompting comment from the Michelin-shod F1 teams that Ferrari was simply a bad loser.

This looked as though it could be a major blow for Williams driver Juan Pablo Montoya and McLaren's Kimi Räikkönen, who trailed Michael Schumacher by one and two points respectively after the race at Budapest. Initially, Ferrari rejected claims that it was behind the complaint.

Bridgestone took the same view. 'The size of the front tyre contact patch does not concern us,' said a company spokesperson. 'Bridgestone did not complain, either formally or informally, to the FIA about this issue.' It did, however, advise Ferrari of its suspicions.

Subsequently, Charlie Whiting, the FIA's technical delegate, wrote to all the team principals outlining changes in the way the tread patterns on the front tyres would be checked in future. The purpose of this was to ensure that no tyre maker gained an unfair advantage by having more rubber gripping the track surface than was permitted.

But the FIA's ruling implied that Michelin-shod cars had benefited from having more than the prescribed tread area in contact with the road. However, Michelin claimed that it had confirmation in writing from the FIA that its current F1 tyre profile was within the regulations and called for any changes to the application of the regulations to be deferred until 2004. It was becoming an ugly and confused business.

Whiting advised the teams, 'It has become clear that under certain circumstances the total front tyre contact patch on some cars can exceed 270 mm in width, despite the fact that when measured statically on a new tyre, the apparent tread width does not exceed the maximum stipulated in the sporting regulations.

'With immediate effect, any part of a front tyre which we consider has been in regular or systematic contact with the track will be deemed tread and will be taken into account when measuring the width of the tyre as defined in the regulations.'

Sam Michael, chief operations engineer for the BMW Williams team commented, 'The FIA have changed the way they measure the front tyre contact patch. We are reviewing the consequences of that.'

McLaren's operations director, Jonathan Neil, made the point that it was more difficult to take accurate measurements of the contact patch after the race. 'When the tyres are hot and covered in debris, it obviously has a much less well-defined surface,' he said. 'Even if you remove all the debris, you often get a degree of scuffing in one direction, so we are urgently seeking clarification of what this means from the FIA.'

In the end, Michelin made a new batch of tyres in time for the Italian Grand Prix, just to ensure that the company erred on the safe side of the FIA's edict. They worked extremely well and the race passed without any scrutineering unpleasantness. But what could not be expunged was a ratcheting up of the tension and an increase in the sense of mutual suspicion between the Michelin front runners – Renault, Williams and McLaren – and their sparring partner, Ferrari, over the manner in which the entire episode had been conducted.

MICHAEL Schumacher delivered one of the finest drives of his career at Monza in a race run at an all-time record average of 153.8 mph, to beat Juan Pablo Montoya's Williams-BMW after an epic chase on this classic circuit. Michael's success was the fastest ever grand prix victory, beating Peter Gethin's average speed set when he won the 1971 Italian race at the wheel of a BRM P160, at a time when Monza was one unfettered, flat-out blast, free of any chicanes whatsoever.

Montoya pressed hard in the early stages, but was never quite in a position to mount a serious attack. By the time an inattentive Heinz-Harald Frentzen balked the Colombian 14 laps from the end of the 53-lap race, it was all done and dusted.

Bridgestone and Ferrari were always going to be very strong at Monza, but there was a degree of speculation as to whether the older Michelins, which the company had replaced the previous week in the wake of a huge post-Hungarian GP controversy (see sidebar), might have offered Montoya a better chance.

Montoya, however, certainly didn't think that the recent rule clarification by the FIA, which forced Williams's tyre supplier, Michelin, to make new rubber for this race, had any adverse outcome. 'I don't think it had anything to do with it,' he said. 'We were still very strong; this is a very low-downforce circuit. At the end of the day, we came out of here with the least loss possible.' Referring to his own championship prospects, he added, 'Nothing's over yet.'

Michelin played safe by producing some modified tyres with slightly-stepped shoulders to ensure that there was no possibility of infringing the 270-mm maximum allowable width now that the measurements were being taken after the race rather than before, following the FIA's recent clarification.

However, Ferrari continued to take an extremely aggressive and defensive attitude about blowing the whistle on Michelin, Ross Brawn in particular refusing to be cowed by criticism from Ron Dennis, Flavio Briatore and Patrick Head during a lively Friday media conference.

'Sometimes you can get a situation where something needs to be clarified from FIA, and I think it's fair what my people have done,' said Luca di Montezemolo, the Ferrari chairman. 'They have some pictures. We went to the FIA and said, "This is the situation. What is your opinion?" If the FIA had said, "Sorry, we don't see anything strange," then it's finish. I think it was necessary to clarify. Now it's cleared up. Full stop. We look ahead.

'The FIA examined the situation, okay. Michelin brought new tyres, so maybe in the past there was something wrong. But we must look ahead, we must be realistic. Sometimes in this matter, I have seen the English press coming close to the Italians.'

The first lap of the race saw some spine-tingling wheel-to-wheel confrontation between the two leading contenders. Michael Schumacher got off the line just ahead of Montoya, but as they braked for the tricky Variante della Roggia, just prior to the first Lesmo right-hander, Montoya took his Williams down the outside of the Ferrari, pulled level and turned in alongside the Italian car.

For a few tense seconds, they were absolutely side by side, but Michael kept his nerve – and his line – to edge ahead into what eventually would prove a decisive lead. At this point, Jarno Trulli's Renault was running third after a great start, but suddenly it slowed and pulled off a couple of corners later with a suspected hydraulic failure. 'It's a real shame,' shrugged Trulli, 'because the car was good today.'

Montoya was heartened by that opening lap. 'I think it was pretty good,' he said. 'Michael went for the inside, I went for the outside. He braked quite a bit earlier than me and I made up a lot of ground. But when I came out of the chicane, I was a lot tighter than him to make the corner so I didn't hit him and he just had better acceleration.'

All in all, it was a bad first lap for the Renault squad. While Trulli accelerated away for his brief moment of glory, Fernando Alonso, starting from the back of the grid, hit Jos Verstappen's Minardi, which, in turn, was attempting to avoid Justin Wilson's slow-starting Jaguar. Wilson had lost first gear on the warm-up lap and was attempting to get away using the Jag's long Monza second ratio. He was push-started away and retired soon afterward, while Alonso pitted after completing the opening lap,

Above: Kimi Räikkönen explores late braking points in his McLaren-Mercedes.

Top left: Luca de Montezemolo tried to calm the tyre controversy.

Centre left: Treading the depths. Thankfully, the issue of tyres did not overshadow proceedings at the Italian GP.

Bottom left: Still feeling the after-effects of his testing shunt, Ralf Schumacher withdrew from the meeting.
Photographs: Darren Heath

when the car was inspected for damage before resuming, now with a full tank of fuel for a one-stop strategy.

At the end of the opening lap, Schumacher's Ferrari led by 0.7s from Montoya, Rubens Barrichello's Ferrari, the McLaren-Mercedes of Kimi Räikkönen and David Coulthard, Olivier Panis's Toyota TF103 and Williams test driver Marc Gené, who was subbing for the unwell Ralf Schumacher. By lap four, Michael Schumacher was 1.7s ahead, just as Cristiano da Matta's Toyota suffered a left rear tyre deflation approaching Parabolica and spun spectacularly out of the contest.

Ten laps into the race and things were warming up. Michael was 3.5s ahead of Juan Pablo, but Barrichello was edging forward and only another 0.4s behind; Räikkönen was also a threat, hanging on gamely in fourth.

On lap 13, Räikkönen and Gené made their first refuelling stops (9.4s and 9.1s respectively). Barrichello came in to the pits on lap 14 (8.2s), and race leader Schumacher on lap 15 (8.6s), allowing Montoya to lead briefly until the Colombian pitted for an 8.4s service next time around.

After that, the stalemate at the front of the field resumed, Schumacher running consistently around 1.6s ahead of Montoya. As they lapped Giancarlo Fisichella's Jordan on lap 28, Schumacher's advantage dropped momentarily to under a second, but the strategic manner in which he passed the Italian driver put him 1.3s ahead of Montoya by the end of lap 30.

On lap 31, Barrichello made his second stop (9.8s), while Montoya (9.0s) and Coulthard in the fifth-place McLaren (8.7s) followed suit on lap 32. Schumacher (9.2s) and Räikkönen came in at the end of lap 34, allowing Marc Gené one glorious lap in the lead before he took on his second batch of fuel on lap 35. The outcome of all this short-term shuffling was to leave the leading bunch in exactly the same order, albeit with Räikkönen a fraction closer to Barrichello's third-place Ferrari.

Montoya admitted that at one point he had been edging closer to the leading Ferrari, but had experienced problems lapping slower cars in heavy traffic.

'I was about a second behind Michael and the team told me I was taking two- or three-tenths of a lap from him. Then I got to [lap] Frentzen and suddenly I found myself four seconds behind him,' he said, referring to the Sauber driver's apparent reluctance to use his mirrors when a faster car appeared behind him.

'Then we were quite even, then I got to, what's his name, the new Jordan guy [Baumgartner]… You know, I lost about another two or three or four seconds, but then I knew we had to finish and fight for another day, really.'

Completing lap 45, David Coulthard coasted to a standstill just beyond the pit-lane exit, his McLaren MP4/17D having been sidelined with a fuel pressure problem. 'I had a pretty quiet and uneventful race in fifth place until the engine began to sound a bit rough and my pace dropped, which allowed Marc Gené to close up,' he said. 'I was struggling with the balance throughout

the race with lots of oversteer, which made it hard to attack the corners. We tried to rectify the problem by dropping some wing at the pit stops, but no luck.'

Eight laps later, Michael Schumacher took the chequered flag for his 69th career victory and his 50th as a Ferrari driver. 'It is quite a while ago that we won the last race,' he enthused, reflecting on Barrichello's victory at Silverstone and his own previous win in Canada in June.

'We have had tough races behind us,' he continued, 'not just winning, but we failed to score the points we thought we would score. And then we had all this summer break and a big push in the team, in the factory, everywhere, everyone, really over the top, motivated and giving more than 100 per cent of work. That's something which is unbelievable.

'I was able to pay that back a little with pole position yesterday, but I think that this is one of the greatest days in my career, honestly. I'm so thankful to everyone in the team because those guys have done a tremendous job.'

Montoya reckoned that his second place was the best he could have done under the circumstances, crossing the line only 5.2s behind the Ferrari after easing back to conserve his car in the closing stages of the race. Barrichello, by contrast, had his hands full in fending off Räikkönen, a task he just managed to do by 0.999s.

'To be honest, my first set [of tyres] was the best one,' he said. 'I had a little too much understeer to begin with and I lost time with Trulli. He seemed to think that he wanted to pass even Michael at the second chicane, so I lost time and, all of a sudden, I almost crashed into him when he had a problem and slowed down, so I had quite a first lap.

'Then I was running quite fast. I caught Montoya up and it was really good, but then after I put on my second set of tyres, it was never as competitive. The third one was even worse and I had a little bit of a problem with the rears, and unfortunately my pace wasn't so fast. It was good enough to hold Kimi and so I did.'

Marc Gené finished fifth after an excellent performance, keeping the second Williams-BMW out of trouble and helping the team retain its lead in the constructors' world championship. BAR Honda experienced mixed fortunes: Jenson Button suffered gearbox failure after 24 laps, but Jacques Villeneuve drove a fine race to take sixth.

'The race was a great team effort and the guys did a fantastic job during the pit stops,' said the Canadian. 'We didn't qualify as well as we hoped yesterday, but we were working for the race, so it was great to stay reliable and be able to make the most of a good race set-up.'

Mark Webber was seventh for Jaguar, despite forgetting to switch on the R4's traction control until he reached the second chicane on the opening lap. The brilliant Alonso climbed back through the field superbly to pip Nick Heidfeld's Sauber C22 for eighth place on the final lap, while the Jordans of Fisichella and Baumgartner were followed home by Nicolas Kiesa in the sole surviving Minardi, Jos Verstappen having retired on lap 28 with a split oil radiator.

Now Michael led the championship by four crucial points, seemingly stemming the adverse tide against which he had been swimming since Silverstone. Ahead lay Indianapolis and Suzuka, two very different tracks with very specific technical challenges. If he could get through Indianapolis unscathed, he might well be home and dry.

Heinz-Harald Frentzen sets his Sauber's discs aglow approaching one of Monza's chicanes, a circuit notorious for heavy braking.
Photograph: Bryn Williams/crash.net

Photograph: Darren Heath

FIA F1 WORLD CHAMPIONSHIP • ROUND 14

GRAN PREMIO
VODAFONE D'ITALIA
MONZA 12–14 SEPTEMBER 2003

MONZA – GRAND PRIX CIRCUIT

CIRCUIT LENGTH: 3.600 miles/5.793 km

CURVA DI LESMO 100/161 (3)
90/145 (2)
CURVA DEL SERRAGLIO 205/330 (6)
mph/km/h (gear)
SECONDA VARIANTE 70/113 (2)
VARIANTE ASCARI 100/161 (3)
RETTILINEO PARABOLICA 205/330 (6)
210/338 (6)
CURVA GRANDE 180/290 (5)
PRIMA VARIANTE 60/97 (2)
CURVA PARABOLICA 155/250 (4)

RACE DISTANCE: 53 laps, 190.587 miles/306.720 km   RACE WEATHER: Sunny and hot (track 40°C, air 28°C)

Pos.	Driver	Nat.	No.	Entrant	Car/Engine	Tyres	Laps	Time/Retirement	Speed (mph/km/h)	Gap to leader	Fastest race lap	
1	Michael Schumacher	D	1	Scuderia Ferrari Marlboro	Ferrari F2003-GA-051 V10	B	53	1h 14m 19.838s	153.842/247.585		1m 21.832s	14
2	Juan Pablo Montoya	COL	3	BMW WilliamsF1 Team	Williams FW25-BMW P83 V10	M	53	1h 14m 25.132s	153.660/247.292	+5.294s	1m 22.126s	31
3	Rubens Barrichello	BR	2	Scuderia Ferrari Marlboro	Ferrari F2003-GA-051 V10	B	53	1h 14m 31.673s	153.435/246.930	+11.835s	1m 22.171s	13
4	Kimi Räikkönen	FIN	6	West McLaren Mercedes	McLaren MP4/17D-Mercedes F0110M V10	M	53	1h 14m 32.672s	153.401/246.875	+12.834s	1m 22.032s	32
5	Marc Gené	E	4	BMW WilliamsF1 Team	Williams FW25-BMW P83 V10	M	53	1h 14m 47.729s	152.886/246.046	+27.891s	1m 22.413s	12
6	Jacques Villeneuve	CDN	16	Lucky Strike BAR Honda	BAR 005-Honda RA003E V10	B	52			+1 lap	1m 23.039s	13
7	Mark Webber	AUS	14	Jaguar Racing	Jaguar R4-Cosworth CR5 V10	M	52			+1 lap	1m 23.778s	10
8	Fernando Alonso	E	8	Mild Seven Renault F1 Team	Renault R3-RS23 V10	M	52			+1 lap	1m 23.195s	47
9	Nick Heidfeld	D	9	Sauber Petronas	Sauber C22-Petronas 03C V10	B	52			+1 lap	1m 24.225s	9
10	Giancarlo Fisichella	I	11	Jordan Ford	Jordan EJ-13-Ford Cosworth RS1 V10	B	52			+1 lap	1m 25.133s	52
11	Zsolt Baumgartner	H	12	Jordan Ford	Jordan EJ-13-Ford Cosworth RS1 V10	B	51			+2 laps	1m 25.549s	38
12	Nicolas Kiesa	DK	18	European Minardi Cosworth	Minardi PS03-Cosworth CR3 V10	B	51			+2 laps	1m 26.127s	49
13	Heinz-Harald Frentzen	D	10	Sauber Petronas	Sauber C22-Petronas 03C V10	B	50	Transmission		DNF	1m 23.518s	14
	David Coulthard	GB	5	West McLaren Mercedes	McLaren MP4/17D-Mercedes F0110M V10	M	45	Fuel pressure			1m 22.427s	10
	Olivier Panis	F	20	Panasonic Toyota Racing	Toyota TF103-RVX-03 V10	M	35	Brakes			1m 23.303s	10
	Jos Verstappen	NL	19	European Minardi Cosworth	Minardi PS03-Cosworth CR3 V10	B	27	Oil leak			1m 25.816s	22
	Jenson Button	GB	17	Lucky Strike BAR Honda	BAR 005-Honda RA003E V10	B	24	Gearbox			1m 23.225s	13
	Cristiano da Matta	BR	21	Panasonic Toyota Racing	Toyota TF103-RVX-03 V10	M	3	Puncture/spin			1m 26.148s	3
	Justin Wilson	GB	15	Jaguar Racing	Jaguar R4-Cosworth CR5 V10	M	2	Gearbox			1m 59.265s	2
	Jarno Trulli	I	7	Mild Seven Renault F1 Team	Renault R3-RS23 V10	M	0	Throttle				

Fastest lap: Michael Schumacher, on lap 14, 1m 21.832s, 158.355 mph/254.848 km/h (record).

Previous lap record: Rubens Barrichello (F1 Ferrari F2002-051 V10), 1m 23.657s, 154.901 mph/249.289 km/h (2002).

19th: NICOLAS KIESA Minardi-Cosworth

17th: JOS VERSTAPPEN Minardi-Cosworth

15th: JUSTIN WILSON Jaguar-Cosworth

13th: GIANCARLO FISICHELLA Jordan-Ford Cosworth

11th: MARK WEBBER Jaguar-Cosworth

20th: FERNANDO ALONSO Renault

18th: ZSOLT BAUMGARTNER Jordan-Ford Cosworth

16th: NICK HEIDFELD Sauber-Petronas

14th: HEINZ-HARALD FRENTZEN Sauber-Petronas

12th: CRISTIANO DA MATTA Toyota

Grid order	1	2	3	4	5	6	7	8	9	10	11	12	13	14	15	16	17	18	19	20	21	22	23	24	25	26	27	28	29	30	31	32	33	34	35	36	37	38	39	40	41
1 M. SCHUMACHER	1	1	1	1	1	1	1	1	1	1	1	1	1	1	1	3	1	1	1	1	1	1	1	1	1	1	1	1	1	1	1	1	1	1	1	1	1	1	1	1	1
3 MONTOYA	3	3	3	3	3	3	3	3	3	3	3	3	3	3	3		3	3	3	3	3	3	3	3	3	3	3	3	3	3	3	3	6	3	3	3	3	3	3	3	3
2 BARRICHELLO	2	2	2	2	2	2	2	2	2	2	2	2	2	16	16		2	2	2	2	2	2	2	2	2	2	2	2	2	2	6	4	4	4	2	2	2	2	2	2	2
6 RÄIKKÖNEN	6	6	6	6	6	6	6	6	6	6	6	16	17	2		6	6	6	6	6	6	6	6	6	6	6	6	6	6	5	3	3	2	6	6	6	6	6	6		
4 GENÉ	5	5	5	5	5	5	5	5	5	5	4	17	2		5	5	5	5	5	5	5	5	5	5	5	5	5	5	5	4	2	6	5	5	5	5	5				
7 TRULLI	20	4	4	4	4	4	4	4	16	16	10	6	5	4	4	4	4	4	4	4	4	4	4	4	4	4	2	5	5	4	4	4	4	4							
17 BUTTON	4	20	20	20	20	20	20	20	20	16	17	16	6	5	4	16	16	16	16	16	16	16	16	16	16	16	16	16	10	9	16	16	16	16	16						
5 COULTHARD	16	16	16	16	16	16	16	16	16	17	14	14	5	10	20	20	20	20	20	20	20	20	20	20	20	20	10	10	9	16	10	10	10	10	10						
20 PANIS	17	17	17	17	17	17	17	17	17	20	9	10	4	4	17	17	17	17	17	10	10	10	10	10	10	10	14	14	16	10	14	14	14	14	14						
16 VILLENEUVE	14	14	14	14	14	14	14	14	10	9	20	20	10	10	10	10	10	10	10	14	14	14	14	14	14	14	9	9	20	14	9	9	9	9	9						
14 WEBBER	9	9	9	9	9	9	9	9	5	14	14	14	14	14	9	9	9	9	9	9	9	20	20	14	8	8	8	8	8												
21 DA MATTA	21	21	21	10	10	10	10	10	20	20	12	9	9	17	11	11	8	9	8	8	8	8	11	11	11	11	11	11	11												
11 FISICHELLA	12	12	10	12	12	12	12	12	12	12	9	12	12	11	11	11	11	8	8	11	12	12	12	12	12	12	12	12	12												
10 FRENTZEN	18	18	18	18	18	18	18	18	18	18	11	11	11	11	12	8	8	8	8	12	12	11	11	11	11	11	20	18	18	18	18	18									
15 WILSON	10	10	18	11	11	11	11	11	11	11	11	18	8	8	8	8	8	12	12	12	12	18	18	18	18	18	18	18													
9 HEIDFELD	11	11	11	8	8	8	8	8	8	8	8	8	19	19	19	18	18	18	18	18	19	19	19																		
19 VERSTAPPEN	8	8	8	19	19	19	19	19	19	19	19	19	19	19	19	19	19	19	19	19																					
12 BAUMGARTNER	19	19	19																																						
18 KIESA	15	15																																							
8 ALONSO																																									

Pit stop
One lap behind leader

TIME SHEETS

SATURDAY QUALIFYING determines race grid order
Dry and hot (track 36/39°C, air 25/27°C)

Pos.	Driver	Lap time	Sector 1	Sector 2	Sector 3
1	Michael Schumacher	1m 20.963s	25.995s	27.793s	27.175
2	Juan Pablo Montoya	1m 21.014s	25.992s	27.720s	27.302s
3	Rubens Barrichello	1m 21.242s	26.219s	27.838s	27.185s
4	Kimi Räikkönen	1m 21.466s	26.202s	28.021s	27.243s
5	Marc Gené	1m 21.834s	26.261s	28.000s	27.573s
6	Jarno Trulli	1m 21.944s	26.528s	28.036s	27.380s
7	Jenson Button	1m 22.301s	26.528s	28.029s	27.744s
8	David Coulthard	1m 22.471s	26.300s	28.432s	27.739s
9	Olivier Panis	1m 22.488s	26.332s	28.333s	27.823s
10	Jacques Villeneuve	1m 22.717s	26.610s	28.411s	27.696s
11	Mark Webber	1m 22.754s	26.854s	28.281s	27.619s
12	Cristiano da Matta	1m 22.914s	26.423s	28.379s	28.112s
13	Giancarlo Fisichella	1m 22.992s	26.756s	28.343s	27.893s
14	Heinz-Harald Frentzen	1m 23.216s	26.469s	28.477s	28.270s
15	Justin Wilson	1m 23.484s	26.977s	28.607s	27.900s
16	Nick Heidfeld	1m 23.803s	26.937s	28.872s	27.994s
17	Jos Verstappen	1m 25.078s	26.870s	29.295s	28.913s
18	Zsolt Baumgartner	1m 25.881s	27.312s	29.744s	28.825s
19	Nicolas Kiesa	1m 26.778s	27.301s	29.730s	29.747s
20	Fernando Alonso	1m 40.405s	33.022s	31.952s	29.185s

FRIDAY QUALIFYING determines Sat running order
Dry and hot (track 38 °C, air 24/26°C)

Pos.	Driver	Lap time
1	Juan Pablo Montoya	1m 20.656s
2	Rubens Barrichello	1m 20.784s
3	Michael Schumacher	1m 21.268s
4	Cristiano da Matta	1m 21.829s
5	Kimi Räikkönen	1m 21.966s
6	Mark Webber	1m 21.966s
7	Jarno Trulli	1m 22.034s
8	Fernando Alonso	1m 22.103s
9	Heinz-Harald Frentzen	1m 22.203s
10	Olivier Panis	1m 22.372s
11	Jenson Button	1m 22.495s
12	Nick Heidfeld	1m 22.547s
13	Jacques Villeneuve	1m 22.858s
14	David Coulthard	1m 23.154s
15	Justin Wilson	1m 23.609s
16	Giancarlo Fisichella	1m 24.179s
17	Zsolt Baumgartner	1m 24.872s
18	Nicolas Kiesa	1m 26.299s
19	Ralf Schumacher	No time

POINTS TABLES: CONSTRUCTORS

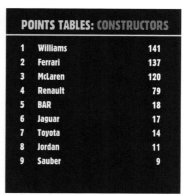

1	Williams	141
2	Ferrari	137
3	McLaren	120
4	Renault	79
5	BAR	18
6	Jaguar	17
7	Toyota	14
8	Jordan	11
9	Sauber	9

PRIVATE TESTING
Dry and warm (track: 34 °C, air 24°C)

Pos.	Driver	Laps	Time
1	Jarno Trulli	44	1m 22.083s
2	Fernando Alonso	40	1m 22.507s
3	Allan McNish	40	1m 22.533s
4	Mark Webber	45	1m 23.191s
5	Justin Wilson	35	1m 23.541s
6	Jos Verstappen	28	1m 23.999s
7	Giancarlo Fisichella	39	1m 24.026s
8	Gianmaria Bruni	27	1m 24.318s
9	Zsolt Baumgartner	34	1m 25.210s
10	Nicolas Kiesa	11	1m 26.296s

FRIDAY FREE PRACTICE
Dry and warm (track 36°C, air 26°C)

Pos.	Driver	Laps	Time
1	Rubens Barrichello	18	1m 21.001s
2	Michael Schumacher	15	1m 21.152s
3	Kimi Räikkönen	19	1m 21.318s
4	Juan Pablo Montoya	22	1m 21.556s
5	David Coulthard	24	1m 21.675s
6	Cristiano da Matta	24	1m 21.881s
7	Jenson Button	27	1m 21.913s
8	Fernando Alonso	18	1m 22.100s
9	Ralf Schumacher	22	1m 22.312s
10	Jarno Trulli	17	1m 22.335s
11	Mark Webber	22	1m 22.368s
12	Olivier Panis	20	1m 22.584s
13	Nick Heidfeld	16	1m 22.821s
14	Heinz-Harald Frentzen	13	1m 22.929s
15	Jacques Villeneuve	13	1m 23.151s
16	Justin Wilson	11	1m 23.478s
17	Giancarlo Fisichella	16	1m 23.794s
18	Jos Verstappen	14	1m 24.652s
19	Zsolt Baumgartner	22	1m 24.891s
20	Nicolas Kiesa	3	1m 26.903s

SATURDAY FIRST FREE PRACTICE
Dry and hot (track 36/38°C, air 24/26°C)

Pos.	Driver	Laps	Time
1	Michael Schumacher	13	1m 21.623s
2	Rubens Barrichello	15	1m 22.146s
3	David Coulthard	17	1m 22.552s
4	Jenson Button	19	1m 22.642s
5	Juan Pablo Montoya	18	1m 22.646s
6	Marc Gené	21	1m 22.685s
7	Kimi Räikkönen	14	1m 22.718s
8	Fernando Alonso	18	1m 22.731s
9	Jarno Trulli	16	1m 22.735s
10	Jacques Villeneuve	19	1m 23.120s
11	Cristiano da Matta	12	1m 23.312s
12	Heinz-Harald Frentzen	17	1m 23.572s
13	Justin Wilson	16	1m 23.955s
14	Nick Heidfeld	13	1m 24.134s
15	Mark Webber	17	1m 24.454s
16	Giancarlo Fisichella	12	1m 25.194s
17	Nicolas Kiesa	18	1m 25.870s
18	Jos Verstappen	15	1m 25.934s
19	Zsolt Baumgartner	17	1m 26.295s
20	Olivier Panis	4	No time

SATURDAY SECOND FREE PRACTICE
Dry and hot (track 36/38°C, air 24/26°C)

Pos.	Driver	Laps	Time
1	Juan Pablo Montoya	11	1m 21.468s
2	Michael Schumacher	15	1m 21.586s
3	Marc Gené	16	1m 21.928s
4	Kimi Räikkönen	15	1m 22.091s
5	Rubens Barrichello	15	1m 22.108s
6	David Coulthard	10	1m 22.134s
7	Olivier Panis	14	1m 22.321s
8	Jarno Trulli	16	1m 22.333s
9	Jenson Button	21	1m 22.378s
10	Fernando Alonso	16	1m 22.399s
11	Jacques Villeneuve	18	1m 22.906s
12	Cristiano da Matta	20	1m 23.195s
13	Mark Webber	22	1m 23.294s
14	Heinz-Harald Frentzen	20	1m 23.461s
15	Nick Heidfeld	17	1m 23.846s
16	Justin Wilson	24	1m 24.049s
17	Giancarlo Fisichella	18	1m 24.627s
18	Jos Verstappen	17	1m 24.837s
19	Zsolt Baumgartner	17	1m 25.916s
20	Nicolas Kiesa	11	1m 26.160s

WARM-UP
Dry and hot (track 35/38°C, air 24/26°C)

Pos.	Driver	Laps	Time
1	Rubens Barrichello	4	1m 21.633s
2	Juan Pablo Montoya	5	1m 21.819s
3	Jenson Button	7	1m 22.462s
4	Jacques Villeneuve	7	1m 22.472s
5	David Coulthard	5	1m 22.480s
6	Kimi Räikkönen	4	1m 22.512s
7	Marc Gené	4	1m 22.534s
8	Jarno Trulli	4	1m 22.581s
9	Fernando Alonso	6	1m 22.591s
10	Olivier Panis	5	1m 23.095s
11	Giancarlo Fisichella	7	1m 23.270s
12	Mark Webber	6	1m 23.378s
13	Heinz-Harald Frentzen	6	1m 23.382s
14	Cristiano da Matta	6	1m 23.467s
15	Justin Wilson	6	1m 23.601s
16	Nick Heidfeld	6	1m 24.157s
17	Zsolt Baumgartner	7	1m 26.363s
18	Nicolas Kiesa	4	1m27.384s
19	Michael Schumacher	4	1m 27.906s
20	Jos Verstappen	3	No time

9th: OLIVIER PANIS Toyota

7th: JENSON BUTTON BAR-Honda

5th: MARC GENÉ Williams-BMW

3rd: RUBENS BARRICHELLO Ferrari

Pole: MICHAEL SCHUMACHER Ferrari

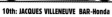

10th: JACQUES VILLENEUVE BAR-Honda

8th: DAVID COULTHARD McLaren-Mercedes

6th: JARNO TRULLI Renault

4th: KIMI RÄIKKÖNEN McLaren-Mercedes

2nd: JUAN PABLO MONTOYA Williams-BMW

42	43	44	45	46	47	48	49	50	51	52	53	•
1	1	1	1	1	1	1	1	1	1	1	1	1
3	3	3	3	3	3	3	3	3	3	3	3	3
2	2	2	2	2	2	2	2	2	2	2	2	2
6	6	6	6	6	6	6	6	6	6	6	6	4
5	5	5	5	4	4	4	4	4	4	4	4	5
4	4	4	4	16	16	16	16	16	16	16		6
16	16	16	16	10	10	10	10	10	14	14		7
10	10	10	10	14	14	14	14	14	9	8		8
14	14	14	14	9	9	9	9	9	8	9		
9	9	9	9	8	8	8	8	8	11	11		
8	8	8	8	11	11	11	11	11	12			
11	11	11	11	12	12	12	12	12	18			
12	12	12	12	18	18	18	18	18				
18	18	18	18									

CHASSIS LOG BOOK

1	Michael Schumacher	F2003-GA/229
2	Rubens Barrichello	F2003-GA/233
	Spare	F2003-GA/231/228
3	Juan Pablo Montoya	FW25/05
4	Marc Gené	FW25/07
	Spare	FW25/04
5	David Coulthard	MP4/17D-08
6	Kimi Räikkönen	MP4/17D-09
	Spare	MP4/17D-07
7	Jarno Trulli	R23/05
8	Fernando Alonso	R23/06
	Allan McNish	R23/03
	Spare	R23/03
9	Nick Heidfeld	C22/01
10	Heinz-Harald Frentzen	C22/02
	Spare	C22/03
11	Giancarlo Fisichella	EJ-13/05
12	Zsolt Baumgartner	EJ-13/04
	Spare	EJ-13/02
14	Mark Webber	R4/03
15	Justin Wilson	R4/05
	Spare	R4/03
16	Jacques Villeneuve	BAR005/6
17	Jenson Button	BAR005/4
	Spare	BAR005/3
18	Justin Wilson	PS03/01
19	Jos Verstappen	PS03/03
	Spare	PS03/02
20	Olivier Panis	TF103/07
21	Cristiano da Matta	TF103/04
	Spare	TF103/08

POINTS TABLES: DRIVERS

1	Michael Schumacher	82
2	Juan Pablo Montoya	79
3	Kimi Räikkönen	75
4	Ralf Schumacher	58
5=	Rubens Barrichello	55
5=	Fernando Alonso	55
7	David Coulthard	45
8	Jarno Trulli	24
9	Mark Webber	17
10	Jenson Button	12
11	Giancarlo Fisichella	10
12	Cristiano da Matta	8
13	Heinz-Harald Frentzen	7
14=	Olivier Panis	6
14=	Jacques Villeneuve	6
16	Marc Gené	4
17	Nick Heidfeld	2
18	Ralph Firman	1

FIA F1 WORLD CHAMPIONSHIP • ROUND 15

UNITED STATESGP
INDIANAPOLIS

Above: The defining moment in Juan Pablo Montoya's championship bid as he muscles his Williams-BMW into Rubens Barrichello's Ferrari.

Far left: Final stop. Armed with dry-weather Bridgestones, Ferrari mechanics await Michael Schumacher.

Left: The champion is sent back into the fray to record a crushing win.

Photographs: Patrick Gosling

INDIANAPOLIS QUALIFYING

Kimi Räikkönen's pole-winning effort at Indianapolis was one of the great laps of the season. He was quick in all three sectors, running in low-drag configuration to touch 211 mph as he hurtled down the main straight to post a 1m 11.670s best. That meant he would share the front row of the grid with Rubens Barrichello, who was a scant 0.124s behind the Finn.

Rubens made no secret of the fact that he felt his Ferrari 2003-GA had been good enough to challenge for the pole. 'My flying lap was a good one, even though the car felt a bit different to the way it did in the warm-up and was loose all the way round,' he said. 'It was quite windy this afternoon, which I am sure affected everyone, so I had to gamble a bit on the car's set-up in the hope that it will be good tomorrow.'

By contrast, Michael Schumacher had a disappointing session, and his 1m 12.194s best earned him only seventh place. He was fastest on the main straight, at 214 mph, but the car felt wayward through the turns and simply was sliding about too much. 'This was a very average qualifying session for me today and naturally I am not at all satisfied with the way it went,' he said.

Olivier Panis did a fine job in the Toyota TF103, lapping in 1m 11.920s to take third-fastest time ahead of the Williams-BMWs of Juan Pablo Montoya (1m 11.948s) and Ralf Schumacher (1m 12.078s).

'My first sector was okay,' said Montoya, 'but I had quite a bit of oversteer in the second and third sectors, and this wasn't ideal, as I lost about three-tenths there.'

For his part, Ralf added, 'The very first part of my lap was very weak, as one can see from my sector time. Besides this, we had to change the car a lot from the warm-up to qualifying because of the accident I had in this morning's free practice when I braked too late and went off the track, which lost me a lot of time.'

Renault's Fernando Alonso lined up sixth on 1m 12.087s, although he reported that his R23 felt nervous with understeer and oversteer in some of the corners. Jarno Trulli did well to make tenth in the other Renault on 1m 12.566s, as the team had to work hard repairing his machine after he crashed during the warm-up. 'Nothing felt quite right all the way around the lap,' he sighed.

Eighth place fell to David Coulthard's McLaren (1m 12.297s), ahead of Cristiano da Matta (1m 12.326s) in the other Toyota. For BAR Honda, Jenson Button (1m 12.695s) and Jacques Villeneuve (1m 13.050s) wound up a closely matched 11th and 12th.

Nick Heidfeld managed a 1m 13.083s for 13th on the grid, two places ahead of team-mate Heinz-Harald Frentzen (1m 13.447s); the two Sauber C22s sandwiched Mark Webber's Jaguar (1m 13.269s). 'I was happier with my lap today than I was with yesterday's in comparable conditions,' said Heidfeld. 'The car felt better balanced. Unfortunately, the tyres had started to "grain" before the end of my lap, otherwise I could have finished in front of Villeneuve.'

Webber was disappointed slightly. 'You win some, you lose some, and today wasn't our day,' he said. 'We lost a bit of balance and grip going into the qualifying session, and it became quite apparent as I came out of turn ten from my out lap. As I came out, the car understeered considerably and I began worrying about what was in store for me today. The brakes going into turn one were fine, but then the understeer kicked in again and stayed with me for the whole lap.'

Justin Wilson, who recorded a 1m 13.585s, agreed precisely with Webber's assessment of the situation. He lined up in 16th place, a whisker ahead of the other Cosworth-engined cars on the starting grid — the two Jordans and two Minardis.

WHAT promised to be an epic battle between Michael Schumacher and Juan Pablo Montoya for victory in the US Grand Prix – and the possible implications for the World Championship battle – turned out to be something of a damp squib, as the Colombian driver's challenge fell apart almost from the start of the 73-lap race. While Schumacher surged to his 70th career victory after a finely judged, opportunistic performance in his Ferrari F2003-GA, Montoya slipped and slid his Williams-BMW to an inconsequential sixth place, which wrote him out of the championship equation.

Schumacher also had benefited from the superior performance of the Bridgestone rain tyres fitted to his Ferrari. Their Michelin opposition, used by both McLaren and Williams, had been far less effective when intermittent downpours transformed the circuit into a skating rink.

Montoya started the day feeling confident. He'd qualified fourth, three places ahead of Schumacher, but by the end of the opening lap, their positions had been reversed and he had lost the initiative to his key rival.

Pushing hard to stay in contention, Montoya ran down the outside of Rubens Barrichello's sixth-place Ferrari as they braked for the right-hander after the pits, going into lap three. Then, he tried to squeeze ahead of the Brazilian as they went into the following left-hander. In an excessively ambitious manoeuvre, he forced his Williams up the kerb on the inside and made firm contact with Barrichello, spinning the Ferrari into the gravel trap and out of the race. Montoya lost a couple more places, but was reported immediately to the stewards for investigation for a possible driving infringement. Eventually, it was decided that he was to blame for the incident and he was forced to serve a drive-through penalty, which effectively wiped him out of contention.

'It was a very disappointing race, basically decided by the penalty I was given for the accident with Rubens and the moment I had to pay for it,' said the Colombian. 'Due to the changeable weather conditions, in fact, it started to rain just when I was given my drive-through penalty, which forced me to delay by one lap my pit stop to change on to wet tyres.

'It is sad to lose my drivers' championship chances in this way, especially knowing that I needed to finish fifth today to keep my hopes open.'

Barrichello was more philosophical than one might have expected. 'I did not get the best of starts and, after that, my gears were not working,' he shrugged. 'After that, I hit Montoya. I went into the corner and, all of a sudden, I felt a bang. I thought I had given him sufficient room.'

The race settled down with Kimi Räikkönen's McLaren-Mercedes MP4/17D leading confidently by just over 2s from Ralf Schumacher, who'd winged past Olivier Panis's second-place Toyota TF103 at the end of the third lap. Next in the queue behind the Japanese car was Michael Schumacher's Ferrari, and as they approached the yellow flags for the Barrichello incident at the start of lap five, the world champion pulled out and overtook the Frenchman.

After the race, Panis accused Michael of passing him under waved yellow warning flags. Had it gone to a protest and Schumacher been disqualified, Räikkönen would have been right back in the championship race.

On examining the videos, however, McLaren chairman Ron Dennis made it clear that he felt Schumacher had no case to answer. He accepted that the Ferrari driver had completed the overtaking manoeuvre before reaching the yellow-flag area and the whole matter was allowed to drop.

Panis's race ended on an unfortunate note. As a light rain shower brushed the circuit, he came in for wet-weather tyres at the end of lap six, but then four laps later had to return to the pits for slicks, as the rain had passed quickly. Cristiano da Matta did the same on laps seven and 11, effectively writing the team out of the equation.

'Even by this early point, we were one lap down and our race was effectively over,' explained da Matta, whose previous visit to Indianapolis had been crowned by a superb victory in the Indy 500. 'After we stopped again, I got a drive-through penalty for speeding in the pit lane, but we were so far back that it made little difference.'

By contrast, Michael Schumacher kept his Ferrari pretty well out of trouble, although by the end of the race there was a conspicuous tyre mark on one of his side-pods, which bore testimony to a slight brush with an unidentified rival, probably David Coulthard's McLaren.

Going into lap 15, Montoya surged ahead of Coulthard to take

RENAULT DROPS F1 TESTER MCNISH

A year after being made redundant from F1 competition by Toyota, Allan McNish received a second helping of the same treatment when Renault announced that the highly rated Scot would be replaced as F1 test driver for 2004.

His place would be taken by Franck Montagny, although inevitably there was some question as to whether the far less experienced French driver would be able to generate such worthwhile technical input for the team.

McNish commented, 'I'm obviously disappointed that I won't be with the team next year, particularly having seen the results of all our hard work with Fernando's first win in Hungary.'

He continued, 'I am in the fortunate position of having a number of options open to me, and my management team and I are assessing which path to take at the moment. I don't want to rush into anything, but I am more determined than ever to succeed, and ultimately I will make the choice that gives me the best chance of success.'

Left: Olivier Panis was encouraged by third place in qualifying.

Below: Dominant in qualifying, Kimi Räikkönen lost out in the race when the weather spoiled his chances of a win.

Photographs: Darren Heath

This page: Justin Wilson claimed eighth place and a valuable FIA F1 World Championship point.
Photograph: Darren Heath

Right: Out of luck once more. Jenson Button returns on foot after losing a seemingly safe podium place.
Photograph: Patrick Gosling

Below right: Different emotions on the podium from Kimi Räikkönen, Michael Schumacher and Heinz-Harald Frentzen.
Photograph: Darren Heath

fourth place, and with Schumacher's Ferrari back in fifth, the Colombian was emerging as a very strong contender – had it not been for that drive-through penalty hanging over his head.

Suddenly, the track was doused by a serious downpour and the cars began slipping and sliding in all directions, team managers desperately attempting to reduce the impact of the dramatically changing conditions – and trying to anticipate whether or not the surface would remain wet or start drying again.

The shower even caught out the Ferrari team. At the end of lap 20, Michael came in from fifth place for another set of dry-weather Bridgestones, although he admitted later to having second thoughts about this decision as he drove down the pit lane. Heinz-Harald Frentzen, on the other hand, read the conditions perfectly and suspected that it was likely to rain for some time to come.

Schumacher returned to the pits from 11th on lap 21 for a set of 'wets'. He resumed eighth, still well in play.

Mark Webber's Jaguar R4 had been leading on that lap, but he spun off next time around, as did Ralf Schumacher from second place. With Michael Schumacher making his unscheduled tyre stop, Coulthard assumed the lead briefly from Räikkönen.

Later, Ralf would slam his team for what he termed 'an avoidable error', claiming that without the mistake, he might have won the race.

'After the pit stop, I was even in the lead, but then there was nothing but chaos,' reported the German driver on his personal website. 'For two laps I tried to find out via the radio what their view on the weather was in order to possibly make [another] tyre change. Nothing. No information. Everyone was drowning each other with chatter. And when the order finally came to come into the pits, I had already gone 100 metres past the entrance. It was a mistake that we could have avoided.'

However, BMW motorsport director Mario Theissen wholly rejected the driver's comments, adding, 'This criticism we can throw straight back at him. It was the other way around. We were waiting for an answer from Ralf, but there was nothing from him. He stayed out for another lap, then spun off on his own.'

At this point, the well-placed Jenson Button, profiting from the performance of the Bridgestone rain tyres, took over at the head of the pack in his BAR-Honda, leading from Heinz-Harald Frentzen's Sauber and Räikkönen, whose Michelin rubber was less well-suited to the wet conditions, although he began to come back at the leaders as the circuit started to dry again.

At the start of lap 38, Schumacher's Ferrari passed Button to take the lead, and the hapless British driver stopped three laps later when his engine expired spectacularly on the main straight. From then on, Michael cruised home to win, leaving Räikkönen to

pass Frentzen, but not allowing his rival to get within sight of his bullet-proof scarlet machine, which never missed a beat from start to finish.

Understandably, Jenson was exasperated, as he had looked extremely confident running at the head of the pack. 'Leading the US Grand Prix was a great feeling and a fantastic moment in my career, but it's massively disappointing to lose out on the best chance I've had at my first podium.

'The team were aware for a few laps that I was losing hydraulic pressure, but there was nothing they could do about it. Before this affected the car, we had an engine problem and as I came round the last corner, the engine gave way. Realistically, Michael was going to get past me sooner or later, but I was hanging in well behind him and I'm confident that, all things being equal, we could have stayed there for the rest of the race. We badly needed points here and instead missed out on a great opportunity.'

Button's retirement handed the number-two spot back to Räikkönen, although on the drying track surface he might well have got back ahead of the BAR in the closing stages. Either way, Kimi came home a strong second.

'For sure, we lost the race because we got very unlucky with the weather today,' he said. 'But what can you do? I was fighting as much as I could, and we only got second place. Of course, it's not the best because Michael won and we came in second. But we gained second in the championship. It's a lot more difficult now, but you never know. Maybe we will have another very difficult race in the last one of the year and it all can happen. Yeah, I think so.'

He was circumspect when it came to commenting on the difference between the Bridgestone tyres fitted to Schumacher's Ferrari and the Michelins on his own McLaren-Mercedes.

'When it is just a little bit wet, we can run with the dry-weather tyres and feel more stronger,' he said. 'But if it gets really heavy rain, I think Bridgestone is having a good chance. Our tyres are not working as well as Bridgestone in the rain. But it is an improvement over last year and we hope it will get better still.'

Heinz-Harald Frentzen finished an excellent third in his Sauber-Petronas, with Jarno Trulli's Renault fourth and the other Sauber driven by Nick Heidfeld fifth, ahead of Montoya, wiping out the Colombian's chances of challenging for the championship. In a double blow, Williams lost its lead in the constructors' championship, dropping three points behind Ferrari, now on 147.

As for the drivers' championship, Räikkönen had it all to do. To take the title, he would have to win at Suzuka, with Michael Schumacher failing to score a single point. It was a long shot indeed, but as a McLaren insider remarked, 'At Suzuka, we have nothing to lose. But Ferrari has everything to lose.'

VILLENEUVE MISSES LAST RACE FOR BAR HONDA

Jacques Villeneuve was absent from the starting line-up at the Japanese Grand Prix, having told BAR Honda chairman David Richards that he wanted to miss what was scheduled to be his last race for the British team. He cited 'lack of motivation' following the announcement a few days earlier that he would be replaced by Takuma Sato for 2004.

Richards had been on the Bullet Train travelling from Tokyo to Nagoya, en route to Suzuka, when Villeneuve's manager, Craig Pollock, had phoned him with the news that Villeneuve did not want to compete.

'I've agreed to this,' said Richards. 'If somebody doesn't want to drive, they don't want to drive, and so Takuma will be driving on Sunday.' Sato's inclusion in the team for 2004 was widely interpreted within the F1 community as an indication that Honda was preparing to exert a greater influence over the way in which the team was run, prior to reviewing its partnership with BAR at the end of that season.

'We received a call from BAR managing director David Richards on Friday [a week before the Suzuka race], informing us of their decision,' said Pollock. 'What is so disappointing is the fact that this team was built for and around Jacques, and he underwent all sorts of trials and tribulations over the years as BAR struggled to find its place in F1.

'Jacques never wavered and his loyalty to British American Racing was constant. He had other opportunities, and no one would have blamed him for going elsewhere, but he preferred to see this project through, despite a car that did not live up to its expectations.'

He added, 'Our primary emotions right now are sadness and disappointment. Jacques has given everything to British American Racing in its first five years, and always with a view to building a team that would be front of the grid some day.'

Pollock might usefully have added that Villeneuve had earned more than £40 million in that five-year period, during which his best results were two third places. However, the Canadian driver and his current team-mate, Jenson Button, had been extremely disappointed with the BAR-Honda's performance in 2003.

Villeneuve was openly critical of Honda after both he and Button had been forced to retire from the US Grand Prix at Indianapolis with engine failures.

'At the end of the day, it doesn't matter how good or bad we are in performance, we have problem after problem,' said the Canadian. 'I don't see why we would want more power when this engine already blows up. We are not quick enough at the moment. We keep getting a little more power, but what we really want is less weight.'

Villeneuve's future in F1 now looked bleak, with the prospect that his front-line racing career might have come to an end. It was certainly a major blow to the Canadian grand prix organisers as they sought a way of having their race reinstated on the 2004 FIA F1 World Championship calendar after a dispute over tobacco advertising restrictions.

Could Indianapolis have been the sunset of Jacques Villeneuve's grand prix career?
Photograph: Darren Heath

UNITED STATES GRAND PRIX
INDIANAPOLIS
26–28 SEPTEMBER 2003

Photograph: Darren Heath

INDIANAPOLIS – GRAND PRIX CIRCUIT
CIRCUIT LENGTH: 2.605 miles/4.192 km

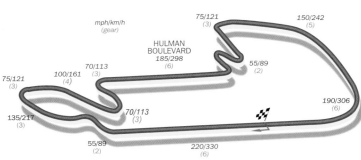

RACE DISTANCE: 73 laps, 190.150 miles/306.016 km   RACE WEATHER: Variable – dry/damp/very wet (track 20°C, air 19°C)

Pos.	Driver	Nat.	No.	Entrant	Car/Engine	Tyres	Laps	Time/Retirement	Speed (mph/km/h)	Gap to leader	Fastest race lap	
1	Michael Schumacher	D	1	Scuderia Ferrari Marlboro	Ferrari F2003-GA-051 V10	B	73	1h 33m 35.997s	121.890/196.164		1m 11.473s	13
2	Kimi Räikkönen	FIN	6	West McLaren Mercedes	McLaren MP4/17D-Mercedes F0110M V10	M	73	1h 33m 54.255s	121.495/195.528	+18.258s	1m 11.617s	9
3	Heinz-Harald Frentzen	D	10	Sauber Petronas	Sauber C22-Petronas 03C V10	B	73	1h 34m 13.961s	121.072/194.847	+37.964s	1m 13.338s	71
4	Jarno Trulli	I	7	Mild Seven Renault F1 Team	Renault R3-RS23 V10	M	73	1h 34m 24.326s	120.850/194.490	+48.329s	1m 12.015s	14
5	Nick Heidfeld	D	9	Sauber Petronas	Sauber C22-Petronas 03C V10	B	73	1h 34m 32.400s	120.678/194.213	+56.403s	1m 13.085s	13
6	Juan Pablo Montoya	COL	3	BMW WilliamsF1 Team	Williams FW25-BMW P83 V10	M	72			+1 lap	1m 11.595s	9
7	Giancarlo Fisichella	I	11	Jordan Ford	Jordan EJ-13-Ford Cosworth RS1 V10	B	72			+1 lap	1m 13.630s	13
8	Justin Wilson	GB	15	Jaguar Racing	Jaguar R4-Cosworth CR5 V10	M	71			+2 laps	1m 13.324s	12
9	Cristiano da Matta	BR	21	Panasonic Toyota Racing	Toyota TF103-RVX-03 V10	M	71			+2 laps	1m 13.231s	13
10	Jos Verstappen	NL	19	European Minardi Cosworth	Minardi PS03-Cosworth CR3 V10	B	69			+4 laps	1m 15.257s	68
11	Nicolas Kiesa	DK	18	European Minardi Cosworth	Minardi PS03-Cosworth CR3 V10	B	69			+4 laps	1m 14.737s	67
	Jacques Villeneuve	CDN	16	Lucky Strike BAR Honda	BAR 005-Honda RA003E V10	B	63	Engine			1m 13.538s	62
	Ralph Firman	IRL	12	Jordan Ford	Jordan EJ-13-Ford Cosworth RS1 V10	B	48	Spin			1m 14.687s	11
	David Coulthard	GB	5	West McLaren Mercedes	McLaren MP4/17D-Mercedes F0110M V10	M	45	Gearbox			1m 12.009s	12
	Fernando Alonso	E	8	Mild Seven Renault F1 Team	Renault R3-RS23 V10	M	44	Engine			1m 11.525s	9
	Jenson Button	GB	17	Lucky Strike BAR Honda	BAR 005-Honda RA003E V10	B	41	Hydraulics			1m 13.038s	10
	Olivier Panis	F	20	Panasonic Toyota Racing	Toyota TF103-RVX-03 V10	M	27	Accident			1m 13.340s	12
	Mark Webber	AUS	14	Jaguar Racing	Jaguar R4-Cosworth CR5 V10	M	21	Accident			1m 13.099s	12
	Ralf Schumacher	D	4	BMW WilliamsF1 Team	Williams FW25-BMW P83 V10	M	21	Accident			1m 11.655s	13
	Rubens Barrichello	BR	2	Scuderia Ferrari Marlboro	Ferrari F2003-GA-051 V10	B	2	Accident			1m 13.905s	2

Fastest lap: Michael Schumacher, on lap 13, 1m 11.473s, 131.199 mph/211.145 km/h (record).

Previous lap record: Rubens Barrichello (F1 Ferrari F2002-051 V10), 1m 12.738s, 128.918 mph/207.473 km/h (2002).

19th: JOS VERSTAPPEN Minardi-Cosworth

17th: GIANCARLO FISICHELLA Jordan-Ford Cosworth

15th: HEINZ-HARALD FRENTZEN Sauber-Petronas

13th: NICK HEIDFELD Sauber-Petronas

11th: JENSON BUTTON BAR-Honda

20th: NICOLAS KIESA Minardi-Cosworth

18th: RALPH FIRMAN Jordan-Ford Cosworth

16th: JUSTIN WILSON Jaguar-Cosworth

14th: MARK WEBBER Jaguar-Cosworth

12th: JACQUES VILLENEUVE BAR-Honda

Grid order	1	2	3	4	5	6	7	8	9	10	11	12	13	14	15	16	17	18	19	20	21	22	23	24	25	26	27	28	29	30	31	32	33	34	35	36	37	38	39	40	41	42	43	44	45	46	47	48	49	50	51	52	53	54	55
6 RÄIKKÖNEN	6	6	6	6	6	6	6	6	6	6	6	6	6	6	6	6	6	6	1	14	14	5	17	17	17	17	17	17	17	17	17	17	17	17	17	17	1	1	1	1	1	1	1	1	1	1	10	1	1	1	1	1	1	1	1
2 BARRICHELLO	20	20	4	4	4	4	4	4	4	4	4	4	4	3	8	1	7	17	4	6	10	10	10	10	10	10	10	10	10	10	1	1	1	1	1	17	17	17	10	10	10	10	10	1	9	9	10	10	10	10	6
20 PANIS	4	4	20	20	1	1	5	5	5	5	5	5	5	8	1	7	14	15	6	10	15	15	6	6	1	1	1	1	10	10	10	10	10	10	10	9	9	9	9	9	9	10	6	6	6	10					
3 MONTOYA	1	1	1	1	20	5	3	3	3	3	3	3	3	5	7	14	17	4	8	17	6	6	15	1	1	6	6	6	6	6	6	6	6	6	6	6	6	6	6	6	6	6	6	6	6	9	9	9	9					
4 R. SCHUMACHER	2	5	5	5	8	3	8	8	8	8	8	8	8	1	14	17	6	1	5	8	5	8	8	8	15	8	8	8	8	8	8	9	9	9	9	6	11	7	7	7	7	7	7	7	7	7	7	7	7					
8 ALONSO	5	2	8	8	5	8	1	1	1	1	1	1	1	7	17	8	15	6	3	15	8	1	8	15	15	15	9	9	9	9	8	7	7	7	7	7	7	11	11	11	11	11	11	11	11	11	11	11	11					
1 M. SCHUMACHER	3	3	7	3	3	7	7	7	7	7	7	7	7	9	15	15	4	8	7	3	1	5	9	9	9	9	9	15	15	7	7	7	11	11	11	11	11	8	8	3	3	3	3	3	3	3	3	3	3					
5 COULTHARD	8	8	3	7	7	21	9	9	9	9	9	9	9	14	10	4	8	7	15	1	9	9	5	7	7	7	7	7	11	11	11	11	8	8	8	8	8	3	3	16	15	15	15	15	15	15	15	15	15					
21 DA MATTA	7	7	21	21	21	17	14	14	14	14	14	14	14	17	17	4	10	5	17	9	7	7	11	11	11	11	11	11	3	3	3	3	3	3	3	3	16	16	15	16	16	16	16	16	16	16									
7 TRULLI	21	21	17	17	9	17	17	17	17	17	17	17	17	4	15	5	5	3	3	10	7	11	11	11	5	3	3	3	3	15	15	16	16	16	15	15	15	21	21	21	21	21	21	21	21	21	21								
17 BUTTON	17	17	9	9	17	15	15	15	15	15	15	15	15	15	10	3	3	11	11	11	3	3	3	5	21	21	21	21	21	21	15	16	16	15	19	21	19	19	19	19	19	19	19	19											
16 VILLENEUVE	9	9	10	10	10	15	10	10	10	10	10	10	10	4	11	11	9	9	21	21	21	21	21	5	16	16	16	16	16	15	15	21	19	19	18	5	19	18	18	18	18	18	18	18											
9 HEIDFELD	10	10	14	14	14	10	11	11	11	11	11	11	11	9	10	10	11	20	20	20	20	20	16	16	5	19	19	19	19	19	19	21	5	19	12	12	12																	
14 WEBBER	14	14	15	15	15	11	21	21	21	21	21	21	21	21	21	21	21	5	5	5	5	19	19	19	19	19	21	5	5	18	18	18	5	19	19	12																		
10 FRENTZEN	15	15	16	16	16	20	20	20	20	16	20	20	20	16	16	16	20	16	16	16	16	18	18	18	18	18	18	18	18	5	5	5	5	5	5	12	12	12																
15 WILSON	16	16	11	11	11	16	16	16	16	20	16	16	16	20	20	12	12	12	12	12	12	12	12	12	12	12																												
11 FISICHELLA	11	11	18	18	18	18	18	16	18	18	19	19	19	18	18	18	18	20	16	12	12	12	12	12	12																													
12 FIRMAN	18	18	12	12	12	12	12	12	12	19	18	18	18	18	18	18	20	20	19	18	18																																	
19 VERSTAPPEN	19	12	19	19	19	19	19	12	12	12	12	12	12	12	12	12	12																																					
18 KIESA	12	19																																																					

Pit stop
One lap behind leader

TIME SHEETS

SATURDAY QUALIFYING determines race grid order

Dry and sunny (track 30/34°C, air 20/22°C)

Pos.	Driver	Lap time	Sector 1	Sector 2	Sector 3
1	Kimi Räikkönen	1m 11.670s	22.348s	29.411s	19.911s
2	Rubens Barrichello	1m 11.794s	22.128s	29.755s	19.911s
3	Olivier Panis	1m 11.920s	22.378s	29.416s	20.126s
4	Juan Pablo Montoya	1m 11.948s	22.273s	29.741s	19.672s
5	Ralf Schumacher	1m 12.078s	22.610s	29.647s	19.814s
6	Fernando Alonso	1m 12.087s	22.287s	29.572s	20.175s
7	Michael Schumacher	1m 12.194s	22.377s	29.814s	20.003s
8	David Coulthard	1m 12.297s	22.517s	29.704s	19.972s
9	Cristiano da Matta	1m 12.326s	22.586s	29.413s	20.327s
10	Jarno Trulli	1m 12.566s	22.391s	29.930s	20.096s
11	Jenson Button	1m 12.695s	22.585s	29.865s	20.245s
12	Jacques Villeneuve	1m 13.050s	22.813s	29.941s	20.296s
13	Nick Heidfeld	1m 13.083s	22.660s	29.999s	20.424s
14	Mark Webber	1m 13.269s	22.886s	30.047s	20.336s
15	Heinz-Harald Frentzen	1m 13.447s	22.755s	30.278s	20.414s
16	Justin Wilson	1m 13.585s	22.987s	30.233s	20.365s
17	Giancarlo Fisichella	1m 13.798s	23.094s	30.274s	20.430s
18	Ralph Firman	1m 14.027s	23.200s	30.351s	20.444s
19	Jos Verstappen	1m 15.360s	23.517s	30.228s	20.615s
20	Nicolas Kiesa	1m 15.644s	23.860s	30.023s	20.761s

FRIDAY QUALIFYING determines Sat running order

Initially dry, then wet (track 18/20°C, air 16°C)

Pos.	Driver	Lap time
1	Jarno Trulli	1m 09.566s
2	Rubens Barrichello	1m 09.835s
3	Mark Webber	1m 10.081s
4	Ralf Schumacher	1m 10.222s
5	Juan Pablo Montoya	1m 10.372s
6	David Coulthard	1m 10.450s
7	Fernando Alonso	1m 10.556s
8	Michael Schumacher	1m 10.736s
9	Kimi Räikkönen	1m 10.756s
10	Jenson Button	1m 11.847s
11	Cristiano da Matta	1m 11.949s
12	Giancarlo Fisichella	1m 12.227s
13	Heinz-Harald Frentzen	1m 13.541s
14	Olivier Panis	1m 17.666s
15	Nick Heidfeld	1m 17.768s
16	Jacques Villeneuve	1m 18.547s
17	Ralph Firman	1m 19.383s
18	Justin Wilson	1m 19.491s
19	Nicolas Kiesa	1m 21.973s
20	Jos Verstappen	No time

POINTS TABLES: CONSTRUCTORS

1	Ferrari	147
2	Williams	144
3	McLaren	128
4	Renault	84
5	Sauber	19
6 =	BAR	18
6 =	Jaguar	18
8	Toyota	14
9	Jordan	13

PRIVATE TESTING

Dry and overcast (track 17/18°C, air 15/16°C)

Pos.	Driver	Laps	Time
1	Jarno Trulli	43	1m 10.986s
2	Fernando Alonso	50	1m 10.987s
3	Allan McNish	47	1m 11.253s
4	Mark Webber	49	1m 11.586s
5	Justin Wilson	55	1m 12.142s
6	Giancarlo Fisichella	17	1m 12.263s
7	Ralph Firman	46	1m 12.762s
8	Gianmaria Bruni	33	1m 13.129s
9	Jos Verstappen	23	1m 13.196s
10	Nicolas Kiesa	39	1m 13.655s
11	Björn Wirdheim	44	1m 13.678s

FRIDAY FREE PRACTICE

Dry and overcast (track 18/20°C, air 16°C)

Pos.	Driver	Laps	Time
1	Jarno Trulli	18	1m 11.153s
2	Ralf Schumacher	22	1m 11.339s
3	Olivier Panis	20	1m 11.388s
4	Rubens Barrichello	22	1m 11.499s
5	Michael Schumacher	22	1m 11.656s
6	Fernando Alonso	24	1m 11.692s
7	Mark Webber	21	1m 11.794s
8	Juan Pablo Montoya	19	1m 11.842s
9	Kimi Räikkönen	26	1m 11.876s
10	David Coulthard	27	1m 11.967s
11	Cristiano da Matta	23	1m 12.084s
12	Jenson Button	28	1m 12.331s
13	Justin Wilson	18	1m 12.387s
14	Jacques Villeneuve	29	1m 12.656s
15	Giancarlo Fisichella	8	1m 12.849s
16	Ralph Firman	19	1m 13.167s
17	Nicolas Kiesa	19	1m 13.537s
18	Nick Heidfeld	20	1m 13.601s
19	Heinz-Harald Frentzen	22	1m 13.881s
20	Jos Verstappen	15	1m 18.255s

SATURDAY FIRST FREE PRACTICE

Wet, then dry (track 22/24°C, air 18/19°C)

Pos.	Driver	Laps	Time
1	Jarno Trulli	6	1m 12.408s
2	Ralf Schumacher	15	1m 12.468s
3	Juan Pablo Montoya	15	1m 12.495s
4	Rubens Barrichello	14	1m 12.510s
5	Fernando Alonso	6	1m 12.741s
6	Cristiano da Matta	17	1m 13.098s
7	Olivier Panis	10	1m 13.306s
8	Heinz-Harald Frentzen	7	1m 13.363s
9	Mark Webber	14	1m 13.573s
10	Justin Wilson	8	1m 13.781s
11	Jacques Villeneuve	7	1m 13.960s
12	Jos Verstappen	7	1m 14.411s
13	Nick Heidfeld	9	1m 14.439s
14	Nicolas Kiesa	6	1m 14.493s
15	Jenson Button	7	1m 14.911s
16	Giancarlo Fisichella	4	1m 18.267s
17	Michael Schumacher	1	No time
18	Ralph Firman	3	No time
19	Kimi Räikkönen	1	No time
20	David Coulthard	1	No time

SATURDAY SECOND FREE PRACTICE

Dry and bright (track 25/26°C, air 19°C)

Pos.	Driver	Laps	Time
1	Rubens Barrichello	18	1m 11.112s
2	Jarno Trulli	23	1m 11.124s
3	Michael Schumacher	16	1m 11.139s
4	Juan Pablo Montoya	17	1m 11.232s
5	David Coulthard	20	1m 11.355s
6	Kimi Räikkönen	22	1m 11.493s
7	Olivier Panis	21	1m 11.758s
8	Mark Webber	27	1m 11.800s
9	Ralf Schumacher	11	1m 12.060s
10	Fernando Alonso	18	1m 12.135s
11	Jenson Button	23	1m 12.186s
12	Nick Heidfeld	22	1m 12.380s
13	Cristiano da Matta	15	1m 12.671s
14	Heinz-Harald Frentzen	17	1m 12.680s
15	Jacques Villeneuve	19	1m 12.931s
16	Justin Wilson	27	1m 13.275s
17	Giancarlo Fisichella	15	1m 13.458s
18	Ralph Firman	20	1m 13.749s
19	Jos Verstappen	12	1m 14.335s
20	Nicolas Kiesa	20	1m 14.781s

WARM-UP

Dry and sunny (track 28/29°C, air 20°C)

Pos.	Driver	Laps	Time
1	Fernando Alonso	7	1m 12.079s
2	Juan Pablo Montoya	4	1m 12.083s
3	Olivier Panis	5	1m 12.127s
4	Kimi Räikkönen	4	1m 12.177s
5	Rubens Barrichello	5	1m 12.537s
6	Michael Schumacher	4	1m 12.688s
7	Cristiano da Matta	5	1m 12.699s
8	David Coulthard	6	1m 12.951s
9	Ralf Schumacher	3	1m 12.958s
10	Mark Webber	5	1m 13.019s
11	Jenson Button	6	1m 13.203s
12	Jacques Villeneuve	7	1m 13.600s
13	Nick Heidfeld	4	1m 13.612s
14	Heinz-Harald Frentzen	4	1m 13.925s
15	Justin Wilson	6	1m 13.982s
16	Giancarlo Fisichella	8	1m 14.347s
17	Ralph Firman	7	1m 14.608s
18	Jos Verstappen	6	1m 14.985s
19	Nicolas Kiesa	5	1m 15.258s
20	Jarno Trulli	3	No time

9th: CRISTIANO DA MATTA Toyota

7th: MICHAEL SCHUMACHER Ferrari

5th: RALF SCHUMACHER Williams-BMW

3rd: OLIVIER PANIS Toyota

Pole: KIMI RÄIKKÖNEN McLaren-Mercedes

10th: JARNO TRULLI Renault

8th: DAVID COULTHARD McLaren-Mercedes

6th: FERNANDO ALONSO Renault

4th: JUAN PABLO MONTOYA Williams-BMW

2nd: RUBENS BARRICHELLO Ferrari

57	58	59	60	61	62	63	64	65	66	67	68	69	70	71	72	73	
1	1	1	1	1	1	1	1	1	1	1	1	1	1	1	1	1	1
6	6	6	6	6	6	6	6	6	6	6	6	6	6	6	6	6	2
10	10	10	10	10	10	10	10	10	10	10	10	10	10	10	10	10	3
9	9	9	9	9	9	7	7	7	7	7	7	7	7	7	7	7	4
7	7	7	7	7	7	9	9	9	9	9	9	9	9	9	9	9	5
11	11	11	11	11	11	11	11	11	11	3	3	3	3	3	3		6
3	3	3	3	3	3	3	3	3	3	11	11	11	11	11	11		7
15	15	15	15	15	15	15	15	15	15	15	15	15	15	15			8
16	16	16	16	16	16	16	21	21	21	21	21	21	21	21			
21	21	21	21	21	21	21	19	19	19	19	19	19					
19	19	19	19	19	19	19	18	18	18	18	18	18					
18	18	18	18	18	18	18											

CHASSIS LOG BOOK

1	Michael Schumacher	F2003-GA/229
2	Rubens Barrichello	F2003-GA/233
	Spare	F2003-GA/231/228
3	Juan Pablo Montoya	FW25/05
4	Ralf Schumacher	FW25/07
	Spare	FW25/02/04
5	David Coulthard	MP4/17D-08
6	Kimi Räikkönen	MP4/17D-09
	Spare	MP4/17D-07
7	Jarno Trulli	R23/05
8	Fernando Alonso	R23/06
	Allan McNish	R23/03
	Spare	R23/03
9	Nick Heidfeld	C22/01
10	Heinz-Harald Frentzen	C22/03
	Spare	C22/02
11	Giancarlo Fisichella	EJ-13/05
12	Ralph Firman	EJ-13/04
	Spare	EJ-13/01
14	Mark Webber	R4/03
15	Antonio Pizzonia	R4/05
	Spare	R4/04
16	Jacques Villeneuve	BAR005/6
17	Jenson Button	BAR005/4
	Spare	BAR005/5
18	Nicolas Kiesa	PS03/01
19	Jos Verstappen	PS03/02
	Gianmaria Bruni	PS03/03
	Spare	PS03/02
20	Olivier Panis	TF103/08
21	Cristiano da Matta	TF103/02
	Spare	TF103/04

POINTS TABLES: DRIVERS

1	Michael Schumacher	92
2	Kimi Räikkönen	83
3	Juan Pablo Montoya	82
4	Ralf Schumacher	58
5 =	Rubens Barrichello	55
5 =	Fernando Alonso	55
7	David Coulthard	45
8	Jarno Trulli	29
9	Mark Webber	17
10	Heinz-Harald Frentzen	13
11 =	Giancarlo Fisichella	12
11 =	Jenson Button	12
13	Cristiano da Matta	8
14 =	Nick Heidfeld	6
14 =	Olivier Panis	6
14 =	Jacques Villeneuve	6
17	Marc Gené	4
18 =	Ralph Firman	1
18 =	Justin Wilson	1

FIA F1 WORLD CHAMPIONSHIP • ROUND 16

JAPANESEGP
SUZUKA

Jean Todt is elated with Rubens Barrichello's victory which helped to ensure Michael Schumacher's sixth title.
Photograph: Darren Heath

SUZUKA QUALIFYING

With the prospect of intermittent rain poised to inject a really unpredictable dimension into the second qualifying session, it was all a question of position in the overall running order that determined whether or not a driver achieved an ideal run on a dry track surface.

Rubens Barrichello did a terrific job as the first raindrops began to fall on the circuit, taking the pole with a 1m 31.713s after the Ferrari team elected to change his settings back to those used on Friday, following a trouble-free practice session on Saturday morning.

'Rubens did a super job,' said Ross Brawn. 'The circuit conditions were already pretty difficult, but we had a different dry tyre to the ones in Indianapolis and it was a relief to see that they worked much better in damp conditions.'

Barrichello added, 'It was the best lap I had ever done at Suzuka. Nevertheless, I have to say that it was very difficult to drive in the conditions, and I was too optimistic in 130R and had a little slide.'

For Michael Schumacher, things were more fraught. The rain was falling quite heavily when the moment came for his run, the result being that he qualified 14th on 1m 34.302s. It looked pretty depressing on the face of it, but historians were quick to remind everyone that he'd won the 1995 Belgian GP from 16th on the grid at the wheel of a Benetton-Renault.

Michael may have fallen victim to the unpredictable Japanese weather, but his arch-rival in the title battle, Kimi Räikkönen, had also endured his share of problems.

At just before 9.30 on Saturday morning, it seemed as though the championship might have been settled prematurely when Räikkönen's McLaren MP4/17D speared off the road on the first right-hander after the pits. He wrestled to keep it under control, but the car skittered across the 'kitty litter' before slamming into the tyre barrier, shedding its left front wheel.

The Finn was unhurt, but his unexpected excursion left McLaren facing a ticklish dilemma. With the rules forbidding the use of spare cars before the 15-minute warm-up session prior to second qualifying, the only way that Räikkönen could continue running in the remainder of the free practice session was to commandeer team-mate David Coulthard's race car.

In the interests of Räikkönen's World Championship bid,

Coulthard gracefully stood aside. Ironically, however, the unpredictable qualifying session, peppered by rain showers, saw the Scot (1m 33.137s) eventually line up one place ahead of his colleague (1m 33.272s) in seventh.

Juan Pablo Montoya's Williams-BMW FW25 joined Barrichello on the front row with a 1m 32.412s best, the Colombian aiming to do his utmost in attempting to wrest back the lead of the constructors' championship from Ferrari. Yet Ralf Schumacher, who had been second fastest on Friday, found the circuit very wet by the time he made his run and did not complete it, thereby saving a lap's fuel for the race.

'It was really a shame,' he said as he contemplated the prospect of starting from the back row of the grid, alongside a similarly disappointed Jarno Trulli. 'I have been strong in all the sessions, and the rain destroyed everything. I aborted the lap so as to have more flexibility with my strategy tomorrow. Maybe I can score a few points from down there.'

Trulli had been quickest on Friday, relishing the challenge of one of his favourite circuits. In the event, however, the Renault team's challenge was spearheaded by Fernando Alonso, who qualified fifth on 1m 33.044s. 'Despite the weather, I was able to limit the damage with a good lap,' said Alonso by way of consolation. 'This time does not reflect the potential of the car and so I am confident for tomorrow.'

The Toyota TF103s of Cristiano da Matta (1m 32.419s) and Olivier Panis (1m 32.862s) buttoned up the second row of the grid, benefiting from the changeable weather, which handicapped some of their key rivals. Jaguar's Mark Webber did an excellent job to line up sixth on 1m 33.106s, while Justin Wilson (1m 33.558s) wound up tenth after an excellent showing.

The BAR Honda squad was guardedly satisfied with the performances of Jenson Button (1m 33.474s) and Takuma Sato (1m 33.924s), both of whom had lucky breaks with the weather. 'Even so, neither driver was able really to make the most of it,' said technical director Geoff Willis. 'Jenson had a moment where there had been some oil at the Degner [curve] and lost another couple of tenths at the chicane. The pressure of the excitement got to Takuma and he over-drove for most of the lap. That said, we're happy with ninth and 13th, but it's going to be a tough race.'

MICHAEL Schumacher could never have imagined that clinching his all-time record sixth world championship would turn into such a nerve-wracking affair. At the end of the Japanese Grand Prix, which was won superbly by his Ferrari team-mate, Rubens Barrichello, Michael trailed home in eighth place.

It was enough to give him the title by two points over Kimi Räikkönen, who finished second, dutifully followed across the line by fellow McLaren-Mercedes driver David Coulthard. The young Finn had done a brilliant job, but had been battling with unpredictable handling for at least part of the race, so beating Barrichello had been out of the question.

It was also a historic day for Ferrari, the famous Italian team becoming the first in history to have clinched five consecutive constructors' championship titles, on this occasion after a strong challenge from the BMW Williams squad had faded.

Michael had survived against the odds. He'd come through a lurid collision with his brother Ralf's Williams-BMW. He'd lost his Ferrari's nose-cone in a bump with F1 returnee Takuma Sato's BAR-Honda. He'd even had a big off-track excursion at the Spoon curve early in the race.

It seemed a low-key way for Fangio's record of five world championships to be erased from the record book. In the gathering gloom at this most magnificent of circuits, Michael had become the most statistically successful driver of all time – six world championships, 70 race wins.

Yet while Michael confirmed his place in the upper reaches of the F1 deity, the hero of the day was Rubens Barrichello. The Brazilian had qualified his Ferrari F2003-GA on pole position and, after Michael had been consigned briefly to a position outside the top ten following his brush with Sato, it looked as though he was

the only one standing between Michael and a title defeat at the hands of outsider Kimi Räikkönen.

'I am proud of what I have achieved this year, even though I haven't achieved so many points as in 2002,' said Barrichello. 'The team has done a fantastic job providing Michael and I with such reliable cars. Four years with the team has given me a lot and it is something I have been proud of.'

At the start, Barrichello surged into an immediate lead ahead of Montoya, with Fernando Alonso vaulting through to take third place. Mid-way around the opening lap, Montoya neatly outbraked the Ferrari to take the lead and accelerated across the timing line 1.3s ahead of the Brazilian.

Alonso remained in third, ahead of Cristiano da Matta's Toyota TF103, then came the two McLaren-Mercedes of David Coulthard and Räikkönen, Olivier Panis's slow-starting Toyota and Jenson Button's BAR-Honda 005. Farther back, Michael Schumacher was taking things cautiously, moving up from 14th to 12th, while Jarno Trulli (Renault R23) and Ralf Schumacher (Williams FW25), who had shared the back row of the grid after catching a rain shower during second qualifying, were already up to 13th and 14th.

By the end of lap two, Montoya was 3.4s ahead, but back in the mid-field ruck his team-mate spun at the chicane before the pits, dropping from 14th to 19th. The slip hardly aided the Williams team's aspirations for the constructors' championship.

Montoya looked supremely confident at the head of the pack, running strongly to open a 4.4s advantage over Barrichello by the end of lap three, and although thereafter Rubens steadied the gap and began to come back at the Williams, it looked as though Montoya had the edge with both cars on a three-stop strategy.

'I thought I just had to pace myself,' said Juan Pablo. 'I was

very pleased with the way the car was performing and we had a really good strategy. Then, bad luck. On lap nine, I felt a loss of some controls and that was that.' The Williams suddenly slowed dramatically with a hydraulic problem that affected the gearchange, and Montoya limped back to the pits to retire.

Meanwhile, by lap six, Michael Schumacher had moved up to tenth and was challenging Sato's BAR-Honda under braking for the pits chicane. He judged that there was a gap and went for it, but the Japanese driver stuck to his line with the result that the Ferrari's nose-wing was shredded in the inevitable impact. Michael drove straight into the pits for repairs, a job that saw his car stationary for 18.3s, after which he rejoined last, 59.8s behind his leading team-mate.

Schumacher blamed Sato for the collision. 'In Formula 1, you accept that if somebody leaves the door open like he did, you are allowed to go through,' he said. 'But obviously [Sato] saw it differently and decided at the last moment to slam the door shut on me. It was hard to avoid him and I lost my nose.'

Sato responded, 'It was not the right distance for Michael to overtake me perfectly, so I just took my usual line.'

Montoya's retirement also coincided with another blow for Williams. Ralf Schumacher, climbing back through the field, tapped the back of Heinz-Harald Frentzen's Sauber C22 at the chicane. 'He hit me so hard that I had to go into the pits where we found that oil was leaking from a damaged cooler,' shrugged Frentzen. 'Later, the engine broke, so that was it.'

On lap 12, Barrichello, Alonso and Coulthard made their first refuelling stops, propelling Räikkönen's McLaren into the lead, with the BARs of Button and Sato running second and third, both on a two-stop strategy. After a lap at the front, Räikkönen made his own way into the pits, leaving a BAR-Honda 1-2 at the head of the field,

Above: Barrichello takes the lead from Montoya and the rest, while Michael Schumacher is marooned in mid-field.

Left: The unlucky Jarno Trulli lost out in his shot at pole when the rain scuppered his run. Starting from the back of the grid, the Italian drove superbly in the race to take fifth place.
Photographs: Darren Heath

which lasted until Sato (lap 15) and Button (lap 16) came in to refuel, allowing Barrichello back into the lead, ahead of Alonso.

The Spaniard was just 2.3s behind the Ferrari on lap 17 and had narrowed that to 1.4s next time around. But the Renault V10 suddenly started to smoke, and Alonso was forced to pull off, thumping the trackside barrier with his fist in sheer frustration after climbing from the cockpit.

'It's a big disappointment to retire,' he commented. 'I was fighting for victory, and we were probably going to make one less stop than Rubens. We have had a great season, but the opportunity was there to win at the last race and it's not a nice feeling to have lost it.'

Alonso's departure really took the pressure off Barrichello. He was just over 15s ahead of Coulthard, while Räikkönen was running third, and when he and David made their second stops at the end of lap 26, Rubens was able to get back out on to the circuit without losing his lead, some 8s ahead of Räikkönen.

Farther back, the Schumacher brothers were running close together in 11th and 12th places, After the next round of refuelling stops, they found themselves behind da Matta's Toyota in fifth and sixth places, but as Michael went to pass the Brazilian under braking for the chicane, at the end of lap 41, he locked up his Ferrari and almost skidded into the Japanese machine.

A few yards behind, Ralf, by now smarting from a 180-mph 'chop' he'd received at the hands of his brother a couple of laps before, also locked up his Williams and skidded into the back of the Ferrari. One of the Williams's front wing end-plates touched the Ferrari's left rear tyre, but Michael, with his usual luck, continued unscathed while Ralf had to head for the pits for a new nose section to be fitted.

Ultimately, it was clear that Barrichello had the edge over the pursuing McLarens. After Coulthard made his final pit stop, he tucked in dutifully behind Räikkönen in third place. Their handling balance hadn't been perfect throughout and they had to settle for the remaining places on the podium.

'I think it is hard to say really whether it would have been quicker on a three-stop strategy,' said Räikkönen, 'but I think overall we would not have been as quick as Rubens and it would not have helped much.'

Suzuka was also a weekend for potential goodbyes. Even before practice got under way, Jacques Villeneuve had bowed out at BAR, to be replaced by the extremely civil Takuma Sato, a newcomer whose grasp of the English language probably eclipses that of anybody in the paddock.

Come the race, the BARs simply flew. Jenson Button drove superbly, leading briefly, to finish fourth, while Takuma Sato delighted the crowd in sixth. Jenson certainly stepped up to the plate in terrific style as *de facto* team leader following Villeneuve's abrupt departure.

'Every lap around here keeps you pretty alert,' said Button. 'We get the best out of the car setting it up for oversteer, and it was certainly a little edgy with flick-oversteer on some of the fast corners, particularly on the odd damp patch.'

Jarno Trulli made up for his disappointment at qualifying last with one of his best ever drives through the field to take fifth, avoiding the skirmishes with other cars that had blighted the progress of some of his more exalted rivals. Cristiano da Matta finished seventh, and the remarkable Michael Schumacher edged unobtrusively home in eighth place to crown that most momentous achievement.

Ralf Schumacher, who finished 12th, commented tersely, 'I am obviously massively disappointed about the result of this race, as the outcome could have been completely different. I started the race from a difficult last position, and I was able to pass several cars getting into the points positions, but in the end I didn't take any reward from it. The whole team has now been rewarded for their great effort in the end.' As for his elder brother, the emotion of the moment overwhelmed him. It was simply too much for him to comprehend.

There was no media conference for Michael Schumacher. The top three finishers – his team-mate, Rubens Barrichello, and the McLaren pair, Räikkönen and Coulthard – were on parade for that little side-show. Michael simply appeared on the TV broadcasts. He looked strangely calm, almost unmoved. It was as if he could hear the words, yet make no sense of his achievement.

'It's probably not appropriate for me to say anything, honestly,' he admitted. 'It's been a tough year, a tough late stage of the season. It has been a tough race, probably one of my toughest.

'I have to repeat again, it is the team who have given us this fantastic car on both occasions. For myself, it was a little bit messy after a couple of incidents. After what happened with da Matta and Ralf hitting me in the back, it was a strange race. I am empty and exhausted. I am proud for the team, but I just cannot think for the moment.'

DIARY

A group of Irish investors purchases a 49.9-per-cent stake in the Jordan F1 team by acquiring the shareholding of Warburg Pincus, the investment bankers who paid around $45 million for a share in the Silverstone-based operation five years ago.

Talks take place between the Jaguar F1 team and the Red Bull energy drink maker about possible future sponsorship arrangements.

Gil de Ferran wins his final IRL race in Texas for the Penske team before retiring from racing at the age of 35. Scott Dixon takes second place to clinch the IRL title.

Allan McNish tipped as a possible candidate for a Jordan drive in 2004.

Left: The celebrations for Michael Schumacher and the Ferrari team.

Below left: What might have been. Fernando Alonso holds his helmet after being forced into retirement when his Renault failed.

Below: Takuma Sato came up with the goods for BAR, securing sixth place and precious points.
Photographs: Darren Heath

FIA F1 WORLD CHAMPIONSHIP • ROUND 16

FUJI TELEVISION JAPANESE GRAND PRIX
SUZUKA 10–12 OCTOBER 2003

Photograph: Darren Heath

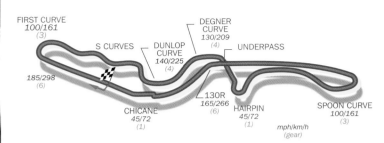

SUZUKA RACING CIRCUIT
CIRCUIT LENGTH: 3.617 miles/5.821 km

FIRST CURVE 100/161 (3)
DEGNER CURVE 130/209 (4)
UNDERPASS
S CURVES
DUNLOP CURVE 140/225 (4)
185/298 (6)
130R 165/266 (6)
HAIRPIN 45/72 (1)
SPOON CURVE 100/161 (3)
CHICANE 45/72 (1)
mph/km/h (gear)

RACE DISTANCE: 53 laps, 191.117 miles/307.573 km RACE WEATHER: Overcast, light rain (track 25/26°C, air 22/23°C)

Pos.	Driver	Nat.	No.	Entrant	Car/Engine	Tyres	Laps	Time/Retirement	Speed (mph/km/h)	Gap to leader	Fastest race lap	
1	Rubens Barrichello	BR	2	Scuderia Ferrari Marlboro	Ferrari F2003-GA-051 V10	B	53	1h 25m 11.743s	134.599/216.611		1m 33.703s	18
2	Kimi Räikkönen	FIN	6	West McLaren Mercedes	McLaren MP4/17D-Mercedes F0110M V10	M	53	1h 25m 22.828s	134.304/216.142	+11.085s	1m 34.488s	12
3	David Coulthard	GB	5	West McLaren Mercedes	McLaren MP4/17D-Mercedes F0110M V10	M	53	1h 25m 23.357s	134.291/216.120	+11.614s	1m 33.416s	14
4	Jenson Button	GB	17	Lucky Strike BAR Honda	BAR 005-Honda RA003E V10	B	53	1h 25m 44.849s	133.729/215.217	+33.106s	1m 34.605s	14
5	Jarno Trulli	I	7	Mild Seven Renault F1 Team	Renault R3-RS23 V10	M	53	1h 25m 46.012s	133.700/215.169	+34.269s	1m 34.546s	26
6	Takuma Sato	J	16	Lucky Strike BAR Honda	BAR 005-Honda RA003E V10	B	53	1h 26m 03.435s	133.248/214.443	+51.692s	1m 35.290s	28
7	Cristiano da Matta	BR	21	Panasonic Toyota Racing	Toyota TF103 RVX-03 V10	M	53	1h 26m 08.537s	133.117/214.231	+56.794s	1m 35.192s	16
8	Michael Schumacher	D	1	Scuderia Ferrari Marlboro	Ferrari F2003-GA-051 V10	B	53	1h 26m 11.230s	133.047/214.119	+59.487s	1m 33.553s	14
9	Nick Heidfeld	D	9	Sauber Petronas	Sauber C22-Petronas 03C V10	B	53	1h 26m 11.902s	133.030/214.091	+60.159s	1m 34.991s	31
10	Olivier Panis	F	20	Panasonic Toyota Racing	Toyota TF103-RVX-03 V10	M	53	1h 26m 13.587s	132.987/214.022	+61.844s	1m 35.023s	53
11	Mark Webber	AUS	14	Jaguar Racing	Jaguar R4-Cosworth CR5 V10	M	53	1h 26m 22.748s	132.751/213.643	+71.005s	1m 34.635s	24
12	Ralf Schumacher	D	4	BMW WilliamsF1 Team	Williams FW25-BMW P83 V10	M	52			+1 lap	1m 33.408s	43
13	Justin Wilson	GB	15	Jaguar Racing	Jaguar R4-Cosworth CR5 V10	M	52			+1 lap	1m 35.014s	11
14	Ralph Firman	IRL	12	Jordan Ford	Jordan EJ-13-Ford Cosworth RS1 V10	B	51			+2 laps	1m 36.662s	15
15	Jos Verstappen	NL	19	European Minardi Cosworth	Minardi PS03-Cosworth CR3 V10	B	51			+2 laps	1m 37.869s	51
16	Nicolas Kiesa	DK	18	European Minardi Cosworth	Minardi PS03-Cosworth CR3 V10	B	50			+3 laps	1m 38.754s	6
	Giancarlo Fisichella	I	11	Jordan Ford	Jordan EJ-13-Ford Cosworth RS1 V10	B	33	Spun off			1m 35.824s	33
	Fernando Alonso	E	8	Mild Seven Renault F1 Team	Renault R3-RS23 V10	M	17	Engine			1m 34.255s	8
	Heinz-Harald Frentzen	D	10	Sauber Petronas	Sauber C22-Petronas 03C V10	B	9	Engine			1m 36.601s	7
	Juan Pablo Montoya	COL	3	BMW WilliamsF1 Team	Williams FW25-BMW P83 V10	M	9	Hydraulics			1m 33.830s	2

All results and data © FOM 2003

Fastest lap: Ralf Schumacher, on lap 43, 1m 33.408s, 139.069 mph/223.805 km/h (record for modified track layout).
Previous lap record: Michael Schumacher (F1 Ferrari F2002-051 V10), 1m 36.125s, 132.576 mph/213.361 km/h (2002).

19th: JARNO TRULLI Renault

17th: JOS VERSTAPPEN Minardi-Cosworth

15th: RALPH FIRMAN Jordan-Ford Cosworth

13th: TAKUMA SATO BAR-Honda

11th: NICK HEIDFELD Sauber-Petronas

20th: RALF SCHUMACHER Williams-BMW

18th: NICOLAS KIESA Minardi-Cosworth

16th: GIANCARLO FISICHELLA Jordan-Ford Cosworth

14th: MICHAEL SCHUMACHER Ferrari

12th: HEINZ-HARALD FRENTZEN Sauber-Petronas

Grid order	1	2	3	4	5	6	7	8	9	10	11	12	13	14	15	16	17	18	19	20	21	22	23	24	25	26	27	28	29	30	31	32	33	34	35	36	37	38	39	40
2 BARRICHELLO	3	3	3	3	3	3	3	2	2	2	2	2	6	17	17	17	2	2	2	2	2	2	2	2	2	2	2	2	2	2	2	2	2	2	2	2	2	2	2	2
3 MONTOYA	2	2	2	2	2	2	2	8	8	8	8	8	17	16	2	2	8	5	5	5	5	5	5	5	6	6	6	6	6	6	5	5	5	5	5	5
21 DA MATTA	8	8	8	8	8	8	8	21	6	6	6	16	2	8	5	6	6	6	6	6	6	6	17	17	17	17	17	5	6	6	6	6	6	6
20 PANIS	21	21	21	21	21	21	21	6	5	5	5	2	16	5	6	21	21	21	21	21	17	17	7	7	7	7	5	17	21	21	21	21	17	17
8 ALONSO	5	5	6	6	6	6	6	5	20	17	17	8	9	9	6	21	17	17	17	17	7	7	5	5	5	5	7	9	4	4	4	4
14 WEBBER	6	6	5	5	5	5	5	20	21	16	16	9	4	5	21	20	20	20	20	20	16	16	16	16	16	16	21	1	1	1	17	20	19
5 COULTHARD	20	20	20	20	20	20	20	17	17	20	9	4	5	6	20	14	14	14	7	7	9	9	9	9	4	17	17	17	7	16	21	2
6 RÄIKKÖNEN	17	17	17	17	17	17	17	16	16	7	4	5	6	21	14	14	7	7	16	16	9	21	21	21	21	21	1	14	7	7	7	20	21	1
17 BUTTON	14	14	14	14	16	16	16	16	7	7	9	11	11	21	20	7	7	16	16	16	4	4	4	21	14	14	14	14	14	14	7	14	20	20	16	1
15 WILSON	15	16	16	16	14	7	7	7	14	4	21	21	20	14	16	16	4	4	14	1	14	20	20	20	4	4	4	7	20	20	16	16	1	4	9
9 HEIDFELD	16	15	15	1	1	14	14	14	9	11	11	12	9	4	15	15	1	1	9	4	4	4	20	1	20	16	16	9	9	9	20	1
10 FRENTZEN	1	1	1	15	7	15	15	15	4	14	7	15	15	15	1	1	15	9	14	14	1	1	1	15	20	20	16	9	14	14	14	14
16 SATO	7	7	7	7	15	4	4	4	11	21	14	7	7	11	4	9	9	15	15	1	15	15	15	15	15	15	15	15	15	15
1 M. SCHUMACHER	4	9	9	9	10	10	10	12	14	7	12	15	7	7	7	11	11	11	11	11	11	11	12	12	12	12	12	12	12	12	12	12
12 FIRMAN	9	10	10	10	9	11	4	4	15	15	15	1	12	11	12	12	12	12	12	12	12	12	12	12	12	12	12	12	19	19	19	19
11 FISICHELLA	10	11	11	11	11	1	11	11	18	1	1	1	12	19	19	19	19	19	19	19	19	19	19	18	18	18	18	18
19 VERSTAPPEN	11	12	12	12	4	12	10	1	18	19	19	19	18	18	18	18	18	18	18	18	18	18	18	18	18
18 KIESA	12	18	18	4	12	18	1	19	19	18	18	18	18	18
7 TRULLI	18	4	4	18	18	18	19	1	3
4 R. SCHUMACHER	19	19	19	19	19	1	19	19

SATURDAY QUALIFYING determines race grid order
Overcast, light rain (track 25/26°C, air 22/23°C)

Pos.	Driver	Lap time	Sector 1	Sector 2	Sector 3
1	Rubens Barrichello	1m 31.713s	31.414s	41.271s	19.028s
2	Juan Pablo Montoya	1m 32.412s	31.764s	41.551s	19.097s
3	Cristiano da Matta	1m 32.419s	31.638s	41.682s	19.099s
4	Olivier Panis	1m 32.862s	31.661s	41.937s	19.264s
5	Fernando Alonso	1m 33.044s	31.841s	41.897s	19.306s
6	Mark Webber	1m 33.106s	32.065s	41.675s	19.366s
7	David Coulthard	1m 33.137s	32.143s	41.912s	19.082s
8	Kimi Räikkönen	1m 33.272s	32.338s	41.966s	18.968s
9	Jenson Button	1m 33.474s	31.984s	42.145s	19.345s
10	Justin Wilson	1m 33.558s	32.533s	41.790s	19.235s
11	Nick Heidfeld	1m 33.632s	32.181s	42.093s	19.358s
12	Heinz-Harald Frentzen	1m 33.896s	31.898s	42.728s	19.270s
13	Takuma Sato	1m 33.924s	32.293s	42.045s	19.586s
14	Michael Schumacher	1m 34.302s	32.422s	42.296s	19.584s
15	Ralph Firman	1m 34.771s	32.593s	42.558s	19.458s
16	Giancarlo Fisichella	1m 34.912s	32.622s	42.692s	19.598s
17	Jos Verstappen	1m 34.975s	32.800s	42.516s	19.659s
18	Nicolas Kiesa	1m 37.226s	34.030s	43.320s	19.876s
19	Ralf Schumacher	No time	–	–	–
20	Jarno Trulli	No time	–	–	–

FRIDAY QUALIFYING determines Sat running order
Sunny and bright (track 32°C, air 24°C)

Pos.	Driver	Lap time
1	Jarno Trulli	1m 30.281s
2	Ralf Schumacher	1m 30.343s
3	Michael Schumacher	1m 30.464s
4	David Coulthard	1m 30.482s
5	Kimi Räikkönen	1m 30.558s
6	Fernando Alonso	1m 30.624s
7	Rubens Barrichello	1m 30.758s
8	Juan Pablo Montoya	1m 31.201s
9	Mark Webber	1m 31.305s
10	Nick Heidfeld	1m 31.783s
11	Takuma Sato	1m 31.832s
12	Heinz-Harald Frentzen	1m 31.892s
13	Olivier Panis	1m 31.908s
14	Cristiano da Matta	1m 32.256s
15	Justin Wilson	1m 32.291s
16	Jenson Button	1m 32.374s
17	Ralph Firman	1m 33.057s
18	Giancarlo Fisichella	1m 33.313s
19	Jos Verstappen	1m 34.836s
20	Nicolas Kiesa	1m 36.181s

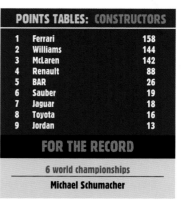

POINTS TABLES: CONSTRUCTORS

1	Ferrari	158
2	Williams	144
3	McLaren	142
4	Renault	88
5	BAR	26
6	Sauber	19
7	Jaguar	18
8	Toyota	16
9	Jordan	13

FOR THE RECORD

6 world championships
Michael Schumacher

PRIVATE TESTING
Sunny, light wind (track: 29°C, air 23°C)

Pos.	Driver	Laps	Time
1	Allan McNish	38	1m 32.170s
2	Fernando Alonso	45	1m 32.367s
3	Jarno Trulli	24	1m 32.891s
4	Giancarlo Fisichella	35	1m 33.497s
5	Mark Webber	40	1m 33.897s
6	Ralph Firman	40	1m 34.054s
7	Justin Wilson	41	1m 34.297s
8	Satoshi Motoyama	40	1m 35.044s
9	Jos Verstappen	24	1m 35.579s
10	Gianmaria Bruni	27	1m 35.695s
11	Nicolas Kiesa	32	1m 36.558s

FRIDAY FREE PRACTICE
Sunny, light wind (track 30°C, air 24°C)

Pos.	Driver	Laps	Time
1	Jarno Trulli	15	1m 30.727s
2	Michael Schumacher	18	1m 31.009s
3	David Coulthard	21	1m 31.019s
4	Rubens Barrichello	19	1m 31.217s
5	Fernando Alonso	19	1m 31.276s
6	Kimi Räikkönen	21	1m 31.303s
7	Juan Pablo Montoya	9	1m 31.654s
8	Mark Webber	23	1m 31.977s
9	Olivier Panis	21	1m 32.011s
10	Cristiano da Matta	25	1m 32.133s
11	Ralf Schumacher	18	1m 32.208s
12	Takuma Sato	20	1m 32.295s
13	Heinz-Harald Frentzen	18	1m 32.422s
14	Nick Heidfeld	17	1m 32.694s
15	Justin Wilson	21	1m 32.735s
16	Giancarlo Fisichella	17	1m 33.956s
17	Jenson Button	9	1m 34.445s
19	Jos Verstappen	13	1m 35.180s
20	Nicolas Kiesa	14	1m 35.900s

SATURDAY FIRST FREE PRACTICE
Cloudy (track 25/28°C, air 22/24°C)

Pos.	Driver	Laps	Time
1	Ralf Schumacher	15	1m 32.931s
2	Michael Schumacher	14	1m 32.989s
3	Rubens Barrichello	15	1m 33.350s
4	Juan Pablo Montoya	13	1m 33.405s
5	Nick Heidfeld	19	1m 33.749s
6	Cristiano da Matta	19	1m 33.963s
7	Justin Wilson	17	1m 34.119s
8	Jenson Button	18	1m 34.171s
9	David Coulthard	15	1m 34.309s
10	Jarno Trulli	13	1m 34.349s
11	Fernando Alonso	15	1m 34.398s
12	Kimi Räikkönen	7	1m 34.523s
13	Olivier Panis	14	1m 34.541s
14	Takuma Sato	8	1m 34.554s
15	Mark Webber	20	1m 34.599s
16	Heinz-Harald Frentzen	13	1m 34.718s
17	Ralph Firman	13	1m 36.368s
18	Giancarlo Fisichella	10	1m 36.705s
19	Jos Verstappen	13	1m 36.928s
20	Nicolas Kiesa	14	1m 38.075s

SATURDAY SECOND FREE PRACTICE
Cloudy (track 25/28°C, air 22/24°C)

Pos.	Driver	Laps	Time
1	Ralf Schumacher	10	1m 31.149s
2	Juan Pablo Montoya	15	1m 31.422s
3	Michael Schumacher	12	1m 31.705s
4	Jarno Trulli	19	1m 32.343s
5	Rubens Barrichello	11	1m 32.796s
6	Kimi Räikkönen	7	1m 32.930s
7	Olivier Panis	16	1m 33.082s
8	Fernando Alonso	15	1m 33.107s
9	Cristiano da Matta	17	1m 33.133s
10	Jenson Button	22	1m 33.411s
11	Takuma Sato	10	1m 33.662s
12	Heinz-Harald Frentzen	16	1m 33.694s
13	Mark Webber	15	1m 33.807s
14	Justin Wilson	18	1m 33.952s
15	Nick Heidfeld	19	1m 34.558s
16	Giancarlo Fisichella	15	1m 35.476s
17	Ralph Firman	15	1m 35.620s
18	Jos Verstappen	6	1m 37.379s
19	Nicolas Kiesa	18	1m 37.884s

WARM-UP
Cloudy (track 25/28°C, air 22/24°C)

Pos.	Driver	Laps	Time
1	Juan Pablo Montoya	5	1m 33.211s
2	Cristiano da Matta	5	1m 33.481s
3	Rubens Barrichello	7	1m 33.963s
4	Fernando Alonso	4	1m 33.972s
5	Takuma Sato	6	1m 34.138s
6	Mark Webber	5	1m 34.504s
7	Ralf Schumacher	5	1m 34.750s
8	Jenson Button	6	1m 34.757s
9	David Coulthard	6	1m 34.790s
10	Giancarlo Fisichella	5	1m 34.869s
11	Nick Heidfeld	4	1m 35.450s
12	Justin Wilson	6	1m 35.778s
13	Jos Verstappen	5	1m 35.853s
14	Ralph Firman	4	1m 36.515s
15	Nicolas Kiesa	4	1m 38.929s
16	Heinz-Harald Frentzen	5	1m 47.062s
17	Olivier Panis	4	No time
18	Jarno Trulli	3	No time
19	Michael Schumacher	6	No time
20	Kimi Räikkönen	2	No time

9th: JENSON BUTTON BAR-Honda

7th: DAVID COULTHARD McLaren-Mercedes

5th: FERNANDO ALONSO Renault

3rd: CRISTIANO DA MATTA Toyota

Pole: RUBENS BARRICHELLO Ferrari

10th: JUSTIN WILSON Jaguar-Cosworth

8th: KIMI RÄIKKÖNEN McLaren-Mercedes

6th: MARK WEBBER Jaguar-Cosworth

4th: OLIVIER PANIS Toyota

2nd: JUAN PABLO MONTOYA Williams-BMW

Lap chart (laps 42–53)

42	43	44	45	46	47	48	49	50	51	52	53	
2	2	2	2	2	2	2	2	2	2	2	2	1
6	6	6	6	6	6	6	6	6	6	6	6	2
5	5	5	5	5	5	5	5	5	5	5	5	3
17	17	17	17	17	17	17	17	17	17	17	17	4
7	7	7	7	7	7	7	7	7	7	7	7	5
16	16	16	16	16	16	16	16	16	16	16	16	6
21	21	21	21	21	21	21	21	21	21	21	21	7
1	1	1	1	1	1	1	1	1	1	1	1	8
9	9	9	9	9	9	9	9	9	9	9	9	
20	20	20	20	20	20	20	20	20	20	20	20	
14	14	14	14	14	14	14	14	14	14	14	14	
15	15	15	15	4	4	4	4	4	4	4		
4	4	4	4	15	15	15	15	15	15			
12	12	12	12	12	12	12	12	12	12			
19	19	19	19	19	19	19	19	19				
18	18	18	18	18	18	18	18	18				

Pit stop
One lap behind leader

CHASSIS LOG BOOK

1	Michael Schumacher	F2003-GA/229	11	Giancarlo Fisichella	EJ-13/05
2	Rubens Barrichello	F2003-GA/233	12	Ralph Firman	EJ-13/04
	Spare	F2003-GA/230/231		Spare	EJ-13/02
3	Juan Pablo Montoya	FW25/06	14	Mark Webber	R4/03
4	Ralf Schumacher	FW25/07	15	Justin Wilson	R4/05
	Spare	FW25/02/04		Spare	R4/04
5	David Coulthard	MP4/17D-06	16	Takuma Sato	BAR005/6
6	Kimi Räikkönen	MP4/17D-09	17	Jenson Button	BAR005/4
	Spare	MP4/17D-07		Spare	BAR005/5
7	Jarno Trulli	R23/05	18	Nicolas Kiesa	PS03/01
8	Fernando Alonso	R23/06	19	Jos Verstappen	PS03/02
	Allan McNish	R23/03		Gianmaria Bruni	PS03/03
	Spare	R23/03		Spare	PS03/03
9	Nick Heidfeld	C22/01	20	Olivier Panis	TF103/08
10	Heinz-Harald Frentzen	C22/03	21	Cristiano da Matta	TF103/07
	Spare	C22/02		Spare	TF103/02

POINTS TABLES: DRIVERS

1	Michael Schumacher	93
2	Kimi Räikkönen	91
3	Juan Pablo Montoya	82
4	Rubens Barrichello	65
5	Ralph Schumacher	58
6	Fernando Alonso	55
7	David Coulthard	51
8	Jarno Trulli	33
9 =	Jenson Button	17
9 =	Mark Webber	17
11	Heinz-Harald Frentzen	13
12	Giancarlo Fisichella	12
13	Cristiano da Matta	10
14 =	Nick Heidfeld	6
14 =	Olivier Panis	6
14 =	Jacques Villeneuve	6
17	Marc Gené	4
18	Takuma Sato	3
19 =	Ralph Firman	1
19 =	Justin Wilson	1

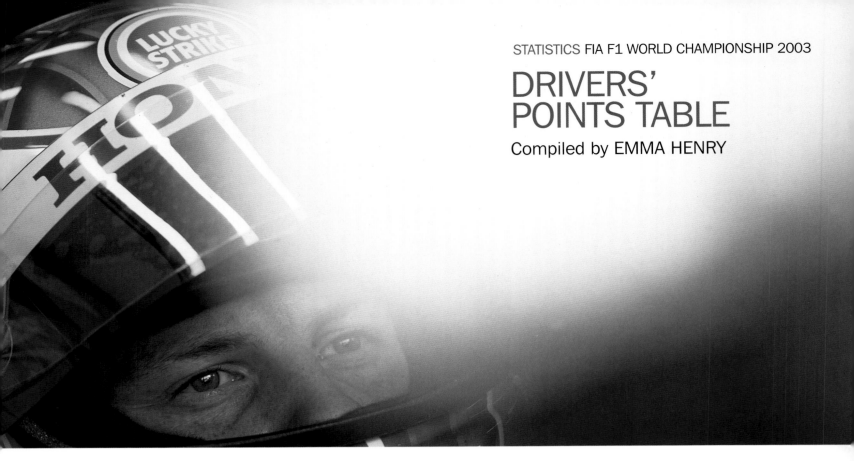

DRIVERS' POINTS TABLE

Compiled by EMMA HENRY

Place	Driver	Nationality	Date of birth	Car	Australia	Malaysia	Brazil	San Marino	Spain	Austria	Monaco	Canada	Europe	France	Britain	Germany	Hungary	Italy	USA	Japan	Points total
1	Michael Schumacher	D	3/1/69	Ferrari	4p	6f	R	1pf	1p	1pf	3	1	5	3	4	7	8	1pf	1f	8	93
2	Kimi Räikkönen	FIN	17/10/79	McLaren-Mercedes	3f	1	2	2	R	2	2f	6	Rpf	4	3	R	2	4	2p	2	91
3	Juan Pablo Montoya	COL	20/9/75	Williams-BMW	2	12	R	7	4	R	1	3	2	2f	2	1pf	3f	2	6	R	82
4	Rubens Barrichello	BR	23/5/72	Ferrari	R	2	Rpf	3	3f	3	8	5	3	7	1pf	R	R	3	R	1p	65
5	Ralf Schumacher	D	30/6/75	Williams-BMW	8	4	7	4	5	6	4p	2p	1	1p	9	R	4	–	R	12f	58
6	Fernando Alonso	E	29/7/81	Renault	7	3p	3	6	2	R	5	4f	4	R	R	4	1p	8	R	R	55
7	David Coulthard	GB	27/3/71	McLaren-Mercedes	1	R	4	5	R	5	7	R	15*	5	5	2	5	R	R	3	51
8	Jarno Trulli	I	13/7/74	Renault	5	5	8	13	R	8	6	R	R	R	6	3	7	R	4	5	33
9 =	Jenson Button	GB	19/1/80	BAR-Honda	10	7	R	8	9	4	DNS	R	7	R	8	8	10	R	R	4	17
9 =	Mark Webber	AUS	27/8/76	Jaguar-Cosworth	R	R	9*	R	7	7	R	7	6	6	14	11*	6	7	R	11	17
11	Heinz-Harald Frentzen	D	18/5/67	Sauber-Petronas	6	9	5	11	R	DNS	R	R	9	12	12	R	R	13*	3	R	13
12	Giancarlo Fisichella	I	14/1/73	Jordan-Ford Cosworth	12*	R	1	15*	R	R	10	R	12	R	R	13*	R	10	7	R	12
13	Cristiano da Matta	BR	19/9/73	Toyota	R	11	10	12	6	10	9	11*	R	11	7	6	11	R	9	7	10
14 =	Nick Heidfeld	D	10/5/77	Sauber-Petronas	R	8	R	10	10	R	11	R	8	13	17	10	9	9	5	9	6
14 =	Olivier Panis	F	2/9/66	Toyota	R	R	R	9	R	R	13	R	R	8	11	5	R	R	R	10	6
14 =	Jacques Villeneuve	CDN	9/4/71	BAR-Honda	9	DNS	6	R	R	12	R	R	R	9	10	9	R	6	R	–	6
17	Marc Gené	E	29/3/74	Williams-BMW	–	–	–	–	–	–	–	–	–	–	–	–	5	–	–	–	4
18	Takuma Sato	J	28/1/77	BAR-Honda	–	–	–	–	–	–	–	–	–	–	–	–	–	–	–	6	3
19 =	Ralph Firman	IRL	20/5/75	Jordan-Ford Cosworth	R	10	R	R	8	11	12	R	11	15	13	R	–	–	R	14	1
19 =	Justin Wilson	GB	31/7/78	Minardi-Cosworth	R	R	R	R	11	13	R	R	13	14	16	–	–				1
				Jaguar-Cosworth												R	R	R	8	13	
21 =	Antonio Pizzonia	BR	11/9/80	Jaguar-Cosworth	13*	R	R	14	R	9	R	10*	10	10	R	–	–	–	–	–	0
21 =	Jos Verstappen	NL	4/3/72	Minardi-Cosworth	11	13	R	R	12	R	R	9	14	16	15	R	12	R	10	15	0
21 =	Nicolas Kiesa	DK	3/3/78	Minardi-Cosworth	–	–	–	–	–	–	–	–	–	–	–	12	13	12	11	16	0
21 =	Zsolt Baumgartner	H	1/1/81	Jordan-Ford Cosworth	–	–	–	–	–	–	–	–	–	–	–	–	R	11	–	–	0

The following drivers took part in Private Testing on the Friday morning of each grand prix:

Matteo Bobbi	I	2/7/78	Minardi-Cosworth
Gianmaria Bruni	I	30/5/81	Minardi-Cosworth
Allan McNish	GB	29/12/69	Renault
Franck Montagny	F	5/1/78	Renault
Satoshi Motoyama	J	4/3/71	Jordan-Ford Cosworth
Björn Wirdheim	S	4/4/80	Jordan-Ford Cosworth

KEY

p	pole position	DNS	did not start
f	fastest lap	*	classified, but not running
R	retired		at the finish

STATISTICS FIA F1 WORLD CHAMPIONSHIP 2003

POINTS & PERCENTAGES
Compiled by DAVID HAYHOE

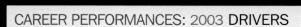

Photograph: Darren Heath

GRID POSITIONS: 2003

Pos	Driver	Starts	Best	Worst	Average
1	Rubens Barrichello	16	1	8	3.63
2	Juan Pablo Montoya	16	1	9	4.19
3	Michael Schumacher	16	1	14	4.25
4	Marc Gené	1	5	5	5.00
5	Ralf Schumacher	15	1	20	6.00
6	Kimi Räikkönen	16	1	20	6.81
7	Jarno Trulli	16	2	19	7.25
8	Fernando Alonso	16	1	20	7.88
9	David Coulthard	16	2	14	8.50
10	Olivier Panis	16	3	17	9.00
11	Mark Webber	16	3	17	9.88
12	Cristiano da Matta	16	3	18	11.25
13	Jenson Button	15	5	20	11.33
14	Jacques Villeneuve	14	6	17	11.64
15	Nick Heidfeld	16	4	20	12.31
16	Takuma Sato	1	13	13	13.00
17	Heinz-Harald Frentzen	16	4	17	13.25
18	Antonia Pizzonia	11	8	18	13.82
19	Giancarlo Fisichella	16	8	17	13.88
20	Ralph Firman	14	14	20	17.00
21	Justin Wilson	16	10	20	17.19
22	Jos Verstappen	16	15	20	18.44
23	Zsolt Baumgartner	2	18	19	18.50
24	Nicolas Kiesa	5	18	20	19.40

CAREER PERFORMANCES: 2003 DRIVERS

Driver	Nationality	Races	Championships	Wins	2nd places	3rd places	4th places	5th places	6th places	7th places	8th places	Pole positions	Fastest laps	Points
Fernando Alonso	E	33	–	1	1	2	1	1	1	1	2	1	55
Rubens Barrichello	BR	178	–	7	17	19	14	13	4	6	3	9	11	337
Zsolt Baumgartner	H	2	–	–	–	–	–	–	–	–	–	–	–	–
Jenson Button	GB	66	–	–	–	5	8	3	5	5	–	–	45
David Coulthard	GB	157	–	13	26	21	8	16	7	8	1	12	18	451
Cristiano da Matta	BR	16	–	–	–	–	2	2	–	–	–	10
Ralph Firman	IRL	14	–	–	–	–	–	1	–	–	1
Giancarlo Fisichella	I	123	–	1	5	4	5	8	5	9	7	1	1	94
Heinz-Harald Frentzen	D	157	–	3	3	12	12	10	16	8	9	2	6	174
Marc Gené	E	34	–	–	–	–	1	1	–	3	–	–	5
Nick Heidfeld	D	66	–	–	1	2	2	7	4	4	–	–	25
Nicolas Kiesa	DK	5	–	–	–	–	–	–	–	–	–	–	–
Juan Pablo Montoya	COL	50	–	3	12	5	6	1	1	1	2	11	9	163
Olivier Panis	F	141	–	1	3	1	4	7	8	11	9	–	–	70
Antonio Pizzonia	BR	11	–	–	–	–	–	–	–	–	–	–	–
Kimi Räikkönen	FIN	50	–	1	8	5	6	1	2	3	1	2	4	124
Takuma Sato	J	18	–	–	–	–	1	1	–	1	–	–	5
Michael Schumacher	D	195	6	70	34	18	9	7	5	2	3	55	56	1038
Ralf Schumacher	D	115	–	6	5	12	15	15	5	5	2	4	7	235
Jarno Trulli	I	113	–	–	1	1	7	7	8	6	8	–	–	71
Jos Verstappen	NL	107	–	–	–	2	1	2	2	2	4	–	–	17
Jacques Villeneuve	CDN	130	1	11	5	7	9	6	8	8	8	13	9	219
Mark Webber	AUS	32	–	–	–	–	–	1	3	4	1	–	–	19
Justin Wilson	GB	16	–	–	–	–	–	–	–	1	–	–	1

Drivers beginning the formation lap are deemed to have made a start. Also, where races have been subject to a restart, those retiring during the initial race are included as having started.

UNLAPPED: 2003

Number of cars on same lap as leader

Grand Prix	Starters	at 1/4 distance	at 1/2 distance	at 3/4 distance	at full distance
Australia	20	17	14	12	10
Malaysia	19	13	9	7	4
Brazil	20	19	13	11	8
San Marino	20	19	11	7	7
Spain	20	16	8	6	4
Austria	20	17	14	7	5
Monaco	19	16	11	8	8
Canada	20	14	11	6	6
Europe	20	18	14	7	5
France	20	19	11	7	6
Britain	20	20	19	15	12
Germany	20	12	7	7	4
Hungary	20	17	11	8	6
Italy	20	14	12	7	5
USA	20	13	7	5	5
Japan	20	18	14	13	11

LAP LEADERS: 2003

Grand Prix	Michael Schumacher	Ralf Schumacher	Juan Pablo Montoya	Kimi Räikkönen	Fernando Alonso	Rubens Barrichello	David Coulthard	Jenson Button	Cristiano da Matta	Jarno Trulli	Mark Webber	Giancarlo Fisichella	Heinz-Harald Frentzen	Total
Australia	10	–	21	16	–	–	11	–	–	–	–	–	–	58
Malaysia	–	–	–	40	13	3	–	–	–	–	–	–	–	56
Brazil	–	–	–	17	–	10	26	–	–	–	1	–	54
San Marino	42	15	–	4	–	1	–	–	–	–	–	–	–	62
Spain	60	–	–	–	3	2	–	–	–	–	–	–	–	65
Austria	53	–	8	7	–	1	–	–	–	–	–	–	–	69
Monaco	10	20	40	6	–	–	–	–	2	–	–	–	–	78
Canada	40	19	–	–	11	–	–	–	–	–	–	–	–	70
Europe	–	40	–	20	–	–	–	–	–	–	–	–	–	60
France	–	70	–	–	–	–	–	–	–	–	–	–	–	70
Britain	–	–	–	8	–	23	–	–	–	17	12	–	–	60
Germany	–	–	66	–	1	–	–	–	–	–	–	–	–	67
Hungary	–	–	–	1	69	–	–	–	–	–	–	–	–	70
Italy	52	–	1	–	–	–	–	–	–	–	–	–	–	53
USA	36	–	–	18	–	–	1	15	–	2	–	1	73
Japan	–	–	8	1	–	40	1	3	–	–	–	–	–	53
Total	303	164	144	138	97	80	39	18	17	14	2	1	1	1018
Per cent	29.8	16.1	14.1	13.6	9.5	7.9	3.8	1.8	1.7	1.4	0.2	0.1	0.1	100

RETIREMENTS: 2003

Number of cars that retired

Grand Prix	Starters	at 1/4 distance	at 1/2 distance	at 3/4 distance	at full distance	percentage
Australia	20	3	6	7	9	55.0
Malaysia	19	3	3	6	6	68.4
Brazil	20	1	7	9	11	45.0
San Marino	20	–	2	3	6	70.0
Spain	20	4	5	8	8	60.0
Austria	20	3	4	6	7	65.0
Monaco	19	3	5	5	6	68.4
Canada	20	2	5	8	11	45.0
Europe	20	–	1	3	6	70.0
France	20	–	1	4	4	80.0
Britain	20	–	2	3	85.0
Germany	20	6	7	7	9	55.0
Hungary	20	1	5	7	7	65.0
Italy	20	3	4	6	7	65.0
USA	20	1	4	8	9	55.0
Japan	20	2	3	4	4	80.0

F3000 REVIEW

VIRTUOSO
PERFORMANCE

By SIMON ARRON

Above: Ricardo Sperafico took the runner-up slot for Coloni, but blotted his copybook at Monaco.

Below: Nicolas Kiesa found himself in Formula 1 sooner than expected following a mid-season call from Minardi.

Photographs: Darren Heath

FOR a moment, Björn Wirdheim looked as though he might let slip his customary veil of calm. The runaway FIA Formula 3000 champion – ten starts, three wins, six second places – had just completed his 22nd and final race for Arden International, at Monza. On the anniversary of his maiden F3000 success, he'd signed off a remarkably consistent campaign with a flawless victory drive and his top lip was on the cusp of a tremble.

'It has been a fantastic season,' he said, 'but I feel quite sad that it has come to an end. I don't just regard the guys at Arden as a team, I regard them as friends. I accept that the time has come to move on, but otherwise I would be happy to stick around and race with these guys in F3000. I have learned a lot during the past two seasons and have enjoyed every moment. I'll definitely be keeping in touch.'

The feeling was mutual. His engineer, Mick Cook, had guided BMW Williams star Juan Pablo Montoya to the FIA F3000 title in 1998 and said, 'Björn has been a pleasure to work with. I don't think I've ever made so few engineering changes to a car during the course of a season – in fact, we've hardly modified the basic set-up for the past 18 months. We've made standard wing and ride height adjustments from track to track, but Björn has always

jumped in, got on with the job and left me with relatively little to do. His level of confidence is amazing.

'I was chatting to Juan Pablo towards the end of the season and teased him about how much easier it had been to deal with Björn than it had been to work with him. He laughed and said, "Yeah, but I was more spectacular." That's perfectly true, but both approaches are effective. Juan perhaps had a bit more flair at this stage of his career, but Björn has an abundance of natural talent and is very intelligent both in and out of the car.'

Wirdheim was bundled off the track in an opening-lap collision at the Nürburgring – the only race in which he finished outside the top two – but that apart he scarcely put a scratch on the car all season. His most conspicuous error, though, was one of the most spectacular in the formula's 19-season history. The Swede obliterated his rivals in Monte Carlo, but stopped to acknowledge the Arden crew a few metres short of a finishing line he thought he had already crossed. While he was busy looking for his perplexed team, distant Dane Nicolas Kiesa (Den Blå Avis) sneaked through and took the flag. The Swede didn't fully appreciate his error until he saw the results on a giant video screen during his cooling-off lap. His reaction, though, spoke volumes for his pragmatic, unflappable nature. 'It was an incredibly stupid mistake,' he said, half grinning because even he could see the funny side, 'but the bottom line is that it cost me two points. There's nothing I can do to change what happened, so there's no point wasting energy worrying about it.' Team boss Christian Horner promised to forgive him if he won Arden's home race at Silverstone. He did, at a canter.

Wirdheim secured the title at Hockenheim on 2 August – earlier than any driver had clinched it previously. He didn't lack for credible rivals, but none was able to match him consistently for speed or composure.

It was a travesty that Giorgio Pantano felt obliged to continue at this level of competition for a third season. Runner-up in 2002, the Italian had nothing to prove, but clinched a last-minute deal with Durango after a proposed switch to the US-based CART series fell through (largely because the individual who offered him a drive didn't actually possess a team, a fact that took several weeks to percolate). While Wirdheim had the benefit of continuity, Pantano had to start afresh for the third time in as many seasons. He conjured two wins, to take his tally in the series to six, but was denied second place in the championship when his car coughed to a halt while he was pressing the Swede at Monza. 'I don't know what I'll do next season,' he said, 'but I think I'd rather stop racing than go through another season of this.' Sadly, he was only half joking. Motor sport tends to value drivers only on hard results or the number of zeros on their backers' quarterly sponsorship cheques – not necessarily in that order. Pantano was in a no-win situation. Nothing less than the title would garnish his reputation; the fact that he failed to deliver the goods should not be allowed to camouflage his natural spark.

Ricardo Sperafico (Coloni) also won twice and pipped the Italian to the runner-up slot, but the Brazilian – also in his third season – sullied his reputation in Monaco where, a lap in arrears, he ran second-placed Pantano off the road. This incident ought not to have been the focus of a competent campaign, but it tended to stick in the mind more than either of his victories.

Star rookie Vitantonio Liuzzi (Red Bull Junior) would have outscored both of them had his admirable sense of adventure not earned him a harsh time penalty in Budapest. His crime was to clatter into Pantano while trying to overtake two cars in a single, last-lap manoeuvre. 'I didn't appeal against the decision because I didn't have enough money,' Liuzzi said. 'All season, people have been saying they want to see more exciting racing. I thought a bit of overtaking might help. I'm a racer, not a taxi driver.'

The Italian qualified on pole by more than half a second in Budapest on what was only the 12th flying lap he had completed at the circuit (a brief, scooter-powered reconnaissance trip notwithstanding). He scored six top-four finishes – including two podiums – and had established himself as F3000's most wanted man by the end of the season.

Liuzzi's team-mate, Patrick Friesacher, was expected to be a title contender, but after finishing second to Wirdheim in the Imola season-opener, he sustained a broken wrist in a first-lap pile-up in Barcelona. He missed the next two races and only truly got back into his stride at the end of the campaign, when he signed off with three straight podium finishes. He scored his maiden win in fine style in Budapest, which was the first F3000 race to feature mandatory tyre stops. These were introduced on a trial basis for the last two races, after the title had been settled, and proved sufficiently popular that they are likely to become a regular feature for the 2004 season.

Defending champion Super Nova had a miserable campaign. Italian recruit Enrico Toccacelo won once, at the Nürburgring, but otherwise was inconsistent, with a tendency to have the kind of accidents most eight-year-olds shake out of their systems within a couple of months of their first Cadet kart race. He was lucky to escape censure after tripping up Liuzzi in Monaco – and luckier still that he didn't injure anybody.

Two Americans – CART refugee Townsend Bell (Arden) and the relatively unknown Phil Giebler, a former Spanish F3 racer who appeared on a handful of occasions with Den Blå Avis – created a favourable impression, and there were signs that young Czech Jaroslav Janis (ISR Charouz) could mature into a capable racer, but the series was missing its time honoured strength in depth. Expected contender Rob Nguyen more or less vanished from the sport's radar, for instance. In 2002, the Australian had emerged as an occasional FIA F3000 front-runner just 18 months after stepping out of an indoor kart. This time, he showed fleeting promise with Spanish newcomer BCN, only for his funds to run dry within a couple of races.

During the past four seasons, F3000 entry lists have slipped from 40-plus to an average of just 17. Part of that is due to global tightening of purse strings (regular race winner Den Blå Avis was forced to quit the series mid-season for financial reasons), but mostly it's a consequence of having too many similar sub-F1 series competing for drivers' attention. Renault is poised to step in from 2005 with a new-look category that will assume the FIA F3000 Championship's role as grand prix racing's approved finishing school. The French giant's intervention should help streamline motor sport's pointlessly cluttered ladder.

For all its recent difficulties, however, F3000 remains a valid academy. Half the 2003 F1 grid cut their teeth here, and recent graduates include Juan Pablo Montoya, Fernando Alonso, Mark Webber, Justin Wilson and Nick Heidfeld. This year, Kiesa (generally unimpressive prior to his inherited Monaco victory) and Zsolt Baumgartner (wholly unimpressive throughout his career, frankly) graduated directly to F1 during the season. In that sense, the series continues to do its job, but progress founded on merit remains an elusive target.

Below: Accident-prone Enrico Toccacelo shone briefly for Super Nova at the Nürburgring.

Bottom: Having lost a potential CART seat, Giorgio Pantano rued the fact that he was forced to continue in F3000 for a third season.
Photographs: Darren Heath

BATTLE FOR SUPREMACY

By MARCUS SIMMONS

Top and inset: Alan van der Merwe showed his talent during a wet practice at Spa.
Both photographs: Glenn Dunbar/LAT Photographic

Above: A chip of the old block. Nelson Angelo Piquet inherited his father's looks and talent.
Photograph: Jeff Bloxham/LAT Photograph

THE 2003 season was a funny old year for Formula 3. Both major championships – the British and Euroseries – were dominated by fine drivers who wrapped up their respective titles before the final round. At the same time, however, Alan van der Merwe and Ryan Briscoe found their thunder – and some of their headlines – being stolen by talented young newcomers Nelson Angelo Piquet and Christian Klien.

And, if there wasn't much dispute over the destiny of the titles, there *was* a battle for supremacy between the two championships themselves, and that perhaps will go down as the story of 2003.

The Euroseries, a merger between the German and French championships, was new for the season, and predictably gained a full and competitive field of 30 cars. Occupying the prime support slot on the German-based DTM touring car package, as well as three stand-alone rounds in France, it enjoyed strong manufacturer support and a relatively solid field.

At the same time, the traditionally strong British championship continued to boast a good entry (generally in the low 20s, with a handful of older Scholarship Class cars boosting the grid to nearly 30), but there was so much chopping and changing among the entry list that it was almost impossible to keep up. As an example, Alan Docking Racing, winner of the title in 2002 with Robbie Kerr, ran no fewer than seven different drivers in its two-car line-up during the course of the season, and that was before another complete change in pilots prior to the last races of the year in Macau and Korea.

Some of the best young talent appeared to be deserting the British championship in favour of the Euroseries, due mainly to the fact that the manufacturers can offer good deals to snap 'em up young. A junior-driver contract from Mercedes or Opel would remove the need to fork out 400 grand to race in the UK, so why not take it? Even so, the independent nature of the British championship should ensure that it's not subject to the whims of the men around the boardroom tables of the big manufacturers, and that it remains on solid ground. That is, at least as long as the nature of F3 remains the same.

The current regulations – for two-litre, production-based engines pushing out around 220 bhp – have remained largely unchanged since 1974, but Mercedes has been lobbying the Euroseries organisers to change to a 'high-mileage' formula (with engines lasting half a season between rebuilds) to cut costs.

At present, the Euroseries could be strong enough to veer away from the FIA regulations without any adverse effect in the short term. But that move could consign the other championships

(Britain, Japan, Italy and the lower-level German F3 Cup) plus the international races to their own ghetto if they don't adopt the same regulations. So, effectively, the Euroseries could end up holding F3 to ransom.

Adding further to the intrigue was a complete absence of Mercedes teams from the prestige end-of-term events in Macau and Korea. Granted, they supported the mid-summer Marlboro Masters at Zandvoort, where Piquet put the British championship one up by grabbing pole position before Klien equalled the score by taking the race win. But Macau and Korea?

Well, Klien's team, Mücke Motorsport, has never contested those races, but the other top Merc squad – ASM – won both events with Renault engines in 2002, but opted to stay away in '03. The official reason was that the team needed to concentrate on testing for the '04 Euroseries. A prime case of putting the cart before the horse – missing races to test? Whatever next?

Macau and Korea seem to be suffering all round in the present climate. What also doesn't help is the current Formula 1 testing ban, so that when testing resumes *just* after the late-November Far East races, some F3 hopefuls feel they have to be on standby, just in case of a call-up or a deal being struck for 2004.

At the time of writing, this looked set to account for van der Merwe, which was a shame because it would have been good to see him take on Briscoe around the streets of Macau. The articulate and highly-intelligent South African had a fantastic year in the British championship with Carlin Motorsport, taking nine wins from the 24 races, a far cry from his 2002 season, when the only predictable thing was that he'd get involved in a silly accident while battling for eighth place.

Instead, van der Merwe recommitted early to a second year with Carlin, took himself away for the winter, gave himself a talking to and burst out of the blocks with consistently excellent preseason testing times. On the eve of the season, he began to be eclipsed by his rookie team-mate, Jamie Green, and it was the British Formula Renault runner-up who dominated the opening round at Donington Park. But then Green suffered a frightening roll in qualifying for round two at Snetterton, and that seemed to dent his confidence.

From then on, van der Merwe's most regular rival was Piquet. The teenage Brazilian had moved to Britain with the same team, Piquet Sports, with which he had dominated the South American championship (for cars built between 1999 and 2001). So the squad was in a new country, on unfamiliar tracks, running in much colder weather on much harder Avon control tyres, and fielding a brand-spanking-new Dallara F303. (The chassis was actually a variable, because only one other driver used an F303 in the UK. Although it was primarily a tidy-up of the F302, it featured a new twin-shock system and had different track and wheelbase.)

Once he found his rhythm, Piquet was stunning. The British tracks, with their long, fast, flowing corners, suit his style perfectly, and it was he who scored the most pole positions – eight to van der Merwe's six.

Unfortunately, Piquet struggled to get to grips with his starts (he was used to just dumping the clutch on the sticky Pirellis used in South America), and seemed to lack a bit of race craft early in the season. Just as Piquet kept improving, so did van der Merwe. The older man won through, although both gave a superb account of themselves.

Green pipped Piquet for the runner-up spot in the championship by dint of regaining some of his form late in the season. He looked much more his old self at Rockingham and Spa, and by stealth scored a great win at Thruxton – from eighth on the grid! The top three in the rankings all used Mugen Honda engines to power their Dallara chassis.

Others to win included Britons Danny Watts (with a Dallara-Renault run by the new Hitech Racing team) and Rob Austin (Menu Motorsport Dallara-Opel), Australian Will Davison (Docking Dallara-Mugen), Swede Robert Dahlgren (Fortec Motorsport Dallara-Renault) and Monegasque Clivio Piccione (Manor Motorsport Dallara-Mugen). But it was a non-winner, Adam Carroll, who impressed more than any of them.

The Ulsterman started the season doing wonders in the troublesome Lola-Dome, which proved unreliable and weak in slow corners, before the money ran out. Then, he was picked up by Menu and went on a mid-season spree of podium finishes, but there was still no budget. Finally, team patron Alain Menu himself used his DTM connections to plonk Carroll into the closing rounds of the Euroseries with Opel Team KMS. Considering his lack of testing and funding, he had been superb during his time in the British championship.

The Scholarship Class provided some amusement, and flamboyant Venezuelan Ernesto Viso took the title at the final race after a controversial clash with Damon Hill protégé Steven Kane. Those two plus Indian Karun Chandhok will all be strong in the top class.

In the Euroseries, Briscoe built up a big advantage in the first half of the season. Still a Toyota junior, the Australian made the most of remaining with the Italian Prema Powerteam, got in some good winter testing with the squad's Dallara-Opel and scored four wins in the first five races.

In the middle of the year, Briscoe lost some ground to his principal Mercedes rivals Klien and Olivier Pla (ASM), but another late-summer purple patch put the crown beyond doubt.

Austrian Klien, the reigning German Formula Renault champion, looked particularly tasty and blew away his more experienced Mücke team-mate, Markus Winkelhock. Similarly, Pla was overshadowed from time to time by spectacular ASM partner Alexandre Premat, who stepped up as French F/Renault champ.

Nico Rosberg proved that Nelsinho Piquet wasn't the only talented teenage 'son of' in the game by taking a win in his Team Rosberg Dallara-Opel, while others to taste victory were German Timo Glock (KMS Dallara-Opel), Poland's Robert Kubica (Prema Dallara-Opel) and Brazilian Fabio Carbone, who took the Pau Grand Prix street race in his Signature Dallara-Renault.

Making it a good year for Australians, James Courtney steamrollered the Japanese championship in his TOM'S Dallara-Toyota. Italian veteran Paolo Montin was runner-up after a fine season in the Nissan-powered Three Bond Racing Dallara.

In Italy, Fausto Ippoliti enjoyed a steady season to claim the title in his Target Racing Dallara-Opel, but one more race could have given it to the resurgent Christian Montanari, driving Coloni Motorsport's much modified Lola-Dome.

Germany also retained an F3 Cup, which was blitzed by Brazilian Joao de Oliveira in a JB Motorsport Dallara-Opel. This championship is rumoured to be on the verge of gaining lower-level teams from the big-money Euroseries for 2004. Another Brazilian to dominate was Danilo Dirani, who cruised to the title in the poorly supported South American series in his Cesario Formula Dallara-Mugen.

Dirani now wants to join Piquet and compete in the British championship for 2004 – but who's going to beat Nelsinho? And will most of the rest of the big names be in the Euroseries? Certainly the on-track stuff looks more predictable than what might go on off track.

Left: A trio of future Grand Prix stars? Piquet, Klien and Briscoe on the podium at Zandvoort.

Below: Under-financed Ulsterman Adam Carroll showed his talent.
Photographs: Glenn Dunbar/LAT Photographic

Above: Christian Klien beats Piquet at Zandvoort. With Red Bull sponsorship, the Austrian driver could be elevated to Formula 1 in 2004.

Above centre: Another famous name. Nico Rosberg took a win in his Dallara-Opel.

Left: Ryan Briscoe was the Euroseries Champion.
All photographs: Glenn Dunbar/LAT Photographic

DRAWING THE LINE

By GARY WATKINS

The Number 7 Bentley driven by Tom Kristensen,
Rinaldo Capello and Guy Smith took the top place
on the podium.
Photograph: Mike Weston/LAT Photographic

THREE or four years before the 2003 Le Mans 24 Hours, you'd have been laughed out of town if you'd suggested that one day Bentley would return to Le Mans and win the world's biggest sports car race for a sixth time. Three or four months before the race, no one would have believed that one of the historic marque's pair of British Racing Green coupés would win. At least, not within the organisation running the cars at La Sarthe.

Bentley may have pitched up at Le Mans as pre-event favourite, and the manufacturer's PR machine may have suggested that endurance testing in the run-up to the race had been a success. Privately, however, those most deeply involved in the design and development of the Speed 8 weren't hopeful. They knew their baby would be the fastest thing on the track, but they weren't so sure about its ability to go the distance without the minor reliability niggles that can prevent a car from winning the event in the modern era.

However, Bentley did win Le Mans, and what's more it claimed the runner-up spot as well. The winning car ran through the 24 hours without a single glitch, and no one could quite believe it within the Team Bentley camp.

True, there had been problems, but only with the second-placed car. The winning Bentley, driven by Tom Kristensen, Rinaldo Capello and Guy Smith, lost only 12 seconds in the pits when the rear body had to be removed so that the water system could be bled. It was an amazing run that put even Audi's domination of the previous three Le Mans races in the shade.

Forget the cynics who suggested that this had been an empty win. It is true that there was no opposition able to take the fight to the British cars, yet the manner of Bentley's victory made it special and at least as worthy of merit as any of sister marque Audi's hat trick of wins.

Had Bentley been required to overcome the Audi factory squad to win the race, almost certainly those cynics would have taken a different view. The absence of the German manufacturer's own team, Joest Racing, was deliberate. As was its policy not to develop the four-year-old R8 prototype or the 3.6-litre version of the same twin-turbo V8 that powered the Speed 8. Volkswagen-Audi group politics dictated that this was the season – the third in a three-year programme – that the green cars would be victorious.

There was never any suggestion that the three customer teams running 2002-spec R8s would be asked to move aside to facilitate a Bentley victory. In reality, they were just too slow to challenge. Predictions that the Audi's lower thirst for fuel and tyres might prove decisive ended up being wide of the mark.

This was Bentley's race from the outset, and it remained just that – a race. The British cars may have had things all their own way, but there was no sign of any team orders, even in the closing stages, as the two evenly matched crews were allowed to fight it out almost to the end.

It was also a battle that was won, not out on the track, but back in the pits.

Whereas the Bentley driven by Kristensen, Capello and Smith ran straight through the 24-hour period, Johnny Herbert, David Brabham and Mark Blundell in the second car endured a run of small problems that never quite allowed them to get to grips with their team-mates.

Herbert, who had qualified second to Kristensen, overtook the Dane twice in the opening two hours, but each time his car spent longer at rest in the pits. Brabham took over at the second stop, then had to return to the pits two laps into his stint when the headrest on the door worked loose and started to swing about disconcertingly in the cockpit. The car was stationary for a matter of seconds, but when he returned to the track, he was nearly three-quarters of a minute behind Capello. The race was barely two hours old, and the winning Bentley would never be headed again.

The gap grew to almost two minutes in the fourth hour, when Blundell lost ground through no fault of his own during a safety-car period. With little to choose between the two driving squads, Blundell and his team-mates were never quite able to get back on terms, more so after a flat battery at 5.00 am delayed them again. Five minutes were lost, allowing the leading car to open the gap to more than a lap. That advantage doubled four hours later, when the number-eight car required a second change of driver.

Herbert, Brabham and Blundell never gave up the chase, but they knew they were relying on the leaders to hit problems of their own. 'Twenty-four hours may be a long time, but you can't afford

to drop any time here,' said Blundell. 'Not when you are up against such a good group of drivers. We had the pace, but we also had the niggly problems.'

The winning margin at the end was two laps. A further three laps separated the second-place car from the 'best of the rest', Champion Racing's customer Audi. The US-entered car, driven by JJ Lehto, Emanuele Pirro and Stefan Johansson, also needed two new batteries and lost time with a brace of punctures. Apart from these minor delays, it ran without fault.

The other two customer Audis weren't so lucky. The Japanese Goh squad's car was often the fastest of the R8s, but two long stops for repairs – caused when Marco Werner crashed during the night – left the German driver and team-mates Jan Magnussen and Seiji Ara a distant fourth. The Audi Sport UK car didn't even make the finish. Frank Biela, winner of the previous three races at Le Mans, missed the pit entry when he was due to stop for fuel in the second hour and ground to a halt two-thirds of the way around the lap. The British Audi's race was run.

Panoz claimed a surprise fifth spot with one of its ageing, front-engined LMP-01 Evos driven by Olivier Beretta, Gunnar Jeanette and Max Papis. Jan Lammers' Racing for Holland team had looked secure in that position for the first two-thirds of the race, but a puncture and then an electrical problem dropped the Judd-engined Dome S101, co-driven by Andy Wallace and John Bosch, to eighth. The squad fought back and was able to claim sixth on the final lap from the Courage-Judd driven by Jean-Marc Gounon, Jonathan Cochet and Stephan Gregoire.

Audi may not have been a force in the 24 Hours, but the R8 was still the car to have in the American Le Mans Series, which remained the world's premier sports car championship in 2003. The title chase came down to a straight fight between the two teams running the German car full-time in the US: Joest Racing – winner of the previous three ALMS titles, but now without factory backing – and Champion.

For once, Joest didn't have things all its own way. Champion, a true Audi customer squad, was a contender right through the season, with Lehto and Herbert driving. The team broke its victory duck at Road Atlanta in June and went on to claim three more wins, but that wasn't quite enough to stop Biela and Marco Werner from giving Joest a fourth straight ALMS title.

There was another contender in the ALMS in 2003, and it wasn't Panoz as in previous years. The American marque had down-sized its assault, which left the way open for the Dyson Racing squad of Lola-MGs to carry the fight to Audi. One of the most successful teams in US racing, Dyson had developed the fragile LMP675 'baby' prototype into a real contender and was unlucky to win only one of the nine rounds.

The FIA GT Championship took another step forward following its relaunch in 2000, although a new level of competitiveness wasn't reflected in the results. The lead pairing at the Scuderia Italia Ferrari squad, Thomas Biagi and Matteo Bobbi, won the first five races on the trot, although one of those was inherited after the disqualification of the winning car. Not surprisingly, they went on to take the title, despite claiming only one more victory

Biagi and Bobbi were worthy champions. They were arguably the best pairing in the championship's top category; the Scuderia Italia team was probably the best in the series; and their Prodrive-built 550 Maranello was most definitely the best car, although not necessarily always the fastest. Scuderia Italia drivers filled out the next four spots in the championship.

Fabrizio Gollin and Luca Cappellari scored one victory and were genuine front-runners, while Enzo Calderari and Lilian Bryner owed their championship positions to consistency.

The FIA Sports Car Championship limped through what soon became obvious was its final season. What had started life as the International Sports Racing Series back in 1998 attracted grids that often failed to break into double figures. Lammers claimed a second FIA crown with Racing for Holland, this time sharing the lead entry with Bosch.

Even Lammers reckoned that the title didn't mean so much. That's no surprise given that the Dutchman had helped Jaguar to its comeback Le Mans victory in 1988. The Coventry marque had hung around in sports car racing to win the 24 Hours again. Bentley, however, never had any plans to return after 2003. Such a stunning Le Mans victory allowed it to draw the line under an all too short revival.

Left: JJ Lehto driving the US-entered Champion Racing Audi. Sharing the driving duties in the third-placed car were Stefan Johansson and Emanuele Pirro.
Photograph: Glenn Dunbar/LAT Photographic

Below; far left: Le Mans perennial Henri Pescarolo in charge of the Courage Team.
Photograph: Jeff Bloxham/LAT Photographic

Below, centre left: The fifth-placed Panoz driven by Olivier Beretta, Gunnar Jeanette and Max Papis.
Photograph: Mike Weston/LAT Photographic

Below left: Exhaustion sets in during the night for this trio of mechanics in the Corvette pit.
Photograph: Glenn Dunbar/LAT Photographic

Below: Scuderia Italia's Ferrari, driven by Matteo Bobbi and Thomas Biagi, took the FIA GT Championship.
Photograph: J Atley/LAT Photographic

Bottom left: Pit stop for the second-placed Bentley of Johnny Herbert, Mark Blundell and Geoff Brabham.
Photograph: Mike Weston/LAT Photographic

Bottom right: Frank Biela heads the field in the Joest Audi at the start of the ALMS race at Laguna Seca.
Photograph: Richard Dole/LAT Photographic

TOURING CARS REVIEW
A FINE VINTAGE
By CHARLES BRADLEY

Above: Yvan Muller's Vauxhall Astra leads the BTCC pack through the first turn at Rockingham.
Photograph: Malcolm Griffiths/LAT Photographic

A HEADY mixture of hectic on-track action combined with some interesting behind-the-scenes developments made 2003 a memorable season for touring cars across Europe. Yvan Muller finally nailed the British championship after six years of trying, Bernd Schneider won the DTM for a record fourth time, and the European title went down to the wire in a fascinating BMW-versus-Alfa Romeo tussle.

For Muller, his fifth year with the Triple Eight Racing Engineering works Vauxhall outfit produced a long awaited title after two years as runner-up to his respective team-mates, Jason Plato and James Thompson. The latter was his closest rival once again, but despite six pole positions, Thompson wasn't quite able to match the Frenchman in the races. He was beaten six-to-four when it really mattered. Perhaps the key to Muller's success was that he dealt with the all-important ballast of success more effectively than his team-mate.

Muller came close to throwing it away, however, when he reacted angrily to a collision with MG's Anthony Reid during the penultimate round at Brands Hatch. Yvan grabbed the Scot in *parc fermé* after the race and shoved him over the bonnet of another car. He was fortunate to get away with an 11-day licence ban for the assault, which meant that he missed the free practice session at the Donington finale. Even worse was to come, as an electrical problem in qualifying put him in last place on the grid for the first Donington race, but then he charged up to third, which was enough to seal the title.

Once again, Vauxhall had a relatively easy run through the season, thanks to its rivals' inability to mount a sustained challenge. Arena's Honda Racing squad was by far the best of the rest, and lead driver Matt Neal won six times – just as many as the champion. But he was let down by a series of niggling mechanical problems and was over 50 points shy of the runner-up spot in third place.

The third works Vauxhall of fan favourite Paul O'Neill was fourth in the championship, the affable scouser taking his now customary solitary race win, this time at Snetterton. That was one more than Honda's Alan Morrison managed, although the consistent Ulsterman did bag a place in the top five overall.

But what of MG? Its drivers – Anthony Reid, Warren Hughes and Colin Turkington – won a race each, but the car's weighty V6 powerplant caused more front-tyre wear than its opponents, and a string of early engine problems also blunted its challenge.

MG fared much better than Proton, though, whose programme was blighted by mechanical woes, the catalyst of which was a lack of pre-season testing due to major personnel changes. Things

were so bad that both David Leslie, a former series runner-up no less, and Phil Bennett were soundly outscored by Independents' champion Robert Collard in his family-run Vauxhall Astra.

Another disappointment was the lack of pace from the privately entered Peugeot 307s of Vic Lee Racing. Penned by former F1 designer Sergio Rinland, once again a lack of testing hampered the car's development when, on paper, it should have been a serious challenger.

In the Production class, Luke Hines beat Barwell Motorsport Honda Accord team-mate Alan Blencowe, while Michael Bentwood's challenge in an Edenbridge BMW was dented by a couple of big crashes, the most notable on the banking at Rockingham.

Off the track, touring car racing received a major boost when former series boss Alan Gow returned to his role. The man who guided the championship through its mid-'90s heyday has been charged with making it great once again, and he has already had a big influence by decreeing a new three-races-per-weekend format for 2004.

Another major change will be the integration of the ETCC Super 2000-specification cars into the series. This is part of a larger effort to incorporate the FIA's regulations into the various national championships, much like it managed to achieve with its previous Super Touring rulebook. As well as the ETCC and BTCC, Super 2000 machinery will appear in Denmark, Germany (in the DTC), Italy and Sweden next year.

With its rules now firmly established, the European Touring Car Championship became a straight fight between heavyweights Alfa Romeo and BMW. Their duel went down to the wire, with Alfa's Gabriele Tarquini, who replaced its multiple champion Fabrizio Giovanardi in 2003, tied on points with BMW's Jörg Müller.

Tarquini appeared to have blown his chances after three non-scores on the trot at Spa-Francorchamps and Anderstorp, but he rallied at Oschersleben and then dominated at Estoril to set up the tense season finale at Monza. Another highlight of the final round would be the racing return of former CART champion Alex Zanardi, who had lost both legs in a crash at Eurospeedway Lausitz in 2001.

Back in the title race, the honour of second-best Alfa and BMW was fought out by Nicola Larini and Britain's Andy Priaulx respectively. The latter was a revelation after switching from the Honda BTCC team to Bart Mampaey's RBM squad, taking race wins at Brno, Spa and Oschersleben in his rookie ETCC season.

It was a disappointing season for the third-string drivers, however, as both Dirk Müller (BMW) and Roberto Colciago (Alfa) didn't match their speed with a high level of consistency. Giovanardi's switch to BMW didn't go as planned either. After a runner-up spot in the Barcelona opener, only the Brno weekend came close to repeating that form in his 320I run by fellow former-ETCC champ Roberto Ravaglia.

Suffering an even worse year was ex-BTCC champion Rickard Rydell, whose loyalty to Volvo was stretched 12 months too far when he raced an S60 for the privateer ART Engineering squad. Somehow, he managed to drag the car to a podium place at Donington Park and Anderstorp, but that was nothing short of a miracle.

It was also a testing first season in the ETCC for SEAT, who entered a pair of its pretty Toledos for Jordi Gene (older brother of Williams F1 tester Mark) and German single-seater convert Frank Diefenbacher. Its main problem was an ineffective rear axle, which took time to rectify, as one of its rivals balked its attempts to claim dispensation to run a new component.

Once that hurdle had been overcome, Diefenbacher claimed a podium finish on home ground of Oschersleben. The marque also drafted in BTCC winner Yvan Muller for the Estoril race weekend, sparking rumours that a full-time drive might come his way for 2004.

In Germany, the DTM enjoyed another successful season, despite the lack of further manufacturer interest beyond stalwarts Audi, Opel and Mercedes-Benz. After its surprise title success of 2002, the Abt Sportsline Audi team suffered a backlash from the AMG Mercedes squad this time around. As ever, Bernd Schneider led the Three-pointed Star's charge, but there was another shock in store as Christijan Albers, a last-minute replacement for Uwe Alzen, blended into the AMG set-up seamlessly and gave the 'Schneidermeister' a run for his money.

After Bernd won the season-opener at Hockenheim, Albers struck back in the next two at Adria (the DTM's first trip to Italy since its rebirth in 2000) and the Nürburgring. Schneider reasserted his authority at Eurospeedway Lausitz, where Albers was uncharacteristically lacklustre, but Christijan came back with a splendid win at the DTM's 'jewel-in-the-crown' event at the Norisring in front of 120,000 fans.

Then the title chasers were forced to take a back seat as star turn Jean Alesi repeated his 2002 win for Mercedes at Donington Park, before last year's champion, Laurent Aiello, proved that the Abt Audi TT-R is still a force to be reckoned with around the Nürburgring. That meeting featured night-time qualifying and a world championship boxing bout in the paddock afterward, one of many innovations that gave the spectators more bang for their bucks. No wonder attendances and TV viewing figures were up this year.

Albers's hugely popular home win at Zandvoort set up a thrilling title finale at Hockenheim, where he needed to finish one place ahead of the more consistent Schneider to take the title. Despite a poor qualifying performance, Christijan was quick in the race and was right on Schneider's tail after Bernd suffered a puncture – fortunately in the Motordrome section near the pits.

Just as he looked set to make his move, Albers also had a left rear tyre blow out, which almost sent him straight into the back of his title nemesis. The Dutchman was forced to limp half a lap back to the pits, and his title shot was gone. Later, Schneider was moved to admit, 'The racing gods smiled on me.'

For Albers, the runner-up spot was much more than ever he could have dreamed of before the start of the season. He had appeared set to race a year-old Mercedes until Alzen's sudden departure – because he didn't take kindly to being paired with Schneider. Christijan proved that you can take the fight to Bernd from within, despite his almost family-like ties with the prime movers at AMG.

Marcel Fässler enjoyed a much more consistent season than in previous years and went one better than his usual habit of finishing fourth in the championship in his AMG Mercedes. Only one victory, at the A1-Ring, came his way, however, but he scored it in fine style ahead of Schneider, who exerted all the pressure in the world on the Swiss driver. The fourth AMG Merc, that of Alesi, was only fifth in the points, but at least the crowd favourite won the final race at Hockenheim and extended his contract for another two years.

Despite his Nürburgring victory and a raft of podium finishes early on, Aiello was outshone at Audi by young Swede Mattias Ekström, who scored a couple of runner-up finishes after storming drives at Adria and Hockenheim. Abt's big problem was that the TT-R's rear wing was effectively clipped over the winter, and its efforts to claw back downforce cost it dear in a straight line. Once again, support from Audi was limited to back-door help, although

it received extra assistance in the second half of the season after a lacklustre display in front of a huge number of corporate guests at the Norisring.

The under-achiever of the series in recent years, Opel, almost got back to winning ways in 2003, but fell short once again. Its best move was signing Peter Dumbreck, whom Mercedes had allowed to slip into its year-old car ranks. The Scot drove his Astra Coupé as if his life depended on it, scoring points in the first six races, including a runner-up spot at Lausitz. Three disastrous races followed, but a front-row start and fourth place in the season finale at Hockenheim ensured that he scored more points than his five Opel colleagues combined.

That statistic is harsh, given the calibre of former BTCC champion Alain Menu and ITC victor Manuel Reuter. Tough, too, on Timo Scheider, who had a Zandvoort race win virtually in his pocket until the team failed to attach one of his wheels in the final pit stop… The fact that Dumbreck, Scheider, Menu and Reuter filled out the top ten showed that at least Opel is heading in the right direction.

Mention must be made of the impressive showing by young Briton Gary Paffett, who took Albers's place in Keke Rosberg's year-old Mercedes squad. Despite a complete lack of experience in touring cars and left-hand drive (he also missed the first two races), Gary simply wrung the car's neck and even finished in the top six at the A1-Ring.

Next year, the DTM will adopt four-door cars for the first time, which will run alongside its existing coupés. It's a facelift that should rejuvenate interest in the Continent's fastest touring car series and could attract that all-important fourth manufacturer to take it to another level. With the multifarious two-litre series putting their house in order, and the DTM looking more attractive than ever, these are exciting times for tin-top racing.

Top right: Gabriele Tarquini took the ETC for Alfa by virtue of winning more races than the BMW of Jörg Müller (above centre).
Photographs: Peter Spinney and J Atley/LAT Photographic

Above: Christian Albers took the battle with his team-mate for the DTM championship to the wire.
Photograph: Malcolm Griffiths/LAT Photographic

Left: Mercedes favourite son Bernd Schneider finally emerged as the champion, but it had been a close call.
Photograph: John Tingle/LAT Photographic

THE BIGGEST SHOW IN TOWN

By GORDON KIRBY

A S ever, NASCAR dominated the headlines and airwaves across America in 2003. There were stories aplenty, including a string of much-publicised on- and off-track confrontations between Kurt Busch and Jimmy Spencer, and Kevin Harvick and Ricky Rudd. Truly, it was a case of young bloods against old bucks, complete with pushing, shoving and name-calling, and penalties from NASCAR. Vintage stock car racing, in fact.

There was also the usual stream of different winners. Sixteen drivers won races in 2003 (the record is 19 winners from 2001), including newcomers like Busch, Harvick, Jimmie Johnson and Penske's stock car superstar, Ryan Newman, who won twice as many races (8) as anyone else. And there was also a quiet, self-effacing new champion in Matt Kenseth, 'Mr Consistency', a 31-year-old from Wisconsin in the upper Midwest. In his fourth full Winston Cup season, Kenseth won only one of the 36 races, but he was a dogged top-ten finisher, controlling the points battle for most of the year. Clearly, the latest youth revolution has overtaken NASCAR, with the old guard like Rusty Wallace, Bill Elliott, Mark Martin, Ricky Rudd and Dale Jarrett relegated to bit-player roles.

Off track, there was just as much news and even more intrigue. Long-time series sponsor (since 1971) Winston confirmed that it was pulling out, to be replaced in 2004 by mobile-phone giant Nextel. The R.J. Reynolds cigarette brand had been a bastion of NASCAR's growth over the previous three decades, spending like only a cigarette company could on advertising, marketing and prize money, and contributing in a major way to the grass-roots growth of NASCAR's extensive farm system. Nextel strikes a whole new image for NASCAR, and it will be interesting to see how the rebranded Nextel Cup evolves over the next few years.

This is particularly true in light of the momentous change announced in September that Bill France Jnr was stepping down as NASCAR's chairman and handing over the reins to his 41-year-old son, Brian. Bill Jnr's father, Bill Snr, founded NASCAR in 1949, built the Daytona International Speedway – which opened in 1959 – and developed the stock car organising body into the United States' most respected racing group. Bill Jnr took over the running of NASCAR in 1972, and the son proved every bit the equal of his father, ruling with an iron fist and a street-smart, business-savvy mind.

Bill Jnr propelled NASCAR to unimagined heights, transforming the Winston Cup series from a largely regional, south-eastern championship into a truly national series, and presiding over stock car racing's historic overtaking of Indy or Champ car racing as America's most important form of motor sport. In recent years, in fact, NASCAR has broken into the mainstream like never before, aided by a six-year, $2.4-billion TV deal with NBC and Fox, which has helped the series become the fastest growing sport in America today.

Like his father and grandfather before him, Brian France grew up in racing, working for NASCAR around the country in various capacities during the past 20 years. But unlike his father, Brian has never been a regular face in the garage area. He has attended fewer than half the races, although he says that will change now that he's been elevated to NASCAR's top job. His strong suit is considered to be marketing and business development rather than the rough and tumble politics of running a racing series.

Those things are left to Mike Helton, who took over as NASCAR's president at the end of 2000, becoming the first person outside the France family to take a powerful executive role with the organisation. It is Helton who runs the races and enforces the rules. Bill Jnr's brother, Jim, and daughter, Lesa France Kennedy, comprise the board of directors with Bill Jnr, Brian and Helton. Another important player is senior vice president George Pyne, a marketing man who runs many of NASCAR's business affairs.

With people like Helton and Pyne behind him, Brian France should be well served as he steps into his father's substantial shoes. 'My father is just down the hallway with all his experience I can draw on,' said the younger France. 'He was so successful and is so experienced. I'm more of a consensus builder. We're very different personalities. I view him more as a legend. He pioneered things. There is no way for me to walk in his footsteps.'

For better or worse, there's no doubt that NASCAR's 21st-century style will be very different to the tough, old dictatorial ways of founder 'Big Bill' and his equally powerful son, Bill Jnr.

On the track, the big star of our times is Dale Earnhardt Jnr, 29-year-old son of the late Dale Snr, the seven-times NASCAR champion who was killed on the last lap of the 2001 Daytona 500. Dale Jnr was starting his second full Winston Cup season when his father died and has accepted the legendary driver's mantle with

Facing page, top: Matt Kenseth heads a pack of cars in his Ford. Consistency was the key to his successful title bid.

Facing page, bottom: A new breed of young guns are making their names in NASCAR. From left to right: Kevin Harvick, Matt Kenseth, Ryan Newman and Jimmy Johnson.

Below left: Dale Earnhardt Jr remains a massive favourite with the fans.

Below: Kurt Busch emerged as a top-ten runner.

Below centre: NASCAR fans in the Pocono infield show their allegience.

Bottom: Jeff Gordon was still a winner, but found it tough to regain his crown.
Photographs: LAT Photographic

style and bravado. He's become a regular race winner and front-runner, and was in contention for the 2003 championship through most of the year, eventually finishing second in points.

Earnhardt Jr drives a Chevrolet for the three-car family team, DEI (Dale Earnhardt Incorporated) Racing, and his car number 8 is just as popular as his late father's retired number 3. In every corner of the United States, you will see all manner of vehicles proudly displaying stickers bearing those numbers. The big test for Junior lays ahead as he tries to become a champion, like his father, no small task among today's deeply competitive field.

Four-times champion Jeff Gordon is the most accomplished active NASCAR driver, but in the popularity and celebrity stakes he's overshadowed by Dale Jr and seriously threatened by the rest of the new generation – Newman at Penske, Harvick at Richard Childress Racing, Johnson with Rick Hendrick, and Busch and Kenseth with Jack Roush's five-car operation. In his 11th Winston Cup season, all with Rick Hendrick's Chevrolet team, Gordon struggled to regain his glory years of 1995–99, but was able to win only one race and finished fourth in the championship.

Harvick replaced Earnhardt Sr after his death, and has been fast and fiery from the start. Stepping into Childress's number-one car was a big opportunity, but also carried lots of pressure and scrutiny. Many of Earnhardt Sr's fans just couldn't warm to Californian Harvick, who had a tough 2002 season, winning just once and finishing 21st in points. But he showed his stuff in 2003, charging from 11th in points at mid-season to occupy second for a while until eventually ending up sixth.

Most prolific winner of the year was Ryan Newman, who had joined Roger Penske's NASCAR team in 2001 on a part-time basis. He had risen through USAC midgets and sprint cars, switching to stock cars in 1999 and graduating from engineering school in 2001. He scored his first Winston Cup win in 2002 and narrowly beat Jimmie Johnson to Rookie of the Year. In 2003, Indiana native Newman started to come into his own, winning eight races while veteran team leader Rusty Wallace failed to win any for the second year in a row. The newcomer clearly overshadowed his boss, but Newman had too many crashes and other DNFs to muster a championship challenge, eventually taking fifth in points.

Like Harvick, Jimmie Johnson is from California and is Jeff Gordon's protégé. His Hendrick Chevrolet team is co-owned by Gordon, in fact, and Johnson was in the thick of the battle in most races in 2003. He won three, and topped Newman and mentor Gordon by finishing third in points.

Another multiple winner in 2003 was Kurt Busch, a 25-year-old from Las Vegas in his third full Winston Cup season with Jack Roush's team. Busch won four races, and became famous for his aggressive driving style and sharp tongue following a series of incidents with crowd favourite Jimmy Spencer.

Out of luck in 2003 was 2002 champion Tony Stewart, who had too many DNFs to mount a serious defence of his title. He won just once and finished seventh in points after signing a new five-year contract with team owner Joe Gibbs, although he had considered a lucrative offer from Chip Ganassi's team beforehand.

In the final quarter of the year, there was also a debate over the points system, as Kenseth had dominated the championship despite winning only one race. Many pundits suddenly decided that the system favoured consistency too much over winning, a fact that has long been obvious and trumpeted by NASCAR. In fact, Kenseth collected more points than some previous NASCAR champions, including 2002 winner Stewart, who actually scored a record low number of points per start. Although Brian France has said that he expects to refine the points system, no major changes are expected.

A more challenging prospect for NASCAR's new boss will be Toyota's arrival in stock car racing. It will be interesting to see if France can keep Toyota from outspending its American rivals. The Japanese manufacturing giant is the world's most successful car maker and has been expanding rapidly in the United States for many years. It has seven manufacturing plants in America and will start racing in NASCAR's entry-level Craftsman Truck series in 2004. Toyota's pick-up trucks are built in the USA, and Toyota will promote the 'made-in-America' label as they warm up for an expected move into the Nextel Cup series in 2007.

Toyota has been resoundingly successful in American racing, first in IMSA, then in CART and now IRL, as well as making a quick start in F1. The Japanese company has unmatched financial and engineering resources, and is sure to change the balance of power in NASCAR. Will the beleaguered American manufacturers – all of them struggling to contend with Toyota in both global and domestic markets – have the wherewithal and commitment to respond to the challenge?

The Civil War – Year Eight

While NASCAR has become part of America's popular culture, with all the top stock car stars household names, open-wheel and sports car racing, both weakened by internal disagreements and competing series, have struggled to pick up the crumbs. Eight years ago, few people could have imagined how much damage the CART/IRL split would wreak on Indy or Champ car racing, but as we've documented in recent editions of *AUTOCOURSE*, the situation has hardly improved as the two categories battle to establish their own individual identities.

These days, the national media largely ignore both CART and IRL. Sad to say, but open-wheel racing now takes second billing to NASCAR.

CART survives because of its street and road races, as well as its three successful events in Canada (Toronto, Vancouver and, most recently, Montreal), two rounds in Mexico (Monterrey, near the Texas border, and the refurbished F1 circuit in Mexico City) and, of course, the well-established and very popular Surfers Paradise street race on Australia's Gold Coast. In 2003, Mexico City drew a record CART race-day crowd of 221,911, while the three-day gate of 402,403 was also a CART record.

The IRL holds the Indianapolis 500 as its 'Ace of Spades', although the month-long attendance and TV ratings are not what they once were. A handful of other IRL races – Texas most notably – are popular, too, but most draw poor crowds and, like CART events, receive little serious coverage by other than the local and enthusiast media.

Where will it go from here? Indy boss and IRL founder Tony George has spent $300 million on the IRL so far, paying the prize money for all the races, underwriting teams, large and small, and paying some driver salaries, too. Responding in kind, amid a failing marketplace, CART was compelled last year to spend some $40 million underwriting its own teams and races as socialism was introduced to this most capitalistic, sponsor-driven of sports.

The IRL benefited in 2003 from Toyota and Honda's switch from CART following the disputes over engine rules and pop-off valves in 2001. The two Japanese rivals took with them to the IRL a trio of top CART teams – Chip Ganassi, Mo Nunn and Andretti-Green – giving the series a substantial boost at CART's expense. There was a down-side to this, however. Some of the smaller teams that had formed the backbone of the original IRL have begun to struggle in the face of the arrival of the CART teams and big-budget engine manufacturers.

In his Toyota-powered team's first full year in the IRL, Chip Ganassi was able to add the championship to his four CART titles from 1996–99. After a relatively slow start to the year, his number-one driver, Scott Dixon, became the man to beat. The taciturn 23-year-old Antipodean ultimately eked out the championship by finishing second in the season-closer amid a five-way points battle with Helio Castroneves, Gil de Ferran, Tony Kanaan and Sam Hornish. Dixon won three races and took five more podiums on the way to winning the IRL title.

De Ferran won the Indy 500, beating team-mate and 2001/2002 winner Castroneves in a Penske 1-2. It was Penske's 12th win at Indy, as well as his third in a row and the team's first 1-2 sweep. Quite an achievement. Before the end of the season, de Ferran decided to retire. He had been badly bruised and beaten about in a series of oval-track accidents in recent years, in both CART and IRL, and sensibly decided that, at 35, with two CART titles and an Indy 500 win in his pocket, the time had come to quit. The popular Brazilian went out on a high, winning his last race at Texas.

Replacing de Ferran at Penske, alongside Castroneves, was Sam Hornish, who had won the 2001 and 2002 IRL titles driving for the Chevy-powered Panther team. He challenged again in the closing stages of 2003. Hornish had appeared to be a non-contender during the first half of the season, his Chevrolet engine soundly dominated by Toyota and Honda. Then came the 'Gen IV' Chevrolet, which was, in fact, a Cosworth! The engine manufacturer had designed and developed an IRL engine, but with Ford committed to CART, a decision had been taken to sell the programme to arch-rival Chevrolet. The engine was competitive right off the bat, and Hornish was able to win three races with it and fight for the championship until a late-race engine failure in the season-closer.

Also retiring in 2003 was Michael Andretti, who had become a team owner at the end of 2002, having bought a controlling interest in former CART outfit Andretti-Green Racing. The 40-year-old Andretti reckoned he could not drive and run a team at the same time, so decided to retire after the Indy 500 in May. Although he

Top: The consistent Scott Dixon emerged as the IRL champion.

Above: Two-time IRL champion Sam Hornish, who was only able to show his talent late in the year after his Panther Team gained a competitive engine package.

Right: Huge crowds rolled up for the IRL race held in Kansas.

Photographs: Phil Abbott/LAT Photographic

Overleaf: The excitement of a mass pit stop at the Indianapolis 500. To the left, Al Unser Jr, Scott Sharp and Tony Kanaan head out down the pit road, while on the right, Dan Wheldon and Kenny Bräck leave their pit boxes.

Left: Gil de Ferran leads team-mate Helio Castroneves to a Penske 1-2 at the famed Indianapolis 500.
Photographs: Phil Abbott/LAT Photographic

Below: Tony Renna, just signed to Chip Ganassi Racing, was tragically killed in testing at Indianapolis in October.
Photograph: Greg Bauders/LAT Photographic

had led many laps at Indy, Michael was never able to win the 500. In the last start of his career, he charged to the front and led for a while before pulling into the pits with a broken throttle linkage, which ended his race.

A fact that cannot be avoided is that the IRL is more dangerous than CART in terms of frequency of accidents and severity of injuries. Seventy-six IRL drivers have been hospitalised with serious injuries over eight years, while 32 CART drivers have been seriously injured over 25 years. Being a restrictor-plate, Indy Lights-style formula, IRL races are close, thanks to the lack of horsepower versus downforce, but running in close packs can lead to accidents, like the spectacular crash Kenny Bräck was fortunate to survive in the closing laps of the IRL's last race of the year at the notorious Texas Motor Speedway. Such accidents raise questions about racing open-wheel cars on high-banked ovals, questions the IRL is trying to address with technical developments to improve safety. However, some argue that it is a form of racing whose time may have passed.

Tracy is The Man

On the CART side, Chris Pook pedalled hard to keep the weakened team owners group afloat. Long Beach founder Pook had taken charge of CART at the end of 2001 following Joe Heitzler's disastrous tenure. After it became clear in the spring of 2002 that Toyota and Honda were off to the IRL in 2003, Pook reversed a decision for CART to adopt IRL-like engine rules. Instead, he worked out a deal with Ford and Cosworth to retain the existing turbo V8 engine formula for 2003 and 2004, with Cosworth supplying the entire field with a 'spec' version of its successful 2.65-litre XF turbo V8 fitted with a 12,500-rpm rev limiter (down from 16,000+ rpm in unrestricted form) and built to last 1,200 miles.

The new high-mileage engine formula proved a godsend, Cosworth producing a couple of hundred remarkably reliable and equally-matched engines. A great by-product of having a single-engine formula meant that the dreaded traction control was eliminated, making the cars very difficult to drive, but at the same time exciting to watch.

With the spec Cosworth formula and a multi-million-dollar Entrant Support Programme, Pook was able to muster a field of 19 cars, just enough to stay in business, because most contracts with TV, sponsors and race promoters required a minimum of 18 cars. The year was dominated by Paul Tracy, who had become a CART stalwart, refusing to move to the IRL with Andretti-Green and joining Jerry Forsythe's Player's team. Tracy started the season with three wins in a row, and despite a few mistakes and crashes at Elkhart Lake and Miami, he was the man to beat all year. In the

end, he won seven of 18 races and took the CART title for the first time after 13 years of trying.

Tracy's biggest competition came from Bruno Junqueira, who had taken over 2002 champion Cristiano da Matta's seat at Newman/Haas. Junqueira kept the pressure on Tracy for most of the year, but was never the equal of the Canadian veteran. His Newman/Haas team-mate, Sébastien Bourdais, was a runaway winner of CART's Rookie of the Year award, taking the chequered flag in three races and finishing fourth in the championship.

Other race winners included Michel Jourdain Jr, Patrick Carpentier, Adrian Fernandez and Mario Dominguez. Jourdain Jr finally scored the first victory of his career at Milwaukee in June, then won again at Montreal in August, and for a while he was a championship challenger to Tracy and Junqueira. Carpentier, Fernandez and Dominguez each won a race apiece, but weren't consistently quick, although Dominguez began to emerge more and more as a serious front-runner.

Some insiders believed that CART boss Chris Pook had convinced Bernie Ecclestone to buy the beleaguered sanctioning body, and that he would use the Champ car formula as a North American promotional adjunct and/or 'feeder series' for F1. Yet others thought that Tony George would buy out CART. George's strategy, it was believed, would be to fold CART's best road and street races into the all-oval IRL series and euthanise the remaining races.

The true picture began to emerge in August, when a small group of Champ car team owners, led by Jerry Forsythe, made a bid to buy all outstanding shares in the company for 50 cents per share. At the time of the offer, CART's share price had dwindled to around $1.50 after the company had lost $43.5 million in the first half of 2003 because it had to spend to keep its teams in business, buy television time and subsidise many of its races.

Forsythe's team has been one of CART's top squads during the last ten years, and he became CART's largest shareholder with 22.9 per cent of the company's common stock. His primary business is Indeck Power, a global supplier of portable powerplants, and his partners in the holding company called Open Wheel Racing Series, which made the late-August bid to buy CART, were fellow team owners Paul Gentilozzi and Kevin Kalkhoven. Gentilozzi is a multiple TransAm champion and owner of the TransAm series; also, he is a property developer in central Michigan. Kalkhoven made his fortune in Silicon Valley and is worth $1.8 billion; he is Craig Pollock's partner in the PK Racing Champ car team.

'I'm willing to spend money to make CART a viable sanctioning body for the future,' Forsythe said. 'I'm very optimistic and confident. I've been very, very positive on CART for the past several years. There isn't anybody who has been more positive on CART than me. I want to see it survive. I want to see it succeed.'

Threats of shareholder suits continued into the autumn, when

Top: Bryan Herta, substituting for the injured Dario Franchitti, came up trumps for his recently retired team boss Michael Andretti by winning in Kansas.
Photograph: Walt Kuhn/LAT Photographic

Top left: Sébastien Bourdais was Rookie of the Year in CART Champ Car.
Photograph: Mike Levitt/LAT Photographic

Above: Bourdais's Newman/Haas team-mate, Bruno Junqueira, was Tracy's nearest title challenger.

Right: Driving for Bobby Rahal, Michel Jourdain Jr took a popular first win during the season.
Photographs: Phil Abbott/LAT Photographic

Facing page: Loyalty rewarded. Paul Tracy stayed with Champ Car and deservedly took the championship crown.
Photograph: Gavin Lawrence/LAT Photographic

Above: Briton Mark Taylor dominated the IRL Infiniti Pro series and was rewarded with a seat at Panther in the IRL for 2004.

Above right: AJ Allmendinger was the class of the Toyota/Atlantic Championship.
Photographs: LAT Photographic

Below: Mexico proved to be a big draw for the Champ cars. Huge crowds turned up at Monterrey to support local heroes such as Mario Dominguez.
Photograph: Gavin Lawrence/LAT Photographic

Forsythe, Gentilozzi and Kalkhoven presented their buy-out proposal to the US government's Securities and Exchange Commission. Approval was expected to take a month or two, meaning late November or December. Assuming the deal goes through, CART's new owners plan to privatise the company swiftly and get on with the business of running a racing series rather than appealing to shareholder interests.

Former F1 and Indy driver, and current CART TV commentator, Derek Daly is optimistic about CART's future. 'The new owner group are very bright, very successful businessmen,' he said. 'From conversations I've had with each of them, I'm beginning to buy into the belief that CART has a stronger future than it's ever had.'

'There was a racer's mentality that drove CART,' he added. 'Despite the fact that they will tell you they made business decisions, I don't think the owners ever made business decisions. They made racing decisions. They made short-term racing decisions that suited their team at that particular time. I don't think anyone of them ever made a business decision about CART.'

Daly sees considerable potential in the fresh view of Forsythe, Gentilozzi and Kalkhoven. 'Now, there's different thinking,' he observed. 'There's business thinking. There's long-term thinking. They're viewing this racing product from multiple angles, not just from the racing angle, and that's probably the reason it will survive and flourish.'

Pat Patrick co-founded CART with Roger Penske in 1979. Patrick's money and Penske's people and organisation got CART rolling through the early years, and Patrick reflected on an important similarity between CART's formative days and the latest regime. 'It's the first time since I ran the organisation back at the beginning, before we handed it over to John Frasco, that somebody has invested in the series,' he observed. 'That's a very important point.'

Unification Unlikely

As the year wore on, there was constant talk from IRL notables about the need for a single, unified series. Michael Andretti said it repeatedly. So did Roger Penske, reiterating a point he had made in 2002. Even Tony George began to say it, suggesting that the IRL had always been open to road and street racing.

Their hope was that CART would die and the IRL would take over the best CART races. But thanks to messrs Forsythe, Gentilozzi and Kalkhoven, that apparently will not happen. This trio has invested many millions of dollars in buying and relaunching CART, and while Gentilozzi in particular opened talks with Tony George to see if the two groups could come together, the new owners are hardly going to hand over the keys to him.

Another issue is that, between the two series, there are too many races – more than 30 in all. The weak events, as far as spectator numbers are concerned, are almost invariably oval races, and the type of audience – the demographics – that sponsors are looking for makes road and street racing essential. George, Penske and Andretti have admitted that gaining street races like Long Beach and Toronto is the key to the IRL's future, but a move to embrace street racing and reduce the number of ovals may not receive unqualified support from the International Speedway Corporation, which provides the IRL with many of its tracks. The last thing ISC, or NASCAR, wants to see is a revitalised Indy or Champ car series, least of all a series centred on successful street and road races capable of drawing fans, sponsors and media interest away from NASCAR.

Allmendinger Stands Out

One of the most promising American single-seater drivers to emerge in recent years is AJ Allmendinger. Driving for Carl Russo's RuSports team, the 21-year-old Californian swept the Toyota/Atlantic championship in 2003, winning seven of 12 races after gaining the Barber/Dodge title in similar fashion in 2002. Allmendinger is set to move up to CART in 2004 with RuSports. Champion of the IRL's Infiniti-Pro series was Briton Mark Taylor, while Brazilian/American Leo Maia won CART's Barber/Dodge title.

In sports car racing, Don Panoz's American Le Mans Series continued to rule the roost ahead of the NASCAR-backed Grand American series. The latter has created a new, dumbed-down car built around a stock car-like, tube-frame chassis, but has generated little fan or media following. The ALMS, on the other hand, featured a championship battle between the Joest Audi R8 of Frank Biela/Marco Werner and the Champion R8 driven by JJ Lehto/Johnny Herbert. The GTS class was dominated by a pair of Corvette C5Rs piloted by Johnny O'Connell/Ron Fellows and Kelly Collins/Oliver Gavin, which were challenged in the second half of the season by a ProDrive Ferrari 550 Maranello driven by David Brabham/Jan Magnussen. Scott Pruett, now retired from Champ cars, returned to the TransAm series, which he dominated driving a Jaguar for series boss Paul Gentilozzi.

GOLD COAST QUEENSLAND AUSTRALIA

Above left: Bridgestone and Ford became sole tyre and engine suppliers in the Champ Car series.
Photograph: Phil Abbott/LAT Photographic

Left: Jimmy Vasser, Ryan Hunter-Reay and Darren Manning on the podium at Surfers Paradise.
Photograph: Phil Abbott/LAT Photographic

Below: Craig Pollock set up his own Champ Car team, PK Racing.
Photograph: Gavin Lawrence/LAT Photographic

Far left: Patrick Carpentier was a winner, but largely overshadowed by team-mate Paul Tracy.
Photograph: Gavin Lawrence/LAT Photographic

Left: Alex Zanardi made an emotional return to Lausitz, symbolically completing the 13 laps that were left at the time of his accident in 2001.

Below: Bruno Junqueira guides his Newman/Haas Lola through the Elkhart Lake curves.
Photographs: Phil Abbott/LAT Photographic

MAJOR RESULTS

OTHER CHAMPIONSHIP RACING SERIES WORLDWIDE

Compiled by DAVID HAYHOE

International Formula 3000 Championship

All cars are Lola B2/50-Zytek Judd KV.

2002

After AUTOCOURSE 2002–2003 went to press, Antonio Pizzonia was disqualified from 2nd place at Monza for running a rear wing element upside-down.

Consequently, the final championship points were as follows:

Drivers
1 Sébastien Bourdais, F, 56; **2** Giorgio Pantano, I, 54; **2** Tomas Enge, CZ, 50; **4** Björn Wirdheim, S, 29; **5** Ricardo Sperafico, BR, 22; **6** Rodrigo Sperafico, BR, 20; **7=** Mario Haberfeld, BR, 18; **7=** Antonio Pizzonia, BR, 18; **9=** Enrico Toccacelo, I, 14; **9=** Patrick Freisacher, A, 14; **11** Ricardo Mauricio, BR, 9; **12** Nicolas Kiesa, DK, 3; **13=** Rob Nguyen, AUS, 2; **13=** Tiago Monteiro, P, 2; **15** Zsolt Baumgartner, H, 1.

Teams
1 Arden Team Russia, 79; **2** Coloni, 68; **2** Super Nova Racing, 58; **4** Petrobras Junior Team, 40; **5** Red Bull Junior Team, 23; **6=** Durango Formula, 20; **6=** Team Astromega, 20; **8** PSM Racing Line, 3; **9** Nordic Racing, 1.

2003

FIA INTERNATIONAL FORMULA 3000 CHAMPIONSHIP, Autodromo Enzo e Dino Ferrari, Imola, Italy, 19 April. Round 1. 31 laps of the 3.065-mile/4.933-km circuit, 94.875 miles/152.686 km.
1 Björn Wirdheim, S, 52m 15.743s, 108.921 mph/175.292 km/h; **2** Patrick Friesacher, A, 52m 16.050s; **2** Ricardo Sperafico, BR, 52m 39.892s; **4** Vitantonio Liuzzi, I, 52m 52.813s; **5** Enrico Toccacelo, I, 52m 53.107s; **6** Yannick Schroeder, F, 52m 56.753s; **7** Raffaele Giammaria, I, 53m 11.740s; **8** Rob Nguyen, AUS, 53m 20.153s; **9** Townsend Bell, USA, 53m 21.796s; **10** Zsolt Baumgartner, H, 53m 36.997s; **11** Nicolas Minassian, F, 53m 51.141s; **12** Nicolas Kiesa, DK, 53m 58.972s*; **13** Valerio Scassellati, I, 30 laps; **14** Gary Paffett, GB, 30; **15** Derek Hill, USA, 30; **16** Jeffrey van Hooydonk, B, 18 (DNF – accident damage); **17** Tony Schmidt, D, 15 (DNF – accident damage); **18** Giorgio Pantano, I, 14 (DNF – accident damage); **19** Jaroslav Janis, CZ, 0 (DNF – stopped on parade lap).
* finished 10th in 53m 33.972s, but received a 25-second penalty for causing an accident.
Did not start: Robbie Kerr, GB (fuel pump).
Fastest race lap: Wirdheim, 1m 39.645s, 110.741 mph/178.221 km/h.
Fastest qualifying lap: Wirdheim, 1m 38.153s, 112.425 mph/180.930 km/h.
Championship points: **1** Wirdheim, 10; **2** Friesacher, 8; **2** Sperafico, 6; **4** Liuzzi, 5; **5** Toccacelo, 4; **6** Schroeder, 3.
Teams: **1** Red Bull, 13; **2** Arden, 10; **3** Coloni, 6.

FIA INTERNATIONAL FORMULA 3000 CHAMPIONSHIP, Circuit de Catalunya, Montmeló, Barcelona, Spain, 3 May. Round 2. 32 laps of the 2.939-mile/4.730-km circuit, 93.972 miles/151.234 km.
1 Giorgio Pantano, I, 52m 50.428s, 106.705 mph/171.725 km/h; **2** Björn Wirdheim, S, 52m 53.706s; **2** Enrico Toccacelo, I, 53m 11.181s; **4** Jaroslav Janis, CZ, 53m 19.770s; **5** Rob Nguyen, AUS, 53m 27.773s; **6** Tony Schmidt, D, 53m 28.046s; **7** Zsolt Baumgartner, H, 53m 28.878s; **8** Yannick Schroeder, F, 53m 35.192s; **9** Alessandro Piccolo, I, 53m 46.912s; **10** Nicolas Kiesa, DK, 54m 27.477s; **11** Derek Hill, USA, 31 laps; **12** Townsend Bell, USA, 31; **13** Ricardo Sperafico, BR, 25 (DNF – handling); **14** Vitantonio Liuzzi, I, 16 (DNF – accident damage); **15** Jeffrey van Hooydonk, B, 6 (DNF – accident damage); **16** Raffaele Giammaria, I, 1 (DNF – accident); **17** Philip 'Phil' Giebler, USA, 1 (DNF – accident); **18** Patrick Friesacher, A, 1 (DNF – driver injury).
Fastest race lap: Pantano, 1m 35.998s, 110.218 mph/177.379 km/h.
Fastest qualifying lap: Pantano, 1m 33.958s, 112.611 mph/181.230 km/h.
Championship points: **1** Wirdheim, 18; **2=** Pantano, 10; **2=** Toccacelo, 10; **4** Friesacher, 8; **5** Sperafico, 6; **6=** Liuzzi, 5; **6=** Janis, 5; **6=** Nguyen, 5.
Teams: **1** Arden, 18; **2** Red Bull, 13; **3** Durango, 12.

FIA INTERNATIONAL FORMULA 3000 CHAMPIONSHIP, A1-Ring, Spielberg, Austria, 17 May. Round 3. 35 laps of the 2.688-mile/4.326-km circuit, 94.082 miles/151.410 km.
1 Ricardo Sperafico, BR, 49m 08.128s, 114.885 mph/184.889 km/h; **2** Björn Wirdheim, S, 49m 11.799s; **2** Giorgio Pantano, I, 49m 18.183s; **4** Vitantonio Liuzzi, I, 49m 27.371s; **5** Enrico Toccacelo, I, 49m 29.658s; **6** Nicolas Kiesa, DK, 49m 35.531s; **7** Townsend Bell, USA, 49m 38.344s; **8** Philip 'Phil' Giebler, USA, 49m 39.165s; **9** Jaroslav Janis, CZ, 49m 39.575s; **10** Zsolt Baumgartner, H, 50m 03.221s; **11** Bernhard Auinger, A, 50m 07.632s; **12** Alessandro Piccolo, I, 50m 24.887s; **13** Rob Nguyen, AUS, 50m 35.525s; **14** Raffaele Giammaria, I, 34 laps; **15** Tony Schmidt, D, 31 (DNF – gearbox); **16** Yannick Schroeder, F, 19 (DNF – accident); **17** Derek Hill, USA, 19 (DNF – accident damage).
Fastest race lap: Wirdheim, 1m 23.473s, 115.930 mph/186.571 km/h.
Fastest qualifying lap: Sperafico, 1m 22.036s, 117.960 mph/189.839 km/h.
Championship points: **1** Wirdheim, 26; **2=** Pantano, 16; **2=** Sperafico, 16; **4** Toccacelo, 14; **5** Liuzzi, 10; **6** Friesacher, 8.
Teams: **1** Arden, 28; **2=** Red Bull, 18; **2=** Durango, 18; **2=** Coloni, 18.

FIA INTERNATIONAL FORMULA 3000 CHAMPIONSHIP, Monte Carlo Street Circuit, Monaco, 31 May. Round 4. 45 laps of the 2.075-mile/3.340-km circuit, 93.392 miles/150.300 km.
1 Nicolas Kiesa, DK, 1h 09m 21.483s, 80.791 mph/130.021 km/h; **2** Björn Wirdheim, S, 1h 09m 22.376s; **2** Raffaele Giammaria, I, 1h 09m 24.886s; **4** Jaroslav Janis, CZ, 1h 09m 25.328s; **5** Zsolt Baumgartner, H, 1h 09m 26.033s; **6** Townsend Bell, USA, 1h 09m 26.837s; **7** Yannick Schroeder, F, 1h 09m 37.341s; **8** Jeffrey van Hooydonk, B, 1h 09m 38.318s; **9** Bernhard Auinger, A, 44 laps; **10** Will Langhorne, USA, 43; **11** Giorgio Pantano, I, 39 (DNF – accident); **12** Ricardo Sperafico, BR, 39 (DNF – black flagged); **13** Enrico Toccacelo, I, 34 (DNF – accident); **14** Vitantonio Liuzzi, I, 34 (DNF – accident); **15** Tony Schmidt, D, 25 (DNF – vibration); **16** Derek Hill, USA, 17 (DNF – black flagged); **17** Philip 'Phil' Giebler, USA, 0 (DNF – spin).
Did not start: Alessandro Piccolo, I (injured in qualifying).
Fastest race lap: Wirdheim, 1m 27.384s, 85.500 mph/137.600 km/h.
Fastest qualifying lap: Wirdheim, 1m 25.881s, 86.997 mph/140.008 km/h.
Championship points: **1** Wirdheim, 34; **2=** Pantano, 16; **2=** Sperafico, 16; **4** Toccacelo, 14; **5** Kiesa, 13; **6=** Janis, 10; **6=** Liuzzi, 10.
Teams: **1** Arden, 39; **2** Durango, 24; **2** Coloni, 22.

FIA INTERNATIONAL FORMULA 3000 CHAMPIONSHIP, Nürburgring Grand Prix Circuit, Nürburg/Eifel, Germany, 28 June. Round 5. 30 laps of the 3.199-mile/5.148-km circuit, 95.954 miles/154.423 km.
1 Enrico Toccacelo, I, 55m 17.457s, 104.126 mph/167.575 km/h; **2** Vitantonio Liuzzi, I, 55m 17.940s; **2** Nicolas Kiesa, DK, 55m 31.987s; **4** Yannick Schroeder, F, 55m 43.369s; **5** Derek Hill, USA, 55m 44.234s; **6** Jaroslav Janis, CZ, 55m 44.547s; **7** Raffaele Giammaria, I, 55m 58.886s; **8** Jeffrey van Hooydonk, B, 56m 01.678s; **9** Philip 'Phil' Giebler, USA, 56m 01.841s; **10** Tony Schmidt, D, 56m 02.353s; **11** Zsolt Baumgartner, H, 56m 02.872s; **12** Will Langhorne, USA, 56m 23.734s; **13** Björn Wirdheim, S, 56m 36.674s; **14** Ricardo Sperafico, BR, 56m 39.666s; **15** Valerio Scassellati, I, 29 laps; **16** Giorgio Pantano, I, 28; **17** Townsend Bell, USA, 4 (DNF – accident damage); **18** Patrick Friesacher, A, 4 (DNF – accident damage).
Fastest race lap: Wirdheim, 1m 49.026s, 105.624 mph/169.985 km/h.
Fastest qualifying lap: Wirdheim, 1m 48.123s, 106.506 mph/171.405 km/h.
Championship points: **1** Wirdheim, 34; **2** Toccacelo, 24; **3** Kiesa, 19; **4** Liuzzi, 18; **5=** Sperafico, 16; **5=** Pantano, 16.
Teams: **1** Arden, 39; **2** Super Nova, 28; **3=** Durango, 26; **3=** Red Bull Jr, 26.

FIA INTERNATIONAL FORMULA 3000 CHAMPIONSHIP, Circuit de Nevers, Magny-Cours, France, 5 July. Round 6. 35 laps of the 2.741-mile/4.411-km circuit, 95.816 miles/154.201 km.
1 Giorgio Pantano, I, 53m 23.683s, 107.669 mph/173.278 km/h; **2** Björn Wirdheim, S, 53m 28.481s; **3** Ricardo Sperafico, BR, 53m 40.697s; **4** Vitantonio Liuzzi, I, 53m 52.858s; **5** Tony Schmidt, D, 53m 55.790s; **6** Jeffrey van Hooydonk, B, 53m 56.492s; **7** Yannick Schroeder, F, 54m 07.664s; **8** Raffaele Giammaria, I, 54m 13.486s; **9** Zsolt Baumgartner, H, 54m 22.825s; **10** Derek Hill, USA, 54m 23.451s; **11** Patrick Friesacher, A, 54m 23.658s; **12** Townsend Bell, USA, 54m 25.361s; **13** Enrico Toccacelo, I, 54m 27.106s; **14** Will Langhorne, USA, 34 laps; **15** Valerio Scassellati, I, 34; **16** Nicolas Kiesa, DK, 17 (DNF – gearbox); **17** Jaroslav Janis, CZ, 2 (DNF – gearbox).
Did not start: Philip 'Phil' Giebler, USA (practised, but unable to continue due to injury).
Fastest race lap: Pantano, 1m 30.924s, 108.521 mph/174.647 km/h.
Fastest qualifying lap: Pantano, 1m 28.888s, 111.006 mph/178.647 km/h.
Championship points: **1** Wirdheim, 42; **2** Pantano, 26; **3** Toccacelo, 24; **4** Liuzzi, 23; **5** Sperafico, 22; **6** Kiesa, 19.
Teams: **1** Arden, 47; **2** Durango, 37; **3** Red Bull, 31.

FIA INTERNATIONAL FORMULA 3000 CHAMPIONSHIP, Silverstone Grand Prix Circuit, Towcester, Northamptonshire, Great Britain, 19 July. Round 7. 30 laps of the 3.194-mile/5.141-km circuit, 95.769 miles/154.125 km.
1 Björn Wirdheim, S, 50m 25.858s, 113.941 mph/183.369 km/h; **2** Giorgio Pantano, I, 50m 34.793s; **3** Vitantonio Liuzzi, I, 50m 46.508s; **4** Ricardo Sperafico, BR, 50m 46.939s; **5** Patrick Friesacher, A, 50m 47.466s; **6** Enrico Toccacelo, I, 50m 49.105s; **7** Townsend Bell, USA, 50m 49.773s; **8** Nicolas Kiesa, DK, 50m 58.386s; **9** Yannick Schroeder, F, 51m 07.267s; **10** Jaroslav Janis, CZ, 51m 07.782s; **11** Zsolt Baumgartner, H, 51m 16.465s; **12** Michael Keohane, IRL, 51m 22.993s; **13** Will Langhorne, USA, 51m 43.331s; **14** Marc Hynes, GB, 51m 49.941s; **15** Tony Schmidt, D, 19 laps (DNF – drive-train); **16** Raffaele Giammaria, I, 11 (DNF – spin).
Fastest race lap: Wirdheim, 1m 39.471s, 115.612 mph/186.060 km/h.
Fastest qualifying lap: Wirdheim, 1m 36.541s, 119.121 mph/191.707 km/h.
Championship points: **1** Wirdheim, 52; **2** Pantano, 34; **3** Liuzzi, 29; **4=** Sperafico, 27; **4=** Toccacelo, 27; **6** Kiesa, 20.
Teams: **1** Arden, 59; **2** Durango, 45; **3** Red Bull, 41.

FIA INTERNATIONAL FORMULA 3000 CHAMPIONSHIP, Hockenheimring Grand Prix Circuit, Heidelberg, Germany, 2 August. Round 8. 33 laps of the 2.842-mile/4.574-km circuit, 93.791 miles/150.942 km.
1 Ricardo Sperafico, BR, 50m 25.250s, 111.610 mph/179.619 km/h; **2** Björn Wirdheim, S, 50m 28.483s; **3** Patrick Friesacher, A, 50m 30.744s; **4** Vitantonio Liuzzi, I, 50m 38.734s; **5** Townsend Bell, USA, 50m 39.941s; **6** Tony Schmidt, D, 50m 43.722s; **7** Giorgio Pantano, I, 50m 47.193s; **8** Jaroslav Janis, CZ, 50m 59.715s; **9** Zsolt Baumgartner, H, 51m 03.389s; **10** Raffaele Giammaria, I, 51m 06.549s; **11** Yannick Schroeder, F, 51m 07.724s; **12** Will Langhorne, USA, 51m 44.033s; **13** Sam Hancock, GB, 51m 45.375s; **14** Valerio Scassellati, I, 32 laps; **15** Michael Keohane, IRL, 2 (DNF – transmission); **16** Enrico Toccacelo, I, 1 (DNF – accident damage).
Fastest race lap: Wirdheim, 1m 31.098s, 112.316 mph/180.755 km/h.
Fastest qualifying lap: Sperafico, 1m 29.829s, 113.902 mph/183.308 km/h.
Championship points: **1** Wirdheim, 60; **2** Sperafico, 37; **3** Pantano, 36; **4** Liuzzi, 34; **5** Toccacelo, 27; **6** Kiesa, 20.
Teams: **1** Arden, 71; **2** Red Bull, 52; **3** Durango, 47.

FIA INTERNATIONAL FORMULA 3000 CHAMPIONSHIP, Hungaroring, Mogyorod, Budapest, Hungary, 23 August. Round 9. 35 laps of the 2.722-mile/4.381-km circuit, 95.274 miles/153.328 km.
1 Patrick Friesacher, A, 58m 02.294s, 98.494 mph/158.511 km/h; **2** Björn Wirdheim, S, 58m 26.040s; **3** Townsend Bell, USA, 58m 26.600s; **4** Giorgio Pantano, I, 58m 28.734s; **5** Jaroslav Janis, CZ, 58m 29.375s; **6** Raffaele Giammaria, I, 58m 34.383s; **7** Enrico Toccacelo, I, 58m 39.794s; **8** Tony Schmidt, D, 58m 42.257s; **9** Vitantonio Liuzzi, I, 58m 53.593s*; **10** Giovanni Beron, I, 34 laps; **11** Sam Hancock, GB, 34; **12** Ferdinando Monfardini, I, 30 (DNF – gearbox); **13** Ricardo Sperafico, BR, 11 (DNF – suspension).
* finished 4th in 58m 28.593s, but received a 25-second penalty for driving into Pantano.
Did not start: Zsolt Baumgartner, H (replaced Ralph Firman in the Grand Prix).
Fastest race lap: Friesacher, 1m 36.809s, 101.230 mph/162.915 km/h.
Fastest qualifying lap: Liuzzi, 1m 36.092s, 101.986 mph/164.130 km/h.
Championship points: **1** Wirdheim, 68; **2** Pantano, 41; **3** Sperafico, 37; **4** Liuzzi, 34; **5** Toccacelo, 29; **6** Friesacher, 28.
Teams: **1** Arden, 85; **2** Red Bull, 62; **3** Durango, 55.

FIA INTERNATIONAL FORMULA 3000 CHAMPIONSHIP, Autodromo Nazionale di Monza, Milan, Italy, 13 September. Round 10. 26 laps of the 3.600-mile/5.793-km circuit, 93.398 miles/150.309 km.
1 Björn Wirdheim, S, 44m 01.863s, 127.271 mph/204.822 km/h; **2** Patrick Friesacher, A, 44m 10.379s; **3** Ricardo Sperafico, BR, 44m 11.895s; **4** Vitantonio Liuzzi, I, 44m 38.834s; **5** Jeffrey van Hooydonk, B, 44m 39.972s; **6** Tony Schmidt, D, 44m 40.787s; **7** Jaroslav Janis, CZ, 44m 41.044s; **8** Enrico Toccacelo, I, 44m 42.844s; **9** Christian Montanari, RSM, 25 laps; **10** Ferdinando Monfardini, I, 24; **11** Alessandro Piccolo, I, 24; **12** Giorgio Pantano, I, 14 (DNF – electrics); **13** Raffaele Giammaria, I, 2 (DNF – accident damage); **14** Townsend Bell, USA, 2 (DNF – accident).
Did not start: Sam Hancock, GB, 0 (injury from pre-race accident).
Fastest race lap: Wirdheim, 1m 38.881s, 131.052 mph/210.908 km/h.
Fastest qualifying lap: Wirdheim, 1m 38.457s, 131.617 mph/211.816 km/h.

Final championship points

Drivers
1 Björn Wirdheim, S, 78; **2** Ricardo Sperafico, BR, 43; **3** Giorgio Pantano, I, 41; **4** Vitantonio Liuzzi, I, 39; **5** Patrick Friesacher, A, 36; **6** Enrico Toccacelo, I, 30; **7=** Nicolas Kiesa, DK, 20; **7=** Jaroslav Janis, CZ, 20; **9** Townsend Bell, USA, 17; **10=** Raffaele Giammaria, I, 14; **10=** Tony Schmidt, D, 14; **12** Yannick Schroeder, F, 13; **13** Jeffrey van Hooydonk, B, 9; **14** Zsolt Baumgartner, H, 6; **15** Rob Nguyen, AUS, 5; **16** Derek Hill, USA, 4; **17** Philip 'Phil' Giebler, 1.

Teams
1 Arden International, 95; **2** Red Bull Junior Team, 75; **3** Durango Formula, 55; **4** Coloni Motorsport, 49; **5** Super Nova Racing, 35; **6** Superfund-I.S.R.-Charouz, 33; **7** Team Astromega, 23; **8** Den Blå Avis, 20; **9** BCN F3000, 5.

Euro Formula 3000 Series

All cars are Lola B99/50-Zytek Judd KV.

2002

The following race was run after AUTOCOURSE 2002–2003 went to press.

EURO F3000 SERIES, Autodromo di Cagliari, Sardinia, Italy, 10 November. Round 9. 62 laps.
1 Jaroslav Janis, CZ, 1h 13m 13.349s; **2** Jaime Melo Jr, BR, 1h 13m 19.658s; **3** Matteo Grassotto, I, 1h 13m 21.324s; **4** Alessandro Piccolo, I, 1h 24.093s; **5** Romain Dumas, F, 1h 13m 56.764s; **6** Christian Montanari, RSM, 1h 14m 15.487s; **7** Martin Basso, RA, 1h 14m 22.083s; **8** Michael Bentwood, GB, 61 laps; **9** Gabriele Gardel, CH, 61; **10** Fabrizio del Monte, I, 61.
Fastest qualifying lap: Janis.

Final championship points

1 Jaime Melo Jr, BR, 49; **2** Romain Dumas, F, 42; **3** Jaroslav Janis, CZ, 36; **4** Alessandro Piccolo, I, 28; **5** Thomas Biagi, I, 15; **6** Yannick Schroeder, F, 14; **7** Matteo Grassotto, I, 12; **8** Martin Basso, RA, 10; **9** Augusto Farfus, BR, 8; **10** Massimiliano 'Max' Busnelli, I, 7; **11** Julien Vidot, F, 6; **12** Gianmaria Bruni, I, 5; **13=** Valerio Scassellati, I, 1; **13=** Christian Montanari, RSM, 1.

2003

EURO F3000 SERIES, Nürburgring Grand Prix Circuit, Nürburg/Eifel, Germany, 4 May. Round 1. 30 laps of the 3.194-mile/5.141-km circuit, 95.834 miles/154.230 km.
1 Gianmaria Bruni, I, 56m 20.557s, 102.055 mph/164.242 km/h; **2** Augusto Farfus, BR, 56m 23.959s; **3** Matteo Grassotto, I, 56m 25.848s; **4** 'Babalus', I, 56m 53.576s; **5** Peter Boss, USA, 56m 58.437s; **6** Roman Rusinov, RUS, 57m 01.368s; **7** Milos Pavlovic, YU, 57m 06.840s; **8** Nicky Pastorelli, I, 57m 07.057s; **9** Rafael Sperafico, BR, 58m 12.037s; **10** Joel Nelson, USA, 29 laps.
Fastest race lap: Farfus, 1m 51.152s, 103.463 mph/166.507 km/h.
Fastest qualifying lap: Rusinov, 1m 48.915s, 105.588 mph/169.927 km/h.

EURO F3000 SERIES, Circuit de Nevers, Magny-Cours, France, 11 May. Round 2. 35 laps of the 2.641-mile/4.251-km circuit, 92.451 miles/148.785 km.
1 Gianmaria Bruni, I, 52m 46.007s, 105.124 mph/169.180 km/h; **2** Matteo Grassotto, I, 52m 48.898s; **3** Augusto Farfus, BR, 52m 50.040s; **4** Roman Rusinov, RUS, 52m 50.778s; **5** Nicky Pastorelli, I, 53m 02.303s; **6** Colin Brown, GB, 53m 19.657s; **7** 'Babalus', I, 53m 20.070s; **8** Sven Heidfeld, D, 53m 20.586s; **9** Fabrizio del Monte, I, 53m 22.967s; **10** Peter Boss, USA, 53m 24.186s.
Fastest race lap: Bruni, 1m 31.844s, 103.537 mph/166.626 km/h.
Fastest qualifying lap: Farfus, 1m 30.190s, 105.435 mph/169.682 km/h.

EURO F3000 SERIES, Ente Autodromo di Pergusa, Enna-Pergusa, Sicily, 25 May. Round 3. 31 laps of the 3.076-mile/4.950-km circuit, 95.349 miles/153.450 km.
1 Augusto Farfus, BR, 48m 37.392s, 117.659 mph/189.354 km/h; **2** Nicky Pastorelli, I, 48m 43.754s; **3** Peter Boss, USA, 48m 54.284s; **4** Matteo Grassotto, I, 48m 56.094s; **5** 'Babalus', I, 49m 07.756s; **6** Fabrizio del Monte, I, 49m 31.352s; **7** Sven Heidfeld, D, 49m 54.653s; **8** Rafael Sperafico, BR; **9** Gianmaria Bruni, I; **10** Roman Rusinov, RUS.
Fastest race lap: Farfus, 1m 33.188s, 118.823 mph/191.226 km/h.
Fastest qualifying lap: Farfus, 1m 30.578s, 122.246 mph/196.737 km/h.

EURO F3000 SERIES, Autodromo Nazionale di Monza, Milan, Italy, 29 June. Round 4. 25 laps of the 3.600-mile/5.793-km circuit, 89.990 miles/144.825 km.
1 Augusto Farfus, BR, 42m 45.087s, 126.298 mph/203.256 km/h; **2** Matteo Grassotto, I, 42m 50.720s; **2** Fabrizio del Monte, I, 42m 51.290s; **4** Peter Boss, USA, 43m 11.765s; **5** Gabriele Lancieri, I, 43m 15.382s; **6** Colin Brown, GB, 43m 16.888s; **7** Nicky Pastorelli, I, 43m 21.983s; **8** Rafael Sperafico, BR; **9** Sven Heidfeld, D; **10** Roman Rusinov, RUS.
Fastest race lap: del Monte, 1m 41.646s, 127.487 mph/205.171 km/h.
Fastest qualifying lap: Farfus, 1m 39.840s, 129.793 mph/208.882 km/h.

EURO F3000 SERIES, Circuit de Spa-Francorchamps, Stavelot, Belgium, 20 July. Round 5. 19 laps of the 4.317-mile/6.947-km circuit, 82.017 miles/131.993 km.
1 Augusto Farfus, BR, 41m 54.281s, 117.433 mph/188.990 km/h; **2** Joel Nelson, USA, 41m 56.525s; **3** Fabrizio del Monte, I, 42m 05.712s; **4** Peter Boss, USA, 42m 09.676s; **5** Jaime Melo Jr, BR, 42m 11.304s; **6** Colin Brown, GB, 42m 20.978s; **7** Nicky Pastorelli, I, 42m 23.139s; **8** Jean de Pourtales, F, 42m 58.856s; **9** Gianmaria Bruni, I, 42m 59.500s; **10** Matteo Grassotto, I.
Fastest race lap: Farfus, 2m 09.984s, 119.553 mph/192.402 km/h.
Fastest qualifying lap: Farfus, 2m 06.260s, 123.079 mph/198.077 km/h.

DONINGTON PARK GOLD CUP, Donington Park Grand Prix Circuit, Castle Donington, Derbyshire, Great Britain, 10 August. Round 6. 38 laps of the 2.500-mile/4.023-km circuit, 95.000 miles/152.888 km.
1 Gianmaria Bruni, I, 1h 05m 21.400s, 87.214 mph/140.357 km/h; **2** Nicky Pastorelli, I, 1h 06m 07.606s; **3** Augusto Farfus, BR, 1h 06m 16.932s; **4** Fabrizio del Monte, I, 1h 06m 38.758s; **5** Roman Rusinov, RUS, 1h 06m 48.313s; **6** Colin Brown, GB, 1h 06m 55.561s; **7** Joel Nelson, USA, 1h 06m 56.568s; **8** Sven Heidfeld, D, 37 laps; **9** Rafael Sperafico, BR, 37; **10** Matteo Grassotto, I, 36.
Fastest race lap: Heidfeld, 1m 40.425s, 89.619 mph/144.228 km/h.

Fastest qualifying lap: Bruni, 1m 23.723s, 107.497 mph/173.000 km/h.

EURO F3000 SERIES, Automotodrom Brno Masaryk Circuit, Brno, Czech Republic, 21 September. Round 7. 27 laps of the 3.357-mile/5.403-km circuit, 90.646 miles/145.881 km.
1 Fabrizio del Monte, I, 51m 04.514s, 106.486 mph/171.372 km/h; 2 Joel Nelson, USA, 51m 09.795s; 3 Matteo Grassotto, I, 51m 24.410s; 4 Matteo Cressoni, I, 51m 41.293s; 5 Rafael Sperafico, BR, 51m 52.586s; 6 Jean de Pourtales, F, 52m 00.288s; 7 Sven Heidfeld, D, 26 laps; 8 Peter Boss, USA, 26; 9 Nicky Pastorelli, I, DNF; 10 Augusto Farfus, BR, DNF.
Fastest race lap: del Monte, 1m 55.392s, 104.740 mph/168.562 km/h.
Fastest qualifying lap: Augusto Farfus, BR, 1m 48.505s, 111.388 mph/179.262 km/h.

EURO F3000 SERIES, Circuito Permanente de Jerez, Jerez de la Frontera, Spain, 12 October. Round 8. 34 laps of the 2.748-mile/4.423-km circuit, 93.443 miles/150.382 km.
1 Augusto Farfus, BR, 56m 27.791s, 99.296 mph/159.802 km/h; 2 Fabrizio del Monte, I, 56m 28.120s; 2 Sven Heidfeld, D; 4 Nicky Pastorelli, I; 5 Jaime Melo Jr, BR; 6 Nicolas Dalli, E; 7 Peter Boss, USA, DNF; 8 Maxime Hodencq, B, DNF; 9 Joel Nelson, USA, DNF; 10 Matteo Grassotto, I, DNF.
Fastest race lap: Farfus, 1m 36.707s, 102.309 mph/164.650 km/h.
Fastest qualifying lap: Nelson, 1m 33.495s, 105.824 mph/170.306 km/h.

CAGLIARI GRAND PRIX, Autodromo di Cagliari, Sardinia, Italy, 2 November. Round 9. 60 laps of the 1.500-mile/2.414-km circuit, 89.999 miles/144.840 km.
1 Jaime Melo Jr, BR, 1h 09m 14.803s, 77.982 mph/125.499 km/h; 2 Augusto Farfus, BR, 1h 10m 17.582s; 3 Norbert Siedler, D; 4 Fabrizio del Monte, I; 5 Nicky Pastorelli, I; 6 Jean de Pourtales, F; 7 Giacomo Vargiu, I; 8 Peter Boss, USA; 9 Mauro Contu, I; 10 Vitaly Petrov, RUS.
Fastest qualifying lap: Melo Jr, 1m 06.416s, 81.305 mph/130.848 km/h.

Final championship points

1 Augusto Farfus, BR, 60; 2 Fabrizio del Monte, I, 31; 3 Gianmaria Bruni, I, 30; 4 Matteo Grassotto, I, 23; 5 Nicky Pastorelli, I, 19; 6 Jaime Melo Jr, BR, 14; 7= Joel Nelson, USA, 12; 7= Peter Boss, USA, 12; 9 Roman Rusinov, RUS, 6; 10 'Babalus', I, 5.

BRDC British Formula 3 Championship

BRDC BRITISH FORMULA 3 CHAMPIONSHIP, Donington Park National Circuit, Castle Donington, Derbyshire, Great Britain, 6 April. 2 x 20 laps of the 1.9573-mile/3.149-km circuit.
Round 1 (39.146 miles/62.999 km)
1 Jamie Green, GB (Dallara F303-Mugen Honda), 21m 46.590s, 107.858 mph/173.580 km/h; 2 Alan van der Merwe, ZA (Dallara F303-Mugen Honda), 21m 47.099s; 3 Michael Keohane, IRL (Dallara F303-Mugen Honda), 21m 52.203s; 4 Rob Austin, GB (Dallara F303-Opel), 21m 54.708s; 5 Richard Antinucci, USA (Dallara F303-Mugen Honda), 21m 55.220s; 6 Ronnie Bremer, DK (Dallara F303-Mugen Honda), 21m 55.687s; 7 Fairuz Fauzy, MAL (Dallara F303-Opel), 21m 59.955s; 8 Clivio Piccione, MC (Dallara F303-Mugen Honda), 22m 00.565s; 9 Ernani Judice, BR (Dallara F303-Mugen Honda), 22m 05.699s; 10 Karun Chandhok, IND (Dallara F301-Mugen Honda), 22m 10.325s (1st Scholarship class).
Green and Antinucci were originally disqualified, but later reinstated following an appeal.
Fastest race lap: van der Merwe, 1m 04.699s, 108.909 mph/175.271 km/h.
Fastest qualifying lap: Green, 1m 04.167s, 109.812 mph/176.725 km/h.

Round 2 (39.146 miles/62.999 km)
1 Jamie Green, GB (Dallara F303-Mugen Honda), 21m 40.071s, 108.398 mph/174.450 km/h; 2 Alan van der Merwe, ZA (Dallara F303-Mugen Honda), 21m 41.712s; 3 Nelson Angelo Piquet, BR (Dallara F303-Mugen Honda), 21m 42.411s; 4 Rob Austin, GB (Dallara F303-Opel), 21m 51.217s; 5 Ronnie Bremer, DK (Dallara F303-Mugen Honda), 21m 51.742s; 6 Adam Carroll, GB (Lola-Dome F106/03-Opel), 21m 55.214s; 7 Robert Dahlgren, S (Dallara F303-Renault), 21m 55.549s; 8 Danny Watts, GB (Dallara F303-Renault), 21m 55.881s; 9 Ernani Judice, BR (Dallara F303-Mugen Honda), 21m 57.282s; 10 Fabio Carbone, BR (Dallara F303-Renault), 21m 57.750s.
Winner Scholarship Class: Steven Kane, GB (Dallara F301-Mugen Honda), 22m 05.608s (15th).
Fastest race lap: Green, 1m 04.269s, 109.637 mph/176.444 km/h.
Fastest qualifying lap: Green, 1m 04.314s, 109.561 mph/176.321 km/h.
Championship points: 1 van der Merwe, 36; 2 Austin, 22; 3 Green, 21; 4 Bremer, 18; 5 Keohane, 15; 6 Piquet, 12.
Scholarship Class: 1 Chandhok, 35; 2 Kane, 33; 3 Christian England, GB, 22.

BRDC BRITISH FORMULA 3 CHAMPIONSHIP, Snetterton Circuit, Norfolk, Great Britain, 19/20 April. 2 x 23 laps of the 1.952-mile/3.141-km circuit.
Round 3 (44.896 miles/72.253 km)
1 Alan van der Merwe, ZA (Dallara F303-Mugen Honda), 30m 25.377s, 88.544 mph/142.497 km/h; 2 Nelson Angelo Piquet, BR (Dallara F303-Mugen Honda), 30m 29.829s; 3 Ronnie Bremer, DK (Dallara F303-Mugen Honda), 30m 30.430s; 4 Danny Watts, GB (Dallara F303-Renault), 30m 32.932s; 5 Jamie Green, GB (Dallara F303-Mugen Honda), 30m 34.743s; 6 Robert Dahlgren, S (Dallara F303-Renault), 30m 34.838s; 7 Clivio Piccione, MC (Dallara F303-Mugen Honda), 30m 35.368s; 8 Fairuz Fauzy, MAL (Dallara F303-Opel), 30m 35.854s; 9 Scott Speed, USA (Dallara F303-Mugen Honda), 30m 36.939s; 10 Ernesto Viso, YV (Dallara F301-Mugen Honda), 30m 38.121s (1st Scholarship class).
Fastest race lap: Richard Antinucci, USA (Dallara F303-Mugen Honda), 1m 02.412s, 112.594 mph/181.202 km/h.
Fastest qualifying lap: van der Merwe, 1m 01.845s, 113.626 mph/182.863 km/h.

Round 4 (44.896 miles/72.253 km)
1 Alan van der Merwe, ZA (Dallara F303-Mugen Honda), 36m 30.419s, 73.788 mph/118.750 km/h; 2 Jamie Green, GB (Dallara F303-Mugen Honda), 36m 32.898s; 3 Rob Austin, GB (Dallara F303-Opel), 36m 33.514s; 4 Richard Antinucci, USA (Dallara F303-Mugen Honda), 36m 34.977s; 5 Nelson Angelo Piquet, BR (Dallara F303-Mugen Honda), 36m 35.052s; 6 Ernani Judice, BR (Dallara F303-Mugen Honda), 36m 37.052s; 7 Danny Watts, GB (Dallara F303-Renault), 36m 37.959s; 8 Michael Keohane, IRL (Dallara F303-Mugen Honda), 36m 38.291s; 9 Clivio Piccione, MC (Dallara F303-Mugen Honda), 36m 38.772s; 10 Steven Kane, GB (Dallara F301-Mugen Honda), 36m 39.545s (1st Scholarship class).
Fastest race lap: Antinucci, 1m 02.769s, 111.953 mph/180.171 km/h.
Fastest qualifying lap: van der Merwe, 1m 01.678s, 113.934 mph/183.358 km/h.
Championship points: 1 van der Merwe, 76; 2 Green, 44; 3 Piquet, 35; 4 Austin, 34; 5 Bremer, 30; 6= Keohane, 18; 6= Watts, 18.
Scholarship Class: 1 Kane, 65; 2 Chandhok, 60; 3 Justin Sherwood, GB, 38.

BRDC BRITISH FORMULA 3 CHAMPIONSHIP, Croft Circuit, Croft-on-Tees, North Yorkshire, Great Britain, 4 May. 17 and 20 laps of the 2.127-mile/3.423-km circuit.
Round 5 (36.159 miles/58.192 km)
1 Will Davison, AUS (Dallara F303-Mugen Honda), 21m 34.629s, 100.548 mph/161.816 km/h; 2 Rob Austin, GB (Dallara F303-Opel), 21m 39.242s; 3 Alan van der Merwe, ZA (Dallara F303-Mugen Honda), 21m 41.996s; 4 Ronnie Bremer, DK (Dallara F303-Mugen Honda), 21m 43.266s; 5 Richard Antinucci, USA (Dallara F303-Mugen Honda), 21m 44.203s; 6 Danny Watts, GB (Dallara F303-Renault), 21m 52.607s; 7 Stefano Fabi, I (Dallara F303-Mugen Honda), 21m 55.297s; 8 Nelson Angelo Piquet, BR (Dallara F303-Mugen Honda), 21m 57.317s; 9 Ernani Judice, BR (Dallara F303-Mugen Honda), 21m 57.722s; 10 Fairuz Fauzy, MAL (Dallara F303-Opel), 21m 58.222s.
Winner Scholarship Class: Karun Chandhok, IND (Dallara F301-Mugen Honda), 22m 09.235s (15th).
Fastest race lap: Davison, 1m 15.296s, 101.695 mph/163.662 km/h.
Fastest qualifying lap: Davison, 1m 15.232s, 101.781 mph/163.801 km/h.

Round 6 (42.540 miles/68.461 km)
1 Alan van der Merwe, ZA (Dallara F303-Mugen Honda), 29m 15.548s, 87.234 mph/140.390 km/h; 2 Jamie Green, GB (Dallara F303-Mugen Honda), 29m 19.138s; 3 Richard Antinucci, USA (Dallara F303-Mugen Honda), 29m 20.096s; 4 Michael Keohane, IRL (Dallara F303-Mugen Honda), 29m 24.430s; 5 Rob Austin, GB (Dallara F303-Opel), 29m 25.593s; 6 Ronnie Bremer, DK (Dallara F303-Mugen Honda), 29m 26.194s; 7 Robert Dahlgren, S (Dallara F303-Renault), 29m 27.358s; 8 Billy Asaro, CDN (Dallara F303-Opel), 29m 36.383s; 9 Christian England, GB (Dallara F301-Mugen Honda), 29m 37.706s (1st Scholarship class); 10 Stefano Fabi, I (Dallara F303-Mugen Honda), 29m 39.607s.
Fastest race lap: van der Merwe, 1m 15.733s, 101.108 mph/162.717 km/h.
Fastest qualifying lap: van der Merwe, 1m 14.602s, 102.641 mph/165.184 km/h.
Championship points: 1 van der Merwe, 109; 2 Green, 59; 3 Austin, 57; 4 Bremer, 46; 5 Piquet, 38; 6 Antinucci, 32.
Scholarship Class: 1 Chandhok, 80; 2 Kane, 79; 3 Viso, 62.

BRDC BRITISH FORMULA 3 CHAMPIONSHIP, Knockhill Racing Circuit, By Dunfermline, Fife, Scotland, Great Britain, 11 May. 26 and 21 laps of the 1.2986-mile/2.090-km circuit.
Round 7 (33.764 miles/54.337 km)
1 Clivio Piccione, MC (Dallara F303-Mugen Honda), 21m 27.485s, 94.409 mph/151.937 km/h; 2 Nelson Angelo Piquet, BR (Dallara F303-Mugen Honda), 21m 30.917s; 3 Richard Antinucci, USA (Dallara F303-Mugen Honda), 21m 37.206s; 4 Ronnie Bremer, DK (Dallara F303-Mugen Honda), 21m 39.732s; 5 Will Davison, AUS (Dallara F303-Mugen Honda), 21m 40.017s; 6 Alan van der Merwe, ZA (Dallara F303-Mugen Honda), 21m 48.434s; 7 Steven Kane, GB (Dallara F301-Mugen Honda), 21m 49.057s (1st Scholarship class); 8 Stefano Fabi, I (Dallara F303-Mugen Honda), 21m 50.327s; 9 Billy Asaro, CDN (Dallara F303-Opel), 21m 50.664s; 10 Fairuz Fauzy, MAL (Dallara F303-Opel), 21m 50.911s.
Fastest race lap: Piccione, 47.606s, 98.201 mph/158.039 km/h.
Fastest qualifying lap: Piccione, 47.378s, 98.674 mph/158.800 km/h.

Round 8 (27.271 miles/43.888 km)
1 Nelson Angelo Piquet, BR (Dallara F303-Mugen Honda), 16m 53.390s, 96.878 mph/155.911 km/h; 2 Jamie Green, GB (Dallara F303-Mugen Honda), 16m 57.978s; 3 Michael Keohane, IRL (Dallara F303-Mugen Honda), 16m 58.851s; 4 Alan van der Merwe, ZA (Dallara F303-Mugen Honda), 17m 02.236s; 5 Will Davison, AUS (Dallara F303-Mugen Honda), 17m 02.607s; 6 Robert Dahlgren, S (Dallara F303-Renault), 17m 05.256s; 7 Steven Kane, GB (Dallara F301-Mugen Honda), 17m 06.818s (1st Scholarship class); 8 Ronnie Bremer, DK (Dallara F303-Mugen Honda), 17m 09.944s; 9 Ernesto Viso, YV (Dallara F301-Mugen Honda), 17m 10.415s; 10 Danny Watts, GB (Dallara F303-Renault), 17m 14.993s.
Fastest race lap: Piquet, 47.578s, 98.259 mph/158.132 km/h.
Fastest qualifying lap: Piquet, 47.366s, 98.699 mph/158.840 km/h.
Championship points: 1 van der Merwe, 120; 2 Green, 94; 3 Piquet, 74; 4 Bremer, 56; 5 Austin, 55; 6 Antinucci, 54.
Scholarship Class: 1 Kane, 120; 2 Viso, 93; 3 Chandhok, 92.

BRDC BRITISH FORMULA 3 CHAMPIONSHIP, Silverstone Grand Prix Circuit, Towcester, Northamptonshire, Great Britain, 25/26 May. 2 x 15 laps of the 3.194-mile/5.140-km circuit.
Round 9 (47.910 miles/77.104 km)
1 Nelson Angelo Piquet, BR (Dallara F303-Mugen Honda), 26m 37.031s, 107.998 mph/173.806 km/h; 2 Adam Carroll, GB (Dallara F303-Opel), 26m 38.014s; 3 Danny Watts, GB (Dallara F303-Renault), 26m 41.992s; 4 Will Davison, AUS (Dallara F303-Mugen Honda), 26m 44.048s; 5 Richard Antinucci, USA (Dallara F303-Mugen Honda), 26m 45.503s; 6 Rob Austin, GB (Dallara F303-Opel), 26m 46.400s; 7 Alan van der Merwe, ZA (Dallara F303-Mugen Honda), 26m 48.334s; 8 Karun Chandhok, IND (Dallara F301-Mugen Honda), 26m 54.620s (1st Scholarship class); 9 Clivio Piccione, MC (Dallara F303-Mugen Honda), 26m 55.511s; 10 Ronnie Bremer, DK (Dallara F303-Mugen Honda), 26m 56.167s.
Fastest race lap: Piquet, 1m 45.572s, 108.915 mph/175.282 km/h.
Fastest qualifying lap: Piquet, 1m 44.502s, 110.030 mph/177.077 km/h.

Round 10 (47.910 miles/77.104 km)
1 Alan van der Merwe, ZA (Dallara F303-Mugen Honda), 26m 43.815s, 107.541 mph/173.071 km/h; 2 Richard Antinucci, USA (Dallara F303-Mugen Honda), 26m 49.150s; 3 Rob Austin, GB (Dallara F303-Opel), 26m 52.045s; 4 Jamie Green, GB (Dallara F303-Mugen Honda), 26m 53.179s; 5 Danny Watts, GB (Dallara F303-Renault), 26m 54.793s; 6 Nelson Angelo Piquet, BR (Dallara F303-Mugen Honda), 26m 55.233s; 7 Will Davison, AUS (Dallara F303-Mugen Honda), 26m 55.641s; 8 Ernani Judice, BR (Dallara F303-Mugen Honda), 26m 56.878s; 9 Clivio Piccione, MC (Dallara F303-Mugen Honda), 26m 58.059s; 10 Ronnie Bremer, DK (Dallara F303-Mugen Honda), 26m 59.121s.
Winner Scholarship Class: Karun Chandhok, IND (Dallara F301-Mugen Honda), 27m 05.127s (14th).
Fastest race lap: van der Merwe, 1m 45.884s, 108.594 mph/174.766 km/h.
Fastest qualifying lap: Piquet, 1m 44.039s, 110.520 mph/177.865 km/h.
Championship points. 1 van der Merwe, 145; 2 Green, 105; 3 Piquet, 101; 4 Antinucci, 77; 5 Austin, 73; 6 Bremer, 59. **Scholarship Class:** 1 Kane, 151; 2 Chandhok, 133; 3 Viso, 107.

BRDC BRITISH FORMULA 3 CHAMPIONSHIP, Castle Combe Circuit, Wiltshire, Great Britain, 22 June. 23 and 16 laps of the 1.850-mile/2.977-km circuit.
Round 11 (42.550 miles/68.478 km)
1 Alan van der Merwe, ZA (Dallara F303-Mugen Honda), 25m 51.523s, 98.729 mph/158.889 km/h; 2 Adam Carroll, GB (Dallara F303-Opel), 25m 51.784s; 3 Robert Dahlgren, S (Dallara F303-Renault), 25m 54.984s; 4 Ronnie Bremer, DK (Dallara F303-Mugen Honda), 25m 55.287s; 5 Will Power, AUS (Dallara F303-Renault), 25m 58.670s; 6 Clivio Piccione, MC (Dallara F303-Mugen Honda), 25m 59.007s; 7 Jamie Green, GB (Dallara F303-Mugen Honda), 25m 59.763s; 8 Eric Salignon, F (Dallara F303-Renault), 26m 00.564s; 9 Nelson Angelo Piquet, BR (Dallara F303-Mugen Honda), 26m 01.058s; 10 Scott Speed, USA (Dallara F303-Mugen Honda), 26m 03.398s.
Winner Scholarship Class: Ernesto Viso, YV (Dallara F301-Mugen Honda), 26m 08.499s (12th).
Fastest race lap: Carroll, 1m 00.901s, 109.358 mph/175.994 km/h.
Fastest qualifying lap: Danny Watts, GB (Dallara F303-Renault), 1m 00.291s, 110.464 mph/177.775 km/h.

Round 12 (29.600 miles/47.637 km)
1 Danny Watts, GB (Dallara F303-Renault), 16m 20.990s, 108.625 mph/174.815 km/h; 2 Robert Dahlgren, S (Dallara F303-Renault), 16m 23.575s; 3 Adam Carroll, GB (Dallara F303-Opel), 16m 24.349s; 4 Alan van der Merwe, ZA (Dallara F303-Mugen Honda), 16m 26.238s; 5 Ronnie Bremer, DK (Dallara F303-Mugen Honda), 16m 27.526s; 6 Clivio Piccione, MC (Dallara F303-Mugen Honda), 16m 28.053s; 7 Rob Austin, GB (Dallara F303-Opel), 16m 28.701s; 8 Richard Antinucci, USA (Dallara F303-Mugen Honda), 16m 30.188s; 9 Jamie Green, GB (Dallara F303-Mugen Honda), 16m 32.959s; 10 Ernesto Viso, YV (Dallara F301-Mugen Honda), 16m 36.434s (1st Scholarship class).
Fastest race lap: Watts, 1m 00.598s, 109.905 mph/176.874 km/h.
Fastest qualifying lap: Watts, 1m 00.022s, 110.959 mph/178.572 km/h.
Championship points: 1 van der Merwe, 175; 2 Green, 111; 3 Piquet, 103; 4 Antinucci, 80; 5= Austin, 77; 5= Bremer, 77. **Scholarship Class:** 1 Kane, 182; 2 Viso, 148; 3 Chandhok, 145.

BRDC BRITISH FORMULA 3 CHAMPIONSHIP, Oulton Park International Circuit, Tarporley, Cheshire, Great Britain, 13 July. 17 and 12 laps of the 2.692-mile/4.332-km circuit.
Round 13 (45.764 miles/73.650 km)
1 Alan van der Merwe, ZA (Dallara F303-Mugen Honda), 28m 42.100s, 95.668 mph/153.963 km/h; 2 Danny Watts, GB (Dallara F303-Renault), 28m 45.163s; 3 Adam Carroll, GB (Dallara F303-Opel), 28m 45.907s; 4 Jamie Green, GB (Dallara F303-Mugen Honda), 28m 51.884s; 5 Will Davison, AUS (Dallara F303-Mugen Honda), 28m 52.327s; 6 Robert Dahlgren, S (Dallara F303-Renault), 28m 54.481s; 7 Richard Antinucci, USA (Dallara F303-Mugen Honda), 28m 55.806s; 8 Ronnie Bremer, DK (Dallara F303-Mugen Honda), 28m 57.228s; 9 Billy Asaro, CDN (Dallara F303-Opel), 29m 05.136s; 10 Rob Austin, GB (Dallara F303-Opel), 29m 08.828s.
Winner Scholarship Class: Karun Chandhok, IND (Dallara F301-Mugen Honda), 29m 17.245s (14th).
Fastest race lap: Watts, 1m 31.883s, 105.473 mph/169.743 km/h.
Fastest qualifying lap: Nelson Angelo Piquet, BR (Dallara F303-Mugen Honda), 1m 30.583s, 106.987 mph/172.179 km/h.

Round 14 (32.304 miles/51.988 km)
1 Alan van der Merwe, ZA (Dallara F303-Mugen Honda), 18m 30.029s, 104.767 mph/168.606 km/h; 2 Adam Carroll, GB (Dallara F303-Opel), 18m 32.709s; 3 Jamie Green, GB (Dallara F303-Mugen Honda), 18m 33.843s; 4 Nelson Angelo Piquet, BR (Dallara F303-Mugen Honda), 18m 34.430s; 5 Richard Antinucci, USA (Dallara F303-Mugen Honda), 18m 36.924s; 6 Clivio Piccione, MC (Dallara F303-Mugen Honda), 18m 40.774s; 7 Danny Watts, GB (Dallara F303-Renault), 18m 43.066s; 8 Will Davison, AUS (Dallara F303-Mugen Honda), 18m 43.568s; 9 Will Power, AUS (Dallara F303-Renault), 18m 47.730s; 10 Fairuz Fauzy, MAL (Dallara F303-Opel), 18m 47.842s.
Winner Scholarship Class: Karun Chandhok, IND (Dallara F301-Mugen Honda), 18m 55.184s (12th).
Fastest race lap: van der Merwe, 1m 31.710s, 105.672 mph/170.063 km/h.
Fastest qualifying lap: Piquet, 1m 31.267s, 106.185 mph/170.888 km/h.
Championship points. 1 van der Merwe, 216; 2 Green, 133; 3 Piquet, 113; 4 Antinucci, 92; 5 Watts, 87; 6 Bremer, 80.
Scholarship Class: 1 Kane, 196; 2 Chandhok, 185; 3 Viso, 163.

BRDC BRITISH FORMULA 3 CHAMPIONSHIP, Rockingham International Road Course, Corby, Northamptonshire, Great Britain, 3 August. 15 and 18 laps of the 2.443-mile/3.931-km circuit.
Round 15 (36.645 miles/58.974 km)
1 Nelson Angelo Piquet, BR (Dallara F303-Mugen Honda), 22m 32.631s, 97.530 mph/156.959 km/h; 2 Clivio Piccione, MC (Dallara F303-Mugen Honda), 22m 35.994s; 3 Ronnie Bremer, DK (Dallara F303-Mugen Honda), 22m 42.350s; 4 Alan van der Merwe, ZA (Dallara F303-Mugen Honda), 22m 43.959s; 5 Will Power, AUS (Dallara F303-Renault), 22m 51.888s; 6 Stefano Fabi, I (Dallara F303-Mugen Honda), 22m 53.969s; 7 Jamie Green, GB (Dallara F303-Mugen Honda), 22m 55.028s; 8 Billy Asaro, CDN (Dallara F303-Mugen Honda), 22m 58.208s; 9 Will Davison, AUS (Dallara F303-Mugen Honda), 22m 58.290s; 10 Adam Carroll, GB (Dallara F303-Opel), 23m 00.007s.
Winner Scholarship Class: Karun Chandhok, IND (Dallara F301-Mugen Honda), 23m 04.051s (12th).
Fastest race lap: Piquet, 1m 29.183s, 98.615 mph/158.706 km/h.
Fastest qualifying lap: Piquet, 1m 28.652s, 99.206 mph/159.656 km/h.

Round 16 (43.974 miles/70.769 km)
1 Jamie Green, GB (Dallara F303-Mugen Honda), 31m 29.211s, 83.795 mph/134.855 km/h; 2 Nelson Angelo Piquet, BR (Dallara F303-Mugen Honda), 31m 29.709s; 3 Alan van der Merwe, ZA (Dallara F303-Mugen Honda), 31m 32.260s; 4 Clivio Piccione, MC (Dallara F303-Mugen Honda), 31m 34.062s; 5 Fairuz Fauzy, MAL (Dallara F303-Mugen Honda), 31m 35.924s; 6 Robert Dahlgren, S (Dallara F303-Renault), 31m 37.232s; 7 Ernesto Viso, YV (Dallara F301-Mugen Honda), 31m 38.794s (1st Scholarship class); 8 Billy Asaro, CDN (Dallara F303-Mugen Honda), 31m 39.588s; 9 Richard Antinucci, USA (Dallara F303-Mugen Honda), 31m 46.112s; 10 Karun Chandhok, IND (Dallara F301-Mugen Honda), 31m 46.580s.
Fastest race lap: Piquet, 1m 29.217s, 98.578 mph/158.645 km/h.
Fastest qualifying lap: Green, 1m 28.765s, 99.080 mph/159.453 km/h.
Championship points: 1 van der Merwe, 238; 2 Green, 157; 3 Piquet, 150; 4 Antinucci, 95; 5 Bremer, 92; 6 Watts, 87.
Scholarship Class. 1 Chandhok, 220; 2 Kane, 218; 3 Viso, 200.

BRDC BRITISH FORMULA 3 CHAMPIONSHIP, Thruxton Circuit, Andover, Hampshire, Great Britain, 17 August. 21 and 18 laps of the 2.356-mile/3.792-km circuit.
Round 17 (49.476 miles/79.624 km)
1 Robert Dahlgren, S (Dallara F303-Renault), 26m 43.775s, 111.059 mph/178.732 km/h; 2 Alan van der Merwe, ZA (Dallara F303-Mugen Honda), 26m 45.260s; 3 Jamie Green, GB (Dallara F303-Mugen Honda), 26m 50.856s; 4 Fairuz Fauzy, MAL (Dallara F303-Mugen Honda), 26m 51.743s; 5 Eric Salignon, F (Dallara F303-Renault), 26m 52.085s; 6 Danny Watts, GB (Dallara F303-Renault), 26m 53.773s; 7 Ronnie Bremer, DK (Dallara F303-Mugen Honda), 26m 54.198s; 8 Steven Kane, GB (Dallara F301-Mugen Honda), 26m 56.698s (1st Scholarship class); 9 Ernesto Viso, YV (Dallara F301-Mugen Honda), 26m 57.002s; 10 Michael Keohane, IRL (Dallara F303-Mugen Honda), 26m 57.244s.
Fastest race lap: Dahlgren, 1m 08.714s, 123.433 mph/198.647 km/h.
Fastest qualifying lap: Watts, 1m 07.589s, 125.488 mph/201.953 km/h.

Round 18 (42.408 miles/68.249 km)
1 Jamie Green, GB (Dallara F303-Mugen Honda), 20m 50.714s, 122.065 mph/196.445 km/h; 2 Will Power, AUS (Dallara F303-Renault), 20m 52.308s; 3 Adam Carroll, GB (Dallara F303-Opel), 20m 54.373s; 4 Ronnie Bremer, DK (Dallara F303-Mugen Honda), 20m 56.332; 5 Andrew Thompson, GB (Dallara F303-Renault), 20m 57.306s; 6 Richard Antinucci, USA (Dallara F303-Mugen Honda), 20m 57.383s; 7 Will Davison, AUS (Dallara F303-Mugen Honda), 20m 57.671s; 8 Ernesto Viso, YV (Dallara F301-Mugen Honda), 20m 58.426s (1st Scholarship class); 9 Stefano Fabi, I (Dallara F303-Mugen Honda), 21m 05.121s; 10 Steven Kane, GB (Dallara F301-Mugen Honda), 21m 06.533s.
Fastest race lap: Salignon, 1m 08.368s, 124.058 mph/199.652 km/h.
Fastest qualifying lap: Salignon, 1m 07.369s, 125.898 mph/202.613 km/h.
Championship points: 1 van der Merwe, 253; 2 Green, 189; 3 Piquet, 151; 4 Bremer, 106; 5 Antinucci, 101; 6 Watts, 93.
Scholarship Class: 1 Kane, 253; 2 Chandhok, 244; 3 Viso, 237.

BRDC BRITISH FORMULA 3 CHAMPIONSHIP, Circuit de Spa-Francorchamps, Stavelot, Belgium, 30/31 August. 5 and 11 laps of the 4.317-mile/6.947-km circuit.
First race scheduled for 11 laps, but shortened due to rain.
Round 19 (21.583 miles/34.735 km)
1 Alan van der Merwe, ZA (Dallara F303-Mugen Honda), 11m 46.358s, 110.001 mph/177.029 km/h; 2 Jamie Green, GB (Dallara F303-Mugen Honda), 11m 46.794s; 3 Nelson Angelo Piquet, BR (Dallara F303-Mugen Honda), 11m 49.835s; 4 Will Power, AUS (Dallara F303-Renault), 11m 50.344s; 5 Ronnie Bremer, DK (Dallara F303-Mugen Honda), 11m 52.853s; 6 Ryan Briscoe, AUS (Dallara F303-Opel), 11m 54.098s; 7 Alvaro Parente, P (Dallara F303-Mugen Honda), 11m 54.370s; 8 Eric Salignon, F (Dallara F303-Renault), 11m 56.663s; 9 Richard Antinucci, USA (Dallara F303-Mugen Honda), 11m 56.921s; 10 Adam Carroll, GB (Dallara F303-Mugen Honda), 11m 58.511s.
Winner Scholarship Class: Ernesto Viso, YV (Dallara F301-Mugen Honda), 12m 12.042s (20th).
Fastest race lap: Green, 2m 18.954s, 111.836 mph/179.982 km/h.
Fastest qualifying lap: van der Merwe, 2m 35.001s, 100.257 mph/161.349 km/h.

Round 20 (47.483 miles/76.417 km)
1 Alan van der Merwe, ZA (Dallara F303-Mugen Honda), 28m 43.486s, 99.183 mph/159.619 km/h; 2 Eric Salignon, F (Dallara F303-Renault), 28m 44.909s; 3 Jamie Green, GB (Dallara F303-Mugen Honda), 28m 49.977s; 4 Ryan Briscoe, AUS (Dallara F303-Opel), 28m 51.299s; 5 Robert Doornbos, NL (Dallara F303-Opel), 28m 54.332s; 6 Danny Watts, GB (Dallara F303-Renault), 28m 57.843s; 7 Nelson Angelo Piquet, BR (Dallara F303-Mugen Honda), 29m 00.745s; 8 Alvaro Parente, P (Dallara F303-Mugen Honda), 29m 05.524s; 9 Robert Dahlgren, S (Dallara F303-Renault), 29m 09.058s; 10 Joao Paulo de Oliveira, BR (Dallara F302-Opel), 29m 11.988s.
Winner Scholarship Class: Ernesto Viso, YV (Dallara F301-Mugen Honda), 29m 29.718s (16th).
Fastest race lap: Green, 2m 35.304s, 100.062 mph/161.034 km/h.
Fastest qualifying lap: Doornbos, 2m 16.745s, 113.642 mph/182.889 km/h.
Championship points: 1 van der Merwe, 283; 2 Green, 210;

3 Piquet, 163; 4 Bremer, 110; 5 Antinucci, 102.5; 6 Watts, 101. **Scholarship Class:** 1 Kane, 270.5; 2 Chandhok, 267.5; 3 Viso, 267.

BRDC BRITISH FORMULA 3 CHAMPIONSHIP, Donington Park National Circuit, Castle Donington, Derbyshire, Great Britain, 7 September. 22 and 18 laps of the 1.9573-mile/3.150-km circuit.
Round 21 (43.061 miles/69.299 km)
1 Nelson Angelo Piquet, BR (Dallara F303-Mugen Honda), 29m 53.409s, 86.439 mph/139.109 km/h; 2 Richard Antinucci, USA (Dallara F303-Mugen Honda), 29m 54.914s; 3 Rob Austin, GB (Dallara F303-Opel), 29m 56.078s; 4 Will Davison, AUS (Dallara F303-Opel), 30m 07.808s; 5 Rizal Ramli, MAL (Dallara F303-Opel), 30m 08.548s; 6 Robert Dahlgren, S (Dallara F303-Renault), 30m 09.452s; 7 Jamie Green, GB (Dallara F303-Mugen Honda), 30m 11.619s; 8 Steven Kane, GB (Dallara F301-Mugen Honda), 30m 11.852s (1st Scholarship class); 9 Clivio Piccione, MC (Dallara F303-Mugen Honda), 30m 14.652s; 10 Andrew Thompson, GB (Dallara F303-Renault), 30m 16.088s.
Fastest race lap: Piquet, 1m 06.078s, 106.636 mph/171.614 km/h.
Fastest qualifying lap: Alan van der Merwe, ZA (Dallara F303-Mugen Honda), 1m 04.499s, 109.246 mph/175.815 km/h.

Round 22 (35.231 miles/56.699 km)
1 Rob Austin, GB (Dallara F303-Opel), 19m 34.692s, 107.970 mph/173.761 km/h; 2 Alan van der Merwe, ZA (Dallara F303-Mugen Honda), 19m 35.666s; 3 Danny Watts, GB (Dallara F303-Renault), 19m 38.196s; 4 Jamie Green, GB (Dallara F303-Mugen Honda), 19m 38.583s; 5 Ronnie Bremer, DK (Dallara F303-Mugen Honda), 19m 44.723s; 6 Nelson Angelo Piquet, BR (Dallara F303-Mugen Honda), 19m 45.113s; 7 Will Davison, AUS (Dallara F303-Opel), 19m 45.721s; 8 Richard Antinucci, USA (Dallara F303-Mugen Honda), 19m 46.259s; 9 Ernesto Viso, YV (Dallara F301-Mugen Honda), 19m 51.260s (1st Scholarship class); 10 Andrew Thompson, GB (Dallara F303-Renault), 19m 52.225s.
Fastest race lap: Green, 1m 04.780s, 108.772 mph/175.052 km/h.
Fastest qualifying lap: Austin, 1m 04.025s, 110.055 mph/177.117 km/h.
Championship points: 1 van der Merwe, 298; 2 Green, 225; 3 Piquet, 190; 4 Antinucci, 120.5; 5 Bremer, 118; 6 Watts, 113. **Scholarship Class:** 1 Viso, 303; 2 Kane, 301.5; 3 Chandhok, 282.5.

BRDC BRITISH FORMULA 3 CHAMPIONSHIP, Brands Hatch Grand Prix Circuit, West Kingsdown, Dartford, Kent, Great Britain, 27/28 September. 15 and 12 laps of the 2.6082-mile/4.197-km circuit.
Round 23 (39.123 miles/62.962 km)
1 Nelson Angelo Piquet, BR (Dallara F303-Mugen Honda), 20m 04.063s, 116.972 mph/188.250 km/h; 2 Will Davison, AUS (Dallara F303-Opel), 20m 09.642s; 3 Danny Watts, GB (Dallara F303-Renault), 20m 13.751s; 4 Billy Asaro, CDN (Dallara F303-Mugen Honda), 20m 15.894s; 5 Eric Salignon, F (Dallara F303-Renault), 20m 19.738s; 6 Robert Dahlgren, S (Dallara F303-Renault), 20m 20.307s; 7 Andrew Thompson, GB (Dallara F303-Renault), 20m 20.642s; 8 Richard Antinucci, USA (Dallara F303-Mugen Honda), 20m 21.494s; 9 Ronnie Bremer, DK (Dallara F303-Mugen Honda), 20m 21.906s; 10 Michael Keohane, IRL (Dallara F303-Mugen Honda), 20m 24.496s.
Winner Scholarship Class: Ernesto Viso, YV (Dallara F301-Mugen Honda), 20m 28.249s (13th).
Fastest race lap: Robert Doornbos, NL (Dallara F303-Opel), 1m 19.127s, 118.664 mph/190.971 km/h.
Fastest qualifying lap: Piquet, 1m 19.073s, 118.745 mph/191.101 km/h.

Round 24 (31.298 miles/50.370 km)
Race stopped after 2 laps following an accident and restarted for a further 9 laps, with times being aggregated.
1 Nelson Angelo Piquet, BR (Dallara F303-Mugen Honda), 16m 05.169s, 116.739 mph/187.873 km/h; 2 Robert Doornbos, NL (Dallara F303-Opel), 16m 16.967s; 3 Jamie Green, GB (Dallara F303-Mugen Honda), 16m 19.476s; 4 Alan van der Merwe, ZA (Dallara F303-Mugen Honda), 16m 21.375s; 5 Billy Asaro, CDN (Dallara F303-Mugen Honda), 16m 23.895s; 6 Robert Dahlgren, S (Dallara F303-Renault), 16m 26.453s; 7 Will Davison, AUS (Dallara F303-Opel), 16m 26.538s; 8 Eric Salignon, F (Dallara F303-Renault), 16m 26.811s; 9 Richard Antinucci, USA (Dallara F303-Mugen Honda), 16m 30.294s; 10 Ronnie Bremer, DK (Dallara F303-Mugen Honda), 16m 31.230s.
Winner Scholarship Class: Karun Chandhok, IND (Dallara F301-Mugen Honda), 16m 52.278s (15th).
Fastest race lap: Piquet, 1m 18.865s, 119.058 mph/191.605 km/h.
Fastest qualifying lap: Piquet, 1m 18.823s, 119.122 mph/191.708 km/h.

Final championship points

1 Alan van der Merwe, ZA, 308; 2 Jamie Green, GB, 237; 3 Nelson Angelo Piquet, BR, 231; 4 Richard Antinucci, USA, 125.5; 5 Danny Watts, GB, 125; 6 Ronnie Bremer, DK, 121; 7 Rob Austin, GB, 110; 8 Will Davison, AUS, 103; 9 Robert Dahlgren, S, 102; 10 Adam Carroll, GB, 90; 11 Clivio Piccione, MC, 84; 12 Eric Salignon, F, 63; 13 Michael Keohane, IRL, 42; 14 Will Power, AUS, 40; 15 Billy Asaro, CDN, 34; 16 Fairuz Fauzy, MAL, 30.5; 17 Robert Doornbos, NL, 26; 18= Stefano Fabi, I, 19; 18= Andrew Thompson, GB, 19; 20 Ernani Judice, BR, 15; 21 Rizal Ramli, MAL, 9; 22 Alvaro Parente, P, 7; 23 Scott Speed, USA, 3; 24 Tuka Rocha, BR, 2; 25 Fabio Carbone, BR, 1.

Scholarship Class
1 Ernesto Viso, YV, 324; 2 Steven Kane, GB, 316.5; 3 Karun Chandhok, IND, 314.5; 4 Justin Sherwood, GB, 178; 5 Christian England, GB, 94.

Formula 3 Euro Series

FORMULA 3 EURO SERIES, Hockenheimring Grand Prix Circuit, Heidelberg, Germany, 26/27 April. 2 x 18 laps of the 2.842-mile/4.574-km circuit.
Round 1 (51.159 miles/82.332 km)
1 Ryan Briscoe, AUS (Dallara F303-Opel), 28m 48.613s, 106.543 mph/171.464 km/h; 2 Robert Doornbos, NL (Dallara F302-Mugen Honda), 28m 50.548s; 3 Markus Winkelhock, D (Dallara F302-Mercedes-Benz), 28m 50.960s; 4 Christian Klien, A (Dallara F302-Mercedes-Benz), 28m 53.085s; 5 Nicolas Lapierre, F (Dallara F302-Renault), 29m 02.226s; 6 Timo Glock, D (Dallara F303-Opel), 29m 02.917s; 7 Simon Abadie, F (Dallara F302-Renault), 29m 06.676s; 8 Alexandros 'Alex' Margaritis, GR (Dallara F303-Opel), 29m 07.417s; 9 Alvaro Parente, P (Dallara F302-Mugen Honda), 29m 09.931s; 10 Charles Zwolsman, NL (Dallara F303-Mercedes-Benz), 29m 10.809s. Alexandre Prémat, F and Olivier Pla, F (both Dallara F303-Mercedes-Benz), finished 5th and 6th, but were disqualified for front wing infringements.
Fastest race lap: Winkelhock, 1m 35.050s, 107.646 mph/173.239 km/h.
Fastest qualifying lap: Pla, 1m 33.996s, 108.853 mph/175.182 km/h.

Round 2 (51.159 miles/82.332 km)
1 Ryan Briscoe, AUS (Dallara F303-Opel), 28m 52.705s, 106.291 mph/171.059 km/h; 2 Olivier Pla, F (Dallara F303-Mercedes-Benz), 29m 06.026s; 3 Nico Rosberg, FIN (Dallara F303-Opel), 29m 09.969s; 4 Markus Winkelhock, D (Dallara F302-Mercedes-Benz), 29m 10.985s; 5 Christian Klien, A (Dallara F302-Mercedes-Benz), 29m 11.521s; 6 César Campanico, P (Dallara F302-Opel), 29m 12.669s; 7 Timo Glock, D (Dallara F303-Opel), 29m 14.297s; 8 Robert Doornbos, NL (Dallara F302-Mugen Honda), 29m 15.300s; 9 Andreas Zuber, A (Dallara F303-Opel), 29m 17.023s; 10 Sakon Yamamoto, J (Dallara F303-TOM'S Toyota), 29m 20.087s.
Fastest race lap: Glock, 1m 34.430s, 108.353 mph/174.377 km/h.
Fastest qualifying lap: Pla, 1m 34.515s, 108.255 mph/174.220 km/h.

FORMULA 3 EURO SERIES, Autodromo di Adria, Italy, 10/11 May. 24 and 26 laps of the 1.679-mile/2.702-km circuit.
Round 3 (40.295 miles/64.848 km)
1 Timo Glock, D (Dallara F303-Opel), 30m 12.461s, 80.035 mph/128.804 km/h; 2 Fabio Carbone, BR (Dallara F302-Renault), 30m 13.385s; 3 Christian Klien, A (Dallara F302-Mercedes-Benz), 30m 14.509s; 4 César Campanico, P (Dallara F302-Opel), 30m 15.462s; 5 Ryan Briscoe, AUS (Dallara F303-Opel), 30m 15.800s; 6 Nicolas Lapierre, F (Dallara F302-Renault), 30m 16.767s; 7 Alexandre Prémat, F (Dallara F303-Mercedes-Benz), 30m 17.468s; 8 Olivier Pla, F (Dallara F303-Mercedes-Benz), 30m 18.063s; 9 Alexandros 'Alex' Margaritis, GR (Dallara F303-Opel), 30m 29.152s; 10 Robert Doornbos, NL (Dallara F302-Mugen Honda), 30m 33.092s.
Fastest race lap: Briscoe, 1m 11.600s, 84.416 mph/135.855 km/h.
Fastest qualifying lap: Klien, 1m 25.578s, 70.628 mph/113.665 km/h.

Round 4 (43.653 miles/70.252 km)
1 Ryan Briscoe, AUS (Dallara F303-Opel), 30m 48.472s, 85.016 mph/136.820 km/h; 2 Nico Rosberg, FIN (Dallara F303-Opel), 30m 54.441s; 3 Olivier Pla, F (Dallara F303-Mercedes-Benz), 31m 01.549s; 4 Bernhard Auinger, A (Dallara F302-TOM'S Toyota), 31m 07.297s; 5 Alexandre Prémat, F (Dallara F303-Mercedes-Benz), 31m 07.936s; 6 Robert Doornbos, NL (Dallara F302-Mugen Honda); 7 Charles Zwolsman, NL (Dallara F303-Mercedes-Benz), 31m 12.996s; 8 Richard Lietz, A (Dallara F302-Opel), 31m 15.360s; 9 Sakon Yamamoto, J (Dallara F303-TOM'S Toyota), 31m 15.748s; 10 Fabio Carbone, BR (Dallara F302-Renault), 31m 16.169s.
Fastest race lap: Briscoe, 1m 10.425s, 85.825 mph/138.121 km/h.
Fastest qualifying lap: Rosberg, 1m 10.345s, 85.922 mph/138.278 km/h.

63rd GRAND PRIX DE PAU, FIA FORMULA 3 EUROPE CUP, Circuit de Pau Ville, France. 8/9 June. 21 and 23 laps of the 1.715-mile/2.760-km circuit.
Round 5 (36.015 miles/57.960 km)
1 Ryan Briscoe, AUS (Dallara F303-Opel), 30m 31.386s, 70.795 mph/113.933 km/h.; 2 Olivier Pla, F (Dallara F303-Mercedes-Benz), 30m 38.492s; 3 Timo Glock, D (Dallara F303-Opel), 30m 49.172s; 4 Fabio Carbone, BR (Dallara F302-Renault), 30m 53.000s; 5 Simon Abadie, F (Dallara F302-Renault), 30m 59.371s; 6 Katsuyuki Hiranaka, J (Dallara F303-Opel), 30m 59.442s; 7 Alexandros 'Alex' Margaritis, GR (Dallara F303-Opel), 31m 03.613s; 8 Robert Doornbos, NL (Dallara F302-Mugen Honda), 31m 03.680s; 9 Lucas di Grassi, BR (Dallara F303-Opel), 31m 09.313s; 10 Jan Heylen, B (Dallara F302-Mercedes-Benz), 31m 13.035s.
Fastest race lap: Hiranaka, 1m 21.556s, 75.702 mph/121.830 km/h.
Fastest qualifying lap: Nicolas Lapierre, F (Dallara F302-Renault), 1m 11.999s, 85.750 mph/138.002 km/h.

Round 6 (39.445 miles/63.480 km)
1 Fabio Carbone, BR (Dallara F302-Renault), 28m 40.032s, 82.557 mph/132.863 km/h; 2 Ryan Briscoe, AUS (Dallara F303-Opel), 28m 47.040s; 3 Jamie Green, GB (Dallara F303-Mercedes-Benz), 28m 49.312s; 4 Lucas di Grassi, BR (Dallara F303-Opel), 28m 54.832s; 5 Simon Abadie, F (Dallara F302-Renault), 28m 57.437s; 6 Charles Zwolsman, NL (Dallara F303-Mercedes-Benz), 28m 57.910s; 7 Christian Klien, A (Dallara F302-Mercedes-Benz), 28m 58.934s; 8 César Campanico, P (Dallara F302-Opel), 28m 59.500s; 9 Richard Lietz, A (Dallara F302-Opel), 29m 05.517s; 10 Bernhard Auinger, A (Dallara F302-TOM'S Toyota), 29m 07.524s.
Fastest race lap: Alexandre Prémat, F (Dallara F303-Mercedes-Benz), 1m 12.999s, 84.576 mph/136.111 km/h.
Fastest qualifying lap: Briscoe, 1m 12.528s, 85.125 mph/136.995 km/h.

FORMULA 3 EURO SERIES, Norisring, Nürnberg, Germany, 21/22 June. 2 x 35 laps of the 1.429-mile/2.300-km circuit.
Round 7 (50.020 miles/80.500 km)
1 Robert Kubica, PL (Dallara F303-Opel), 29m 20.379s, 102.292 mph/164.624 km/h; 2 Timo Glock, D (Dallara F303-Opel), 29m 24.534s; 3 Olivier Pla, F (Dallara F303-Mercedes-Benz), 29m 25.749s; 4 Ryan Briscoe, AUS (Dallara F303-Opel), 29m 25.829s; 5 Fabio Carbone, BR (Dallara F302-Renault), 29m 29.109s; 6 Nicolas Lapierre, F (Dallara F302-Renault), 29m 40.436s; 7 César Campanico, P (Dallara F302-Opel), 29m 43.369s; 8 Nico Rosberg, FIN (Dallara F303-Opel), 29m 45.527s; 9 Marcel Lasée, D (Dallara F302-Opel), 29m 46.381s; 10 James Manderson, AUS (Dallara F302-Opel), 29m 49.603s.
Fastest race lap: Katsuyuki Hiranaka, J (Dallara F303-Opel), 49.567s, 103.798 mph/167.047 km/h.
Fastest qualifying lap: Alexandre Prémat, F (Dallara F303-Mercedes-Benz), 49.310s, 104.339 mph/167.917 km/h.

Round 8 (50.020 miles/80.500 km)
1 Alexandre Prémat, F (Dallara F303-Mercedes-Benz), 29m 06.177s, 103.124 mph/165.963 km/h; 2 Robert Kubica, PL (Dallara F303-Opel), 29m 08.893s; 3 Timo Glock, D (Dallara F303-Opel), 29m 17.487s; 4 Robert Doornbos, NL (Dallara F302-Mugen Honda), 29m 21.282s; 5 Markus Winkelhock, D (Dallara F302-Mercedes-Benz), 29m 24.729s; 6 Nicolas Lapierre, F (Dallara F302-Renault), 29m 27.818s; 7 César Campanico, P (Dallara F302-Opel), 29m 33.032s; 8 Daniel la Rosa, D (Dallara F302-Opel), 29m 37.072s; 9 Charles Zwolsman, NL (Dallara F303-Mercedes-Benz), 29m 38.272s; 10 Christian Klien, A (Dallara F302-Mercedes-Benz), 29m 38.934s.
Fastest race lap: Kubica, 49.348s, 104.259 mph/167.788 km/h.
Fastest qualifying lap: Prémat, 49.358s, 104.237 mph/167.754 km/h.

FORMULA 3 EURO SERIES, Circuit Le Mans-Bugatti, France, 13/14 July. 2 x 18 laps of the 2.597-mile/4.180-km circuit.
Round 9 (46.752 miles/75.240 km)
1 Nico Rosberg, FIN (Dallara F303-Opel), 28m 15.515s, 99.266 mph/159.753 km/h; 2 Christian Klien, A (Dallara F302-Mercedes-Benz), 28m 16.305s; 3 Ryan Briscoe, AUS (Dallara F303-Opel), 28m 23.515s; 4 Olivier Pla, F (Dallara F303-Mercedes-Benz), 28m 24.122s; 5 Alexandre Prémat, F (Dallara F303-Mercedes-Benz), 28m 25.240s; 6 Fabio Carbone, BR (Dallara F302-Renault), 28m 26.700s; 7 Andreas Zuber, A (Dallara F303-Opel), 28m 32.868s; 8 Markus Winkelhock, D (Dallara F302-Mercedes-Benz), 28m 34.290s; 9 Sakon Yamamoto, J (Dallara F303-TOM'S Toyota), 28m 39.207s; 10 Charles Zwolsman, NL (Dallara F303-Mercedes-Benz), 28m 41.166s.
Fastest race lap: Rosberg, 1m 33.159s, 100.370 mph/161.530 km/h.
Fastest qualifying lap: Klien, 1m 31.494s, 102.197 mph/164.470 km/h.

Round 10 (46.752 miles/75.240 km)
1 Christian Klien, A (Dallara F302-Mercedes-Benz), 28m 40.814s, 97.807 mph/157.405 km/h; 2 Fabio Carbone, BR (Dallara F302-Renault), 28m 41.819s; 3 Bruno Spengler, CDN (Dallara F303-Mercedes-Benz), 28m 42.314s; 4 Bernhard Auinger, A (Dallara F302-TOM'S Toyota), 28m 54.204s; 5 Nicolas Lapierre, F (Dallara F302-Renault), 28m 54.660s; 6 Simon Abadie, F (Dallara F302-Renault), 28m 55.233s; 7 Robert Kubica, PL (Dallara F303-Opel), 28m 56.007s; 8 Robert Doornbos, NL (Dallara F302-Mugen Honda), 29m 00.818s; 9 Alexandros 'Alex' Margaritis, GR (Dallara F303-Opel), 29m 03.292s; 10 Alvaro Parente, P (Dallara F302-Mugen Honda), 29m 03.570s.
Fastest race lap: Kubica, 1m 34.438s, 99.011 mph/159.343 km/h.
Fastest qualifying lap: Pla, 1m 32.893s, 100.658 mph/161.993 km/h.

FORMULA 3 EURO SERIES, Nürburgring Sprint Circuit, Nürburg/Eifel, Germany, 16/17 August. 17 and 19 laps of the 2.252-mile/3.625-km circuit.
Round 11 (38.292 miles/61.625 km)
1 Markus Winkelhock, D (Dallara F302-Mercedes-Benz), 27m 00.295s, 85.078 mph/136.920 km/h; 2 Olivier Pla, F (Dallara F303-Mercedes-Benz), 27m 04.992s; 3 Robert Doornbos, NL (Dallara F302-Mugen Honda), 27m 07.501s; 4 Bernhard Auinger, A (Dallara F302-TOM'S Toyota), 27m 08.712s; 5 Alexandre Prémat, F (Dallara F303-Mercedes-Benz), 27m 09.290s; 6 Fabio Carbone, BR (Dallara F302-Renault), 27m 10.221s; 7 Marcel Lasée, D (Dallara F302-Opel), 27m 11.018s; 8 Katsuyuki Hiranaka, J (Dallara F303-Opel), 27m 12.990s; 9 Robert Kubica, PL (Dallara F303-Opel), 27m 13.564s; 10 Alexandros 'Alex' Margaritis, GR (Dallara F303-Opel), 27m 16.523s.
Fastest race lap: Winkelhock, 1m 24.338s, 96.148 mph/154.735 km/h.
Fastest qualifying lap: Christian Klien, A (Dallara F302-Mercedes-Benz), 1m 23.315s, 97.328 mph/156.634 km/h.

Round 12 (42.797 miles/68.875 km)
1 Christian Klien, A (Dallara F302-Mercedes-Benz), 30m 26.990s, 84.329 mph/135.715 km/h; 2 Markus Winkelhock, D (Dallara F302-Mercedes-Benz), 30m 27.700s; 3 Nico Rosberg, FIN (Dallara F303-Opel), 30m 30.137s; 4 Bruno Spengler, CDN (Dallara F303-Mercedes-Benz), 30m 30.637s; 5 Richard Lietz, A (Dallara F302-Opel), 30m 31.236s; 6 Robert Kubica, PL (Dallara F303-Opel), 30m 31.671s; 7 Ryan Briscoe, AUS (Dallara F303-Opel), 30m 32.062s; 8 Marcel Lasée, D (Dallara F302-Opel), 30m 32.759s; 9 Olivier Pla, F (Dallara F303-Mercedes-Benz), 30m 34.022s; 10 Simon Abadie, F (Dallara F302-Mugen Honda), 30m 35.535s.
Fastest race lap: Klien, 1m 24.585s, 95.867 mph/154.283 km/h.
Fastest qualifying lap: Klien, 1m 23.300s, 97.346 mph/156.663 km/h.

FORMULA 3 EURO SERIES, A1-Ring, Spielberg, Austria, 6/7 September. 2 x 19 laps of the 2.688-mile/4.326-km circuit.
Round 13 (51.073 miles/82.194 km)
1 Ryan Briscoe, AUS (Dallara F303-Opel), 28m 04.031s, 109.180 mph/175.708 km/h; 2 Alexandre Prémat, F (Dallara F303-Mercedes-Benz), 28m 09.348s; 3 Bruno Spengler, CDN (Dallara F303-Mercedes-Benz), 28m 11.245s; 4 Markus Winkelhock, D (Dallara F302-Mercedes-Benz), 28m 12.505s; 5 Christian Klien, A (Dallara F302-Mercedes-Benz), 28m 13.068s; 6 Adam Carroll, GB (Dallara F303-Opel), 28m 18.436s; 7 Charles Zwolsman, NL (Dallara F303-Mercedes-Benz), 28m 21.211s; 8 Nico Rosberg, FIN (Dallara F303-Opel), 28m 21.729s; 9 Andreas Zuber, A (Dallara F303-Opel), 28m 24.097s; 10 Robert Doornbos, NL (Dallara F302-Mugen Honda), 28m 24.730s.
Fastest race lap: Robert Kubica, PL (Dallara F303-Opel), 1m 27.446s, 110.662 mph/178.094 km/h.
Fastest qualifying lap: Briscoe, 1m 27.066s, 111.145 mph/178.871 km/h.

Round 14 (51.073 miles/82.194 km)
1 Ryan Briscoe, AUS (Dallara F303-Opel), 29m 55.051s, 102.428 mph/164.841 km/h; 2 Alexandre Prémat, F (Dallara F303-Mercedes-Benz), 29m 59.434s; 3 Nico Rosberg, FIN (Dallara F303-Opel), 30m 01.120s; 4 Olivier Pla, F (Dallara F303-Mercedes-Benz), 30m 06.669s; 5 Christian Klien, A (Dallara F302-Mercedes-Benz), 30m 06.925s; 6 Markus Winkelhock, D (Dallara F302-Mercedes-Benz), 30m 07.417s; 7 Bruno Spengler, CDN (Dallara F303-Mercedes-Benz), 30m 11.331s; 8 Robert Doornbos, NL (Dallara F302-Mugen Honda), 30m 11.797s; 9 Timo Glock, D (Dallara F303-Opel), 30m 12.711s; 10 Nicolas Lapierre, F (Dallara F302-Renault), 30m 13.427s.
Fastest race lap: Rosberg, 1m 27.427s, 110.686 mph/178.133 km/h.
Fastest qualifying lap: Briscoe, 1m 27.358s, 110.774 mph/178.273 km/h.

FORMULA 3 EURO SERIES, Circuit Park Zandvoort, Netherlands, 20/21 September. 16 and 17 laps of the 2.672-mile/4.300-km circuit.
Round 15 (42.750 miles/68.800 km)
1 Christian Klien, A (Dallara F302-Mercedes-Benz), 30m 26.609s, 84.255 mph/135.596 km/h; 2 Bruno Spengler, CDN (Dallara F303-Mercedes-Benz), 30m 27.855s; 3 Olivier Pla, F (Dallara F303-Mercedes-Benz), 30m 29.593s; 4 Markus Winkelhock, D (Dallara F302-Mercedes-Benz), 30m 30.463s; 5 Robert Doornbos, NL (Dallara F302-Mugen Honda), 30m 31.068s; 6 Simon Abadie, F (Dallara F302-Mugen Honda), 30m 32.364s; 7 Robert Kubica, PL (Dallara F303-Opel), 30m 32.512s; 8 Alvaro Parente, P (Dallara F302-Mugen Honda), 30m 32.836s; 9 Nicolas Lapierre, F (Dallara F302-Renault), 30m 33.682s; 10 Katsuyuki Hiranaka, J (Dallara F303-Opel), 30m 35.094s.
Fastest race lap: Klien, 1m 34.036s, 102.289 mph/164.618 km/h.
Fastest qualifying lap: Klien, 1m 32.938s, 103.497 mph/166.563 km/h.

Round 16 (45.422 miles/73.100 km)
1 Ryan Briscoe, AUS (Dallara F303-Opel), 30m 31.428s, 89.286 mph/143.691 km/h; 2 Christian Klien, A (Dallara F302-Mercedes-Benz), 30m 37.636s; 3 Olivier Pla, F (Dallara F303-Mercedes-Benz), 30m 38.422s; 4 Markus Winkelhock, D (Dallara F302-Mercedes-Benz), 30m 40.369s; 5 Alexandre Prémat, F (Dallara F303-Mercedes-Benz), 30m 41.143s; 6 Fabio Carbone, BR (Dallara F302-Renault), 30m 47.709s; 7 Robert Doornbos, NL (Dallara F302-Mugen Honda), 30m 47.949s; 8 Nico Rosberg, FIN (Dallara F303-Opel), 30m 48.385s; 9 Nicolas Lapierre, F (Dallara F302-Renault), 30m 50.544s; 10 Katsuyuki Hiranaka, J (Dallara F303-Opel), 30m 51.129s.
Fastest race lap: Briscoe, 1m 34.065s, 102.257 mph/164.567 km/h.
Fastest qualifying lap: Klien, 1m 33.288s, 103.109 mph/165.938 km/h.

FORMULA 3 EURO SERIES, Hockenheimring Grand Prix Circuit, Heidelberg, Germany, 4/5 October. 15 and 18 laps of the 2.842-mile/4.574-km circuit.
Round 17 (42.632 miles/68.610 km)
1 Timo Glock, D (Dallara F303-Opel), 30m 38.015s, 83.501 mph/134.382 km/h; 2 Alexandros 'Alex' Margaritis, GR (Dallara F303-Opel), 30m 38.716s; 3 Nicolas Lapierre, F (Dallara F302-Renault), 30m 39.921s; 4 Fabio Carbone, BR (Dallara F302-Renault), 30m 40.498s; 5 Adam Carroll, GB (Dallara F303-Opel), 30m 40.553s; 6 Bruno Spengler, CDN (Dallara F303-Mercedes-Benz), 30m 40.733s; 7 Nico Rosberg, FIN (Dallara F303-Opel), 30m 42.104s; 8 Simon Abadie, F (Dallara F302-Mugen Honda), 30m 42.289s; 9 Alexandre Prémat, F (Dallara F303-Mercedes-Benz), 30m 43.663s; 10 Olivier Pla, F (Dallara F303-Mercedes-Benz), 30m 45.848s.
Fastest race lap: Ryan Briscoe, AUS (Dallara F303-Opel), 1m 40.806s, 101.499 mph/163.347 km/h.
Fastest qualifying lap: Markus Winkelhock, D (Dallara F302-Mercedes-Benz), 1m 54.236s, 89.567 mph/144.144 km/h.

Round 18 (51.159 miles/82.332 km)
1 Ryan Briscoe, AUS (Dallara F303-Opel), 28m 51.116s, 106.389 mph/171.216 km/h; 2 Markus Winkelhock, D (Dallara F302-Mercedes-Benz), 28m 55.664s; 3 Christian Klien, A (Dallara F302-Mercedes-Benz), 28m 56.426s; 4 Alexandros 'Alex' Margaritis, GR (Dallara F303-Opel), 29m 06.763s; 5 Bruno Spengler, CDN (Dallara F303-Mercedes-Benz), 29m 08.375s; 6 Olivier Pla, F (Dallara F303-Mercedes-Benz), 29m 10.044s; 7 Nicolas Lapierre, F (Dallara F302-Renault), 29m 12.287s; 8 Simon Abadie, F (Dallara F302-Mugen Honda), 29m 18.718s; 9 Charles Zwolsman, NL (Dallara F303-Mercedes-Benz), 29m 19.868s; 10 Robert Kubica, PL (Dallara F303-Opel), 29m 20.268s.
Fastest race lap: Briscoe, 1m 35.017s, 107.683 mph/173.300 km/h.
Fastest qualifying lap: Briscoe, 1m 34.455s, 108.324 mph/174.331 km/h.

FORMULA 3 EURO SERIES, Circuit de Nevers, Magny-Cours, France, 25/26 October. 16 and 19 laps of the 2.741-mile/4.411-km circuit.
Round 19 (43.854 miles/70.576 km).
1 Markus Winkelhock, D (Dallara F302-Mercedes-Benz), 30m 38.126s, 85.889 mph/138.224 km/h; 2 Olivier Pla, F (Dallara F303-Mercedes-Benz), 30m 42.145s; 3 Fabio Carbone, BR (Dallara F302-Renault), 30m 42.848s; 4 Robert Kubica, PL (Dallara F303-Opel), 30m 43.728s; 5 Nicolas Lapierre, F (Dallara F302-Renault), 3m 44.252s; 6 Nico Rosberg, FIN (Dallara F303-Opel), 30m 46.769s; 7 Richard Lietz, A (Dallara F302-Opel), 30m 47.397s; 8 Simon Abadie, F (Dallara F302-Mugen Honda), 30m 48.067s; 9 Robert Doornbos, NL (Dallara F302-Mugen Honda), 30m 48.321s; 10 Jamie Green, GB (Dallara F303-Mercedes-Benz), 30m 49.168s.
Fastest race lap: Winkelhock, 1m 35.507s, 103.313 mph/166.266 km/h.
Fastest qualifying lap: Alexandros 'Alex' Margaritis, GR (Dallara F303-Opel), 1m 34.855s, 104.023 mph/167.409 km/h.

Round 20 (52.076 miles/83.809 km).
1 Timo Glock, D (Dallara F303-Opel), 30m 44.710s, 101.629 mph/163.555 km/h; 2 Robert Doornbos, NL (Dallara F302-Mugen Honda), 30m 45.286s; 3 Christian Klien, A (Dallara F302-Mercedes-Benz), 30m 45.909s; 4 Alexandros 'Alex' Margaritis, GR (Dallara F303-Opel), 30m 49.251s; 5 Alexandre Prémat, F (Dallara F303-Mercedes-Benz), 30m 53.035s; 6 Nicolas Lapierre, F (Dallara F302-Renault), 30m 55.638s; 7 Olivier Pla, F (Dallara F303-Mercedes-Benz), 30m 56.669s; 8 Robert Kubica, PL (Dallara F303-Opel), 30m 56.873s; 9 Markus Winkelhock, D (Dallara F302-Mercedes-Benz), 30m 58.687s; 10 Jamie Green, GB (Dallara F303-Mercedes-Benz), 31m 01.172s.
Fastest race lap: Klien, 1m 35.613s, 103.199 mph/166.082 km/h.
Fastest qualifying lap: Margaritis, 1m 34.678s, 104.218 mph/167.722 km/h.

Final championship points

1 Ryan Briscoe, AUS, 110; **2** Christian Klien, A, 89; **3** Olivier Pla, F, 74; **4** Markus Winkelhock, D, 71; **5=** Timo Glock, D, 55; **5=** Fabio Carbone, BR, 55; **7** Alexandre Prémat, F, 50; **8** Nico Rosberg, FIN, 45; **9** Robert Doornbos, NL, 40; **10** Bruno Spengler, CDN, 34; **11** Nicolas Lapierre, F, 33; **12** Robert Kubica, PL, 31; **13** Alexandros 'Alex' Margaritis, GR, 23; **14** Simon Abadie, F, 19; **15** Berhard Auinger, A, 15; **16** César Campanico, P, 13; **17=** Richard Lietz, A, 7; **17=** Charles Zwolsman, NL, 7; **17=** Adam Carroll, GB, 7; **20** Jamie Green, GB, 6; **21** Lucas di Grassi, BR, 5; **22** Katsuyuki Hiranaka, J, 4; **23** Marcel Lasée, D, 3; **24** Andreas Zuber, A, 2; **25=** Daniel la Rosa, D, 1; **25=** Alvaro Parente, P, 1.

Rookie Cup
1 Christian Klien, 135; **2** Nico Rosberg, 102; **3** Alexandre Prémat, 96.

Nation's Cup
1 France, 166; **2** Germany, 128; **3** Austria, 107.

Recaro Formel-3-Cup

RECARO FORMEL-3-CUP, Motopark Oschersleben, Germany, 3/4 May. 2.279-mile/3.667-km circuit.
Round 1
1 Hannes Neuhauser, A (Dallara F302-Opel), 23m 32.154s; **2** Joao Paulo de Oliveira, BR (Dallara F302-Opel), 23m 32.749s; **3** Catharina Felser, D (Dallara F302-Opel), 23m 51.695s; **4** Franz Schmöller, D (Dallara F302-Opel), 23m 56.600s; **5** Markus Mann, D (Dallara F300-Opel), 23m 56.704s; **6** Diego Romanini, I (Dallara F399-Opel), 24m 10.061s; **7** Sven Barth, D (Dallara F399-Opel), 24m 10.358s; **8** Oliver Muytjens, B (Dallara F302-Opel), 24m 22.511s; **9** Tomás Kostka, CZ (Dallara F302-Opel), 24m 22.855s; **10** Frank Brendecke, D (Dallara F300-Opel), 1 lap behind.
Fastest qualifying lap: Neuhauser, 1m 21.387s, 100.788 mph/162.203 km/h.

Round 2
1 Hannes Neuhauser, A (Dallara F302-Opel), 25m 02.547s; **2** Joao Paulo de Oliveira, BR (Dallara F302-Opel), 25m 02.963s; **3** Tomás Kostka, CZ (Dallara F302-Opel), 25m 11.549s; **4** Catharina Felser, D (Dallara F302-Opel), 25m 12.134s; **5** Sven Barth, D (Dallara F399-Opel), 25m 12.343s; **6** Markus Mann, D (Dallara F300-Opel), 25m 14.445s; **7** Diego Romanini, I (Dallara F399-Opel), 25m 29.155s; **8** Oliver Muytjens, B (Dallara F302-Opel), 25m 52.517s; **9** Franz Schmöller, D (Dallara F302-Opel), 26m 01.803s; **10** Denis Watt, A (Dallara F302-Opel), 25m 10.857s.
Fastest qualifying lap: no qualifying, same grid as for round 1.

RECARO FORMEL-3-CUP, EuroSpeedway Lausitz, Germany, 10/11 May. 2 x 15 laps of the 2.817-mile/4.534-km circuit.
Round 3 (42.259 miles/68.010 km)
1 Joao Paulo de Oliveira, BR (Dallara F302-Opel), 25m 27.070s, 99.625 mph/160.331 km/h; **2** Sven Barth, D (Dallara F399-Opel), 25m 33.055s; **3** Hannes Neuhauser, A (Dallara F302-Opel), 25m 33.316s; **4** Markus Mann, D (Dallara F300-Opel), 25m 36.495s; **5** Franz Schmöller, D (Dallara F302-Opel), 25m 44.517s; **6** Diego Romanini, I (Dallara F399-Opel), 25m 56.865s; **7** Catharina Felser, D (Dallara F302-Opel), 25m 57.046s; **8** André Fibier, D (Dallara F399-Opel), 25m 57.945s; **9** Tomás Kostka, CZ (Dallara F302-Opel), 26m 02.467s; **10** Michael Herich, D (Dallara F399-Opel), 26m 03.253s.
Fastest race lap: de Oliveira, 1m 40.704s, 100.714 mph/162.083 km/h.
Fastest qualifying lap: de Oliveira, 1m 39.748s, 101.679 mph/163.636 km/h.

Round 4 (42.259 miles/68.010 km)
1 Joao Paulo de Oliveira, BR (Dallara F302-Opel), 25m 34.437s, 99.146 mph/159.561 km/h; **2** Hannes Neuhauser, A (Dallara F302-Opel), 25m 39.507s; **3** Sven Barth, D (Dallara F399-Opel), 25m 41.460s; **4** Markus Mann, D (Dallara F300-Opel), 25m 45.462s; **5** Catharina Felser, D (Dallara F302-Opel), 25m 50.599s; **6** Tomás Kostka, CZ (Dallara F302-Opel), 25m 53.812s; **7** Diego Romanini, I (Dallara F399-Opel), 25m 59.333s; **8** Franz Schmöller, D (Dallara F302-Opel), 25m 59.651s; **9** André Fibier, D (Dallara F399-Opel), 26m 00.619s; **10** Michael Herich, D (Dallara F399-Opel), 26m 01.570s.
Fastest race lap: de Oliveira, 1m 40.635s, 100.783 mph/162.194 km/h.
Fastest qualifying lap: de Oliveira, 1m 39.857s, 101.568 mph/163.458 km/h.

RECARO FORMEL-3-CUP. Hockenheimring Grand Prix Circuit, Heidelberg, Germany, 14/15 June. 11 and 16 laps of the 2.842-mile/4.574-km circuit.
Round 5 (31.264 miles/50.314 km)
1 Joao Paulo de Oliveira, BR (Dallara F302-Opel), 21m 40.008s, 86.576 mph/139.330 km/h; **2** Sven Barth, D (Dallara F399-Opel), 22m 05.094s; **3** Markus Mann, D (Dallara F300-Opel), 22m 12.737s; **4** Franz Schmöller, D (Dallara F302-Opel), 22m 13.392s; **5** Diego Romanini, I (Dallara F399-Opel), 22m 19.090s; **6** Hannes Neuhauser, A (Dallara F302-Opel), 22m 19.455s; **7** Jo Zeller, CH (Dallara F301-Opel), 22m 28.278s; **8** Tomás Kostka, CZ (Dallara F302-Opel), 22m 45.990s; **9** Tobias Blätter, CH (Dallara F301-Opel), 22m 46.448s; **10** Frank Brendecke, D (Dallara F300-Opel), 23m 14.418s.
Fastest race lap: de Oliveira, 1m 54.480s, 89.376 mph/143.836 km/h.
Fastest qualifying lap: Zeller, 1m 36.707s, 105.802 mph/170.271 km/h.

Round 6 (45.474 miles/73.184 km)
1 Joao Paulo de Oliveira, BR (Dallara F302-Opel), 26m 07.921s, 104.411 mph/168.033 km/h; **2** Sven Barth, D (Dallara F399-Opel), 26m 20.678s; **3** Jo Zeller, CH (Dallara F301-Opel), 26m 24.689s; **4** Markus Mann, D (Dallara F300-Opel), 26m 25.137s; **5** Marcel Lasée, D (Dallara F399-Opel), 26m 32.575s; **6** Catharina Felser, D (Dallara F302-Opel), 26m 40.370s; **7** Franz Schmöller, D (Dallara F302-Opel), 26m 43.604s; **8** Tobias Blätter, CH (Dallara F301-Opel), 27m 23.692s; **9** Frank Brendecke, D (Dallara F300-Opel), 27m 24.476s; **10** Franz Wöss, A (Dallara F302-Opel), 15 laps.
Fastest race lap: de Oliveira, 1m 36.772s, 105.730 mph/170.157 km/h.
Fastest qualifying lap: de Oliveira, 1m 36.444s, 106.090 mph/170.735 km/h.

RECARO FORMEL-3-CUP. Nürburgring Sprint Circuit, Nürburg/Eifel, Germany, 12/13 July. 2.252-mile/3.625-km circuit.
Round 7
1 Joao Paulo de Oliveira, BR (Dallara F302-Opel), 25m 53.592s; **2** Sven Barth, D (Dallara F399-Opel), 26m 20.118s; **3** Adrian Wolf, D (Dallara F399-Opel), 26m 21.994s; **4** Thomas Holzer, D (Dallara F302-Opel), 26m 23.535s; **5** Michael Frey, CH (Dallara F301-Opel), 26m 30.796s; **6** Franz Schmöller, D (Dallara F302-Opel), 26m 32.070s; **7** Hannes Neuhauser, A (Dallara F302-Opel), 26m 33.480s; **8** Justin Sherwood, GB (Dallara F300-Opel), 26m 40.409s; **9** Tomás Kostka, CZ (Dallara F302-Opel), 24m 41.284s; **10** Ina Fabry, D (Dallara F399-Opel), 26m 55.975s.
Fastest qualifying lap: de Oliveira, 1m 24.614s, 95.834 mph/154.230 km/h.

Round 8
1 Joao Paulo de Oliveira, BR (Dallara F302-Opel), 25m 42.488s; **2** Sven Barth, D (Dallara F399-Opel), 26m 00.446s; **3** Hannes Neuhauser, A (Dallara F302-Opel), 26m 01.738s; **4** Michael Frey, CH (Dallara F301-Opel), 26m 04.236s; **5** Thomas Holzer, D (Dallara F302-Opel), 26m 09.698s; **6** Franz Schmöller, D (Dallara F302-Opel), 26m 10.290s; **7** Adrian Wolf, D (Dallara F399-Opel), 26m 11.260s; **8** Tomás Kostka, CZ (Dallara F302-Opel), 26m 21.398s; **9** Ina Fabry, D (Dallara F399-Opel), 26m 33.593s; **10** Catharina Felser, D (Dallara F302-Opel), 26m 37.395s.
Fastest qualifying lap: de Oliveira, 1m 24.774s, 95.653 mph/153.939 km/h.

RECARO FORMEL-3-CUP, EuroSpeedway Lausitz, Germany, 19/20 July. 2 x 15 laps of the 2.817-mile/4.534-km circuit.
Round 9 (42.259 miles/68.010 km)
1 Joao Paulo de Oliveira, BR (Dallara F302-Opel), 25m 02.029s, 101.286 mph/163.004 km/h; **2** Hannes Neuhauser, A (Dallara F302-Opel), 25m 06.718s; **3** Ross Zwolsman, NL (Dallara F399-Opel), 25m 08.865s; **4** Sven Barth, D (Dallara F399-Opel), 25m 15.380s; **5** Markus Mann, D (Dallara F300-Opel), 25m 15.537s; **6** Thomas Holzer, D (Dallara F302-Opel), 25m 23.541s; **7** Justin Sherwood, GB (Dallara F300-Opel), 25m 25.965s; **8** Tomás Kostka, CZ (Dallara F302-Opel), 25m 30.213s; **9** Diego Romanini, I (Dallara F399-Opel), 25m 31.490s; **10** Catharina Felser, D (Dallara F302-Opel), 25m 40.545s.
Fastest race lap: de Oliveira, 1m 38.873s, 102.579 mph/165.085 km/h.
Fastest qualifying lap: de Oliveira, 1m 38.477s, 102.991 mph/165.748 km/h.

Round 10 (42.259 miles/68.010 km)
1 Joao Paulo de Oliveira, BR (Dallara F302-Opel), 25m 13.648s, 100.508 mph/161.752 km/h; **2** Ross Zwolsman, NL (Dallara F399-Opel), 25m 15.208s; **3** Sven Barth, D (Dallara F399-Opel), 25m 18.456s; **4** Franz Schmöller, D (Dallara F302-Opel), 25m 19.116s; **5** Tomás Kostka, CZ (Dallara F302-Opel), 25m 24.341s; **6** Thomas Holzer, D (Dallara F302-Opel), 25m 24.729s; **7** Hannes Neuhauser, A (Dallara F302-Opel), 25m 25.539s; **8** Diego Romanini, I (Dallara F399-Opel), 25m 35.280s; **9** Justin Sherwood, GB (Dallara F300-Opel), 25m 37.344s; **10** Catharina Felser, D (Dallara F302-Opel), 25m 37.540s.
Fastest race lap: de Oliveira, 1m 38.674s, 102.786 mph/165.417 km/h.
Fastest qualifying lap: de Oliveira, 1m 38.275s, 103.203 mph/166.089 km/h.

RECARO FORMEL-3-CUP, A1-Ring, Spielberg, Austria, 23/24 August. 2.983-mile/4.800-km circuit.
Round 11
1 Joao Paulo de Oliveira, BR (Dallara F302-Opel), 25m 19.242s; **2** Franz Schmöller, D (Dallara F302-Opel), 25m 34.169s; **3** Catharina Felser, D (Dallara F302-Opel), 25m 37.878s; **4** Tomás Kostka, CZ (Dallara F302-Opel), 25m 43.532s; **5** Hannes Neuhauser, A (Dallara F302-Opel), 25m 44.173s; **6** Sven Barth, D (Dallara F399-Opel), 25m 44.762s; **7** Thomas Holzer, D (Dallara F302-Opel), 25m 51.935s; **8** Roman Hoffmann, D (Dallara F301-Opel), 26m 00.835s; **9** Diego Romanini, I (Dallara F399-Opel), 26m 07.798s; **10** Nassim Sidi Said, ALG (Dallara F300-Opel), 26m 18.418s.
Fastest qualifying lap: de Oliveira, 1m 27.387s, 122.871 mph/197.741 km/h.

Round 12
1 Joao Paulo de Oliveira, BR (Dallara F302-Opel), 25m 40.213s; **2** Hannes Neuhauser, A (Dallara F302-Opel), 25m 44.437s; **3** Sven Barth, D (Dallara F399-Opel), 25m 45.311s; **4** Roman Hoffmann, D (Dallara F301-Opel), 25m 50.064s; **5** Franz Schmöller, D (Dallara F302-Opel), 25m 51.083s; **6** Catharina Felser, D (Dallara F302-Opel), 25m 54.118s; **7** Markus Mann, D (Dallara F300-Opel), 25m 54.744s; **8** Thomas Holzer, D (Dallara F302-Opel), 26m 09.196s; **9** Diego Romanini, I (Dallara F399-Opel), 26m 19.283s; **10** Tomas Toth, SK (Dallara F302-Opel), 26m 20.972s.
Fastest qualifying lap: de Oliveira, 1m 27.439s, 122.798 mph/197.623 km/h.

RECARO FORMEL-3-CUP, A1-Ring, Spielberg, Austria, 20/21 September. 2 x 17 laps of the 2.683-mile/4.318-km circuit.
Round 13 (45.612 miles/73.406 km)
1 Sven Barth, D (Dallara F399-Opel), 25m 33.161s, 107.102 mph/172.364 km/h; **2** Thomas Holzer, D (Dallara F302-Opel), 25m 35.151s; **3** Markus Mann, D (Dallara F300-Opel), 25m 36.213s; **4** Adrian Wolf, D (Dallara F302-Opel), 25m 38.348s; **5** Catharina Felser, D (Dallara F302-Opel), 25m 44.380s; **6** Roman Hoffmann, D (Dallara F301-Opel), 25m 46.624s; **7** Franz Schmöller, D (Dallara F302-Opel), 25m 50.065s; **8** Joao Paulo de Oliveira, BR (Dallara F302-Opel), 25m 52.834s; **9** Adam Langley-Khan, GB (Dallara F399-Opel), 25m 59.711s; **10** Tomas Toth, SK (Dallara F302-Opel), 26m 07.347s.
Fastest race lap: de Oliveira, 1m 28.451s, 109.203 mph/175.745 km/h.
Fastest qualifying lap: de Oliveira, 1m 27.417s, 110.494 mph/177.824 km/h.

Round 14 (45.612 miles/73.406 km)
1 Joao Paulo de Oliveira, BR (Dallara F302-Opel), 25m 14.002s, 108.457 mph/174.545 km/h; **2** Hannes Neuhauser, A (Dallara F302-Opel), 25m 25.079s; **3** Sven Barth, D (Dallara F399-Opel), 25m 26.207s; **4** Catharina Felser, D (Dallara F302-Opel), 25m 31.023s; **5** Thomas Holzer, D (Dallara F302-Opel), 25m 35.006s; **6** Markus Mann, D (Dallara F300-Opel), 25m 35.406s; **7** Tomás Kostka, CZ (Dallara F302-Opel), 25m 38.951s; **8** Adrian Wolf, D (Dallara F302-Opel), 25m 39.167s; **9** Tomas Toth, SK (Dallara F302-Opel), 25m 44.876s; **10** Florian Stoll, D (Dallara F399-Opel), 25m 49.767s.
Fastest race lap: de Oliveira, 1m 27.569s, 110.303 mph/177.515 km/h.
Fastest qualifying lap: Neuhauser, 1m 27.629s, 110.227 mph/177.393 km/h.

RECARO FORMEL-3-CUP, Motopark Oschersleben, Germany, 11/12 October. 19 & 15 laps of the 2.279-mile/3.667-km circuit.
Round 15 (43.293 miles/69.673 km)
1 Joao Paulo de Oliveira, BR (Dallara F302-Opel), 26m 03.273s, 99.697 mph/160.447 km/h; **2** Hannes Neuhauser, A (Dallara F302-Opel), 26m 16.976s; **3** Markus Mann, D (Dallara F300-Opel), 26m 19.130s; **4** Sven Barth, D (Dallara F399-Opel), 26m 20.906s; **5** Thomas Holzer, D (Dallara F302-Opel), 26m 21.583s; **6** Franz Schmöller, D (Dallara F302-Opel), 26m 23.795s; **7** Adrian Wolf, D (Dallara F399-Opel), 26m 28.117s; **8** Tomás Kostka, CZ (Dallara F302-Opel), 26m 31.827s; **9** Catharina Felser, D (Dallara F302-Opel), 26m 32.524s; **10** Diego Romanini, I (Dallara F399-Opel), 26m 48.785s.
Fastest race lap: de Oliveira, 1m 21.640s, 100.476 mph/161.700 km/h.
Fastest qualifying lap: de Oliveira, 1m 20.826s, 101.488 mph/163.329 km/h.

Round 16 (34.179 miles/55.005 km)
1 Joao Paulo de Oliveira, BR (Dallara F302-Opel), 20m 32.942s, 99.796 mph/160.606 km/h; **2** Hannes Neuhauser, A (Dallara F302-Opel), 20m 33.861s; **3** Markus Mann, D (Dallara F300-Opel), 20m 43.003s; **4** Sven Barth, D (Dallara F399-Opel), 20m 46.626s; **5** Adrian Wolf, D (Dallara F399-Opel), 20m 50.456s; **6** Tomás Kostka, CZ (Dallara F302-Opel), 20m 51.866s; **7** Thomas Holzer, D (Dallara F302-Opel), 20m 52.527s; **8** Diego Romanini, I (Dallara F399-Opel), 20m 55.992s; **9** Michael Frey, CH (Dallara F300-Opel), 21m 00.069s; **10** Catharina Felser, D (Dallara F302-Opel), 21m 01.895s.
Fastest qualifying lap: de Oliveira, 1m 20.674s, 101.679 mph/163.636 km/h.

Final championship points

1 Joao Paulo de Oliveira, BR, 283; **2** Sven Barth, D, 171; **3** Hannes Neuhauser, A, 155; **4=** Franz Schmöller, D, 86; **4=** Markus Mann, D, 86; **6** Catharina Felser, D, 79; **7** Thomas Holzer, D, 60; **8** Tomás Kostka, CZ, 55; **9** Diego Romanini, I, 37; **10** Adrian Wolf, D, 29; **11** Ross Zwolsman, NL, 27; **12=** Jo Zeller, CH, 19; **12=** Roman Hoffmann, D, 19; **14** Michael Frey, CH, 18; **15** Justin Sherwood, GB, 9; **16** Marcel Lasée, D, 8; **17** Oliver Muytjens, B, 6; **18=** Tobias Blätter, CH, 5; **18=** André Fibier, D, 5; **20=** Frank Brendecke, D, 4; **20=** Tomas Toth, SK, 4; **22** Ina Fabry, D, 3; **23=** Michael Herich, D, 2; **23=** Adam Langley-Khan, GB, 2; **25=** Nassim Sidi Said, ALG, 1; **25=** Denis Watt, A, 1; **25=** Franz Wöss, A, 1; **25=** Florian Stoll, D, 1.

Rookie Cup
1 Sven Barth; **2** Markus Mann; **3** Franz Schmöller.

Italian Formula 3 Championship

ITALIAN FORMULA 3 CHAMPIONSHIP, Circuito Internazionale Santa Monica, Misano, Rimini, Italy, 30 March. Round 1. 20 laps of the 2.523-mile/4.060-km circuit, 50.455 miles/81.200 km.
1 Alvaro Parente, P (Dallara F302-Mugen Honda), 29m 03.785s, 104.164 mph/167.635 km/h; **2** Fausto Ippoliti, I (Dallara F303-Opel), 29m 04.731s; **3** Gregory Franchi, B (Dallara F303-Opel), 29m 14.504s; **4** Giorgio Sernagiotto, I (Dallara F301-Opel), 29m 16.528s; **5** Giovanni Berton, I (Dallara F302-Opel), 29m 17.398s; **6** Robert Doornbos, NL (Dallara F302-Mugen Honda), 29m 27.366s; **7** Davide Mazzoleni, I (Dallara F303-Mugen Honda), 29m 55.296s; **8** Omar Galeffi, I (Dallara F303-Opel), 29m 56.021s; **9** Stefano Gattuso, I (Dallara F302-Mugen Honda), 30m 00.080s; **10** Andrea Michele Tiso, I (Dallara F302-Fiat), 30m 07.339s.
Fastest race lap: Parente, 1m 26.087s, 105.497 mph/169.782 km/h.
Fastest qualifying lap: Parente, 1m 25.366s, 106.389 mph/171.216 km/h.

ITALIAN FORMULA 3 CHAMPIONSHIP, Autodromo del Levante, Binetto, Bari, Italy, 13 April. Round 2. 38 laps of the 0.980-mile/1.577-km circuit, 37.236 miles/59.926 km.
1 Fausto Ippoliti, I (Dallara F303-Opel), 30m 12.533s, 73.958 mph/119.023 km/h; **2** Giacomo Piccini, I (Dallara F303-Opel), 30m 19.363s; **3** Christian Montanari, RSM (Lola/Dome F106/03-Mugen Honda), 30m 21.549s; **4** Davide Mazzoleni, I (Dallara F303-Mugen Honda), 30m 40.864s; **5** Stefano Gattuso, I (Dallara F302-Mugen Honda), 30m 42.442s; **6** Omar Galeffi, I (Dallara F303-Opel), 30m 42.682s; **7** Nicky Pastorelli, I (Dallara F303-Opel), 30m 43.130s; **8** Giovanni Berton, I (Dallara F302-Opel), 30m 50.915s; **9** Andrea Michele Tiso, I (Dallara F302-Fiat), 30m 51.584s; **10** Giampiero Negrotti, I (Dallara F303-Fiat), 35 laps.
Fastest race lap: Ippoliti, 43.944s, 80.276 mph/129.192 km/h.
Fastest qualifying lap: Ippoliti, 43.973s, 80.223 mph/129.106 km/h.

ITALIAN FORMULA 3 CHAMPIONSHIP, Autodromo Mario Umberto Borzacchini, Magione, Perugia, Italy, 27 April. Round 3. 26 laps of the 1.558-mile/2.507-km circuit, 40.502 miles/65.182 km.
1 Fausto Ippoliti, I (Dallara F303-Opel), 29m 45.469s, 81.664 mph/131.425 km/h; **2** Marco Bonanomi, I (Lola/Dome F106/03-Mugen Honda), 29m 48.323s; **3** Omar Galeffi, I (Dallara F303-Opel), 29m 49.376s; **4** Giovanni Berton, I (Dallara F302-Opel), 29m 51.928s; **5** Gregory Franchi, B (Dallara F303-Opel), 29m 52.402s; **6** Leonardo Orecchioni, I (Dallara F303-Opel), 30m 14.187s; **7** Giorgio Sernagiotto, I (Dallara F301-Opel), 30m 14.760s; **8** Giacomo Piccini, I (Dallara F303-Opel), 30m 14.988s; **9** Davide Mazzoleni, I (Dallara F303-Mugen Honda), 30m 21.714s; **10** Imerio Brigliadori, I (Dallara F303-Opel), 30m 32.538s.
Fastest race lap: Ippoliti, 1m 07.814s, 82.697 mph/133.088 km/h.
Fastest qualifying lap: Ippoliti, 1m 06.866s, 83.869 mph/134.974 km/h.

ITALIAN FORMULA 3 CHAMPIONSHIP, Autodromo Internazionale Enzo e Dino Ferrari, Imola, Italy, 18 May. Round 4. 19 laps of the 3.065-mile/4.933-km circuit, 58.239 miles/93.727 km.
1 Marco Bonanomi, I (Lola/Dome F106/03-Mugen Honda), 34m 42.299s, 100.687 mph/162.041 km/h; **2** Giacomo Piccini, I (Dallara F303-Opel), 34m 47.631s; **3** Christian Montanari, RSM (Lola/Dome F106/03-Mugen Honda), 34m 49.159s; **4** Gregory Franchi, B (Dallara F303-Opel), 34m 51.936s; **5** Stefano Gattuso, I (Dallara F302-Mugen Honda), 34m 54.666s; **6** Fausto Ippoliti, I (Dallara F303-Opel), 34m 55.235s; **7** Omar Galeffi, I (Dallara F303-Opel), 35m 01.829s; **8** Matteo Cressoni, I (Dallara F302-Opel), 35m 04.254s; **9** Giovanni Berton, I (Dallara F302-Opel), 35m 04.570s; **10** Philipp Baron, A (Dallara F303-Renault), 35m 23.847s.
Fastest race lap: Davide Mazzoleni, I (Dallara F303-Mugen Honda), 1m 48.521s, 101.684 mph/163.644 km/h.
Fastest qualifying lap: Galeffi, 1m 47.148s, 102.987 mph/165.741 km/h.

14th TROFEO AZIENDA SOGGIORNO E TURISMO, Autodromo di Pergusa, Enna-Pergusa, Sicily, 15 June. Round 5. 18 laps of the 3.076-mile/4.950-km circuit, 55.364 miles/89.100 km.
1 Omar Galeffi, I (Dallara F303-Opel), 30m 06.795s, 110.312 mph/177.530 km/h; **2** Fausto Ippoliti, I (Dallara F303-Opel), 30m 16.070s; **3** Gregory Franchi, B (Dallara F303-Opel), 30m 16.771s; **4** Christian Montanari, RSM (Lola/Dome F106/03-Mugen Honda), 30m 25.225s; **5** Stefano Gattuso, I (Dallara F302-Mugen Honda), 30m 25.607s; **6** Giacomo Piccini, I (Dallara F303-Opel), 30m 37.432s; **7** Davide Mazzoleni, I (Dallara F303-Mugen Honda), 30m 40.327s; **8** Giovanni Berton, I (Dallara F302-Opel), 30m 40.662s; **9** Marco Bonanomi, I (Lola/Dome F106/03-Mugen Honda), 30m 40.884s; **10** Imerio Brigliadori, I (Dallara F303-Opel), 31m 13.182s.
Fastest race lap: Mazzoleni, 1m 38.553s, 112.354 mph/180.816 km/h.
Fastest qualifying lap: Galeffi, 1m 38.205s, 112.752 mph/181.457 km/h.

ITALIAN FORMULA 3 CHAMPIONSHIP, Autodromo Internazionale del Mugello, Scarperia, Firenze (Florence), Italy, 13 July. Round 6. 18 laps of the 3.259-mile/5.245-km circuit, 58.664 miles/94.410 km.
1 Christian Montanari, RSM (Lola/Dome F106/03-Mugen Honda), 32m 54.482s, 106.959 mph/172.134 km/h; **2** Toni Vilander, FIN (Dallara F303-Renault), 32m 55.765s; **3** Gregory Franchi, B (Dallara F303-Opel), 33m 09.048s; **4** Giacomo Piccini, I (Dallara F303-Opel), 33m 20.564s; **5** Marco Bonanomi, I (Lola/Dome F106/03-Mugen Honda), 33m 22.417s; **6** Matteo Cressoni, I (Dallara F302-Opel), 33m 25.113s; **7** Fausto Ippoliti, I (Dallara F303-Opel), 33m 27.906s; **8** Davide Mazzoleni, I (Dallara F303-Mugen Honda), 33m 33.079s; **9** Stefano Gattuso, I (Dallara F303-Mugen Honda), 33m 35.819s; **10** Omar Galeffi, I (Dallara F303-Opel), 33m 37.359s.
Fastest race lap: Montanari, 1m 48.235s, 108.401 mph/174.454 km/h.
Fastest qualifying lap: Vilander, 1m 45.730s, 110.969 mph/178.587 km/h.

42nd TROFEO AUTOMOBILE CLUB PARMA, Autodromo Riccardo Paletti, Varano dei Melegari, Parma, Italy, 7 September. Round 7. 28 laps of the 1.476-mile/2.375-km circuit, 41.321 miles/66.500 km.
1 Davide Mazzoleni, I (Dallara F303-Mugen Honda), 30m 11.335s, 82.125 mph/132.168 km/h; **2** Stefano Gattuso, I (Dallara F303-Mugen Honda), 30m 12.457s; **3** Omar Galeffi, I (Dallara F303-Opel), 30m 23.940s; **4** Gregory Franchi, B (Dallara F303-Opel), 30m 25.836s; **5** Fausto Ippoliti, I (Dallara F303-Opel), 30m 27.370s; **6** Andrea Michele Tiso, I (Dallara F302-Fiat), 30m 29.233s; **7** Giacomo Piccini, I (Dallara F303-Opel), 30m 44.044s; **8** Giacomo Mattei, I (Dallara F303-Opel), 30m 44.606s; **9** Alessandro Bonetti, I (Dallara F303-Opel), 31m 12.090s; **10** Imerio Brigliadori, I (Dallara F303-Opel), 27 laps.
Fastest race lap: Marco Bonanomi, I (Lola/Dome F106/03-Mugen Honda), 1m 03.490s, 83.678 mph/134.667 km/h.
Fastest qualifying lap: Bonanomi, 1m 02.945s, 84.403 mph/135.833 km/h.

ITALIAN FORMULA 3 CHAMPIONSHIP, Autodromo Nazionale Monza, Milan, Italy, 28 September. Round 8. 16 laps of the 3.600-mile/5.793-km circuit, 57.594 miles/92.688 km.
1 Christian Montanari, RSM (Lola/Dome F106/03-Mugen Honda), 29m 20.802s, 117.752 mph/189.503 km/h; **2** Marco Bonanomi, I (Lola/Dome F106/03-Mugen Honda), 29m 22.754s; **3** Gregory Franchi, B (Dallara F303-Opel), 29m 30.723s; **4** Matteo Cressoni, I (Dallara F302-Opel), 29m 41.021s; **5** Giacomo Piccini, I (Dallara F303-Opel), 29m 53.890s; **6** Giovanni Berton, I (Dallara F302-Opel), 29m 55.154s; **7** Alessandro Bonetti, I (Dallara F303-Opel), 29m 55.588s; **8** Philipp Baron, A (Dallara F302-Mugen Honda), 30m 08.361s; **9** Fausto Ippoliti, I (Dallara F303-Opel), 30m 10.513s; **10** Andrea Michele Tiso, I (Dallara F302-Fiat), 30m 11.631s.
Fastest race lap: Franchi, 1m 49.236s, 118.629 mph/190.915 km/h.
Fastest qualifying lap: Montanari, 1m 48.199s, 119.766 mph/192.745 km/h.

ITALIAN FORMULA 3 CHAMPIONSHIP, Autodromo di Vallelunga, Campagnano di Roma, Italy, 12 October. Round 9. 26 laps of the 2.006-mile/3.228-km circuit, 52.150 miles/83.928 km.
1 Christian Montanari, RSM (Lola/Dome F106/03-Mugen Honda), 30m 32.891s, 102.429 mph/164.844 km/h; **2** Marco Bonanomi, I (Lola/Dome F106/03-Mugen Honda), 30m 38.204s; **3** Alvaro Parente, P (Dallara F302-Mugen Honda), 30m 55.568s; **4** Giacomo Piccini, I (Dallara F303-Opel), 31m 00.241s; **5** Fausto Ippoliti, I (Dallara F303-Opel), 31m 01.054s; **6** Philipp Baron, A (Dallara F302-Mugen Honda), 31m 07.070s; **7** Omar Galeffi, I (Dallara F303-Opel), 31m 07.605s; **8** Stefano Gattuso, I (Dallara F303-Mugen Honda), 31m 11.937s; **9** Andrea Michele Tiso, I (Dallara F302-Fiat), 31m 12.056s; **10** Davide Mazzoleni, I (Dallara F303-Mugen Honda), 31m 17.465s.
Fastest race lap: Montanari, 1m 09.621s, 103.716 mph/166.915 km/h.
Fastest qualifying lap: Montanari, 1m 08.799s, 104.955 mph/168.909 km/h.

Final championship points

1 Fausto Ippoliti, I, 93; **2** Gregory Franchi, B, 78; **3** Christian Montanari, RSM, 76; **4** Marco Bonanomi, I, 62; **5=** Omar Galeffi, I, 61; **5=** Giacomo Piccini, I, 61; **7** Davide Mazzoleni, I, 45; **8** Stefano Gattuso, I, 43; **9** Giovanni Berton, I, 32; **10** Alvaro Parente, P, 22; **11** Matteo Cressoni, I, 19; **12** Toni Vilander,

FIN, 16; **13** Giorgio Sernagiotto, I, 14; **14** Andrea Michele Tiso, I, 9; **15=** Alessandro Bonetti, I, 6; **15=** Robert Doornbos, NL, 6; **15=** Leonardo Orecchioni, I, 6; **18=** Philipp Baron, A, 4; **18=** Nicky Pastorelli, I, 4; **20=** Imerio Brigliadori, I, 3; **20=** Giacomo Mattel, I, 3; **22** Giampiero Negrotti, I, 1.

Major Non-Championship Formula 3

2002

The following races were run after AUTOCOURSE 2002–2003 went to press.

FIA F3 WORLD CUP, 49th MACAU GP, Circuito Da Guia, Macau, 17 November. 2 x 15 laps of the 3.803-mile/6.120-km circuit.
Leg 1 (57.042 miles/91.800 km)
1 Paolo Montin, I (Dallara F302-TOM'S Toyota), 39m 45.976s, 86.066 mph/138.509 km/h; **2** Tristan Gommendy, F (Dallara F302-Renault), 39m 46.787s; **3** Narain Karthikeyan, IND (Dallara F302-Mugen Honda), 39m 47.399s; **4** Heikki Kovalainen, FIN (Dallara F302-Renault), 39m 50.935s; **5** Yuji Ide, J (Dallara F302-Renault), 39m 51.898s; **6** Kousuke Matsuura, J (Dallara F302-Opel), 39m 52.510s; **7** Robert Doornbos, NL (Dallara F302-Mugen Honda), 39m 53.725s; **8** Bruce Jouanny, F (Dallara F302-Mugen Honda), 39m 57.486s; **9** Richard Antinucci, USA (Dallara F302-Mugen Honda), 39m 58.256s; **10** Robbie Kerr, GB (Dallara F302-Mugen Honda), 39m 59.540s.
Fastest race lap: Karthikeyan, 2m 14.058s, 102.120 mph/164.347 km/h.
Fastest qualifying lap: Montin, 2m 14.995s, 101.412 mph/163.206 km/h.

Leg 2 (57.042 miles/91.800 km)
1 Tristan Gommendy, F (Dallara F302-Renault), 38m 56.415s, 87.891 mph/141.447 km/h; **2** Heikki Kovalainen, FIN (Dallara F302-Renault), 38m 58.519s; **3** Takashi Kogure, J (Dallara F302-Mugen Honda), 38m 59.513s; **4** Katsuyuki Hiranaka, J (Dallara F302-TOM'S Toyota), 39m 02.028s; **5** James Courtney, AS (Dallara F302-Mugen Honda), 39m 06.548s; **6** Milos Pavlovic, YU (Dallara F302-Opel), 39m 07.479s; **7** Hiroi Yoshimoto, J (Dallara F302-TOM'S Toyota), 39m 09.531s; **8** Vitantonio Liuzzi (Dallara F302-Mugen Honda), 39m 10.486s; **9** Olivier Pla, F (Dallara F302-Renault), 39m 11.410s; **10** Robert Doornbos, NL (Dallara F302-Mugen Honda), 39m 11.546s.
Fastest race lap: Gommendy, 2m 14.036s, 102.137 mph/164.374 km/h.

Combined
1 Tristan Gommendy, F (Dallara F302-Renault), 30 laps; **2** Heikki Kovalainen, FIN (Dallara F302-Renault), 30; **3** Takashi Kogure, J (Dallara F302-Mugen Honda), 30; **4** Katsuyuki Hiranaka, J (Dallara F302-TOM'S Toyota), 30; **5** Hiroi Yoshimoto, J (Dallara F302-TOM'S Toyota), 30; **6** Robert Doornbos, NL (Dallara F302-Mugen Honda), 30; **7** Marchy Lee, PRC (Dallara F302-Mugen Honda), 30; **8** Cristiano Citron, I (Dallara F302-Opel), 30; **9** Michael Ho, PRC (Dallara F302-Mugen Honda), 30; **10** César Campanico, P (Dallara F302-Opel), 30.

INTERNATIONAL F3 KOREA SUPER PRIX, Changwon City Raceway, South Korea, 24 November. 25 and 24 laps of the 1.873-mile/3.014-km circuit.
Provisional Race – Leg 1 (46.820 miles/75.350 km)
1 Olivier Pla, F (Dallara F302-Renault), 30m 41.432s, 91.534 mph/147.309 km/h; **2** Heikki Kovalainen, FIN (Dallara F302-Renault), 30m 43.602s; **3** Kousuke Matsuura, J (Dallara F302-Opel), 30m 44.480s; **4** Takashi Kogure, J (Dallara F302-Mugen Honda), 30m 46.562s; **5** Paolo Montin, I (Dallara F302-TOM'S Toyota), 30m 57.342s; **6** Stefan de Groot, NL (Dallara F302-Mugen Honda), 31m 02.554s; **7** Fabio Carbone, BR (Dallara F302-Renault), 31m 03.377s; **8** Richard Antinucci, USA (Dallara F302-Mugen Honda), 31m 06.546s; **9** James Courtney, AUS (Dallara F302-Mugen Honda), 31m 08.696s; **10** Bernhard Auinger, A (Dallara F302-Mugen Honda), 31m 14.650s.
Fastest race lap: Pla, 1m 12.598s, 92.869 mph/149.459 km/h.
Fastest qualifying lap: Pla, 1m 11.584s, 94.185 mph/151.576 km/h.

Final Race – Leg 2 (44.948 miles/72.336 km)
1 Olivier Pla, F (Dallara F302-Renault), 32m 14.653s, 83.638 mph/134.603 km/h; **2** Takashi Kogure, J (Dallara F302-Mugen Honda), 32m 15.257s; **3** Kousuke Matsuura, J (Dallara F302-Opel), 32m 16.399s; **4** Fabio Carbone, BR (Dallara F302-Renault), 32m 25.596s; **5** Paolo Montin, I (Dallara F302-TOM'S Toyota), 32m 26.026s; **6** Stefan de Groot, NL (Dallara F302-Mugen Honda), 32m 33.586s; **7** Richard Antinucci, USA (Dallara F302-Mugen Honda), 32m 35.436s; **8** Robert Doornbos, NL (Dallara F302-Mugen Honda), 32m 40.253s; **9** Jamie Green, GB (Dallara F302-Mugen Honda), 32m 40.367s; **10** Tristan Gommendy, F (Dallara F302-Renault), 32m 40.501s.
Fastest race lap: Bruce Jouanny, F (Dallara F302-Mugen Honda), 1m 12.406s, 93.116 mph/149.855 km/h.

Aggregate of the two races
1 Olivier Pla, F (Dallara F302-Renault); **2** Takashi Kogure, J (Dallara F302-Mugen Honda); **3** Kousuke Matsuura, J (Dallara F302-Opel); **4** Fabio Carbone, BR (Dallara F302-Renault); **5** Paolo Montin, I (Dallara F302-TOM'S Toyota); **6** Stefan de Groot, NL (Dallara F302-Mugen Honda); **7** Richard Antinucci, USA (Dallara F302-Mugen Honda); **8** Robert Doornbos, NL (Dallara F302-Mugen Honda); **9** Jamie Green, GB (Dallara F302-Mugen Honda); **10** Yuji Ide, J (Dallara F302-Renault).

2003

13th MARLBORO MASTERS OF FORMULA 3, Circuit Park Zandvoort, Netherlands, 10 August. 25 laps of the 2.677-mile/4.3075-km circuit, 66.914 miles/107.688 km.
1 Christian Klien, A (Dallara F302-Mercedes Benz), 44m 32.801s, 90.127 mph/145.045 km/h; **2** Nelson Angelo Piquet, BR (Dallara F303-Mugen Honda), 44m 33.122s; **3** Ryan Briscoe, AUS (Dallara F303-Opel), 44m 35.807s; **4** Nicolas Lapierre, F (Dallara F302-Renault), 44m 42.319s; **5** Jamie Green, GB (Dallara F302-Mugen Honda), 44m 47.939s; **6** Markus Winkelhock, D (Dallara F302-Mercedes Benz), 44m 48.456s; **7** Olivier Pla, F (Dallara F303-Mercedes Benz), 44m 48.532s; **8** Alan van der Merwe, ZA (Dallara F302-Mugen Honda), 44m 49.044s; **9** Alexandre Prémat, F (Dallara F303-Mercedes Benz), 44m 49.386s; **10** Fabio Carbone, BR (Dallara F302-Renault), 44m 50.011s.
Fastest race lap: Briscoe, 1m 35.693s, 100.693 mph/162.049 km/h.
Fastest qualifying lap: Piquet, 1m 33.115s, 103.481 mph/166.536 km/h.

CAGLIARI MASTERS F3 RACE, Autodromo di Cagliari, Sardinia, Italy, 1/2 November. 28 and 29 laps of the 1.500-mile/2.414-km circuit.
Race 1 (42.000 miles/67.592 km)
1 Robert Kubica, PL (Dallara F303-Opel), 32m 57.007s, 76.479 mph/123.081 km/h; **2** Paolo Montin, I (Dallara F302-Mugen Honda), 33m 01.110s; **3** Andrea Belicchi, I (Dallara F302-Opel), 33m 02.136s; **4** Ernesto Viso, YV (Dallara F303-Mugen Honda), 33m 04.103s; **5** Marco Bonanomi, I (Lola/Dome F106/03-Mugen Honda), 33m 24.315s; **6** Michele Rugolo, I (Lola/Dome F106/03-Mugen Honda), 33m 25.031s; **7** Christian Montanari, RSM (Lola/Dome F106/03-Mugen Honda), 33m 25.281s; **8** Gregory Franchi, B (Dallara F302-Opel), 33m 25.455s; **9** Philipp Baron, A (Dallara F303-Mugen Honda), 33m 51.296s; **10** Fairuz Fauzy, MAL (Dallara F303-Mugen Honda), 34m 02.426s.
Fastest race lap: Kubica, 1m 09.160s, 78.079 mph/125.656 km/h.
Fastest qualifying lap: Kubica, 1m 09.400s, 77.809 mph/125.222 km/h.

Race 2 (43.500 miles/70.006 km)
1 Robert Kubica, PL (Dallara F303-Opel), 33m 53.338s, 77.016 mph/123.945 km/h; **2** Paolo Montin, I (Dallara F302-Mugen Honda), 33m 54.237s; **3** Andrea Belicchi, I (Dallara F302-Opel), 34m 23.096s; **4** Marco Bonanomi, I (Lola/Dome F106/03-Mugen Honda), 34m 29.878s; **5** Gregory Franchi, B (Dallara F302-Opel), 34m 30.325s; **6** Fairuz Fauzy, MAL (Dallara F303-Mugn Honda), 34m 57.043s; **7** Fausto Ippoliti, I (Dallara F303-Mugen Honda), 35m 00.021s; **8** Philipp Baron, A (Dallara F303-Mugen Honda), 35m 01.885s; **9** Michele Rugolo, I (Lola/Dome F106/03-Mugen Honda), 35m 03.531s; **10** Matteo Cressoni, I (Dallara F302-Opel), 28 laps.
Fastest race lap: Montin, 1m 09.503s, 77.694 mph/125.036 km/h.

Overall
1 Robert Kubica, PL; **2** Paolo Montin, I; **3** Andrea Belicchi, I; **4** Marco Bonanomi, I; **5=** Ernesto Viso, YV; **5=** Gregory Franchi, B; **7=** Michele Rugolo, I; **7=** Fairuz Fauzy, MAL; **9=** Christian Montanari, RSM; **9=** Fausto Ippoliti, I.

Results of the Macau and Changwon races will be given in AUTOCOURSE 2004–2005.

FIA GT Championship

FIA GT CHAMPIONSHIP, Circuit de Catalunya, Montmeló, Barcelona, Spain, 6 April. Round 1. 96 laps of the 2.939-mile/4.730-km circuit, 282.152 miles/454.080 km.
1 Thomas Biagi/Matteo Bobbi, I/I (Ferrari 550 Maranello), 3h 00m 37.819s, 93.723 mph/150.832 km/h (1st GT class); **2** Luca Cappellari/Fabrizio Gollin, I/I (Ferrari 550 Maranello), 3h 00m 53.482s; **3** Lilian Bryner/Enzo Calderari/Stefano Livio, CH/CH/I (Ferrari 550 Maranello), 95 laps; **4** Jean-Denis Deletraz/Andrea Piccini, F/I (Lister Storm GT), 95; **5** Bobby Verdon-Roe/Peter Snowdon, GB/GB (Lister Storm GT), 95; **6** Magnus Wallinder/Henrik Roos, S/S (Chrysler Viper GTS-R), 94; **7** Arjan van der Zwaan/Rob van der Zwaan/Klaus Abbelen, NL/NL/D (Chrysler Viper GTS-R), 93; **8** Fabrizio de Simone/Andrea Bertolini, I/I (Ferrari 360 Modena), 93 (1st N-GT class); **9** Jamie Davies/Tim Mullen, GB/GB (Ferrari 360 Modena), 92; **10** Kelvin Burt/Darren Turner, GB/GB (Ferrari 360 Modena), 92.
Fastest race lap: Christophe Bouchut/Jean-Philippe Belloc, F/F (Chrysler Viper GTS-R), 1m 45.081s, 100.691 mph/162.046 km/h.
Fastest qualifying lap: Jamie Campbell-Walter/Nathan Kinch, GB/GB (Lister Storm GT), 1m 40.975s, 104.785 mph/168.636 km/h.

FIA GT CHAMPIONSHIP, Circuit de Nevers, Magny-Cours, France, 27 April. Round 2. 104 laps of the 2.741-mile/4.411-km circuit, 285.050 miles/458.744 km.
1 Thomas Biagi/Matteo Bobbi, I/I (Ferrari 550 Maranello), 3h 01m 44.710s, 94.104 mph/151.446 km/h (1st GT class); **2** Luca Cappellari/Fabrizio Gollin, I/I (Ferrari 550 Maranello), 3h 01m 46.094s; **3** Jean-Denis Deletraz/Andrea Piccini, F/I (Lister Storm GT), 3h 02m 10.476s; **4** Magnus Wallinder/Henrik Roos, S/S (Chrysler Viper GTS-R), 101 laps; **5** Ni Amorim/Pedro Chaves/Miguel Ramos, P/P/P (Saleen S7-R), 101; **6** Jamie Davies/Tim Mullen, GB/GB (Ferrari 360 Modena), 101 (1st N-GT class); **7** Stéphane Ortelli/Marc Lieb, MC/D (Porsche 996 GT3-RS), 101; **8** Guillaume Gomez/Steeve Hiesse, F/F (Ferrari 360 Modena), 100; **9** Jamie Campbell-Walter/Nathan Kinch, GB/GB (Lister Storm GT), 100; **10** Bert Longin/Gabriele Gardel, B/CH (Porsche 996 GT3-RS), 99.
Fastest race lap: Biagi/Bobbi, 1m 38.625s, 100.047 mph/161.010 km/h.
Fastest qualifying lap: Biagi/Bobbi, 1m 55.642s, 85.325 mph/137.317 km/h.

FIA GT CHAMPIONSHIP, Ente Autodromo di Pergusa, Enna-Pergusa, Sicily, 11 May. Round 3. 102 laps of the 3.076-mile/4.950-km circuit, 313.730 miles/504.900 km.
1 Thomas Biagi/Matteo Bobbi, I/I (Ferrari 550 Maranello), 2h 56m 47.745s, 106.472 mph/171.350 km/h (1st GT class); **2** Jamie Campbell-Walter/Nathan Kinch, GB/GB (Lister Storm GT), 2h 56m 56.028s; **3** Lilian Bryner/Enzo Calderari/Stefano Livio, CH/CH/I (Ferrari 550 Maranello), 101 laps; **4** Bobby Verdon-Roe/Marco Zadra, GB/MON (Lister Storm GT), 101; **5** Jean-Denis Deletraz/Andrea Piccini, F/I (Lister Storm GT), 100; **6** Philippe Alliot/Steve Zacchia, F/CH (Chrysler Viper GTS-R), 99; **7** Martin Short/Tim Sugden, GB/GB (Porsche 996 GT3-RS), 99 (1st N-GT class); **8** Fabrizio de Simone/Andrea Bertolini, I/I (Ferrari 360 Modena), 99; **9** Ni Amorim/Pedro Chaves/Miguel Ramos, P/P/P (Saleen S7-R), 97; **10** Godfrey Jones/David Jones, GB/GB (Porsche 996 GT3-RS), 97.
Fastest race lap: Franz Konrad/Toni Seiler/Jean-Marc Gounon, D/CH/F (Saleen S7-R), 1m 36.649s, 114.568 mph/184.379 km/h.
The fastest lap was set by Luca Cappellari/Fabrizio Gollin, I/I (Ferrari 550 Maranello), 1m 36.467s, 114.784 mph/184.726 km/h, but this car was excluded for a technical infringement.
Fastest qualifying lap: Konrad/Seiler/Gounon, 1m 34.939s, 116.631 mph/187.699 km/h.

FIA GT CHAMPIONSHIP, Automotodrom Brno Masaryk Circuit, Brno, Czech Republic, 25 May. Round 4. 87 laps of the 3.357-mile/5.403-km circuit, 292.082 miles/470.061 km.
1 Thomas Biagi/Matteo Bobbi, I/I (Ferrari 550 Maranello), 3h 01m 47.256s, 96.403 mph/155.146 km/h (1st GT class); **2** Jean-Denis Deletraz/Andrea Piccini, F/I (Lister Storm GT), 3h 02m 18.312s; **3** Luca Cappellari/Fabrizio Gollin, I/I (Ferrari 550 Maranello), 3h 02m 18.441s; **4** Jamie Campbell-Walter/Nathan Kinch, GB/GB (Lister Storm GT), 3h 02m 22.064s; **5** Lilian Bryner/Enzo Calderari/Stefano Livio, CH/CH/I (Ferrari 550 Maranello), 3h 03m 30.804s; **6** Bobby Verdon-Roe/Marco Zadra, GB/MON (Lister Storm GT), 86 laps; **7** Ni Amorim/Pedro Chaves/Miguel Ramos, P/P/P (Saleen S7-R), 84; **8** Stéphane Ortelli/Marc Lieb, MC/D (Porsche 996 GT3-RS), 84 (1st N-GT class); **9** Fabrizio de Simone/Andrea Bertolini, I/I (Ferrari 360 Modena), 84; **10** Jamie Davies/Tim Mullen, GB/GB (Ferrari 360 Modena), 84.
Thomas Erdos/Mike Newton, BR/GB (Saleen S7-R), finished 7th, but disqualified for a technical infringement.
Fastest race lap: Franz Konrad/Toni Seiler/Jean-Marc Gounon, D/CH/F (Saleen S7-R), 1m 59.171s, 101.419 mph/163.218 km/h.
Fastest qualifying lap: Konrad/Seiler/Gounon, 1m 56.695s, 103.571 mph/166.681 km/h.

LG SUPER RACING WEEKEND, Donington Park Grand Prix Circuit, Castle Donington, Derbyshire, Great Britain, 29 June. Round 5. 112 laps of the 2.498-mile/4.020-km circuit, 279.766 miles/450.240 km.
1 Thomas Biagi/Matteo Bobbi, I/I (Ferrari 550 Maranello), 3h 00m 08.238s, 93.184 mph/149.966 km/h (1st GT class); **2** Lilian Bryner/Enzo Calderari/Stefano Livio, CH/CH/I (Ferrari 550 Maranello), 111 laps; **3** Philippe Alliot/David Hallyday/Steve Zacchia, F/F/CH (Chrysler Viper GTS-R), 111; **4** Thomas Erdos/Mike Newton, BR/GB (Saleen S7-R), 110; **5** Bobby Verdon-Roe/Marco Zadra, GB/MON (Lister Storm GT), 110; **6** Stéphane Ortelli/Marc Lieb, MC/D (Porsche 996 GT3-RS), 109 (1st N-GT class); **7** Franz Konrad/Toni Seiler/Jean-Marc Gounon, D/CH/F (Saleen S7-R), 109; **8** Magnus Wallinder/Henrik Roos, S/S (Chrysler Viper GTS-R), 109; **9** Stéphane Daoudi/Johnny Mowlem, F/GB (Porsche 996 GT3-RS), 108; **10** Bert Longin/Gabriele Gardel, B/CH (Porsche 996 GT3-RS), 108.
Fastest race lap: Konrad/Seiler/Gounon, 1m 30.802s, 99.034 mph/ 159.380 km/h.
Fastest qualifying lap: Alliot/Hallyday/Zacchia, 1m 29.361s, 100.631 mph/161.950 km/h.

FIA GT CHAMPIONSHIP, Circuit de Spa-Francorchamps, Stavelot, Belgium, 26-27 July. Round 6. 479 laps of the 4.317-mile/6.947-km circuit, 2067.683 miles/3327.613 km.
1 Stéphane Ortelli/Marc Lieb/Romain Dumas, MC/D/F (Porsche 996 GT3-RS), 24h 00m 58.410s, 86.095 mph/138.557 km/h (1st N-GT class); **2** Luca Cappellari/Fabrizio Gollin/Lilian Bryner/Enzo Calderari, I/I/CH/CH (Ferrari 550 Maranello), 471 laps (1st GT class); **3** Andrea Chiesa/Alex Caffi/Gabrio Rosa/Luca Drudi, I/I/I/I (Porsche 996 GT3-RS), 470; **4** Christophe Bouchut/Vincent Vosse/Patrick Huisman, F/B/NL (Chrysler Viper GTS-R), 469; **5** Kurt Mollekens/Didier de Radigues/Pedro Lamy, B/B/P (Chrysler Viper GTS-R), 468; **6** Paul Belmondo/Emmanuel Clerico/Yann Clairay/Pirre-Yves Corthals, F/F/F/F (Chrysler Viper GTS-R), 466; **7** Yannick Schroeder/Jaroslav Janis/Robert Pergl, F/CZ/CZ (Ferrari 360 Modena), 466; **8** Luciano Burti/Fabrizio de Simone/Iradj Alexander David, BR/I/CH (Ferrari 360 Modena), 461; **9** Albert Vanierschot/Jos Menten/Koen Wauters/Kris Wauters, B/NL/B/B (Porsche 996 GT3 turbo), 457; **10** Andrea Piccini/Gabriele Lancieri/David Sterckx/Gavin Pickering, I/I/B/GB (Lister Storm GT), 455.
Fastest qualifying lap: Cappellari/Gollin/Bryner/Calderari, 2m 15.718s, 114.502 mph/184.273 km/h.

FIA GT CHAMPIONSHIP, Anderstorp Scandinavian Raceway, Sweden, 7 September. Round 7. 114 laps of the 2.501-mile/4.025-km circuit, 285.116 miles/458.850 km.
1 Jamie Campbell-Walter/Nathan Kinch, GB/GB (Lister Storm GT), 3h 00m 14.477s, 94.911 mph/152.745 km/h (1st GT class); **2** Franz Konrad/Walter Lechner Jr/Toni Seiler, D/D/CH (Saleen S7-R), 114 laps; **3** Andrea Piccini/David Sterckx, I/B (Lister Storm GT), 113; **4** Luca Cappellari/Fabrizio Gollin, I/I (Ferrari 550 Maranello), 113; **5** Lilian Bryner/Enzo Calderari/Stefano Livio, CH/CH/I (Ferrari 550 Maranello), 112; **6** Emmanuel Collard/Tim Sugden, F/GB (Porsche 996 GT3-RS), 111 (1st N-GT class); **7** Arjan van der Zwaan/Rob van der Zwaan/Klaus Abbelen, NL/NL/D (Chrysler Viper GTS-R), 111; **8** Stéphane Ortelli/Marc Lieb, MC/D (Porsche 996 GT3-RS), 110; **9** Jamie Davies/Darren Turner, GB/GB (Ferrari 360 Modena), 110; **10** Stéphane Daoudi/Adam Jones, F/GB (Porsche 996 GT3-RS), 109.
Fastest race lap: Konrad/Lechner Jr/Seiler, 1m 31.424s, 98.483 mph/158.492 km/h.
Fastest qualifying lap: Lechner Jr, 1m 28.899s, 101.280 mph/162.994 km/h.

FIA GT CHAMPIONSHIP, Motopark Oschersleben, Germany, 21 September. Round 8. 119 laps of the 2.279-mile/3.667-km circuit, 271.150 miles/436.373 km.
1 Thomas Biagi/Matteo Bobbi, I/I (Ferrari 550 Maranello), 3h 01m 37.024s, 89.578 mph/144.163 km/h (1st GT class); **2** Bobby Verdon-Roe/Marco Zadra, GB/MON (Lister Storm GT), 118 laps; **3** Lilian Bryner/Enzo Calderari/Stefano Livio, CH/CH/I (Ferrari 550 Maranello), 118; **4** Thomas Erdos/Mike Newton, BR/GB (Saleen S7-R), 117; **5** Fabrizio de Simone/Andrea Bertolini, I/I (Ferrari 360 Modena), 117 (1st N-GT class); **6** Jamie Davies/Darren Turner, GB/GB (Ferrari 360 Modena), 117; **7** Kelvin Burt/Tim Mullen, GB/GB (Ferrari 360 Modena), 117; **8** Emmanuel Collard/Tim Sugden, F/GB (Porsche 996 GT3-RS), 116; **9** Arjan van der Zwaan/Rob van der Zwaan/Klaus Abbelen, NL/NL/D (Chrysler Viper GTS-R), 116; **10** Stéphane Ortelli/Marc Lieb, MC/D (Porsche 996 GT3-RS), 116.
Fastest race lap: Erdos/Newton, 1m 26.361s, 94.687 mph/152.384 km/h.
Fastest qualifying lap: Franz Konrad/Walter Lechner Jr/Toni Seiler, D/D/CH (Saleen S7-R), 1m 23.869s, 97.805 mph/157.403 km/h.

FIA GT CHAMPIONSHIP, Autódromo Fernanda Pires da Silva, Alcabideche, Estoril, Portugal, 5 October. Round 9. 106 laps of the 2.599-mile/4.183-km circuit, 275.515 miles/443.398 km.
1 Fabio Babini/Philipp Peter, I/A (Ferrari 575M Maranello), 3h 00m 47.187s, 91.439 mph/147.156 km/h (1st GT class); **2** Luca Cappellari/Fabrizio Gollin, I/I (Ferrari 550 Maranello), 3h 01m 03.035s; **3** Thomas Biagi/Matteo Bobbi, I/I (Ferrari 550 Maranello), 3h 01m 20.382s; **4** Franz Konrad/Walter Lechner Jr/Toni Seiler, D/D/CH (Saleen S7-R), 104 laps; **5** Arjan van der Zwaan/Rob van der Zwaan/Klaus Abbelen, NL/NL/D (Chrysler Viper GTS-R), 104; **6** Magnus Wallinder/Henrik Roos, S/S (Chrysler Viper GTS-R), 104; **7** Thomas Erdos/Mike Newton, BR/GB (Saleen S7-R), 103; **8** Fabrizio de Simone/Andrea Bertolini, I/I (Ferrari 360 Modena), 103 (1st N-GT class); **9** Jamie Davies/Darren Turner, GB/GB (Ferrari 360 Modena), 103; **10** Emmanuel Collard/Tim Sugden, F/GB (Porsche 996 GT3-RS), 102.
Fastest race lap: Cappellari/Gollin, 1m 37.708s, 95.766 mph/154.120 km/h.
Fastest qualifying lap: Mike Hezemans/Anthony Kumpen/Philippe Alliot, NL/B/F (Chrysler Viper GTS-R), 1m 36.222s, 97.245 mph/156.501 km/h.

FIA GT CHAMPIONSHIP, Autodromo Nazionale di Monza, Milan, Italy, 19 October. Round 10. 87 laps of the 3.600-mile/5.793-km circuit, 313.165 miles/503.991 km.
1 Luca Cappellari/Fabrizio Gollin, I/I (Ferrari 550 Maranello), 2h 40m 08.081s, 117.338 mph/188.838 km/h (1st GT class); **2** Lilian Bryner/Enzo Calderari/Stefano Livio, CH/CH/I (Ferrari 550 Maranello), 2h 40m 45.625s; **3** Jamie Campbell-Walter/Nathan Kinch, GB/GB (Lister Storm GT), 2h 41m 50.511s; **4** Fabio Babini/Philipp Peter, I/A (Ferrari 575M Maranello), 86 laps; **5** Boris Derichebourg/Christian Pescatori, F/I (Ferrari 575M Maranello), 86; **6** Thomas Biagi/Matteo Bobbi, I/I (Ferrari 550 Maranello), 86; **7** Andrea Piccini/David Sterckx/Gabriele Lancieri, I/B/I (Lister Storm GT), 86; **8** Bobby Verdon-Roe/Marco Zadra, GB/MON (Lister Storm GT), 86; **9** Fabrizio de Simone/Andrea Bertolini, I/I (Ferrari 360 Modena), 83 (1st N-GT class); **10** Stéphane Ortelli/Marc Lieb, MC/D (Porsche 996 GT3-RS), 82.
Fastest race lap: Franz Konrad/Walter Lechner Jr/Toni Seiler, D/D/CH (Saleen S7-R), 1m 45.649s, 122.657 mph/197.397 km/h.
Fastest qualifying lap: Mike Hezemans/Anthony Kumpen/Philippe Alliot, NL/B/F (Chrysler Viper GTS-R), 1m 43.559s, 125.132 mph/201.381 km/h.

Final championship points

GT Class
Drivers
1= Thomas Biagi, I, 69; **1=** Matteo Bobbi, I, 69; **3=** Fabrizio Gollin, I, 61; **3=** Luca Cappellari, I, 61; **5=** Lilian Bryner, CH, 57; **5=** Enzo Calderari, CH, 57; **7** Andrea Piccini, I, 39; **8** Stefano Livio, I, 38; **9=** Nathan Kinch, GB, 32; **9=** Jamie Campbell-Walter, GB, 32; **11** Bobby Verdon-Roe, GB, 28; **12=** Philipp Peter, A, 25; **12=** Fabio Babini, I, 25; **14** Marco Zadra, MON, 24; **15** Jean-Denis Deletraz, CH, 23; **16=** Henrik Roos, S, 17; **16=** Franz Konrad, D, 17; **16=** Christophe Bouchut, F, 17; **16=** Magnus Wallinder, S, 17; **16=** Toni Seiler, CH, 17; **16=** Patrick Huisman, NL, 17; **16=** Vincent Vosse, B, 17; **23=** Thomas Erdos, BR, 16.5; **23=** Miguel Ramos, P, 16.5; **23=** Mike Newton, GB, 16.5; **26** David Sterckx, B, 16; **27** Pedro Chaves, P, 15.5; **28=** Rob van der Zwaan, NL, 14; **28=** Steve Zacchia, CH, 14; **28=** Arjan van der Zwaan, NL, 14; **28=** Klaus Abbelen, D, 14; **28=** Boris Derichebourg, F, 14.

Teams
1 BMS Scuderia Italia, I, 117; **2** Lister Racing, GB, 71; **3** Care Racing, 42; **4=** JMB Racing, 30; **4=** Creation Autosportif, 30.

N-GT Class
Drivers
1= Stéphane Ortelli, MC, 73; **1=** Marc Lieb, D, 73; **3** Fabrizio de Simone, I, 65; **4** Andrea Bertolini, I, 59; **5** Jamie Davies, GB, 55.5; **6** Tim Sugden, GB, 43; **7** Tim Mullen, GB, 37.5; **8** Darren Turner, GB, 32.5; **9** Emmanuel Collard, F, 28; **10** Robert Pergl, CZ, 24.5.

Teams
1 Freisinger Motorsport, 92; **2** JMB Racing, 71; **3** Team Maranello Concessionaires, 70; **4** EMKA Racing, 43; **5=** RWS Yukos, 37; **5=** Team Eurotech, 37.

Other Sports Car Race

71st 24 HEURES DU MANS, Circuit International Du Mans, Les Raineries, Le Mans, France, 14–15 June. 377 laps of the 8.482-mile/13.650-km circuit, 3197.607 miles/5146.050 km.
1 Tom Kristensen/Rinaldo Capello/Guy Smith, DK/I/GB (Bentley EXP Speed 8), 133.178 mph/214.330 km/h; (1st LM GTP class); **2** David Brabham/Mark Blundell/Johnny Herbert, AUS/GB/GB (Bentley EXP Speed 8), 375 laps; **3** JJ Lehto/Emanuele Pirro/Stefan Johansson, FIN/I/S (Audi R8), 372 (1st LMP 900 class); **4** Jan Magnussen/Seiji Ara/Marco Werner, DK/J/D (Audi R8), 370; **5** Olivier Beretta/Gunnar Jeannette/Massimiliano 'Max' Papis, MC/USA/I (Panoz Elan LMP-01 Evo), 360; **6** Jan Lammers/Andy Wallace/John Bosch, NL/GB/NL (Dome S101-Judd), 360; **7** Jonathan Cochet/Stéphan Grégoire/Jean-Marc Gounon, F/F/F (Courage C60-Judd), 360; **8** Jean-Christophe Boullion/Franck Lagorce/Stéphane Sarrazin, F/F/F (Courage C60-Peugeot), 356; **9** Nicolas Minassian/Éric Hélary/Soheil Ayari, F/F/F (Courage C60-Peugeot), 352; **10** Jamie Davies/Peter Kox/Tomás Enge, GB/NL/CZ (Ferrari 550 Maranello), 336 (1st LM GTS class); **11** Kelly Collins/Oliver Gavin/Andy Pilgrim, USA/GB/USA (Chevrolet Corvette C5-R), 326; **12** Ron Fellows/Franck Fréon/Johnny O'Connell, CDN/F/USA (Chevrolet Corvette C5-R), 326; **13** Masahiko Kondo/Ukyo Katayama/Ryo Fukuda, J/J/J (Dome S101-Mugen), 322; **14** Sascha Maassen/Lucas Luhr/Emmanuel Collard, D/D/F (Porsche 911 GT3-RS), 320 (1st LM GT class); **15** Christophe Pillon/Didier André/Jean-Luc Maury-Laribiere, CH/F/F (Reynard 2KQ-LM-Volkswagen/Lehmann), 319 (1st LMP 675 class); **16** Christophe Bouchut/Patrice Goueslard/Steve Zacchia, F/F/CH (Chrysler Viper GTS-R), 317; **17** Tristan Gommendy/Beppe Gabbiani/Felipe Ortiz, F/I/BOL (Dome S101-Judd), 316 (DNF – accident); **18** Marc Lieb/Peter Barron/Leo Hindery, D/USA/USA (Porsche 911 GT3-RS), 314; **19**

Nigel Smith/Ian Kahn/Michel Neugarten, GB/GB/B (Porsche 911 GT3-RS), 305; **20** Atsushi Yogo/Akira Iida/Kazuyuki Nishizawa, J/J/J (Porsche 911 GT3-RS), 304; **21** Kevin Buckler/Jörg Bergmeister/Timo Bernhard, USA/D/D (Porsche 911 GT3-RS), 304; **22** Luc Alphand/Jérôme Policand/Frederic Dor, F/F/F (Ferrari 550 Maranello), 298; **23** Thomas Erdos/Pedro Chaves/Mike Newton, BR/P/GB (Saleen S7-R), 292 (DNF – gearbox); **24** John Nielsen/Hayanara Shimoda/Caspar Elsgaard, DK/J/DK (DBA4 03S-Zytek), 288; **25** Robin Liddell/David Warnock/Piers Masarati, GB/GB/GB (Porsche 911 GT3-RS), 285; **26** Jean-Bernard Bouvet/Michele Rugolo/Sylvain Boulay, F/I/F (Durango MG PM 02-Judd), 277; **27** David Terrien/Fabrizio de Simone/Fabio Babini, F/I/I (Ferrari 360 Modena), 273; **28** Anthony Lazzaro/Ralf Kelleners/Terry Borcheller, USA/D/USA (Ferrari 360 Modena), 269; **29** Vanina Ickx/Patrick Bourdais/Roland Berville, B/F/F (Porsche 911 GT3-RS), 264; **30** Yojiro Terada/Olivier Porta/Gavin Pickering, J/F/GB (WR LMP-01-Peugeot), 235; **31** Scott Maxwell/David Saelens/Benjamin Leuenberger, CDN/B/CH (Panoz-Elan LMP-01 Evo), 233 (DNF – accident); **32** Hans Hugenholtz/Norman Simon/Tom Coronel, NL/D/NL (Spyker C8 Double 12-R), 229; **33** Luis Marques/Dominique Dupuy/Denis Dupuis, F/F/F (Chrysler Viper GTS-R), 229 (DNF – engine); **34** Gaël Lesoudier/Michel Ferté/Ange Barde, F/F/F (Ferrari 550 Maranello), 227 (DNF – fire); **35** Jim Matthews/Marc Goossens/Christophe Tinseau, USA/B/F (Riley & Scott Mk IIIC-Ford), 214 (DNF – engine); **36** Stéphane Daoudi/Bastien Brière/Jean-René de Fournoux, F/F/F (WR LMP-02-Peugeot V6), 176 (DNF – engine); **37** Kelvin Burt/Anthony Davidson/Darren Turner, GB/GB/GB (Ferrari 550 Maranello), 176 (DNF – accident); **38** Werner Lupberger/Robbie Stirling/Romain Dumas, ZA/CDN/F (Reynard 01Q-Ford Cosworth XDE), 138 (DNF – fire); **39** Johnny Mowlem/Butch Leitzinger/Shane Lewis, GB/USA/USA (Ferrari 360 Modena), 138 (DNF – engine); **40** Tony Burgess/David Shep/Andrew Bagnall, CDN/CDN/NZ (Porsche 911 GT3-RS), 134 (DNF – transmission); **41** Duncan Dayton/Jon Field/Rick Sutherland, USA/USA/USA (MG Lola EX257), 107 (DNF – engine); **42** Tim Sugden/Mike Jordan/Michael Caine, GB/GB/GB (TVR Tuscan T400R), 93 (DNF – transmission); **43** Franz Konrad/Toni Seiler/Walter Brun, D/CH/CH (Saleen S7-R), 91 (DNF – transmission); **44** Edouard Sezionale/Patrice Roussel/Lucas Lasserre, F/F/F (Norma M2000-2-Ford), 82 (DNF – engine); **45** David Hallyday/Philippe Alliot/Carl Rosenblad, F/F/S (Courage C65-JPX), 41 (DNF – piston); **46** Frank Biela/Mika Salo/Perry McCarthy, D/FIN/GB (Audi R8), 28 (DNF – fuel feed); **47** Jeff Bucknum/Bryan Willman/Chris McMurray, USA/USA/USA (Pilbeam MP91 JPX-IES), 27 (DNF – engine); **48** Richard Stanton/Richard Hay/Rob Barff, GB/GB/GB (TVR Tuscan T400 R), 11 (DNF – accident/transmission); **49** Anthony Kumpen/Mike Hezemans/David Hart, B/NL/NL (Pagani Zonda GT-Mercedes), 10 (DNF – gearbox).

Did not start: Jamie Campbell-Walter/Nathan Kinch/Vincent Vosse, GB/GB/B (Lister Storm LMP-Chevrolet) – accident in qualifying.

Fastest race lap: Herbert, 3m 35.529s, 141.671 mph/227.997 km/h.

Fastest qualifying lap: Kristensen, 3m 32.843s, 143.459 mph/230.874 km/h.

Indy Racing League (IRL) IndyCar Series

TOYOTA INDY 300, Homestead-Miami Speedway, Florida, USA, 2 March. Round 1. 200 laps of the 1.500-mile/2.414-km circuit, 300.000 miles/482.803 km.

1 Scott Dixon, NZ (Panoz G-Force-Toyota), 1h 57m 06.2062s, 153.710 mph/247.373 km/h; **2** Gil de Ferran, BR (Dallara-Toyota), 1h 57m 06.7814s; **3** Helio Castroneves, BR (Dallara-Toyota), 1h 57m 08.8014s; **4** Tony Kanaan, BR (Dallara-Honda), 1h 57m 09.6231s; **5** Scott Sharp, USA (Dallara-Toyota), 1h 57m 10.4363s; **6** Michael Andretti, USA (Dallara-Honda), 1h 57m 20.5964s; **7** Dario Franchitti, GB (Dallara-Honda), 1h 57m 24.1501s; **8** Tomas Scheckter, ZA (Panoz G-Force-Toyota), 1h 57m 26.9633s; **9** Felipe Giaffone, BR (Panoz G-Force-Toyota), 199 laps; **10** Sam Hornish Jr, USA (Dallara-Chevrolet), 199.

Most laps led: de Ferran, 92.

Fastest race lap: Kanaan, 27.6791s, 195.093 mph/313.972 km/h.

Fastest qualifying lap: Kanaan, 26.5278s, 203.560 mph/327.598 km/h.

Championship points: 1 Dixon, 50; **2** de Ferran, 42; **3** Castroneves, 35; **4** Kanaan, 32; **5** Sharp, 30; **6** Andretti, 28.

PUREX DIAL INDY 200, Phoenix International Raceway, Avondale, Arizona, USA, 23 March. Round 2. 200 laps of the 1.000-mile/1.609-km circuit, 200.000 miles/321.869 km.

1 Tony Kanaan, BR (Dallara-Honda), 1h 59m 54.7395s, 100.073 mph/161.052 km/h; **2** Helio Castroneves, BR (Dallara-Toyota), 1h 59m 55.6723s; **3** Felipe Giaffone, BR (Panoz G-Force-Toyota), 1h 59m 56.0352s; **4** Al Unser Jr, USA (Dallara-Toyota), 1h 59m 56.9875s; **5** Kenny Bräck, S (Dallara-Honda), 1h 59m 57.1195s; **6** Jacques Lazier, USA (Dallara-Chevrolet), 1h 59m 57.5662s; **7** Scott Sharp, USA (Dallara-Toyota), 1h 59m 58.3117s; **8** Sarah Fisher, USA (Dallara-Chevrolet), 1h 59m 58.5621s; **9** Buddy Rice, USA (Dallara-Chevrolet), 1h 59m 58.6711s; **10** Shigeaki Hattori, J (Dallara-Toyota), 199 laps.

Most laps led: Kanaan, 79.

Fastest race lap: Scott Dixon, NZ (Panoz G-Force-Toyota), 21.4804s, 167.595 mph/269.717 km/h.

Fastest qualifying lap: Kanaan, 20.1667s, 178.512 mph/287.287 km/h.

Championship points: 1 Kanaan, 84; **2** Castroneves, 75; **2** Dixon, 60; **4** de Ferran, 58; **5** Giaffone, 57; **6** Sharp, 56.

INDY JAPAN 300, Twin Ring Motegi, Motegi, Japan, 13 April. Round 3. 200 laps of the 1.502-mile/2.446-km circuit, 304.000 miles/489.520 km.

1 Scott Sharp, USA (Dallara-Toyota), 2h 21m 17.8256s, 129.090 mph/207.750 km/h; **2** Kenny Bräck, S (Dallara-Honda), 2h 21m 18.1487s (under caution); **3** Felipe Giaffone, BR (Panoz G-Force-Toyota), 2h 21m 19.3717s; **4** Michael Andretti, USA (Dallara-Honda), 2h 21m 21.1242s; **5** Al Unser Jr, USA (Dallara-Toyota), 2h 21m 24.1505s; **6** Sam Hornish Jr, USA (Dallara-Chevrolet), 199 laps; **7** Dan Wheldon, GB (Dallara-Honda), 198; **8** Toranosuke 'Tora' Takagi, J (Panoz G-Force-Toyota), 198; **9** Greg Ray, USA (Panoz G-Force-Honda), 197; **10** Robbie Buhl, USA (Dallara-Chevrolet), 192.

Most laps led: Kanaan, 70.

Fastest race lap: Tomas Scheckter, ZA (Panoz G-Force-Toyota), 27.0977s, 201.936 mph/324.984 km/h.

Fastest qualifying lap: Scott Dixon, NZ (Panoz G-Force-Toyota), 26.4353s, 206.996 mph/333.128 km/h.

Championship points: 1 Sharp, 106; **2** Kanaan, 102; **2** Giaffone, 92; **4** Bräck, 89; **5** Castroneves, 83; **6** Unser Jr, 79.

87th INDIANAPOLIS 500, Indianapolis Motor Speedway, Speedway, Indiana, USA, 25 May. Round 4. 200 laps of the 2.500-mile/4.023-km circuit, 500.000 miles/804.672 km.

1 Gil de Ferran, BR (Panoz G-Force-Toyota), 3h 11m 56.9891s, 156.291 mph/251.526 km/h; **2** Helio Castroneves, BR (Dallara-Toyota), 3h 11m 57.2881s; **3** Tony Kanaan, BR (Dallara-Honda), 3h 11m 58.2366s; **4** Tomas Scheckter, ZA (Panoz G-Force-Toyota), 3h 11m 58.6736s; **5** Toranosuke 'Tora' Takagi, J (Panoz G-Force-Toyota), 3h 11m 58.9497s; **6** Alex Barron, USA (Panoz G-Force-Toyota), 3h 12m 02.9928s; **7** Tony Renna, USA (Dallara-Toyota), 3h 12m 04.4773s; **8** Greg Ray, USA (Panoz G-Force-Honda), 3h 12m 08.5557s; **9** Al Unser Jr, USA (Dallara-Toyota), 200 laps; **10** Roger Yasukawa, J (Dallara-Honda), 199; **11** Buddy Rice, USA (Dallara-Chevrolet), 199; **12** Vitor Meira, BR (Dallara-Chevrolet), 199; **13** Jimmy Kite, USA (Dallara-Chevrolet), 197; **14** Shinji Nakano, J (Dallara-Honda), 196; **15** Sam Hornish Jr, USA (Dallara-Chevrolet), 195 (DNF – engine); **16** Kenny Bräck, S (Dallara-Honda), 195; **17** Scott Dixon, NZ (Panoz G-Force-Toyota), 191 (DNF- accident); **18** AJ Foyt IV, USA (Dallara-Toyota), 189; **19** Dan Wheldon, GB (Dallara-Honda), 186 (DNF – accident); **20** Scott Sharp, USA (Dallara-Toyota), 181 (DNF – accident); **21** Buddy Lazier, USA (Dallara-Chevrolet), 171 (DNF – engine); **22** Robby Gordon, USA (Dallara-Honda), 169 (DNF – gearbox); **23** Robbie Buhl, USA (Dallara-Chevrolet), 147 (DNF – engine); **24** Airton Dare, BR (Panoz G-Force-Toyota), 125 (DNF – accident); **25** Robby McGehee, USA (Dallara-Chevrolet), 125 (DNF – steering); **26** Jimmy Vasser, USA (Dallara-Honda), 102 (DNF – gearbox); **27** Michael Andretti, USA (Dallara-Honda), 94 (DNF – throttle linkage); **28** Richie Hearn, USA (Panoz G-Force-Toyota), 61 (DNF – accident); **29** Jacques Lazier, USA (Dallara-Chevrolet), 61 (DNF – accident); **30** Shigeaki Hattori, J (Dallara-Toyota), 19 (DNF – fuel system); **31** Sarah Fisher, USA (Dallara-Chevrolet), 14 (DNF – engine); **32** Billy Boat, USA (Dallara-Chevrolet), 7 (DNF – engine); **33** Felipe Giaffone, BR (Panoz G-Force-Toyota), 6 (DNF – electrics).

Did not start: Dario Franchitti, GB (Dallara-Honda) – entered, but injured in motorcycle accident; Arie Luyendyk, NL (Panoz G-Force-Toyota) – injured in practice; Scott Mayer, USA (Dallara-Chevrolet).

Most laps led: Scheckter, 63.

Fastest race lap: Kanaan, 39.2692s, 229.187 mph/368.841 km/h.

Fastest leading lap: Castroneves, 39.5982s, 227.283 mph/365.777 km/h.

Pole position/Fastest qualifying lap: Castroneves, 2m 35.3564s, 231.725 mph/372.925 km/h (over four laps).

Championship points: 1 Kanaan, 137; **2** Castroneves, 123; **3** Sharp, 116; **4** de Ferran, 108; **5** Bräck, 103; **6** Unser Jr, 101.

BOMBARDIER 500, Texas Motor Speedway, Fort Worth, Texas, USA, 7 June. Round 5. 200 laps of the 1.455-mile/2.342-km circuit, 291.000 miles/468.319 km.

1 Al Unser Jr, USA (Dallara-Toyota), 1h 43m 47.8051s, 168.213 mph/270.713 km/h; **2** Tony Kanaan, BR (Dallara-Honda), 1h 43m 47.8861s; **3** Toranosuke 'Tora' Takagi, J (Panoz G-Force-Toyota), 1h 43m 47.9646s; **4** Kenny Bräck, S (Dallara-Honda), 1h 43m 48.0637s; **5** Bryan Herta, USA (Dallara-Honda), 1h 43m 48.3780s; **6** Scott Dixon, NZ (Panoz G-Force-Toyota), 1h 43m 49.6241s; **7** Helio Castroneves, BR (Dallara-Toyota), 1h 43m 55.5582s; **8** Gil de Ferran, BR (Panoz G-Force-Toyota), 199 laps; **9** Roger Yasukawa, J (Dallara-Honda), 199; **10** Sam Hornish Jr, USA (Dallara-Chevrolet), 199.

Most laps led: Tomas Scheckter, ZA (Panoz G-Force-Toyota), 145.

Fastest race lap: Felipe Giaffone, BR (Panoz G-Force-Toyota), 23.6646s, 221.343 mph/356.217 km/h.

Fastest qualifying lap: Scheckter, 23.8851s, 219.300 mph/352.929 km/h.

Championship points: 1 Kanaan, 177; **2** Unser Jr, 151; **3** Castroneves, 149; **4** Bräck, 135; **5** de Ferran, 132; **6** Sharp, 130.

HONDA INDY 225, Pikes Peak International Raceway, Fountain, Colorado, USA, 15 June. Round 6. 225 laps of the 1.000-mile/1.609-km circuit, 225.000 miles/362.102 km.

1 Scott Dixon, NZ (Panoz G-Force-Toyota), 1h 32m 19.9594s, 146.210 mph/235.303 km/h; **2** Tony Kanaan, BR (Dallara-Honda), 1h 32m 20.1331s (under yellow); **3** Gil de Ferran, BR (Dallara-Toyota), 1h 32m 21.4290s; **4** Dario Franchitti, GB (Dallara-Honda), 1h 32m 24.8593s; **5** Sam Hornish Jr, USA (Dallara-Chevrolet), 1h 32m 25.8368s; **6** Toranosuke 'Tora' Takagi, J (Panoz G-Force-Toyota), 224 laps; **7** Kenny Bräck, S (Dallara-Honda), 224; **8** Tomas Scheckter, ZA (Panoz G-Force-Toyota), 224; **9** Buddy Rice, USA (Dallara-Chevrolet), 223; **10** Buddy Lazier, USA (Dallara-Chevrolet), 223.

Most laps led: Dixon, 89.

Fastest race lap: Kanaan, 20.7067s, 173.857 mph/279.795 km/h.

Fastest qualifying lap: Kanaan, 19.9743s, 180.232 mph/290.055 km/h.

Championship points: 1 Kanaan, 217; **2** Dixon, 168; **3=** de Ferran, 167; **3=** Castroneves, 167; **3=** Unser Jr, 167; **6** Bräck, 161.

SUNTRUST INDY CHALLENGE, Richmond International Raceway, Virginia, USA, 28 June. Round 7. 206 laps of the 0.750-mile/1.207-km circuit, 154.500 miles/248.644 km.

1 Scott Dixon, NZ (Panoz G-Force-Toyota), 1h 26m 47.9459s, 106.798 mph/171.875 km/h; **2** Helio Castroneves, BR (Dallara-Toyota), 1h 26m 52.9809s (under yellow); **3** Gil de Ferran, BR (Dallara-Toyota), 1h 26m 55.7723s; **4** Sam Hornish Jr, USA (Dallara-Chevrolet), 1h 26m 57.8517s; **5** Tony Kanaan, BR (Dallara-Honda), 1h 27m 07.2705s; **6** Felipe Giaffone, BR (Panoz G-Force-Toyota), 1h 27m 08.1786s; **7** Kenny Bräck, S (Dallara-Honda), 1h 27m 09.5279s; **8** Dan Wheldon, GB (Dallara-Honda), 1h 27m 10.8022s; **9** Buddy Rice, USA (Dallara-Chevrolet), 1h 27m 12.9771s; **10** Al Unser Jr, USA (Dallara-Toyota), 1h 27m 14.9430s.

Most laps led: Dixon, 206.

Fastest race lap: Tomas Scheckter, ZA (Panoz G-Force-Toyota), 17.1403s, 157.523 mph/253.509 km/h.

Fastest qualifying lap: Dixon, 16.0582s, 168.138 mph/270.593 km/h.

Championship points: 1 Kanaan, 247; **2** Dixon, 220; **3** Castroneves, 207; **4** de Ferran, 202; **5=** Bräck, 187; **5=** Unser Jr, 187.

KANSAS INDY 300, Kansas Speedway, Kansas City, Kansas, USA, 6 July. Round 8. 200 laps of the 1.520-mile/2.446-km circuit, 304.000 miles/489.241 km.

1 Bryan Herta, USA (Dallara-Honda), 1h 48m 50.9861s, 167.570 mph/269.678 km/h; **2** Helio Castroneves, BR (Dallara-Toyota), 1h 48m 58.3125s; **3** Gil de Ferran, BR (Dallara-Toyota), 1h 48m 58.4706s; **4** Tony Kanaan, BR (Dallara-Honda), 1h 49m 00.7283; **5** Kenny Bräck, S (Dallara-Honda), 199 laps; **6** Scott Dixon, NZ (Panoz G-Force-Toyota), 199; **7** Roger Yasukawa, J (Dallara-Honda), 198; **8** Greg Ray, USA (Panoz G-Force-Honda), 198; **9** Tomas Scheckter, ZA (Panoz G-Force-Toyota), 198; **10** Jacques Lazier, USA (Dallara-Toyota), 197.

Most laps led: de Ferran, 93.

Fastest race lap: Kanaan, 25.1849s, 217.273 mph/349.667 km/h.

Fastest qualifying lap: Dixon, 25.0911s, 218.085 mph/350.974 km/h.

Championship points: 1 Kanaan, 279; **2** Dixon, 248; **3** Castroneves, 247; **4** de Ferran, 239; **5** Bräck, 217; **6** Unser Jr, 203.

FIRESTONE INDY 200, Nashville Superspeedway, Lebanon, Tennessee, USA, 19 July. Round 9. 200 laps of the 1.300-mile/2.092-km circuit, 260.000 miles/418.429 km.

1 Gil de Ferran, BR (Dallara-Toyota), 1h 53m 18.4386s, 137.679 mph/221.572 km/h; **2** Scott Dixon, NZ (Panoz G-Force-Toyota), 1h 53m 18.5708s (under caution); **3** Helio Castroneves, BR (Dallara-Toyota), 1h 53m 19.6108s; **4** Dan Wheldon, GB (Dallara-Honda), 1h 53m 22.2208s; **5** Alex Barron, USA (Panoz G-Force-Toyota), 1h 53m 22.8257s; **6** Kenny Bräck, S (Dallara-Honda), 1h 53m 23.1500s; **7** Toranosuke 'Tora' Takagi, J (Panoz G-Force-Toyota), 1h 53m 23.3379s; **8** Al Unser Jr, USA (Dallara-Toyota), 1h 53m 26.0199s; **9** Tony Kanaan, BR (Dallara-Honda), 1h 53m 26.1436s; **10** Tomas Scheckter, ZA (Panoz G-Force-Toyota), 1h 53m 27.0141s.

Most laps led: Kanaan, 55.

Fastest race lap: Sam Hornish Jr, USA (Dallara-Chevrolet), 22.9685s, 203.757 mph/327.916 km/h.

Fastest qualifying lap: Dixon, 22.6952s, 206.211 mph/331.864 km/h.

Championship points: 1 Kanaan, 303; **2** de Ferran, 289; **3** Dixon, 288; **4** Castroneves, 282; **5** Bräck, 245; **6** Unser Jr, 227.

FIRESTONE INDY 400, Michigan International Speedway, Brooklyn, Michigan, USA, 27 July. Round 10. 200 laps of the 2.000-mile/3.219-km circuit, 400.000 miles/643.738 km.

1 Alex Barron, USA (Panoz G-Force-Toyota), 2h 12m 39.4413s, 180.917 mph/291.158 km/h; **2** Sam Hornish Jr, USA (Dallara-Chevrolet), 2h 12m 39.4534s; **3** Tomas Scheckter, ZA (Panoz G-Force-Toyota), 2h 12m 40.1099s; **4** Scott Sharp, USA (Dallara-Toyota), 2h 12m 40.1521s; **5** Scott Dixon, NZ (Panoz G-Force-Toyota), 2h 12m 41.7694s; **6** Toranosuke 'Tora' Takagi, J (Panoz G-Force-Toyota), 2h 12m 41.8784s; **7** Gil de Ferran, BR (Dallara-Toyota), 2h 12m 42.3378s; **8** Roger Yasukawa, J (Dallara-Honda), 2h 12m 48.1462s; **9** Al Unser Jr, USA (Dallara-Toyota), 2h 13m 12.8713s; **10** Greg Ray, USA (Panoz G-Force-Honda), 199 laps.

Most laps led: Hornish Jr, 126.

Fastest race lap: Bryan Herta, USA (Dallara-Honda), 32.2730s, 223.097 mph/359.039 km/h.

Fastest qualifying lap: Scheckter, 32.3657s, 222.458 mph/358.011 km/h.

Championship points: 1 Dixon, 318; **2** Kanaan, 317; **3** de Ferran, 315; **4** Castroneves, 295; **5** Bräck, 257; **6** Unser Jr, 249.

EMERSON INDY 250, Gateway International Raceway, Madison, Illinois, USA, 10 August. Round 11. 200 laps of the 1.250-mile/2.012-km circuit, 250.000 miles/402.336 km.

1 Helio Castroneves, BR (Dallara-Toyota), 1h 50m 52.5587s, 135.286 mph/217.722 km/h; **2** Tony Kanaan, BR (Dallara-Honda), 1h 50m 53.4053s; **3** Gil de Ferran, BR (Dallara-Toyota), 1h 50m 53.8344s; **4** Tomas Scheckter, ZA (Panoz G-Force-Toyota), 1h 50m 55.3786s; **5** Dan Wheldon, GB (Dallara-Honda), 1h 50m 56.5855s; **6** Sam Hornish Jr, USA (Dallara-Chevrolet), 1h 50m 57.6448s; **7** Toranosuke 'Tora' Takagi, J (Dallara-Toyota), 1h 51m 00.9901s; **8** Greg Ray, USA (Panoz G-Force-Honda), 1h 51m 01.3264s; **9** Vitor Meira, BR (Dallara-Chevrolet), 198 laps; **10** Scott Sharp, USA (Dallara-Toyota), 197.

Most laps led: Castroneves, 96.

Fastest race lap: Scott Dixon, NZ (Panoz G-Force-Toyota), 26.5592s, 169.433 mph/272.676 km/h.

Fastest qualifying lap: Castroneves, 25.5732s, 175.965 mph/283.189 km/h.

Championship points: 1 Kanaan, 357; **2** de Ferran, 350; **3** Castroneves, 347; **4** Dixon, 333; **5** Bräck, 268; **6** Unser Jr, 259.

BELTERRA CASINO INDY 300, Kentucky Speedway, Sparta, Kentucky, USA, 17 August. Round 12. 200 laps of the 1.480-mile/2.382-km circuit, 296.000 miles/476.366 km.

1 Sam Hornish Jr, USA (Dallara-Chevrolet), 1h 29m 44.6120s, 197.897 mph/318.485 km/h; **2** Scott Dixon, NZ (Panoz G-Force-Toyota), 1h 29m 45.7832s; **3** Bryan Herta, USA (Dallara-Honda), 1h 29m 59.5923s; **4** Al Unser Jr, USA (Dallara-Toyota), 199 laps; **5** Helio Castroneves, BR (Dallara-Toyota), 199; **6** Tony Kanaan, BR (Dallara-Honda), 199; **7** Robbie Buhl, USA (Dallara-Chevrolet), 199; **8** Dan Wheldon, GB (Dallara-Honda), 199; **9** Gil de Ferran, BR (Dallara-Toyota), 199; **10** Tomas Scheckter, ZA (Panoz G-Force-Toyota), 199.

Most laps led: Hornish Jr, 181.

Fastest race lap: Sarah Fisher, USA (Dallara-Chevrolet), 24.2830s, 219.413 mph/353.111 km/h.

Fastest qualifying lap: Hornish Jr, 24.2608s, 219.614 mph/353.434 km/h.

Championship points: 1 Kanaan, 385; **2** Castroneves, 377; **3** Dixon, 373; **4** de Ferran, 372; **5** Hornish Jr, 308; **6** Unser Jr, 291.

FIRESTONE INDY 225, Nazareth Speedway, Pennsylvania, USA. 24 August. Round 13. 225 laps of the 0.935-mile/1.505-km circuit, 210.375 miles/338.566 km.

1 Helio Castroneves, BR (Dallara-Toyota), 1h 42m 07.1375s, 123.606 mph/198.924 km/h; **2** Sam Hornish Jr, USA (Dallara-Chevrolet), 1h 42m 07.3072s; **3** Bryan Herta, USA (Dallara-Honda), 1h 42m 15.7398s; **4** Gil de Ferran, BR (Dallara-Toyota), 1h 42m 17.0835s; **5** Kenny Bräck, S (Dallara-Honda), 1h 42m 17.9090s; **6** Al Unser Jr, USA (Dallara-Toyota), 1h 42m 23.5383s; **7** Dan Wheldon, GB (Dallara-Honda), 1h 42m 25.2027s; **8** Roger Yasukawa, J (Dallara-Honda), 1h 42m 26.2336s; **9** Robbie Buhl, USA (Dallara-Chevrolet), 224 laps; **10** Buddy Rice, USA (Dallara-Chevrolet), 223.

Most laps led: Castroneves, 173.

Fastest race lap: Hornish Jr, 20.6862s, 162.717 mph/261.868 km/h.

Fastest qualifying lap: Scott Dixon, NZ (Panoz G-Force-Toyota), 19.6633s, 171.182 mph/275.490 km/h.

Championship points: 1 Castroneves, 429; **2** de Ferran, 404; **2** Kanaan, 397; **4** Dixon, 387; **5** Hornish Jr, 348; **6** Unser Jr, 319.

DELPHI INDY 300, Chicagoland Speedway, Joliet, Illinois, USA, 7 September. Round 14. 200 of the 1.520-mile/2.446-km circuit, 304.000 miles/489.241 km.

1 Sam Hornish Jr, USA (Dallara-Chevrolet), 1h 38m 58.3310s, 184.294 mph/296.593 km/h; **2** Scott Dixon, NZ (Panoz G-Force-Toyota), 1h 38m 58.3409s; **3** Bryan Herta, USA (Dallara-Honda), 1h 38m 58.3410s; **4** Dan Wheldon, GB (Dallara-Honda), 1h 38m 58.4555s; **5** Tomas Scheckter, ZA (Panoz G-Force-Toyota), 1h 38m 58.5372s; **6** Tony Kanaan, BR (Dallara-Honda), 1h 38m 58.6246s; **7** Alex Barron, USA (Dallara-Chevrolet), 1h 38m 58.7383s; **8** Roger Yasukawa, J (Dallara-Honda), 1h 38m 58.8204s; **9** Toranosuke 'Tora' Takagi, J (Panoz G-Force-Toyota), 1h 38m 59.1219s; **10** Robbie Buhl, USA (Dallara-Chevrolet), 1h 38m 59.3944s.

Most laps led: Scheckter, 76.

Fastest race lap: Herta, 24.4721s, 223.602 mph/359.852 km/h.

Fastest qualifying lap: Richie Hearn, USA (Dallara-Chevrolet), 24.5206s, 223.159 mph/359.140 km/h.

Championship points: 1 Castroneves, 439; **2** Dixon, 427; **3** Kanaan, 425; **4** de Ferran, 422; **5** Hornish Jr, 398; **6** Unser Jr, 330.

TOYOTA INDY 400, California Speedway, Fontana, California, USA, 21 September. Round 15. 200 laps of the 2.000-mile/3.219-km circuit, 400.000 miles/643.738 km.

1 Sam Hornish Jr, USA (Dallara-Chevrolet), 1h 55m 51.4395s, 207.151 mph/333.378 km/h; **2** Scott Dixon, NZ (Panoz G-Force-Toyota), 1h 55m 51.7958s; **3** Tony Kanaan, BR (Dallara-Honda), 1h 55m 55.3992s; **4** Dan Wheldon, GB (Dallara-Honda), 1h 55m 56.7857s; **5** Tomas Scheckter, ZA (Panoz G-Force-Toyota), 1h 56m 00.6258s; **6** Helio Castroneves, BR (Dallara-Toyota), 1h 56m 04.3361s; **7** Roger Yasukawa, J (Dallara-Honda), 1h 56m 13.4493s; **8** Scott Sharp, USA (Dallara-Toyota), 199 laps; **9** Al Unser Jr, USA (Dallara-Toyota), 199; **10** Alex Barron, USA (Dallara-Chevrolet), 199.

Most laps led: Scheckter, 112.

Fastest race lap: Dixon, 32.1208s, 224.154 mph/360.741 km/h.

Fastest qualifying lap: Castroneves, 31.7521s, 226.757 mph/364.929 km/h.

Championship points: 1= Dixon, 467; **1=** Castroneves, 467; **3** Kanaan, 460; **4** Hornish Jr, 448; **5** de Ferran, 437; **6** Unser Jr, 352.

CHEVY 500, Texas Motor Speedway, Fort Worth, Texas, USA, 12 October. Round 16. 195 laps of the 1.455-mile/2.342-km circuit, 283.725 miles/456.611 km.

1 Gil de Ferran, BR (Dallara-Toyota), 1h 48m 56.2674s, 156.268 mph/251.489 km/h; **2** Scott Dixon, NZ (Panoz G-Force-Toyota), 1h 48m 56.4755s; **3** Dan Wheldon, GB (Dallara-Honda), 1h 48m 57.3605s; **4** Vitor Meira, BR (Dallara-Chevrolet), 1h 48m 58.0452s; **5** Bryan Herta, USA (Dallara-Honda), 1h 48m 59.8615s; **6** Scott Sharp, USA (Dallara-Toyota), 1h 49m 01.3388s; **7** Toranosuke 'Tora' Takagi, J (Panoz G-Force-Toyota), 1h 49m 01.7213s; **8** Greg Ray, USA (Panoz G-Force-Honda), 1h 49m 03.0202s; **9** Al Unser Jr, USA (Dallara-Toyota), 1h 49m 05.3763s; **10** Roger Yasukawa, J (Dallara-Honda), 1h 49m 06.0649s.

Most laps led: de Ferran, 68.

Fastest race lap: Tony Kanaan, BR (Dallara-Honda), 23.4413s, 223.452 mph/359.611 km/h.

Fastest qualifying lap: de Ferran, 23.5031s, 222.864 mph/358.665 km/h.

Final championship points

1 Scott Dixon, NZ, 507; **2** Gil de Ferran, BR, 489; **3** Helio Castroneves, BR, 484; **4** Tony Kanaan, BR, 476; **5** Sam Hornish Jr, USA, 461; **6** Al Unser Jr, USA, 374; **7** Tomas Scheckter, ZA, 356; **8** Scott Sharp, USA, 351; **9** Kenny Bräck, S, 342; **10** Toranosuke 'Tora' Takagi, J, 317; **11** Dan Wheldon, GB, 312; **12** Roger Yasukawa, J, 301; **13** Bryan Herta, USA, 277; **14** Robbie Buhl, USA, 261; **15** Greg Ray, USA, 253; **16** Buddy Rice, USA, 229; **17** Alex Barron, USA, 216; **18** Sarah Fisher, USA, 211; **19** Buddy Lazier, USA, 201; **20** Felipe Giaffone, BR, 199; **21** AJ Foyt IV, USA, 198; **22** Vitor Meira, BR, 170; **23** Jacques Lazier, USA, 120; **24** Michael Andretti, USA, 80; **25** Dario Franchitti, GB, 72; **26=** Ed Carpenter, USA, 43; **26=** Shigeaki Hattori, J, 43; **28** Richie Hearn, USA, 39; **29** Shinji Nakano, J, 35; **30=** Tony Renna, USA, 26; **30=** Scott Mayer, USA, 26; **32** Jimmy Kite, USA, 17; **33** Robby Gordon, USA, 8; **34** Airton Dare, BR, 6; **35** Robby McGehee, USA, 5; **36** Jimmy Vasser, USA, 4; **37** Billy Boat, USA, 1.

Bombardier Rookie of the Year

1 Dan Wheldon; **2** Roger Yasukawa; **3** A.J. Foyt Jr; **4** Ed Carpenter; **5** Scott Mayer.

Engine manufacturers

1 Chevrolet; **2** Honda; **3** Toyota.

Chassis manufacturers

1 Dallara; **2** Panoz G-Force.

The ChampCar World Series powered by Ford

2002

The following race was run after AUTOCOURSE 2002–2003 went to press.

GRAN PREMIO TELMEX-GIGANTE PRESENTED BY BANAMEX/VISA, Autodromo Hermanos Rodriguez, Mexico City, Mexico, 17 November. Round 19. 73 laps of the 2.786-mile/4.484-km circuit, 203.378 miles/327.305 km.

1 Kenny Bräck, S (Lola B2/00-Toyota RV8F), 1h 56m 48.475s, 104.468 mph/168.125 km/h; **2** Cristiano da Matta, BR (Lola B2/00-Toyota RV8F), 1h 56m 52.462s; **3** Bruno Junqueira, BR (Lola B2/00-Toyota RV8F), 1h 56m 53.548s; **4** Patrick Carpen-

tier, CDN (Reynard 02I-Ford Cosworth XF), 1h 56m 59.317s; **5** Dario Franchitti, GB (Lola B2/00-Honda HR-2), 1h 57m 01.023s; **6** Toranosuke 'Tora' Takagi, J (Reynard 02I-Toyota RV8F), 1h 57m 05.237s; **7** Scott Dixon, NZ (Lola B2/00-Toyota RV8F), 1h 57m 12.097s; **8** Tony Kanaan, BR (Lola B2/00-Honda HR-2), 1h 57m 14.321s; **9** Oriol Servia, E (Reynard 02I-Toyota RV8F), 1h 57m 16.509s; **10** Alex Tagliani, CDN (Reynard 02I-Ford Cosworth XF), 1h 57m 18.424s.
Most laps led: Kanaan, 40.
Fastest qualifying lap: Junqueira, 1m 25.941s, 116.703 mph/187.816 km/h.

Final championship points

1 Cristiano da Matta, BR, 237; **2** Bruno Junqueira, BR, 164; **3** Patrick Carpentier, CDN, 157; **4** Dario Franchitti, GB, 148; **5** Christian Fittipaldi, BR, 122; **6=** Kenny Bräck, S, 114; **6=** Jimmy Vasser, USA, 114; **8** Alex Tagliani, CDN, 111; **9** Michael Andretti, USA, 110; **10** Michel Jourdain Jr, MEX, 105; **11** Paul Tracy, CDN, 101; **12** Tony Kanaan, BR, 99; **13** Scott Dixon, NZ, 97; **14** Adrian Fernandez, MEX, 59; **15** Toranosuke 'Tora' Takagi, J, 53; **16** Oriol Servia, E, 44; **17** Shinji Nakano, J, 43; **18** Mario Dominguez, MEX, 37; **19** Massimiliano 'Max' Papis, I, 32; **20** Townsend Bell, USA, 19; **21** Darren Manning, GB, 4; **22** Andre Lotterer, D, 1.

Nation's Cup
1 Brazil, 325; **2** Canada, 247; **3** USA, 164; **4** Scotland, 148; **5** Mexico, 142; **6** Sweden, 113; **7** New Zealand, 96; **8** Japan, 73; **9** Catalonia, 44; **10** Italy, 32; **11** England, 4; **12** Germany, 1.

Manufacturer's Cup (engines)
1 Toyota, 333; **2** Honda, 282; **3** Ford Cosworth, 259.

Constructor's Cup
1 Lola, 401; **2** Reynard, 235.

Rookie of the Year
1 Mario Dominguez; **2** Townsend Bell; **3** Darren Manning; **4** Andre Lotterer.

2003

GRAND PRIX OF ST. PETERSBURG, Streets of St. Petersburg, Florida, USA, 23 February. Round 1. 105 laps of the 1.806-mile/2.906-km circuit, 189.630 miles/305.180 km.
1 Paul Tracy, CDN (Lola B2/00-Ford Cosworth XFE), 2h 04m 28.904s, 91.401 mph/147.096 km/h; **2** Michel Jourdain Jr, MEX (Lola B2/00-Ford Cosworth XFE), 2h 04m 41.040s; **3** Bruno Junqueira, BR (Lola B2/00-Ford Cosworth XFE), 2h 04m 45.474s; **4** Mario Haberfeld, BR (Reynard 02ib-Ford Cosworth XFE), 2h 05m 10.264s; **5** Roberto Moreno, BR (Lola B2/00-Ford Cosworth XFE), 2h 05m 25.689s; **6** Jimmy Vasser, USA (Reynard 02ib-Ford Cosworth XFE), 104 laps; **7** Tiago Monteiro, P (Reynard 02ib-Ford Cosworth XFE), 104; **8** Patrick Carpentier, CDN (Lola B2/00-Ford Cosworth XFE), 103; **9** Joel Camathias, CH (Lola B2/00-Ford Cosworth XFE), 103; **10** Patrick Lemarié, F (Lola B2/00-Ford Cosworth XFE), 102.
Most laps led: Tracy, 71.
Fastest qualifying lap: Sébastien Bourdais, F (Lola B2/00-Ford Cosworth XFE), 1m 00.928s, 106.710 mph/171.732 km/h.
Championship points: **1** Tracy, 21; **2** Jourdain Jr, 16; **3** Junqueira, 14; **4** Haberfeld, 12; **5** Moreno, 10; **6** Vasser, 8.

TECATE/TELMEX MONTERREY GRAND PRIX, Parque Fundidora, Monterrey, Nuevo Leon, Mexico, 23 March. Round 2. 85 laps of the 2.104-mile/3.386-km circuit, 178.840 miles/287.815 km.
1 Paul Tracy, CDN (Lola B2/00-Ford Cosworth XFE), 2h 03m 04.677s, 87.184 mph/140.309 km/h; **2** Michel Jourdain Jr, MEX (Lola B2/00-Ford Cosworth XFE), 2h 03m 06.716s; **3** Alex Tagliani, CDN (Lola B2/00-Ford Cosworth XFE), 2h 03m 16.707s; **4** Adrian Fernandez, MEX (Lola B2/00-Ford Cosworth XFE), 2h 03m 18.916s; **5** Bruno Junqueira, BR (Lola B2/00-Ford Cosworth XFE), 2h 03m 19.527s; **6** Roberto Moreno, BR (Lola B2/00-Ford Cosworth XFE), 2h 03m 35.610s; **7** Darren Manning, GB (Reynard 02ib-Ford Cosworth XFE), 2h 03m 39.860s; **8** Patrick Carpentier, CDN (Lola B2/00-Ford Cosworth XFE), 84 laps; **9** Alex Yoong, MAL (Lola B2/00-Ford Cosworth XFE), 84; **10** Patrick Lemarié, F (Lola B2/00-Ford Cosworth XFE), 84.
Most laps led: Tracy, 69.
Fastest qualifying lap: Sébastien Bourdais, F (Lola B2/00-Ford Cosworth XFE), 1m 14.938s, 101.076 mph/162.665 km/h.
Championship points: **1** Tracy, 43; **2** Jourdain Jr, 32; **3** Junqueira, 24; **4** Moreno, 18; **5** Tagliani, 14; **6=** Fernandez, 12; **6=** Haberfeld, 12.

TOYOTA GRAND PRIX OF LONG BEACH, Long Beach Street Circuit, California, USA, 13 April. Round 3. 90 laps of the 1.968-mile/3.167-km circuit, 177.120 miles/285.047 km.
1 Paul Tracy, CDN (Lola B2/00-Ford Cosworth XFE), 1h 56m 01.792s, 91.590 mph/147.400 km/h; **2** Adrian Fernandez, MEX (Lola B2/00-Ford Cosworth XFE), 1h 56m 06.336s; **3** Bruno Junqueira, BR (Lola B2/00-Ford Cosworth XFE), 1h 56m 15.443s; **4** Jimmy Vasser, USA (Reynard 02ib-Ford Cosworth XFE), 1h 56m 22.832s; **5** Mario Dominguez, MEX (Lola B2/00-Ford Cosworth XFE), 1h 56m 23.983s; **6** Patrick Carpentier, CDN (Lola B2/00-Ford Cosworth XFE), 1h 56m 24.452s; **7** Ryan Hunter-Reay, USA (Reynard 02ib-Ford Cosworth XFE), 1h 56m 27.495s; **8** Darren Manning, GB (Reynard 02ib-Ford Cosworth XFE), 1h 56m 35.165s; **9** Mario Haberfeld, BR (Reynard 02ib-Ford Cosworth XFE), 1h 56m 50.363s; **10** Alex Tagliani, CDN (Lola B2/00-Ford Cosworth XFE), 89 laps.
Most laps led: Michel Jourdain Jr, MEX (Lola B2/00-Ford Cosworth XFE), 48.
Fastest qualifying lap: Jourdain Jr, 1m 08.177s, 103.918 mph/167.239 km/h.
Championship points: **1** Tracy, 64; **2** Junqueira, 38; **3** Jourdain Jr, 34; **4** Fernandez, 28; **5** Vasser, 20; **6=** Moreno, 18; **6=** Carpentier, 18.

THE LONDON CHAMP CAR TROPHY, Brands Hatch Indy circuit, West Kingsdown, Dartford, Kent, England, 5 May. Round 4. 165 laps of the 1.192-mile/1.918-km circuit, 196.680 miles/316.526 km.
1 Sébastien Bourdais, F (Lola B2/00-Ford Cosworth XFE), 1h 51m 56.987s, 105.412 mph/169.643 km/h; **2** Bruno Junqueira, BR (Lola B2/00-Ford Cosworth XFE), 1h 52m 04.822s; **3** Mario Dominguez, MEX (Lola B2/00-Ford Cosworth XFE), 1h 52m 08.511s; **4** Oriol Servia, E (Lola B2/00-Ford Cosworth XFE), 1h 52m 11.372s; **5** Patrick Carpentier, CDN (Lola B2/00-Ford Cosworth XFE), 1h 52m 12.022s; **6** Michel Jourdain Jr, MEX (Lola B2/00-Ford Cosworth XFE), 1h 52m 27.690s; **7** Roberto Moreno, BR (Lola B2/00-Ford Cosworth XFE), 1h 52m 33.984s; **8** Alex Tagliani, CDN (Lola B2/00-Ford Cosworth XFE), 1h 52m 35.749s; **9** Mario Haberfeld, BR (Reynard 02ib-Ford Cosworth XFE), 164 laps; **10** Darren Manning, GB (Reynard 02ib-Ford Cosworth XFE), 164.
Most laps led: Bourdais, 95.
Fastest qualifying lap: Paul Tracy, CDN (Lola B2/00-Ford Cosworth XFE), 37.006s, 115.960 mph/186.619 km/h.
Championship points: **1** Tracy, 65; **2** Junqueira, 54; **3** Jourdain Jr, 42; **4** Fernandez, 29; **5** Carpentier, 28; **6** Bourdais, 27.

GERMAN 500, EuroSpeedway Lausitz, Germany, 11 May. Round 5. 154 laps of the 2.023-mile/3.256-km circuit, 311.542 miles/501.378 km.
1 Sébastien Bourdais, F (Lola B2/00-Ford Cosworth XFE), 1h 49m 22.498s, 170.903 mph/275.042 km/h; **2** Mario Dominguez, MEX (Lola B2/00-Ford Cosworth XFE), 1h 49m 22.582s; **3** Michel Jourdain Jr, MEX (Lola B2/00-Ford Cosworth XFE), 1h 49m 22.743s; **4** Bruno Junqueira, BR (Lola B2/00-Ford Cosworth XFE), 1h 49m 34.540s; **5** Oriol Servia, E (Lola B2/00-Ford Cosworth XFE), 1h 49m 34.553s; **6** Darren Manning, GB (Reynard 02ib-Ford Cosworth XFE), 1h 49m 47.100s; **7** Patrick Carpentier, CDN (Lola B2/00-Ford Cosworth XFE), 153 laps; **8** Jimmy Vasser, USA (Reynard 02ib-Ford Cosworth XFE), 153; **9** Rodolfo Lavin, MEX (Reynard 02ib-Ford Cosworth XFE), 153; **10** Roberto Moreno, BR (Lola B2/00-Ford Cosworth XFE), 153.
Most laps led: Bourdais, 74.
Fastest qualifying lap: Bourdais, 37.000s, 196.832 mph/316.771 km/h.
Championship points: **1=** Tracy, 66; **1=** Junqueira, 66; **3** Jourdain Jr, 56; **4** Bourdais, 49; **5** Dominguez, 40; **6** Carpentier, 34.

MILWAUKEE MILE 250, The Milwaukee Mile, Wisconsin State Fair Park, West Allis, Wisconsin, USA, 1 June. Round 6. 250 laps of the 1.032-mile/1.661-km circuit, 258.000 miles/415.211 km.
1 Michel Jourdain Jr, MEX (Lola B2/00-Ford Cosworth XFE), 2h 16m 45.692s, 113.190 mph/182.161 km/h; **2** Oriol Servia, E (Lola B2/00-Ford Cosworth XFE), 2h 16m 46.160s; **3** Patrick Carpentier, CDN (Lola B2/00-Ford Cosworth XFE), 2h 16m 46.396s; **4** Darren Manning, GB (Reynard 02ib-Ford Cosworth XFE), 2h 16m 46.865s; **5** Alex Tagliani, CDN (Lola B2/00-Ford Cosworth XFE), 2h 16m 47.884s; **6** Adrian Fernandez, MEX (Lola B2/00-Ford Cosworth XFE), 2h 16m 48.798s; **7** Mario Haberfeld, BR (Reynard 02ib-Ford Cosworth XFE), 2h 16m 49.918s; **8** Mario Dominguez, MEX (Lola B2/00-Ford Cosworth XFE), 2h 16m 51.281s; **9** Sébastien Bourdais, F (Lola B2/00-Ford Cosworth XFE), 2h 16m 51.575s; **10** Tiago Monteiro, P (Reynard 02ib-Ford Cosworth XFE), 2h 16m 53.379s.
Most laps led: Jourdain Jr, 234.
Fastest qualifying lap: Tagliani, 20.882s, 177.914 mph/286.325 km/h.
Championship points: **1** Jourdain Jr, 77; **2** Tracy, 67; **3** Junqueira, 66; **4** Bourdais, 53; **5** Carpentier, 48; **6** Dominguez, 45.

GRAND PRIX OF MONTEREY, Mazda Raceway Laguna Seca, Monterey, California, USA, 15 June. Round 7. 87 laps of the 2.238-mile/3.602-km circuit, 194.706 miles/313.349 km.
1 Patrick Carpentier, CDN (Lola B2/00-Ford Cosworth XFE), 1h 48m 11.023s, 107.986 mph/173.787 km/h; **2** Bruno Junqueira, BR (Lola B2/00-Ford Cosworth XFE), 1h 48m 11.867s; **3** Paul Tracy, CDN (Lola B2/00-Ford Cosworth XFE), 1h 48m 39.598s; **4** Michel Jourdain Jr, MEX (Lola B2/00-Ford Cosworth XFE), 1h 48m 51.842s; **5** Mario Haberfeld, BR (Reynard 02ib-Ford Cosworth XFE), 1h 48m 53.135s; **6** Oriol Servia, E (Lola B2/00-Ford Cosworth XFE), 1h 49m 11.180s; **7** Adrian Fernandez, MEX (Lola B2/00-Ford Cosworth XFE), 1h 49m 12.451s; **8** Jimmy Vasser, USA (Reynard 02ib-Ford Cosworth XFE), 1h 49m 12.851s; **9** Tiago Monteiro, P (Reynard 02ib-Ford Cosworth XFE), 86 laps; **10** Mario Dominguez, MEX (Lola B2/00-Ford Cosworth XFE), 86.
Most laps led: Carpentier, 87.
Fastest qualifying lap: Carpentier, 1m 09.575s, 115.800 mph/186.362 km/h.
Championship points: **1** Jourdain Jr, 89; **2** Junqueira, 83; **3** Tracy, 81; **4** Carpentier, 70; **5** Bourdais, 53; **6=** Dominguez, 48; **6=** Servia, 48.

THE G.I.JOE'S 200, Portland International Raceway, Oregon, USA, 22 June. Round 8. 100 laps of the 1.969-mile/3.169-km circuit, 196.900 miles/316.880 km.
1 Adrian Fernandez, MEX (Lola B2/00-Ford Cosworth XFE), 1h 56m 16.626s, 101.602 mph/163.513 km/h; **2** Paul Tracy, CDN (Lola B2/00-Ford Cosworth XFE), 1h 56m 18.899s; **3** Alex Tagliani, CDN (Lola B2/00-Ford Cosworth XFE), 1h 56m 21.083s; **4** Bruno Junqueira, BR (Lola B2/00-Ford Cosworth XFE), 1h 56m 25.211s; **5** Oriol Servia, E (Lola B2/00-Ford Cosworth XFE), 1h 56m 26.653s; **6** Darren Manning, GB (Reynard 02ib-Ford Cosworth XFE), 1h 56m 27.516s; **7** Jimmy Vasser, USA (Reynard 02ib-Ford Cosworth XFE), 1h 56m 27.811s; **8** Mario Haberfeld, BR (Reynard 02ib-Ford Cosworth XFE), 1h 56m 29.885s; **9** Roberto Moreno, BR (Lola B2/00-Ford Cosworth XFE), 1h 56m 31.097s; **10** Mario Dominguez, MEX (Lola B2/00-Ford Cosworth XFE), 1h 56m 31.565s.
Most laps led: Tracy & Michel Jourdain Jr, MEX (Lola B2/00-Ford Cosworth XFE), 42.
Fastest qualifying lap: Tracy, 58.793s, 120.565 mph/194.031 km/h.
Championship points: **1** Tracy, 99; **2** Junqueira, 95; **3** Jourdain r., 91; **4** Carpentier, 70; **5** Fernandez, 63; **6** Servia, 58.

U.S. BANK PRESENTS THE CLEVELAND GRAND PRIX, Burke Lakefront Airport Circuit, Cleveland, Ohio, USA, 5 July. Round 9. 115 laps of the 2.106-mile/3.389-km circuit, 242.190 miles/389.767 km.
1 Sébastien Bourdais, F (Lola B2/00-Ford Cosworth XFE), 2h 03m 51.974s, 117.315 mph/188.801 km/h; **2** Paul Tracy, CDN (Lola B2/00-Ford Cosworth XFE), 2h 03m 54.215s; **3** Bruno Junqueira, BR (Lola B2/00-Ford Cosworth XFE), 2h 03m 54.952s; **4** Patrick Carpentier, CDN (Lola B2/00-Ford Cosworth XFE), 2h 03m 59.811s; **5** Mario Dominguez, MEX (Lola B2/00-Ford Cosworth XFE), 2h 04m 00.209s; **6** Oriol Servia, E (Lola B2/00-Ford Cosworth XFE), 2h 04m 01.839s; **7** Michel Jourdain Jr, MEX (Lola B2/00-Ford Cosworth XFE), 2h 04m 02.500s; **8** Alex Tagliani, CDN (Lola B2/00-Ford Cosworth XFE), 2h 04m 04.935s; **9** Ryan Hunter-Reay, USA (Reynard 02ib-Ford Cosworth XFE), 2h 04m 07.333s; **10** Darren Manning, GB (Reynard 02ib-Ford Cosworth XFE), 2h 04m 14.197s.
Most laps led: Tracy, 67.
Fastest qualifying lap: Bourdais, 58.014s, 130.686 mph/210.318 km/h.
Championship points: **1** Tracy, 117; **2** Junqueira, 109; **3** Jourdain Jr, 97; **4** Carpentier, 82; **5** Bourdais, 74; **6** Servia, 66.

MOLSON INDY TORONTO, Canada National Exhibition Place Circuit, Toronto, Ontario, Canada, 13 July. Round 10. 112 laps of the 1.755-mile/2.824-km circuit, 196.560 miles/316.333 km.
1 Paul Tracy, CDN (Lola B2/00-Ford Cosworth XFE), 2h 02m 36.488s, 96.189 mph/154.802 km/h; **2** Michel Jourdain Jr, MEX (Lola B2/00-Ford Cosworth XFE), 2h 02m 41.021s; **3** Bruno Junqueira, BR (Lola B2/00-Ford Cosworth XFE), 2h 02m 45.114s; **4** Sébastien Bourdais, F (Lola B2/00-Ford Cosworth XFE), 2h 02m 47.141s; **5** Oriol Servia, E (Lola B2/00-Ford Cosworth XFE), 2h 02m 47.812s; **6** Roberto Moreno, BR (Lola B2/00-Ford Cosworth XFE), 2h 02m 50.789s; **7** Patrick Carpentier, CDN (Lola B2/00-Ford Cosworth XFE), 2h 02m 51.843s; **8** Darren Manning, GB (Reynard 02ib-Ford Cosworth XFE), 2h 02m 52.224s; **9** Adrian Fernandez, MEX (Lola B2/00-Ford Cosworth XFE), 2h 03m 37.465s; **10** Tiago Monteiro, P (Reynard 02ib-Ford Cosworth XFE), 110 laps.
Most laps led: Tracy, 112.
Fastest qualifying lap: Tracy, 58.839s, 107.378 mph/172.808 km/h.
Championship points: **1** Tracy, 139; **2** Junqueira, 124; **3** Jourdain Jr, 113; **4** Carpentier, 88; **5** Bourdais, 86; **6** Servia, 76.

MOLSON INDY VANCOUVER, Vancouver Street Circuit, Concord Pacific Place, Vancouver, British Columbia, Canada, 27 July. Round 11. 100 laps of the 1.781-mile/2.866-km circuit, 178.100 miles/286.624 km.
1 Paul Tracy, CDN (Lola B2/00-Ford Cosworth XFE), 1h 57m 54.322s, 90.632 mph/145.858 km/h; **2** Bruno Junqueira, BR (Lola B2/00-Ford Cosworth XFE), 1h 58m 12.142s; **3** Sébastien Bourdais, F (Lola B2/00-Ford Cosworth XFE), 1h 58m 20.042s; **4** Michel Jourdain Jr, MEX (Lola B2/00-Ford Cosworth XFE), 1h 58m 39.737s; **5** Darren Manning, GB (Reynard 02ib-Ford Cosworth XFE), 98 laps; **6** Ryan Hunter-Reay, USA (Reynard 02ib-Ford Cosworth XFE), 98; **7** Mario Haberfeld, BR (Reynard 02ib-Ford Cosworth XFE), 98; **8** Rodolfo Lavin, MEX (Reynard 02ib-Ford Cosworth XFE), 98; **9** Massimiliano 'Max' Papis, USA (Lola B2/00-Ford Cosworth XFE), 98; **10** Mario Dominguez, MEX (Lola B2/00-Ford Cosworth XFE), 96.
Most laps led: Tracy, 77.
Fastest qualifying lap: Tracy, 1m 00.926s, 105.236 mph/169.361 km/h.
Championship points: **1** Tracy, 161; **2** Junqueira, 141; **3** Jourdain Jr, 125; **4** Bourdais, 100; **5** Carpentier, 88; **6** Servia, 76.

MARIO ANDRETTI GRAND PRIX AT ROAD AMERICA, Road America Circuit, Elkhart Lake, Wisconsin, USA, 3 August. Round 12. 34 laps of the 4.048-mile/6.515-km circuit, 137.632 miles/221.497 km.
Scheduled for 60 laps, but reduced because of rain delays.
1 Bruno Junqueira, BR (Lola B2/00-Ford Cosworth XFE), 1h 35m 28.491s, 86.493 mph/139.197 km/h; **2** Sébastien Bourdais, F (Lola B2/00-Ford Cosworth XFE), 1h 35m 29.194s; **3** Alex Tagliani, CDN (Lola B2/00-Ford Cosworth XFE), 1h 35m 39.374s; **4** Massimiliano 'Max' Papis, USA (Lola B2/00-Ford Cosworth XFE), 1h 35m 43.434s; **5** Patrick Carpentier, CDN (Lola B2/00-Ford Cosworth XFE), 1h 35m 47.985s; **6** Darren Manning, GB (Reynard 02ib-Ford Cosworth XFE), 1h 35m 48.083s; **7** Roberto Moreno, BR (Lola B2/00-Ford Cosworth XFE), 1h 35m 49.789s; **8** Mario Haberfeld, BR (Reynard 02ib-Ford Cosworth XFE), 1h 36m 00.032s; **9** Jimmy Vasser, USA (Reynard 02ib-Ford Cosworth XFE), 1h 36m 03.473s; **10** Ryan Hunter-Reay, USA (Reynard 02ib-Ford Cosworth XFE), 1h 36m 09.516s.
Most laps led: Junqueira, 34.
Fastest qualifying lap: Junqueira, 1m 43.703s, 140.524 mph/226.152 km/h.
Championship points: **1** Junqueira, 164; **2** Tracy, 161; **3** Jourdain Jr, 125; **4** Bourdais, 116; **5** Carpentier, 98; **6** Servia, 76.

CHAMP CAR GRAND PRIX OF MID-OHIO, Mid-Ohio Sports Car Course, Lexington, Ohio, USA, 10 August. Round 13. 92 laps of the 2.258-mile/3.634-km circuit, 206.769 miles/332.762 km.
1 Paul Tracy, CDN (Lola B2/00-Ford Cosworth XFE), 1h 56m 45.737s, 106.251 mph/170.994 km/h; **2** Patrick Carpentier, CDN (Lola B2/00-Ford Cosworth XFE), 1h 56m 46.347s; **3** Ryan Hunter-Reay, USA (Reynard 02ib-Ford Cosworth XFE), 1h 56m 47.709s; **4** Michel Jourdain Jr, MEX (Lola B2/00-Ford Cosworth XFE), 1h 56m 48.942s; **5** Sébastien Bourdais, F (Lola B2/00-Ford Cosworth XFE), 1h 56m 49.791s; **6** Alex Tagliani, CDN (Lola B2/00-Ford Cosworth XFE), 1h 56m 53.662s; **7** Adrian Fernandez, MEX (Lola B2/00-Ford Cosworth XFE), 1h 56m 54.450s; **8** Darren Manning, GB (Reynard 02ib-Ford Cosworth XFE), 1h 56m 54.899s; **9** Massimiliano 'Max' Papis, USA (Lola B2/00-Ford Cosworth XFE), 1h 56m 56.245s; **10** Mario Haberfeld, BR (Reynard 02ib-Ford Cosworth XFE), 1h 56m 58.151s.
Most laps led: Tracy, 69.
Fastest qualifying lap: Tracy, 1m 07.058s, 121.220 mph/195.085 km/h.
Championship points: **1** Tracy, 184; **2** Junqueira, 164; **3** Jourdain Jr, 137; **4** Bourdais, 126; **5** Carpentier, 114; **6** Fernandez, 77.

MOLSON INDY MONTREAL, Circuit Gilles-Villeneuve, Ile-Notre-Dame, Montréal, Québec, Canada, 24 August. Round 14. 75 laps of the 2.709-mile /4.360-km circuit, 203.175 miles/326.978 km.
1 Michel Jourdain Jr, MEX (Lola B2/00-Ford Cosworth XFE), 1h 54m 23.210s, 106.573 mph/171.512 km/h; **2** Oriol Servia, E (Lola B2/00-Ford Cosworth XFE), 1h 54m 24.487s; **3** Patrick Carpentier, CDN (Lola B2/00-Ford Cosworth XFE), 1h 54m 25.309s; **4** Alex Tagliani, CDN (Lola B2/00-Ford Cosworth XFE), 1h 54m 30.429s; **5** Mario Dominguez, MEX (Lola B2/00-Ford Cosworth XFE), 1h 54m 33.220s; **6** Paul Tracy, CDN (Lola B2/00-Ford Cosworth XFE), 1h 54m 38.121s; **7** Roberto Moreno, BR (Lola B2/00-Ford Cosworth XFE), 1h 54m 40.043s; **8** Adrian Fernandez, MEX (Lola B2/00-Ford Cosworth XFE), 1h 55m 00.405s; **9** Massimiliano 'Max' Papis, USA (Lola B2/00-Ford Cosworth XFE), 1h 55m 00.753s; **10** Darren Manning, GB (Reynard 02ib-Ford Cosworth XFE), 1h 55m 01.627s.
Most laps led: Tagliani, 52.
Fastest qualifying lap: Tagliani, 1m 19.665s, 122.418 mph/197.012 km/h.
Championship points: **1** Tracy, 192; **2** Junqueira, 164; **3** Jourdain Jr, 157; **4** Carpentier, 128; **5** Bourdais, 126; **6** Servia, 93.

CENTRIX FINANCIAL GRAND PRIX OF DENVER, Denver Street Circuit, Colorado, USA, 31 August. Round 15. 106 laps of the 1.647-mile/2.651-km circuit, 174.582 miles/280.962 km.
1 Bruno Junqueira, BR (Lola B2/00-Ford Cosworth XFE), 2h 03m 10.259s, 85.044 mph/136.865 km/h; **2** Sébastien Bourdais, F (Lola B2/00-Ford Cosworth XFE), 2h 03m 10.594s; **3** Oriol Servia, E (Lola B2/00-Ford Cosworth XFE), 2h 03m 22.754s; **4** Paul Tracy, CDN (Lola B2/00-Ford Cosworth XFE), 2h 03m 23.577s; **5** Adrian Fernandez, MEX (Lola B2/00-Ford Cosworth XFE), 2h 03m 27.974s; **6** Michel Jourdain Jr, MEX (Lola B2/00-Ford Cosworth XFE), 2h 03m 29.040s; **7** Mario Dominguez, MEX (Lola B2/00-Ford Cosworth XFE), 2h 03m 29.522s; **8** Darren Manning, GB (Reynard 02ib-Ford Cosworth XFE), 2h 03m 35.849s; **9** Alex Tagliani, CDN (Lola B2/00-Ford Cosworth XFE), 2h 03m 37.175s; **10** Mario Haberfeld, BR (Reynard 02ib-Ford Cosworth XFE), 2h 04m 00.958s.
Most laps led: Junqueira, 76.
Fastest qualifying lap: Junqueira, 1m 01.438s, 96.507 mph/155.313 km/h.
Championship points: **1** Tracy, 204; **2** Junqueira, 186; **3** Jourdain Jr, 165; **4** Bourdais, 142; **5** Carpentier, 128; **6** Servia, 108.

GRAND PRIX AMERICAS PRESENTED BY SPORTSBOOK.COM, Miami Bayfront Park Street Circuit, Miami, Florida, USA, 28 September. Round 16. 135 laps of the 1.150-mile/1.851-km circuit, 155.250 miles/249.851 km.
1 Mario Dominguez, MEX (Lola B2/00-Ford Cosworth XFE), 2h 03m 19.401s, 75.533 mph/121.559 km/h; **2** Roberto Moreno, BR (Lola B2/00-Ford Cosworth XFE), 2h 03m 24.642s; **3** Mika Salo, FIN (Lola B2/00-Ford Cosworth XFE), 2h 03m 27.389s; **4** Jimmy Vasser, USA (Reynard 02ib-Ford Cosworth XFE), 2h 03m 28.609s; **5** Mario Haberfeld, BR (Reynard 02ib-Ford Cosworth XFE), 2h 03m 28.884s; **6** Patrick Carpentier, CDN (Lola B2/00-Ford Cosworth XFE), 2h 03m 29.658s; **7** Michel Jourdain Jr, MEX (Lola B2/00-Ford Cosworth XFE), 2h 03m 38.575s; **8** Adrian Fernandez, MEX (Lola B2/00-Ford Cosworth XFE), 134 laps; **9** Bruno Junqueira, BR (Lola B2/00-Ford Cosworth XFE), 131; **10** Geoff Boss, USA (Lola B2/00-Ford Cosworth XFE), 129.
Most laps led: Fernandez, 88.
Fastest qualifying lap: Fernandez, 44.253s, 93.553 mph/150.559 km/h.
Championship points: **1** Tracy, 204; **2** Junqueira, 191; **3** Jourdain Jr, 171; **4** Bourdais, 142; **5** Carpentier, 136; **6** Servia, 108.

GRAN PREMIO TELMEX/GIGANTE PRESENTED BY BANAMEX/VISA, Autodromo Hermanos Rodriguez, Mexico City, Mexico, 12 October. Round 17. 70 laps of the 2.786-mile/4.484-km circuit, 195.020 miles/313.854 km.
1 Paul Tracy, CDN (Lola B2/00-Ford Cosworth XFE), 1h 56m 51.396s, 100.133 mph/161.148 km/h; **2** Sébastien Bourdais, F (Lola B2/00-Ford Cosworth XFE), 1h 56m 53.178s; **3** Mario Dominguez, MEX (Lola B2/00-Ford Cosworth XFE), 1h 56m 54.650s; **4** Michel Jourdain Jr, MEX (Lola B2/00-Ford Cosworth XFE), 1h 57m 03.514s; **5** Mika Salo, FIN (Lola B2/00-Ford Cosworth XFE), 1h 57m 05.183s; **6** Tiago Monteiro, P (Reynard 02ib-Ford Cosworth XFE), 1h 57m 09.140s; **7** Bruno Junqueira, BR (Lola B2/00-Ford Cosworth XFE), 1h 57m 09.476s; **8** Adrian Fernandez, MEX (Lola B2/00-Ford Cosworth XFE), 1h 57m 11.075s; **9** Darren Manning, GB (Reynard 02ib-Ford Cosworth XFE), 1h 57m 18.872s; **10** Roberto Gonazalez, MEX (Lola B2/00-Ford Cosworth XFE), 1h 57m 34.385s.
Most laps led: Tracy, 64.
Fastest qualifying lap: Tracy, 1m 28.842s, 112.893 mph/181.683 km/h.
Championship points: **1** Tracy, 226; **2** Junqueira, 197; **3** Jourdain Jr, 183; **4** Bourdais, 158; **5** Carpentier, 136; **6** Dominguez, 115.

LEXMARK INDY 300, Surfers Paradise Street Circuit, Southport, Queensland, Australia, 26 October. Round 18. 47 laps of the 2.795-mile/4.498-km circuit, 131.365 miles/211.411 km.
Scheduled for 70 laps but shortened due to rain.
1 Ryan Hunter-Reay, USA (Reynard 02ib-Ford Cosworth XFE), 1h 49m 02.803s, 72.280 mph/116.323 km/h; **2** Darren Manning, GB (Reynard 02ib-Ford Cosworth XFE), 1h 49m 04.349s; **3** Jimmy Vasser, USA (Reynard 02ib-Ford Cosworth XFE), 1h 49m 06.595s; **4** Michel Jourdain Jr, MEX (Lola B2/00-Ford Cosworth XFE), 1h 49m 08.118s; **5** Patrick Carpentier, CDN (Lola B2/00-Ford Cosworth XFE), 1h 49m 08.640s; **6** Gualter Salles, BR (Lola B2/00-Ford Cosworth XFE), 1h 49m 10.983s; **7** Alex Tagliani, CDN (Lola B2/00-Ford Cosworth XFE), 1h 49m 12.934s; **8** Rodolfo Lavin, MEX (Reynard 02ib-Ford Cosworth XFE), 1h 49m 14.476s; **9** Geoff Boss, USA (Lola B2/00-Ford Cosworth XFE), 1h 49m 53.531s; **10** Mario Dominguez, MEX (Lola B2/00-Ford Cosworth XFE), 46 laps.
Most laps led: Junqueira, 29.
Fastest qualifying lap: Bourdais, 1m 31.718s, 109.706 mph/176.554 km/h.

The Champ Car 500 at Fontana scheduled for 2 November was cancelled due to fires in the region.

Final championship points

Drivers
1 Paul Tracy, CDN, 226; **2** Bruno Junqueira, BR, 199; **3** Michel Jourdain Jr, MEX, 195; **4** Sébastien Bourdais, F, 159; **5** Patrick Carpentier, CDN, 146; **6** Mario Dominguez, MEX, 118; **7** Oriol Servia, E, 108; **8** Adrian Fernandez, MEX, 105; **9** Darren Manning, GB, 103; **10** Alex Tagliani, CDN, 97; **11** Jimmy Vasser, USA, 72; **12** Mario Haberfeld, BR, 71; **13** Roberto Moreno, BR, 67; **14** Ryan Hunter-Reay, USA, 64; **15** Tiago Monteiro, P, 29; **16** Mika Salo, FIN, 26; **17** Massimiliano 'Max' Papis, USA, 25; **18** Rodolfo Lavin, MEX, 17; **19** Gualter Salles, BR, 11; **20** Geoff Boss, USA, 8; **21** Patrick Lemarié, F, 8; **22** Joel Camathias, CH, 6; **23** Alex Yoong, MAL, 4; **24** Roberto Gonzalez, MEX, 3; **25** Bryan Herta, USA, 2.

Nation's Cup
1 Canada, 298; **2** Mexico, 262; **3** Brazil, 228; **4** France, 161; **5** United States, 107; **6** Catalonia (Spain), 106; **7** England, 103; **8** Portugal, 28; **9** Finland, 26; **10** Italy, 25; **11** Switzerland, 6; **12** Malaysia, 4.

Manufacturer's Cup (engines)
1 Ford Cosworth, 395.

Constructor's Cup
1 Lola, 387; **2** Reynard, 161.

Rookie of the Year
1 Sébastien Bourdais, 159; **2** Darren Manning, 103; **3** Mario Haberfeld, 71.

NASCAR Winston Cup

2002

The following races were run after AUTOCOURSE 2002–2003 went to press.

CHECKER AUTO PARTS 500 PRESENTED BY PENNZOIL, Phoenix International Raceway, Arizona, USA, 10 November. Round 35. 312 laps of the 1.000-mile/1.609-km circuit, 312.000 miles/502.115 km.
1 Matt Kenseth, USA (Ford Taurus), 2h 44m 25.0s, 113.857 mph/183.235 km/h; **2** Rusty Wallace, USA (Ford Taurus), 2h 44m 26.344s; **3** Jeff Gordon, USA (Chevrolet Monte Carlo), 312 laps; **4** Mark Martin, USA (Ford Taurus), 312; **5** Dale Earnhardt Jr, USA (Chevrolet Monte Carlo), 312; **6** Kurt Busch, USA (Ford Taurus), 312; **7** Dave Blaney, USA (Ford Taurus), 312; **8** Tony Stewart, USA (Pontiac Grand Prix), 312; **9** Dale Jarrett, USA (Ford Taurus), 312; **10** Elliott Sadler, USA (Ford Taurus), 312.
Fastest qualifying lap: Ryan Newman, USA (Ford Taurus), 27.138s, 132.655 mph/213.488 km/h.
Drivers Championship points: 1 Stewart, 4691; **2** Martin, 4602; **3** Busch, 4461; **4** Johnson, 4453; **5** Wallace (Rusty), 4453; **6** Gordon (Jeff), 4452.

FORD 400, Homestead-Miami Speedway, Florida, USA, 17 November. Round 36. 267 laps of the 1.500-mile/2.414-km circuit, 400.500 miles/644.542 km.
1 Kurt Busch, USA (Ford Taurus), 3h 26m 20.0s, 116.462 mph/187.427 km/h; **2** Joe Nemechek, USA (Chevrolet Monte Carlo), 3h 26m 22.070s; **3** Jeff Burton, USA (Ford Taurus), 267 laps; **4** Mark Martin, USA (Ford Taurus), 267; **5** Jeff Gordon, USA (Chevrolet Monte Carlo), 267; **6** Ryan Newman, USA (Ford Taurus), 267; **7** Bill Elliott, USA (Dodge Intrepid), 267; **8** Jimie Johnson, USA (Chevrolet Monte Carlo), 267; **9** Elliott Sadler, USA (Ford Taurus), 267; **10** Bobby Hamilton, USA (Chevrolet Monte Carlo), 267.
Fastest qualifying lap: Busch, 34.982s, 154.365 mph/248.427 km/h.

Final championship points

Drivers
1 Tony Stewart, USA, 4800; **2** Mark Martin, USA, 4762; **3** Kurt Busch, USA, 4641; **4** Jeff Gordon, USA, 4607; **5** Jimmie Johnson, USA, 4600; **6** Ryan Newman, USA, 4593; **7** Rusty Wallace, USA, 4574; **8** Matt Kenseth, USA, 4432; **9** Dale Jarrett, USA, 4415; **10** Ricky Rudd, USA, 4323; **11** Dale Earnhardt Jr, USA, 4270; **12** Jeff Burton, USA, 4259; **13** Bill Elliott, USA, 4158; **14** Michael Waltrip, USA, 3985; **15** Ricky Craven, USA, 3888; **16** Bobby Labonte, USA, 3810; **17** Jeff Green, USA, 3704; **18** Sterling Marlin, USA, 3703; **19** Dave Blaney, USA, 3670; **20** Robby Gordon, USA, 3632; **21=** Kevin Harvick, USA, 3501; **21=** Kyle Petty, USA, 3501; **23** Elliott Sadler, USA, 3418; **24** Terry Labonte, USA, 3417; **25** Ward Burton, USA, 3362; **26** Jeremy Mayfield, USA, 3309; **27** Jimmy Spencer, USA, 3187; **28** John Andretti, USA, 3161; **29** Johnny Benson Jr, USA, 3132; **30** Ken Schrader, USA, 2954.

Manufacturers
1 Ford, 245; **2** Chevrolet, 211; **3** Dodge, 169; **4** Pontiac, 167.

Raybestos Rookie of the Year: Ryan Newman.

Bud Pole Award Winner: Ryan Newman.

2003

45th DAYTONA 500, Daytona International Speedway, Daytona Beach, Florida, USA, 16 February. Round 1. 109 laps of the 2.500-mile/4.023-km circuit, 272.500 miles/438.546 km.
Race scheduled for 200 laps, but shortened due to rain.
1 Michael Waltrip, USA (Chevrolet Monte Carlo), 2h 02m 08.0s, 133.870 mph/215.443 km/h; **2** Kurt Busch, USA (Ford Taurus), 109 laps (under caution); **3** Jimmie Johnson, USA (Chevrolet Monte Carlo), 109; **4** Kevin Harvick, USA (Chevrolet Monte Carlo), 109; **5** Mark Martin, USA (Ford Taurus), 109; **6** Robby Gordon, USA (Chevrolet Monte Carlo), 109; **7** Tony Stewart, USA (Chevrolet Monte Carlo), 109; **8** Jeremy Mayfield, USA (Dodge Intrepid), 109; **9** Mike Wallace, USA (Dodge Intrepid), 109; **10** Dale Jarrett, USA (Ford Taurus), 109.
Pole position: Jeff Green, USA (Chevrolet Monte Carlo).
Drivers Championship points: 1 Waltrip, 185; **2=** Busch, 170; **2=** Johnson, 170; **4** Harvick, 160; **5** Martin, 155; **6** Stewart, 151.

SUBWAY 400, North Carolina Motor Speedway, Rockingham, North Carolina, USA, 23 February. Round 2. 393 laps of the 1.017-mile/1.637-km circuit, 399.681 miles/643.224 km.
1 Dale Jarrett, USA (Ford Taurus), 3h 23m 29.0s, 117.852 mph/189.664 km/h; **2** Kurt Busch, USA (Ford Taurus), 3h 23m 29.966s; **3** Matt Kenseth, USA (Ford Taurus), 393 laps; **4** Ricky Craven, USA (Pontiac Grand Prix), 393; **5** Jamie McMurray, USA (Dodge Intrepid), 393; **6** Rusty Wallace, USA (Dodge Intrepid), 393; **7** Mark Martin, USA (Ford Taurus), 393; **8** Jimmie Johnson, USA (Chevrolet Monte Carlo), 393; **9** Elliott Sadler, USA (Ford Taurus), 393; **10** Dave Blaney, USA (Ford Taurus), 393.
Pole position: Blaney.
Drivers Championship points: 1 Busch, 345; **2** Jarrett, 314; **3** Johnson, 312; **4** Martin, 306; **5** Waltrip, 291; **6** Kenseth, 278.

UAW-DAIMLER CHRYSLER 400, Las Vegas Motor Speedway, Nevada, USA, 2 March. Round 3. 267 laps of the 1.500-mile/2.414-km circuit, 400.500 miles/644.542 km.
1 Matt Kenseth, USA (Ford Taurus), 3h 00m 46.0s, 132.934 mph/213.936 km/h; **2** Dale Earnhardt Jr, USA (Chevrolet Monte Carlo), 3h 00m 54.104s; **3** Michael Waltrip, USA (Chevrolet Monte Carlo), 267 laps; **4** Bobby Labonte, USA (Chevrolet Monte Carlo), 267; **5** Tony Stewart, USA (Chevrolet Monte Carlo), 267; **6** Jeff Burton, USA (Ford Taurus), 267; **7** Ryan Newman, USA (Dodge Intrepid), 267; **8** Sterling Marlin, USA (Dodge Intrepid), 267; **9** Joe Nemechek, USA (Chevrolet Monte Carlo), 267; **10** Steve Park, USA (Chevrolet Monte Carlo), 267.
Pole position: Labonte (Bobby).
Drivers Championship points: 1 Waltrip, 461; **2** Kenseth, 458; **3** Johnson, 447; **4** Burton (Jeff), 412; **5** Stewart, 409; **6** Busch, 399.

BASS PRO SHOPS MBNA 500, Atlanta Motor Speedway, Hampton, Georgia, USA, 9 March. Round 4. 325 laps of the 1.540-mile/2.478-km circuit, 500.000 miles/805.477 km.
1 Bobby Labonte, USA (Chevrolet Monte Carlo), 3h 25m 37.0s, 146.048 mph/235.042 km/h; **2** Jeff Gordon, USA (Chevrolet Monte Carlo), 3h 25m 38.274s; **3** Dale Earnhardt Jr, USA (Chevrolet Monte Carlo), 325 laps; **4** Matt Kenseth, USA (Ford Taurus), 325; **5** Tony Stewart, USA (Chevrolet Monte Carlo), 325; **6** Elliott Sadler, USA (Ford Taurus), 325; **7** Jimmy Spencer, USA (Dodge Intrepid), 325; **8** Dave Blaney, USA (Ford Taurus), 325; **9** Joe Nemechek, USA (Chevrolet Monte Carlo), 325; **10** Ryan Newman, USA (Dodge Intrepid), 324.
Pole position: Newman.
Drivers Championship points: 1 Kenseth, 618; **2** Stewart, 569; **3** Waltrip, 543; **4** Johnson, 519; **5** Labonte (Bobby), 510; **6** Benson Jr, 487.

CAROLINA DODGE DEALERS 400, Darlington Raceway, South Carolina, USA, 16 March. Round 5. 293 laps of the 1.366-mile/2.198-km circuit, 400.238 miles/644.121 km.
1 Ricky Craven, USA (Pontiac Grand Prix), 3h 10m 16.0s, 126.214 mph/203.121 km/h; **2** Kurt Busch, USA (Ford Taurus), 3h 10m 16.002s; **3** Dave Blaney, USA (Ford Taurus), 293 laps; **4** Mark Martin, USA (Ford Taurus), 293; **5** Michael Waltrip, USA (Chevrolet Monte Carlo), 293; **6** Dale Earnhardt Jr, USA (Chevrolet Monte Carlo), 293; **7** Elliott Sadler, USA (Ford Taurus), 293; **8** Matt Kenseth, USA (Ford Taurus), 293; **9** Bill Elliott, USA (Dodge Intrepid), 293; **10** Tony Stewart, USA (Chevrolet Monte Carlo), 293.
Pole position: Sadler.
Drivers Championship points: 1 Kenseth, 760; **2** Stewart, 703; **3** Waltrip, 698; **4** Earnhardt Jr, 634; **5=** Craven, 617; **5=** Busch, 617.

FOOD CITY 500, Bristol Motor Speedway, Tennessee, USA, 23 March. Round 6. 500 laps of the 0.533-mile/0.858-km circuit, 266.500 miles/428.890 km.
1 Kurt Busch, USA (Ford Taurus), 3h 29m 53.0s, 76.185 mph/122.608 km/h; **2** Matt Kenseth, USA (Ford Taurus), 3h 29m 53.390s; **3** Bobby Labonte, USA (Chevrolet Monte Carlo), 500 laps; **4** Ricky Rudd, USA (Ford Taurus), 500; **5** Greg Biffle, USA (Ford Taurus), 500; **6** Sterling Marlin, USA (Dodge Intrepid), 500; **7** Kevin Harvick, USA (Chevrolet Monte Carlo), 499; **8** Jimmie Johnson, USA (Chevrolet Monte Carlo), 499; **9** Jeff Gordon, USA (Chevrolet Monte Carlo), 499; **10** Kenny Wallace, USA (Dodge Intrepid), 499.
Pole position: Ryan Newman, USA (Dodge Intrepid).
Drivers Championship points: 1 Kenseth, 935; **2** Busch, 797; **3** Stewart, 788; **4** Waltrip, 786; **5** Earnhardt Jr, 749; **6** Johnson, 743.

SAMSUNG/RADIO SHACK 500, Texas Motor Speedway, Fort Worth, Texas, USA, 30 March. Round 7. 334 laps of the 1.500-mile/2.414-km circuit, 501.000 miles/806.281 km.
1 Ryan Newman, USA (Dodge Intrepid), 3h 43m 28.0s, 134.517 mph/216.484 km/h; **2** Dale Earnhardt Jr, USA (Chevrolet Monte Carlo), 3h 43m 31.405s; **3** Jeff Gordon, USA (Chevrolet Monte Carlo), 334 laps; **4** Jerry Nadeau, USA (Pontiac Grand Prix), 334; **5** Mark Martin, USA (Ford Taurus), 334; **6** Matt Kenseth, USA (Ford Taurus), 334; **7** Jeff Green, USA (Chevrolet Monte Carlo), 334; **8** Jimmie Johnson, USA (Chevrolet Monte Carlo), 334; **9** Kurt Busch, USA (Ford Taurus), 334; **10** Jamie McMurray, USA (Dodge Intrepid), 334.
Pole position: Bobby Labonte, USA (Chevrolet Monte Carlo).
Drivers Championship points: 1 Kenseth, 1090; **2** Busch, 935; **3** Earhardt Jr, 924; **4** Waltrip, 898; **5** Johnson, 885; **6** Gordon (Jeff), 864.

AARON'S 499, Talladega Superspeedway, Alabama, USA, 6 April. Round 8. 188 laps of the 2.660-mile/4.281-km circuit, 500.080 miles/804.801 km.
1 Dale Earnhardt Jr, USA (Chevrolet Monte Carlo), 3h 27m 28.0s, 144.625 mph/232.751 km/h; **2** Kevin Harvick, USA (Chevrolet Monte Carlo), 3h 27m 28.125s; **3** Elliott Sadler, USA (Ford Taurus), 188 laps; **4** Ricky Craven, USA (Pontiac Grand Prix), 188; **5** Terry Labonte, USA (Chevrolet Monte Carlo), 188; **6** Sterling Marlin, USA (Dodge Intrepid), 188; **7** Ward Burton, USA (Dodge Intrepid), 188; **8** Jeff Gordon, USA (Chevrolet Monte Carlo), 188; **9** Matt Kenseth, USA (Ford Taurus), 188; **10** Robby Gordon, USA (Chevrolet Monte Carlo), 188.
Pole position: Jeremy Mayfield, USA (Dodge Intrepid).
Drivers Championship points: 1 Kenseth, 1233; **2** Earnhardt Jr, 1104; **3** Busch, 1046; **4** Johnson, 1013; **5** Gordon (Jeff), 1011; **6** Craven, 1000.

VIRGINIA 500, Martinsville Speedway, Virginia, USA, 13 April. Round 9. 500 laps of the 0.526-mile/0.847-km circuit, 263.000 miles/423.257 km.
1 Jeff Gordon, USA (Chevrolet Monte Carlo), 3h 28m 51.0s, 75.557 mph/121.597 km/h; **2** Bobby Labonte, USA (Chevrolet Monte Carlo), 500 laps (under caution); **3** Dale Earnhardt Jr, USA (Chevrolet Monte Carlo), 500; **4** Jeff Burton, USA (Ford Taurus), 500; **5** Elliott Sadler, USA (Ford Taurus), 500; **6** Tony Stewart, USA (Chevrolet Monte Carlo), 500; **7** Sterling Marlin, USA (Dodge Intrepid), 500; **8** Rusty Wallace, USA (Dodge Intrepid), 500; **9** Jimmie Johnson, USA (Chevrolet Monte Carlo), 500; **10** Ken Schrader, USA (Dodge Intrepid), 500.
Pole position: Gordon (Jeff).
Drivers Championship points: 1 Kenseth, 1330; **2** Earnhardt Jr, 1279; **3** Gordon (Jeff), 1191; **4** Johnson, 1151; **5** Busch, 1125; **6** Harvick, 1097.

AUTO CLUB 500, California Speedway, Fontana, California, USA, 27 April. Round 10. 250 laps of the 2.000-mile/3.219-km circuit, 500.000 miles/804.672 km.
1 Kurt Busch, USA (Ford Taurus), 3h 34m 07.0s, 140.111 mph/225.486 km/h; **2** Bobby Labonte, USA (Chevrolet Monte Carlo), 3h 34m 09.294s; **3** Rusty Wallace, USA (Dodge Intrepid), 250 laps; **4** Bill Elliott, USA (Dodge Intrepid), 250; **5** Jamie McMurray, USA (Dodge Intrepid), 250; **6** Dale Earnhardt Jr, USA (Chevrolet Monte Carlo), 250; **7** Michael Waltrip, USA (Chevrolet Monte Carlo), 250; **8** John Andretti, USA (Dodge Intrepid), 250; **9** Matt Kenseth, USA (Ford Taurus), 250; **10** Sterling Marlin, USA (Dodge Intrepid), 250.
Pole position: Steve Park, USA (Chevrolet Monte Carlo).
Drivers Championship points: 1 Kenseth, 1473; **2** Earnhardt Jr, 1429; **3** Gordon (Jeff), 1321; **4** Busch, 1305; **5** Johnson, 1266; **6** Waltrip, 1234.

PONTIAC EXCITEMENT 400, Richmond International Raceway, Virginia, USA, 3 May. Round 11. 393 laps of the 0.750-mile/1.207-km circuit, 294.750 miles/474.354 km.
Race scheduled for 400 laps, but shortened due to rain.
1 Joe Nemechek, USA (Chevrolet Monte Carlo), 3h 23m 47.0s, 86.783 mph/139.664 km/h; **2** Bobby Labonte, USA (Chevrolet Monte Carlo), 393 laps (under caution); **3** Dale Earnhardt Jr, USA (Chevrolet Monte Carlo), 393; **4** Robby Gordon, USA (Chevrolet Monte Carlo), 393; **5** Mark Martin, USA (Ford Taurus), 393; **6** Kevin Harvick, USA (Chevrolet Monte Carlo), 393; **7** Matt Kenseth, USA (Ford Taurus), 393; **8** Kurt Busch, USA (Ford Taurus), 393; **9** Jeff Burton, USA (Ford Taurus), 393; **10** Rusty Wallace, USA (Dodge Intrepid), 393.
Pole position: Terry Labonte, USA (Chevrolet Monte Carlo).
Drivers Championship points: 1 Kenseth, 1619; **2** Earnhardt Jr, 1599; **3** Busch, 1452; **4** Gordon (Jeff), 1438; **5** Labonte (Bobby), 1376; **6** Johnson, 1372.

COCA-COLA 600, Lowe's Motor Speedway, Concord, Charlotte, North Carolina, USA, 25 May. Round 12. 276 laps of the 1.500-mile/2.414-km circuit, 414.000 miles/666.268 km.
Race scheduled for 400 laps, but shortened due to rain.
1 Jimmie Johnson, USA (Chevrolet Monte Carlo), 3h 16m 50.0s, 126.198 mph/203.096 km/h; **2** Matt Kenseth, USA (Ford Taurus), 276 laps (under caution); **3** Bobby Labonte, USA (Chevrolet Monte Carlo), 276; **4** Jimmy Spencer, USA (Dodge Intrepid), 276; **5** Ryan Newman, USA (Dodge Intrepid), 276; **6** Michael Waltrip, USA (Chevrolet Monte Carlo), 276; **7** Sterling Marlin, USA (Dodge Intrepid), 276; **8** Jeff Gordon, USA (Chevrolet Monte Carlo), 276; **9** Dale Jarrett, USA (Ford Taurus), 276; **10** Ward Burton, USA (Dodge Intrepid), 276.
Pole position: Newman.
Drivers Championship points: 1 Kenseth, 1799; **2** Earnhardt Jr, 1639; **3** Gordon (Jeff), 1583; **4** Busch, 1575; **5** Johnson, 1552; **6** Labonte (Bobby), 1546.

MBNA ARMED FORCES FAMILY 400, Dover International Speedway, Dover, Delaware, USA, 1 June. Round 13. 400 laps of the 1.000-mile/1.609-km circuit, 400.000 miles/643.738 km.
1 Ryan Newman, USA (Dodge Intrepid), 3h 44m 31.0s, 106.896 mph/172.033 km/h; **2** Jeff Gordon, USA (Chevrolet Monte Carlo), 3h 44m 31.834s; **3** Bobby Labonte, USA (Chevrolet Monte Carlo), 400 laps; **4** Tony Stewart, USA (Chevrolet Monte Carlo), 400; **5** Johnny Benson Jr, USA (Pontiac Grand Prix), 400; **6** Rusty Wallace, USA (Dodge Intrepid), 400; **7** Matt Kenseth, USA (Ford Taurus), 400; **8** Ricky Craven, USA (Pontiac Grand Prix), 400; **9** Robby Gordon, USA (Chevrolet Monte Carlo), 400; **10** Terry Labonte, USA (Chevrolet Monte Carlo), 400.
Pole position: Newman.
Drivers Championship points: 1 Kenseth, 1945; **2** Earnhardt Jr, 1774; **3** Gordon (Jeff), 1758; **4** Labonte (Bobby), 1716; **5** Busch, 1698; **6** Waltrip, 1631.

POCONO 500, Pocono Raceway, Long Pond, Pennsylvania, USA, 8 June. Round 14. 200 laps of the 2.500-mile/4.023-km circuit, 500.000 miles/804.672 km.
1 Tony Stewart, USA (Chevrolet Monte Carlo), 3h 42m 24.0s, 134.892 mph/217.088 km/h; **2** Mark Martin, USA (Ford Taurus), 200 laps (under caution); **3** Matt Kenseth, USA (Ford Taurus), 200; **4** Dale Earnhardt Jr, USA (Chevrolet Monte Carlo), 200; **5** Ryan Newman, USA (Dodge Intrepid), 200; **6** Sterling Marlin, USA (Dodge Intrepid), 200; **7** Terry Labonte, USA (Chevrolet Monte Carlo), 200; **8** Ward Burton, USA (Dodge Intrepid), 200; **9** Elliott Sadler, USA (Ford Taurus), 200; **10** Ricky Craven, USA (Pontiac Grand Prix), 200.
Pole position: Jimmie Johnson, USA (Chevrolet Monte Carlo).
Drivers Championship points: 1 Kenseth, 2115; **2** Earnhardt Jr, 1939; **3** Gordon (Jeff), 1882; **4** Labonte (Bobby), 1828; **5** Busch, 1753; **6** Waltrip, 1745.

SIRIUS 400, Michigan International Speedway, Brooklyn, Michigan, USA, 15 June. Round 15. 200 laps of the 2.000-mile/3.219-km circuit, 400.000 miles/643.738 km.
1 Kurt Busch, USA (Ford Taurus), 3h 02m 54.0s, 131.219 mph/211.177 km/h; **2** Bobby Labonte, USA (Chevrolet Monte Carlo), 3h 02m 54.774s; **3** Jeff Gordon, USA (Chevrolet Monte Carlo), 200 laps; **4** Matt Kenseth, USA (Ford Taurus), 200; **5** Michael Waltrip, USA (Chevrolet Monte Carlo), 200; **6** Sterling Marlin, USA (Dodge Intrepid), 200; **7** Dale Earnhardt Jr, USA (Chevrolet Monte Carlo), 200; **8** Tony Stewart, USA (Chevrolet Monte Carlo), 200; **9** Mark Martin, USA (Ford Taurus), 200; **10** Terry Labonte, USA (Chevrolet Monte Carlo), 200.
Pole position: Labonte (Bobby).
Drivers Championship points: 1 Kenseth, 2275; **2** Earnhardt Jr, 2090; **3** Gordon (Jeff), 2052; **4** Labonte (Bobby), 1998; **5** Busch, 1933; **6** Waltrip, 1900.

DODGE/SAVE MART 350, Infineon Raceway, Sears Point, Sonoma, California, USA, 22 June. Round 16. 110 laps of the 1.990-mile/3.203-km circuit, 218.900 miles/352.285 km.
1 Robby Gordon, USA (Chevrolet Monte Carlo), 2h 57m 55.0s, 73.821 mph/118.804 km/h; **2** Jeff Gordon, USA (Chevrolet Monte Carlo), 2h 57m 55.553s; **3** Kevin Harvick, USA (Chevrolet Monte Carlo), 110 laps; **4** Bill Elliott, USA (Dodge Intrepid), 110; **5** Ryan Newman, USA (Dodge Intrepid), 110; **6** Boris Said, USA (Pontiac Grand Prix), 110; **7** Ron Fellows, USA (Chevrolet Monte Carlo), 110; **8** Rusty Wallace, USA (Dodge Intrepid), 110; **9** Bobby Labonte, USA (Chevrolet Monte Carlo), 110; **10** Jeremy Mayfield, USA (Dodge Intrepid), 110.
Pole position: Said.
Drivers Championship points: 1 Kenseth, 2396; **2** Gordon (Jeff), 2222; **3** Earnhardt Jr, 2220; **4** Labonte (Bobby), 2136; **5** Waltrip, 2024; **6** Busch, 2012.

PEPSI 400, Daytona International Speedway, Daytona Beach, Florida, USA, 5 July. Round 17. 160 laps of the 2.500-mile/4.023-km circuit, 400.000 miles/643.738 km.
1 Greg Biffle, USA (Ford Taurus), 2h 24m 29.0s, 166.109 mph/267.327 km/h; **2** Jeff Burton, USA (Ford Taurus), 2h 24m 33.102s; **3** Ricky Rudd, USA (Ford Taurus), 160 laps; **4** Terry Labonte, USA (Chevrolet Monte Carlo), 160; **5** Bobby Labonte, USA (Chevrolet Monte Carlo), 160; **6** Matt Kenseth, USA (Ford Taurus), 160; **7** Dale Earnhardt Jr, USA (Chevrolet Monte Carlo), 160; **8** Jeremy Mayfield, USA (Dodge Intrepid), 160; **9** Kevin Harvick, USA (Chevrolet Monte Carlo), 160; **10** Dale Jarrett, USA (Ford Taurus), 160.
Pole position: Steve Park, USA (Chevrolet Monte Carlo).
Drivers Championship points: 1 Kenseth, 2551; **2** Earnhardt Jr, 2371; **3** Gordon (Jeff), 2348; **4** Labonte (Bobby), 2296; **5** Waltrip, 2159; **6** Johnson, 2079.

TROPICANA 400, Chicagoland Speedway, Chicago, Illinois, USA, 13 July. Round 18. 267 of the 1.500-mile/2.414-km circuit, 400.500 miles/644.542 km.
1 Ryan Newman, USA (Dodge Intrepid), 2h 59m 15.0s, 134.059 mph/215.746 km/h; **2** Tony Stewart, USA (Chevrolet Monte Carlo), 2h 59m 17.633s; **3** Jimmie Johnson, USA (Chevrolet Monte Carlo), 267 laps; **4** Jeff Gordon, USA (Chevrolet Monte Carlo), 267; **5** Michael Waltrip, USA (Chevrolet Monte Carlo), 267; **6** Jeff Burton, USA (Ford Taurus), 267; **7** Robby Gordon, USA (Chevrolet Monte Carlo), 267; **8** Jamie McMurray, USA (Dodge Intrepid), 267; **9** Elliott Sadler, USA (Ford Taurus), 267; **10** Jeremy Mayfield, USA (Dodge Intrepid), 267.
Pole position: Stewart.
Drivers Championship points: 1 Kenseth, 2678; **2** Gordon (Jeff), 2513; **3** Earnhardt Jr, 2420; **4** Labonte (Bobby), 2351; **5** Waltrip, 2294; **6** Johnson, 2249.

NEW ENGLAND 300, New Hampshire International Speedway, Loudon, New Hampshire, USA, 20 July. Round 19. 300 laps of the 1.058-mile/1.703-km circuit, 317.400 miles/510.806 km.
1 Jimmie Johnson, USA (Chevrolet Monte Carlo), 3h 16m 29.0s, 96.924 mph/155.984 km/h; **2** Kevin Harvick, USA (Chevrolet Monte Carlo), 3h 16m 30.582s; **3** Matt Kenseth, USA (Ford Taurus), 300 laps; **4** Ryan Newman, USA (Dodge Intrepid), 300; **5** Robby Gordon, USA (Chevrolet Monte Carlo), 300; **6** Dale Earnhardt Jr, USA (Chevrolet Monte Carlo), 300; **7** Dale Jarrett, USA (Ford Taurus), 300; **8** Steve Park, USA (Chevrolet Monte Carlo), 300; **9** Jeff Burton, USA (Ford Taurus), 300; **10** Greg Biffle, USA (Ford Taurus), 300.
Pole position: Kenseth.
Drivers Championship points: 1 Kenseth, 2848; **2** Gordon (Jeff), 2614; **3** Earnhardt Jr, 2575; **4** Labonte (Bobby), 2472; **5** Johnson, 2429; **6** Waltrip, 2373.

PENNSYLVANIA 500, Pocono Raceway, Long Pond, Pennsylvania, USA, 27 July. Round 20. 200 laps of the 2.500-mile/4.023-km circuit, 500.000 miles/804.672 km.
1 Ryan Newman, USA (Dodge Intrepid), 3h 54m 55.0s, 127.705 mph/205.521 km/h; **2** Kurt Busch, USA (Ford Taurus), 3h 54m 55.307s; **3** Dale Earnhardt Jr, USA (Chevrolet Monte Carlo), 200 laps; **4** Michael Waltrip, USA (Chevrolet Monte Carlo), 200; **5** Terry Labonte, USA (Chevrolet Monte Carlo), 200; **6** Jeff Burton, USA (Ford Taurus), 200; **7** Joe Nemechek, USA (Chevrolet Monte Carlo), 200; **8** Todd Bodine, USA (Ford Taurus), 200; **9** Dave Blaney, USA (Ford Taurus), 200; **10** Sterling Marlin, USA (Dodge Intrepid), 200.
Pole position: Newman.
Drivers Championship points: 1 Kenseth, 2977; **2** Earnhardt Jr, 2745; **3** Gordon (Jeff), 2669; **4** Johnson, 2547; **5** Labonte (Bobby), 2545; **6** Waltrip, 2538.

BRICKYARD 400, Indianapolis Motor Speedway, Speedway, Indiana, USA, 3 August. Round 21. 160 laps of the 2.500-mile/4.023-km circuit, 400.000 miles/643.738 km.
1 Kevin Harvick, USA (Chevrolet Monte Carlo), 2h 58m 22.0s, 134.554 mph/216.544 km/h; **2** Matt Kenseth, USA (Ford Taurus), 2h 58m 24.758s; **3** Jamie McMurray, USA (Dodge Intrepid), 160 laps; **4** Jeff Gordon, USA (Chevrolet Monte Carlo), 160; **5** Bill Elliott, USA (Dodge Intrepid), 160; **6** Robby Gordon, USA (Chevrolet Monte Carlo), 160; **7** Kurt Busch, USA (Ford Taurus), 160; **8** Jimmy Spencer, USA (Dodge Intrepid), 160; **9** Mark Martin, USA (Ford Taurus), 160; **10** Rusty Wallace, USA (Dodge Intrepid), 160.
Pole position: Harvick.
Drivers Championship points: 1 Kenseth, 3152; **2** Earnhardt Jr, 2866; **3** Gordon (Jeff), 2834; **4** Johnson, 2656; **5** Waltrip, 2653; **6** Labonte (Bobby), 2642.

SIRIUS AT THE GLEN, Watkins Glen International, New York, USA, 10 August. Round 22. 90 laps of the 2.450-mile/3.943-km circuit, 220.500 miles/354.860 km.
1 Robby Gordon, USA (Chevrolet Monte Carlo), 2h 26m 17.0s, 90.441 mph/145.551 km/h; **2** Scott Pruett, USA (Dodge Intrepid), 2h 26m 19.335s; **3** Dale Earnhardt Jr, USA (Chevrolet Monte Carlo), 90 laps; **4** Jimmie Johnson, USA (Chevrolet Monte Carlo), 90; **5** Kevin Harvick, USA (Chevrolet Monte Carlo), 90; **6** Ward Burton, USA (Dodge Intrepid), 90; **7** Dale Jarrett, USA (Ford Taurus), 90; **8** Matt Kenseth, USA (Ford Taurus), 90; **9** Ryan Newman, USA (Dodge Intrepid), 90; **10** Mark Martin, USA (Ford Taurus), 90.
Pole position: Jeff Gordon, USA (Chevrolet Monte Carlo).
Drivers Championship points: 1 Kenseth, 3294; **2** Earnhardt Jr, 3036; **3** Gordon (Jeff), 2898; **4** Johnson, 2816; **5** Harvick, 2778; **6** Waltrip, 2777.

GFS MARKETPLACE 400, Michigan International Speedway, Brooklyn, Michigan, USA, 17 August. Round 23. 200 laps of the 2.000-mile/3.219-km circuit, 400.000 miles/643.738 km.
1 Ryan Newman, USA (Dodge Intrepid), 3h 08m 31.0s, 127.310 mph/204.885 km/h; **2** Kevin Harvick, USA (Chevrolet Monte Carlo), 3h 08m 32.652s; **3** Tony Stewart, USA (Chevrolet Monte Carlo), 200 laps; **4** Greg Biffle, USA (Ford Taurus), 200; **5** Steve Park, USA (Chevrolet Monte Carlo), 200; **6** Robby Gordon, USA (Chevrolet Monte Carlo), 200; **7** Michael Waltrip, USA (Chevrolet Monte Carlo), 200; **8** Ken Schrader, USA (Dodge Intrepid), 200; **9** Matt Kenseth, USA (Ford Taurus), 200; **10** Johnny Benson Jr, USA (Pontiac Grand Prix), 200.
Pole position: Bobby Labonte, USA (Chevrolet Monte Carlo).
Drivers Championship points: 1 Kenseth, 3432; **2** Earnhardt Jr, 3103; **3** Gordon (Jeff), 2971; **4** Harvick, 2953; **5** Waltrip, 2923; **6** Johnson, 2908.

SHARPIE 500, Bristol Motor Speedway, Tennessee, USA, 23 August. Round 24. 500 laps of the 0.533-mile/0.858-km circuit, 266.500 miles/428.890 km.
1 Kurt Busch, USA (Ford Taurus), 3h 26m 32.0s, 77.421 mph/124.597 km/h; **2** Kevin Harvick, USA (Chevrolet Monte Carlo), 3h 26m 32.818s; **3** Jamie McMurray, USA (Dodge Intrepid), 500 laps; **4** Matt Kenseth, USA (Ford Taurus), 500; **5** Jimmie Johnson, USA (Chevrolet Monte Carlo), 500; **6** Ryan Newman, USA (Dodge Intrepid), 500; **7** Dale Jarrett, USA (Ford Taurus), 500; **8** Ricky Craven, USA (Pontiac Grand Prix), 500; **9** Dale Earnhardt Jr, USA (Chevrolet Monte Carlo), 500; **10** Jeremy Mayfield, USA (Dodge Intrepid), 500.
Pole position: Jeff Gordon, USA (Chevrolet Monte Carlo).
Drivers Championship points: 1 Kenseth, 3592; **2** Earn-

hardt Jr, 3241; **3** Harvick, 3128; **4** Johnson, 3063; **5** Gordon (Jeff), 3060; **6** Busch, 2990.

MOUNTAIN DEW SOUTHERN 500, Darlington Raceway, South Carolina, USA, 31 August. Round 25. 367 laps of the 1.366-mile/2.198-km circuit, 501.322 miles/806.800 km.
1 Terry Labonte, USA (Chevrolet Monte Carlo), 4h 09m 07.0s, 120.744 mph/194.318 km/h; **2** Kevin Harvick, USA (Chevrolet Monte Carlo), 4h 09m 08.651s; **3** Jimmie Johnson, USA (Chevrolet Monte Carlo), 367 laps; **4** Jamie McMurray, USA (Dodge Intrepid), 367; **5** Bill Elliott, USA (Dodge Intrepid), 367; **6** Jeremy Mayfield, USA (Dodge Intrepid), 367; **7** Bobby Labonte, USA (Chevrolet Monte Carlo), 367; **8** Ricky Craven, USA (Pontiac Grand Prix), 367; **9** Elliott Sadler, USA (Ford Taurus), 367; **10** Greg Biffle, USA (Ford Taurus), 367.
Pole position: Ryan Newman, USA (Dodge Intrepid).
Drivers Championship points: 1 Kenseth, 3718; **2** Earnhardt Jr, 3329; **3** Harvick, 3303; **4** Johnson, 3233; **5** Gordon (Jeff), 3127; **6** Busch, 3114.

CHEVY ROCK & ROLL 400, Richmond International Raceway, Virginia, USA, 6 September. Round 26. 400 laps of the 0.750-mile/1.207-km circuit, 300.000 miles/482.803 km.
1 Ryan Newman, USA (Dodge Intrepid), 3h 09m 35.0s, 94.945 mph/152.799 km/h; **2** Jeremy Mayfield, USA (Dodge Intrepid), 3h 09m 35.159s; **3** Ricky Rudd, USA (Ford Taurus), 400 laps; **4** Jeff Burton, USA (Ford Taurus), 400; **5** Rusty Wallace, USA (Dodge Intrepid), 400; **6** Bobby Labonte, USA (Chevrolet Monte Carlo), 400; **7** Matt Kenseth, USA (Ford Taurus), 400; **8** Terry Labonte, USA (Chevrolet Monte Carlo), 400; **9** Johnny Benson Jr, USA (Pontiac Grand Prix), 400; **10** Jeff Gordon, USA (Chevrolet Monte Carlo), 400.
Pole position: Mike Skinner, USA (Pontiac Grand Prix).
Drivers Championship points: 1 Kenseth, 3864; **2** Earnhardt Jr, 3446; **3** Harvick, 3423; **4** Johnson, 3363; **5** Gordon (Jeff), 3271; **6** Newman, 3255.

SYLVANIA 300, New Hampshire International Speedway, Loudon, New Hampshire, USA, 14 September. Round 27. 300 laps of the 1.058-mile/1.703-km circuit, 317.400 miles/510.806 km.
1 Jimmie Johnson, USA (Chevrolet Monte Carlo), 2h 58m 41.0s, 106.580 mph/171.523 km/h; **2** Ricky Rudd, USA (Ford Taurus), 2h 58m 47.240s; **3** Joe Nemechek, USA (Chevrolet Monte Carlo), 300 laps; **4** Bill Elliott, USA (Dodge Intrepid), 300; **5** Dale Earnhardt Jr, USA (Chevrolet Monte Carlo), 300; **6** Rusty Wallace, USA (Dodge Intrepid), 300; **7** Matt Kenseth, USA (Ford Taurus), 300; **8** Elliott Sadler, USA (Ford Taurus), 300; **9** Ryan Newman, USA (Dodge Intrepid), 300; **10** Jamie McMurray, USA (Dodge Intrepid), 300.
Pole position: Newman.
Drivers Championship points: 1 Kenseth, 4015; **2** Earnhardt Jr, 3611; **3** Harvick, 3552; **4** Johnson, 3543; **5** Newman, 3398; **6** Gordon (Jeff), 3382.

MBNA AMERICA 400, Dover International Speedway, Dover, Delaware, USA, 21 September. Round 28. 400 laps of the 1.000-mile/1.609-km circuit, 400.000 miles/643.738 km.
1 Ryan Newman, USA (Dodge Intrepid), 3h 40m 35.0s, 108.802 mph/175.101 km/h; **2** Jeremy Mayfield, USA (Dodge Intrepid), 3h 40m 36.152s; **3** Tony Stewart, USA (Chevrolet Monte Carlo), 400 laps; **4** Kevin Harvick, USA (Chevrolet Monte Carlo), 400; **5** Jeff Gordon, USA (Chevrolet Monte Carlo), 400; **6** Jamie McMurray, USA (Dodge Intrepid), 400; **7** Greg Biffle, USA (Ford Taurus), 400; **8** Jimmie Johnson, USA (Chevrolet Monte Carlo), 400; **9** Matt Kenseth, USA (Ford Taurus), 400; **10** Rusty Wallace, USA (Dodge Intrepid), 400.
Pole position: Kenseth.
Drivers Championship points: 1 Kenseth, 4158; **2** Harvick, 3722; **3** Johnson, 3685; **4** Earnhardt Jr, 3668; **5** Newman, 3578; **6** Gordon (Jeff), 3542.

EA SPORTS 500, Talladega Superspeedway, Alabama, USA, 28 September. Round 29. 188 laps of the 2.660-mile/4.281-km circuit, 500.080 miles/804.801 km.
1 Michael Waltrip, USA (Chevrolet Monte Carlo), 3h 12m 17.0s, 156.045 mph/251.130 km/h; **2** Dale Earnhardt Jr, USA (Chevrolet Monte Carlo), 3h 12m 17.095s; **3** Tony Stewart, USA (Chevrolet Monte Carlo), 188 laps; **4** Ryan Newman, USA (Dodge Intrepid), 188; **5** Jeff Gordon, USA (Chevrolet Monte Carlo), 188; **6** Kurt Busch, USA (Ford Taurus), 188; **7** Kevin Harvick, USA (Chevrolet Monte Carlo), 188; **8** Ricky Craven, USA (Pontiac Grand Prix), 188; **9** Rusty Wallace, USA (Dodge Intrepid), 188; **10** Mike Wallace, USA (Dodge Intrepid), 188.
Pole position: Elliott Sadler, USA (Ford Taurus).
Drivers Championship points: 1 Kenseth, 4227; **2** Harvick, 3873; **3** Earnhardt Jr, 3843; **4** Johnson, 3751; **5** Newman, 3738; **6** Gordon (Jeff), 3707.

BANQUET 400 presented by CONAGRA FOODS, Kansas Speedway, Kansas City, Kansas, USA, 5 October. Round 30. 267 laps of the 1.500-mile/2.414-km circuit, 400.500 miles/644.542 km.
1 Ryan Newman, USA (Dodge Intrepid), 3h 17m 34.0s, 121.630 mph/195.744 km/h; **2** Bill Elliott, USA (Dodge Intrepid), 3h 17m 34.863s; **3** Jeremy Mayfield, USA (Dodge Intrepid), 267 laps; **4** Tony Stewart, USA (Chevrolet Monte Carlo), 267; **5** Jeff Gordon, USA (Chevrolet Monte Carlo), 267; **6** Kevin Harvick, USA (Chevrolet Monte Carlo), 267; **7** Jimmie Johnson, USA (Chevrolet Monte Carlo), 267; **8** Jamie McMurray, USA (Dodge Intrepid), 267; **9** Rusty Wallace, USA (Dodge Intrepid), 267; **10** Ricky Rudd, USA (Ford Taurus), 267.
Pole position: Johnson.
Drivers Championship points: 1 Kenseth, 4282; **2** Harvick, 4023; **3** Earnhardt Jr, 3957; **4** Newman, 3918; **5** Johnson, 3902; **6** Gordon (Jeff), 3862.

UAW-GM QUALITY 500, Lowe's Motor Speedway, Concord, Charlotte, North Carolina, USA, 11 October. Round 31. 334 laps of the 1.500-mile/2.414-km circuit, 501.000 miles/806.281 km.
1 Tony Stewart, USA (Chevrolet Monte Carlo), 3h 30m 24.0s, 142.871 mph/229.928 km/h; **2** Ryan Newman, USA (Dodge Intrepid), 3h 30m 24.608s; **3** Jimmie Johnson, USA (Chevrolet Monte Carlo), 334 laps; **4** Bill Elliott, USA (Dodge Intrepid), 334; **5** Jeff Gordon, USA (Chevrolet Monte Carlo), 334; **6** Bobby Labonte, USA (Chevrolet Monte Carlo), 334; **7** Jamie McMurray, USA (Dodge Intrepid), 334; **8** Matt Kenseth, USA (Ford Taurus), 334; **9** Dale Earnhardt Jr, USA (Chevrolet Monte Carlo), 334; **10** Kevin Harvick, USA (Chevrolet Monte Carlo), 334.
Pole position: Newman.

Drivers Championship points: 1 Kenseth, 4424; **2** Harvick, 4157; **3** Earnhardt Jr, 4100; **4** Newman, 4093; **5** Johnson, 4072; **6** Gordon (Jeff), 4017.

SUBWAY 500, Martinsville Speedway, Virginia, USA, 19 October. Round 32. 500 laps of the 0.526-mile/0.847-km circuit, 263.000 miles/423.257 km.
1 Jeff Gordon, USA (Chevrolet Monte Carlo), 3h 53m 14.0s, 67.658 mph/108.884 km/h; **2** Jimmie Johnson, USA (Chevrolet Monte Carlo), 3h 53m 15.036s; **3** Tony Stewart, USA (Chevrolet Monte Carlo), 500 laps; **4** Dale Earnhardt Jr, USA (Chevrolet Monte Carlo), 500; **5** Ryan Newman, USA (Dodge Intrepid), 500; **6** Terry Labonte, USA (Chevrolet Monte Carlo), 500; **7** Kevin Harvick, USA (Chevrolet Monte Carlo), 500; **8** Jamie McMurray, USA (Dodge Intrepid), 500; **9** Bill Elliott, USA (Dodge Intrepid), 500; **10** Jeff Burton, USA (Ford Taurus), 500.
Pole position: Gordon (Jeff).
Drivers Championship points: 1 Kenseth, 4548; **2** Harvick, 4308; **3** Earnhardt Jr, 4265; **4** Newman, 4248; **5** Johnson, 4242; **6** Gordon (Jeff), 4202.

BASS PRO SHOPS MBNA 500, Atlanta Motor Speedway, Hampton, Georgia, USA, 26/27 October. Round 33. 325 laps of the 1.540-mile/2.478-km circuit, 500.500 miles/805.477 km.
Rain delayed the final laps, which were run on the second day.
1 Jeff Gordon, USA (Chevrolet Monte Carlo), 3h 55m 02.0s, 127.769 mph/205.624 km/h; **2** Tony Stewart, USA (Chevrolet Monte Carlo), 325 laps (under caution); **3** Jimmie Johnson, USA (Chevrolet Monte Carlo), 325; **4** Bill Elliott, USA (Dodge Intrepid), 325; **5** Bobby Labonte, USA (Chevrolet Monte Carlo), 325; **6** Dale Earnhardt Jr, USA (Chevrolet Monte Carlo), 325; **7** Jeremy Mayfield, USA (Dodge Intrepid), 325; **8** Kurt Busch, USA (Ford Taurus), 325; **9** Jimmy Spencer, USA (Dodge Intrepid), 325; **10** Joe Nemechek, USA (Pontiac Grand Prix), 325.
Pole position: Newman.
Drivers Championship points: 1 Kenseth, 4678; **2** Earnhardt Jr, 4420; **3** Harvick, 4416; **4** Johnson, 4412; **5** Gordon (Jeff), 4382; **6** Newman, 4329.

CHECKER AUTO PARTS 500 PRESENTED BY HAVOLINE, Phoenix International Raceway, Arizona, USA, 2 November. Round 34. 312 laps of the 1.000-mile/1.609-km circuit, 312.000 miles/502.115 km.
1 Dale Earnhardt Jr, USA (Chevrolet Monte Carlo), 3h 19m 11.0s, 93.984 mph/151.252 km/h; **2** Jimmie Johnson, USA (Chevrolet Monte Carlo), 3h 19m 11.735s; **3** Ryan Newman, USA (Dodge Intrepid), 312 laps; **4** Kurt Busch, USA (Ford Taurus), 312; **5** Michael Waltrip, USA (Chevrolet Monte Carlo), 312; **6** Matt Kenseth, USA (Ford Taurus), 312; **7** Jeff Gordon, USA (Chevrolet Monte Carlo), 312; **8** Jeff Burton, USA (Ford Taurus), 312; **9** Scott Wimmer, USA (Dodge Intrepid), 312; **10** Mark Martin, USA (Ford Taurus), 312.
Pole position: Newman.

Provisional championship points

Drivers
1 Matt Kenseth, USA, 4828; **2** Dale Earnhardt Jr, USA, 4600; **3** Jimmie Johnson, USA, 4587; **4** Jeff Gordon, USA, 4528; **5** Ryan Newman, USA, 4499; **6** Kevin Harvick, USA, 4477; **7** Tony Stewart, USA, 4260; **8** Bobby Labonte, USA, 4055; **9** Kurt Busch, USA, 3983; **10** Bill Elliott, USA, 3966; **11** Terry Labonte, USA, 3912; **12** Michael Waltrip, USA, 3842; **13** Jeff Burton, USA, 3842; **14** Jamie McMurray, USA, 3769; **15** Rusty Wallace, USA, 3757; **16** Robby Gordon, USA, 3680; **17** Mark Martin, USA, 3665; **18** Greg Biffle, USA, 3508; **19** Sterling Marlin, USA, 3477; **20** Jeremy Mayfield, USA, 3411; **21** Ricky Rudd, USA, 3408; **22** Ward Burton, USA, 3369; **23** Elliott Sadler, USA, 3325; **24** Joe Nemechek, USA, 3226; **25** Dale Jarrett, USA, 3224; **26** Ricky Craven, USA, 3212; **27** Johnny Benson Jr., USA, 3207; **28** Dave Blaney, USA, 3033; **29** Jimmy Spencer, USA, 2933; **30** Kenny Wallace, USA, 2894.

Raybestos Rookie of the Year: Jamie McMurray.

Manufacturers
1 Chevrolet, 249; **2** Ford, 193; **3** Dodge, 190; **4** Pontiac, 116.

Bud Pole Award winner: Ryan Newman.

Results of the Rockingham and Homestead races will be given in AUTOCOURSE 2004–2005

Other NASCAR races

THE BUDWEISER SHOOTOUT, Daytona International Speedway, Daytona Beach, Florida, USA, 8 February. 70 laps of the 2.500-mile/4.023-km circuit, 175.000 miles/281.635 km.
1 Dale Earnhardt Jr, USA (Chevrolet Monte Carlo), 70 laps; **2** Jeff Gordon, USA (Chevrolet Monte Carlo), 70; **3** Matt Kenseth, USA (Ford Taurus), 70; **4** Ryan Newman, USA (Dodge Intrepid), 70; **5** Ward Burton, USA (Dodge Intrepid), 70; **6** Ken Schrader, USA (Dodge Intrepid), 70; **7** Jimmie Johnson, USA (Chevrolet Monte Carlo), 70; **8** Ricky Rudd, USA (Ford Taurus), 70; **9** Kevin Harvick, USA (Chevrolet Monte Carlo), 70; **10** Ricky Craven, USA (Pontiac Grand Prix), 70.
Pole position: Geoffrey Bodine, USA (Ford Taurus).

THE WINSTON OPEN, Lowe's Motor Speedway, Concord, Charlotte, North Carolina, USA, 17 May. 30 laps of the 1.500-mile/2.414-km circuit, 135.000 miles/217.261 km.
1 Jeff Burton, USA (Ford Taurus), 32m 23.0s, 83.376 mph/134.181 km/h; **2** Dave Blaney, USA (Ford Taurus), 32m 23.799s; **3** Mike Skinner, USA (Pontiac Grand Prix), 30 laps; **4** Brett Bodine, USA (Ford Taurus), 30; **5** Greg Biffle, USA (Ford Taurus), 30; **6** Jimmy Spencer, USA (Dodge Intrepid), 30; **7** Kenny Wallace, USA (Dodge Intrepid), 30; **8** Steve Park, USA (Chevrolet Monte Carlo), 30; **9** Kyle Petty, USA (Dodge Intrepid), 30; **10** Jack Sprague, USA (Pontiac Grand Prix), 30.
Pole position: Park.

THE WINSTON, Lowe's Motor Speedway, Concord, Charlotte, North Carolina, USA, 17 May. 90 laps of the 1.500-mile/2.414-km circuit, 135.000 miles/217.261 km.
Run over three segments (30, 30 and 30 laps). Aggregate results given.
1 Jimmie Johnson, USA (Chevrolet Monte Carlo), 1h 00m 46.0s, 133.297 mph/214.520 km/h; **2** Kurt Busch, USA (Ford Taurus), 1h 00m 46.888s; **3** Bobby Labonte, USA (Chevrolet Monte Carlo), 90 laps; **4** Joe Nemechek, USA (Chevrolet Monte Carlo), 90; **5** Michael Waltrip, USA (Chevrolet Monte Carlo), 90; **6** Matt Kenseth, USA (Ford Taurus), 90; **7** Kevin Harvick, USA (Chevrolet Monte Carlo), 90; **8** Jeff Gordon, USA (Chevrolet Monte Carlo), 90; **9** Jeff Burton, USA (Ford Taurus), 90; **10** Ricky Craven, USA (Pontiac Grand Prix), 90.
Pole position: Bill Elliott, USA (Dodge Intrepid).

CART Toyota Atlantic Championship

All cars are Swift 014.a chassis with a Toyota 4A-GE engine

MONTERREY TOYOTA ATLANTIC RACE, Parque Fundidora, Monterrey, Nuevo Leon, Mexico, 23 March. Round 1. 32 laps of the 2.104-mile/3.386-km circuit, 67.328 miles/108.354 km.
1 Michael Valiante, CDN, 49m 36.669s, 81.427 mph/131.044 km/h; **2** Jonathan Macri, CDN, 49m 37.117s; **3** Danica Patrick, USA, 49m 41.943s; **4** Ryan Dalziel, GB, 49m 50.626s; **5** Aaron Justus, USA, 49m 55.903s; **6** Alex Figge, USA, 49m 56.903s; **7** Marc DeVellis, CDN, 50m 01.610s; **8** A.J. Allmendinger, USA, 50m 07.735s; **9** Romain Dumas, F, 50m 09.130s; **10** Luis Diaz, MEX, 50m 49.321s.
Most laps led: Valiante, 27.
Fastest race lap: Diaz, 1m 24.708s, 89.418 mph/143.904 km/h.
Fastest qualifying lap: Diaz, 1m 24.960s, 89.153 mph/143.477 km/h.

LONG BEACH TOYOTA ATLANTIC RACE, Long Beach Street Circuit, California, USA, 13 April. Round 2. 32 laps of the 1.968-mile/3.167-km circuit, 62.976 miles/101.350 km.
1 A.J. Allmendinger, USA, 46m 00.773s, 82.119 mph/132.159 km/h; **2** Aaron Justus, USA, 46m 03.152s; **3** Jonathan Macri, CDN, 46m 04.914s; **4** Michael Valiante, CDN, 46m 07.721s; **5** Alex Figge, USA, 46m 08.852s; **6** Luis Diaz, MEX, 46m 08.955s; **7** Joey Hand, USA, 46m 20.308s; **8** Stephan C. Roy, CDN, 46m 21.120s; **9** Kyle Krisiloff, USA, 46m 28.691s; **10** Alex Garcia, YV, 46m 31.767s.
Most laps led: Allmendinger, 32.
Fastest race lap: Allmendinger, 1m 17.016s, 91.991 mph/148.046 km/h.
Fastest qualifying lap: Allmendinger, 1m 16.267s, 92.895 mph/149.500 km/h.

MILWAUKEE TOYOTA ATLANTIC RACE, The Milwaukee Mile, Wisconsin State Fair Park, West Allis, Wisconsin, USA, 31 May. Round 3. 70 laps of the 1.032-mile/1.661-km circuit, 72.240 miles/116.259 km.
1 Ryan Dalziel, GB, 34m 12.338s, 126.716 mph/203.930 km/h; **2** Kyle Krisiloff, USA, 34m 12.677s; **3** A.J. Allmendinger, USA, 34m 23.639s; **4** Jonathan Macri, CDN, 34m 24.196s; **5** Aaron Justus, USA, 34m 26.479s; **6** Danica Patrick, USA, 34m 27.438s; **7** Alex Figge, USA, 34m 33.830s; **8** Stephan C. Roy, CDN, 34m 34.097s; **9** Joey Hand, USA, 69 laps; **10** Tony Ave, USA, 69.
Most laps led: Dalziel, 70.
Fastest race lap: Krisiloff, 24.645s, 150.749 mph/242.606 km/h.
Fastest qualifying lap: Dalziel, 24.839s, 149.571 mph/240.712 km/h.

MONTEREY TOYOTA ATLANTIC RACE, Mazda Raceway at Laguna Seca, Monterey, California, USA, 14 June. Round 4. 30 laps of the 2.238-mile/3.602-km circuit, 67.140 miles/108.051 km.
1 A.J. Allmendinger, USA, 42m 20.641s, 95.135 mph/153.105 km/h; **2** Ryan Dalziel, GB, 42m 38.420s; **3** Jonathan Macri, CDN, 42m 51.031s; **4** Aaron Justus, USA, 42m 56.440s; **5** Alex Figge, USA, 42m 57.801s; **6** Luis Diaz, MEX, 43m 10.834s; **7** Kyle Krisiloff, USA, 43m 21.225s; **8** Alex Garcia, YV, 43m 32.709s; **9** Eric Jensen, CDN, 29 laps; **10** Joey Hand, USA, 26.
Most laps led: Allmendinger, 30.
Fastest race lap: Allmendinger, 1m 17.727s, 103.655 mph/166.817 km/h.
Fastest qualifying lap: Allmendinger, 1m 16.986s, 104.653 mph/168.422 km/h.

PORTLAND TOYOTA ATLANTIC RACE, Portland International Raceway, Oregon, USA, 21 June. Round 5. 35 laps of the 1.969-mile/3.169-km circuit, 68.915 miles/110.908 km.
1 Ryan Dalziel, GB, 40m 23.576s, 102.367 mph/164.744 km/h; **2** Joey Hand, USA, 40m 37.996s; **3** Michael Valiante, CDN, 40m 38.513s; **4** A.J. Allmendinger, USA, 40m 39.412s; **5** Aaron Justus, USA, 40m 50.074s; **6** Danica Patrick, USA, 40m 51.640s; **7** Alex Figge, USA, 40m 51.868s; **8** Jonathan Macri, CDN, 41m 04.672s; **9** Luis Diaz, MEX, 41m 05.256s; **10** Bryan Sellers, USA, 41m 06.961s.
Most laps led: Dalziel, 35.
Fastest race lap: Dalziel, 1m 07.062s, 105.699 mph/170.106 km/h.
Fastest qualifying lap: Dalziel, 1m 06.204s, 107.069 mph/172.311 km/h.

ARGENT MORTGAGE TOYOTA ATLANTIC 100K, Burke Lakefront Airport, Cleveland, Ohio, USA, 5 July. Round 6. 32 laps of the 2.106-mile/3.389-km circuit, 67.392 miles/108.457 km.
1 A.J. Allmendinger, USA, 44m 15.524s, 91.361 mph/147.031 km/h; **2** Jonathan Macri, CDN, 40m 17.328s; **3** Ryan Dalziel, GB, 44m 18.403s; **4** Michael Valiante, CDN, 44m 19.358s; **5** Danica Patrick, USA, 44m 22.242s; **6** Alex Garcia, YV, 44m 23.308s; **7** Kyle Krisiloff, USA, 44m 28.329s; **8** Eric Jensen, CDN, 44m 28.847s; **9** Philip Fayer, CDN, 44m 29.995s; **10** Joey Hand, USA, 31 laps.
Most laps led: Allmendinger, 17.
Fastest race lap: Allmendinger, 1m 05.885s, 115.073 mph/185.192 km/h.
Fastest qualifying lap: Allmendinger, 1m 04.927s, 116.771 mph/187.925 km/h.

TORONTO TOYOTA ATLANTIC RACE, Canada National Exhibition Place Circuit, Toronto, Ontario, Canada, 12 July. Round 7. 35 laps of the 1.755-mile/2.824-km circuit, 61.425 miles/98.854 km.
1 A.J. Allmendinger, USA, 40m 43.450s, 90.499 mph/145.644 km/h; **2** Aaron Justus, USA, 40m 45.476s; **3** Jonathan Macri, CDN, 40m 46.054s; **4** Michael Valiante, CDN, 40m 46.576s; **5** Ryan Dalziel, GB, 40m 47.274s; **6** Joey Hand, USA, 40m 47.955s; **7** Bryan Sellers, USA, 40m 49.012s; **8** Alex Figge, USA, 40m 50.645s; **9** Luis Diaz, MEX, 40m 53.037s; **10** Danica Patrick, USA, 40m 55.517s.
Most laps led: Allmendinger, 26.
Fastest race lap: Allmendinger, 1m 05.829s, 95.976 mph/154.458 km/h.
Fastest qualifying lap: Allmendinger, 1m 04.920s, 97.320 mph/156.621 km/h.

TROIS-RIVIÈRES TOYOTA ATLANTIC RACE, Trois-Rivières street circuit, Québec, Canada, 3 August. Round 8. 45 laps of the 1.521-mile/2.448-km circuit, 68.445 miles/110.152 km.
1 A.J. Allmendinger, USA, 45m 14.076s, 90.787 mph/146.107 km/h; **2** Ryan Dalziel, GB, 45m 14.541s; **3** Michael Valiante, CDN, 45m 19.750s; **4** Joey Hand, USA, 45m 39.700s; **5** Danica Patrick, USA, 45m 41.040s; **6** Luis Diaz, MEX, 45m 48.716s; **7** Jonathan Macri, CDN, 45m 58.973s; **8** Stephan C. Roy, CDN, 46m 04.897s; **9** Louis-Philippe Dumoulin, CDN, 46m 23.962s; **10** Philip Fayer, CDN, 43 laps.
Most laps led: Allmendinger, 45.
Fastest race lap: Allmendinger, 59.521s, 91.994 mph/148.051 km/h.
Fastest qualifying lap: Allmendinger, 59.296s, 92.343 mph/148.612 km/h.

MID-OHIO TOYOTA ATLANTIC RACE, Mid-Ohio Sports Car Course, Lexington, Ohio, USA, 10 August. Round 9. 30 laps of the 2.258-mile/3.634-km circuit, 66.773 miles/107.461 km.
1 Michael Valiante, CDN, 41m 50.941s, 95.734 mph/154.069 km/h; **2** Ryan Dalziel, GB, 41m 51.613s; **3** Aaron Justus, USA, 41m 52.344s; **4** Joey Hand, USA, 41m 53.209s; **5** Jonathan Macri, CDN, 41m 55.586s; **6** Bryan Sellers, USA, 41m 56.630s; **7** Luis Diaz, MEX, 41m 57.494s; **8** Alex Figge, USA, 41m 57.883s; **9** Kyle Krisiloff, USA, 41m 58.712s; **10** Danica Patrick, USA, 42m 10.908s.
Most laps led: Valiante, 29.
Fastest race lap: Macri, 1m 16.405s, 106.391 mph/171.220 km/h.
Fastest qualifying lap: A.J. Allmendinger, USA, 1m 15.668s, 107.427 mph/172.887 km/h.

MONTRÉAL TOYOTA ATLANTIC RACE, Circuit Gilles-Villeneuve, Ile-Notre-Dame, Montréal, Québec, Canada, 23 August. Round 10. 25 laps of the 2.709-mile/4.360-km circuit, 67.725 miles/108.993 km.
1 A.J. Allmendinger, USA, 40m 23.476s, 100.603 mph/161.906 km/h; **2** Ryan Dalziel, GB, 40m 27.223s; **3** Aaron Justus, USA, 40m 35.153s; **4** Michael Valiante, CDN, 40m 35.817s; **5** Joey Hand, USA, 40m 36.159s; **6** Jonathan Macri, CDN, 40m 39.709s; **7** Danica Patrick, USA, 40m 39.859s; **8** Alex Figge, USA, 40m 48.523s; **9** Kyle Krisiloff, USA, 40m 56.615s; **10** Stephan C. Roy, CDN, 40m 57.680s.
Most laps led: Allmendinger, 25.
Fastest race lap: Allmendinger, 1m 31.259s, 106.865 mph/171.983 km/h.
Fastest qualifying lap: Allmendinger, 1m 31.839s, 106.190 mph/170.897 km/h.

DENVER TOYOTA ATLANTIC RACE, Denver Street Circuit, Colorado, USA, 31 August. Round 11. 37 laps of the 1.647-mile/2.651-km circuit, 60.939 miles/98.072 km.
1 A.J. Allmendinger, USA, 44m 43.705s, 81.745 mph/131.556 km/h; **2** Michael Valiante, CDN, 44m 45.951s; **3** Ryan Dalziel, GB, 44m 46.602s; **4** Jon Fogarty, USA, 44m 49.241s; **5** Danica Patrick, USA, 44m 50.248s; **6** Jonathan Macri, CDN, 44m 51.655s; **7** Kyle Krisiloff, USA, 44m 53.553s; **8** Luis Diaz, MEX, 45m 11.443s; **9** Joey Hand, USA, 45m 26.557s; **10** Marc Breuers, USA, 36 laps.
Most laps led: Allmendinger, 37.
Fastest race lap: Allmendinger, 1m 07.294s, 88.109 mph/141.798 km/h.
Fastest qualifying lap: Allmendinger, 1m 06.966s, 88.540 mph/142.492 km/h.

ARGENT MORTGAGE TOYOTA ATLANTIC 100k, Miami Bayfront Park Street Circuit, Miami, Florida, USA, 28 September. Round 12. 55 laps of the 1.150-mile/1.851-km circuit, 63.250 miles/101.791 km.
1 Michael Valiante, CDN, 48m 05.360s, 78.916 mph/127.002 km/h; **2** Danica Patrick, USA, 48m 06.569s; **3** Ryan Dalziel, GB, 48m 07.122s; **4** Jon Fogarty, USA, 48m 17.259s; **5** Jonathan Macri, CDN, 48m 40.060s; **6** Joey Hand, USA, 48m 56.193s; **7** Aaron Justus, USA, 54 laps; **8** Alex Figge, USA, 54; **9** Luis Diaz, MEX, 53; **10** Eric Jensen, CDN, 52.
Most laps led: Valiante, 55.
Fastest race lap: Dalziel, 47.599s, 86.977 mph/139.975 km/h.
Fastest qualifying lap: A.J. Allmendinger, USA, 47.717s, 86.762 mph/139.629 km/h.

Final championship points

1 A.J. Allmendinger, USA, 201; **2** Ryan Dalziel, GB, 175; **3** Michael Valiante, CDN, 161; **4** Jonathan Macri, CDN, 145; **5** Aaron Justus, USA, 123; **6** Danica Patrick, USA, 109; **7** Joey Hand, USA, 108; **8** Luis Diaz, MEX, 88; **9** Alex Figge, USA, 87; **10** Kyle Krisiloff, USA, 77; **11** Alex Garcia, YV, 60; **12** Eric Jensen, CDN, 49; **13** Stephan C. Roy, CDN, 48; **14** Bryan Sellers, USA, 30; **15=** Jon Fogarty, USA, 24; **15=** Philip Fayer, CDN, 24; **17** Marc Breuers, USA, 12; **18** Louis-Philippe Dumoulin, CDN, 11; **19** Marc DeVellis, CDN, 9; **20** Romain Dumas, F, 7; **21** Tony Ave, USA, 6; **22** Dan Selznick, USA, 5; **23=** Hoover Orsi, BR, 2; **23=** Eduardo Figueroa, MEX, 2.

Nation's Cup
1 United States, 215; **2** Canada, 168; **3** Scotland, 148; **4** Mexico, 85; **5** Venezuela, 57; **6** France, 7; **7** Brazil, 2.

Rookie of the Year
1 A.J. Allmendinger; **2** Aaron Justus; **3** Danica Patrick; **4** Bryan Sellers.